Transactions of the Association for Computational Linguistics

(TACL 2013)

TACL Volume 1, Issue 1

ISBN: 978-1-62748-394-0

Printed from e-media with permission by:

Curran Associates, Inc.
57 Morehouse Lane
Red Hook, NY 12571

Some format issues inherent in the e-media version may also appear in this print version.

Printed by Curran Associates, Inc. (2013)

For permission requests, please contact the Association for Computational Linguistics at the address below.

Association for Computational Linguistics
209 N. Eighth Street
Stroudsburg, Pennsylvania 18360

Phone: 1-570-476-8006
Fax: 1-570-476-0860

acl@aclweb.org

Additional copies of this publication are available from:

Curran Associates, Inc.
57 Morehouse Lane
Red Hook, NY 12571 USA
Phone: 845-758-0400
Fax: 845-758-2634
Email: curran@proceedings.com
Web: www.proceedings.com

TABLE OF CONTENTS

Token and Type Constraints for Cross-Lingual Part-of-Speech Tagging

Oscar Täckström[◇†*] **Dipanjan Das**[‡] **Slav Petrov**[‡] **Ryan McDonald**[‡] **Joakim Nivre**[†*]

[◇] Swedish Institute of Computer Science
[†] Department of Linguistics and Philology, Uppsala University
[‡] Google Research, New York

oscar@sics.se
{dipanjand|slav|ryanmcd}@google.com
joakim.nivre@lingfil.uu.se

Abstract

We consider the construction of part-of-speech taggers for resource-poor languages. Recently, manually constructed tag dictionaries from Wiktionary and dictionaries projected via bitext have been used as *type constraints* to overcome the scarcity of annotated data in this setting. In this paper, we show that additional *token constraints* can be projected from a resource-rich source language to a resource-poor target language via word-aligned bitext. We present several models to this end; in particular a partially observed conditional random field model, where coupled token and type constraints provide a partial signal for training. Averaged across eight previously studied Indo-European languages, our model achieves a 25% relative error reduction over the prior state of the art. We further present successful results on seven additional languages from different families, empirically demonstrating the applicability of coupled token and type constraints across a diverse set of languages.

1 Introduction

Supervised part-of-speech (POS) taggers are available for more than twenty languages and achieve accuracies of around 95% on in-domain data (Petrov et al., 2012). Thanks to their efficiency and robustness, supervised taggers are routinely employed in many natural language processing applications, such as syntactic and semantic parsing, named-entity recognition and machine translation. Unfortunately, the resources required to train supervised taggers are expensive to create and unlikely to exist for the majority of written languages. The necessity of building NLP tools for these resource-poor languages has been part of the motivation for research on unsupervised learning of POS taggers (Christodoulopoulos et al., 2010).

In this paper, we instead take a *weakly* supervised approach towards this problem. Recently, learning POS taggers with *type*-level tag dictionary constraints has gained popularity. Tag dictionaries, noisily projected via word-aligned bitext, have bridged the gap between purely unsupervised and fully supervised taggers, resulting in an average accuracy of over 83% on a benchmark of eight Indo-European languages (Das and Petrov, 2011). Li et al. (2012) further improved upon this result by employing Wiktionary[1] as a tag dictionary source, resulting in the hitherto best published result of almost 85% on the same setup.

Although the aforementioned weakly supervised approaches have resulted in significant improvements over fully unsupervised approaches, they have not exploited the benefits of *token*-level cross-lingual projection methods, which are possible with word-aligned bitext between a *target* language of interest and a resource-rich *source* language, such as English. This is the setting we consider in this paper (§2). While prior work has successfully considered both token- and type-level projection across word-aligned bitext for estimating the model parameters of generative tagging models (Yarowsky and Ngai, 2001; Xi and Hwa, 2005, *inter alia*), a key observation underlying the present work is that token- and type-level information offer different and complementary signals. On the one hand, high confidence token-level projections offer precise constraints on a tag in a particular context. On the other hand, manually cre-

* Work primarily carried out while at Google Research.

[1] http://www.wiktionary.org/.

ated type-level dictionaries can have broad coverage and do not suffer from word-alignment errors; they can therefore be used to filter systematic as well as random noise in token-level projections.

In order to reap these potential benefits, we propose a partially observed conditional random field (CRF) model (Lafferty et al., 2001) that couples token and type constraints in order to guide learning (§3). In essence, the model is given the freedom to push probability mass towards hypotheses consistent with both types of information. This approach is flexible: we can use either noisy projected or manually constructed dictionaries to generate type constraints; furthermore, we can incorporate arbitrary features over the input. In addition to standard (contextual) lexical features and transition features, we observe that adding features from a monolingual word clustering (Uszkoreit and Brants, 2008) can significantly improve accuracy. While most of these features can also be used in a generative feature-based hidden Markov model (HMM) (Berg-Kirkpatrick et al., 2010), we achieve the best accuracy with a globally normalized discriminative CRF model.

To evaluate our approach, we present extensive results on standard publicly available datasets for 15 languages: the eight Indo-European languages previously studied in this context by Das and Petrov (2011) and Li et al. (2012), and seven additional languages from different families, for which no comparable study exists. In §4 we compare various features, constraints and model types. Our best model uses type constraints derived from Wiktionary, together with token constraints derived from high-confidence word alignments. When averaged across the eight languages studied by Das and Petrov (2011) and Li et al. (2012), we achieve an accuracy of 88.8%. This is a 25% relative error reduction over the previous state of the art. Averaged across all 15 languages, our model obtains an accuracy of 84.5% compared to 78.5% obtained by a strong generative baseline. Finally, we provide an in depth analysis of the relative contributions of the two types of constraints in §5.

2 Coupling Token and Type Constraints

Type-level information has been amply used in weakly supervised POS induction, either via pure manually crafted tag dictionaries (Smith and Eisner, 2005; Ravi and Knight, 2009; Garrette and Baldridge, 2012), noisily projected tag dictionaries (Das and Petrov, 2011) or through crowdsourced lexica, such as Wiktionary (Li et al., 2012). At the other end of the spectrum, there have been efforts that project token-level information across word-aligned bitext (Yarowsky and Ngai, 2001; Xi and Hwa, 2005). However, systems that combine both sources of information in a single model have yet to be fully explored. The following three subsections outline our overall approach for coupling these two types of information to build robust POS taggers that do not require any direct supervision in the target language.

2.1 Token Constraints

For the majority of resource-poor languages, there is at least some bitext with a resource-rich source language; for simplicity, we choose English as our source language in all experiments. It is then natural to consider using a supervised part-of-speech tagger to predict part-of-speech tags for the English side of the bitext. These predicted tags can subsequently be projected to the target side via automatic word alignments. This approach was pioneered by Yarowsky and Ngai (2001), who used the resulting partial target annotation to estimate the parameters of an HMM. However, due to the automatic nature of the word alignments and the POS tags, there will be significant noise in the projected tags. To conquer this noise, they used very aggressive smoothing techniques when training the HMM. Fossum and Abney (2005) used similar token-level projections, but instead combined projections from multiple source languages to filter out random projection noise as well as the systematic noise arising from different source language annotations and syntactic divergences.

2.2 Type Constraints

It is well known that given a tag dictionary, even if it is incomplete, it is possible to learn accurate POS taggers (Smith and Eisner, 2005; Goldberg et al., 2008; Ravi and Knight, 2009; Naseem et al., 2009). While widely differing in the specific model structure and learning objective, all of these approaches achieve excellent results. Unfortunately, they rely on tag dictionaries extracted directly from the underlying treebank data. Such dictionaries provide in depth coverage of the test domain and also list all

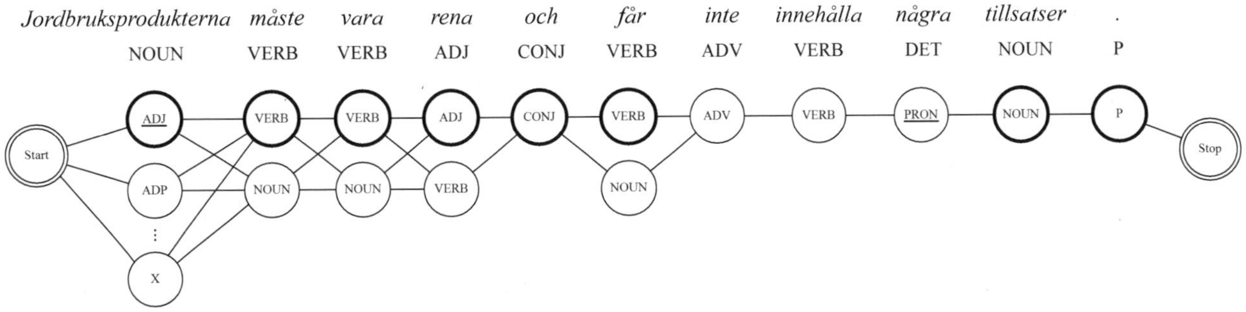

Figure 1: Lattice representation of the inference search space $\mathcal{Y}(x)$ for an authentic sentence in Swedish (*"The farming products must be pure and must not contain any additives"*), after pruning with Wiktionary type constraints. The correct parts of speech are listed underneath each word. Bold nodes show projected token constraints $\tilde{y}$. Underlined text indicates incorrect tags. The coupled constraints lattice $\widehat{\mathcal{Y}}(x, \tilde{y})$ consists of the bold nodes together with nodes for words that are lacking token constraints; in this case, the coupled constraints lattice thus defines exactly one valid path.

inflected forms – both of which are difficult to obtain and unrealistic to expect for resource-poor languages.

In contrast, Das and Petrov (2011) automatically create type-level tag dictionaries by aggregating over projected token-level information extracted from bitext. To handle the noise in these automatic dictionaries, they use label propagation on a similarity graph to smooth (and also expand) the label distributions. While their approach produces good results and is applicable to resource-poor languages, it requires a complex multi-stage training procedure including the construction of a large distributional similarity graph.

Recently, Li et al. (2012) presented a simple and viable alternative: crowdsourced dictionaries from Wiktionary. While noisy and sparse in nature, Wiktionary dictionaries are available for 170 languages.[2] Furthermore, their quality and coverage is growing continuously (Li et al., 2012). By incorporating type constraints from Wiktionary into the feature-based HMM of Berg-Kirkpatrick et al. (2010), Li et al. were able to obtain the best published results in this setting, surpassing the results of Das and Petrov (2011) on eight Indo-European languages.

2.3 Coupled Constraints

Rather than relying exclusively on either token or type constraints, we propose to complement the one with the other during training. For each sentence in our training set, a partially constrained lattice of tag sequences is constructed as follows:

1. For each token whose type is *not* in the tag dictionary, we allow the entire tag set.
2. For each token whose type *is* in the tag dictionary, we prune all tags not licensed by the dictionary and mark the token as dictionary-pruned.
3. For each token that has a tag projected via a high-confidence bidirectional word alignment: if the projected tag is still present in the lattice, then we prune every tag but the projected tag for that token; if the projected tag is not present in the lattice, which can only happen for dictionary-pruned tokens, then we ignore the projected tag.

Figure 1 provides a running example. The lattice shows tags permitted after constraining the words to tags licensed by the dictionary (up until Step 2 from above). There is only a single token "Jordbruksprodukterna" (*"the farming products"*) not in the dictionary; in this case the lattice permits the full set of tags. With token-level projections (Step 3; nodes with bold border in Figure 1), the lattice can be further pruned. In most cases, the projected tag is both correct and is in the dictionary-pruned lattice. We thus successfully disambiguate such tokens and shrink the search space substantially.

There are two cases we highlight in order to show where our model can break. First, for the token "Jordbruksprodukterna", the erroneously projected tag ADJ will eliminate all other tags from the lattice, including the correct tag NOUN. Second, the token "några" (*"any"*) has a single dictionary entry PRON and is missing the correct tag DET. In the case where

[2] `http://meta.wikimedia.org/wiki/Wiktionary` — October 2012.

DET is the projected tag, we will not add it to the lattice and simply ignore it. This is because we hypothesize that the tag dictionary can be trusted more than the tags projected via noisy word alignments. As we will see in §4, taking the union of tags performs worse, which supports this hypothesis.

For *generative* models, such as HMMs (§3.1), we need to define only one lattice. For our best generative model this is the coupled token- and type-constrained lattice.[3] At prediction time, in both the discriminative and the generative cases, we find the most likely label sequence using Viterbi decoding.

For *discriminative* models, such as CRFs (§3.2), we need to define two lattices: one that the model moves probability mass towards and another one defining the overall search space (or partition function). In traditional supervised learning without a dictionary, the former is a trivial lattice containing the gold standard tag sequence and the latter is the set of all possible tag sequences spanning the tokens. With our best model, we will move mass towards the coupled token- and type-constrained lattice, such that the model can freely distribute mass across all paths consistent with these constraints. The lattice defining the partition function will be the full set of possible tag sequences when no dictionary is used; when a dictionary is used it will consist of all dictionary-pruned tag sequences (sans Step 3 above; the full set of possibilities shown in Figure 1 for our running example).

Figures 2 and 3 provide statistics regarding the supervision coverage and remaining ambiguity. Figure 2 shows that more than two thirds of all tokens in our training data are in Wiktionary. However, there is considerable variation between languages: Spanish has the highest coverage with over 90%, while Turkish, an agglutinative language with a vast number of word forms, has less than 50% coverage. Figure 3 shows that there is substantial uncertainty left after pruning with Wiktionary, since tokens are rarely fully disambiguated: 1.3 tags per token are allowed on average for types in Wiktionary.

Figure 2 further shows that high-confidence alignments are available for about half of the tokens for most languages (Japanese is a notable exception with less than 30% of the tokens covered). Intersecting the Wiktionary tags and the projected tags (Step 2 and 3 above) filters out some of the potentially erroneous tags, but preserves the majority of the projected tags; the remaining, presumably more accurate projected tags cover almost half of all tokens, greatly reducing the search space that the learner needs to explore.

[3]Other training methods exist as well, for example, contrastive estimation (Smith and Eisner, 2005).

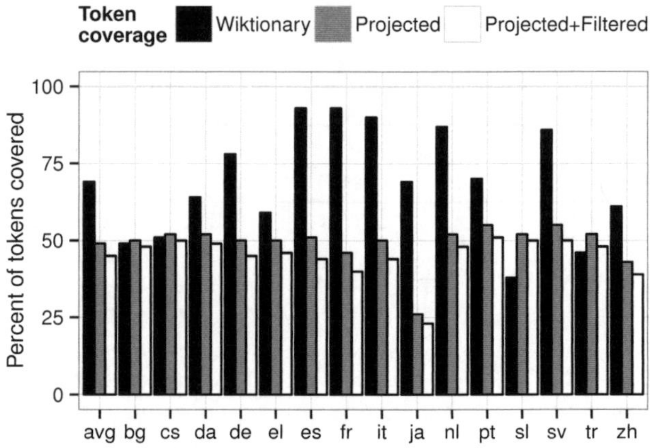

Figure 2: Wiktionary and projection dictionary coverage. Shown is the percentage of tokens in the target side of the bitext that are covered by Wiktionary, that have a projected tag, and that have a projected tag after intersecting the two.

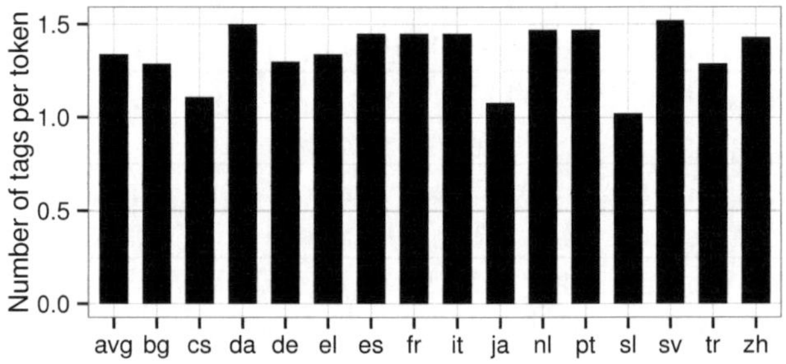

Figure 3: Average number of licensed tags per token on the target side of the bitext, for types in Wiktionary.

3 Models with Coupled Constraints

We now formally present how we couple token and type constraints and how we use these coupled constraints to train probabilistic tagging models. Let $x = (x_1 x_2 \dots x_{|x|}) \in \mathcal{X}$ denote a sentence, where each token $x_i \in \mathcal{V}$ is an instance of a word type from the vocabulary $\mathcal{V}$ and let $y = (y_1 y_2 \dots y_{|x|}) \in \mathcal{Y}$ denote a tag sequence, where $y_i \in \mathcal{T}$ is the tag assigned to token x_i and $\mathcal{T}$ denotes the set of all possible part-of-speech tags. We denote the lattice of all admissible tag sequences for the sentence x by $\mathcal{Y}(x)$. This is the inference search space in which the tagger operates. As we shall see, it is crucial to constrain the size of this lattice in order to simplify learning when only incomplete supervision is available.

A tag dictionary maps a word type $x_j \in \mathcal{V}$ to a set of admissible tags $\mathcal{T}(x_j) \subseteq \mathcal{T}$. For word types not in the dictionary we allow the full set of tags $\mathcal{T}$ (while possible, in this paper we do not attempt to distinguish closed-class versus open-class words). When provided with a tag dictionary, the lattice of admissible tag sequences for a sentence x is $\mathcal{Y}(x) = \mathcal{T}(x_1) \times \mathcal{T}(x_2) \times \ldots \times \mathcal{T}(x_{|x|})$. When no tag dictionary is available, we simply have the full lattice $\mathcal{Y}(x) = \mathcal{T}^{|x|}$.

Let $\tilde{y} = (\tilde{y}_1 \tilde{y}_2 \ldots \tilde{y}_{|x|})$ be the projected tags for the sentence x. Note that $\{\tilde{y}_i\} = \emptyset$ for tokens without a projected tag. Next, we define a piecewise operator $\frown$ that couples $\tilde{y}$ and $\mathcal{Y}(x)$ with respect to every sentence index, which results in a token- and type-constrained lattice. The operator behaves as follows, coherent with the high level description in §2.3:

$$\widehat{\mathcal{T}}(x_i, \tilde{y}_i) = \tilde{y}_i \frown \mathcal{T}(x_i) = \begin{cases} \{\tilde{y}_i\} & \text{if } \tilde{y}_i \in \mathcal{T}(x_i) \\ \mathcal{T}(x_i) & \text{otherwise}\,. \end{cases}$$

We denote the token- and type-constrained lattice as $\widehat{\mathcal{Y}}(x, \tilde{y}) = \widehat{\mathcal{T}}(x_1, \tilde{y}_1) \times \widehat{\mathcal{T}}(x_2, \tilde{y}_2) \times \ldots \times \widehat{\mathcal{T}}(x_{|x|}, \tilde{y}_{|x|})$. Note that when token-level projections are not used, the dictionary-pruned lattice and the lattice with coupled constraints are identical, that is $\widehat{\mathcal{Y}}(x, \tilde{y}) = \mathcal{Y}(x)$.

3.1 HMMs with Coupled Constraints

A first-order hidden Markov model (HMM) specifies the joint distribution of a sentence $x \in \mathcal{X}$ and a tag-sequence $y \in \mathcal{Y}(x)$ as:

$$p_\beta(x, y) = \prod_{i=1}^{|x|} \underbrace{p_\beta(x_i \mid y_i)}_{\text{emission}} \underbrace{p_\beta(y_i \mid y_{i-1})}_{\text{transition}}\,.$$

We follow the recent trend of using a log-linear parametrization of the emission and the transition distributions, instead of a multinomial parametrization (Chen, 2003). This allows model parameters β to be shared across categorical events, which has been shown to give superior performance (Berg-Kirkpatrick et al., 2010). The categorical emission and transition events are represented by feature vectors $\phi(x_i, y_i)$ and $\phi(y_i, y_{i-1})$. Each element of the parameter vector β corresponds to a particular feature; the component log-linear distributions are:

$$p_\beta(x_i \mid y_i) = \frac{\exp\left(\beta^\top \phi(x_i, y_i)\right)}{\sum_{x'_i \in \mathcal{V}} \exp\left(\beta^\top \phi(x'_i, y_i)\right)}\,,$$

and

$$p_\beta(y_i \mid y_{i-1}) = \frac{\exp\left(\beta^\top \phi(y_i, y_{i-1})\right)}{\sum_{y'_i \in \mathcal{T}} \exp\left(\beta^\top \phi(y'_i, y_{i-1})\right)}\,.$$

In maximum-likelihood estimation of the parameters, we seek to maximize the likelihood of the observed parts of the data. For this we need the joint marginal distribution $p_\beta(x, \widehat{\mathcal{Y}}(x, \tilde{y}))$ of a sentence x, and its coupled constraints lattice $\widehat{\mathcal{Y}}(x, \tilde{y})$, which is obtained by marginalizing over all consistent outputs:

$$p_\beta(x, \widehat{\mathcal{Y}}(x, \tilde{y})) = \sum_{y \in \widehat{\mathcal{Y}}(x, \tilde{y})} p_\beta(x, y)\,.$$

If there are no projections and no tag dictionary, then $\widehat{\mathcal{Y}}(x, \tilde{y}) = \mathcal{T}^{|x|}$, and thus $p_\beta(x, \widehat{\mathcal{Y}}(x, \tilde{y})) = p_\beta(x)$, which reduces to fully unsupervised learning. The ℓ_2-regularized *marginal joint* log-likelihood of the constrained training data $\mathcal{D} = \{(x^{(i)}, \tilde{y}^{(i)})\}_{i=1}^n$ is:

$$\mathcal{L}(\beta; \mathcal{D}) = \sum_{i=1}^n \log p_\beta(x^{(i)}, \widehat{\mathcal{Y}}(x^{(i)}, \tilde{y}^{(i)})) - \gamma \|\beta\|_2^2\,. \tag{1}$$

We follow Berg-Kirkpatrick et al. (2010) and take a direct gradient approach for optimizing Eq. 1 with L-BFGS (Liu and Nocedal, 1989). We set $\gamma = 1$ and run 100 iterations of L-BFGS. One could also employ the Expectation-Maximization (EM) algorithm (Dempster et al., 1977) to optimize this objective, although the relative merits of EM versus direct gradient training for these models is still a topic of debate (Berg-Kirkpatrick et al., 2010; Li et al., 2012).[4] Note that since the marginal likelihood is non-concave, we are only guaranteed to find a local maximum of Eq. 1.

After estimating the model parameters β, the tag-sequence $y^* \in \mathcal{Y}(x)$ for a sentence $x \in \mathcal{X}$ is predicted by choosing the one with maximal *joint* probability:

$$y^* \leftarrow \arg\max_{y \in \mathcal{Y}(x)} p_\beta(x, y)\,.$$

[4] We trained the HMM with EM as well, but achieved better results with direct gradient training and hence omit those results.

3.2 CRFs with Coupled Constraints

Whereas an HMM models the joint probability of the input $x \in \mathcal{X}$ and output $y \in \mathcal{Y}(x)$, using locally normalized component distributions, a conditional random field (CRF) instead models the probability of the output conditioned on the input as a globally normalized log-linear distribution (Lafferty et al., 2001):

$$p_\theta(y \mid x) = \frac{\exp\left(\theta^\top \Phi(x, y)\right)}{\sum_{y' \in \mathcal{Y}(x)} \exp\left(\theta^\top \Phi(x, y')\right)} ,$$

where θ is a parameter vector. As for the HMM, $\mathcal{Y}(x)$ is not necessarily the full space of possible tag-sequences; specifically, for us, it is the dictionary-pruned lattice *without* the token constraints.

With a first-order Markov assumption, the feature function factors as:

$$\Phi(x, y) = \sum_{i=1}^{|x|} \phi(x, y_i, y_{i-1}) .$$

This model is more powerful than the HMM in that it can use richer feature definitions, such as joint input/transition features and features over a wider input context. We model a marginal conditional probability, given by the total probability of all tag sequences consistent with the lattice $\widehat{\mathcal{Y}}(x, \tilde{y})$:

$$p_\theta(\widehat{\mathcal{Y}}(x, \tilde{y}) \mid x) = \sum_{y \in \widehat{\mathcal{Y}}(x, \tilde{y})} p_\theta(y \mid x) .$$

The parameters of this constrained CRF are estimated by maximizing the ℓ_2-regularized *marginal conditional* log-likelihood of the constrained data (Riezler et al., 2002):

$$\mathcal{L}(\theta; \mathcal{D}) = \sum_{i=1}^{n} \log p_\theta(\widehat{\mathcal{Y}}(x^{(i)}, \tilde{y}^{(i)}) \mid x^{(i)}) - \gamma \|\theta\|_2^2 . \quad (2)$$

As with Eq. 1, we maximize Eq. 2 with 100 iterations of L-BFGS and set $\gamma = 1$. In contrast to the HMM, after estimating the model parameters θ, the tag-sequence $y^* \in \mathcal{Y}(x)$ for a sentence $x \in \mathcal{X}$ is chosen as the sequence with the maximal *conditional* probability:

$$y^* \leftarrow \arg\max_{y \in \mathcal{Y}(x)} p_\theta(y \mid x) .$$

4 Empirical Study

We now present a detailed empirical study of the models proposed in the previous sections. In addition to comparing with the state of the art in Das and Petrov (2011) and Li et al. (2012), we present models with several combinations of token and type constraints, additional features incorporating word clusters. Both generative and discriminative models are explored.

4.1 Experimental Setup

Before delving into the experimental details, we present our setup and datasets.

Languages. We evaluate on eight target languages used in previous work (Das and Petrov, 2011; Li et al., 2012) and on seven additional languages (see Table 1). While the former eight languages all belong to the Indo-European family, we broaden the coverage to language families more distant from the source language (for example, Chinese, Japanese and Turkish). We use the treebanks from the CoNLL shared tasks on dependency parsing (Buchholz and Marsi, 2006; Nivre et al., 2007) for evaluation.[5] The two-letter abbreviations from the ISO 639-1 standard are used when referring to these languages in tables and figures.

Tagset. In all cases, we map the language-specific POS tags to universal POS tags using the mapping of Petrov et al. (2012).[6] Since we use indirect supervision via projected tags or Wiktionary, the model states induced by all models correspond directly to POS tags, enabling us to compute tagging accuracy without a greedy 1-to-1 or many-to-1 mapping.

Bitext. For all experiments, we use English as the source language. Depending on availability, there are between 1M and 5M parallel sentences for each language. The majority of the parallel data is gathered automatically from the web using the method of Uszkoreit et al. (2010). We further include data from Europarl (Koehn, 2005) and from the UN parallel corpus (UN, 2006), for languages covered by these corpora. The English side of the bitext is POS tagged with a standard supervised CRF tagger, trained on the Penn Treebank (Marcus et al., 1993), with tags mapped to universal tags. The parallel sen-

[5] For French we use the treebank of Abeillé et al. (2003).

[6] We use version 1.03 of the mappings available at `http://code.google.com/p/universal-pos-tags/`.

tences are word aligned with the aligner of DeNero and Macherey (2011). Intersected high-confidence alignments (confidence >0.95) are extracted and aggregated into projected type-level dictionaries. For purely practical reasons, the training data with token-level projections is created by randomly sampling target-side sentences with a total of 500K tokens.

Wiktionary. We use a snapshot of the Wiktionary word definitions, and follow the heuristics of Li et al. (2012) for creating the Wiktionary dictionary by mapping the Wiktionary tags to universal POS tags.[7]

Features. For all models, we use only an identity feature for tag-pair transitions. We use five features that couple the current tag and the observed word (analogous to the emission in an HMM): word identity, suffixes of up to length 3, and three indicator features that fire when the word starts with a capital letter, contains a hyphen or contains a digit. These are the same features as those used by Das and Petrov (2011). Finally, for some models we add a word cluster feature that couples the current tag and the word cluster identity of the word. These (monolingual) word clusters are induced with the exchange algorithm (Uszkoreit and Brants, 2008). We set the number of clusters to 256 across all languages, as this has previously been shown to produce robust results for similar tasks (Turian et al., 2010; Täckström et al., 2012). The clusters for each language are learned on a large monolingual newswire corpus.

	Prior work		HMM with type constraints			
Lang.	D&P	LG&T	$\mathcal{Y}^{\text{HMM}}_{\text{proj.}}$	$\mathcal{Y}^{\text{HMM}}_{\text{wik.}}$	$\mathcal{Y}^{\text{HMM}}_{\text{union}}$	$\mathcal{Y}^{\text{HMM}}_{\text{union}}$+C
bg	–	–	84.2	68.1	87.2	**87.9**
cs	–	–	75.4	70.2	75.4	**79.2**
da	83.2	83.3	87.7	82.0	78.4	**89.5**
de	82.8	85.8	86.6	85.1	80.0	**88.3**
el	82.5	79.2	83.3	83.8	**86.0**	83.2
es	84.2	86.4	83.9	83.7	**88.3**	87.3
fr	–	–	**88.4**	75.7	75.6	86.6
it	86.8	86.5	89.0	85.4	89.9	**90.6**
ja	–	–	45.2	**76.9**	74.4	73.7
nl	79.5	**86.3**	81.7	79.1	83.8	82.7
pt	87.9	84.5	86.7	79.0	83.8	**90.4**
sl	–	–	78.7	64.8	82.8	**83.4**
sv	80.5	86.1	80.6	85.9	85.9	**86.7**
tr	–	–	**66.2**	44.1	65.1	65.7
zh	–	–	59.2	**73.9**	63.2	73.0
avg (8)	83.4	84.8	84.9	83.0	84.5	**87.3**
avg	–	–	78.5	75.9	80.0	**83.2**

Table 1: Tagging accuracies for type-constrained HMM models. D&P is the "With LP" model in Table 2 of Das and Petrov (2011), while LG&T is the "SHMM-ME" model in Table 2 of Li et al. (2012). $\mathcal{Y}^{\text{HMM}}_{\text{proj.}}$, $\mathcal{Y}^{\text{HMM}}_{\text{wik.}}$ and $\mathcal{Y}^{\text{HMM}}_{\text{union}}$ are HMMs trained solely with type constraints derived from the projected dictionary, Wiktionary and the union of these dictionaries, respectively. $\mathcal{Y}^{\text{HMM}}_{\text{union}}$+C is equivalent to $\mathcal{Y}^{\text{HMM}}_{\text{union}}$ with additional cluster features. All models are trained on the treebank of each language, stripped of gold labels. Results are averaged over the 8 languages from Das and Petrov (2011), denoted *avg (8)*, as well as over the full set of 15 languages, denoted *avg*.

4.2 Models with Type Constraints

To examine the sole effect of type constraints, we experiment with the HMM, drawing constraints from three different dictionaries. Table 1 compares the performance of our models with the best results of Das and Petrov (2011, D&P) and Li et al. (2012, LG&T). As in previous work, training is done exclusively on the training portion of each treebank, stripped of any manual linguistic annotation.

We first use all of our parallel data to generate projected tag dictionaries: the English POS tags are projected across word alignments and aggregated to tag distributions for each word type. As in Das and Petrov (2011), the distributions are then filtered with a threshold of 0.2 to remove noisy tags and to create an unweighted tag dictionary. We call this model $\mathcal{Y}^{\text{HMM}}_{\text{proj.}}$; its average accuracy of 84.9% on the eight languages is higher than the 83.4% of D&P and on par with LG&T (84.8%).[8] Our next model ($\mathcal{Y}^{\text{HMM}}_{\text{wik.}}$) simply draws type constraints from Wiktionary. It slightly underperforms LG&T (83.0%), presumably because they used a second-order HMM. As a simple extension to these two models, we take the union of the projected dictionary and Wiktionary to constrain an HMM, which we name $\mathcal{Y}^{\text{HMM}}_{\text{union}}$. This model performs a little worse on the eight Indo-European languages (84.5), but gives an improvement over the projected dictionary when evaluated across all 15 languages (80.0% vs. 78.5%).

[7]The definitions were downloaded on August 31, 2012 from `http://toolserver.org/~enwikt/definitions/`. This snapshot is more recent than that used by Li et al.

[8]Our model corresponds to the weaker, "No LP" projection of Das and Petrov (2011). We found that label propagation was only beneficial when small amounts of bitext were available.

		Token constraints		HMM with coupled constraints			CRF with coupled constraints		
Lang.	$\mathcal{Y}^{\text{HMM}}_{\text{union}}$+C+L	$\tilde{y}^{\text{HMM}}$+C+L	$\tilde{y}^{\text{CRF}}$+C+L	$\widehat{\mathcal{Y}}^{\text{HMM}}_{\text{proj.}}$+C+L	$\widehat{\mathcal{Y}}^{\text{HMM}}_{\text{wik.}}$+C+L	$\widehat{\mathcal{Y}}^{\text{HMM}}_{\text{union}}$+C+L	$\widehat{\mathcal{Y}}^{\text{CRF}}_{\text{proj.}}$+C+L	$\widehat{\mathcal{Y}}^{\text{CRF}}_{\text{wik.}}$+C+L	$\widehat{\mathcal{Y}}^{\text{CRF}}_{\text{union}}$+C+L
bg	87.7	77.9	84.1	84.5	83.9	86.7	86.0	**87.8**	85.4
cs	78.3	65.4	74.9	74.8	**81.1**	76.9	74.7	80.3**	75.0
da	87.3	80.9	85.1	87.2	85.6	88.1	85.5	**88.2***	86.0
de	87.7	81.4	83.3	85.0	89.3	86.7	84.4	**90.5****	85.5
el	85.9	81.1	77.8	80.1	87.0	83.9	79.6	**89.5****	79.7
es	**89.1****	84.1	85.5	83.7	85.9	88.0	85.7	87.1	86.0
fr	**88.4****	83.5	84.7	85.9	86.4	87.4	84.9	87.2	85.6
it	89.6	85.2	88.5	88.7	87.6	**89.8**	88.3	89.3	89.4
ja	72.8	47.6	54.2	43.2	76.1	70.5	44.9	**81.0****	68.0
nl	83.1	78.4	82.4	82.3	84.2	83.2	83.1	**85.9****	83.2
pt	89.1	84.7	87.0	86.6	88.7	88.0	87.9	**91.0****	88.3
sl	**82.4**	69.8	78.2	78.5	81.8	80.1	79.7	82.3	80.0
sv	86.1	80.1	84.2	82.3	87.9	86.9	84.4	**88.9****	85.5
tr	62.4	58.1	64.5	64.6	61.8	64.8	65.0	64.1**	**65.2**
zh	72.6	52.7	39.5	56.0	74.1	73.3	59.7	**74.4****	73.4
avg (8)	87.2	82.0	84.2	84.5	87.0	86.8	84.9	**88.8**	85.4
avg	82.8	74.1	76.9	77.6	82.8	82.3	78.2	**84.5**	81.1

Table 2: Tagging accuracies for models with token constraints and coupled token and type constraints. All models use cluster features (. . . +C) and are trained on large training sets each containing 500k tokens with (partial) token-level projections (. . . +L). The best type-constrained model, trained on the larger datasets, $\mathcal{Y}^{\text{HMM}}_{\text{union}}$+C+L, is included for comparison. The remaining columns correspond to HMM and CRF models trained *only* with token constraints ($\tilde{y}\ldots$) and with coupled token and type constraints ($\widehat{\mathcal{Y}}\ldots$). The latter are trained using the projected dictionary ($\cdot_{\text{proj.}}$), Wiktionary ($\cdot_{\text{wik.}}$) and the union of these dictionaries ($\cdot_{\text{union}}$), respectively. The search spaces of the models trained with coupled constraints ($\widehat{\mathcal{Y}}\ldots$) are each pruned with the respective tag dictionary used to derive the coupled constraints. The observed difference between $\widehat{\mathcal{Y}}^{\text{CRF}}_{\text{wik.}}$+C+L and $\mathcal{Y}^{\text{HMM}}_{\text{union}}$+C+L is statistically significant at $p < 0.01$ (**) and $p < 0.015$ (*) according to a paired bootstrap test (Efron and Tibshirani, 1993). Significance was not assessed for *avg* or *avg (8)*.

We next add monolingual cluster features to the model with the union dictionary. This model, $\mathcal{Y}^{\text{HMM}}_{\text{union}}$+C, significantly outperforms all other type-constrained models, demonstrating the utility of word-cluster features.[9] For further exploration, we train the same model on the datasets containing 500K tokens sampled from the target side of the parallel data ($\mathcal{Y}^{\text{HMM}}_{\text{union}}$+C+L); this is done to explore the effects of large data during training. We find that training on these datasets result in an average accuracy of 87.2% which is comparable to the 87.3% reported for $\mathcal{Y}^{\text{HMM}}_{\text{union}}$+C in Table 1. This shows that the different source domain and amount of training data does not influence the performance of the HMM significantly.

Finally, we train CRF models where we treat type constraints as a partially observed lattice and use the full unpruned lattice for computing the partition function (§3.2). Due to space considerations, the results of these experiments are not shown in table 1. We observe similar trends in these results, but on average, accuracies are much lower compared to the type-constrained HMM models; the CRF model with the union dictionary along with cluster features achieves an average accuracy of 79.3% when trained on same data. This result is not unsurprising. First, the CRF's search space is fully unconstrained. Second, the dictionary only provides a weak set of observation constraints, which do not provide sufficient information to successfully train a discriminative model. However, as we will observe next, coupling the dictionary constraints with token-level information solves this problem.

4.3 Models with Token and Type Constraints

We now proceed to add token-level information, focusing in particular on coupled token and type

[9]These are monolingual clusters. Bilingual clusters as introduced in Täckström et al. (2012) might bring additional benefits.

constraints. Since it is not possible to generate projected token constraints for our monolingual treebanks, we train all models in this subsection on the 500K-tokens datasets sampled from the bitext. As a baseline, we first train HMM and CRF models that use *only* projected token constraints ($\tilde{y}^{\text{HMM}}$+C+L and $\tilde{y}^{\text{CRF}}$+C+L). As shown in Table 2, these models underperform the best type-level model ($\mathcal{Y}^{\text{HMM}}_{\text{union}}$+C+L),[10] which confirms that projected token constraints are not reliable on their own. This is in line with similar projection models previously examined by Das and Petrov (2011).

We then study models with coupled token and type constraints. These models use the same three dictionaries as used in §4.2, but additionally couple the derived type constraints with projected token constraints; see the caption of Table 2 for a list of these models. Note that since we only allow projected tags that are licensed by the dictionary (Step 3 of the transfer, §2.3), the actual token constraints used in these models vary with the different dictionaries.

From Table 2, we see that coupled constraints are superior to token constraints, when used both with the HMM and the CRF. However, for the HMM, coupled constraints do not provide any benefit over type constraints alone, in particular when the projected dictionary or the union dictionary is used to derive the coupled constraints ($\widehat{\mathcal{Y}}^{\text{HMM}}_{\text{proj.}}$+C+L and $\widehat{\mathcal{Y}}^{\text{HMM}}_{\text{union}}$+C+L). We hypothesize that this is because these dictionaries (in particular the former) have the same bias as the token-level tag projections, so that the dictionary is unable to correct the systematic errors in the projections (see §2.1). Since the token constraints are stronger than the type constraints in the coupled models, this bias may have a substantial impact. With the Wiktionary dictionary, the difference between the type-constrained and the coupled-constrained HMM is negligible: $\mathcal{Y}^{\text{HMM}}_{\text{union}}$+C+L and $\widehat{\mathcal{Y}}^{\text{HMM}}_{\text{wik.}}$+C+L both average at an accuracy of 82.8%.

The CRF model, on the other hand, is able to take advantage of the complementary information in the coupled constraints, provided that the dictionary is able to filter out the systematic token-level errors. With a dictionary derived from Wiktionary and projected token-level constraints, $\widehat{\mathcal{Y}}^{\text{CRF}}_{\text{wik.}}$+C+L performs better than all the remaining models, with an average accuracy of 88.8% across the eight Indo-European languages available to D&P and LG&T. Averaged over all 15 languages, its accuracy is 84.5%.

[10]To make the comparison fair vis-a-vis potential divergences in training domains, we compare to the best type-constrained model trained on the same 500K tokens training sets.

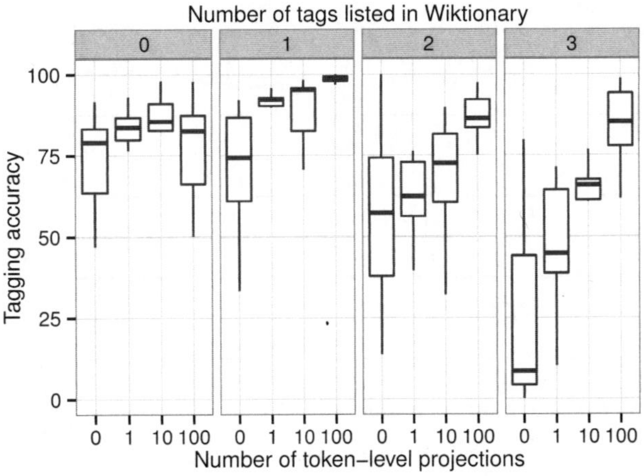

Figure 4: Relative influence of token and type constraints on tagging accuracy in the $\widehat{\mathcal{Y}}^{\text{CRF}}_{\text{wik.}}$+C+L model. Word types are categorized according to a) their number of Wiktionary tags (0,1,2 or 3+ tags, with 0 representing no Wiktionary entry; top-axis) and b) the number of times they are token-constrained in the training set (divided into buckets of 0, 1-9, 10-99 and 100+ occurrences; x-axis). The boxes summarize the accuracy distributions across languages for each word type category as defined by a) and b). The horizontal line in each box marks the median accuracy, the top and bottom mark the first and third quantile, respectively, while the whiskers mark the minimum and maximum values of the accuracy distribution.

5 Further Analysis

In this section we provide a detailed analysis of the impact of token versus type constraints and we study the pruning and filtering mistakes resulting from incomplete Wiktionary entries in detail. This analysis is based on the training portion of each treebank.

5.1 Influence of Token and Type Constraints

The empirical success of the model trained with coupled token and type constraints confirms that these constraints indeed provide complementary signals. Figure 4 provides a more detailed view of the relative benefits of each type of constraint. We observe several interesting trends.

First, word types that occur with more token constraints during training are generally tagged more accurately, regardless of whether these types occur

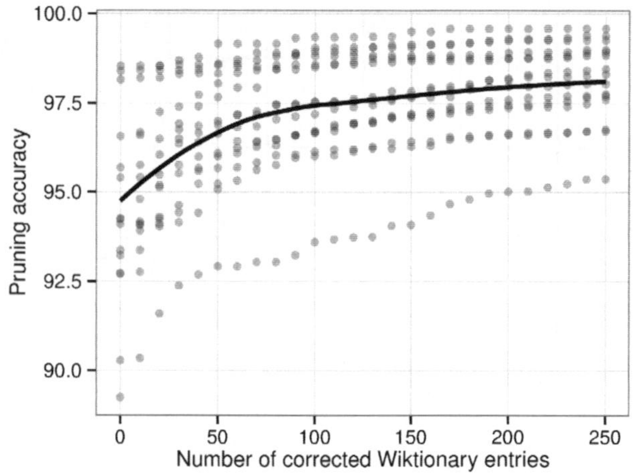

Figure 5: Average pruning accuracy (line) across languages (dots) as a function of the number of hypothetically corrected Wiktionary entries for the k most frequent word types. For example, position 100 on the x-axis corresponds to manually correcting the entries for the 100 most frequent types, while position 0 corresponds to experimental conditions.

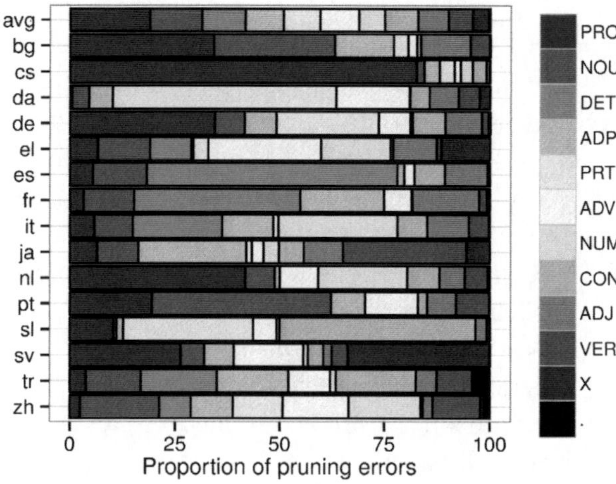

Figure 6: Prevalence of pruning mistakes per POS tag, when pruning the inference search space with Wiktionary.

in Wiktionary. The most common scenario is for a word type to have exactly one tag in Wiktionary and to occur with this projected tag over 100 times in the training set (facet 1, rightmost box). These common word types are typically tagged very accurately across all languages.

Second, the word types that are ambiguous according to Wiktionary (facets 2 and 3) are predominantly frequent ones. The accuracy is typically lower for these words compared to the unambiguous words. However, as the number of projected token constraints is increased from zero to 100+ observations, the ambiguous words are effectively disambiguated by the token constraints. This shows the advantage of intersecting token and type constraints.

Finally, projection generally helps for words that are not in Wiktionary, although the accuracy for these words never reach the accuracy of the words with only one tag in Wiktionary. Interestingly, words that occur with a projected tag constraint less than 100 times are tagged more accurately for types not in the dictionary compared to ambiguous word types with the same number of projected constraints. A possible explanation for this is that the ambiguous words are inherently more difficult to predict and that most of the words that are not in Wiktionary are less common words that tend to also be less ambiguous.

5.2 Wiktionary Pruning Mistakes

The error analysis by Li et al. (2012) showed that the tags licensed by Wiktionary are often valid. When using Wiktionary to prune the search space of our constrained models and to filter token-level projections, it is also important that correct tags are not mistakenly pruned because they are missing from Wiktionary. While the accuracy of filtering is more difficult to study, due to the lack of a gold standard tagging of the bitext, Figure 5 (position 0 on the x-axis) shows that search space pruning errors are not a major issue for most languages; on average the pruning accuracy is almost 95%. However, for some languages such as Chinese and Czech the correct tag is pruned from the search space for nearly 10% of all tokens. When using Wiktionary as a pruner, the upper bound on accuracy for these languages is therefore only around 90%. However, Figure 5 also shows that with some manual effort we might be able to remedy many of these errors. For example, by adding missing valid tags to the 250 most common word types in the worst language, the minimum pruning accuracy would rise above 95% from below 90%. If the same was to be done for all of the studied languages, the mean pruning accuracy would reach over 97%.

Figure 6 breaks down pruning errors resulting from incorrect or incomplete Wiktionary entries across the correct POS tags. From this we observe that, for many languages, the pruning errors are highly skewed towards specific tags. For example, for Czech over 80% of the pruning errors are caused by mistakenly pruned pronouns.

6 Conclusions

We considered the problem of constructing multilingual POS taggers for resource-poor languages. To this end, we explored a number of different models that combine token constraints with type constraints from different sources. The best results were obtained with a partially observed CRF model that effectively integrates these complementary constraints. In an extensive empirical study, we showed that this approach substantially improves on the state of the art in this context. Our best model significantly outperformed the second-best model on 10 out of 15 evaluated languages, when trained on identical data sets, with an insignificant difference on 3 languages. Compared to the prior state of the art (Li et al., 2012), we observed a relative reduction in error by 25%, averaged over the eight languages common to our studies.

Acknowledgments

We thank Alexander Rush for help with the hypergraph framework that was used to implement our models and Klaus Macherey for help with the bitext extraction. This work benefited from many discussions with Yoav Goldberg, Keith Hall, Kuzman Ganchev and Hao Zhang. We also thank the editor and the three anonymous reviewers for their valuable feedback. The first author is grateful for the financial support from the Swedish National Graduate School of Language Technology (GSLT).

References

Anne Abeillé, Lionel Clément, and François Toussenel. 2003. Building a Treebank for French. In A. Abeillé, editor, *Treebanks: Building and Using Parsed Corpora*, chapter 10. Kluwer.

Taylor Berg-Kirkpatrick, Alexandre Bouchard-Côté, John DeNero, and Dan Klein. 2010. Painless unsupervised learning with features. In *Proceedings of NAACL-HLT*.

Sabine Buchholz and Erwin Marsi. 2006. CoNLL-X shared task on multilingual dependency parsing. In *Proceedings of CoNLL*.

Stanley F Chen. 2003. Conditional and joint models for grapheme-to-phoneme conversion. In *Proceedings of Eurospeech*.

Christos Christodoulopoulos, Sharon Goldwater, and Mark Steedman. 2010. Two decades of unsupervised POS induction: How far have we come? In *Proceedings of EMNLP*.

Dipanjan Das and Slav Petrov. 2011. Unsupervised part-of-speech tagging with bilingual graph-based projections. In *Proceedings of ACL-HLT*.

Arthur P. Dempster, Nan M. Laird, and Donald B. Rubin. 1977. Maximum likelihood from incomplete data via the EM algorithm. *Journal of the Royal Statistical Society, Series B*, 39.

John DeNero and Klaus Macherey. 2011. Model-based aligner combination using dual decomposition. In *Proceedings of ACL-HLT*.

Brad Efron and Robert J. Tibshirani. 1993. *An Introduction to the Bootstrap*. Chapman & Hall, New York, NY, USA.

Victoria Fossum and Steven Abney. 2005. Automatically inducing a part-of-speech tagger by projecting from multiple source languages across aligned corpora. In *Proceedings of IJCNLP*.

Dan Garrette and Jason Baldridge. 2012. Type-supervised hidden markov models for part-of-speech tagging with incomplete tag dictionaries. In *Proceedings of EMNLP-CoNLL*.

Yoav Goldberg, Meni Adler, and Michael Elhadad. 2008. EM can find pretty good HMM POS-taggers (when given a good start). In *Proceedings of ACL-HLT*.

Philipp Koehn. 2005. Europarl: A parallel corpus for statistical machine translation. In *MT Summit*.

John D. Lafferty, Andrew McCallum, and Fernando C. N. Pereira. 2001. Conditional random fields: Probabilistic models for segmenting and labeling sequence data. In *Proceedings of ICML*.

Shen Li, João Graça, and Ben Taskar. 2012. Wiki-ly supervised part-of-speech tagging. In *Proceedings of EMNLP-CoNLL*.

Dong C. Liu and Jorge Nocedal. 1989. On the limited memory BFGS method for large scale optimization. *Mathematical Programming*, 45.

Mitchell P. Marcus, Mary Ann Marcinkiewicz, and Beatrice Santorini. 1993. Building a large annotated corpus of English: the Penn treebank. *Computational Linguistics*, 19(2).

Tahira Naseem, Benjamin Snyder, Jacob Eisenstein, and Regina Barzilay. 2009. Multilingual part-of-speech tagging: Two unsupervised approaches. *JAIR*, 36.

Joakim Nivre, Johan Hall, Sandra Kübler, Ryan McDonald, Jens Nilsson, Sebastian Riedel, and Deniz Yuret. 2007. The CoNLL 2007 shared task on dependency parsing. In *Proceedings of EMNLP-CoNLL*.

Slav Petrov, Dipanjan Das, and Ryan McDonald. 2012. A universal part-of-speech tagset. In *Proceedings of LREC*.

Sujith Ravi and Kevin Knight. 2009. Minimized models for unsupervised part-of-speech tagging. In *Proceedings of ACL-IJCNLP*.

Stefan Riezler, Tracy H. King, Ronald M. Kaplan, Richard Crouch, John T. Maxwell, III, and Mark Johnson. 2002. Parsing the wall street journal using a lexical-functional grammar and discriminative estimation techniques. In *Proceedings of ACL*.

Noah Smith and Jason Eisner. 2005. Contrastive estimation: Training log-linear models on unlabeled data. In *Proceedings of ACL*.

Oscar Täckström, Ryan McDonald, and Jakob Uszkoreit. 2012. Cross-lingual word clusters for direct transfer of linguistic structure. In *Proceedings of NAACL-HLT*.

Joseph Turian, Lev-Arie Ratinov, and Yoshua Bengio. 2010. Word representations: A simple and general method for semi-supervised learning. In *Proceedings of ACL*.

UN. 2006. ODS UN parallel corpus.

Jakob Uszkoreit and Thorsten Brants. 2008. Distributed word clustering for large scale class-based language modeling in machine translation. In *Proceedings of ACL-HLT*.

Jakob Uszkoreit, Jay Ponte, Ashok Popat, and Moshe Dubiner. 2010. Large scale parallel document mining for machine translation. In *Proceedings of COLING*.

Chenhai Xi and Rebecca Hwa. 2005. A backoff model for bootstrapping resources for non-English languages. In *Proceedings of HLT-EMNLP*.

David Yarowsky and Grace Ngai. 2001. Inducing multilingual POS taggers and NP bracketers via robust projection across aligned corpora. In *Proceedings of NAACL*.

Finding Optimal 1-Endpoint-Crossing Trees

Emily Pitler, Sampath Kannan, Mitchell Marcus
Computer and Information Science
University of Pennsylvania
Philadelphia, PA 19104
epitler,kannan,mitch@seas.upenn.edu

Abstract

Dependency parsing algorithms capable of producing the types of crossing dependencies seen in natural language sentences have traditionally been orders of magnitude slower than algorithms for projective trees. For 95.8-99.8% of dependency parses in various natural language treebanks, whenever an edge is crossed, the edges that cross it all have a common vertex. The optimal dependency tree that satisfies this 1-Endpoint-Crossing property can be found with an $O(n^4)$ parsing algorithm that recursively combines forests over intervals with one exterior point. 1-Endpoint-Crossing trees also have natural connections to linguistics and another class of graphs that has been studied in NLP.

1 Introduction

Dependency parsing is one of the fundamental problems in natural language processing today, with applications such as machine translation (Ding and Palmer, 2005), information extraction (Culotta and Sorensen, 2004), and question answering (Cui et al., 2005). Most high-accuracy graph-based dependency parsers (Koo and Collins, 2010; Rush and Petrov, 2012; Zhang and McDonald, 2012) find the highest-scoring *projective* trees (in which no edges cross), despite the fact that a large proportion of natural language sentences are non-projective. Projective trees can be found in $O(n^3)$ time (Eisner, 2000), but cover only 63.6% of sentences in some natural language treebanks (Table 1).

The class of directed spanning trees covers all treebank trees and can be parsed in $O(n^2)$ with edge-based features (McDonald et al., 2005), but it is NP-hard to find the maximum scoring such tree with grandparent or sibling features (McDonald and Pereira, 2006; McDonald and Satta, 2007).

There are various existing definitions of mildly non-projective trees with better empirical coverage than projective trees that do not have the hardness of extensibility that spanning trees do. However, these have had parsing algorithms that are orders of magnitude slower than the projective case or the edge-based spanning tree case. For example, well-nested dependency trees with block degree 2 (Kuhlmann, 2013) cover at least 95.4% of natural language structures, but have a parsing time of $O(n^7)$ (Gómez-Rodríguez et al., 2011).

No previously defined class of trees simultaneously has high coverage and low-degree polynomial algorithms for parsing, allowing grandparent or sibling features.

We propose *1-Endpoint-Crossing* trees, in which for any edge that is crossed, all other edges that cross that edge share an endpoint. While simple to state, this property covers 95.8% or more of dependency parses in natural language treebanks (Table 1). The optimal 1-Endpoint-Crossing tree can be found in faster asymptotic time than any previously proposed mildly non-projective dependency parsing algorithm. We show how any 1-Endpoint-Crossing tree can be decomposed into isolated sets of intervals with one exterior point (Section 3). This is the key insight that allows efficient parsing; the $O(n^4)$ parsing algorithm is presented in Section 4. 1-Endpoint-Crossing trees are a subclass of 2-planar graphs (Section 5.1), a class that has been studied in NLP. 1-Endpoint-Crossing trees also have some linguistic interpretation (pairs of cross serial verbs produce 1-Endpoint-Crossing trees, Section 5.2).

2 Definitions of Non-Projectivity

Definition 1. *Edges e and f* cross *if e and f have distinct endpoints and exactly one of the endpoints of f lies between the endpoints of e.*

Definition 2. *A dependency tree is **1-Endpoint-Crossing** if for any edge e, all edges that cross e share an endpoint p.*

Table 1 shows the percentage of dependency parses in the CoNLL-X training sets that are 1-Endpoint-Crossing trees. Across six languages with varying amounts of non-projectivity, 95.8-99.8% of dependency parses in treebanks are 1-Endpoint-Crossing trees.[1]

We next review and compare other relevant definitions of non-projectivity from prior work: well-nested with block degree 2, gap-minding, projective, and 2-planar.

The definitions of block degree and well-nestedness are given below:

Definition 3. *For each node u in the tree, a* block *of the node is "a longest segment consisting of descendants of u." (Kuhlmann, 2013). The* block-degree *of u is "the number of distinct blocks of u". The block degree of a tree is the maximum block degree of any of its nodes. The* gap degree *is the number of gaps between these blocks, and so by definition is one less than the block degree. (Kuhlmann, 2013)*

Definition 4. *Two trees "T_1 and T_2* interleave *iff there are nodes l_1,$r_1 \in T_1$ and l_2,$r_2 \in T_2$ such that $l_1 < l_2 < r_1 < r_2$." A tree is* well-nested *if no two disjoint subtrees interleave. (Bodirsky et al., 2005)*

As can be seen in Table 1, 95.4%-99.9% of dependency parses across treebanks are both well-nested and have block degree 2. The optimal such tree can be found in $O(n^7)$ time and $O(n^5)$ space (Gómez-Rodríguez et al., 2011).

[1] Conventional edges from the artificial root node to the root(s) of the sentence reduce the empirical coverage of 1-Endpoint-Crossing trees. Excluding these artificial root edges, the empirical coverage for Dutch rises to 12949 (97.0%). These edges have no effect on the coverage of well-nested trees with block degree at most 2, gap-minding trees, or projective trees.

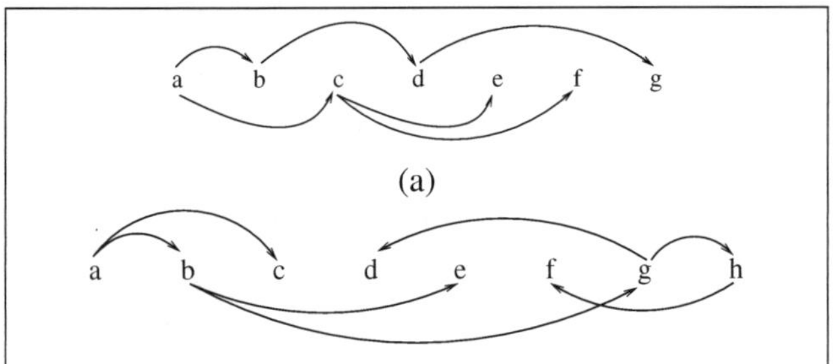

Figure 1: 1a is 1-Endpoint-Crossing, but is neither block degree 2 nor well-nested; 1b is gap-minding but not 2-planar.

Definition 5. *A tree is **gap-minding** if it is well-nested, has gap degree at most 1, and has* gap inheritance degree 0. Gap inheritance degree 0 *requires that there are no child nodes with descendants in more than one of their parent's blocks. (Pitler et al., 2012)*

Gap-minding trees can be parsed in $O(n^5)$ (Pitler et al., 2012). They have slightly less empirical coverage, however: 90.4-97.7% (Table 1).

Definition 6. *A tree is **projective** if it has block degree 1 (gap degree 0).*

This definition has the least coverage (as low as 63.6% for Dutch), but can be parsed in $O(n^3)$ (Eisner, 2000).

Definition 7. *A tree is **2-planar** if each edge can be drawn either above or below the sentence such that no edges cross (Gómez-Rodríguez and Nivre, 2010).*

Gómez-Rodríguez and Nivre (2010) presented a transition-based parser for 2-planar trees, but there is no known globally optimal parsing algorithm for 2-planar trees.

Clearly *projective $\subsetneq$ gap-minding $\subsetneq$ well-nested with block degree at most 2*. In Section 5.1, we prove the somewhat surprising fact that *1-Endpoint-Crossing $\subsetneq$ 2-planar*. These are two distinct hierarchies capturing different dimensions of non-projectivity: *1-Endpoint-Crossing $\not\subseteq$ well-nested with block degree 2* (Figure 1a), and *gap-minding $\not\subseteq$ 2-planar* (Figure 1b).

3 Edges (and their Crossing Point) Define Isolated Crossing Regions

We introduce notation to facilitate the discussion:

	Arabic	Czech	Danish	Dutch	Portuguese	Swedish	Parsing
1-Endpoint-Crossing	1457 (99.8)	71810 (98.8)	5144 (99.1)	12785 (95.8)	9007 (99.3)	10902 (98.7)	$O(n^4)$
Well-nested, block degree 2	1458 (99.9)	72321 (99.5)	5175 (99.7)	12896 (96.6)	8650 (95.4)	10955 (99.2)	$O(n^7)$
Gap-Minding	1394 (95.5)	70695 (97.2)	4985 (96.1)	12068 (90.4)	8481 (93.5)	10787 (97.7)	$O(n^5)$
Projective	1297 (88.8)	55872 (76.8)	4379 (84.4)	8484 (63.6)	7353 (81.1)	9963 (90.2)	$O(n^3)$
Sentences	1460	72703	5190	13349	9071	11042	

Table 1: Over 95% of the dependency parse trees in the CoNLL-X training sets are 1-Endpoint-Crossing trees. Coverage statistics and parsing times of previously proposed properties are shown for comparison.

Definition 8. *Within a 1-Endpoint-Crossing tree, the* **(crossing) pencil**[2] *of an edge e ($\mathcal{P}(e)$) is defined as the set of edges (sharing an endpoint) that cross e. The* **(crossing pencil) point** *of an edge e ($\mathcal{P}t(e)$) is defined as the endpoint that all edges in $\mathcal{P}(e)$ share.*

We will use e_{uv} to indicate an edge in either direction between u and v, i.e., either $u \rightarrow v$ or $u \leftarrow v$.

Before defining the parsing algorithm, we first give some intuition by analogy to parsing for projective trees. (This argument mirrors that of Eisner (2000, pps.38-39).) Projective trees can be produced using dynamic programming over *intervals*. Intervals are sufficient for projective trees: consider any edge e_{uv} in a projective tree.

The vertices in (u, v) must *only* have edges to vertices in $[u, v]$. If there were an edge between a vertex in (u, v) and a vertex outside $[u, v]$, such an edge would cross e_{uv}, which would contradict the assumption of projectivity. Thus every edge in a projective tree creates one interior interval isolated from the rest of the tree, allowing dynamic programming over intervals. We can analyze the case of 1-Endpoint-Crossing trees in a similar fashion:

Definition 9. *An* isolated interval *$[i, j]$ has no edges between the vertices in (i, j) and the vertices outside of $[i, j]$. An interval and one exterior vertex $[i, j] \cup \{x\}$ is called an* **isolated crossing region** *if the following two conditions are satisfied:*

1. *There are no edges between the vertices $\in (i, j)$ and vertices $\notin [i, j] \cup \{x\}$*
2. *None of the edges between x and vertices $\in (i, j)$ are crossed by any edges with both endpoints $\in (i, j)$*

[2]This notation comes from an analogy to geometry: "A set of distinct, coplanar, concurrent lines is a **pencil** of lines" (Ringenberg, 1967, p. 221); concurrent lines all intersect at the same single point.

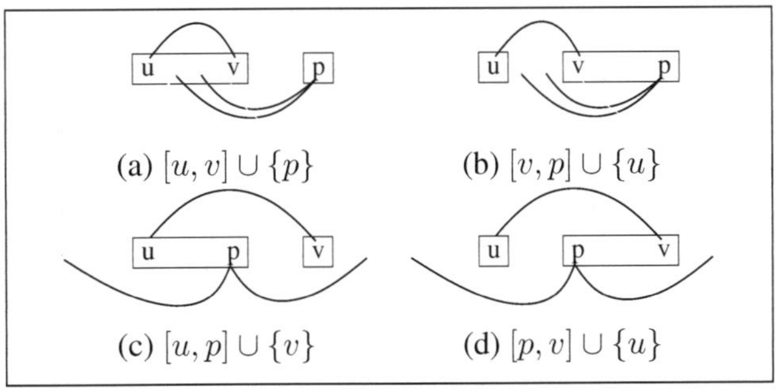

Figure 2: An edge e_{uv} and $\mathcal{P}t(e_{uv}) = p$ form two sets of isolated crossing regions (Lemma 1). 2a and 2b show $p \notin (u, v)$; 2c and 2d show $p \in (u, v)$.

Lemma 1. *Consider any edge e_{uv} and $\mathcal{P}t(e_{uv}) = p$ in a 1-Endpoint-Crossing forest F. Let l, r, and m denote the leftmost, rightmost, and middle point out of $\{u, v, p\}$, respectively. Then the three points u, v, and p define two isolated crossing regions: (1) $[l, m] \cup \{r\}$, and (2) $[m, r] \cup \{l\}$.*

Proof. First note that as $p = \mathcal{P}t(e_{uv})$, $\mathcal{P}(e_{uv})$ is non-empty: there must be at least one edge between vertices $\in (u, v)$ and vertices $\notin [u, v]$. p is either $\notin [u, v]$ (i.e., $p = l \vee p = r$) or $\in (u, v)$ (i.e., $p = m$):

Case 1: $\mathbf{p = l \vee p = r}$: Assume without loss of generality that $u < v < p$ (i.e., $p = r$).

(a) $[u, v] \cup \{p\}$ **is an isolated crossing region (Figure 2a)**: Condition 1: Assume for the sake of contradiction that there were an edge between a vertex $\in (u, v)$ and a vertex $\notin [u, v] \cup \{p\}$. Then such an edge would cross e_{uv} without having an endpoint at p, which contradicts the 1-Endpoint-Crossing property for e_{uv}.

Condition 2: Assume that for some e_{pa} such that $a \in (u, v)$, e_{pa} was crossed by an edge in the interior of (u, v). The interior edge would not share an endpoint with e_{uv}; since e_{uv} also crosses e_{pa}, this contradicts the 1-Endpoint-Crossing property for e_{pa}.

(b) $[v, p] \cup \{u\}$ **is an isolated crossing region (Figure 2b)**: Condition 1: Assume there were an edge e_{ab} with $a \in (v, p)$ and $b \notin [v, p] \cup \{u\}$. b cannot be in (u, v) (by above). Thus, $b \notin [u, p]$, which implies that e_{ab} crosses the edges in $\mathcal{P}(e_{uv})$; as e_{uv} does not share a vertex with e_{ab}, this contradicts the 1-Endpoint-Crossing property for all edges in $\mathcal{P}(e_{uv})$.

Condition 2: Assume that for some e_{ua} such that $a \in (v, p)$, e_{ua} was crossed by an edge in the interior of (v, p). e_{ua} would also be crossed by all the edges in $\mathcal{P}(e_{uv})$; as the interior edge would not share an endpoint with any of the edges in $\mathcal{P}(e_{uv})$, this would contradict the 1-Endpoint-Crossing property for e_{ua}.

Case 2: $\mathbf{p = m}$:

(a) $[u, p] \cup \{v\}$ **is an isolated crossing region (Figure 2c)**: Condition 1: Assume there were an edge e_{ab} with $a \in (u, p)$ and $b \notin [u, p] \cup \{v\}$ $(b \in (p, v) \vee b \notin [u, v])$. First assume $b \in (p, v)$. Then e_{ab} crosses all edges in $\mathcal{P}(e_{uv})$; as e_{ab} does not share an endpoint with e_{uv}, this contradicts the 1-Endpoint-Crossing property for the edges in $\mathcal{P}(e_{uv})$. Next assume $b \notin [u, v]$. Then e_{ab} crosses e_{uv}; since $a \neq p \wedge b \neq p$, this violates the 1-Endpoint-Crossing property for e_{uv}.

Condition 2: Assume that for some e_{va} with $a \in (u, p)$, e_{va} was crossed by an edge in the interior of (u, v). e_{va} is also crossed by all the edges in $\mathcal{P}(e_{uv})$; as the interior edge will not share an endpoint with the edges in $\mathcal{P}(e_{uv})$, this contradicts the 1-Endpoint-Crossing property for e_{va}.

(b) $[p, v] \cup \{u\}$ **is an isolated crossing region (Figure 2d)**: Symmetric to the above.

□

4 Parsing Algorithm

The optimal 1-Endpoint-Crossing tree can be found using a dynamic programming algorithm that exploits the fact that edges and their crossing points define intervals and isolated crossing regions. This section assumes an arc-factored model, in which the score of a tree is defined as the sum of the scores of its edges; scoring functions for edges are generally learned from data.

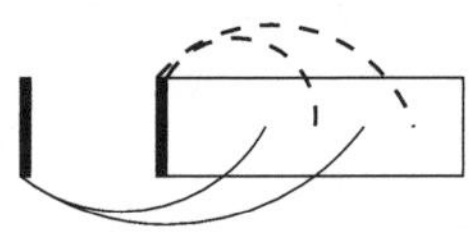

(a) Only edges incident to the **L**eft point of the interval may cross the edges from the exterior point

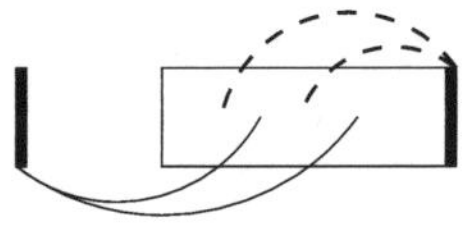

(b) Only edges incident to the **R**ight point of the interval may cross the edges from the exterior point

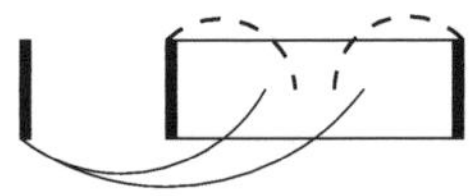

(c) both (**LR**)

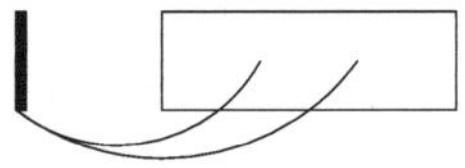

(d) **N**either

Figure 3: Isolated crossing region sub-problems.

The dynamic program uses five types of sub-problems: interval sub-problems for each interval $[i, j]$, denoted $Int[i, j]$, and four types of isolated crossing region sub-problems for each interval and exterior point $[i, j] \cup \{x\}$, which differ in whether edges from the exterior point may be crossed by edges with an endpoint at the **L**eft point of the interval, the **R**ight point, both **LR**, or **N**either (Figure 3). $L[i, j, x]$, for example, refers to an isolated crossing region over the interval $[i, j]$ with an exterior point of x, in which edges incident to i (the left boundary point) can cross edges between x and (i, j).

These distinctions allow the 1-Endpoint-Crossing property to be globally enforced; crossing edges in one region may constrain edges in another. For example, consider that Figure 2a allows edges with an endpoint at v to cross the edges from p, while Figure 2b allows edges from u into (v, p). Both *simultaneously* would cause a 1-Endpoint-Crossing violation for the edges in $\mathcal{P}(e_{uv})$. Figures 4 and 5 show valid combinations of the sub-problems in Figure 3.

The full dynamic program is shown in Appendix A. The final answer must be a valid dependency tree, which requires each word to have exactly one parent and prohibits cycles. We use booleans (b_i, b_j, b_x) for each sub-problem, in which the boolean is set to true if and only if the solution to the sub-problem must contain the incoming (parent) edge for the corresponding boundary point. We use the suffix *AFromB* for a sub-problem to enforce that a boundary point A must be descended from boundary point B (to avoid cycles). We will occasionally mention these issues,

(a) If $l \in (k, j]$:

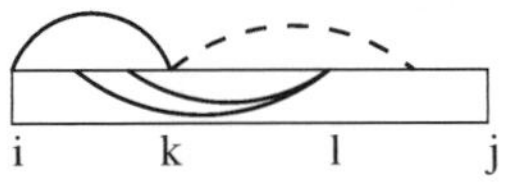

(i) **If the dashed edge exists**:
All the edges from l into (i, k) must choose k as their $\mathcal{P}t$. The interval decomposes into $S[e_{ik}] + R[i, k, l] + Int[k, l] + L[l, j, k]$:

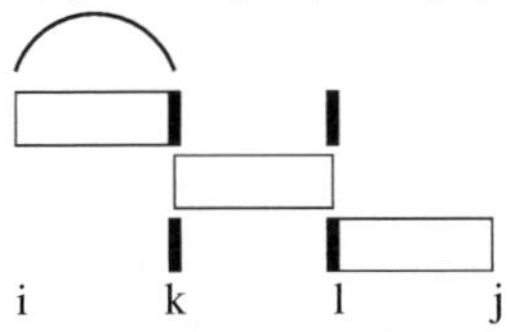

(ii) **If no edges like the dashed edge exist**:
All edges from l into (i, k) may choose either i or k as their $\mathcal{P}t$. The interval decomposes into $S[e_{ik}] + LR[i, k, l] + Int[k, l] + Int[l, j]$:

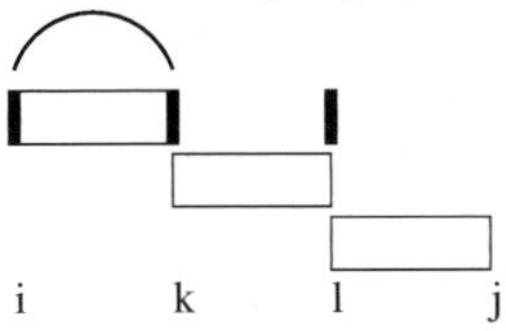

(b) If $l \in (i, k)$:

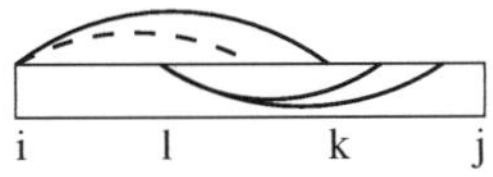

(i) **If dashed edge exists**: All the edges from l into $(k, j]$ must choose i as their $\mathcal{P}t$. The interval decomposes into $S[e_{ik}] + Int[i, l] + L[l, k, i] + N[k, j, l]$:

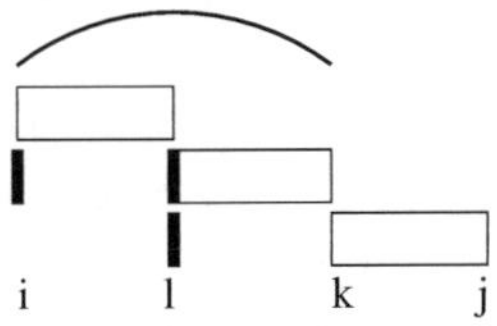

(ii) **If no edges like the dashed edge exist**: All edges from l may choose k as their $\mathcal{P}t$. The interval decomposes into $S[e_{ik}] + R[i, l, k] + Int[l, k] + L[k, j, l]$:

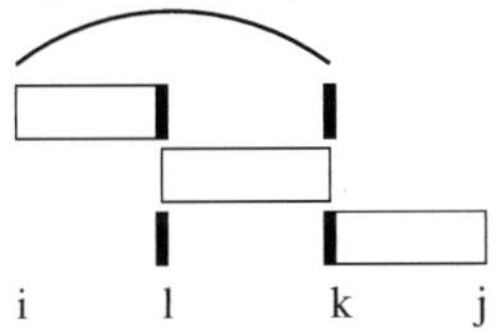

Figure 4: Decomposing an $Int[i, j]$ sub-problem, with $\mathcal{P}t(e_{ik}) = l$

but for simplicity focus the discussion on the decomposition into crossing regions and the maintenance of the 1-Endpoint-Crossing property. Edge direction does not affect these points of focus, and so we will refer simply to $S[e_{uv}]$ to mean the score of either the edge from u to v or vice-versa.

In the following subsections, we show that the optimal parse for each type of sub-problem can be decomposed into smaller valid sub-problems. If we take the maximum over all these possible combinations of smaller solutions, we can find the maximum scoring parse for that sub-problem. Note that the overall tree is a valid sub-problem (over the interval $[0, n]$), so the argument will also hold for finding the optimal overall tree. Each individual vertex and each pair of adjacent vertices (with no edges) trivially form isolated intervals (as there is no interior); this forms the base case of the dynamic program.

The overall dynamic program takes $O(n^4)$ time: there are $O(n^2)$ interval sub-problems, each of which needs two free split points to find the maximum, and $O(n^3)$ region sub-problems, each of which is a maximization over one free split point.

4.1 Decomposing an Int sub-problem

Consider an isolated interval sub-problem $Int[i, j]$. There are three cases: (1) there are no edges between i and the rest of the interval, (2) the longest edge incident to i is not crossed, (3) the longest edge incident to i is crossed. An Int sub-problem can be decomposed into smaller valid sub-problems in each of these three cases. Finding the optimal Int forest can be done by taking the maximum over these cases:

No edges between i and $[i + 1, j]$: The same set of edges is also a valid $Int[i + 1, j]$ sub-problem. b_i must be true for the $Int[i + 1, j]$ sub-problem to ensure $i + 1$ receives a parent.

Furthest edge from i is not crossed: If the furthest edge is to j, the problem can be decomposed into $S[e_{ij}] + Int[i, j]$, as that edge has no effect on the interior of the interval. Clearly, this is only applicable if the boundary point needed a parent (as indicated by the booleans) and the boolean must then be updated accordingly. If the furthest edge is to some k in (i, j), the problem is decomposed into $S[e_{ik}] + Int[i, k] + Int[k, j]$.

Furthest edge from i is crossed: This is the most

interesting case, which uses two split points: the other endpoint of the edge (k), and $l = \mathcal{P}t(e_{ik})$. The dynamic program depends on the order of k and l.

$\mathbf{l \notin (i, k)}$ **(Figure 4a)**: By Lemma 1, $[i, k] \cup \{l\}$ and $[k, l] \cup \{i\}$ form isolated regions. $(l, j]$ is the remainder of the interval, and the only vertex from $[i, l)$ that can have edges into $(l, j]$ is k: (i, k) and (k, l) are part of isolated regions, and i is ruled out because k was i's furthest neighbor.

If at least one edge from k into $(l, j]$ (the dashed line in Figure 4a) exists, the decomposition is as in Figure 4a, Case i; otherwise, it is as in Figure 4a, Case ii. In Case i, e_{ik} and the edge(s) between k and $(l, j]$ force all of the edges between l and (i, k) to have k as their $\mathcal{P}t$. Thus, the region $[i, k] \cup \{l\}$ must be a sub-problem of type R (Figure 3b), as these edges from l can only be crossed by edges with an endpoint at k (the right endpoint of $[i, k]$). All of the edges between k and $(l, j]$ have l as their $\mathcal{P}t$, as they are crossed by all the edges in $\mathcal{P}(e_{ik})$, and so the sub-problem corresponding to the region $[l, j] \cup \{k\}$ is of type L (Figure 3a). In Case ii, each of the edges in $\mathcal{P}(e_{ik})$ may choose either i or k as their $\mathcal{P}t$, so the sub-problem $[i, k] \cup \{l\}$ is of type LR (Figure 3c). Note that $l = j$ is a special case of Case ii in which the rightmost interval $Int[l, j]$ is empty.

$\mathbf{l \in (i, k)}$ **(Figure 4b)**: $[i, l] \cup \{k\}$ and $[l, k] \cup \{i\}$ form isolated crossing regions by Lemma 1. There cannot both be edges between i and (l, k) and between k and (i, l), as this would violate 1-Endpoint-Crossing for the edges in $\mathcal{P}(e_{ik})$. If there are *any* edges between i and (l, k) (i.e., Case i in Figure 4b), then all of the edges in $\mathcal{P}(e_{ik})$ must choose i as their $\mathcal{P}t$, and so these edges cannot be crossed at all in the region $[k, j] \cup \{l\}$, and there cannot be any edges from k into (i, l). If there are no such edges (Case ii in 4b), then k must be a valid $\mathcal{P}t$ for all edges in $\mathcal{P}(e_{ik})$, and so there can both be edges from k into (i, l) and $[k, j] \cup \{l\}$ may be of type L (allowing crossings with an endpoint at k).

4.2 Decomposing an LR sub-problem

An LR sub-problem is over an isolated crossing region $[i, j] \cup \{x\}$, such that edges from x into (i, j) may be crossed by edges with an endpoint at either i or j. This sub-problem is only defined when neither i nor j get their parent from this sub-problem. From a top-down perspective, this case is only used when there will be an edge between i and j (as in one of the sub-problems in Figure 4a, Case ii).

If none of the edges from x are crossed by any edges with an endpoint at i, this can be considered an R problem. Similarly, if none are crossed by any edges with an endpoint at j, this may be considered an L sub-problem. The only case which needs discussion is when both edges with an endpoint at i and also at j cross edges from x; see Figure 3c for a schematic. In that scenario, there must exist a split point such that: (1) to the left of the point, all edges crossing x-edges have an endpoint at i, and to the right of the point, all such edges have an endpoint at j, and (2) no edges in the region cross the split point.

Let r_i be i's rightmost child in (i, j); let l_j be j's leftmost child in (i, j). Every edge from x into (i, r_i) is crossed by e_{ir_i}; every edge between x and (l_j, j) is crossed by $e_{l_j j}$. e_{ir_i} cannot cross $e_{l_j j}$, as that would either violate 1-Endpoint-Crossing (because of the x-interior edges) or create a cycle (if both children are also connected by an edge to x). r_i and l_j also cannot be equal: as neither i nor j may be assigned a parent, they must both be in the direction of the child, and the child cannot have multiple parents. Thus, r_i is to the left of l_j.

Any split point between r_i and l_j clearly satisfies (1). There is at least one point within $[r_i, l_j]$ that satisfies (2) as long as there is not a chain of crossing edges from e_{ir_i} to $e_{l_j j}$. The proof is omitted for space reasons, but such a chain can be ruled out using a counting argument similar to that in the proof in Section 5.1. The decomposition is: $L[i, k, x] + R[k, j, x]$ for some $k \in (i, j)$.

4.3 Decomposing an N sub-problem

Consider the maximum scoring forest of type N over $[i, j] \cup \{x\}$ (Figure 3d; *no* edges from x are crossed in this sub-problem). If there are no edges from x, then it is also a valid $Int[i, j]$ sub-problem. If there are edges between x and the endpoints i or j, then the forest with that edge removed is still a valid N sub-problem (with the ancestor and parent book-keeping updated). Otherwise, if there are edges between x and (i, j), choose the neighbor of x closest to j (call it k). Since the edge e_{xk} is not crossed, there are no edges from $[i, k)$ into $(k, j]$; since k was the neighbor of x closest to j, there are no edges from x into $(k, j]$. Thus, the region decomposes into

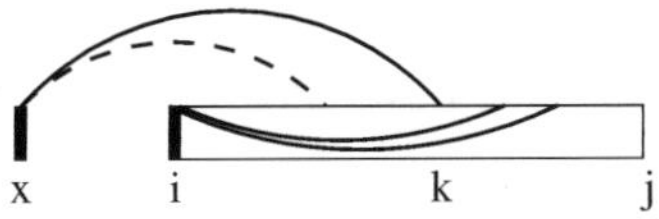

(i) **If dashed edge exists**: All the edges from i into $(k, j]$ must choose x as their $\mathcal{P}t$. The interval decomposes into $S[e_{xk}] + L[i, k, x] + N[k, j, i]$:

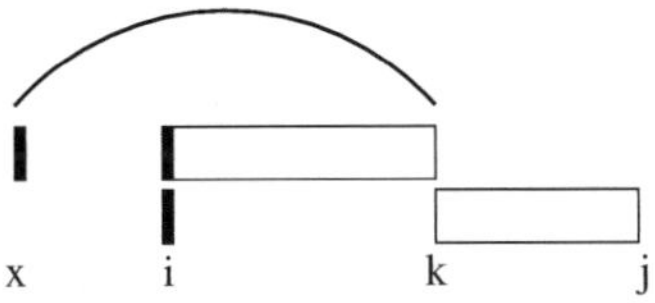

(ii) **If no edges like the dashed edge exist**: Edges from i into $(k, j]$ may choose k as their $\mathcal{P}t$. The interval decomposes into $S[e_{xk}] + Int[i, k] + L[k, j, i]$:

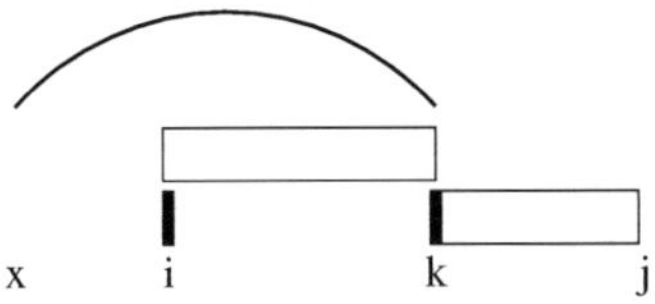

Figure 5: An L sub-problem over $[i, j] \cup \{x\}$, k is the neighbor of x furthest from i in the interval.

$S[e_{ik}] + Int[k, j] + N[i, k, x]$.

As an aside, if b_x was true (x needed a parent from this sub-problem), and k was a child of x, then x's parent must come from the $[i, k] \cup \{x\}$ sub-problem. However, it cannot be a descendant of k, as that would cause a cycle. Thus in this case, we call the sub-problem a N_XFromI problem, to indicate that x needs a parent, i and k do not, and x must be descended from i, not k.

4.4 Decomposing an L or R sub-problem

An L sub-problem over $[i, j] \cup \{x\}$ requires that any edges in this region that cross an edge with an endpoint at x have an endpoint at i (the *left* endpoint). If there are no edges between x and $[i, j]$ in an L sub-problem, then it is also a valid Int sub-problem over $[i, j]$. If there are edges between x and i or j, then the sub-problem can be decomposed into that edge plus the rest of the forest with that edge removed.

The interesting case is when there are edges between x and the interior (Figure 5). Let k be the neighbor of x within (i, j) that is furthest from i. As all edges that cross e_{xk} will have an endpoint at i, there are no edges between (i, k) and $(k, j]$. Combined with the fact that k was the neighbor of x closest to j, we have that $[i, k] \cup \{x\}$ must form an isolated crossing region, as must $[k, j] \cup \{i\}$.

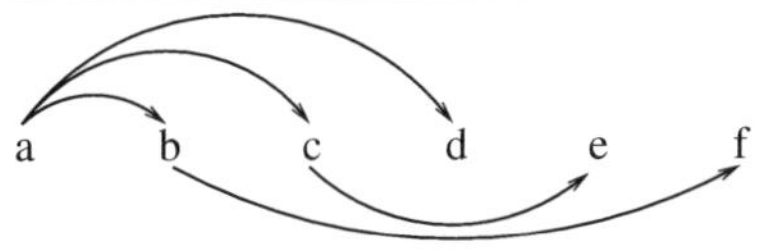

Figure 6: 2-planar but not 1-Endpoint-Crossing

If there are additional edges between x and the interior (Case i in 5), all of the edges from i into $(k, j]$ cross both the edge e_{xk} and the other edges from x into (i, k). The $\mathcal{P}t$ for all these edges must therefore be x, and as x is not in the region $[k, j] \cup \{i\}$, those edges cannot be crossed at all in that region (i.e., $[k, j] \cup \{i\}$ must be of type N). If there are no additional edges from x into (i, k) (Case ii in Figure 5), then all of the edges from i into (k, j) must choose either x or k as their $\mathcal{P}t$. As there will be no more edges from x, choosing k as their $\mathcal{P}t$ allows strictly more trees, and so $[k, j] \cup \{i\}$ can be of type L (allowing edges from i to be crossed in that region by edges with an endpoint at k).

An R sub-problem is identical, with k instead chosen to be the neighbor of x furthest from j.

5 Connections

5.1 Graph Theory: All 1-Endpoint-Crossing Trees are 2-Planar

The 2-planar characterization of dependency structures in Gómez-Rodríguez and Nivre (2010) exactly correspond to *2-page book embeddings* in graph theory: an embedding of the vertices in a graph onto a line (by analogy, along the *spine* of a book), and the edges of the graph onto one of 2 (more generally, k) half-planes (*pages* of the book) such that no edges on the same page cross (Bernhart and Kainen, 1979). The problem of finding an embedding that minimizes the number of pages required is a natural formulation of many problems arising in disparate areas of computer science, for example, sorting a sequence using the minimum number of stacks (Even and Itai, 1971), or constructing fault-tolerant layouts in VLSI design (Chung et al., 1987).

In this section we prove *1-Endpoint-Crossing* $\subseteq$ *2-planar*. These classes are not equal (Figure 6). We first prove some properties about the *crossings graphs* (Gómez-Rodríguez and Nivre, 2010) of 1-Endpoint-Crossing trees. The crossings graph of a

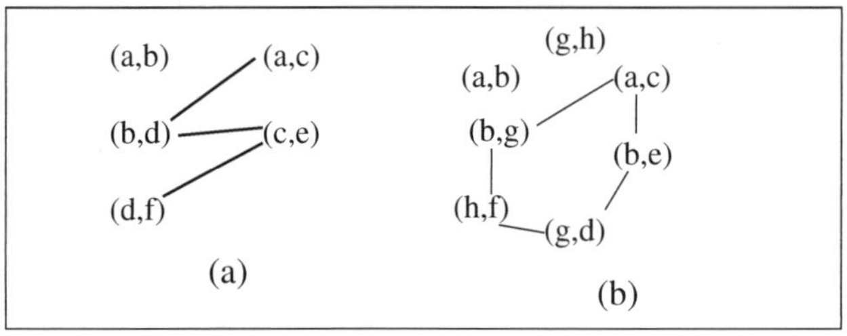

Figure 7: The crossing graphs for Figures 1a and 1b.

graph has a vertex corresponding to each edge in the original, and an edge between two vertices if the two edges they correspond to cross. The crossings graphs for the dependency trees in Figures 1a and 1b are shown in Figures 7a and 7b, respectively.

Lemma 2. *No 1-Endpoint-Crossing tree has a cycle of length* 3 *in its crossings graph.*

Proof. Assume there existed a cycle e_1, e_2, e_3. e_1 and e_3 must share an endpoint, as they both cross e_2. Since e_1 and e_3 share an endpoint, e_1 and e_3 do not cross. Contradiction. □

Lemma 3. *Any odd cycle of size* n $(n \geq 4)$ *in a crossings graph of a 1-Endpoint-Crossing tree uses at most* n *distinct vertices in the original graph.*

Proof. Let e_1, e_2, ..., e_n be an odd cycle in a crossings graph of a 1-Endpoint-Crossing tree with $n \geq 4$. Since $n \geq 4$, e_1, e_2, e_{n-1}, and e_n are distinct edges. Let a be the vertex that e_1 and e_{n-1} share (because they both cross e_n) and let b be the vertex that e_2 and e_n share (both cross e_1). Note that e_1 and e_{n-1} cannot contain b and that e_2 and e_n cannot contain a (otherwise they would not cross an edge adjacent to them along the cycle).

We will now consider how many vertices each edge can introduce that are distinct from all vertices previously seen in the cycle. e_1 and e_2 necessarily introduce two distinct vertices each.

Let e_o be the first odd edge that contains b (we know one exists since e_n contains b). (o is at least 3, since e_1 does not contain b.) e_o's other vertex must be the one shared with e_{o-2} (e_{o-2} does not contain b, since e_o was the first odd edge to contain b). Therefore, both of e_o's vertices have already been seen along the cycle.

Similarly, let e_e be the first even edge that contains an a. By the same reasoning, e_e must not introduce any new vertices.

All other edges e_i such that $i > 2$ and $e_i \neq e_o$ and $e_i \neq e_e$ introduce at most one new vertex, since one must be shared with the edge e_{i-2}. There are $n - 4$ such edges.

Counting up all possibilities, the maximum number of distinct vertices is $4 + (n - 4) = n$. □

Theorem 1. *1-Endpoint-Crossing trees* $\subseteq$ *2-planar.*

Proof. Assume there existed an odd cycle in the crossings graph of a 1-Endpoint-Crossing tree. The cycle has size at least 5 (by Lemma 2). There are at least as many edges as vertices in the subgraph of the forest induced by the vertices used in the cycle (by Lemma 3). That implies the existence of a cycle in the original graph, contradicting that the original graph was a tree.

Since there are no odd cycles in the crossings graph, the crossings graph of edges is bipartite. Each side of the bipartite graph can be assigned to a page, such that no two edges on the same page cross. Therefore, the original graph was 2-planar. □

5.2 Linguistics: Cross-serial Verb Constructions and Successive Cyclicity

Cross-serial verb constructions were used to provide evidence for the "non-context-freeness" of natural language (Shieber, 1985). Cross-serial verb constructions with two verbs form 1-Endpoint-Crossing trees. Below is a cross-serial sentence from Swiss-German, from (1) in Shieber (1985):

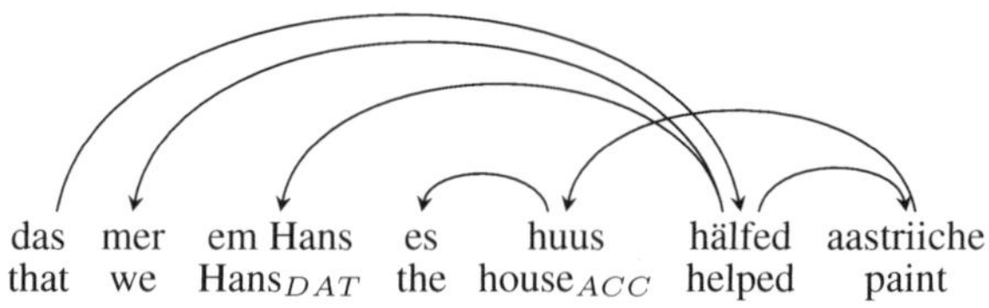

The edges $(\textit{that}, \textit{helped})$, $(\textit{helped}, \textit{we})$, and $(\textit{helped}, \textit{Hans})$ are each only crossed by an edge with an endpoint at *paint*; the edge $(\textit{paint}, \textit{house})$ is only crossed by edges with an endpoint at *helped*. More generally, with a set of two cross serial verbs in a subordinate clause, each verb should suffice as the crossing point for all edges incident to the other verb that are crossed.

Cross-serial constructions with three or more verbs would have dependency trees that violate 1-

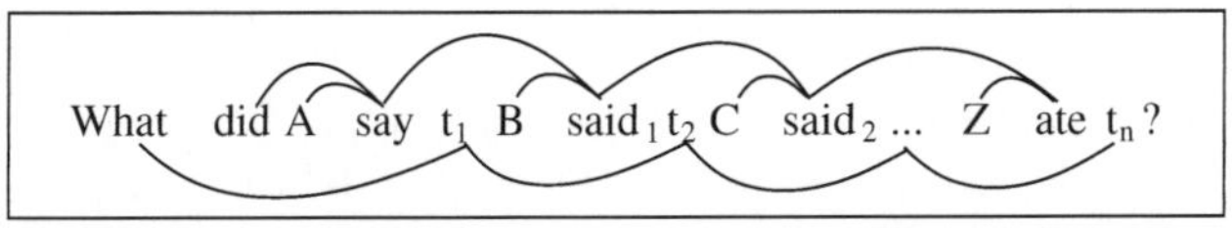

Figure 8: An example of *wh-movement* over a potentially unbounded number of clauses. The edges between the heads of each clause cross the edges from trace to trace, but all obey 1-Endpoint-Crossing.

Endpoint-Crossing. Psycholinguistically, between two and three verbs is exactly where there is a large change in the sentence processing abilities of *human* listeners (based on both grammatical judgments and scores on a comprehension task) (Bach et al., 1986).

More speculatively, there may be a connection between the form of 1-Endpoint-Crossing trees and *phases* (roughly, propositional units such as clauses) in Minimalism (Chomsky et al., 1998). Figure 8 shows an example of *wh-movement* over a potentially unbounded number of clauses. The *phase-impenetrability condition* (PIC) states that only the head of the phase and elements that have moved to its edge are accessible to the rest of the sentence (Chomsky et al., 1998, p.22). Movement is therefore required to be *successive cyclic*, with a moved element leaving a *chain* of traces at the edge of each clause on its way to its final pronounced location (Chomsky, 1981). In Figure 8, notice that the crossing edges form a repeated pattern that obeys the 1-Endpoint-Crossing property. More generally, we suspect that trees satisfying the PIC will tend to also be 1-Endpoint-Crossing. Furthermore, if the traces were *not* at the edge of each clause, and instead were positioned between a head and one of its arguments, 1-Endpoint-Crossing would be violated. For example, if t_2 in Figure 8 were between *C* and *said*$_2$, then the edge (t_1, t_2) would cross $(say, said_1)$, $(said_1, said_2)$, and $(C, said_2)$, which do not all share an endpoint. An exploration of these linguistic connections may be an interesting avenue for further research.

6 Conclusions

1-Endpoint-Crossing trees characterize over 95% of structures found in natural language treebank, and can be parsed in only a factor of n more time than projective trees. The dynamic programming algorithm for projective trees (Eisner, 2000) has been extended to handle higher order factors (McDonald and Pereira, 2006; Carreras, 2007; Koo and Collins, 2010), adding at most a factor of n to the edge-based running time; it would be interesting to extend the algorithm presented here to include higher order factors. 1-Endpoint-Crossing is a condition on *edges*, while properties such as well-nestedness or block degree are framed in terms of *subtrees*. Three edges will always suffice as a certificate of a 1-Endpoint-Crossing violation (two vertex-disjoint edges that both cross a third). In contrast, for a property like ill-nestedness, two nodes might have a least common ancestor arbitrarily far away, and so one might need the entire graph to verify whether the sub-trees rooted at those nodes are disjoint and ill-nested. We have discussed cross-serial dependencies; a further exploration of which linguistic phenomena would and would not have 1-Endpoint-Crossing dependency trees may be revealing.

Acknowledgments

We would like to thank Julie Legate for an interesting discussion. This material is based upon work supported under a National Science Foundation Graduate Research Fellowship, NSF Award CCF 1137084, and Army Research Office MURI grant W911NF-07-1-0216.

A Dynamic Program to find the maximum scoring 1-Endpoint-Crossing Tree

Input: Matrix S: $S[i, j]$ is the score of the directed edge (i, j)
Output: Maximum score of a 1-Endpoint-Crossing tree over vertices $[0, n]$, rooted at 0
Init: $\forall i \quad Int[i, i, F, F] = Int[i, i+1, F, F] = 0$
$Int[i, i, T, F] = Int[i, i, F, T] = Int[i, i, T, T] = -\infty$
Final: $Int[0, n, F, T]$
Shorthand for booleans: $\mathcal{TF}(x, S) :=$
  if $x = T$, exactly one of the set S is true
  if $x = F$, all of the set S must be false
b_i, b_j, b_x are true iff the corresponding boundary point has its incoming edge (parent) in that sub-problem. For the LR sub-problem, b_i and b_j are always false, and so omitted. For all sub-problems with the suffix $AFromB$, the boundary point A has its parent edge in the sub-problem solution; the other two boundary points do not. For example, L_XFromI would correspond to having booleans $b_i = b_j = F$ and $b_x = T$, with the restriction that x must be a descendant of i.

$$
Int[i,j,F,b_j] \leftarrow \max
\begin{cases}
Int[i+1,j,T,F] & \text{if } b_j = F \\
S[i,j] + Int[i,j,F,F] & \text{if } b_j = T \\
\max\limits_{k \in (i,j)} S[i,k] + \\
\quad \begin{cases}
Int[i,k,F,F] + Int[k,j,F,b_j] \\
\max\limits_{\mathcal{TF}(b_j,\{b_l,b_r\})} LR[i,k,j,b_l] + Int[k,j,F,b_r] \\
\max_{l \in (k,j), \mathcal{TF}(T,\{b_l,b_m,b_r\})} \\
\quad \begin{cases}
R[i,k,l,F,F,b_l] + Int[k,l,F,b_m] + L[l,j,k,b_r,b_j,F] \\
LR[i,k,l,b_l] + Int[k,l,F,b_m] + Int[l,j,b_r,b_j]
\end{cases} \\
\max_{l \in (i,k), \mathcal{TF}(T,\{b_l,b_m,b_r\})} \\
\quad \begin{cases}
Int[i,l,F,b_l] + L[l,k,i,b_m,F,F] + N[k,j,l,F,b_j,b_r] \\
R[i,l,k,F,b_l,F] + Int[l,k,b_m,F] + L[k,j,l,F,b_j,b_r]
\end{cases}
\end{cases}
\end{cases}
$$

$Int[i,j,T,F] \leftarrow$ symmetric to $Int[i,j,F,T]$
$Int[i,j,T,T] \leftarrow -\infty$

$$
LR[i,j,x,b_x] \leftarrow \max
\begin{cases}
L[i,j,x,F,F,b_x] \\
R[i,j,x,F,F,b_x] \\
\max_{k \in (i,j), \mathcal{TF}(b_x,\{b_{xl},b_{xr}\}), \mathcal{TF}(T,\{b_{kl},b_{kr}\})} \\
\quad L[i,k,x,F,b_{kl},b_{xl}] + R[k,j,x,b_{kr},F,b_{xr}]
\end{cases}
$$

$$
N[i,j,x,b_i,b_j,F] \leftarrow \max
\begin{cases}
Int[i,j,b_i,b_j] \\
S[x,i] + N[i,j,x,F,b_j,F] & \text{if } b_i = T \\
S[x,j] + N[i,j,x,b_i,F,F] & \text{if } b_j = T \\
\max\limits_{k \in (i,j)} S[x,k] + N[i,k,x,b_i,F,F] + Int[k,j,F,b_j]
\end{cases}
$$

$$
N[i,j,x,F,b_j,T] \leftarrow \max
\begin{cases}
S[i,x] + N[i,j,x,F,b_j,F] \\
S[x,j] + N\_XFromI[i,j,x] & \text{if } b_j = T \\
S[j,x] + N[i,j,x,F,F,F] & \text{if } b_j = F \\
S[j,x] + Int[i,j,F,T] & \text{if } b_j = T \\
\max\limits_{k \in (i,j)} S[x,k] + N\_XFromI[i,k,x] + Int[k,j,F,b_j] \\
\max\limits_{k \in (i,j)} S[k,x] + \\
\quad \begin{cases}
Int[i,k,F,T] + Int[k,j,F,b_j] \\
N[i,k,x,F,F,F] + Int[k,j,T,b_j]
\end{cases}
\end{cases}
$$

$N[i,j,x,T,F,T] \leftarrow$ symmetric to $N[i,j,x,F,T,T]$
$N[i,j,x,T,T,T] \leftarrow -\infty$

$$
N\_XFromI[i,j,x] \leftarrow \max
\begin{cases}
S[i,x] + N[i,j,x,F,F,F] \\
\max_{k \in (i,j)} \\
\quad \begin{cases}
S[x,k] + N\_XFromI[i,k,x] + Int[k,j,F,F] \\
S[k,x] + Int[i,k,F,T] + Int[k,j,F,F]
\end{cases}
\end{cases}
$$

$$
N\_IFromX[i,j,x] \leftarrow \max
\begin{cases}
S[x,i] + N[i,j,x,F,F,F] \\
\max\limits_{k \in (i,j)} S[x,k] + N[i,k,x,T,F,F] + Int[k,j,F,F]
\end{cases}
$$

$N\_XFromJ[i,j,x] \leftarrow$ symmetric to $N\_XFromI[i,j,x]$
$N\_JFromX[i,j,x] \leftarrow$ symmetric to $N\_IFromX[i,j,x]$

$$
L[i,j,x,b_i,b_j,F] \leftarrow \max
\begin{cases}
Int[i,j,b_i,b_j] \\
S[x,i] + L[i,j,x,F,b_j,F] & \text{if } b_i = T \\
S[x,j] + L[i,j,x,b_i,F,F] & \text{if } b_j = T \\
\max\limits_{k \in (i,j), \mathcal{TF}(b_i,\{b_l,b_r\})} S[x,k] + \\
\quad \begin{cases}
L[i,k,x,b_l,F,F] + N[k,j,i,F,b_j,b_r] \\
Int[i,k,b_l,F] + L[k,j,i,F,b_j,b_r]
\end{cases}
\end{cases}
$$

$$
L[i,j,x,F,b_j,T] \leftarrow \max
\begin{cases}
S[i,x] + L[i,j,x,F,b_j,F] \\
S[x,j] + L\_XFromI[i,j,x] & \text{if } b_j = T \\
S[j,x] + L[i,j,x,F,F,F] & \text{if } b_j = F \\
S[j,x] + L\_JFromI[i,j,x] & \text{if } b_j = T \\
\max\limits_{k \in (i,j)} S[x,k] + L\_XFromI[i,k,x] + N[k,j,i,F,b_j,F] \\
\max\limits_{k \in (i,j)} S[k,x] + \\
\quad \begin{cases}
L\_JFromI[i,k,x] + N[k,j,i,F,b_j,F] \\
L[i,k,x,F,F,F] + N[k,j,i,T,b_j,F] \\
\max\limits_{\mathcal{TF}(T,\{b_l,b_r\})} Int[i,k,F,b_l] + L[k,j,i,b_r,b_j,F]
\end{cases}
\end{cases}
$$

$L[i,j,x,T,b_j,T] \leftarrow$ not reachable

$$
L\_XFromI[i,j,x] \leftarrow \max
\begin{cases}
S[i,x] + L[i,j,x,F,F,F] \\
\max\limits_{k \in (i,j)} S[x,k] + L\_XFromI[i,k,x] + N[k,j,i,F,F,F] \\
\max\limits_{k \in (i,j)} S[k,x] + \\
\quad \begin{cases}
L\_JFromI[i,k,x] + N[k,j,i,F,F,F] \\
L[i,k,x,F,F,F] + N\_IFromX[k,j,i] \\
Int[i,k,F,T] + L[k,j,i,F,F,F] \\
Int[i,k,F,F] + L\_IFromX[k,j,i]
\end{cases}
\end{cases}
$$

$$
L\_IFromX[i,j,x] \leftarrow \max
\begin{cases}
S[x,i] + L[i,j,x,F,F,F] \\
\max\limits_{k \in (i,j)} S[x,k] + \\
\quad \begin{cases}
L[i,k,x,T,F,F] + N[k,j,i,F,F,F] \\
L[i,k,x,F,F,F] + N\_XFromI[k,j,i] \\
Int[i,k,T,F] + L[k,j,i,F,F,F] \\
Int[i,k,F,F] + L\_XFromI[k,j,i]
\end{cases}
\end{cases}
$$

$$
L\_JFromX[i,j,x] \leftarrow \max
\begin{cases}
S[x,j] + L[i,j,x,F,F,F] \\
\max\limits_{k \in (i,j)} S[x,k] + \\
\quad \begin{cases}
L[i,k,x,F,F,F] + Int[k,j,F,T] \\
Int[i,k,F,F] + L\_JFromI[k,j,i]
\end{cases}
\end{cases}
$$

$$
L\_JFromI[i,j,x] \leftarrow \max
\begin{cases}
Int[i,j,F,T] \\
\max\limits_{k \in (i,j)} S[x,k] + \\
\quad \begin{cases}
L[i,k,x,F,F,F] + N\_JFromX[k,j,i] \\
Int[i,k,F,F] + L\_JFromX[k,j,i]
\end{cases}
\end{cases}
$$

$R[i,j,x,b_i,b_j,F] \leftarrow$ symmetric to $L[i,j,x,b_i,b_j,F]$
$R[i,j,x,b_i,F,T] \leftarrow$ symmetric to $L[i,j,x,F,b_j,T]$
$R[i,j,x,b_i,T,T] \leftarrow$ not reachable
$R\_XFromJ[i,j,x] \leftarrow$ symmetric to $L\_XFromI[i,j,x]$
$R\_JFromX[i,j,x] \leftarrow$ symmetric to $L\_IFromX[i,j,x]$
$R\_IFromX[i,j,x] \leftarrow$ symmetric to $L\_JFromX[i,j,x]$
$R\_IFromJ[i,j,x] \leftarrow$ symmetric to $L\_JFromI[i,j,x]$

References

E. Bach, C. Brown, and W. Marslen-Wilson. 1986. Crossed and nested dependencies in german and dutch: A psycholinguistic study. *Language and Cognitive Processes*, 1(4):249–262.

F. Bernhart and P.C. Kainen. 1979. The book thickness of a graph. *Journal of Combinatorial Theory, Series B*, 27(3):320 – 331.

M. Bodirsky, M. Kuhlmann, and M. Möhl. 2005. Well-nested drawings as models of syntactic structure. In *In Tenth Conference on Formal Grammar and Ninth Meeting on Mathematics of Language*, pages 88–1. University Press.

X. Carreras. 2007. Experiments with a higher-order projective dependency parser. In *Proceedings of the CoNLL Shared Task Session of EMNLP-CoNLL*, volume 7, pages 957–961.

N. Chomsky, Massachusetts Institute of Technology. Dept. of Linguistics, and Philosophy. 1998. *Minimalist inquiries: the framework*. MIT occasional papers in linguistics. Distributed by MIT Working Papers in Linguistics, MIT, Dept. of Linguistics.

N. Chomsky. 1981. *Lectures on Government and Binding*. Dordrecht: Foris.

F. Chung, F. Leighton, and A. Rosenberg. 1987. Embedding graphs in books: A layout problem with applications to VLSI design. *SIAM Journal on Algebraic Discrete Methods*, 8(1):33–58.

H. Cui, R. Sun, K. Li, M.Y. Kan, and T.S. Chua. 2005. Question answering passage retrieval using dependency relations. In *Proceedings of the 28th annual international ACM SIGIR conference on Research and development in information retrieval*, pages 400–407. ACM.

A. Culotta and J. Sorensen. 2004. Dependency tree kernels for relation extraction. In *Proceedings of the 42nd Annual Meeting on Association for Computational Linguistics*, page 423. Association for Computational Linguistics.

Y. Ding and M. Palmer. 2005. Machine translation using probabilistic synchronous dependency insertion grammars. In *Proceedings of the 43rd Annual Meeting on Association for Computational Linguistics*, pages 541–548. Association for Computational Linguistics.

J. Eisner. 2000. Bilexical grammars and their cubic-time parsing algorithms. In Harry Bunt and Anton Nijholt, editors, *Advances in Probabilistic and Other Parsing Technologies*, pages 29–62. Kluwer Academic Publishers, October.

S. Even and A. Itai. 1971. Queues, stacks, and graphs. In *Proc. International Symp. on Theory of Machines and Computations*, pages 71–86.

C. Gómez-Rodríguez and J. Nivre. 2010. A transition-based parser for 2-planar dependency structures. In *Proceedings of ACL*, pages 1492–1501.

C. Gómez-Rodríguez, J. Carroll, and D. Weir. 2011. Dependency parsing schemata and mildly non-projective dependency parsing. *Computational Linguistics*, 37(3):541–586.

T. Koo and M. Collins. 2010. Efficient third-order dependency parsers. In *Proceedings of ACL*, pages 1–11.

M. Kuhlmann. 2013. Mildly non-projective dependency grammar. *Computational Linguistics*, 39(2).

R. McDonald and F. Pereira. 2006. Online learning of approximate dependency parsing algorithms. In *Proceedings of EACL*, pages 81–88.

R. McDonald and G. Satta. 2007. On the complexity of non-projective data-driven dependency parsing. In *Proceedings of the 10th International Conference on Parsing Technologies*, pages 121–132.

R. McDonald, F. Pereira, K. Ribarov, and J. Hajič. 2005. Non-projective dependency parsing using spanning tree algorithms. In *Proceedings of the conference on Human Language Technology and Empirical Methods in Natural Language Processing*, pages 523–530. Association for Computational Linguistics.

E. Pitler, S. Kannan, and M. Marcus. 2012. Dynamic programming for higher order parsing of gap-minding trees. In *Proceedings of EMNLP*, pages 478–488.

L.A. Ringenberg. 1967. *College geometry*. Wiley.

A. Rush and S. Petrov. 2012. Vine pruning for efficient multi-pass dependency parsing. In *Proceedings of NAACL*, pages 498–507.

S.M. Shieber. 1985. Evidence against the context-freeness of natural language. *Linguistics and Philosophy*, 8(3):333–343.

H. Zhang and R. McDonald. 2012. Generalized higher-order dependency parsing with cube pruning. In *Proceedings of EMNLP*, pages 320–331.

Grounding Action Descriptions in Videos

Michaela Regneri *, **Marcus Rohrbach** ◇, **Dominikus Wetzel** *,
Stefan Thater *, **Bernt Schiele** ◇ and **Manfred Pinkal** *

* Department of Computational Linguistics, Saarland University, Saarbrücken, Germany
(regneri|dwetzel|stth|pinkal)@coli.uni-saarland.de

◇ Max Planck Institute for Informatics, Saarbrücken, Germany
(rohrbach|schiele)@mpi-inf.mpg.de

Abstract

Recent work has shown that the integration of visual information into text-based models can substantially improve model predictions, but so far only visual information extracted from static images has been used. In this paper, we consider the problem of grounding *sentences describing actions* in visual information extracted from *videos*. We present a general purpose corpus that aligns high quality videos with multiple natural language descriptions of the actions portrayed in the videos, together with an annotation of how similar the action descriptions are to each other. Experimental results demonstrate that a text-based model of similarity between actions improves substantially when combined with visual information from videos depicting the described actions.

1 Introduction

The estimation of semantic similarity between words and phrases is a basic task in computational semantics. Vector-space models of meaning are one standard approach. Following the distributional hypothesis, frequencies of context words are recorded in vectors, and semantic similarity is computed as a proximity measure in the underlying vector space. Such distributional models are attractive because they are conceptually simple, easy to implement and relevant for various NLP tasks (Turney and Pantel, 2010). At the same time, they provide a substantially incomplete picture of word meaning, since they ignore the relation between language and extralinguistic information, which is constitutive for linguistic meaning. In the last few years, a growing amount of work has been devoted to the task of grounding meaning in visual information, in particular by extending the distributional approach to jointly cover texts and images (Feng and Lapata, 2010; Bruni et al., 2011). As a clear result, visual information improves the quality of distributional models. Bruni et al. (2011) show that visual information drawn from images is particularly relevant for concrete common nouns and adjectives.

A natural next step is to integrate visual information from *videos* into a semantic model of event and action verbs. Psychological studies have shown the connection between action semantics and videos (Glenberg, 2002; Howell et al., 2005), but to our knowledge, we are the first to provide a suitable data source and to implement such a model.

The contribution of this paper is three-fold:

- We present a *multimodal corpus* containing textual descriptions aligned with high-quality videos. Starting from the video corpus of Rohrbach et al. (2012b), which contains high-resolution video recordings of basic cooking tasks, we collected multiple textual descriptions of each video via Mechanical Turk. We also provide an accurate sentence-level alignment of the descriptions with their respective videos. We expect the corpus to be a valuable resource for computational semantics, and moreover helpful for a variety of purposes, including video understanding and generation of text from videos.

- We provide a *gold-standard dataset* for the evaluation of similarity models for action verbs and phrases. The dataset has been designed as analogous to the Usage Similarity dataset of

Erk et al. (2009) and contains pairs of natural-language action descriptions plus their associated video segments. Each of the pairs is annotated with a similarity score based on several manual annotations.

- We report an experiment on *similarity modeling of action descriptions* based on the video corpus and the gold standard annotation, which demonstrates the impact of scene information from videos. Visual similarity models outperform text-based models; the performance of combined models approaches the upper bound indicated by inter-annotator agreement.

The paper is structured as follows: We first place ourselves in the landscape of related work (Sec. 2), then we introduce our corpus (Sec. 3). Sec. 4 reports our action similarity annotation experiment and Sec. 5 introduces the similarity measures we apply to the annotated data. We outline the results of our evaluation in Sec. 6, and conclude the paper with a summary and directions for future work (Sec. 7).

2 Related Work

A large multimodal resource combining language and visual information resulted from the ESP game (von Ahn and Dabbish, 2004). The dataset contains many images tagged with several one-word labels.

The Microsoft Video Description Corpus (Chen and Dolan, 2011, MSVD) is a resource providing textual descriptions of videos. It consists of multiple crowd-sourced textual descriptions of short video snippets. The MSVD corpus is much larger than our corpus, but most of the videos are of relatively low quality and therefore too challenging for state-of-the-art video processing to extract relevant information. The videos are typically short and summarized with a single sentence. Our corpus contains coherent textual descriptions of longer video sequences, where each sentence is associated with a timeframe.

Gupta et al. (2009) present another useful resource: their model learns the alignment of predicate-argument structures with videos and uses the result for action recognition in videos. However, the corpus contains no natural language texts.

The connection between natural language sentences and videos has so far been mostly explored by the computer vision community, where different methods for improving action recognition by exploiting linguistic data have been proposed (Gupta and Mooney, 2010; Motwani and Mooney, 2012; Cour et al., 2008; Tzoukermann et al., 2011; Rohrbach et al., 2012b, among others). Our resource is intended to be used for action recognition as well, but in this paper, we focus on the inverse effect of visual data on language processing.

Feng and Lapata (2010) were the first to enrich topic models for newspaper articles with visual information, by incorporating features from article illustrations. They achieve better results when incorporating the visual information, providing an enriched model that pairs a single text with a picture.

Bruni et al. (2011) used the ESP game data to create a visually grounded semantic model. Their results outperform purely text-based models using visual information from pictures for the task of modeling noun similarities. They model single words, and mostly visual features lead only to moderate improvements, which might be due to the mixed quality and random choice of the images. Dodge et al. (2012) recently investigated which words can actually be grounded in images at all, producing an automatic classifier for visual words.

An interesting in-depth study by Mathe et al. (2008) automatically learnt the semantics of motion verbs as abstract features from videos. The study captures 4 actions with 8-10 videos for each of the actions, and would need a perfect object recognition from a visual classifier to scale up.

Steyvers (2010) and later Silberer and Lapata (2012) present an alternative approach to incorporating visual information directly: they use so-called *feature norms*, which consist of human associations for many given words, as a proxy for general perceptual information. Because this model is trained and evaluated on those feature norms, it is not directly comparable to our approach.

The *Restaurant Game* by Orkin and Roy (2009) grounds written chat dialogues in actions carried out in a computer game. While this work is outstanding from the social learning perspective, the actions that ground the dialogues are clicks on a screen rather than real-world actions. The dataset has successfully been used to model determiner meaning (Reckman et al., 2011) in the context of the *Restaurant Game*, but it is unclear how this approach could scale up to content words and other domains.

3 The TACOS Corpus

We build our corpus on top of the "MPII Cooking Composite Activities" video corpus (Rohrbach et al., 2012b, *MPII Composites*), which contains videos of different activities in the cooking domain, e.g., *preparing carrots* or *separating eggs*. We extend the existing corpus with multiple textual descriptions collected by crowd-sourcing via Amazon Mechanical Turk[1] *(MTurk)*. To facilitate the alignment of sentences describing activities with their proper video segments, we also obtained approximate timestamps, as described in Sec. 3.2.

MPII Composites comes with timed gold-standard annotation of low-level activities and participating objects (e.g. OPEN [HAND,DRAWER] or TAKE OUT [HAND,KNIFE,DRAWER]). By adding textual descriptions (e.g., *The person takes a knife from the drawer*) and aligning them on the sentence level with videos and low-level annotations, we provide a rich multimodal resource (cf. Fig. 2), the "Saarbrücken Corpus of Textually Annotated Cooking Scenes" (TACOS). In particular, the TACOS corpus provides:

- A collection of coherent *textual descriptions for video recordings* of activities of medium complexity, as as a basis for empirical discourse-related research, e.g., the selection and granularity of action descriptions in context
- A high-quality *alignment of sentences with video segments*, supporting the grounding of action descriptions in visual information
- *Collections of paraphrases* describing the same scene, which result as a by-product from the text-video alignment and can be useful for text generation from videos (among other things)
- The alignment of textual activity descriptions with *sequences of low-level activities*, which may be used to study the decomposition of action verbs into basic activity predicates

We expect that our corpus will encourage and enable future work on various topics in natural language and video processing. In this paper, we will make use of the second aspect only, demonstrating the usefulness of the corpus for the grounding task.

After a more detailed description of the basic video corpus and its annotation (Sec. 3.1) we describe the collection of textual descriptions with MTurk (Sec. 3.2), and finally show the assembly and some benchmarks of the final corpus (Sec. 3.3).

3.1 The video corpus

MPII Composites contains 212 high resolution video recordings of 1-23 minutes length (4.5 min. on average). 41 basic cooking tasks such as *cutting a cucumber* were recorded, each between 4 and 8 times. The selection of cooking tasks is based on those proposed at "Jamie's Home Cooking Skills".[2] The corpus is recorded in a kitchen environment with a total of 22 subjects. Each video depicts a single task executed by an individual subject.

The dataset contains expert annotations of low-level activity tags. Annotations are provided for segments containing a semantically meaningful cooking related movement pattern. The action must go beyond single body part movements (such as *move arm up*) and must have the goal of changing the state or location of an object. 60 different activity labels are used for annotation (e.g. PEEL, STIR, TRASH). Each low-level activity tag consists of an activity label (PEEL), a set of associated objects (CARROT, DRAWER,...), and the associated timeframe (starting and ending points of the activity). Associated objects are the participants of an activity, namely tools (e.g. KNIFE), patient (CARROT) and location (CUTTING-BOARD). We provide the coarse-grained role information for *patient*, *location* and *tool* in the corpus data, but we did not use this information in our experiments. The dataset contains a total of 8818 annotated segments, on average 42 per video.

3.2 Collecting textual video descriptions

We collected textual descriptions for a subset of the videos in *MPII Composites*, restricting collection to tasks that involve manipulation of cooking ingredients. We also excluded tasks with fewer than four

[1] mturk.com

[2] www.jamieshomecookingskills.com

video recordings in the corpus, leaving 26 tasks to be described. We randomly selected five videos from each task, except the three tasks for which only four videos are available. This resulted in a total of 127 videos. For each video, we collected 20 different textual descriptions, leading to 2540 annotation assignments. We published these assignments (HITs) on MTurk, using an adapted version[3] of the annotation tool Vatic (Vondrick et al., 2012).

In each assignment, the subject saw one video specified with the task title (e.g. *How to prepare an onion*), and then was asked to enter at least five and at most 15 complete English sentences to describe the events in the video. The annotation instructions contained example annotations from a kitchen task not contained in our actual dataset.

Annotators were encouraged to watch each video several times, skipping backward and forward as they wished. They were also asked to take notes while watching, and to sketch the annotation before entering it. Once familiarized with the video, subjects did the final annotation by watching the entire video from beginning to end, without the possibility of further non-sequential viewing. Subjects were asked to enter each sentence as soon as the action described by the sentence was completed. The video playback paused automatically at the beginning of the sentence input. We recorded pause onset for each sentence annotation as an approximate ending timestamp of the described action. The annotators resumed the video manually.

The tasks required a HIT approval rate of 75% and were open only to workers in the US, in order to increase the general language quality of the English annotations. Each task paid 1.20 USD. Before paying we randomly inspected the annotations and manually checked for quality. The total costs of collecting the annotations amounted to 3,353 USD. The data was obtained within a time frame of 3.5 weeks.

3.3 Putting the TACOS corpus together

Our corpus is a combination of the MTurk data and MPII Composites, created by filtering out inappropriate material and computing a high-quality alignment of sentences and video segments. The alignment is done by matching the approximate timestamps of the MTurk data to the accurate timestamps in MPII Composites.

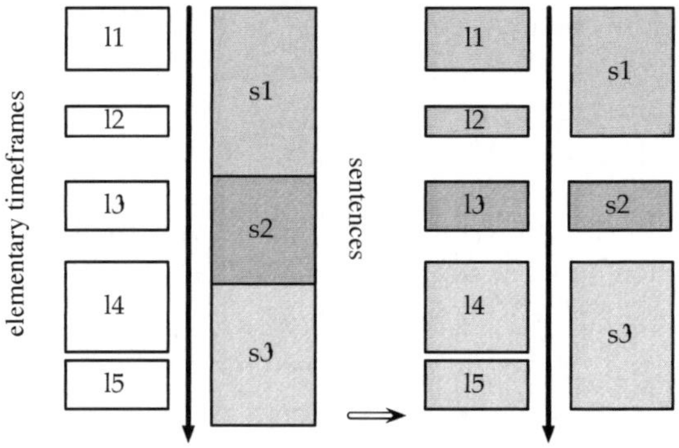

Figure 1: Aligning action descriptions with the video.

We discarded text instances if people did not time the sentences properly, taking the association of several (or even all) sentences to a single timestamp as an indicator. Whenever we found a timestamp associated with two or more sentences, we discarded the whole instance. Overall, we had to filter out 13% of the text instances, which left us with 2206 textual video descriptions.

For the alignment of sentence annotations and video segments, we assign a precise timeframe to each sentence in the following way: We take the timeframes given by the low-level annotation in MPII Composites as a gold standard micro-event segmentation of the video, because they mark all distinct frames that contain activities of interest. We call them *elementary frames*. The sequence of elementary frames is not necessarily continuous, because idle time is not annotated.

The MTurk sentences have end points that constitute a coarse-grained, noisy video segmentation, assuming that each sentence spans the time between the end of the previous sentence and its own ending point. We refine those noisy timeframes to gold frames as shown in Fig. 1: Each elementary frame (*l1-l5*) is mapped to a sentence (*s1-s3*) if its noisy timeframe covers at least half of the elementary frame. We define the final gold sentence frame then as the timespan between the starting point of the first and the ending point of the last elementary frame.

The alignment of descriptions with low-level activities results in a table as given in Fig. 3. Columns contain the textual descriptions of the videos; rows

[3] github.com/marcovzla/vatic/tree/bolt

Top 10 Verbs	cut, take, get, put, wash, place, rinse, remove, **pan*, peel
Top 10 Activities	move, take out, cut, wash, take apart, add, shake, screw, put in, peel

Figure 4: 10 most frequent verbs and low-level actions in the TACOS corpus. *pan* is probably often mis-tagged.

correspond to low-level actions, and each sentence is aligned with the last of its associated low-level actions. As a side effect, we also obtain multiple paraphrases for each sentence, by considering all sentences with the same associated time frame as equivalent realizations of the same action.

The corpus contains 17,334 action descriptions (tokens), realizing 11,796 different sentences (types). It consists of 146,771 words (tokens), 75,210 of which are content word instances (i.e. nouns, verbs and adjectives). The verb vocabulary comprises 28,292 verb tokens, realizing 435 lemmas. Since verbs occurring in the corpus typically describe actions, we can note that the linguistic variance for the 58 different low-level activities is quite large. Fig. 4 gives an impression of the action realizations in the corpus, listing the most frequent verbs from the textual data, and the most frequent low-level activities.

On average, each description covers 2.7 low-level activities, which indicates a clear difference in granularity. 38% of the descriptions correspond to exactly one low-level activity, about a quarter (23%) covers two of them; 16% have 5 or more low-level elements, 2% more than 10. The corpus shows how humans vary the granularity of their descriptions, measured in time or number of low-level activities, and it shows how they vary the linguistic realization of the same action. For example, Fig. 3 contains *dice* and *chop into small pieces* as alternative realizations of the low-level activity sequence SLICE - SCRATCH OFF - SLICE.

The descriptions are of varying length (9 words on average), reaching from two-word phrases to detailed descriptions of 65 words. Most sentences are short, consisting of a reference to the person in the video, a participant and an action verb (*The person rinses the carrot*, *He cuts off the two edges*). People often specified an instrument (*from the faucet*), or the resulting state of the action (*chop the carrots in small pieces*). Occasionally, we find more complex constructions (support verbs, coordinations).

As Fig. 3 indicates, the timestamp-based alignment is pretty accurate; occasional errors occur like *He starts chopping the carrot...* in NL Sequence 3. The data contains some typos and ungrammatical sentences (*He washed carrot*), but for our own experiments, the small number of such errors did not lead to any processing problems.

4 The Action Similarity Dataset

In this section, we present a gold standard dataset, as a basis for the evaluation of visually grounded models of action similarity. We call it the "Action Similarity Dataset" (ASim) in analogy to the Usage Similarity dataset (USim) of Erk et al. (2009) and Erk et al. (2012). Similarly to USim, ASim contains a collection of sentence pairs with numerical similarity scores assigned by human annotators. We asked the annotators to focus on the similarity of the activities described rather than on assessing semantic similarity in general. We use sentences from the TACOS corpus and record their timestamps. Thus each sentence comes with the video segment which it describes (these were not shown to the annotators).

4.1 Selecting action description pairs

Random selection of annotated sentences from the corpus would lead to a large majority of pairs which are completely dissimilar, or difficult to grade (e.g., *He opens the drawer – The person cuts off the ends of the carrot*). We constrained the selection process in two ways: First, we consider only sentences describing activities of manipulating an ingredient. The low-level annotation of the video corpus helps us identify candidate descriptions. We exclude rare and special activities, ending up with CUT, SLICE, CHOP, PEEL, TAKE APART, and WASH, which occur reasonably frequently, with a wide distribution over different scenarios. We restrict the candidate set to those sentences whose timespan includes one of these activities. This results in a conceptually more focussed repertoire of descriptions, and at the same time admits full linguistic variation (*wash an apple under the faucet – rinse an apple*, *slice the cucumber – cut the cucumber into slices*).

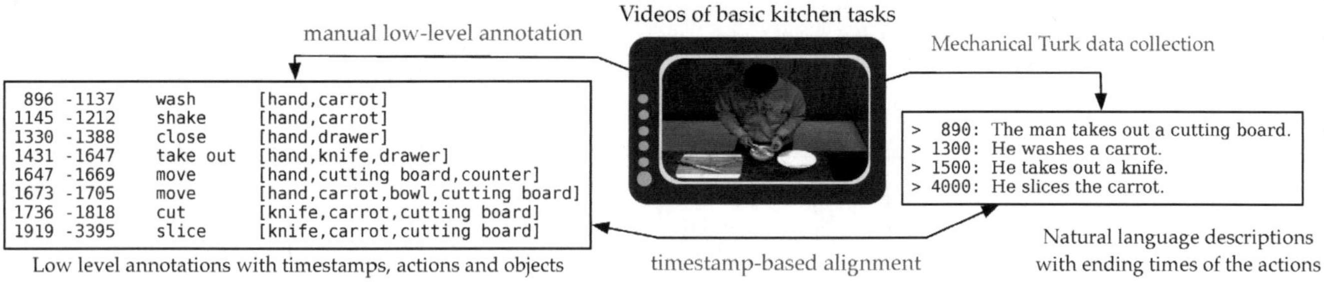

Figure 2: Corpus Overview

Sample frame	Start	End	Action	Participants	NL Sequence 1	NL Sequence 2	NL Sequence 3
	743	911	wash	hand, carrot	He washed carrot	The person rinses the carrot.	He rinses the carrot from the faucet.
	982	1090	cut	knife, carrot, cutting board	He cut off ends of carrots	The person cuts off the ends of the carrot.	He cuts off the two edges.
	1164	1257	open	hand, drawer			
	1679	1718	close	hand, drawer			He searches for something in the drawer, failed attempt, he throws away the edges in trash.
	1746	1799	trash	hand, carrot		The person searches for the trash can, then throws the ends of the carrot away.	
	1854	2011	wash	hand, carrot			He rinses the carrot again.
	2011	2045	shake	hand, carrot	He washed carrot	The person rinses the carrot again.	He starts chopping the carrot in small pieces.
	2083	2924	slice	knife, carrot, cutting board			
	2924	2959	scratch off	hand, carrot, knife, cutting board			
	3000	3696	slice	knife, carrot, cutting board	He diced carrots		He finished chopping the carrots in small pieces.

Figure 3: Excerpt from the corpus for a video on PREPARING A CARROT. Example frames, low-level annotation (*Action* and *Participants*) is shown along with three of the MTurk sequences (*NL Sequence 1-3*).

Second, we required the pairs to share some lexical material, either the head verb or the manipulated ingredient (or both).[4] More precisely, we composed the ASim dataset from three different subsets:

Different activity, same object: This subset contains pairs describing different types of actions carried out on the same type of object (e.g. *The man washes the carrot. – She dices the carrot.*). Its focus is on the central task of modeling the semantic relation between *actions* (rather than the objects involved in the activity), since the object head nouns in the descriptions are the same, and the respective video segments show the same type of object.

Same activity, same object: Description pairs of this subset will in many cases, but not always, agree in their head verbs. The dataset is useful for exploring the degree to which action descriptions are underspecified with respect to the precise manner of their practical realization. For example, peeling an onion will mostly be done in a rather uniform way, while *cut* applied to *carrot* can mean that the carrot is chopped up, or sliced, or cut in halves.

Same activity & verb, different object: Description pairs in this subset share head verb and low-level activity, but have different objects (e.g. *The man washes the carrot. – A girl washes an apple under the faucet.*). This dataset enables the exploration of the objects' meaning contribution to the complete action, established by the variation of equivalent actions that are done to different objects.

We assembled 900 action description pairs for annotation: 480 pairs share the object; 240 of which have different activities, and the other 240 pairs share the same activity. We included paraphrases describing the same video segment, but we excluded pairs of identical sentences. 420 additional pairs share their head verb, but have different objects.

4.2 Manual annotation

Three native speakers of English were asked to judge the similarity of the action pairs with respect to *how they are carried out*, rating each sentence pair with a score from 1 (not similar at all) to 5 (the same or nearly the same). They did not see the respective videos, but we noted the relevant kitchen task (i.e. which vegetable was prepared). We asked the annotators explicitly to ignore the actor of the action (e.g. whether it is a man or a woman) and score the similarities of the underlying actions rather than their verbalizations. Each subject rated all 900 pairs, which were shown to them in completely random order, with a different order for each subject.

We compute inter-annotator agreement (and the forthcoming evaluation scores) using Spearman's rank correlation coefficient (ρ), a non-parametric test which is widely used for similar evaluation tasks (Mitchell and Lapata, 2008; Bruni et al., 2011; Erk and McCarthy, 2009). Spearman's ρ evaluates how the samples are ranked relative to each other rather than the numerical distance between the rankings.

Part of Gold Standard	**Sim**	σ	ρ
DIFF. ACTIVITY, SAME OBJECT	2.20	1.07	0.73
SAME ACTIVITY, SAME OBJECT	4.19	1.04	0.73
ALL WITH SAME OBJECT	3.20	1.44	0.84
SAME VERB, DIFF. OBJECT	3.34	0.69	0.43
COMPLETE DATASET	3.27	1.15	0.73

Figure 5: Average similarity ratings (*Sim*), their standard deviation (σ)) and annotator agreement (ρ) for ASim.

Fig. 5 shows the average similarity ratings in the different settings and the inter-annotator agreement. The average inter-rater agreement was $\rho = 0.73$ (averaged over pairwise rater agreements), with pairwise results of $\rho = 0.77$, 0.72, and 0.69, respectively, which are all highly significant at $p < 0.001$.

As expected, pairs with the same activity and object are rated very similar (4.19) on average, while the similarity of different activities on the same object is the lowest (2.2). For both subsets, inter-rater agreement is high ($\rho = 0.73$), and even higher for both SAME OBJECT subsets together (0.84).

Pairs with identical head verbs and different objects have a small standard deviation, at 0.69. The inter-annotator agreement on this set is much lower than for pairs from the SAME OBJECT set. This indicates that similarity assessment for different variants of the same activity is a hard task even for humans.

[4] We refer to the latter with the term *object*; we don't require the ingredient term to be the actual grammatical object in the action descriptions, we rather use "object" in its semantic role sense as the entity affected by an action.

5 Models of Action Similarity

In the following, we demonstrate that visual information contained in videos of the kind provided by the TACOS corpus (Sec. 3) substantially contributes to the semantic modeling of action-denoting expressions. In Sec. 6, we evaluate several methods for predicting action similarity on the task provided by the ASim dataset. In this section, we describe the models considered in the evaluation. We use two different models based on visual information, and in addition two text based models. We will also explore the effect of combining linguistic and visual information and investigate which mode is most suitable for which kinds of similarity.

5.1 Text-based models

We use two different models of textual similarity to predict action similarity: a simple word-overlap measure (Jaccard coefficient) and a state-of-the-art model based on "contextualized" vector representations of word meaning (Thater et al., 2011).

Jaccard coefficient. The Jaccard coefficient gives the ratio between the number of (distinct) words common to two input sentences and the total number of (distinct) words in the two sentences. Such simple surface-oriented measures of textual similarity are often used as baselines in related tasks such as recognizing textual entailment (Dagan et al., 2005) and are known to deliver relatively strong results.

Vector model. We use the vector model of Thater et al. (2011), which "contextualizes" vector representations for individual words based on the particular sentence context in which the target word occurs. The basic intuition behind this approach is that the words in the syntactic context of the target word in a given input sentence can be used to refine or disambiguate its vector. Intuitively, this allows us to discriminate between different actions that a verb can refer to, based on the different objects of the action.

We first experimented with a version of this vector model which predicts action similarity scores of two input sentences by computing the cosine similarity of the contextualized vectors of the verbs in the two sentences only. We achieved better performance with a variant of this model which computes vectors for the two sentences by summing over the contextualized vectors of all constituent content words.

In the experiments reported below, we only use the second variant. We use the same experimental setup as Thater et al. (2011), as well as the parameter settings that are reported to work best in that paper.

5.2 Video-based models

We distinguish two approaches to compute the similarity between two video segments. In the first, unsupervised approach we extract a video descriptor and compute similarities between these raw features (Wang et al., 2011). The second approach builds upon the first by additionally learning higher level attribute classifiers (Rohrbach et al., 2012b) on a held out training set. The similarity between two segments is then computed between the classifier responses. In the following we detail both approaches:

Raw visual features. We use the state-of-the-art video descriptor *Dense Trajectories* (Wang et al., 2011) which extracts visual video features, namely histograms of oriented gradients, flow, and motion boundary histograms, around densely sampled and tracked points.

This approach is especially suited for this data as it ignores non-moving parts in the video: we are interested in activities and manipulation of objects, and this type of feature implicitly uses only information in relevant image locations. For our setting this feature representation has been shown to be superior to human pose-based approaches (Rohrbach et al., 2012a). Using a bag-of-words representation we encode the features using a 16,000 dimensional codebook. Features and codebook are provided with the publicly available video dataset.

We compute the similarity between two encoded features by computing the intersection of the two (normalized) histograms.

Visual classifiers. Visual raw features tend to have several dimensions in the feature space which provide unreliable, noisy values and thus degrade the strength of the similarity measure. Intermediate level attribute classifiers can learn which feature dimensions are distinctive and thus significantly improve performance over raw features. Rohrbach et al. (2012b) showed that using such an attribute classifier representation can significantly improve per-

MODEL		SAME OBJECT	SAME VERB	OVERALL
TEXT	JACCARD	0.28	0.25	0.25
	TEXTUAL VECTORS	0.30	0.25	0.27
	TEXT COMBINED	0.39	**0.35**	0.36
VIDEO	VISUAL RAW VECTORS	0.53	-0.08	0.35
	VISUAL CLASSIFIER	0.60	0.03	0.44
	VIDEO COMBINED	0.61	-0.04	0.44
MIX	ALL UNSUPERVISED	0.58	0.32	0.48
	ALL COMBINED	**0.67**	0.28	**0.55**
UPPER BOUND		0.84	0.43	0.73

Figure 6: Evaluation results in Spearman's ρ. All values > 0.11 are significant at $p < 0.001$.

formance for composite activity recognition. The relevant attributes are all activities and objects annotated in the video data (cf. Section 3.1). For the experiments reported below we use the same setup as Rohrbach et al. (2012b) and use all videos in MPII Composites and MPII Cooking (Rohrbach et al., 2012a), excluding the 127 videos used during evaluation. The real-valued SVM-classifier output provides a confidence how likely a certain attribute appeared in a given video segment. This results in a 218-dimensional vector of classifier outputs for each video segment. To compute the similarity between two vectors we compute the cosine between them.

6 Evaluation

We evaluate the different similarity models introduced in Sec. 5 by calculating their correlation with the gold-standard similarity annotations of ASim (cf. Sec. 4). For all correlations, we use Spearman's ρ as a measure. We consider the two textual measures (JACCARD and TEXTUAL VECTORS) and their combination, as well as the two visual models (VISUAL RAW VECTORS and VISUAL CLASSIFIER) and their combination. We also combined textual and visual features, in two variants: The first includes all models (ALL COMBINED), the second only the unsupervised components, omitting the visual classifier (ALL UNSUPERVISED). To combine multiple similarity measures, we simply average their normalized scores (using z-scores).

Figure 6 shows the scores for all of these measures on the complete ASim dataset (OVERALL), along with the two subparts, where description pairs share either the object (SAME OBJECT) or the head verb (SAME VERB). In addition to the model results, the table also shows the average human inter-annotator agreement as UPPER BOUND.

On the complete set, both visual and textual measures have a highly significant correlation with the gold standard, whereas the combination of both clearly leads to the best performance (0.55). The results on the SAME OBJECT and SAME VERB subsets shed light on the division of labor between the two information sources. While the textual measures show a comparable performance over the two subsets, there is a dramatic difference in the contribution of visual information: On the SAME OBJECT set, the visual models clearly outperform the textual ones, whereas the visual information has no positive effect on the SAME VERB set. This is clear evidence that the visual model does not capture the similarity of the participating objects but rather genuine action similarity, which the visual features (Wang et al., 2011) we employ were designed for. A direction for future work is to learn dedicated visual object detectors to recognize and capture similarities between objects more precisely.

The numbers shown in Figure 7 support this hypothesis, showing the two groups in the SAME OBJECT class: For sentence pairs that share the same activity, the textual models seem to be much more suitable than the visual ones. In general, visual models perform better on actions with different activity types, textual models on closely related activities.

	Model (Same Object)	*same action*	*diff. action*
Text	Jaccard	0.44	0.14
	Text Vectors	0.42	0.05
	Text Combined	**0.52**	0.14
Video	Vis. Raw Vectors	0.21	0.23
	Vis. Classifier	0.21	**0.45**
	Video Combined	0.26	0.38
Mix	All Unsupervised	0.49	0.24
	All Combined	0.48	0.41
Upper Bound		0.73	0.73

Figure 7: Results for sentences with the same object, with either the same or different low-level activity.

Overall, the supervised classifier contributes a good part to the final results. However, the supervision is not strictly necessary to arrive at a significant correlation; the raw visual features alone are sufficient for the main performance gain seen with the integration of visual information.

7 Conclusion

We presented the TACOS corpus, which provides coherent textual descriptions for high-quality video recordings, plus accurate alignments of text and video on the sentence level. We expect the corpus to be beneficial for a variety of research activities in natural-language and visual processing.

In this paper, we focused on the task of grounding the meaning of action verbs and phrases. We designed the ASim dataset as a gold standard and evaluated several text- and video-based semantic similarity models on the dataset, both individually and in different combinations.

We are the first to provide semantic models for action-describing expressions, which are based on information extracted from videos. Our experimental results show that these models are of considerable quality, and that predictions based on a combination of visual and textual information even approach the upper bound given by the agreement of human annotators.

In this work we used existing similarity models that had been developed for different applications. We applied these models without any special training or optimization for the current task, and we combined them in the most straightforward way. There is room for improvement by tuning the models to the task, or by using more sophisticated approaches to combine modality-specific information (Silberer and Lapata, 2012).

We built our work on an existing corpus of high-quality video material, which is restricted to the cooking domain. As a consequence, the corpus covers only a limited inventory of activity types and action verbs. Note, however, that our models are fully unsupervised (except the Visual Classifier model), and thus can be applied without modification to arbitrary domains and action verbs, given that they are about observable activities. Also, corpora containing information comparable to the TACOS corpus but with wider coverage (and perhaps a bit noisier) can be obtained with a moderate amount of effort. One needs videos of reasonable quality and some sort of alignment with action descriptions. In some cases such alignments even come for free, e.g. via subtitles, or descriptions of short video clips that depict just a single action.

For future work, we will further investigate the compositionality of action-describing phrases. We also want to leverage the multimodal information provided by the TACOS corpus for the improvement of high-level video understanding, as well as for generation of natural-language text from videos.

The TACOS corpus and all other data described in this paper (videos, low-level annotation, aligned textual descriptions, the ASim-Dataset and visual features) are publicly available. [5]

Acknowledgements

We'd like to thank Asad Sayeed, Alexis Palmer and Prashant Rao for their help with the annotations. We're indebted to Carl Vondrick and Marco Antonio Valenzuela Escrcega for their extensive support with the video annotation tool. Further we thank Alexis Palmer and in particular three anonymous reviewers for their helpful comments on this paper. – This work was funded by the Cluster of Excellence "Multimodal Computing and Interaction" of the German Excellence Initiative and the DFG project SCHI989/2-2.

[5] `http://www.coli.uni-saarland.de/projects/smile/page.php?id=tacos`

References

Luis von Ahn and Laura Dabbish. 2004. Labeling images with a computer game. In *Proceedings of SIGCHI 2004*.

Elia Bruni, Giang Binh Tran, and Marco Baroni. 2011. Distributional semantics from text and images. In *Proceedings of GEMS 2011*.

David L. Chen and William B. Dolan. 2011. Collecting highly parallel data for paraphrase evaluation. In *Proceedings of ACL 2011*.

Timothee Cour, Chris Jordan, Eleni Miltsakaki, and Ben Taskar. 2008. Movie/script: Alignment and parsing of video and text transcription. In *Computer Vision – ECCV 2008*, volume 5305 of *Lecture Notes in Computer Science*, pages 158–171. Springer Berlin Heidelberg.

Ido Dagan, Oren Glickman, and Bernardo Magnini. 2005. The PASCAL recognising textual entailment challenge. In *Proceedings of MLCW 2005*.

Jesse Dodge, Amit Goyal, Xufeng Han, Alyssa Mensch, Margaret Mitchell, Karl Stratos, Kota Yamaguchi, Yejin Choi, Hal Daumé III, Alexander C. Berg, and Tamara L. Berg. 2012. Detecting visual text. In *HLT-NAACL*, pages 762–772.

Katrin Erk and Diana McCarthy. 2009. Graded word sense assignment. In *Proceedings of EMNLP 2009*.

Katrin Erk, Diana McCarthy, and Nicholas Gaylord. 2009. Investigations on word senses and word usages. In *Proceedings of ACL/AFNLP 2009*.

Katrin Erk, Diana McCarthy, and Nick Gaylord. 2012. Measuring word meaning in context. *CL*.

Yansong Feng and Mirella Lapata. 2010. Visual information in semantic representation. In *Proceedings of HLT-NAACL 2010*.

A. M. Glenberg. 2002. Grounding language in action. *Psychonomic Bulletin & Review*.

Sonal Gupta and Raymond J. Mooney. 2010. Using closed captions as supervision for video activity recognition. In *Proceedings of the Twenty-Fourth AAAI Conference on Artificial Intelligence (AAAI-2010)*, pages 1083–1088, Atlanta, GA, July.

Abhinav Gupta, Praveen Srinivasan, Jianbo Shi, and Larry S. Davis. 2009. Understanding videos, constructing plots learning a visually grounded storyline model from annotated videos. In *Proceedings of CVPR 2009*.

Steve R. Howell, Damian Jankowicz, and Suzanna Becker. 2005. A model of grounded language acquisition: Sensorimotor features improve lexical and grammatical learning. *JML*.

S. Mathe, A. Fazly, S. Dickinson, and S. Stevenson. 2008. Learning the abstract motion semantics of verbs from captioned videos. pages 1–8.

Jeff Mitchell and Mirella Lapata. 2008. Vector-based models of semantic composition. In *Proceedings of ACL 2008*.

Tanvi S. Motwani and Raymond J. Mooney. 2012. Improving video activity recognition using object recognition and text mining. In *Proceedings of the 20th European Conference on Artificial Intelligence (ECAI-2012)*, pages 600–605, August.

Jeff Orkin and Deb Roy. 2009. Automatic learning and generation of social behavior from collective human gameplay. In *Proceedings of AAMAS 2009*.

Hilke Reckman, Jeff Orkin, and Deb Roy. 2011. Extracting aspects of determiner meaning from dialogue in a virtual world environment. In *Proceedings of CCS 2011*, IWCS '11.

Marcus Rohrbach, Sikandar Amin, Mykhaylo Andriluka, and Bernt Schiele. 2012a. A database for fine grained activity detection of cooking activities. In *Proceedings of CVPR 2012*.

Marcus Rohrbach, Michaela Regneri, Micha Andriluka, Sikandar Amin, Manfred Pinkal, and Bernt Schiele. 2012b. Script data for attribute-based recognition of composite activities. In *Proceedings of ECCV 2012*.

Carina Silberer and Mirella Lapata. 2012. Grounded models of semantic representation. In *Proceedings of EMNLP-CoNLL 2012*.

Mark Steyvers. 2010. Combining feature norms and text data with topic models. *Acta Psychologica*, 133(3):234 – 243. ¡ce:title¿Formal modeling of semantic concepts¡/ce:title¿.

Stefan Thater, Hagen Fürstenau, and Manfred Pinkal. 2011. Word meaning in context: A simple and effective vector model. In *Proceedings of IJCNLP 2011*.

Peter D. Turney and Patrick Pantel. 2010. From frequency to meaning. vector space models for semantics. *JAIR*.

E. Tzoukermann, J. Neumann, J. Kosecka, C. Fermuller, I. Perera, F. Ferraro, B. Sapp, R. Chaudhry, and G. Singh. 2011. Language models for semantic extraction and filtering in video action recognition. In *AAAI Workshop on Language-Action Tools for Cognitive Artificial Agents*.

Carl Vondrick, Donald Patterson, and Deva Ramanan. 2012. Efficiently scaling up crowdsourced video annotation. *IJCV*.

Heng Wang, Alexander Kläser, Cordelia Schmid, and Cheng-Lin Liu. 2011. Action Recognition by Dense Trajectories. In *Proceedings of CVPR 2011*.

Branch and Bound Algorithm for Dependency Parsing with Non-local Features

Xian Qian and **Yang Liu**
Computer Science Department
The University of Texas at Dallas
{qx,yangl}@hlt.utdallas.edu

Abstract

Graph based dependency parsing is inefficient when handling non-local features due to high computational complexity of inference. In this paper, we proposed an exact and efficient decoding algorithm based on the Branch and Bound (B&B) framework where non-local features are bounded by a linear combination of local features. Dynamic programming is used to search the upper bound. Experiments are conducted on English PTB and Chinese CTB datasets. We achieved competitive Unlabeled Attachment Score (UAS) when no additional resources are available: 93.17% for English and 87.25% for Chinese. Parsing speed is 177 words per second for English and 97 words per second for Chinese. Our algorithm is general and can be adapted to non-projective dependency parsing or other graphical models.

1 Introduction

For graph based projective dependency parsing, dynamic programming (DP) is popular for decoding due to its efficiency when handling local features. It performs cubic time parsing for arc-factored models (Eisner, 1996; McDonald et al., 2005a) and biquadratic time for higher order models with richer sibling and grandchild features (Carreras, 2007; Koo and Collins, 2010). However, for models with general non-local features, DP is inefficient.

There have been numerous studies on global inference algorithms for general higher order parsing. One popular approach is reranking (Collins, 2000; Charniak and Johnson, 2005; Hall, 2007). It typically has two steps: the low level classifier generates the top k hypotheses using local features, then the high level classifier reranks these candidates using global features. Since the reranking quality is bounded by the oracle performance of candidates, some work has combined candidate generation and reranking steps using cube pruning (Huang, 2008; Zhang and McDonald, 2012) to achieve higher oracle performance. They parse a sentence in bottom up order and keep the top k derivations for each span using k best parsing (Huang and Chiang, 2005). After merging the two spans, non-local features are used to rerank top k combinations. This approach is very efficient and flexible to handle various non-local features. The disadvantage is that it tends to compute non-local features as early as possible so that the decoder can utilize that information at internal spans, hence it may miss long historical features such as long dependency chains.

Smith and Eisner modeled dependency parsing using Markov Random Fields (MRFs) with global constraints and applied loopy belief propagation (LBP) for approximate learning and inference (Smith and Eisner, 2008). Similar work was done for Combinatorial Categorial Grammar (CCG) parsing (Auli and Lopez, 2011). They used posterior marginal beliefs for inference to satisfy the tree constraint: for each factor, only legal messages (satisfying global constraints) are considered in the partition function.

A similar line of research investigated the use of integer linear programming (ILP) based parsing (Riedel and Clarke, 2006; Martins et al., 2009). This method is very expressive. It can handle arbitrary non-local features determined or bounded by linear inequalities of local features. For local models, LP is less efficient than DP. The reason is that, DP works on a small number of dimensions in each recursion, while for LP, the popular revised simplex method needs to solve a m dimensional linear system in each iteration (Nocedal and Wright, 2006), where m is the number of constraints, which is quadratic in sentence length for projective dependency parsing (Martins et al., 2009).

Dual Decomposition (DD) (Rush et al., 2010; Koo et al., 2010) is a special case of Lagrangian relaxation. It relies on standard decoding algorithms as oracle solvers for sub-problems, together with a simple method for forcing agreement between the different oracles. This method does not need to consider the tree constraint explicitly, as it resorts to dynamic programming which guarantees its satisfaction. It works well if the sub-problems can be well defined, especially for joint learning tasks. However, for the task of dependency parsing, using various non-local features may result in many overlapped sub-problems, hence it may take a long time to reach a consensus (Martins et al., 2011).

In this paper, we propose a novel Branch and Bound (B&B) algorithm for efficient parsing with various non-local features. B&B (Land and Doig, 1960) is generally used for combinatorial optimization problems such as ILP. The difference between our method and ILP is that the sub-problem in ILP is a relaxed LP, which requires a numerical solution, while ours bounds the non-local features by a linear combination of local features and uses DP for decoding as well as calculating the upper bound of the objective function. An exact solution is achieved if the bound is tight. Though in the worst case, time complexity is exponential in sentence length, it is practically efficient especially when adopting a pruning strategy.

Experiments are conducted on English PennTree Bank and Chinese Tree Bank 5 (CTB5) with standard train/develop/test split. We achieved 93.17% Unlabeled Attachment Score (UAS) for English at a speed of 177 words per second and 87.25% for Chinese at a speed of 97 words per second.

2 Graph Based Parsing

2.1 Problem Definition

Given a sentence $x = x_1, x_2, \ldots, x_n$ where x_i is the ith word of the sentence, dependency parsing assigns exactly one head word to each word, so that dependencies from head words to modifiers form a tree. The root of the tree is a special symbol denoted by x_0 which has exactly one modifier. In this paper, we focus on unlabeled projective dependency parsing but our algorithm can be adapted for labeled or non-projective dependency parsing (McDonald et al., 2005b).

The inference problem is to search the optimal parse tree y^*

$$y^* = \arg\max_{y \in \mathcal{Y}(x)} \phi(x, y)$$

where $\mathcal{Y}(x)$ is the set of all candidate parse trees of sentence x. $\phi(x, y)$ is a given score function which is usually decomposed into small parts

$$\phi(x, y) = \sum_{c \subseteq y} \phi_c(x) \tag{1}$$

where c is a subset of edges, and is called a factor. For example, in the all grandchild model (Koo and Collins, 2010), the score function can be represented as

$$\phi(x, y) = \sum_{e_{hm} \in y} \phi_{e_{hm}}(x) + \sum_{e_{gh}, e_{hm} \in y} \phi_{e_{gh}, e_{hm}}(x)$$

where the first term is the sum of scores of all edges $x_h \rightarrow x_m$, and the second term is the sum of the scores of all edge chains $x_g \rightarrow x_h \rightarrow x_m$.

In discriminative models, the score of a parse tree y is the weighted sum of the fired feature functions, which can be represented by the sum of the factors

$$\phi(x, y) = \mathbf{w}^T \mathbf{f}(x, y) = \sum_{c \subseteq y} \mathbf{w}^T \mathbf{f}(x, c) = \sum_{c \subseteq y} \phi_c(x)$$

where $\mathbf{f}(x, c)$ is the feature vector that depends on c. For example, we could define a feature for grandchild $c = \{e_{gh}, e_{hm}\}$

$$f(x, c) = \begin{cases} 1 & \text{if } x_g = \text{would} \wedge x_h = \text{be} \\ & \wedge x_m = \text{happy} \wedge c \text{ is selected} \\ 0 & \text{otherwise} \end{cases}$$

2.2 Dynamic Programming for Local Models

In first order models, all factors c in Eq(1) contain a single edge. The optimal parse tree can be derived by DP with running time $O(n^3)$ (Eisner, 1996). The algorithm has two types of structures: complete span, which consists of a headword and its descendants on one side, and incomplete span, which consists of a dependency and the region between the head and modifier. It starts at single word spans, and merges the spans in bottom up order.

For second order models, the score function $\phi(x, y)$ adds the scores of siblings (adjacent edges with a common head) and grandchildren

$$\begin{aligned} \phi(x,y) &= \sum_{e_{hm}\in y} \phi_{e_{hm}}(x) \\ &+ \sum_{e_{gh},e_{hm}\in y} \phi_{e_{hm},e_{gh}}(x) \\ &+ \sum_{e_{hm},e_{hs}\in y} \phi_{e_{hm},e_{hs}}(x) \end{aligned}$$

There are two versions of second order models, used respectively by Carreras (2007) and Koo et al. (2010). The difference is that Carreras' only considers the outermost grandchildren, while Koo and Collin's allows all grandchild features. Both models permit $O(n^4)$ running time.

Third-order models score edge triples such as three adjacent sibling modifiers, or grand-siblings that score a word, its modifier and its adjacent grandchildren, and the inference complexity is $O(n^4)$ (Koo and Collins, 2010).

In this paper, for all the factors/features that can be handled by DP, we call them the local factors/features.

3 The Proposed Method

3.1 Basic Idea

For general high order models with non-local features, we propose to use Branch and Bound (B&B) algorithm to search the optimal parse tree. A B&B algorithm has two steps: branching and bounding. The branching step recursively splits the search space $\mathcal{Y}(x)$ into two disjoint subspaces $\mathcal{Y}(x) = \mathcal{Y}_1 \bigcup \mathcal{Y}_2$ by fixing assignment of one edge. For each subspace $\mathcal{Y}_i$, the bounding step calculates the upper bound of the optimal parse tree score in the subspace: $UB\mathcal{Y}_i \geq \max_{y\in\mathcal{Y}_i} \phi(x, y)$. If this bound is no more than any obtained parse tree score $UB\mathcal{Y}_i \leq \phi(x, y')$, then all parse trees in subspace $\mathcal{Y}_i$ are no more optimal than y', and $\mathcal{Y}_i$ could be pruned safely.

The efficiency of B&B depends on the branching strategy and upper bound computation. For example, Sun et al. (2012) used B&B for MRFs, where they proposed two branching strategies and a novel data structure for efficient upper bound computation. Klenner and Ailloud (2009) proposed a variation of Balas algorithm (Balas, 1965) for coreference resolution, where candidate branching variables are sorted by their weights.

Our bounding strategy is to find an upper bound for the score of each non-local factor c containing multiple edges. The bound is the sum of new scores of edges in the factor plus a constant

$$\phi_c(x) \leq \sum_{e\in c} \psi_e(x) + \alpha_c$$

Based on the new scores $\{\psi_e(x)\}$ and constants $\{\alpha_c\}$, we define the new score of parse tree y

$$\psi(x,y) = \sum_{c\subseteq y} \left(\sum_{e\in c} \psi_e(x) + \alpha_c \right)$$

Then we have

$$\psi(x,y) \geq \phi(x,y), \forall y \in \mathcal{Y}(x)$$

The advantage of such a bound is that, it is the sum of new edge scores. Hence, its optimum tree $\max_{y\in\mathcal{Y}(x)} \psi(x, y)$ can be found by DP, which is the upper bound of $\max_{y\in\mathcal{Y}(x)} \phi(x, y)$, as for any $y \in \mathcal{Y}(x)$, $\psi(x, y) \geq \phi(x, y)$.

3.2 The Upper Bound Function

In this section, we derive the upper bound function $\psi(x, y)$ described above. To simplify notation, we drop x throughout the rest of the paper. Let z_c be a binary variable indicating whether factor c is selected in the parse tree. We reformulate the score function in Eq(1) as

$$\phi(y) \equiv \phi(z) = \sum_{c} \phi_c z_c \tag{2}$$

Correspondingly, the tree constraint is replaced by $z \in \mathcal{Z}$. Then the parsing task is

$$z^* = \arg\max_{z \in \mathcal{Z}} \phi_c z_c \tag{3}$$

Notice that, for any z_c, we have

$$z_c = \min_{e \in c} z_e$$

which means that factor c appears in parse tree if and only if all its edges $\{e|e \in c\}$ are selected in the tree. Here z_e is short for $z_{\{e\}}$ for simplicity.

Our bounding method is based on the following fact: for a set $\{a^1, a^2, \ldots a^r\}$ (a^j denotes the jth element) , its minimum

$$\min\{a^j\} = \min_{p \in \Delta} \sum_j p^j a^j \tag{4}$$

where Δ is probability simplex

$$\Delta = \{p | p^j \geq 0, \sum_j p^j = 1\}$$

We discuss the bound for $\phi_c z_c$ in two cases: $\phi_c \geq 0$ and $\phi_c < 0$.

If $\phi_c \geq 0$, we have

$$\begin{aligned}
\phi_c z_c &= \phi_c \min_{e \in c} z_e \\
&= \phi_c \min_{p_c \in \Delta} \sum_{e \in c} p_c^e z_e \\
&= \min_{p_c \in \Delta} \sum_{e \in c} \phi_c p_c^e z_e
\end{aligned}$$

The second equation comes from Eq(4). For simplicity, let

$$g_c(p_c, z) = \sum_{e \in c} \phi_c p_c^e z_e$$

with domain $\mathbf{dom} g_c = \{p_c \in \Delta; z_e \in \{0,1\}, \forall e \in c\}$. Then we have

$$\phi_c z_c = \min_{p_c} g_c(p_c, z) \tag{5}$$

If $\phi_c < 0$, we have two upper bounds. One is commonly used in ILP when all the variables are binary

$$\begin{aligned}
a^* &= \min_j \{a^j\}_{j=1}^r \\
&\Leftrightarrow \\
a^* &\leq a^j \\
a^* &\geq \sum_j a^j - (r-1)
\end{aligned}$$

According to the last inequality, we have the upper bound for negative scored factors

$$\phi_c z_c \leq \phi_c \left(\sum_{e \in c} z_e - (r_c - 1) \right) \tag{6}$$

where r_c is the number of edges in c. For simplicity, we use the notation

$$\sigma_c(z) = \phi_c \left(\sum_{e \in c} z_e - (r_c - 1) \right)$$

The other upper bound when $\phi_c < 0$ is simple

$$\phi_c z_c \leq 0 \tag{7}$$

Notice that, for any parse tree, one of the upper bounds must be tight. Eq(6) is tight if c appears in the parse tree: $z_c = 1$, otherwise Eq(7) is tight. Therefore

$$\phi_c z_c = \min\{\sigma_c(z), 0\}$$

Let

$$h_c(p_c, z) = p_c^1 \sigma_c(z) + p_c^2 \cdot 0$$

with $\mathbf{dom} h_c = \{p_c \in \Delta; z_e \in \{0,1\}, \forall e \in c\}$. According to Eq(4), we have

$$\phi_c z_c = \min_{p_c} h_c(p_c, z) \tag{8}$$

Let

$$\psi(p, z) = \sum_{c, \phi_c \geq 0} g_c(p_c, z) + \sum_{c, \phi_c < 0} h_c(p_c, z)$$

Minimize ψ with respect to p, we have

$$\begin{aligned}
& \min_p \psi(p, z) \\
= & \min_p \left(\sum_{c, \phi_c \geq 0} g_c(p_c, z) + \sum_{c, \phi_c < 0} h_c(p_c, z) \right) \\
= & \sum_{c, \phi_c \geq 0} \min_{p_c} g_c(p_c, z) + \sum_{c, \phi_c < 0} \min_{p_c} h_c(p_c, z) \\
= & \sum_{c, \phi_c \geq 0} \phi_c z_c + \sum_{c, \phi_c < 0} \phi_c z_c \\
= & \phi(z)
\end{aligned}$$

The second equation holds since, for any two factors, c and c', g_c (or h_c) and $g_{c'}$ (or $h_{c'}$) are separable. The third equation comes from Eq(5) and Eq(8).

Based on this, we have the following proposition:

Proposition 1. *For any* $p, p_c \in \Delta$, *and* $z \in \mathcal{Z}$, $\psi(p, z) \geq \phi(z)$.

Therefore, $\psi(p, z)$ is an upper bound function of $\phi(z)$. Furthermore, fixing p, $\psi(p, z)$ is a linear function of z_e , see Eq(5) and Eq(8), variables z_c for large factors are eliminated. Hence $z' = \arg\max_z \psi(p, z)$ can be solved efficiently by DP.

Because

$$\psi(p, z') \geq \psi(p, z^*) \geq \phi(z^*) \geq \phi(z')$$

after obtaining z' , we get the upper bound and lower bound of $\phi(z^*)$: $\psi(p, z')$ and $\phi(z')$.

The upper bound is expected to be as tight as possible. Using min-max inequality, we get

$$\begin{aligned} \max_{z \in \mathcal{Z}} \phi(z) &= \max_{z \in \mathcal{Z}} \min_{p} \psi(p, z) \\ &\leq \min_{p} \max_{z \in \mathcal{Z}} \psi(p, z) \end{aligned}$$

which provides the tightest upper bound of $\phi(z^*)$.

Since ψ is not differentiable w.r.t p, projected sub-gradient (Calamai and Moré, 1987; Rush et al., 2010) is used to search the saddle point. More specifically, in each iteration, we first fix p and search z using DP, then we fix z and update p by

$$p_{new} = P_\Delta \left(p + \frac{\partial \psi}{\partial p} \alpha \right)$$

where $\alpha > 0$ is the step size in line search, function $P_\Delta(q)$ denotes the projection of q onto the probability simplex Δ. In this paper, we use Euclidean projection, that is

$$P_\Delta(q) = \min_{p \in \Delta} \|p - q\|_2$$

which can be solved efficiently by sorting (Duchi et al., 2008).

3.3 Branch and Bound Based Parsing

As discussed in Section 3.1, the B&B recursive procedure yields a binary tree structure called Branch and Bound tree. Each node of the B&B tree has some fixed z_e, specifying some must-select edges and must-remove edges. The root of the B&B tree has no constraints, so it can produce all possible parse trees including z^*. Each node has two children. One adds a constraint $z_e = 1$ for a free edge e and the other fixes $z_e = 0$. We can explore the search space $\{z | z_e \in \{0, 1\}\}$ by traversing the B&B tree in breadth first order.

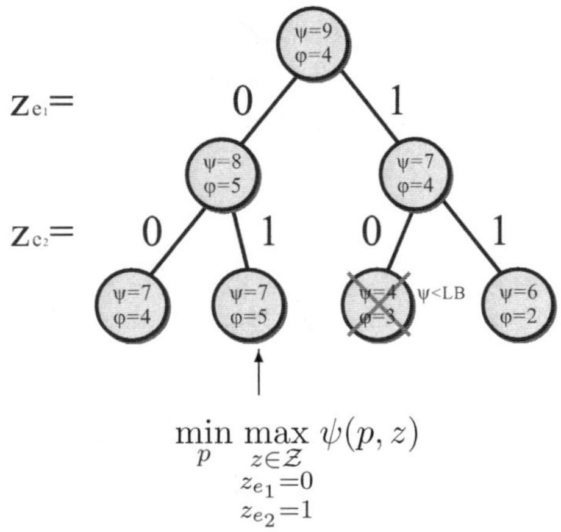

Figure 1: A part of B&B tree. ϕ, ψ are short for $\phi(z')$ and $\psi(p', z')$ respectively. For each node, some edges of the parse tree are fixed. All parse trees that satisfy the fixed edges compose the subset of $S \subseteq \mathcal{Z}$. A min-max problem is solved to get the upper bound and lower bound of the optimal parse tree over S. Once the upper bound ψ is less than LB, the node is removed safely.

Let $S \subseteq \mathcal{Z}$ be subspace of parse trees satisfying the constraint, i.e., in the branch of the node. For each node in B&B tree, we solve

$$p', z' = \arg\min_{p} \max_{z \in S} \psi(p, z)$$

to get the upper bound and lower bound of the best parse tree in S. A global lower bound LB is maintained which is the maximum of all obtained lower bounds. If the upper bound of the current node is lower than the global lower bound, the node can be pruned from the B&B tree safely. An example is shown in Figure 1.

When the upper bound is not tight: $\psi > LB$, we need to choose a good branching variable to generate the child nodes. Let $G(z') = \psi(p', z') - \phi(z')$ denote the gap between the upper bound and lower bound. This gap is actually the accumulated gaps of all factors c. Let G_c be the gap of c

$$G_c = \begin{cases} g_c(p'_c, z') - \phi_c z'_c & \text{if } \phi_c \geq 0 \\ h_c(p'_c, z') - \phi_c z'_c & \text{if } \phi_c < 0 \end{cases}$$

We choose the branching variable heuristically: for each edge e, we define its gap as the sum of the gaps of factors that contain it

$$G^e = \sum_{c, e \in c} G_c$$

The edge with the maximum gap is selected as the branching variable.

Suppose there are N nodes on a level of B&B tree, and correspondingly, we get N branching variables, among which, we choose the one with the highest lower bound as it likely reaches the optimal value faster.

3.4 Lower Bound Initialization

A large lower bound is critical for efficient pruning. In this section, we discuss an alternative way to initialize the lower bound LB. We apply the similar trick to get the lower bound function of $\phi(z)$.

Similar to Eq(8), for $\phi_c \geq 0$, we have

$$\begin{aligned}\phi_c z_c &= \max\{\phi_c \left(\sum_{e \in c} z_e - (r_c - 1)\right), 0\} \\ &= \max\{\sigma_c(z), 0\}\end{aligned}$$

Using the fact that

$$\max\{a^j\} = \max_{p \in \Delta} \sum_j p^j a^j$$

we have

$$\begin{aligned}\phi_c z_c &= \max_{p_c \in \Delta} p_c^1 \sigma_c(z) + p_c^2 \cdot 0 \\ &= \max_{p_c} h_c(p_c, z)\end{aligned}$$

For $\phi_c < 0$, we have

$$\begin{aligned}\phi_c z_c &= \max_{e \in c}\{\phi_c z_e\} \\ &= \max_{p_c \in \Delta} \sum_{e \in c} p_c^e \phi_c z_e \\ &= \max_{p_c} g_c(p_c, z)\end{aligned}$$

Put the two cases together, we get the lower bound function

$$\pi(p, z) = \sum_{c, \phi_c \geq 0} h_c(p_c, z) + \sum_{c, \phi_c < 0} g_c(p_c, z)$$

Algorithm 1 Branch and Bound based parsing

Require: $\{\phi_c\}$
Ensure: Optimal parse tree z^*
  Solve $p^*, z^* = \arg\max_{p,z} \pi(p, z)$
  Initialize $\mathcal{S} = \{\mathcal{Z}\}$, $LB = \pi(p^*, z^*)$
  while $\mathcal{S} \neq \emptyset$ **do**
    Set $\mathcal{S}' = \emptyset$\{nodes that survive from pruning\}
    foreach $S \in \mathcal{S}$
      Solve $\min_p \max_z \psi(p, z)$ to get LB_S, UB_S
    $LB = \max\{LB, LB_{S \in \mathcal{S}}\}$, update z^*
    foreach $S \in \mathcal{S}$, add S to $\mathcal{S}'$, if $UB_S > LB$
    Select a branching variable z_e.
    Clear $\mathcal{S} = \emptyset$
    foreach $S \in \mathcal{S}'$
      Add $S_1 = \{z | z \in S, z_e = 1\}$ to $\mathcal{S}$
      Add $S_2 = \{z | z \in S, z_e = 0\}$ to $\mathcal{S}$.
  end while

For any $p, p_c \in \Delta$, $z \in \mathcal{Z}$

$$\pi(p, z) \leq \phi(z)$$

$\pi(p, z)$ is not concave, however, we could alternatively optimize z and p to get a good approximation, which provides a lower bound for $\phi(z^*)$.

3.5 Summary

We summarize our B&B algorithm in Algorithm 1.

It is worth pointing out that so far in the above description, we have used the assumption that the backbone DP uses first order models, however, the backbone DP can be the second or third order version. The difference is that, for higher order DP, higher order factors such as adjacent siblings, grandchildren are directly handled as local factors.

In the worst case, all the edges are selected for branching, and the complexity grows exponentially in sentence length. However, in practice, it is quite efficient, as we will show in the next section.

4 Experiments

4.1 Experimental Settings

The datasets we used are the English Penn Tree Bank (PTB) and Chinese Tree Bank 5.0 (CTB5). We use the standard train/develop/test split as described in Table 1.

We extracted dependencies using Joakim Nivre's Penn2Malt tool with standard head rules: Yamada and Matsumoto's (Yamada and Matsumoto, 2003)

	Train	*Develop*	*Test*
PTB	sec. 2-21	sec. 22	sec. 23
CTB5	sec. 001-815 1001-1136	sec. 886-931 1148-1151	sec. 816-885 1137-1147

Table 1: Data split in our experiment

for English, and Zhang and Clark's (Zhang and Clark, 2008) for Chinese. Unlabeled attachment score (UAS) is used to evaluate parsing quality[1]. The B&B parser is implemented with C++. All the experiments are conducted on the platform Intel Core i5-2500 CPU 3.30GHz.

4.2 Baseline: DP Based Second Order Parser

We use the dynamic programming based second order parser (Carreras, 2007) as the baseline. Averaged structured perceptron (Collins, 2002) is used for parameter estimation. We determine the number of iterations on the validation set, which is 6 for both corpora.

For English, we train the POS tagger using linear chain perceptron on training set, and predict POS tags for the development and test data. The parser is trained using the automatic POS tags generated by 10 fold cross validation. For Chinese, we use the gold standard POS tags.

We use five types of features: unigram features, bigram features, in-between features, adjacent sibling features and outermost grand-child features. The first three types of features are firstly introduced by McDonald et al. (2005a) and the last two types of features are used by Carreras (2007). All the features are the concatenation of surrounding words, lower cased words (English only), word length (Chinese only), prefixes and suffixes of words (Chinese only), POS tags, coarse POS tags which are derived from POS tags using a simple mapping table, distance between head and modifier, direction of edges. For English, we used 674 feature templates to generate large amounts of features, and finally got $86.7M$ non-zero weighted features after training. The baseline parser got 92.81% UAS on the testing set. For Chinese, we used 858 feature templates, and finally got $71.5M$ non-zero weighted features after training. The baseline parser got 86.89% UAS on the testing set.

[1]For English, we follow Koo and Collins (2010) and ignore any word whose gold-standard POS tag is one of { “ ” : , .}. For Chinese, we ignore any word whose POS tag is *PU*.

4.3 B&B Based Parser with Non-local Features

We use the baseline parser as the backbone of our B&B parser. We tried different types of non-local features as listed below:

- All grand-child features. Notice that this feature can be handled by Koo's second order model (Koo and Collins, 2010) directly.
- All great grand-child features.
- All sibling features: all the pairs of edges with common head. An example is shown in Figure 2.
- All tri-sibling features: all the 3-tuples of edges with common head.
- Comb features: for any word with more than 3 consecutive modifiers, the set of all the edges from the word to the modifiers form a comb.[2]
- Hand crafted features: We perform cross validation on the training data using the baseline parser, and designed features that may correct the most common errors. We designed 13 hand-craft features for English in total. One example is shown in Figure 3. For Chinese, we did not add any hand-craft features, as the errors in the cross validation result vary a lot, and we did not find general patterns to fix them.

4.4 Implementation Details

To speed up the solution of the min-max subproblem, for each node in the B&B tree, we initialize p with the optimal solution of its parent node, since the child node fixes only one additional edge, its optimal point is likely to be closed to its parent's. For the root node of B&B tree, we initialize $p_c^e = \frac{1}{r_c}$ for factors with non-negative weights and $p_c^1 = 0$ for

[2]In fact, our algorithm can deal with non-consecutive modifiers; however, in such cases, factor detection (detect regular expressions like $x_1. * x_2. * \ldots$) requires the longest common subsequence algorithm (LCS), which is time-consuming if many comb features are generated. Similar problems arise for sub-tree features, which may contain many non-consecutive words.

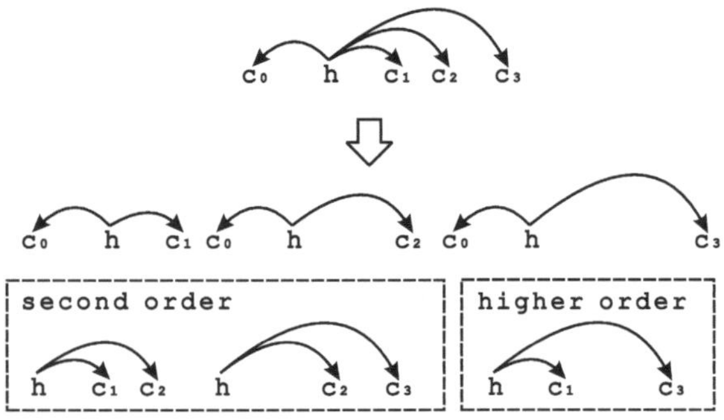

Figure 2: An example of all sibling features. Top: a sub-tree; Bottom: extracted sibling features. Existing higher order DP systems can not handle the siblings on both sides of head.

Figure 3: An example of hand-craft feature: for the word sequence A ... *rather than* A, where A is a preposition, the first A is the head of *than*, *than* is the head of *rather* and the second A.

negative weighted factors. Step size α is initialized with $\max_{c,\phi_c \neq 0}\{\frac{1}{|\phi_c|}\}$, as the vector p is bounded in a unit box. α is updated using the same strategy as Rush et al. (2010). Two stopping criteria are used. One is $0 \leq \psi_{old} - \psi_{new} \leq \epsilon$, where $\epsilon > 0$ is a given precision[3]. The other checks if the bound is tight: $UB = LB$. Because all features are boolean (note that they can be integer), their weights are integer during each perceptron update, hence the scores of parse trees are discrete. The minimal gap between different scores is $\frac{1}{N \times T}$ after averaging, where N is the number of training samples, and T is the iteration number for perceptron training. Therefore the upper bound can be tightened as $UB = \frac{\lfloor NT\psi \rfloor}{NT}$.

During testing, we use the pre-pruning method as used in Martins et al. (2009) for both datasets to balance parsing quality and speed. This method uses a simple classifier to select the top k candidate heads for each word and exclude the other heads from search space. In our experiment, we set $k = 10$.

[3]we use $\epsilon = 10^{-8}$ in our implementation

System	*PTB*	*CTB*
Our baseline	92.81	86.89
B&B +all grand-child	92.97	87.02
+all great grand-child	92.78	86.77
+all sibling	93.00	87.05
+all tri-sibling	92.79	86.81
+comb	92.86	86.91
+hand craft	92.89	N/A
+all grand-child + all sibling + comb + hand craft	**93.17**	**87.25**
3rd order re-impl.	93.03	87.07
TurboParser (reported)	92.62	N/A
TurboParser (our run)	92.82	86.05
Koo and Collins (2010)	93.04	N/A
Zhang and McDonald (2012)	93.06	86.87
Zhang and Nivre (2011)	92.90	86.00
System integration		
Bohnet and Kuhn (2012)	93.39	87.5
Systems using additional resources		
Suzuki et al. (2009)	93.79	N/A
Koo et al. (2008)	93.5	N/A
Chen et al. (2012)	92.76	N/A

Table 2: Comparison between our system and the-state-of-art systems.

4.5 Main Result

Experimental results are listed in Table 2. For comparison, we also include results of representative state-of-the-art systems. For the third order parser, we re-implemented Model 1 (Koo and Collins, 2010), and removed the longest sentence in the CTB dataset, which contains 240 words, due to the $O(n^4)$ space complexity [4]. For ILP based parsing, we used TurboParser[5], a speed-optimized parser toolkit. We trained full models (which use all grandchild features, all sibling features and head bigram features (Martins et al., 2011)) for both datasets using its default settings. We also list the performance in its documentation on English corpus.

The observation is that, the all-sibling features are most helpful for our parser, as some good sibling features can not be encoded in DP based parser. For example, a matched pair of parentheses are always siblings, but their head may lie between them. An-

[4]In fact, Koo's algorithm requires only $O(n^3)$ space. Our implementation is $O(n^4)$ because we store the feature vectors for fast training.

[5]http://www.ark.cs.cmu.edu/TurboParser/

other observation is that all great grandchild features and all tri-sibling features slightly hurt the performance and we excluded them from the final system.

When no additional resource is available, our parser achieved competitive performance: 93.17% Unlabeled Attachment Score (UAS) for English at a speed of 177 words per second and 87.25% for Chinese at a speed of 97 words per second. Higher UAS is reported by joint tagging and parsing (Bohnet and Nivre, 2012) or system integration (Bohnet and Kuhn, 2012) which benefits from both transition based parsing and graph based parsing. Previous work shows that combination of the two parsing techniques can learn to overcome the shortcomings of each non-integrated system (Nivre and McDonald, 2008; Zhang and Clark, 2008). System combination will be an interesting topic for our future research. The highest reported performance on English corpus is 93.79%, obtained by semi-supervised learning with a large amount of unlabeled data (Suzuki et al., 2009).

4.6 Tradeoff Between Accuracy and Speed

In this section, we study the trade off between accuracy and speed using different pre-pruning setups. In Table 3, we show the parsing accuracy and inference time in testing stage with different numbers of candidate heads k in pruning step. We can see that, on English dataset, when $k \geq 10$, our parser could gain $2-3$ times speedup without losing much parsing accuracy. There is a further increase of the speed with smaller k, at the cost of some accuracy. Compared with TurboParser, our parser is less efficient but more accurate. Zhang and McDonald (2012) is a state-of-the-art system which adopts cube pruning for efficient parsing. Notice that, they did not use pruning which seems to increase parsing speed with little hit in accuracy. Moreover, they did labeled parsing, which also makes their speed not directly comparable.

For each node of B&B tree, our parsing algorithm uses projected sub-gradient method to find the saddle point, which requires a number of calls to a DP, hence the efficiency of Algorithm 1 is mainly determined by the number of DP calls. Figure 4 and Figure 5 show the averaged parsing time and number of calls to DP relative to the sentence length with different pruning settings. Parsing time grows smoothly when sentence length ≤ 40. There is some fluctuation for the long sentences. This is because there are very few sentences for a specific long length (usually 1 or 2 sentences), and the statistics are not stable or meaningful for the small samples.

	PTB		*CTB*	
System	*UAS*	*w/s*	*UAS*	*w/s*
Ours (no prune)	93.18	52	87.28	73
Ours ($k = 20$)	93.17	105	87.28	76
Ours ($k = 10$)	93.17	177	87.25	97
Ours ($k = 5$)	93.10	264	86.94	108
Ours ($k = 3$)	92.68	493	85.76	128
TurboParser(full)	92.82	402	86.05	192
TurboParser(standard)	92.68	638	85.80	283
TurboParser(basic)	90.97	4670	82.28	2736
Zhang and McDonald (2012)†	93.06	220	86.87	N/A

Table 3: Trade off between parsing accuracy (UAS) and speed (words per second) with different pre-pruning settings. k denotes the number of candidate heads of each word preserved for B&B parsing. †Their speed is not directly comparable as they performs labeled parsing without pruning.

Without pruning, there are in total $132,161$ calls to parse $2,416$ English sentences, that is, each sentence requires 54.7 calls on average. For Chinese, there are $84,645$ calls for $1,910$ sentences, i.e., 44.3 calls for each sentence on average.

5 Discussion

5.1 Polynomial Non-local Factors

Our bounding strategy can handle a family of non-local factors that can be expressed as a polynomial function of local factors. To see this, suppose

$$z_c = \sum_i \alpha_i \prod_{e \in E_i} z_e$$

For each i, we introduce new variable $z_{E_i} = \min_{e \in E_i} z_e$. Because z_e is binary, $z_{E_i} = \prod_{e \in E_i} z_e$. In this way, we replace z_c by several z_{E_i} that can be handled by our bounding strategy.

We give two examples of these polynomial non-local factors. First is the OR of local factors: $z_c = \max\{z_e, z'_e\}$, which can be expressed by $z_c = z_e + z'_e - z_e z'_e$. The second is the factor of valency feature

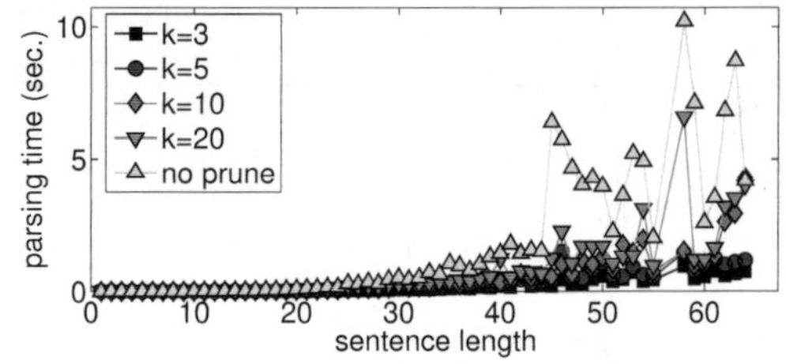

(a) PTB corpus

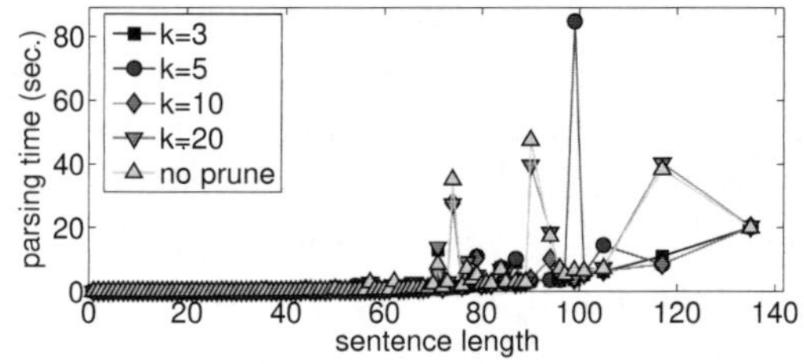

(b) CTB corpus

Figure 4 Averaged parsing time (seconds) relative to sentence length with different pruning settings, k denotes the number of candidate heads of each word in pruning step.

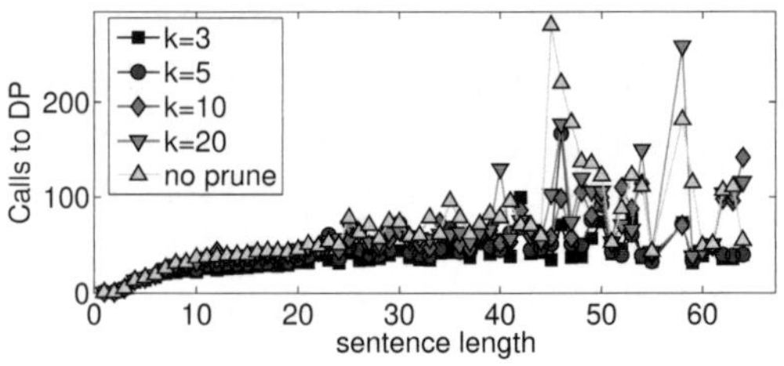

(a) PTB corpus

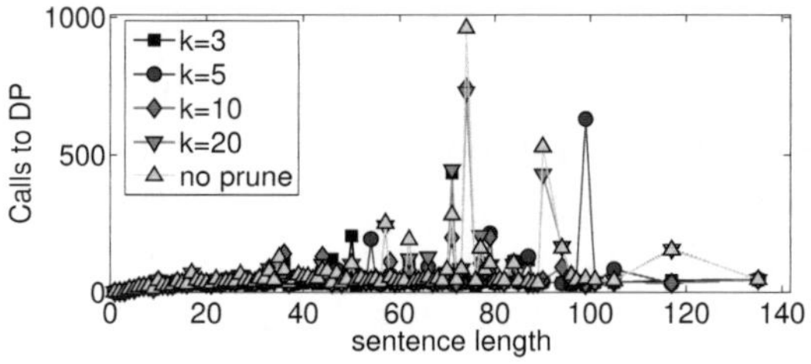

(b) CTB corpus

Figure 5 Averaged number of Calls to DP relative to sentence length with different pruning settings, k denotes the number of candidate heads of each word in pruning step.

(Martins et al., 2009). Let binary variable v_{ik} indicate whether word i has k modifiers. Given $\{z_e\}$ for the edges with head i, then $\{v_{ik}|k = 1, \ldots, n-1\}$ can be solved by

$$\sum_k k^j v_{ik} = \left(\sum_e z_e\right)^j \qquad 0 \leq j \leq n-1$$

The left side of the equation is the linear function of v_{ik}. The right side of the equation is a polynomial function of z_e. Hence, v_{ik} could be expressed as a polynomial function of z_e.

5.2 k Best Parsing

Though our B&B algorithm is able to capture a variety of non-local features, it is still difficult to handle many kinds of features, such as the depth of the parse tree. Hence, a reranking approach may be useful in order to incorporate such information, where k parse trees can be generated first and then a second pass model is used to rerank these candidates based on more global or non-local features. In addition, k-best parsing may be needed in many applications to use parse information and especially utilize information from multiple candidates to optimize task-specific performance. We have not conducted any experiment for k best parsing, hence we only discuss the algorithm.

According to proposition 1, we have

Proposition 2. *Given p and subset $S \subseteq \mathcal{Z}$, let z^k denote the kth best solution of $\max_{z \in S} \psi(p,z)$. If a parse tree $z' \in S$ satisfies $\phi(z') \geq \psi(p, z^k)$, then z' is one of the k best parse trees in subset S.*

Proof. Since z^k is the kth best solution of $\psi(p,z)$, for z^j, $j > k$, we have $\psi(p,z^k) \geq \psi(p,z^j) \geq \phi(z^j)$. Since the size of the set $\{z^j | j > k\}$ is $|S| - k$, hence there are at least $|S| - k$ parse trees whose scores $\phi(z^j)$ are less than $\psi(p, z^k)$. Because $\phi(z') \geq \psi(p, z^k)$, hence z' is at least the kth best parse tree in subset S. □

Therefore, we can search the k best parse trees in this way: for each sub-problem, we use DP to derive the k best parse trees. For each parse tree z, if $\phi(z) \geq \psi(p, z^k)$, then z is selected into the k best set. Algorithm terminates until the kth bound is tight.

6 Conclusion

In this paper we proposed a new parsing algorithm based on a Branch and Bound framework. The motivation is to use dynamic programming to search for the bound. Experimental results on PTB and CTB5 datasets show that our method is competitive in terms of both performance and efficiency. Our method can be adapted to non-projective dependency parsing, as well as the k best MST algorithm (Hall, 2007) to find the k best candidates.

Acknowledgments

We'd like to thank Hao Zhang, Andre Martins and Zhenghua Li for their helpful discussions. We also thank Ryan McDonald and three anonymous reviewers for their valuable comments. This work is partly supported by DARPA under Contract No. HR0011-12-C-0016 and FA8750-13-2-0041. Any opinions expressed in this material are those of the authors and do not necessarily reflect the views of DARPA.

References

Michael Auli and Adam Lopez. 2011. A comparison of loopy belief propagation and dual decomposition for integrated CCG supertagging and parsing. In *Proc. of ACL-HLT*.

Egon Balas. 1965. An additive algorithm for solving linear programs with zero-one variables. *Operations Research*, 39(4).

Bernd Bohnet and Jonas Kuhn. 2012. The best of bothworlds – a graph-based completion model for transition-based parsers. In *Proc. of EACL*.

Bernd Bohnet and Joakim Nivre. 2012. A transition-based system for joint part-of-speech tagging and labeled non-projective dependency parsing. In *Proc. of EMNLP-CoNLL*.

Paul Calamai and Jorge Moré. 1987. Projected gradient methods for linearly constrained problems. *Mathematical Programming*, 39(1).

Xavier Carreras. 2007. Experiments with a higher-order projective dependency parser. In *Proc. of EMNLP-CoNLL*.

Eugene Charniak and Mark Johnson. 2005. Coarse-to-fine n-best parsing and maxent discriminative reranking. In *Proc. of ACL*.

Wenliang Chen, Min Zhang, and Haizhou Li. 2012. Utilizing dependency language models for graph-based dependency parsing models. In *Proc. of ACL*.

Michael Collins. 2000. Discriminative reranking for natural language parsing. In *Proc. of ICML*.

Michael Collins. 2002. Discriminative training methods for hidden markov models: Theory and experiments with perceptron algorithms. In *Proc. of EMNLP*.

John Duchi, Shai Shalev-Shwartz, Yoram Singer, and Tushar Chandra. 2008. Efficient projections onto the l1-ball for learning in high dimensions. In *Proc. of ICML*.

Jason M. Eisner. 1996. Three new probabilistic models for dependency parsing: an exploration. In *Proc. of COLING*.

Keith Hall. 2007. K-best spanning tree parsing. In *Proc. of ACL*.

Liang Huang and David Chiang. 2005. Better k-best parsing. In *Proc. of IWPT*.

Liang Huang. 2008. Forest reranking: Discriminative parsing with non-local features. In *Proc. of ACL-HLT*.

Manfred Klenner and Étienne Ailloud. 2009. Optimization in coreference resolution is not needed: A nearly-optimal algorithm with intensional constraints. In *Proc. of EACL*.

Terry Koo and Michael Collins. 2010. Efficient third-order dependency parsers. In *Proc. of ACL*.

Terry Koo, Xavier Carreras, and Michael Collins. 2008. Simple semi-supervised dependency parsing. In *Proc. of ACL-HLT*.

Terry Koo, Alexander M. Rush, Michael Collins, Tommi Jaakkola, and David Sontag. 2010. Dual decomposition for parsing with non-projective head automata. In *Proc. of EMNLP*.

Ailsa H. Land and Alison G. Doig. 1960. An automatic method of solving discrete programming problems. *Econometrica*, 28(3):497–520.

Andre Martins, Noah Smith, and Eric Xing. 2009. Concise integer linear programming formulations for dependency parsing. In *Proc. of ACL*.

Andre Martins, Noah Smith, Mario Figueiredo, and Pedro Aguiar. 2011. Dual decomposition with many overlapping components. In *Proc. of EMNLP*.

Ryan McDonald, Koby Crammer, and Fernando Pereira. 2005a. Online large-margin training of dependency parsers. In *Proc. of ACL*.

Ryan McDonald, Fernando Pereira, Kiril Ribarov, and Jan Hajic. 2005b. Non-projective dependency parsing using spanning tree algorithms. In *Proc. of HLT-EMNLP*.

Joakim Nivre and Ryan McDonald. 2008. Integrating graph-based and transition-based dependency parsers. In *Proc. of ACL-HLT*.

Jorge Nocedal and Stephen J. Wright. 2006. *Numerical Optimization*. Springer, 2nd edition.

Sebastian Riedel and James Clarke. 2006. Incremental integer linear programming for non-projective dependency parsing. In *Proc. of EMNLP*.

Alexander M Rush, David Sontag, Michael Collins, and Tommi Jaakkola. 2010. On dual decomposition and linear programming relaxations for natural language processing. In *Proc. of EMNLP*.

David Smith and Jason Eisner. 2008. Dependency parsing by belief propagation. In *Proc. of EMNLP*.

Min Sun, Murali Telaprolu, Honglak Lee, and Silvio Savarese. 2012. Efficient and exact MAP-MRF inference using branch and bound. In *Proc. of AISTATS*.

Jun Suzuki, Hideki Isozaki, Xavier Carreras, and Michael Collins. 2009. An empirical study of semi-supervised structured conditional models for dependency parsing. In *Proc. of EMNLP*.

Hiroyasu Yamada and Yuji Matsumoto. 2003. Statistical dependency analysis with support vector machines. In *Proc. of IWPT*.

Yue Zhang and Stephen Clark. 2008. A tale of two parsers: Investigating and combining graph-based and transition-based dependency parsing. In *Proc. of EMNLP*.

Hao Zhang and Ryan McDonald. 2012. Generalized higher-order dependency parsing with cube pruning. In *Proc. of EMNLP*.

Yue Zhang and Joakim Nivre. 2011. Transition-based dependency parsing with rich non-local features. In *Proc. of ACL-HLT*.

Weakly Supervised Learning of Semantic Parsers for Mapping Instructions to Actions

Yoav Artzi and **Luke Zettlemoyer**
Computer Science & Engineering
University of Washington
Seattle, WA 98195
{yoav,lsz}@cs.washington.edu

Abstract

The context in which language is used provides a strong signal for learning to recover its meaning. In this paper, we show it can be used within a grounded CCG semantic parsing approach that learns a joint model of meaning and context for interpreting and executing natural language instructions, using various types of weak supervision. The joint nature provides crucial benefits by allowing situated cues, such as the set of visible objects, to directly influence learning. It also enables algorithms that learn while executing instructions, for example by trying to replicate human actions. Experiments on a benchmark navigational dataset demonstrate strong performance under differing forms of supervision, including correctly executing 60% more instruction sets relative to the previous state of the art.

1 Introduction

The context in which natural language is used provides a strong signal to reason about its meaning. However, using such a signal to automatically learn to understand unrestricted natural language remains a challenging, unsolved problem.

For example, consider the instructions in Figure 1. Correct interpretation requires us to solve many subproblems, such as resolving all referring expressions to specific objects in the environment (including, "the corner" or "the third intersection"), disambiguating word sense based on context (e.g., "the chair" could refer to a chair or sofa), and finding executable action sequences that satisfy stated constraints (such as "twice" or "to face the blue hall").

move forward twice to the chair
$\lambda a.move(a) \land dir(a, forward) \land len(a, 2) \land$
$to(a, \iota x.chair(x))$
at the corner turn left to face the blue hall
$\lambda a.pre(a, \iota x.corner(x)) \land turn(a) \land dir(a, left) \land$
$post(a, front(you, \iota x.blue(x) \land hall(x)))$
move to the chair in the third intersection
$\lambda a.move(a) \land to(a, \iota x.sofa(x)) \land$
$intersect(order(\lambda y.junction(y), frontdist, 3), x)$

Figure 1: A sample navigation instruction set, paired with lambda-calculus meaning representations.

We must also understand implicit requests, for example from the phrase "at the corner," that describe goals to be achieved without specifying the specific steps. Finally, to do all of this robustly without prohibitive engineering effort, we need *grounded* learning approaches that jointly reason about meaning and context to learn directly from their interplay, with as little human intervention as possible.

Although many of these challenges have been studied separately, as we will review in Section 3, this paper represents, to the best of our knowledge, the first attempt at a comprehensive model that addresses them all. Our approach induces a weighted Combinatory Categorial Grammar (CCG), including both the parameters of the linear model and a CCG lexicon. To model complex instructional language, we introduce a new semantic modeling approach that can represent a number of key linguistic constructs that are common in spatial and instructional language. To learn from indirect supervision, we define the notion of a validation function, for example that tests the state of the agent after interpreting an instruction. We then show how this function can be used to drive online learning. For that purpose, we adapt the loss-sensitive Perceptron algorithm (Singh-Miller & Collins, 2007; Artzi & Zettlemoyer, 2011) to use a validation function and coarse-to-fine inference for lexical induction.

The joint nature of this approach provides crucial benefits in that it allows situated cues, such as the set of visible objects, to directly influence parsing and learning. It also enables the model to be learned while executing instructions, for example by trying to replicate actions taken by humans. In particular, we show that, given only a small seed lexicon and a task-specific executor, we can induce high quality models for interpreting complex instructions.

We evaluate the method on a benchmark navigational instructions dataset (MacMahon et al., 2006; Chen & Mooney, 2011). Our joint approach successfully completes 60% more instruction sets relative to the previous state of the art. We also report experiments that vary supervision type, finding that observing the final position of an instruction execution is nearly as informative as observing the entire path. Finally, we present improved results on a new version of the MacMahon et al. (2006) corpus, which we filtered to include only executable instructions paired with correct traces.

2 Technical Overview

Task Let $\mathcal{S}$ be the set of possible environment states and $\mathcal{A}$ be the set of possible actions. Given a start state $s \in \mathcal{S}$ and a natural language instruction x, we aim to generate a sequence of actions $\vec{a} = \langle a_1, \ldots, a_n \rangle$, with each $a_i \in \mathcal{A}$, that performs the steps described in x.

For example, in the navigation domain (MacMahon et al., 2006), $\mathcal{S}$ is a set of positions on a map. Each state $s = (x, y, o)$ is a triple, where x and y are integer grid coordinates and $o \in \{0, 90, 180, 270\}$ is an orientation. Figure 2 shows an example map with 36 states; the ones we use in our experiments contain an average of 141. The space of possible actions $\mathcal{A}$ is $\{\text{LEFT}, \text{RIGHT}, \text{MOVE}, \text{NULL}\}$. Actions change the state of the world according to a transition function $T : \mathcal{A} \times \mathcal{S} \rightarrow \mathcal{S}$. In our navigation example, moving forward can change the x or y coordinates while turning changes the orientation o.

Model To map instructions to actions, we jointly reason about linguistic meaning and action execution. We use a weighted CCG grammar to rank possible meanings z for each instruction x. Section 6 defines how to design such grammars for instructional language. Each logical form z is mapped to a sequence of actions $\vec{a}$ with a deterministic executor, as described in Section 7. The final *grounded CCG* model, detailed in Section 6.3, jointly constructs and scores z and $\vec{a}$, allowing for robust situated reasoning during semantic interpretation.

Learning We assume access to a training set containing n examples $\{(x_i, s_i, \mathcal{V}_i) : i = 1 \ldots n\}$, each containing a natural language sentence x_i, a start state s_i, and a validation function $\mathcal{V}_i$. The validation function $\mathcal{V}_i : A \rightarrow \{0, 1\}$ maps an action sequence $\vec{a} \in A$ to 1 if it's correct according to available supervision, or 0 otherwise. This training data contains no direct evidence about the logical form z_i for each x_i, or the grounded CCG analysis used to construct z_i. We model all these choices as latent variables. We experiment with two validation functions. The first, $\mathcal{V}^D(\vec{a})$, has access to an observable demonstration of the execution $\vec{a}_i$, a given $\vec{a}$ is valid iff $\vec{a} = \vec{a}_i$. The second, $\mathcal{V}_i^S(\vec{a})$, only encodes the final state s'_i of the execution of x, therefore $\vec{a}$ is valid iff its final state is s'_i. Since numerous logical forms often execute identically, both functions provide highly ambiguous supervision.

Evaluation We evaluate task completion for single instructions on a test set $\{(x_i, s_i, s'_i) : i = 1 \ldots n\}$, where s'_i is the final state of an oracle agent following the execution of x_i starting at state s_i. We will also report accuracies for correctly interpreting instruction sequences $\vec{x}$, where a single error can cause the entire sequence to fail. Finally, we report accuracy on recovering correct logical forms z_i on a manually annotated subset of the test set.

3 Related Work

Our learning is inspired by the reinforcement learning (RL) approach of Branavan et al. (2009), and related methods (Vogel & Jurafsky, 2010), but uses latent variable model updates within a semantic parser. Branavan et al. (2010) extended their RL approach to model high-level instructions, which correspond to implicit actions in our domain. Wei et al. (2009) and Kollar et al. (2010) used shallow linguistic representations for instructions. Recently, Tellex et al. (2011) used a graphical model semantics representation to learn from instructions paired with demonstrations. In contrast, we model significantly more complex linguistic phenomena than these approaches, as required for the navigation domain.

Other research has adopted expressive meaning representations, with differing learning approaches. Matuszek et al. (2010, 2012) describe supervised algorithms that learn semantic parsers for navigation instructions. Chen and Mooney (2011), Chen (2012) and Kim and Mooney (2012) present state-of-the-art algorithms for the navigation task, by training a supervised semantic parser from automatically induced labels. Our work differs in the use of joint learning and inference approaches.

Supervised approaches for learning semantic parsers have received significant attention, e.g. Kate and Mooney (2006), Wong and Mooney (2007), Muresan (2011) and Kwiatkowski et al. (2010, 2012). The algorithms we develop in this paper combine ideas from previous supervised CCG learning work (Zettlemoyer & Collins, 2005, 2007; Kwiatkowski et al., 2011), as we describe in Section 4. Recently, various alternative forms of supervision were introduced. Clarke et al. (2010), Goldwasser and Roth (2011) and Liang et al. (2011) describe approaches for learning semantic parsers from sentences paired with responses, Krishnamurthy and Mitchell (2012) describe using distant supervision, Artzi and Zettlemoyer (2011) use weak supervision from conversational logs and Goldwasser et al. (2011) present work on unsupervised learning. We discuss various forms of supervision that complement these approaches. There has also been work on learning for semantic analysis tasks from grounded data, including event streams (Liang et al., 2009; Chen et al., 2010) and language paired with visual perception (Matuszek et al., 2012).

Finally, the topic of executing instructions in non-learning settings has received significant attention (e.g., Winograd (1972), Di Eugenio and White (1992), Webber et al. (1995), Bugmann et al. (2004), MacMahon et al. (2006) and Dzifcak et al. (2009)).

4 Background

We use a weighted linear CCG grammar for semantic parsing, as briefly reviewed in this section.

Combinatory Categorial Grammars (CCGs) CCGs are a linguistically-motivated formalism for modeling a wide range of language phenomena (Steedman, 1996, 2000). A CCG is defined by a lexicon and a set of combinators. The lexicon contains entries that pair words or phrases with categories. For example, the lexical entry chair $\vdash N : \lambda x.chair(x)$ for the word "chair" in the parse in Figure 4 pairs it with a category that has syntactic type N and meaning $\lambda x.chair(x)$. Figure 4 shows how a CCG parse builds a logical form for a complete sentence in our example navigation domain. Starting from lexical entries, each intermediate parse node, including syntax and semantics, is constructed with one of a small set of CCG combinators (Steedman, 1996, 2000). We use the application, composition and coordination combinators, and three others described in Section 6.3.

Factored CCG Lexicons Recently, Kwiatkowski et al. (2011) introduced a factored CCG lexicon representation. Each lexical item is composed of a lexeme and a template. For example, the entry chair $\vdash N : \lambda x.chair(x)$ would be constructed by combining the lexeme chair $\vdash [chair]$, which contains a word paired with logical constants, with the template $\lambda v.[N : \lambda x.v(x)]$, that defines the rest of the category by abstracting over logical constants. This approach allows the reuse of common syntactic structures through a small set of templates. Section 8 describes how we learn such lexical entries.

Weighted Linear CCGs A weighted linear CCG (Clark & Curran, 2007) ranks the space of possible parses under the grammar, and is closely related to several other approaches (Lafferty et al., 2001; Collins, 2004; Taskar et al., 2004). Let x be a sentence, y be a CCG parse, and GEN$(x; \Lambda)$ be the set of all possible CCG parses for x given the lexicon Λ. Define $\phi(x, y) \in \mathbb{R}^d$ to be a d-dimensional *feature–vector* representation and $\theta \in \mathbb{R}^d$ to be a parameter vector. The optimal parse for sentence x is

$$y^*(x) = \arg \max_{y \in \text{GEN}(x;\Lambda)} \theta \cdot \phi(x, y)$$

and the final output logical form z is the λ-calculus expression at the root of $y^*(x)$. Section 7.2 describes how we efficiently compute an approximation to $y^*(x)$ within the joint interpretation and execution model.

Supervised learning with GENLEX Previous work (Zettlemoyer & Collins, 2005) introduced a function GENLEX(x, z) to map a sentence x and its meaning z to a large set of potential lexical entries. These entries are generated by rules that consider the logical form z and guess potential CCG categories. For example, the rule $p \rightarrow N : \lambda x.p(x)$ introduces categories commonly used to model certain types of nouns. This rule would, for example, introduce the category $N : \lambda x.chair(x)$ for any logical form z that contains the constant $chair$. GENLEX uses a small set of such rules to generate categories that are paired with all possible substrings in x, to create a large set of lexical entries. The complete learning algorithm then simultaneously selects a small subset of these entries and estimates parameter values θ. In Section 8, we will introduce a new way of using GENLEX to learn from different signals that, crucially, do not require a labeled logical form z.

5 Spatial Environment Modeling

We will execute instructions in an environment, see Section 2, which has a set of positions. A position is a triple (x, y, o), where x and y are horizontal and vertical coordinates, and $o \in O = \{0, 90, 180, 270\}$ is an orientation. A position also includes properties indicating the object it contains, its floor pattern and its wallpaper. For example, the square at $(4, 3)$ in Figure 2 has four positions, one per orientation.

Because instructional language refers to objects and other structures in an environment, we introduce the notion of a position set. For example, in Figure 2, the position set $D = \{(5, 3, o) : o \in O\}$ represents a chair, while $B = \{(x, 3, o) : o \in O, x \in [0 \ldots 5]\}$ represents the blue floor. Both sets contain all orientations for each (x, y) pair, thereby representing properties of regions. Position sets can have many properties. For example, E, in addition to being a chair, is also an intersection because it overlaps with the neighboring halls A and B. The set of possible entities includes all position sets and a few additional entries. For example, set $C = \{(4, 3, 90)\}$ in Figure 2 represents the agent's position.

6 Modeling Instructional Language

We aim to design a semantic representation that is learnable, models grounded phenomena such as spatial relations and object reference, and is executable.

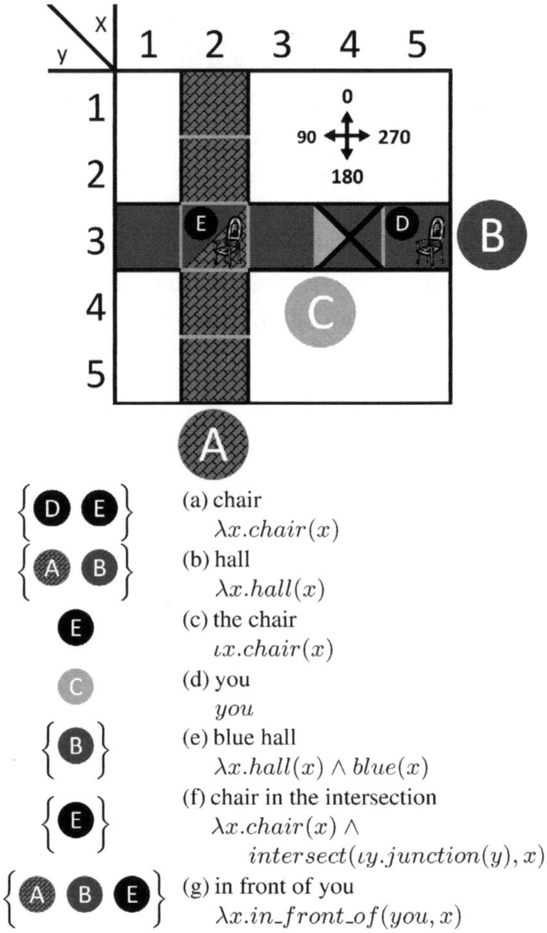

Figure 2: Schematic diagram of a map environment and example of semantics of spatial phrases.

Our semantic representation combines ideas from Carpenter (1997) and Neo-Davidsonian event semantics (Parsons, 1990) in a simply typed λ-calculus. There are four basic types: (1) entities e that are objects in the world, (2) events ev that specify actions in the world, (3) truth values t, and (4) meta-entities m, such as numbers or directions. We also allow functional types, which are defined by input and output types. For example, $\langle e, t\rangle$ is the type of function from entities to truth values.

6.1 Spatial Language Modeling

Nouns and Noun Phrases Noun phrases are paired with e-type constants that name specific entities and nouns are mapped to $\langle e, t\rangle$-type expressions that define a property. For example, the noun "chair" (Figure 2a) is paired with the expression $\lambda x.chair(x)$, which defines the set of objects for which the constant $chair$ returns true. The denotation of this expression is the set $\{D, E\}$ in Figure 2 and the denotation of $\lambda x.hall(x)$ (Figure 2b) is $\{A, B\}$. Also, the noun phrase "you" (Figure 2d), which names the agent, is represented by the constant you with denotation C, the agent's position.

Determiners Noun phrases can also be formed by combining nouns with determiners that pick out specific objects in the world. We consider both definite reference, which names contextually unique objects, and indefinites, which are less constrained.

The definite article is paired with a logical expression ι of type $\langle\langle e,t\rangle,e\rangle$,[1] which will name a single object in the world. For example, the phrase "the chair" in Figure 2c will be represented by $\iota x.chair(x)$ which will denote the appropriate chair. However, computing this denotation is challenging when there is perceptual ambiguity, for positions where multiple chairs are visible. We adopt a simple heuristic approach that ranks referents based on a combination of their distance from the agent and whether they are in front of it. For our example, from position C our agent would pick the chair E in front of it as the denotation. The approach differs from previous, non-grounded models that fail to name objects when faced with such ambiguity (e.g., Carpenter (1997), Heim and Kratzer (1998)).

To model the meaning of indefinite articles, we depart from the Frege-Montague tradition of using existential quantifiers (Lewis, 1970; Montague, 1973; Barwise & Cooper, 1981), and instead introduce a new quantifier $\mathcal{A}$ that, like ι, has type $\langle\langle e,t\rangle,e\rangle$. For example, the phrase "a chair" would be paired with $\mathcal{A}x.chair(x)$ which denotes an arbitrary entry from the set of chairs in the world. Computing the denotation for such expressions in a world will require picking a specific object, without further restrictions. This approach is closely related to Steedman's generalized Skolem terms (2011).[2]

Meta Entities We use m-typed terms to represent non-physical entities, such as numbers (1, 2, etc.) and directions ($left$, $right$, etc.) whose denotations are fixed. The ability to refer to directions allows us to manipulate position sets. For example, the phrase "your left" is mapped to the logical expression $orient(you, left)$, which denotes the position set containing the position to the left of the agent.

Prepositions and Adjectives Noun phrases with modifiers, such as adjectives and prepositional phrases are $\langle e,t\rangle$-type expressions that implement set intersection with logical conjunctions. For example in Figure 2, the phrase "blue hall" is paired with $\lambda x.hall(x) \wedge blue(x)$ with denotation $\{B\}$ and the phrase "chair in the intersection" is paired with $\lambda x.chair(x) \wedge intersect(\iota y.junction(y), x)$ with denotation $\{E\}$. Intuitively, the adjective "blue" introduces the constant $blue$ and "in the" adds a $intersect$. We will describe the full details of how these expressions are constructed in Section 6.3.

Spatial Relations The semantic representation allows more complex reasoning over position sets and the relations between them. For example, the binary relation in_front_of (Figure 2g) tests if the first argument is in front of the second from the point of view of the agent. Additional relations are used to model set intersection, relative direction, relative distance, and relative position by distance.

6.2 Modeling Instructions

To model actions in the world, we adopt Neo-Davidsonian event semantics (Davidson, 1967; Parsons, 1990), which treats events as ev-type primitive objects. Such an approach allows for a compact lexicon where adverbial modifiers introduce predicates, which are linked by a shared event argument.

Instructional language is characterized by heavy usage of imperatives, which we model as functions from events to truth values.[3] For example, an imperative such as "move" would have the meaning $\lambda a.move(a)$, which defines a set of events that match the specified constraints. Here, this set would include all events that involve moving actions.

The denotation of ev-type terms is a sequence of n instances of the same action. In this way, an event defines a function $ev : s \rightarrow s'$, where s is the start state and s' the end state. For example, the

[1] Although quantifiers are logical constants with type $\langle\langle e,t\rangle,e\rangle$ or $\langle\langle e,t\rangle,t\rangle$, we use a notation similar to that used for first-order logic. For example, the notation $\iota x.f(x)$ represents the logical expression $\iota(\lambda x.f(x))$

[2] Steedman (2011) uses generalized Skolem terms as a tool for resolving anaphoric pronouns, which we do not model.

[3] Imperatives are $\langle ev,t\rangle$-type, much like $\langle e,t\rangle$-type wh-interrogatives. Both define sets, the former includes actions to execute, the later defines answers to a question.

denotation of $\lambda a.move(a)$ is the set of move action sequences $\{\langle \text{MOVE}_1, \ldots, \text{MOVE}_n \rangle : n \geq 1\}$. Although performing actions often require performing additional ones (e.g., the agent might have to $turn$ before being able to $move$), we treat such actions as implicit (Section 7.1), and don't model them explicitly within the logical form.

Predicates such as $move$ (seen above) and $turn$ are introduced by verbs. Events can also be modified by adverbials, which are intersective, much like prepositional phrases. For example in the imperative, logical form (LF) pair:

Imp.: move from the sofa to the chair
LF: $\lambda a.move(a) \wedge to(a, \iota x.chair(x)) \wedge from(a, \iota y.sofa(y))$

Each adverbial phrase provides a constraint, and changing their order will not change the LF.

6.3 Parsing Instructional Language with CCG

To compose logical expressions from sentences we use CCG, as described in Section 4. Figures 3 and 4 present a sample of lexical entries and how they are combined, as we will describe in this section. The basic syntactic categories are N (noun), NP (noun phrase), S (sentence), PP (prepositional phrase), AP (adverbial phrase), ADJ (adjective) and C (a special category for coordinators).

Type Raising To compactly model syntactic variations, we follow Carpenter (1997), who argues for polymorphic typing. We include the more simple, or lower type, entry in the lexicon and introduce type-raising rules to reconstruct the other when necessary at parse time. We use four rules:

$$PP : g \rightarrow N\backslash N : \lambda f.\lambda x.f(x) \wedge g(x)$$
$$ADJ : g \rightarrow N/N : \lambda f.\lambda x.f(x) \wedge g(x)$$
$$AP : g \rightarrow S\backslash S : \lambda f.\lambda a.f(a) \wedge g(a)$$
$$AP : g \rightarrow S/S : \lambda f.\lambda a.f(a) \wedge g(a)$$

where the first three are for prepositional, adjectival and adverbial modifications, and the fourth models the fact that adverbials are often topicalized.[4] Figures 3 and 4 show parses that use type-raising rules.

Indefinites As discussed in Section 6.1, we use a new syntactic analysis for indefinites, following Steedman (2011). Previous approaches would build parses such as

with	a	lamp
PP/NP $\lambda x.\lambda y.intersect(x,y)$	$PP\backslash(PP/NP)/N$ $\lambda f.\lambda g.\lambda y.\exists x.g(x,y) \wedge f(x)$	N $\lambda x.lamp(x)$
	$PP\backslash(PP/NP)$ $\lambda g.\lambda y.\exists x.g(x,y) \wedge lamp(x)$ (>)	
PP $\lambda y.\exists x.intersect(x,y) \wedge lamp(x)$ (<)		

where "a" has the relatively complex syntactic category $PP\backslash(PP/NP)/N$ and where similar entries would be needed to quantify over different types of verbs (e.g., $S\backslash(S/NP)/N$) and adverbials (e.g., $AP\backslash(AP/NP)/N$). Instead, we include a single lexical entry $a \vdash NP/N : \lambda f.\mathcal{A}x.f(x)$ which can be used to construct the correct meaning in all cases.

chair	in	the	corner
N $\lambda x.chair(x)$	PP/NP $\lambda x.\lambda y.intersect(x,y)$	NP/N $\lambda f.\mathcal{A}x.f(x)$	N $\lambda x.corner(x)$
		NP $\iota x.corner(x)$ (>)	
	PP $\lambda y.intersect(\iota x.corner(x), y)$ (>)		
	$N\backslash N$ $\lambda f.\lambda y.f(y) \wedge intersect(\iota x.chair(x), y)$		
N $\lambda y.chair(y) \wedge intersect(\iota x.chair(x), y)$ (<)			

Figure 3: A CCG parse with a prepositional phrase.

7 Joint Parsing and Execution

Our inference includes an execution component and a parser. The parser maps sentences to logical forms, and incorporates the grounded execution model. We first discuss how to execute logical forms, and then describe the joint model for execution and parsing.

7.1 Executing Logical Expressions

Dynamic Models In spatial environments, such as the ones in our task, the agent's ability to observe the world depends on its current state. Taking this aspect of spatial environments into account is challenging, but crucial for correct evaluation.

To represent the agent's point of view, for each state $s \in \mathcal{S}$, as defined in Section 2, let M_s be the state-dependent logical model. A model M consists of a domain $D_{M,T}$ of objects for each type T and an interpretation function $\mathcal{I}_{M,T} : O_T \rightarrow D_{M,T}$, where O_T is the set of T-type constants. $\mathcal{I}_{M,T}$ maps logical symbols to T-type objects, for example, it will map you to the agent's position. We have domains for position sets, actions and so on. Finally, let V_T be the set of variables of type T, and

[4]Using type-raising rules can be particularly useful when learning from sparse data. For example, it will no longer be necessary to learn three lexical entries for each adverbial phrase (with syntax AP, $S\backslash S$, and S/S).

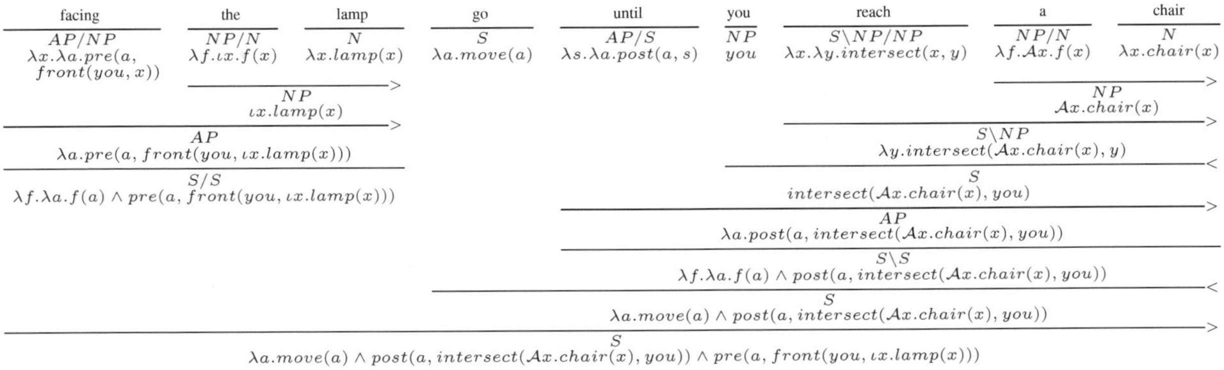

Figure 4: A CCG parse showing adverbial phrases and topicalization.

$A_T : V_T \rightarrow \bigcup_{s \in \mathcal{S}} D_{Ms,T}$ be the assignment function, which maps variables to domain objects.

For each model M_s the domain $D_{M_s,ev}$ is a set of action sequences $\{\langle a_1, ..., a_n\rangle : n \geq 1\}$. Each $\vec{a}$ defines a sequences of states s_i, as defined in Section 6.2, and associated models M_{s_i}. The key challenge for execution is that modifiers of the event will need to be evaluated under different models from this sequence. For example, consider the sentence in Figure 4. To correctly execute, the *pre* literal, introduced by the "facing" phrase, it must be evaluated in the model M_{s_0} for the initial state s_0. Similarly, the literal including *post* requires the final model $M_{s_{n+1}}$. Such state dependent predicates, including *pre* and *post*, are called *stateful*. The list of stateful predicates is pre-defined and includes event modifiers, as well the ι quantifier, which is evaluated under M_{s_0}, since definite determiners are assumed to name objects visible from the start position. In general, a logical expression is traversed depth first and the model is updated every time a stateful predicate is reached. For example, the two e-type *you* constants in Figure 4 will be evaluated under different models: the one within the *pre* literal under M_{s_0}, and the one inside the *post* literal under $M_{s_{n+1}}$.

Evaluation Given a logical expression l, we can compute the interpretation $\mathcal{I}_{M_{s_0},T}(l)$ by recursively mapping each subexpression to an entry on the appropriate model M.

To reflect the changing state of the agent during evaluation, we define the function $update(\vec{a}, pred)$. Given an action sequence $\vec{a}$ and a stateful predicate $pred$, $update$ returns a model M_s, where s is the state under which the literal containing $pred$ should be interpreted, either the initial state or one visited while executing $\vec{a}$. For example, given the predicate $post$ and the action sequence $\langle a_1, \ldots, a_n\rangle$, $update(\langle a_1, \ldots, a_n\rangle, post) = M_{s_{n+1}}$, where s_{n+1} the state of the agent following action a_n. By convention, we place the event variable as the first argument in literals that include one.

Given a T-type logical expression l and a starting state s_0, we compute its interpretation $\mathcal{I}_{M_{s_0},T}(l)$ recursively, following these three base cases:

- If l is a λ operator of type $\langle T_1, T_2\rangle$ binding variable v and body b, $\mathcal{I}_{M_s,T}(l)$ is a set of pairs from $D_{T_1} \times D_{T_2}$, where $D_{T_1}, D_{T_2} \in M_s$. For each object $o \in D_{T_1}$, we create a pair (o, i) where i is the interpretation $\mathcal{I}_{M_s,T_2}(b)$ computed under a variable assignment function extended to map $A_{T_2}(v) = o$.
- If l is a literal $c(c_1, \ldots, c_n)$ with n arguments where c has type P and each c_i has type P_i, $\mathcal{I}_{M_s,T}(l)$ is computed by first interpreting the predicate c to the function $f = \mathcal{I}_{M_s,T}(c)$. In most cases, $\mathcal{I}_{M_s,T}(l) = f(\mathcal{I}_{M_s,P_1}(c_1), \ldots, \mathcal{I}_{M_s,P_n}(c_n))$. However, if c is a stateful predicate, such as pre or $post$, we instead first retrieve the appropriate new model $M_{s'} = update(\mathcal{I}_{M_s,P_1}(c_1), c)$, where c_1 is the event argument and $\mathcal{I}_{M_s,P_1}(c_1)$ is its interpretation. Then, the final results is $\mathcal{I}_{M_s,T}(l) = f(\mathcal{I}_{M_{s'},P_1}(c_1), \ldots, \mathcal{I}_{M_{s'},P_n}(c_n))$.
- If l is a T-type constant or variable, $\mathcal{I}_{M_s,T}(l)$.

The worst case complexity of the process is exponential in the number of bound variables. Although in practice we observed tractable evaluation in the majority of development cases we considered, a more comprehensive and tractable evaluation procedure is an issue that we leave for future work.

Implicit Actions Instructional language rarely specifies every action required for execution, see MacMahon (2007) for a detailed discussion in the maps domain. For example, the sentence in Figure 4 can be said even if the agent is not facing a blue hallway, with the clear implicit request that it should turn to face such a hallway before moving. To allow our agent to perform implicit actions, we extend the domain of ev-type variables by allowing the agent to prefix up to k_I action sequences before each explicit event. For example, in the agent's position in Figure 2 (set C), the set of possible events includes $\langle \text{MOVE}^I, \text{MOVE}^I, \text{RIGHT}^I, \text{MOVE}\rangle$, which contains two implicit sequences (marked by I).

Resolving Action Ambiguity Logical forms often fail to determine a unique action sequences, due to instruction ambiguity. For example, consider the instruction "go forward" and the agent state as specified in Figure 2 (set C). The instruction, which maps to $\lambda a.move(a) \wedge forward(a)$, evaluates to the set containing $\langle \text{MOVE}\rangle$, $\langle \text{MOVE}, \text{MOVE}\rangle$ and $\langle \text{MOVE}, \text{MOVE}, \text{MOVE}\rangle$, as well as five other sequences that have implicit prefixes followed by explicit MOVE actions. To resolve such ambiguity, we prefer shorter actions without implicit actions. In the example above, we will select $\langle \text{MOVE}\rangle$, which includes a single action and no implicit actions.

7.2 Joint Inference

We incorporate the execution procedure described above with a linear weighted CCG parser, as described in Section 4, to create a joint model of parsing and execution. Specifically, we execute logical forms in the current state and observe the result of their execution. For example, the word "chair" can be used to refer to different types of objects, including chairs, sofas, and barstools, in the maps domains. Our CCG grammar would include a lexical item for each meaning, but execution might fail depending on the presence of objects in the world, influencing the final parse output. Similarly, allowing implicit actions provides robustness when resolving these and other ambiguities. For example, an instruction with the precondition phrase "from the chair" might require additional actions to reach the position with the named object.

To allow such joint reasoning we define an execution e to include a parse tree e^y and trace $e^{\vec{a}}$, and define our feature function to be $\Phi(x_i, s_i, e)$, where x_i is an instruction and s_i is the start state. This approach allows joint dependencies: the state of the world influences how the agent interprets words, phrases and even complete sentences, while language understanding determines actions.

Finally, to execute sequences of instructions, we execute each starting from the end state of the previous one, using a beam of size k_s.

8 Learning

Figure 5 presents the complete learning algorithm. Our approach is online, considering each example in turn and performing two steps: expanding the lexicon and updating parameters. The algorithm assumes access to a training set $\{(x_i, s_i, \mathcal{V}_i) : i = 1 \dots n\}$, where each example includes an instruction x_i, starting state s_i and a validation function $\mathcal{V}_i$, as defined in Section 2. In addition the algorithm takes a seed lexicon Λ_0. The output is a joint model, that includes a lexicon Λ and parameters θ.

Coarse Lexical Generation To generate potential lexical entries we use the function $GENLEX(x, s, \mathcal{V}; \Lambda, \theta)$, where x is an instruction, s is a state and $\mathcal{V}$ is a validation function. Λ is the current lexicon and θ is a parameter vector. In $GENLEX$ we use coarse logical constants, as described below, to efficiently prune the set of potential lexical entries. This set is then pruned further using more precise inference in Step 1.

To compute $GENLEX$, we initially generate a large set of lexical entries and then prune most of them. The full set is generated by taking the cross product of a set of templates, computed by factoring out all templates in the seed lexicon Λ_0, and all logical constants. For example, if Λ_0 has a lexical item with the category $AP/NP : \lambda x.\lambda a.to(a, x)$ we would create entries $w \vdash AP/NP : \lambda x.\lambda a.p(a, x)$ for every phrase w in x and all constants p with the same type as to.[5]

In our development work, this approach often generated nearly 100k entries per sentence. To ease

[5]Generalizing previous work (Kwiatkowski et al., 2011), we allow templates that abstract subsets of the constants in a lexical item. For example, the seed entry $facing \vdash AP/NP : \lambda x.\lambda a.pre(a, front(you, x))$ would create 7 templates.

Inputs: Training set $\{(x_i, s_i, \mathcal{V}_i) : i = 1 \dots n\}$ where x_i is a sentence, s_i is a state and $\mathcal{V}_i$ is a validation function, as described in Section 2. Initial lexicon Λ_0. Number of iterations T. Margin γ. Beam size k for lexicon generation.

Definitions: Let an execution e include a parse tree e^y and a trace $e^{\vec{a}}$. GEN$(x, s; \Lambda)$ is the set of all possible executions for the instruction x and state s, given the lexicon Λ. $LEX(y)$ is the set of lexical entries used in the parse tree y. Let $\Phi_i(e)$ be shorthand for the feature function $\Phi(x_i, s_i, e)$ defined in Section 7.2. Define $\Delta_i(e, e') = |\Phi_i(e) - \Phi_i(e')|_1$. $GENLEX(x, s, \mathcal{V}; \lambda, \theta)$ takes as input an instruction x, state s, validation function $\mathcal{V}$, lexicon λ and model parameters θ, and returns a set of lexical entries, as defined in Section 8. Finally, for a set of executions E let $MAXV_i(E; \theta)$ be $\{e | \forall e' \in E, \langle \theta, \Phi_i(e') \rangle \leq \langle \theta, \Phi_i(e) \rangle \wedge \mathcal{V}_i(e^{\vec{a}}) = 1\}$, the set of highest scoring valid executions.

Algorithm:

Initialize θ using Λ_0 , $\Lambda \leftarrow \Lambda_0$

For $t = 1 \dots T, i = 1 \dots n$:

Step 1: (Lexical generation)

a. Set $\lambda_G \leftarrow GENLEX(x_i, s_i, \mathcal{V}_i; \Lambda, \theta)$, $\lambda \leftarrow \Lambda \cup \lambda_G$

b. Let E be the k highest scoring executions from $GEN(x_i, s_i; \lambda)$ which use at most one entry from λ_G

c. Select lexical entries from the highest scoring valid parses: $\lambda_i \leftarrow \bigcup_{e \in MAXV_i(E;\theta)} LEX(e^y)$

d. Update lexicon: $\Lambda \leftarrow \Lambda \cup \lambda_i$

Step 2: (Update parameters)

a. Set $G_i \leftarrow MAXV_i(GEN(x_i, s_i; \Lambda); \theta)$ and $B_i \leftarrow \{e | e \in GEN(x_i, s_i; \Lambda) \wedge \mathcal{V}_i(e^{\vec{a}}) \neq 1\}$

b. Construct sets of margin violating good and bad parses:
$R_i \leftarrow \{g | g \in G_i \wedge \exists b \in B_i \ s.t. \ \langle \theta, \Phi_i(g) - \Phi_i(b) \rangle < \gamma \Delta_i(g, b)\}$
$E_i \leftarrow \{b | b \in B_i \wedge \exists g \in G_i \ s.t. \ \langle \theta, \Phi_i(g) - \Phi_i(b) \rangle < \gamma \Delta_i(g, b)\}$

c. Apply the additive update:
$\theta \leftarrow \theta + \frac{1}{|R_i|} \sum_{r \in R_i} \Phi_i(r) - \frac{1}{|E_i|} \sum_{e \in E_i} \Phi_i(e)$

Output: Parameters θ and lexicon Λ

Figure 5: The learning algorithm.

the cost of parsing at this scale, we developed a coarse-to-fine two-pass parsing approach that limits the number of new entries considered. The algorithm first parses with coarse lexical entries that abstract the identities of the logical constants in their logical forms, thereby greatly reducing the search space. It then uses the highest scoring coarse parses to constrain the lexical entries for a final, fine parse.

Formally, we construct the coarse lexicon λ_a by replacing all constants of the same type with a single newly created, temporary constant. We then parse to create a set of trees A, such that each $y \in A$

1. is a parse for sentence x, given the world state s with the combined lexicon $\Lambda \cup \lambda_a$,
2. scored higher than e^y by at least a margin of δ_L, where e^y is the tree of e, the highest scoring execution of x, at position s under the current model, s.t. $\mathcal{V}(e^{\vec{a}}) = 1$,
3. contains at most one entry from λ_a.

Finally, from each entry $l \in \{l | l \in \lambda_a \wedge l \in y \wedge y \in A\}$, we create multiple lexical entries by replacing all temporary constants with all possible appropriately typed constants from the original set. $GENLEX$ returns all these lexical entries, which will be used to form our final fine-level analysis.

Step 1: Lexical Induction To expand our model's lexicon, we use $GENLEX$ to generate candidate lexical entries and then further refine this set by parsing with the current model. Step 1(a) in Figure 5 uses $GENLEX$ to create a temporary set of potential lexical entries λ_G. Steps (b-d) select a small subset of these lexical entries to add to the current lexicon Λ: we find the k-best executions under the model, which use at most one entry from λ_G, find the entries used in the best valid executions and add them to the current lexicon.

Step 2: Parameter Update We use a variant of a loss-driven perceptron (Singh-Miller & Collins, 2007; Artzi & Zettlemoyer, 2011) for parameter updates. However, instead of taking advantage of a loss function we use a validation signal. In step (a) we collect the highest scoring valid parses and all invalid parses. Then, in step (b) we construct the set R_i of valid analyses and E_i of invalid ones, such that their model scores are not separated by a margin δ scaled by the number of wrong features (Taskar et al., 2003). Finally, step (f) applies the update.

Discussion The algorithm uses the validation signal to drive both lexical induction and parameter updates. Unlike previous work (Zettlemoyer & Collins, 2005, 2007; Artzi & Zettlemoyer, 2011), we have no access to a set of logical constants, either through the the labeled logical form or the weak supervision signal, to guide the $GENLEX$ procedure. Therefore, to avoid over-generating lexical entries, thereby making parsing and learning intractable, we leverage typing for coarse parsing to prune the generated set. By allowing a single

	Oracle	SAIL
# of instruction sequences	501	706
# of instruction sequences with implicit actions	431	
Total # of sentences	2679	3233
Avg. sentences per sequence	5.35	4.61
Avg. tokens per sentence	7.5	7.94
Vocabulary size	373	522

Table 1: Corpora statistics (lower-cased data).

	Single Sentence	Sequence
Final state validation		
Complete system	81.98 (2.33)	59.32 (6.66)
No implicit actions	77.7 (3.7)	38.46 (1.12)
No joint execution	73.27 (3.98)	31.51 (6.66)
Trace validation		
Complete system	82.74 (2.53)	58.95 (6.88)
No implicit actions	77.64 (3.46)	38.34 (6.23)
No joint execution	72.85 (4.73)	30.89 (6.08)

Table 2: Cross-validation development accuracy and standard deviation on the oracle corpus.

new entry per parse, we create a conservative, cascading effect, whereas a lexical entry that is introduced opens the way for many other sentence to be parsed and introduce new lexical entries. Furthermore, grounded features improve parse selection, thereby generating higher quality lexical entries.

9 Experimental Setup

Data For evaluation, we use the navigation task from MacMahon et al. (2006), which includes three environments and the SAIL corpus of instructions and follower traces. Chen and Mooney (2011) segmented the data, aligned traces to instructions, and merged traces created by different subjects. The corpus includes raw sentences, without any form of linguistic annotation. The original collection process (MacMahon et al., 2006) created many uninterpretable instructions and incorrect traces. To focus on the learning and interpretation tasks, we also created a new dataset that includes only accurate instructions labeled with a single, correct execution trace. From this *oracle* corpus, we randomly sampled 164 instruction sequences (816 sentences) for evaluation, leaving 337 (1863 sentences) for training. This simple effort will allow us to measure the effects of noise on the learning approach and provides a resource for building more accurate algorithms. Table 1 compares the two sets.

Features and Parser Following Zettlemoyer and Collins (2005), we use a CKY parser with a beam of k. To boost recall, we adopt a two-pass strategy, which allows for word skipping if the initial parse fails. We use features that indicate usage of lexical entries, templates, lexemes and type-raising rules, as described in Section 6.3, and repetitions in logical coordinations. Finally, during joint parsing, we consider only parses executable at s_i as complete.

Seed Lexicon To construct our seed lexicon we labeled 12 instruction sequences with 141 lexical entries. The sequences were randomly selected from the training set, so as to include two sequences for each participant in the original experiment. Figures 3 and 4 include a sample of our seed lexicon.

Initialization and Parameters We set the weight of each template indicator feature to the number of times it is used in the seed lexicon and each repetition feature to -10. Learning parameters were tuned using cross-validation on the training set: the margin δ is set to 1, the $GENLEX$ margin δ_L is set to 2, we use 6 iterations (8 for experiments on SAIL) and take the 250 top parses during lexical generation (step 1, Figure 5). For parameter update (step 2, Figure 5) we use a parser with a beam of 100. $GENLEX$ generates lexical entries for token sequences up to length 4. k_s, the instruction sequence execution beam, is set to 10. Finally, k_I is set to 2, allowing up to two implicit action sequences per explicit one.

Evaluation Metrics To evaluate single instructions x, we compare the agent's end state to a labeled state s', as described in Section 2. We use a similar method to evaluate the execution of instruction sequences $\vec{x}$, but disregard the orientation, since end goals in MacMahon et al. (2006) are defined without orientation. When evaluating logical forms we measure exact match accuracy.

10 Results

We repeated each experiment five times, shuffling the training set between runs. For the development cross-validation runs, we also shuffled the folds. As our learning approach is online, this allows us to account for performance variations arising from training set ordering. We report mean accuracy and standard deviation across all runs (and all folds).

	Single Sentence	Sequence
Chen and Mooney (2011)	54.4	16.18
Chen (2012)	57.28	19.18
+ additional data	57.62	20.64
Kim and Mooney (2012)	57.22	20.17
Trace validation	**65.28** (5.09)	**31.93** (3.26)
Final state validation	**64.25** (5.12)	**30.9** (2.16)

Table 3: Cross-validation accuracy and standard deviation for the SAIL corpus.

Table 2 shows accuracy for 5-fold cross-validation on the oracle training data. We first varied the validation signal by providing the complete action sequence or the final state only, as described in Section 2. Although the final state signal is weaker, the results are similar. The relatively large difference between single sentence and sequence performance is due to (1) cascading errors in the more difficult task of sequential execution, and (2) corpus repetitions, where simple sentences are common (e.g., "turn left"). Next, we disabled the system's ability to introduce implicit actions, which was especially harmful to the full sequence performance. Finally, ablating the joint execution decreases performance, showing the benefit of the joint model.

Table 3 lists cross validation results on the SAIL corpus. To compare to previous work (Chen & Mooney, 2011), we report cross-validation results over the three maps. The approach was able to correctly execute 60% more sequences then the previous state of the art (Kim & Mooney, 2012). We also outperform the results of Chen (2012), which used 30% more training data.[6] Using the weaker validation signal creates a marginal decrease in performance. However, we still outperform all previous work, despite using weaker supervision. Interestingly, these increases were achieved with a relatively simple executor, while previous work used MARCO (MacMahon et al., 2006), which supports sophisticated recovery strategies.

Finally, we evaluate our approach on the held out test set for the oracle corpus (Table 4). In contrast to experiments on the Chen and Mooney (2011) corpus, we use a held out set for evaluation. Due to this discrepancy, all development was done on the training set only. The increase in accuracy over learning with the original corpus demonstrates the significant impact of noise on our performance. In addition to

[6]This additional training data isn't publicly available.

Validation	Single Sentence	Sequence	LF
Final state	77.6 (1.14)	54.63 (3.5)	44 (6.12)
Trace	78.63 (0.84)	58.05 (3.12)	51.05 (1.14)

Table 4: Oracle corpus test accuracy and standard deviation results.

execution results, we also report exact match logical form (LF) accuracy results. For this purpose, we annotated 18 instruction sequences (105 sentences) with logical forms. The gap between execution and LF accuracy can be attributed to the complexity of the linguistic representation and redundancy in instructions. These results provide a new baseline for studying learning from cleaner supervision.

11 Discussion

We showed how to do grounded learning of a CCG semantic parser that includes a joint model of meaning and context for executing natural language instructions. The joint nature allows situated cues to directly influence parsing and also enables algorithms that learn while executing instructions.

This style of algorithm, especially when using the weaker end state validation, is closely related to reinforcement learning approaches (Branavan et al., 2009, 2010). However, we differ on optimization and objective function, where we aim for minimal loss. We expect many RL techniques to be useful to scale to more complex environments, including sampling actions and using an exploration strategy.

We also designed a semantic representation to closely match the linguistic structure of instructional language, combining ideas from many semantic theories, including, for example, Neo-Davidsonian events (Parsons, 1990). This approach allowed us to learn a compact and executable grammar that generalized well. We expect, in future work, that such modeling can be reused for more general language.

Acknowledgments

The research was supported in part by DARPA under the DEFT program through the AFRL (FA8750-13-2-0019) and the CSSG (N11AP20020), the ARO (W911NF-12-1-0197), and the NSF (IIS-1115966). The authors thank Tom Kwiatkowski, Nicholas FitzGerald and Alan Ritter for helpful discussions, David Chen for providing the evaluation corpus, and the anonymous reviewers for helpful comments.

References

Artzi, Y., & Zettlemoyer, L. (2011). Bootstrapping Semantic Parsers from Conversations. In *Proceedings of the Conference on Empirical Methods in Natural Language Processing*.

Barwise, J., & Cooper, R. (1981). Generalized Quantifiers and Natural Language. *Linguistics and Philosophy*, *4*(2), 159–219.

Branavan, S., Chen, H., Zettlemoyer, L., & Barzilay, R. (2009). Reinforcement learning for mapping instructions to actions. In *Proceedings of the Joint Conference of the Association for Computational Linguistics and the International Joint Conference on Natural Language Processing*.

Branavan, S., Zettlemoyer, L., & Barzilay, R. (2010). Reading between the lines: learning to map high-level instructions to commands. In *Proceedings of the Conference of the Association for Computational Linguistics*.

Bugmann, G., Klein, E., Lauria, S., & Kyriacou, T. (2004). Corpus-based robotics: A route instruction example. In *Proceedings of Intelligent Autonomous Systems*.

Carpenter, B. (1997). *Type-Logical Semantics*. The MIT Press.

Chen, D. L. (2012). Fast Online Lexicon Learning for Grounded Language Acquisition. In *Proceedings of the Annual Meeting of the Association for Computational Linguistics*.

Chen, D., Kim, J., & Mooney, R. (2010). Training a multilingual sportscaster: using perceptual context to learn language. *Journal of Artificial Intelligence Research*, *37*(1), 397–436.

Chen, D., & Mooney, R. (2011). Learning to Interpret Natural Language Navigation Instructions from Observations. In *Proceedings of the National Conference on Artificial Intelligence*.

Clark, S., & Curran, J. (2007). Wide-coverage efficient statistical parsing with CCG and log-linear models. *Computational Linguistics*, *33*(4), 493–552.

Clarke, J., Goldwasser, D., Chang, M., & Roth, D. (2010). Driving Semantic Parsing from the World's Response. In *Proceedings of the Conference on Computational Natural Language Learning*.

Collins, M. (2004). Parameter estimation for statistical parsing models: Theory and practice of distribution-free methods. In *New Developments in Parsing Technology*.

Davidson, D. (1967). The logical form of action sentences. *Essays on actions and events*, 105–148.

Di Eugenio, B., & White, M. (1992). On the Interpretation of Natural Language Instructions. In *Proceedings of the Conference of the Association of Computational Linguistics*.

Dzifcak, J., Scheutz, M., Baral, C., & Schermerhorn, P. (2009). What to Do and How to Do It: Translating Natural Language Directives Into Temporal and Dynamic Logic Representation for Goal Management and Action Execution. In *Proceedings of the IEEE International Conference on Robotics and Automation*.

Goldwasser, D., Reichart, R., Clarke, J., & Roth, D. (2011). Confidence Driven Unsupervised Semantic Parsing. In *Proceedings of the Association of Computational Linguistics*.

Goldwasser, D., & Roth, D. (2011). Learning from Natural Instructions. In *Proceedings of the International Joint Conference on Artificial Intelligence*.

Heim, I., & Kratzer, A. (1998). *Semantics in Generative Grammar*. Blackwell Oxford.

Kate, R., & Mooney, R. (2006). Using String-Kernels for Learning Semantic Parsers. In *Proceedings of the Conference of the Association for Computational Linguistics*.

Kim, J., & Mooney, R. J. (2012). Unsupervised PCFG Induction for Grounded Language Learning with Highly Ambiguous Supervision. In *Proceedings of the Conference on Empirical Methods in Natural Language Processing*.

Kollar, T., Tellex, S., Roy, D., & Roy, N. (2010). Toward Understanding Natural Language Directions. In *Proceedings of the ACM/IEEE International Conference on Human-Robot Interaction*.

Krishnamurthy, J., & Mitchell, T. (2012). Weakly Supervised Training of Semantic Parsers. In *Proceedings of the Joint Conference on Empirical Methods in Natural Language Processing and Computational Natural Language Learning*.

Kwiatkowski, T., Goldwater, S., Zettlemoyer, L., & Steedman, M. (2012). A probabilistic model of syntactic and semantic acquisition from child-directed utterances and their meanings. *Proceedings of the Conference of the European Chapter of the Association of Computational Linguistics*.

Kwiatkowski, T., Zettlemoyer, L., Goldwater, S., & Steedman, M. (2010). Inducing probabilistic CCG grammars from logical form with higher-order unification. In *Proceedings of the Conference on Empirical Methods in Natural Language Processing*.

Kwiatkowski, T., Zettlemoyer, L., Goldwater, S., & Steedman, M. (2011). Lexical Generalization in CCG Grammar Induction for Semantic Parsing. In *Proceedings of the Conference on Empirical Methods in Natural Language Processing*.

Lafferty, J., McCallum, A., & Pereira, F. (2001). Conditional Random Fields: Probabilistic Models for Segmenting and Labeling Sequence Data. In *Proceedings of the International Conference on Machine Learning*.

Lewis, D. (1970). General Semantics. *Synthese*, *22*(1), 18–67.

Liang, P., Jordan, M., & Klein, D. (2009). Learning semantic correspondences with less supervision. In *Proceedings of the Joint Conference of the Association for Computational Linguistics the International Joint Conference on Natural Language Processing*.

Liang, P., Jordan, M., & Klein, D. (2011). Learning Dependency-Based Compositional Semantics. In *Proceedings of the Conference of the Association for Computational Linguistics*.

MacMahon, M. (2007). *Following Natural Language Route Instructions*. Ph.D. thesis, University of Texas at Austin.

MacMahon, M., Stankiewics, B., & Kuipers, B. (2006). Walk the Talk: Connecting Language, Knowledge, Action in Route Instructions. In *Proceedings of the National Conference on Artificial Intelligence*.

Matuszek, C., FitzGerald, N., Zettlemoyer, L., Bo, L., & Fox, D. (2012). A Joint Model of Language and Perception for Grounded Attribute Learning. *Proceedings of the International Conference on Machine Learning*.

Matuszek, C., Fox, D., & Koscher, K. (2010). Following directions using statistical machine translation. In *Proceedings of the international conference on Human-robot interaction*.

Matuszek, C., Herbst, E., Zettlemoyer, L. S., & Fox, D. (2012). Learning to Parse Natural Language Commands to a Robot Control System. In *Proceedings of the International Symposium on Experimental Robotics*.

Montague, R. (1973). The Proper Treatment of Quantification in Ordinary English. *Approaches to natural language*, *49*, 221–242.

Muresan, S. (2011). Learning for Deep Language Understanding. In *Proceedings of the International Joint Conference on Artificial Intelligence*.

Parsons, T. (1990). *Events in the Semantics of English*. The MIT Press.

Singh-Miller, N., & Collins, M. (2007). Trigger-based language modeling using a loss-sensitive perceptron algorithm. In *IEEE International Conference on Acoustics, Speech and Signal Processing*.

Steedman, M. (1996). *Surface Structure and Interpretation*. The MIT Press.

Steedman, M. (2000). *The Syntactic Process*. The MIT Press.

Steedman, M. (2011). *Taking Scope*. The MIT Press.

Taskar, B., Guestrin, C., & Koller, D. (2003). Max-Margin Markov Networks. In *Proceedings of the Conference on Neural Information Processing Systems*.

Taskar, B., Klein, D., Collins, M., Koller, D., & Manning, C. (2004). Max-Margin Parsing. In *Proceedings of the Conference on Empirical Methods in Natural Language Processing*.

Tellex, S., Kollar, T., Dickerson, S., Walter, M., Banerjee, A., Teller, S., & Roy, N. (2011). Understanding Natural Language Commands for Robotic Navigation and Mobile Manipulation. In *Proceedings of the National Conference on Artificial Intelligence*.

Vogel, A., & Jurafsky, D. (2010). Learning to follow navigational directions. In *Proceedings of the Conference of the Association for Computational Linguistics*.

Webber, B., Badler, N., Di Eugenio, B., Geib, C., Levison, L., & Moore, M. (1995). Instructions, Intentions and Expectations. *Artificial Intelligence*, *73*(1), 253–269.

Wei, Y., Brunskill, E., Kollar, T., & Roy, N. (2009). Where To Go: Interpreting Natural Directions Using Global Inference. In *Proceedings of the IEEE International Conference on Robotics and Automation*.

Winograd, T. (1972). Understanding Natural Language. *Cognitive Psychology*, *3*(1), 1–191.

Wong, Y., & Mooney, R. (2007). Learning Synchronous Grammars for Semantic Parsing with Lambda Calculus. In *Proceedings of the Conference of the Association for Computational Linguistics*.

Zettlemoyer, L., & Collins, M. (2005). Learning to map sentences to logical form: Structured classification with probabilistic categorial grammars. In *Proceedings of the Conference on Uncertainty in Artificial Intelligence*.

Zettlemoyer, L., & Collins, M. (2007). Online learning of relaxed CCG grammars for parsing to logical form. In *Proceedings of the Joint Conference on Empirical Methods in Natural Language Processing and Computational Natural Language Learning*.

Unsupervised Dependency Parsing with Acoustic Cues

John K Pate[†‡]
j.k.pate@sms.ed.ac.uk

Sharon Goldwater[†]
sgwater@inf.ed.ac.uk

[†]ILCC, School of Informatics
University of Edinburgh
Edinburgh, EH8 9AB, UK

[‡]Department of Computing
Macquarie University
Sydney, NSW 2109, Australia

Abstract

Unsupervised parsing is a difficult task that infants readily perform. Progress has been made on this task using text-based models, but few computational approaches have considered how infants might benefit from acoustic cues. This paper explores the hypothesis that *word duration* can help with learning syntax. We describe how duration information can be incorporated into an unsupervised Bayesian dependency parser whose only other source of information is the words themselves (without punctuation or parts of speech). Our results, evaluated on both adult-directed and child-directed utterances, show that using word duration can improve parse quality relative to words-only baselines. These results support the idea that acoustic cues provide useful evidence about syntactic structure for language-learning infants, and motivate the use of word duration cues in NLP tasks with speech.

1 Introduction

Unsupervised learning of syntax is difficult for NLP systems, yet infants perform this task routinely. Previous work in NLP has focused on using the implicit syntactic information available in part-of-speech (POS) tags (Klein and Manning, 2004), punctuation (Seginer, 2007; Spitkovsky et al., 2011b; Ponvert et al., 2011), and syntactic similarities between related languages (Cohen and Smith, 2009; Cohen et al., 2011). However, these approaches likely use the data in a very different way from children: neither POS tags nor punctuation are observed during language acquisition (although see Spitkovsky et al. (2011a) and Christodoulopoulos et al. (2012) for encouraging results using unsupervised POS tags), and many children learn in a broadly monolingual environment. This paper explores a possible source of information that NLP systems typically ignore: word duration, or the length of time taken to pronounce each word.

There are good reasons to think that word duration might be useful for learning syntax. First, the well-established *Prosodic Bootstrapping* hypothesis (Gleitman and Wanner, 1982) proposes that infants use acoustic-prosodic cues (such as word duration) to help them identify syntactic structure, because prosodic and syntactic structures sometimes coincide. More recently, we proposed (Pate and Goldwater, 2011) that infants might use word duration as a direct cue to syntactic structure (i.e., without requiring intermediate prosodic structure), because words in high-probability syntactic structures tend to be pronounced more quickly (Gahl and Garnsey, 2004; Gahl et al., 2006; Tily et al., 2009).

Like most recent work on unsupervised parsing, we focus on learning syntactic dependencies. Our work is based on Headden et al. (2009)'s Bayesian version of the Dependency Model with Valence (DMV) (Klein and Manning, 2004), using interpolated backoff techniques to incorporate multiple information sources per token. However, whereas Headden et al. used words and POS tags as input, we use words and word duration information, presenting three variants of their model that use this information in slightly different ways.[1]

[1]By using neither gold-standard nor learned POS tags as input, our work differs from nearly all previous work on unsupervised dependency parsing. While learned tags might be plausible

To our knowledge, this is the first work to incorporate acoustic cues into an unsupervised system for learning full syntactic parses. The methods in this paper were inspired by our previous approach (Pate and Goldwater, 2011), which showed that word duration measurements could improve the performance of an unsupervised lexicalized syntactic chunker over a words-only baseline. However, that work was limited to HMM-like sequence models, tested on adult-directed speech (ADS) only, and none of the models outperformed uniform-branching baselines. Here, we extend our results to full dependency parsing, and experiment on transcripts of both spontaneous ADS and child-directed speech (CDS). Our models using word duration outperform words-only baselines, along with the Common Cover Link parser of Seginer (2007), and the Unsupervised Partial Parser of Ponvert et al. (2011), unsupervised lexicalized parsers that have obtained state-of-the-art results on standard newswire treebanks (though their performance here is worse, as our input lacks punctuation). We also outperform uniform-branching baselines.

2 Syntax and Word Duration

Before presenting our models and experiments, we first discuss why word duration might be a useful cue to syntax. This section reviews the two possible reasons mentioned above: duration as a cue to prosodic structure, or as a cue to predictability.

2.1 Prosodic Bootstrapping

Prosody is the structure of speech as conveyed by rhythm and intonation, which are, in turn, conveyed by such measurable phenomena as variation in fundamental frequency, word duration, and spectral tilt. Prosodic structure is typically analyzed as imposing a shallow, hierarchical grouping structure on speech, with the ends of prosodic phrases (constituents) being cued in part by lengthening the last word of the phrase (Beckman and Pierrehumbert, 1986).

The *Prosodic Bootstrapping* hypothesis (Gleitman and Wanner, 1982) points out that prosodic phrases are often also syntactic phrases, and proposes that language-acquiring infants exploit this correlation. Specifically, if infants can learn about prosodic phrase structure using word duration (and fundamental frequency), they may be able to identify syntactic phrases more easily using word strings and prosodic trees than using word strings alone.

Several behavioral experiments support the connection between prosody and syntax and the prosodic bootstrapping hypothesis specifically. For example, there is evidence that adults use prosodic information for syntactic disambiguation (Millotte et al., 2007; Price et al., 1991) and to help in learning the syntax of an artificial language (Morgan et al., 1987), while infants can use acoustic-prosodic cues for utterance-internal clause segmentation (Seidl, 2007).

On the computational side, we are aware of only our previous HMM-based chunkers (Pate and Goldwater, 2011), which learned shallow syntax from words, words and word durations, or words and hand-annotated prosody. Using these chunkers, we found that using words plus prosodic annotation worked better than just words, and words plus word duration worked even better. While these results are consistent with the prosodic bootstrapping hypothesis, we suggested that predictability bootstrapping (see below) might be a more plausible explanation.

Other computational work has combined prosody with syntax, but only in supervised systems, and typically using hand-annotated prosodic information. For example, Huang and Harper (2010) used annotated prosodic breaks as a kind of punctuation in a supervised PCFG, while prosodic breaks learned in a semi-supervised way have been used as features for parse reranking (Kahn et al., 2005) or PCFG state-splitting (Dreyer and Shafran, 2007). In contrast to these methods, our approach observes neither parse trees nor prosodic annotations.

2.2 Predictability Bootstrapping

On the basis of our HMM chunkers, we introduced the *predictability bootstrapping* hypothesis (Pate and Goldwater, 2011): the idea that word durations could be a useful cue to syntactic structure not (or not only) because they provide information about prosodic structure, but because they are a direct cue to syntactic predictability. It is well-established that talkers tend to pronounce words more quickly when they are more predictable, as measured by, e.g., word frequency, n-gram probability, or whether or not the word has been previously mentioned (Aylett and Turk, 2004; Bell et al., 2009). However, syntactic proba-

in a model of language acquisition, gold tags certainly are not.

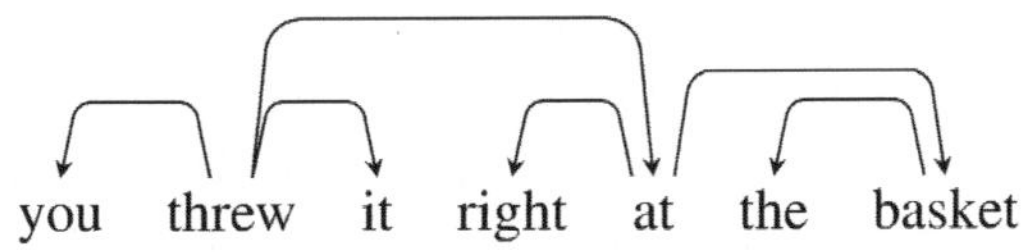

Figure 1: Example unlabeled dependency parse.

bility also seems to matter, with studies showing that verbs tend to be pronounced more quickly when they are in their preferred syntactic frame—transitive vs. intransitive or direct object vs. sentential complement (Gahl and Garnsey, 2004; Gahl et al., 2006; Tily et al., 2009). While this syntactic evidence is only for verbs, together with the evidence that effects of other notions of predictability, it suggests that such syntactic effects may also be widespread. If so, the duration of a word could give clues as to whether it is being used in a high-probability or low-probability structure, and thus what the correct structure is.

We found that our syntactic chunkers benefited more from duration information than prosodic annotations, providing some preliminary evidence in favor of predictability bootstrapping, but not ruling out prosodic bootstrapping. So, we are left with two plausible mechanisms by which word duration could help with learning syntax. Slow pronunciations may cue the end of a prosodic phrase, which is sometimes also the end of a syntactic phrase. Alternatively, slow pronunciations may indicate that the hidden syntactic structure is low probability, facilitating the induction of a probabilistic grammar. This paper will not seek to determine which mechanism is useful, instead taking the presence of two possible mechanisms as encouraging for the prospect of incorporating word duration into unsupervised parsing.

3 Models[2]

As mentioned, we will be incorporating word duration into unsupervised dependency parsing, producing analyses like the one in Figure 1. Each arc is between two words, with the *head* at the non-arrow end of the arc, and the *dependent* at the arrow end. One word, the *root*, depends on no word, and all other words depend on exactly one word. Following previous work on unsupervised dependency parsing, we will not label the arcs.

3.1 Dependency Model with Valence

All of our models are ultimately based on the Dependency Model with Valence (DMV) of Klein and Manning (2004), a generative, probabilistic model for projective (i.e. no crossing arcs), unlabeled dependency parses, such as the one in Figure 1.

The DMV generates dependency parses using three probability distributions, which together comprise model parameters θ. First, the root of the sentence is drawn from P_{root}. Second, we decide whether to stop generating dependents of the head h in direction $dir \in \{\text{left}, \text{right}\}$ with probability $P_{stop}(\cdot|h, dir, v)$, where v is T if h has a dir-ward dependent and F otherwise. If we decide to stop, then h takes no more dependents in the direction of dir. If we don't stop, we use the third probability distribution $P_{choose}(d|h, dir)$ to determine *which* dependent d to generate. The second and third step repeat for each generated word until all words have stopped generating in both directions.

The DMV was the first unsupervised parsing model to outperform a uniform-branching baseline on the Wall Street Journal corpus. It was trained using EM to obtain a maximum-likelihood estimate of the parameters θ, and learned from POS tags to avoid rare events. However, all work on syntactic predictability effects on word duration has been lexicalized (looking at, e.g., the transitivity bias of *particular* verbs). In addition, it is unlikely that children have access to the correct parts of speech when first learning syntactic structure. Thus, we want a DMV variant that learns from words rather than POS tags. We therefore adopt several extensions to the DMV due to Headden et al. (2009), described next.

3.2 The DMV with Backoff

Headden et al. (2009) sought to improve the DMV by incorporating lexical information in addition to POS tags. However, arcs between particular words are rare, so they modified the DMV in two ways to deal with this sparsity. First, they switched from MLE to a Bayesian approach, estimating a probability distribution over model parameters θ and dependency trees T given the training corpus C and a prior distribution $\boldsymbol{\alpha}$ over models: $P(T, \theta|C, \boldsymbol{\alpha})$.

Headden et al. avoided overestimating the probability of rare events that happen to occur in the train-

[2]The implementation of these models is available at http://github.com/jpate/predictabilityParsing

ing data by picking $\boldsymbol{\alpha}$ to assign low probability to models θ which give high probability to rare events. Accordingly, models that overcommit to rare events will contribute little to the final average over models. Specifically, Headden et al. use Dirichlet priors, with $\boldsymbol{\alpha}$ being the Dirichlet hyperparameters.

Headden et al.'s second innovation was to adapt interpolated backoff methods from language modeling with n-grams, where one can estimate the probability of word w_n given word w_{n-1} by interpolating between unigram and bigram probability estimates:

$$\hat{P}(w_n|w_{n-1}) = \lambda P(w_n|w_{n-1}) + (1-\lambda)P(w_n)$$

with $\lambda \in [0,1]$. Ideally, λ should be large when w_{n-1} is frequent, and small when w_{n-1} is rare. Headden et al. (2009) apply this method to the DMV by backing off from Choose and Stop distributions that condition on both head word and POS to distributions that condition on only the head POS.

In the equation above, λ is a scalar parameter. However, it actually specifies a probability distribution over the decision to back off (B) or not back off (¬B), and we can use different notation to reflect this view. Specifically, $\lambda_{stop}(\cdot)$ and $\lambda_{choose}(\cdot)$ will represent our backoff distributions for the Stop and Choose decision, respectively. Using h_p and d_p to represent head and dependent POS tag and h_w and d_w to represent head and dependent word, one of the models Headden et al. explored estimates:

$$\begin{aligned}\hat{P}_{choose}(d_p|h_w, h_p, dir, val) = \\ \lambda_{choose}(\neg\mathrm{B}|h_w, h_p, dir)P_{choose}(d_p|h_w, h_p, dir) \\ +\lambda_{choose}(\mathrm{B}|h_w, h_p, dir)P_{choose}(d_p|h_p, dir)\end{aligned} \quad (1)$$

with an analogous backoff for P_{stop}. We can see from Equation 1 that $\hat{P}_{choose}$ backs off from a distribution that conditions on h_w to a distribution that marginalizes out h_w, and that the extent of backoff varies across h_w; we can use this to back off more when we have less evidence about h_w. This model only conditions on words; it does not generate them in the dependents. This means it is actually a conditional, rather than fully generative, model of observed POS tags and unobserved syntax conditioned on the observed words.

Since identifying the true posterior distribution $P(T, \theta|C, \boldsymbol{\alpha})$ is intractable, Headden et al. use Meanfield Variational Bayes (Kurihara and Sato, 2006; Johnson, 2007), which finds an approximation to the posterior using an iterative EM-like algorithm. In the E-step of VBEM, expected counts $E(r_i)$ are gathered for each latent variable using the Inside-Outside algorithm, exactly as in the E-step of traditional EM. The Maximization step differs from the M-Step of EM in two ways. First, the expected counts for each value of the latent variable r_i are incremented by the hyperparameter α_i. Second, the numerator and denominator are scaled by the function $\exp(\psi(\cdot))$, which reduces the probability of rare events. Specifically, the P_{choose} distribution is estimated using expectations for each arc $a_{d_p,h,dir}$ from head h to dependent POS tag d_p in direction dir, and the update equation for P_{choose} from iteration n to $n+1$ is:

$$\begin{aligned}\hat{P}^{n+1}_{choose}(d_p|h, dir) = \\ \frac{\exp(\psi(E^n(a_{d_p,h,dir}) + \alpha_{d_p,h,dir}))}{\exp(\psi(\sum_c(E^n(a_{c,h,dir}) + \alpha_{c,h,dir})))}\end{aligned} \quad (2)$$

where h is the head POS tag for the backoff distribution, and the head (word, POS) pair for the no backoff distribution. The update equation for P_{stop} is analogous.

Now consider the update equations for λ_{choose}:

$$\hat{\lambda}^{n+1}_{choose}(\neg\mathrm{B}|h_w, h_p, dir) = \frac{\exp(\psi(\alpha_{\neg\mathrm{B}} + \sum_c(E^n(a_{c,h_w,h_p,dir}))))}{\exp(\psi(\alpha_{\mathrm{B}} + \alpha_{\neg\mathrm{B}} + \sum_c(E^n(a_{c,h_w,h_p,dir}))))}$$

$$\hat{\lambda}^{n+1}_{choose}(\mathrm{B}|h_w, h_p, dir) = \frac{\exp(\psi(\alpha_{\mathrm{B}}))}{\exp(\psi(\alpha_{\mathrm{B}} + \alpha_{\neg\mathrm{B}} + \sum_c(E^n(a_{c,h_w,h_p,dir}))))}$$

Only the ¬B numerator includes the expected counts, so as we see h_w in direction dir more often, the ¬B numerator will swamp the B numerator. By picking α_{B} larger than $\alpha_{\neg\mathrm{B}}$, we can bias our λ distribution to prefer backing off until we expect at least $\alpha_{\mathrm{B}} - \alpha_{\neg\mathrm{B}}$ arcs out of h_w with tag h_p in the direction of dir.

To obtain good performance, Headden et al. replaced each word that appeared fewer than 100 times in the training data with the token "UNK." We will also use such an UNK cutoff.

3.3 DMV with Duration

We explore three models. One is a straightforward application of the DMV with Backoff to words and (quantized) word duration, and the other two are fully-generative variants. We also consider using words and POS tags as input to these models. Backoff models are given two streams of information, providing two of word identity, POS tag, or word duration for each observed token. We call one stream the "backoff" stream, and the other the "extra" stream. Backoff models learn a probability distribution conditioning on both streams, backing off to condition on only the backoff stream.

Our first words and duration model takes the duration as the extra stream and the word identity as the backoff stream, and, using h_a to represent the acoustic information for the head, defines:

$$\begin{aligned}\hat{P}_{choose}(d_w|h_w, h_a, dir) = \\ \lambda_{choose}(\neg\mathtt{B}|h_w, h_a, dir)P_{choose}(d_w|h_w, h_a, dir) \\ +\lambda_{choose}(\mathtt{B}|h_w, h_a, dir)P_{choose}(d_w|h_w, dir)\end{aligned} \quad (3)$$

with an analogous backoff scheme for P_{stop}. We will refer to this conditional model as "Cond." in our experiments. This equation is similar to Equation 1, except it uses words and duration instead of words and POS tags, and backs off *to*, not *away* from, words. We back off to the sparse words, rather than the less sparse duration, because duration provides almost no information about syntax in isolation.[3]

Directly modelling the extra stream among the dependents may allow us to capture selectional restrictions in POS and words models, or exploit effects of syntactic predictability on dependent duration. We therefore explore variants that generate both streams in the dependents. First, we examine a model ("Joint") that generates them jointly:

$$\begin{aligned}\hat{P}_{choose}(d_w, d_a|h_w, h_p, dir) = \\ \lambda_{choose}(\neg\mathtt{B}|h_w, h_a, dir) \\ P_{choose}(d_w, d_a|h_w, h_a, dir) \\ +\lambda_{choose}(\mathtt{B}|h_w, h_a, dir) \\ P_{choose}(d_w, d_a|h_w, dir)\end{aligned} \quad (4)$$

However, this joint model will have a very large state-space and may suffer from the same data sparsity, so we also explore a model ("Indep.") that generates the extra and backoff independently:

$$\begin{aligned}\hat{P}_{choose}(d_w, d_a|h_w, h_p, dir) = \\ \lambda_{choose}(\neg\mathtt{B}|h_w, h_a, dir) \\ P_{choose\_backoff}(d_w|h_w, h_a, dir) \\ P_{choose\_extra}(d_a|h_w, h_a, dir) \\ + \quad \lambda_{choose}(\mathtt{B}|h_w, h_a, dir) \\ P_{choose\_backoff}(d_w|h_w, dir) \\ P_{choose\_extra}(d_a|h_w, dir)\end{aligned} \quad (5)$$

We also modified the DMV with Backoff to handle heavily lexicalized models. In Headden et al. (2009), arcs between words that never appear in the same sentence are given probability mass only by virtue of the backoff distribution to POS tags, which all appear in the same sentence at least once. We want to avoid relying on POS tags, and we also want to use held-out development and test sets to avoid implicitly overfitting the data when exploring different model structures. To this end, we add one extra α_{UNK} hyperparameter to the Dirichlet prior of P_{choose} for each combination of conditioning events. This hyperparameter reserves probability mass for a head h to take a word d_w as a dependent if h and d_w never appeared together in the training data. The amount of probability mass reserved decreases as we see h_w more often. This is implemented in training by adding α_{UNK} to the denominator of the P_{choose} update equation for each h and dir. At test time, if a word d_w appears as an unseen dependent for head h, h takes d_w as a dependent with probability:

$$\hat{P}_{choose}(d_w|h, dir) = \quad (6)$$
$$\frac{\exp(\psi(\alpha_{\text{UNK}}))}{\exp(\psi(\alpha_{\text{UNK}} + \sum_c (E^{last}(r_{c,h,dir}) + \alpha_{c,h,dir})))}$$

Here, h may be a word, (word, POS) pair, or (word, duration) pair. Since this event by definition never occurs in the training data, α_{UNK} does not appear in the numerator during training. [4]

Finally, the conditional model ignores the extra stream in P_{root}, and the generative models estimate

[3]Preliminary dev-set experiments confirmed this intuition, as models that backed off to word duration performed poorly.

[4]Note also that α_{UNK} is different from a global UNK cutoff, which is imposed in preprocessing, and so effects every occurrence of an an UNK'd word in the model. α_{UNK} affects only dependents in P_{choose}, and treats a dependent as UNK iff it did not occur on that particular side of that particular head word in any sentence. We used both global UNK cutoffs (optimized on the dev set) and these α_{UNK} hyperparameters.

		Train	Dev	Test
wsj10	Word tokens	42,505	1,765	2,571
	Word types	7,804	818	1,134
	Sentences	6,007	233	357
swbdnxt10	Word tokens	24,998	2,980	3,052
	Word types	2,647	760	767
	Sentences	3,998	488	491
brent	Word tokens	20,954	2,127	2,206
	Word types	1,390	482	488
	Sentences	6,249	424	449

Table 1: Statistics for our three corpora.

P_{root} over both streams jointly and independently, respectively.

4 Experimental Setup

4.1 Datasets

We evaluate on three datasets: `wsj10`, sentences of length 10 or less from the Wall Street Journal portion of the Penn Treebank; `swbdnxt10`, sentences of length 10 or less from the Switchboard dataset of ADS used by Pate and Goldwater (2011); and `brent`, part of the Brent corpus of CDS (Brent and Siskind, 2001). Table 1 presents corpus statistics.

4.1.1 wsj10

We present a new evaluation of the DMV with Backoff on `wsj10`, which does not have any acoustic information, simply to verify that α_{UNK} performs sensibly on a standard corpus. Additionally, Headden et al. (2009) use an intensive initializer that relies on dozens of random restarts, and so, strictly speaking, only show that the backoff technology is useful for good initializations. Our new evaluation will show that the backoff technology provides a substantial benefit even for harmonic initialization.

`wsj10` was created in the standard way; all punctuation and traces were removed, and sentences containing more than ten tokens were discarded. For our fully lexicalized version of `wsj10`, all words were lowercased, and numbers were replaced with the token "NUMBER."[5] Following standard practice, we used sections 2-21 for training, section 22 for development, and section 23 for test. `wsj10` contains hand-annotated constituency parses, not dependency parses, so we used the standard "constituency-to-dependency" conversion tool of Johansson and Nugues (2007) to obtain high-quality CoNLL-style dependency parses.

[5]Numbers were treated in this way only in `wsj10`.

4.1.2 swbdnxt10

Next, we evaluate on `swbdnxt10`, which contains all sentences up to length 10 from the same sections of the `swbdnxt` version of Switchboard used by Pate and Goldwater (2011). Short sentences are usually formulaic discourse responses (e.g. "oh ok"), so this dataset also excludes sentences shorter than three words. As our models successfully use word durations, this evaluation provides an important replication of the basic result from Pate and Goldwater (2011) with a different kind of syntactic model.

`swbdnxt10` has a forced alignment of a dictionary-based phonetic transcription of each utterance to audio, providing our word duration information. As a very simple model of hyper-articulation and hypo-articulation, we classify a word as in the longest third duration, shortest third, or middle third. To minimize effects of word form, this classification was based on vowel count (counting a diphthong as one vowel): each word with n vowels is classified as in the shortest, longest, or middle tercile of duration among words with n vowels.

Like `wsj10`, `swbdnxt10` is annotated only with constituency parses, so to provide approximate "gold-standard" dependencies, we used the same constituency-to-dependency conversion tool as for `wsj10`. We evaluated 200 randomly-selected sentences to check the accuracy of the conversion tool, which was designed for newspaper text. Excluding arcs involving words with no clear role in dependency structure (such as "um"), about 86% of the arcs were correct. While this rate is uncomfortably low, it is still much higher than unsupervised dependency parsers typically achieve, and so may provide a reasonable measure of *relative* dependency parse quality among competing systems.

4.1.3 brent

We also evaluated our models on the "Large Brent" dataset introduced in Rytting et al. (2010), a portion of the Brent corpus of child-directed speech (Brent and Siskind, 2001). We call this corpus `brent`. It consists of utterances from four of the mothers in Brent and Siskind's (2001) study, and, like swbdnxt10, has a forced alignment from which we obtain duration terciles. Rytting et al. (2010) used a 90%/10% train/test partition. We extracted every ninth utterance from the original training partition to create a dev set, producing an 80%/10%/10% partition. We also separated clitics from their base word. This dataset only has 186 sentences longer than ten words, with a maximum length of 22 words, so we discarded only sentences shorter than three words from the evaluation sets.

The Brent corpus is distributed via CHILDES (MacWhinney, 2000) with automatic dependency annotations. However, these are not hand-corrected, and rely on a different tokenization of the dataset than is present on the transcription tier. To produce a reliable gold-standard,[6] we annotated all sentences of length 2 or greater from the development and test sets with dependencies drawn from the Stanford Typed Dependency set (de Marneffe and Manning, 2008) using the annotation tool used for the Copenhagen Dependency Treebank (Kromann, 2003).

4.2 Parameters

In all experiments, hyperparameters for P_{root}, P_{stop}, and P_{choose} (and their backed-off distributions, and including α_{UNK}) were 1, α_{B} was 10, and $\alpha_{\neg\text{B}}$ was 1. VBEM was run on the training set until the data log-likelihood changed by less than 0.001%, and then the parameters were held fixed and used to obtain Viterbi parses for the evaluation sentences. Finally, we explored different global UNK cutoffs, replacing each word that appeared less than c times with the token UNK. We ran each model for each $c \in \{0, 1, 25, 50, 100\}$, and picked the best-scoring c on the development set for running on the test set and presentation here. We used a harmonic initializer similar to the one in Klein and Manning (2004).

4.3 Evaluation

In addition to evaluating the various incarnations of the DMV with backoff and input types, we compare to uniform branching baselines, the Common Cover Link (CCL) parser of Seginer (2007), and the Unsupervised Partial Parser (UPP) of Ponvert et al. (2011). The UPP produces a constituency parse from words and punctuation using a series of finite-state chunkers; we use the best-performing (Probabilistic Right Linear Grammar) version. The CCL parser produces a constituency parse using a novel "Cover Link" representation, scoring these links heuristically. Both CCL and UPP rely on punctuation (though according to Ponvert et al. (2011), UPP less so), which our input is missing. The left-headed "LH" (right-headed "RH") baseline assumes that each word takes the first word to its right (left) as a dependent, and corresponds to a uniform right-branching (left-branching) constituency baseline.

We evaluate the output of all models in terms of both constituency scores and dependency accuracy. Our wsj10 and swbdnxt10 corpora are originally annotated for constituency structure, with the dependency gold standard derived as described above, while our brent corpus is originally annotated for dependency structure, with the constituency gold standard derived by defining a constituent to span a head and each of its dependents (ignoring any one-word "constituents"). As the CCL and UPP parsers don't produce dependencies, only constituency scores are provided.

For constituency scores, we present the standard unlabeled Precision, Recall, and F-measure scores. For dependency scores, we present Directed attachment accuracy, Undirected attachment accuracy, and the "Neutral Edge Detection" (NED) score introduced by Schwartz et al. (2011). Directed attachment accuracy counts an arc as a true positive if it correctly identifies both a head and a dependent, whereas undirected attachment accuracy ignores arc direction in counting true positives. NED counts an arc as a true positive if it would be a true positive under the Undirected attachment score, or if the proposed head is the gold-standard grandparent of the proposed dependent. This avoids penalizing parses for flipping an arc, such as making determiners, rather than nouns, the head of noun phrases.

To assess statistical significance, we carried out stratified shuffling tests, with $10,000$ random shuffles, for all measures. Tables indicate significance differences between the backoff models and the most competitive baseline model on that measure, indicated by an italic score. A star (*) indicates $p < 0.05$, and a dagger (†) indicates $p < 0.01$. To see the direction of a significant difference (i.e. whether the backoff model is better or worse than the baseline),

[6] Available at http://homepages.inf.ed.ac.uk/s0930006/brentDep/

			wsj10						swbdnxt10						
			Dependency			Constituency				Dependency			Constituency		
		UNK	Dir.	Undir.	NED	P	R	F	UNK	Dir.	Undir.	NED	P	R	F
EM	Wds	25	32.5	52.5	67.0	49.5	48.5	49.0	25	30.6	50.9	66.8	45.4	47.1	46.3
	POS	—	*46.4*	*63.8*	*78.1*	59.2	*58.1*	*58.6*	—	*53.0*	*65.0*	*76.8*	*52.5*	*52.9*	*52.7*
VB	Wds	25	29.4	52.4	70.5	51.3	52.6	52.0	25	36.1	54.9	72.7	49.0	50.0	49.5
	POS	—	43.5	61.9	77.3	*59.7*	57.1	58.4	—	51.3	62.5	74.3	47.1	46.6	46.8
Wds+POS	Cond.	50	49.9†	66.1†	79.6*	**64.2**†	**61.9**†	**63.0**†	100	45.5†	62.4†	77.8	58.4†	58.9†	58.7†
	Joint	50	46.0	63.7	79.0	62.0†	59.1	60.5*	1	49.4†	63.7	**79.6**†	60.0†	52.9	56.3†
	Indep.	25	**52.5**†	**68.0**†	**83.5**†	63.5†	61.5†	62.5†	100	**55.7**†	**65.8**	74.6†	**61.5**†	57.9†	59.6†
	LH	—	26.0	55.8	74.3	53.1	69.6	60.3	—	24.1	50.8	72.7	60.8	**82.5**	**70.0**
	RH	—	31.2	56.4	61.4	25.8	33.8	29.3	—	29.2	52.0	57.9	22.2	30.1	25.5
	CCL	—	—	—	—	50.8	40.7	45.2	—	—	—	—	53.6	47.4	50.3
	UPP	—	—	—	—	52.8	37.2	43.7	—	—	—	—	60.0	46.6	52.4

Table 2: Performance on wsj10 and swbdnxt10 for models using words and POS tags only. Bold scores indicate the best performance of all models and baselines on that measure.
† Significantly different from best non-uniform baseline (italics) by a stratified shuffling test, $p < 0.01$; *: $p < 0.05$.

look to the scores themselves.

5 Results

In all results, when a model sees only one kind of information, that is expressed by writing out the abbreviation for the relevant stream: "Wds" for words, "POS" for Part-Of-Speech, "Dur" for word duration. For baseline models that see two streams, the abbreviations are joined by a "×" symbol (as they treat input pairs as atoms drawn in the cross-product of the two streams' vocabulary). For the backoff models, the abbreviations are joined by a "+" symbol (as they combine the information sources with a weighted sum), with the "extra" stream name first.

5.1 Results: wsj10

The left half of Table 2 presents results on wsj10. For the baseline models, the first column with horizontal text indicates the *input*, while for the backoff (Wds+POS) models, the first column with horizontal text indicates whether and how the extra stream is modeled in dependents (as described in Section 3.3). The EM model with POS input is largely a replication of the original DMV, differing in the use of separate train, dev, and test sets, and possibly the details of the harmonic initializer. Our replication achieves an undirected attachment score of 63.8 on the test set, similar to the score of 64.5 reported by Klein and Manning (2004) when training and evaluating on all of wsj10. Cohen et al. (2008) use the same train/dev/test partition that we do, and report a directed attachment score of 45.8, similar to our directed attachment score of 46.4.

The VB model which learns from POS tags does not outperform the EM model which learns from POS tags, suggesting that data sparsity does not hurt the DMV when using POS tags. As expected, the words-only models perform much worse than both the POS input models and the uniform LH baseline. VB does improve the words-only constituency performance.

The Cond. and Indep. backoff models outperform the POS-only baseline on all measures, but the Joint backoff model does not demonstrate a clear advantage over the POS-only baseline on any measure. The success of the Indep. model indicates that modelling dependent word identity does provide enough information to justify the increase in sparsity. The failure of the Joint model to provide a further improvement indicates that the extra information in the full joint over dependents does not justify the large increase in parameters. We also see that several models outperform the LH baseline on dependencies, but the advantage is much less in F-Score, underscoring the loss of information in the conversion of dependencies to constituencies. Finally, all models outperform CCL and UPP on F-score, emphasizing their reliance on the punctuation we removed.

			Dependency			Constituency		
		UNK	Dir.	Undir.	NED	P	R	F
EM	Wds	25	30.6	50.9	66.8	45.4	47.1	46.3
	Wds×Dur	25	26.1	46.5	62.0	45.6	48.7	47.1
VB	Wds	25	*36.4*	*55.1*	*73.0*	49.1	50.0	49.6
	Wds×Dur	25	31.8	51.7	71.3	*49.2*	*55.9*	*52.3*
Dur+Wds	Cond.	25	32.6†	55.1	74.5†	59.1†	71.4†	64.7†
	Joint	50	31.8†	51.8†	70.8*	54.4†	60.5†	57.3†
	Indep.	50	**40.3**†	**59.1**†	**76.0**†	56.1†	61.7†	58.8†
	LH	—	24.1	50.8	72.7	**60.8**	**82.5**	**70.0**
	RH	—	29.2	52.0	57.9	22.2	30.1	25.5
	CCL	—	—	—	—	53.6	47.4	50.3
	UPP	—	—	—	—	60.0	46.6	52.4

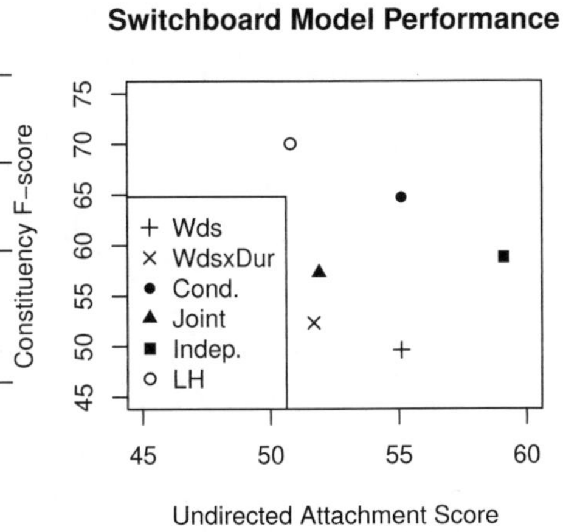

Table 3: Performance on swbdnxt10 for models using words and duration. The scatterplot includes a subset of the information in the table: F-score and undirected attachment accuracy for backoff models and VB and LH baseline. Bold, italics, and significance annotations as in Table 2.

5.2 Results: `swbdnxt10`

The right half of Table 2 presents performance figures on swbdnxt10 for input involving words and POS tags. As expected, the EM and VB baselines perform best when learning from gold-standard POS tags, and we again see no benefit for the VB POS-only model compared to the EM POS-only model. The POS-only baselines far outperform the uniform-attachment baselines on the dependency measures; to our knowledge this is the first demonstration outside the newspaper domain that the DMV outperforms a uniform branching strategy on these measures.

The other comparisons among systems listed in Table 2 are largely inconclusive. Models do comparatively well on *either* the constituency or dependency evaluation, but not both. The backoff models outperform the baseline POS-only models in the constituency evaluation, but underperform or match those same models in the dependency evaluation. Conversely, most models outperform the LH baseline in the dependency evaluation, but not in the constituency evaluation. There are probably two causes for the ambiguity in these results. First, the noise in the dependency gold-standard may have overwhelmed any advantage from backoff. Second, as we saw with wsj10, the conversion from dependencies to constituencies removes information, which may explain the failure of any model to outperform the LH baseline in the constituency evaluation.

Table 3 presents performance figures on swbdnxt10 for input involving words and duration, including a scatter-plot of Undirected attachment against constituency F-Score for the interesting comparisons. In the scatter-plot, models up and to the right performed better, and we see that the negative correlation between the dependency and constituency evaluations persists in words and duration input. VB substantially outperforms EM in the baselines, indicating that good smoothing is helpful when learning from words. Other comparisons are again ambiguous; the dependency evaluation is noisy, and backoff models outperform baseline models on the constituency evaluation but not the LH baseline. Still, the backoff models outperform all words-only baselines in constituency score, with two performing slightly worse in dependency score and one performing much better. So there is some evidence that word duration is useful, but we will find clearer evidence on the brent corpus.

5.3 Results: `brent`

Table 4 presents results on the brent dataset. VB is even more effective than in the other datasets for improving performance among baseline models, leading to double-digit improvements on some measures. Moreover, the best dev-set UNK cutoff drops to 1 for all VB models, indicating that, on this dataset, VB provides good smoothing even in models without backoff. This difference between datasets is likely related to differences in vocabulary diversity; the

			Dependency			Constituency		
		UNK	Dir.	Undir.	NED	P	R	F
EM	Wds	25	36.9	56.3	70.7	52.4	69.5	59.8
	Wds×Dur	25	31.3	51.1	66.9	50.7	64.7	56.9
VB	Wds	1	*51.2*	*64.2*	*77.3*	63.3	*68.1*	*66.0*
	Wds×Dur	1	47.0	60.5	74.0	***66.2***	64.9	65.5
Dur+Wds	Cond.	1	53.1*	65.5*	78.7*	65.4	68.6	**67.0***
	Joint	1	50.7	63.0	76.3	65.6	65.4†	65.5
	Indep.	1	**53.2**	**66.7†**	**79.6†**	61.5†	67.9	64.5
	LH	—	28.3	53.6	78.3	47.9	**85.6**	61.4
	RH	—	27.2	48.8	61.1	26.2	46.8	33.6
	CCL	—	—	—	—	41.7	58.8	48.8
	UPP	—	—	—	—	56.8	63.8	60.1

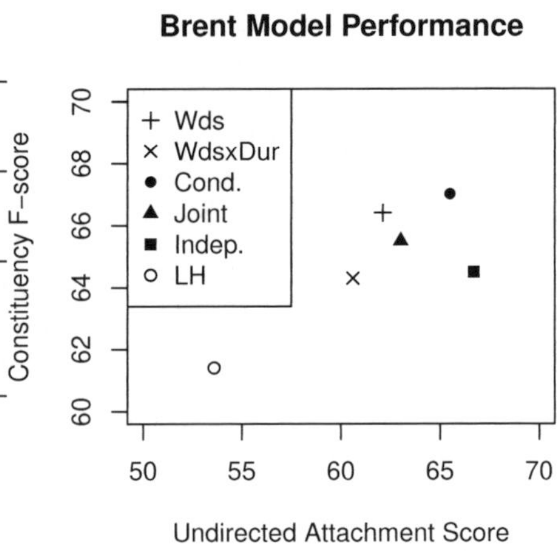

Table 4: Performance on `brent` for models using words and duration. The scatterplot includes a subset of the information in the table: F-score and undirected attachment accuracy for backoff models and VB and LH baseline. Bold, italics, and significance annotations as in Table 2.

type:token ratio in the `brent` training set is about 1:15, compared to 1:5 and 1:9 in the `wsj10` and `swbdnxt10` training sets, respectively.

More importantly for our main hypothesis, all three backoff models using words and duration outperform the words-only baselines (including CCL and UPP) on all dependency measures—the most accurate measures on this corpus, which has hand-annotated dependencies—and the Cond. model also wins on F-score.

6 Conclusion

In this paper, we showed how to use the DMV with Backoff and two fully-generative variants to explore the utility of word duration in fully lexicalized unsupervised dependency parsing. Although other researchers have incorporated features beyond words and POS tags into DMV-like models (e.g., semantics: Naseem and Barzilay (2011); morphology: Berg-Kirkpatrick et al. (2009)), we believe this is the first example based on Headden et al. (2009)'s backoff method. As far as we know, our work is also the first test of a DMV-based model on transcribed conversational speech and the first to outperform uniform-branching baselines without using either POS tags or punctuation in the input. Our results show that fully-lexicalized models can do well if they are smoothed properly and exploit multiple cues.

Our experiments also suggest that CDS is especially easy to learn from. Model performance on the `brent` dataset was generally higher than on `swbdnxt10`, with a much lower UNK threshold. This latter point, and the fact that `brent` has a much lower word type/token ratio than the other datasets, suggest that CDS provides more and clearer evidence about words' syntactic behavior.

Finally, our results provide more evidence, using a different, more powerful syntactic model than that of Pate and Goldwater (2011), that word duration is a useful cue for unsupervised parsing. We found that several ways of incorporating duration were useful, although the extra sparsity of Joint emissions was not justified in any of our investigations. Our results are consistent with both the prosodic and predictability bootstrapping hypotheses of language acquisition, providing the first computational support for these using a full syntactic parsing model and tested on child-directed speech. While our models do not provide a mechanistic account of how children might use duration information to help with learning syntax, they do show that this information is useful in principle, even without any knowledge of latent prosodic structure or its relationship to syntax. In addition, our results suggest it may be useful to explore using word duration to enrich NLP tasks in speech-related technologies, such as syntactically-inspired language models for text-to-speech generation. In the future, we also hope to investigate *why* duration is helpful, designing experiments to tease apart the role of prosody and predictability in learning syntax.

References

Matthew Aylett and Alice Turk. 2004. The smooth signal redundancy hypothesis: A functional explanation for relationships between redundancy, prosodic prominence, and duration in spontaneous speech. *Language and Speech*, 47(1):31–56.

Mary Beckman and Janet Pierrehumbert. 1986. Intonational structure in Japanese and English. *Phonology Yearbook*, 3:255–309.

Alan Bell, Jason M Brenier, Michelle Gregory, Cynthia Girand, and Dan Jurafsky. 2009. Predictability effects on durations of content and function words in conversational English. *Journal of Memory and Language*, 60:92–111.

Taylor Berg-Kirkpatrick, Alexandre Bouchard-Côté, John DeNero, and Dan Klein. 2009. Painless unsupervised learning with features. In *Proceedings of NAACL*.

Michael R Brent and Jeffrey M Siskind. 2001. The role of exposure to isolated words in early vocabulary development. *Cognition*, 81:31–44.

Christos Christodoulopoulos, Sharon Goldwater, and Mark Steedman. 2012. Turning the pipeline into a loop: Iterated unsupervised dependency parsing and PoS induction. In *Proceedings of the NAACL-HLT Workshop on the Induction of Linguistic Structure*, pages 96–99, Montréal, Canada, June. Association for Computational Linguistics.

Shay B Cohen and Noah A Smith. 2009. Shared logistic normal distributions for soft parameter tying in unsupervised grammar induction. In *Proceedings of NAACL*.

Shay B Cohen, Kevin Gimpel, and Noah A Smith. 2008. Logistic normal priors for unsupervised probabilistic grammar induction. In *Advances in Neural Information Processing Systems 22*.

Shay B Cohen, Dipanjan Das, and Noah A Smith. 2011. Unsupervised structure prediction with non-parallel multilingual guidance. In *Proceedings of EMNLP*.

Marie-Catherine de Marneffe and Christopher D Manning. 2008. Stanford typed dependencies manual. Technical report.

Markus Dreyer and Izhak Shafran. 2007. Exploiting prosody for PCFGs with latent annotations. In *Proceedings of Interspeech*, Antwerp, Belgium, August.

Susanne Gahl and Susan M Garnsey. 2004. Knowledge of grammar, knowledge of usage: Syntactic probabilities affect pronunciation variation. *Language*, 80:748–775.

Susanne Gahl, Susan M Garnsey, Cynthia Fisher, and Laura Matzen. 2006. "That sounds unlikely": Syntactic probabilities affect pronunciation. In *Proceedings of the 27th meeting of the Cognitive Science Society*.

Lila Gleitman and Eric Wanner. 1982. Language acquisition: The state of the art. In Eric Wanner and Lila Gleitman, editors, *Language acquisition: The state of the art*, pages 3–48. Cambridge University Press, Cambridge, UK.

Will Headden, Mark Johnson, and David McClosky. 2009. Improved unsupervised dependency parsing with richer contexts and smoothing. In *Proceedings of NAACL-HLT*.

Zhongqiang Huang and Mary Harper. 2010. Appropriately handled prosodic breaks help PCFG parsing. In *Proceedings of NAACL-HLT*, pages 37–45, Los Angeles, California, June. Association for Computational Linguistics.

Richard Johansson and Pierre Nugues. 2007. Extended constituent-to-dependency conversion for English. In *Proceedings of NODALIDA 2007*.

Mark Johnson. 2007. Why doesn't EM find good HMM POS-taggers. In *Proceedings of EMNLP-CoNLL*, pages 296–305.

Jeremy G Kahn, Matthew Lease, Eugene Charniak, Mark Johnson, and Mari Ostendorf. 2005. Effective use of prosody in parsing conversational speech. In *Proceedings of HLT-EMNLP*, pages 233–240.

Dan Klein and Christopher D. Manning. 2004. Corpus-based induction of syntactic structure: Models of dependency and constituency. In *Proceedings of ACL*, pages 479–486.

Matthias Trautner Kromann. 2003. The Danish Dependency Treebank and the DTAG treebank tool. In *Proceedings of the Second Workshop on Treebanks and Linguistic Theories*, pages 217–220.

Kenichi Kurihara and Taisuke Sato. 2006. Variational Bayesian grammar induction for natural language. In *Proceedings of the International Colloquium on Grammatical Inference*, pages 84–96.

Brian MacWhinney. 2000. *The CHILDES project: Tools for analyzing talk.* Lawrence Erlbaum Associates, Mahwah, NJ, third edition.

Séverine Millotte, Roger Wales, and Anne Christophe. 2007. Phrasal prosody disambiguates syntax. *Language and Cognitive Processes*, 22(6):898–909.

James L Morgan, Richard P Meier, and Elissa L Newport. 1987. Structural packaging in the input to language learning: contributions of prosodic and morphological marking of phrases to the acquisition of language. *Cognitive Psychology*, 19:498–550.

Tahira Naseem and Regina Barzilay. 2011. Using semantic cues to learn syntax. In *Proceedings of AAAI*.

John K Pate and Sharon Goldwater. 2011. Unsupervised syntactic chunking with acoustic cues: computational models for prosodic bootstrapping. In *Proceedings of the 2nd ACL workshop on Cognitive Modeling and Computational Linguistics*.

Elias Ponvert, Jason Baldridge, and Katrin Erk. 2011. Simple unsupervised grammar induction from raw text with cascaded finite state models. In *Proceedings of ACL-HLT*.

Patti J Price, Mari Ostendorf, Stefanie Shattuck-Hufnagel, and Cynthia Fong. 1991. The use of prosody in syntactic disambiguation. In *Proceedings of the HLT workshop on Speech and Natural Language*, pages 372–377, Morristown, NJ, USA. Association for Computational Linguistics.

C Anton Rytting, Chris Brew, and Eric Fosler-Lussier. 2010. Segmenting words from natural speech: subsegmental variation in segmental cues. *Journal of Child Language*, 37(3):513–543.

Roy Schwartz, Omri Abend, Roi Reichart, and Ari Rappoport1. 2011. Neutralizing linguistically problematic annotations in unsupervised dependency parsing evaluation. In *Proceedings of the 49th ACL*, pages 663–672.

Yoav Seginer. 2007. Fast unsupervised incremental parsing. In *Proceedings of ACL*.

Amanda Seidl. 2007. Infants' use and weighting of prosodic cues in clause segmentation. *Journal of Memory and Language*, 57(1):24–48.

Valentin I Spitkovsky, Hiyan Alshawi, Angel X Chang, and Daniel Jurafsky. 2011a. Unsupervised dependency parsing without gold part-of-speech tags. In *Proceedings of EMNLP*.

Valentin I Spitkovsky, Hiyan Alshawi, and Daniel Jurafsky. 2011b. Punctuation: Making a point in unsupervised dependency parsing. In *Proceedings of CoNLL*.

Harry Tily, Susanne Gahl, Inbal Arnon, Neal Snider, Anubha Kothari, and Joan Bresnan. 2009. Syntactic probabilities affect pronunciation variation in spontaneous speech. *Language and Cognition*, 1(2):147–165.

An HDP Model for Inducing Combinatory Categorial Grammars

Yonatan Bisk and **Julia Hockenmaier**
Department of Computer Science
The University of Illinois at Urbana-Champaign
201 N Goodwin Ave Urbana, IL 61801
{bisk1, juliahmr}@illinois.edu

Abstract

We introduce a novel nonparametric Bayesian model for the induction of Combinatory Categorial Grammars from POS-tagged text. It achieves state of the art performance on a number of languages, and induces linguistically plausible lexicons.

1 Introduction

What grammatical representation is appropriate for unsupervised grammar induction? Initial attempts with context-free grammars (CFGs) were not very successful (Carroll and Charniak, 1992; Charniak, 1993). One reason may be that CFGs require the specification of a finite inventory of nonterminal categories and rewrite rules, but unless one adopts linguistic principles such as X-bar theory (Jackendoff, 1977), these nonterminals are essentially arbitrary labels that can be combined in arbitrary ways. While further CFG-based approaches have been proposed (Clark, 2001; Kurihara and Sato, 2004), most recent work has followed Klein and Manning (2004) in developing models for the induction of projective dependency grammars. It has been shown that more sophisticated probability models (Headden III et al., 2009; Gillenwater et al., 2011; Cohen and Smith, 2010) and learning regimes (Spitkovsky et al., 2010), as well as the incorporation of prior linguistic knowledge (Cohen and Smith, 2009; Berg-Kirkpatrick and Klein, 2010; Naseem et al., 2010) can lead to significant improvement over Klein and Manning's baseline model. The use of dependency grammars circumvents the question of how to obtain an appropriate inventory of categories, since dependency parses are simply defined by unlabeled edges between the lexical items in the sentence. But dependency grammars make it also difficult to capture non-local structures, and Blunsom and Cohn (2010) show that it may be advantageous to reformulate the underlying dependency grammar in terms of a tree-substitution grammar (TSG) which pairs words with treelets that specify the number of left and right dependents they have. In this paper, we explore yet another option: instead of dependency grammars, we use Combinatory Categorial Grammar (CCG, Steedman (1996; 2000)), a linguistically expressive formalism that pairs lexical items with rich categories that capture all language-specific information. This may seem a puzzling choice, since CCG requires a significantly larger inventory of categories than is commonly assumed for CFGs. However, unlike CFG nonterminals, CCG categories are not arbitrary symbols: they encode, and are determined by, the basic word order of the language and the number of arguments each word takes. CCG is very similar to TSG in that it also pairs lexical items with rich items that capture all language-specific information. Like TSG and projective dependency grammars, we restrict ourselves to a weakly context-free fragment of CCG. But while TSG does not distinguish between argument and modifier dependencies, CCG makes an explicit distinction between the two. And while the elementary trees of Blunsom and Cohn (2010)'s TSG and their internal nodel labels have no obvious linguistic interpretation, the syntactic behavior of any CCG constituent can be directly inferred from its category. To see whether the algorithm has identified the basic syntactic properties of the language, it is hence sufficient to inspect the induced lexicon. Conversely, Boonkwan and Steedman (2011) show that knowledge of these basic syntactic properties makes it very easy to create a language-specific lexicon for accurate unsupervised CCG parsing. We have recently proposed an algorithm for inducing CCGs (Bisk and Hockenmaier, 2012b) that has been shown to be competitive with other approaches even when paired with a very simple probability model (Gelling et al., 2012). In this paper, we pair this induction algorithm with a novel nonparametric Bayesian model that is based on a different factorization of CCG derivations, and show that it outperforms our original model and many other approaches on a large number of languages. Our results indicate that the use of CCG yields grammars that are significantly more robust when dealing with longer sentences than most dependency grammar-based approaches.

2 Combinatory Categorial Grammar

Combinatory Categorial Grammar (Steedman, 2000) is a linguistically expressive, lexicalized grammar formalism that associates rich syntactic types with words and constituents. For simplicity, we restrict ourselves to the standard two atomic types S (sentences) and N (encompassing both nouns and noun phrases) from which we recursively build categories. Complex categories are of the form X/Y or X\Y, and represent functions which return a result of type X when combined with an argument of type Y. The directionality of the slash indicates whether the argument precedes or follows the functor. We write X|Y when the direction of the slash does not matter.

The CCG lexicon encodes all language-specific information. It pairs every word with a set of categories that define both its specific syntactic behavior as well as the overall word order of the language:

$$
\begin{array}{ll}
\mathsf{N}: \{he, girl, lunch, ...\} & \mathsf{N/N}: \{good, the, eating, ...\} \\
\mathsf{S\backslash N}: \{sleeps, ate, eating, ...\} & \mathsf{(S\backslash N)/N}: \{sees, ate, ...\} \\
\mathsf{S\backslash S}: \{quickly, today...\} & \mathsf{(S\backslash N)/(S\backslash N)}: \{good, the, ...\}
\end{array}
$$

To draw a simple contrast, in Spanish we would expect adjectives to take the category N\N because Spanish word ordering dictates that the adjective follow the noun. The lexical categories also capture word-word dependencies: head-argument relations are captured by the lexical category of the head (e.g. (S\N)/N), whereas head-modifier relations are captured by the lexical category of the modifier, which is of the form X\X or X/X, and may take further arguments of its own. Our goal will be to automatically learn these types of lexicons for a language. In Figure 3, we juxtapose several such lexicons which were automatically discovered by our system.

The rules of CCG are defined by a small set of of combinatory rules, which are traditionally written as schemas that define how constituents can be combined in a bottom-up fashion (although generative probability models for CCG view them in a top-down manner, akin to CFG rules). The first, and most obvious, of these rules is function application:

$$
\begin{array}{lll}
\mathsf{X/Y} \;\; \mathsf{Y} & \Rightarrow \mathsf{X} & (\mathsf{B}^0_>) \\
\mathsf{Y} \;\; \mathsf{X\backslash Y} & \Rightarrow \mathsf{X} & (\mathsf{B}^0_<)
\end{array}
$$

Here the functor X/Y or X\Y is applied to an argument Y resulting in X. While standard CCG has a number of additional combinatory rules (type-raising, generalized variants of composition and substitution) that increase its generative capacity beyond context-free grammars and allow an elegant treatment of non-local dependencies arising in extraction, coordination and scrambling, we follow Bisk and Hockenmaier (2012b) and use a restricted fragment, without type-raising, that allows only basic composition and is context-free:

$$
\begin{array}{lll}
\mathsf{X/Y} \;\; \mathsf{Y/Z} & \Rightarrow \mathsf{X/Z} & (\mathsf{B}^1_>) \\
\mathsf{X/Y} \;\; \mathsf{Y\backslash Z} & \Rightarrow \mathsf{X\backslash Z} & (\mathsf{B}^1_{\mathsf{X}>}) \\
\mathsf{Y\backslash Z} \;\; \mathsf{X\backslash Y} & \Rightarrow \mathsf{X\backslash Z} & (\mathsf{B}^1_<) \\
\mathsf{Y/Z} \;\; \mathsf{X\backslash Y} & \Rightarrow \mathsf{X/Z} & (\mathsf{B}^1_{\mathsf{X}<})
\end{array}
$$

The superscript 1 denotes the arity of the composition which is too low to recover non-projective dependencies, and our grammar is thus weakly equivalent to the dependency grammar representations that are commonly used for grammar induction. The main role of composition in our fragment is that it allows sentential and verb modifiers to both take categories of the form S\S and S/S. Composition introduces spurious ambiguities, which we eliminate by using Eisner (1996)'s normal form.[1]

Coordinating conjunctions have a special category conj, and we binarize coordination as follows (Hockenmaier and Steedman, 2007):

$$\begin{array}{llcll} \mathsf{X} & \mathsf{X[conj]} & \Rightarrow_{\&1} & \mathsf{X} & (\&1) \\ \mathrm{conj} & X & \Rightarrow_{\&2} & \mathsf{X[conj]} & (\&2) \end{array}$$

3 Category induction

Unlike dependency grammars, CCG requires an inventory of lexical categories. Given a set of lexical categories, the combinatory rules define the set of parses for each sentence. We follow the algorithm proposed by Bisk and Hockenmaier (2012b) to automatically induce these categories. The lexicon is initialized by pairing all nominal tags (nouns, pronouns and determiners) with the category N, all verb tags with the category S, and coordinating conjunctions with the category conj:

$$\begin{array}{lcl} \text{CONJ} & \rightarrow & \mathsf{conj} \\ \text{DET, NOUN, NUM, PRON} & \rightarrow & \mathsf{N} \\ \text{VERB} & \rightarrow & \mathsf{S} \end{array}$$

Although our lexicons are defined over corpus-specific POS tags, we use a slightly modified version of Petrov et al. (2012)'s Universal POS tagset to categorize them into these broad classes. The primary changes we make to their mappings are the addition of a distinction (where possible) between subordinating and coordinating conjunctions and between main and auxiliary verbs[2].

Since the initial lexicon consists only of atomic categories, it cannot parse any complex sentences:

The	*man*	*ate*	*quickly*
DT	NNS	VBD	RB
-	N	S	-

Complex lexical categories are induced by considering the local context in which tokens appear. Given an input sentence, and a current lexicon which assigns categories to at least some of the tokens in the sentence, we apply the following two rules to add new categories to the lexicon: The argument rule allows any lexical tokens that have categories other than N and conj to take immediately adjacent Ns as arguments. The modifier rule allows any token (other than coordinating conjunctions that appear in the middle of sentences) to modify an immediate neighbor that has the category S or N or is a modifier (S|S or N|N) itself.

The	*man*	*ate*	*quickly*
DT	NNS	VBD	RB
N/N	N, **S/S**	S, **N\N** **S\N**	**S\S**

These rules can be applied iteratively to form more complex categories. We restrict lexical categories to a maximal arity of 2, and disallow the category (S/N)\N, since it is equivalent to (S\N)/N.

The	*man*	*ate*	*quickly*
DT	NNS	VBD	RB
N/N, (**S**/**S**)/(**S**/**S**)	N, S/S (**N****N**)/(**N****N**) (**N**/**N**)\\(**N**/**N**)	S, N\N, S\N (**S**/**S**)\\(**S**/**S**) (**S****S**)/(**S****S**)	S\S, (**N****N**)\\(**N****N**)

The resultant, overly general, lexicon is then used to parse the training data. Each complete parse has to be of category S or N, with the constraint that sentences that contain a main verb can only form parses of category S.

4 A new probability model for CCG

Generative models define the probability of a parse tree τ as the product of individual rule probabilities. Our previous work (Bisk and Hockenmaier, 2012b) uses the most basic model of Hockenmaier and Steedman (2002), which first generates the head direction (left, right, unary, or lexical), followed by the head category, and finally the sister category. [3]

This factorization does not take advantage of the unique functional nature of CCG. We therefore introduce a new factorization we call the Argument Model. It exploits the fact that CCG imposes strong constraints on a category's left and right children, since these must combine to create the parent type via one of the combinators. In practice this means that given the parent X/Z, the choice of combinator[4] c and an argument Y we can uniquely determine the categories of the left and right children:

[1]The normal-form of Hockenmaier and Bisk (2010) is not required for this fragment of CCG.

[2]This distinction was suggested by the authors (p.c.)

[3]Huang et al. (2012) present a (deficient) variant and Bayesian extension of the Bisk and Hockenmaier (2012b) model without k-best smoothing that both underperform our published results.

[4]If X is an atomic category, only application is possible.

Parent	c	$\Rightarrow$	Left	Right
X/Z	$B^0_>$		(X/Z)/Y	Y
	$B^0_<$		Y	(X/Z)\Y
	$B^1_>$		X/Y	Y/Z
	$B^1_<$		Y/Z	X\Y

and correspondingly for X\Z:

Parent	c	$\Rightarrow$	Left	Right
X\Z	$B^0_>$		(X\Z)/Y	Y
	$B^0_<$		Y	(X\Z)\Y
	$B^1_>$		X/Y	Y\Z
	$B^1_<$		Y\Z	X\Y

While type-changing and raising are not used in this work the model's treatment of root productions extends easily to handle these other unary cases. We simply treat the argument Y as the unary outcome so that the parent, combinator and argument uniquely specify every detail of the unary rule:

Parent	c	$\Rightarrow$	Y
TOP	TOP		$\in \{\mathsf{S}, \mathsf{N}\}$
S/(S\N)	$T_<$		N
S\(S/N)	$T_>$		N

We still distinguish the same rule types as before (lexical, unary, binary with head left/right), leading us to the following model definition:

Given: $\mathsf{P} := \mathsf{X/Z}$
where $\text{type}(t) \in \{\text{Left,Right,Unary,Lex}\}$

$$p(t|\mathsf{P}) \times \begin{cases} p(w|\mathsf{P}, t) & \text{Lex} \\ \underbrace{p(\mathsf{Y}|\mathsf{P}, t)}_{\text{Argument}} \times \underbrace{p(c|\mathsf{P}, t, \mathsf{Y})}_{\text{Combinator}} & \text{o.w.} \end{cases}$$

Note that this model generates only one CCG category but uniquely defines the two children of a parent node. We will see below that this greatly simplifies the development of non-parametric extensions.

5 HDP-CCG: a nonparametric model

Simple generative models such as PCFGs or Bisk and Hockenmaier (2012b)'s CCG model are not robust in the face of sparsity, since they assign zero probability to any unseen event. Sparsity is a particular problem for formalisms like CCG that have a rich inventory of object types. Nonparametric Bayesian models, e.g. Dirichlet Processes (Teh, 2010) or their hierarchical variants (Teh et al., 2006) and generalizations (Teh, 2006) overcome this problem in a very elegant manner, and are used by many state-of-the-art grammar induction systems (Naseem et al., 2010; Blunsom and Cohn, 2010; Boonkwan and Steedman, 2011). They also impose a rich-getting-richer behavior that seems to be advantageous in many modeling applications. By contrast, Bisk and Hockenmaier (2012b) propose a weighted top-k scheme to address these issues in an ad-hoc manner.

The argument model introduced above lends itself particularly well to nonparametric extensions such as the standard Hierarchical Dirichlet Processes (HDP). In this work the size of the grammar and the number of productions are fixed and small, but we present the formulation as infinite to allow for easy extension in the future. Specifically, this framework allows for extensions which grow the grammar during parsing/training or fully lexicalize the productions. Additionally, while our current work uses only a restricted fragment of CCG that has only a finite set of categories, the literature's generalized variants of composition make it possible to generate categories of unbounded arity. We therefore believe that this is a very natural probabilistic framework for CCG, since HDPs make it possible to consider a potentially infinite set of categories that can instantiate the Y slot, while allowing the model to capture language-specific preferences for the set of categories that can appear in this position.

The HDP-CCG model In Bayesian models, multinomials are drawn from a corresponding n-dimensional Dirichlet distribution. The Dirichlet Process (DP) generalizes the Dirichlet distribution to an infinite number of possible outcomes, allowing us to deal with a potentially infinite set of categories or words. DPs are defined in terms of a base distribution H that corresponds to the mean of the DP, and a concentration or shape parameter α. In a Hierarchical Dirichlet Process (Teh et al., 2006), there is a hierarchy of DPs, such that the base distribution of a DP at level n is a DP at level $n-1$.

The HDP-CCG (Figure 1) is a reformulation of the Argument Model introduced above in terms of Hierarchical Dirichlet Processes.[5] At the heart of the model is a distribution over CCG categories. By combining a stick breaking process with a multinomial over categories we can define a DP over CCG

[5]An alternative HDP model for semantic parsing with CCG is proposed by Kwiatkowski et al. (2012).

HDP-CCG

1) Draw global parameters
- Define MLE root parameter — θ_{TOP}
- Draw top-level symbol weights — $\beta^Y \sim \text{GEM}(\alpha^Y)$
- Draw top-level lexical weights — $\beta^L \sim \text{GEM}(\alpha^L)$
- For each grammar symbol $z \in \{1, 2, ...\}$:
  - Define MLE rule type parameters — θ^T_z
  - Draw argument parameters — $\phi^Y_z \sim \text{DP}(\alpha^Y, \beta^Y)$
  - Draw lexical emission parameters — $\phi^L_z \sim \text{DP}(\alpha^L, \beta^L)$
  - For each grammar symbol $y \in \{1, 2, ...\}$:
    - Define MLE combinator parameters — $\theta^C_{z,y}$

2) For each parse tree:
- Generate root node — $z_{TOP} \sim \text{Binomial}(\theta_{TOP})$
- For each node i in the parse tree:
  - Choose rule type — $t_i \sim \text{Multinomial}(\theta^T_{z_i})$
  - If t_i == Lex:
    - Emit terminal symbol — $x_i \sim \text{Multinomial}(\phi^L_{z_i})$
  - If t_i == Left/Right/Unary:
    - Generate argument category — $y_i \sim \text{Multinomial}(\phi^Y_{z_i})$
    - Generate combinator — $c_i \sim \text{Multinomial}(\theta^C_{z_i,y_i})$
    - Deterministically create $z_{L(i)}$ (and $z_{R(i)}$ if binary)

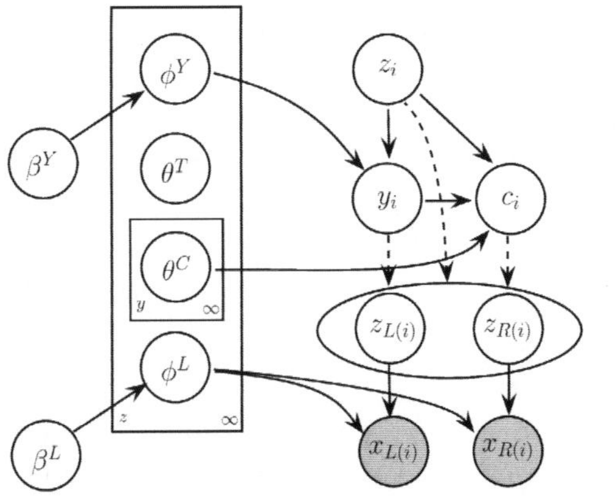

Because we are working with CCG, the parent z_i, argument y_i and combinator c_i uniquely define the two children categories $(z_{L(i)}, z_{R(i)})$. The dashed arrows here represent the deterministic process used to generate these two categories.

Figure 1: The HDP-CCG has two base distributions, one over the space of categories and the other over words (or tags). For every grammar symbol, an argument distribution and emission distribution is drawn from the corresponding Dirichlet Processes. In addition, there are several MLE distributions tied to a given symbol for generating rule types, combinators and lexical tokens.

categories whose stick weights (β^Y) correspond to the frequency of the category in the corpus. Next we build the hierarchical component of our model by choosing an argument distribution (ϕ^Y), again over the space of categories, for every parent X/Z. This argument distribution is drawn from the previously defined base DP, allowing for an important level of parameter tying across all argument distributions.

While the base DP does define the mean around which all argument distributions are drawn, we also require a notion of variance or precision which determines how similar individual draws will be. This precision is determined by the magnitude of the hyperparameter α^Y. This hierarchy is paralleled for lexical productions which are drawn from a unigram base DP over terminal symbols controlled by α^L. For simplicity we use the same scheme for setting the values for α^L as α^Y. We present experimental results in which we vary the value of α^Y as a function of the number of outcomes allowed by the grammar for argument categories or the corpus in the case of terminal symbols. Specifically, we set $\alpha^Y = n^p$ for conditioning contexts with n outcomes. Since Liang et al. (2009) found that the ideal value for alpha appears to be superlinear but subquadratic in n, we present results where p takes the values 0, 1.0, 1.5, and 2.0 to explore the range from uniform to quadratic. This setting for α is the only free parameter in the model. By controlling precision we can tell the model to what extent global corpus statistics should be trusted. We believe this has a similar effect to Bisk and Hockenmaier (2012b)'s top-k upweighting and smoothing scheme.

One advantage of the argument model is that it only requires a single distribution over categories for each binary tree. In contrast to similar proposals for CFGs (Liang et al., 2007), which impose no formal restrictions on the nonterminals X, Y, Z that can appear in a rewrite rule X $\rightarrow$ Y Z, this greatly simplifies the modeling problem (yielding effectively a model that is more akin to nonparametric HMMs), since it avoids the need to capture correlations between different base distributions for Y and Z.

Variational Inference HDPs need to be estimated with approximate techniques. As an alternative to Gibbs sampling (Teh et al., 2006), which is exact, but typically very slow and has no clear convergence criteria, variational inference algorithms (Bishop, 2006; Blei and Jordan, 2004) estimate the parameters of a truncated model to maximize a lower bound of the likelihood of the actual model. This allows for factorization of the model and a training procedure analogous to the Inside-Outside algorithm (Lari and Young, 1991), allowing training to run very quickly and in a trivially parallelizable manner.

To initialize the base DP's stick weights, we follow the example of Kurihara et al. (2007) and use an MLE model initialized with uniform distributions to compute global counts for the categories in our grammar. When normalized these provide a better initialization than a uniform set of weights. Updates to the distributions are then performed in a coordinate descent manner which includes re-estimation of the base DPs.

In variational inference, multinomial weights W take the place of probabilities. The weights for an outcome Y with conditioning variable P are computed by summing pseudocounts with a scaled mean vector from the base DP. The computation involves moving in the direction of the gradient of the Dirichlet distribution which results in the following difference of Digammas (Ψ):

$$W_P(Y) = \Psi(C(P,Y) + \alpha^P \beta_Y) \\ - \Psi(C(P,*) + \alpha^P)$$

Importantly, the Digamma and multinomial weights comprise a righ-get-richer scheme, biasing the model against rare outcomes. In addition, since variational inference is done by coordinate descent, it is trivially parallelizeable. In practice, training and testing our models on the corpora containing sentences up to length 15 used in this paper takes between one minute to at most three hours on a single 12-core machine depending on their size.

6 Evaluation

As is standard for this task, we evaluate our systems against a number of different dependency treebanks, and measure performance in terms of the accuracy of directed dependencies (i.e. the percentage of words in the test corpus that are correctly attached). We use the data from the PASCAL challenge for grammar induction (Gelling et al., 2012), the data from the CoNLL-X shared task (Buchholz and Marsi, 2006) and Goldberg (2011)'s Hebrew corpus.

Converting CCG derivations into dependencies is mostly straightforward, since the CCG derivation identifies the root word of each sentence, and head-argument and head-modifier dependencies are easily read off of CCG derivations, since the lexicon defines them explicitly. Unlike dependency grammar, CCG is designed to recover non-local dependencies that arise in control and binding constructions as well as in wh-extraction and non-standard coordination, but since this requires re-entrancies, or co-indexation of arguments (Hockenmaier and Steedman, 2007), within the lexical categories that trigger these constructions, our current system returns only local dependencies. But since dependency grammars also captures only local dependencies, this has no negative influence on our current evaluation.

However, a direct comparison between dependency treebanks and dependencies produced by CCG is more difficult (Clark and Curran, 2007), since dependency grammars allow considerable freedom in how to analyze specific constructions such as verb clusters (which verb is the head?) prepositional phrases and particles (is the head the noun or the preposition/particle?), subordinating conjunctions (is the conjunction a dependent of the head of the main clause and the head of the embedded clause a dependent of the conjunction, or vice versa?) and this is reflected in the fact that the treebanks we consider often apply different conventions for these cases. Although remedying this issue is beyond the scope of this work, these discrepancies very much hint at the need for a better mechanism to evaluate linguistically equivalent structures or treebank standardization.

The most problematic construction is coordination. In standard CCG-to-dependency schemes, both conjuncts are independent, and the conjunction itself is not attached to the dependency graph, whereas dependency grammars have to stipulate that either one of the conjuncts or the conjunction itself is the head, with multiple possibilities of where the remaining constituents attach. In addition to the standard CCG scheme, we have identified five main styles of conjunction in our data (Figure 2), although several corpora distinguish multiple types of coordinating conjunctions which use different styles (not all shown here). Since our system has explicit rules for coordination, we transform its output into the desired target representation that is specific to each language.

7 Experiments

We evaluate our system on 13 different languages. In each case, we follow the test and training regimes that were used to obtain previously published results in order to allow a direct comparison. We compare our system to the results presented at the PASCAL Challenge on Grammar Induction (Gelling et al., 2012)[6], as well as to Gillenwater et al. (2011) and Naseem et al. (2012). We use Nivre (2006)'s Penn2Malt implementation of Collins (2003)'s head rules to translate the WSJ Penn Treebank (Marcus et al., 1993) into dependencies. Finally, when training the MLE version of our model we use a simple smoothing scheme which defines a small rule probability (e^{-15}) to prevent any rule used during training from going to zero.

7.1 PASCAL Challenge on Grammar Induction

In Table 1, we compare the performance of the basic Argument model (MLE), of our HDP model with four different settings of the hyperparameters (as explained above) and of the systems presented in the PASCAL Challenge on Grammar Induction (Gelling et al., 2012). The systems in this competition were instructed to train over the full dataset, including the unlabelled test data, and include Bisk and Hockenmaier (2012a)'s CCG-based system (BH) to Cohn et al. (2010)'s reimplementation of Klein and Manning (2004)'s DMV model in a tree-substitution grammar framework (BC), as well as three other dependency based systems which either incorporate Naseem et al. (2010)'s rules in a deterministic fashion (Søgaard, 2012), rely on extensive tuning on the development set (Tu, 2012) or incorporate millions of additional tokens from Wikipedia to estimate model parameters (Marecek and Zabokrtsky, 2012). We ignore punctuation for all experiments reported in this paper, but since the training data (but not the evaluation) includes punctuation marks, participants were free to choose whether to include punctuation or ignore it.

While BH is the only other system with directly interpretable linguistic output, we also include a direct comparison with BC, whose TSG representation is equally expressive to ours. Finally we present a row with the maximum performance among the other three models. As we have no knowledge of how much data was used in the training of other systems we simply present results for systems trained on length 15 (not including punctuation) sentences and then evaluated at lengths 10 and 15.

The MLE version of our model shows rather variable performance: although its results are particularly bad on Basque (Eu), it outperforms both BH and BC on some other settings. By contrast, the HDP system is always better than the MLE model. It outperforms all other systems on half of the corpora. On average, it outperforms BH and BC by 10.3% and 9.3% on length 10, or 9.7% and 7.8 % on length 15 respectively. The main reason why our system does not outperform BC by an even higher margin is the very obvious 11.4%/11.5% deficit on Slovene. However, the Slovene dependency treebank seems to follow a substantially different annotation scheme. In particular, the gold standard annotation of the 1,000 sentences in the Slovene development set treats many of them as consisting of independent sentences (often separated by punctuation marks that our system has no access to), so that the average number of roots per sentence is 2.7:

>>	*verjeti*	*ti*	,	⟨⟨	*je*	*mehko*	*rekla*
"	believe	I	,	"	is	soft	said

When our system is presented with these short components in isolation, it oftentimes analyzes them correctly, but since it has to return a tree with a single root, its performance degrades substantially.

We believe the HDP performs so well as compared to the MLE model because of the influence of the shared base distribution, which allows the

[6] Numbers are from personal correspondence with the organizers. The previously published numbers are not comparable to literature due to an error in the evaluation. http://wiki.cs.ox.ac.uk/InducingLinguisticStructure/ResultsDepComparable

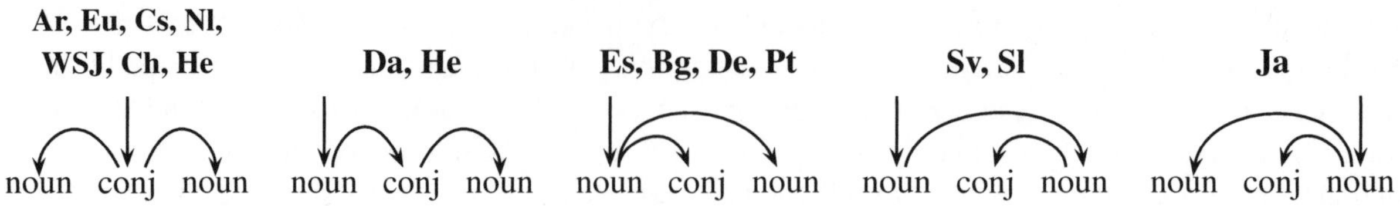

Figure 2: In the treebanks used for evaluation different standards exist for annotating coordination. While not exhaustive, this table demonstrates five of the most common schemes used in the literature. Syntactically these are identical and traditionally CCG draws arcs only to the arguments without attaching the conjunction. For the purposes of comparison with the literature we have implemented these five translation schemes.

		Arabic	Danish	Slovene	Swedish	Dutch	Basque	Portuguese	WSJ	Childes	Czech
	# Tokens	5,470	25,341	54,032	61,877	78,737	81,345	158,648	163,727	290,604	436,126
	# Tags	20	24	36	30	304	14	23	36	69	62
PASCAL	**BC**	60.8/58.4	44.7/39.4	62.6/57.9	63.2/56.6	**51.8/52.0**	53.0/**48.9**	52.4/50.2	68.6/63.3	47.4/46.1	47.9/43.1
	Max	**67.2/66.8**	**60.1/56.0**	**65.6/61.8**	**72.8/63.4**	51.1/47.6	**53.7**/47.8	67.0/61.8	**71.2/64.8**	56.0/54.5	**58.3/54.4**
	BH	41.6/43.7	46.4/43.8	49.6/43.9	63.7/57.0	49.7/43.6	45.1/39.6	**70.8/67.2**	68.2/59.6	**61.4/59.8**	45.0/38.9
This work	**MLE**	41.6/42.9	43.4/39.2	46.1/41.1	70.1/59.7	52.2/47.2	29.6/26.5	62.2/59.7	59.5/52.4	53.3/51.9	50.5/45.8
	$HDP_{0.0}$	48.0/50.0	**63.9/58.5**	44.8/39.8	67.6/62.1	45.0/33.9	41.6/39.1	71.0/66.0	59.8/52.9	56.3/55.2	54.0/49.0
	$HDP_{1.0}$	45.6/47.1	45.7/42.3	53.9/46.9	**74.5/66.9**	**58.5/54.4**	50.1/44.6	65.1/60.6	64.3/56.5	71.5/70.3	**55.8/50.7**
	$HDP_{1.5}$	49.6/50.4	58.7/54.4	53.2/48.2	74.3/67.1	57.4/54.5	**50.6/45.0**	70.0/64.7	65.5/57.2	69.6/68.6	55.6/50.3
	$HDP_{2.0}$	**66.4/65.1**	56.5/49.5	**54.2/46.4**	71.6/64.1	51.7/48.3	49.4/43.3	**76.3/70.5**	**70.7/62.9**	**74.1/73.3**	54.4/48.5
	+/−	-0.8/-1.7	+3.8/+2.5	-11.4/-15.4	+1.7/+3.5	+6.7/+2.4	-3.1/-3.9	+5.5/+3.3	-0.5/-1.9	+12.7/+13.5	-2.5/-3.7

Table 1: A comparison of the basic Argument model (MLE) and four hyper-parameter settings of the HDP-CCG against two syntactic formalisms that participated in the PASCAL Challenge (Gelling et al., 2012), BH (Bisk and Hockenmaier, 2012a) and BC (Blunsom and Cohn, 2010), in addition to a max over all other participants. We trained on length 15 data (punctuation removed), including the test data as recommended by the organizers. The last row indicates the difference between our best system and the competition.

global category distribution to influence each of the more specific distributions. Further, it provides a very simple knob in the choice of hyperparameters, which has a substantial effect on performance. A side effect of the hyperparameters is that their strength also determines the rate of convergence. This may be one of the reasons for the high variance seen in the four settings tested, although we note that since our initialization is always uniform, and not random, consecutive runs do not introduce variance in the model's performance.

7.2 Comparison with systems that capture linguistic constraints

Since our induction algorithm is based on the knowledge of which POS tags are nouns and verbs, we compare in Table 2 our system to Naseem et al. (2010), who present a nonparametric dependency model that incorporates thirteen universal linguistic constraints. Three of these constraints correspond to our rules that verbs are the roots of sentences and may take nouns as dependents, but the other ten constraints (e.g. that adjectives modify nouns, adverbs modify adjectives or verbs, etc.) have no equivalent in our system. Although our system has less prior knowledge, it still performs competitively.

On the WSJ, Naseem et al. demonstrate the importance and effect of the specific choice of syntactic rules by comparing the performance of their system with hand crafted universal rules (71.9), with English specific rules (73.8), and with rules proposed by Druck et al. (2009) (64.9). The performance of Naseem et al.'s system drops very significantly as sentence length (and presumable parse complexity)

	Sl	Es	Da	Pt	Sv
~#Tokens	3.8K	4.2K	9.5K	15K	24K
N10	50.9	**67.2**	**51.9**	71.5	63.3
HDP	**56.6**	62.1	51.5	**74.7**	**69.8**

Table 2: A comparison of our system with Naseem et al. (2010), both trained and tested on the length 10 training data from the CoNLL-X Shared Task.

increases, whereas our system shows significantly less decline, and outperforms their universal system by a significant margin.[7]

	≤ 10	≤ 20
Naseem Universal Rules	71.9	50.4
Naseem English Rules	**73.8**	**66.1**
HDP-CCG	68.2	64.2
HDP-CCG (train $\leq$ 20)	71.9	

In contrast to Spitkovsky et al. (2010), who reported that performance of their dependency based system degrades when trained on longer sentences, our performance on length 10 sentences increases to **71.9** when we train on sentences up to length 20.

Another system that is also based on CCG, but captures significantly more linguistic knowledge than ours, was presented by Boonkwan and Steedman (2011), who achieve an accuracy of 74.5 on WSJ10 section 23 (trained on sections 02-22). Using the same settings, our system achieves an accuracy of 68.4. Unlike our approach, Boonkwan and Steedman do not automatically induce an appropriate inventory of lexical category, but use an extensive questionnaire that defines prototype categories for various syntactic constructions, and requires significant manual engineering of which POS tags are mapped to what categories to generate a language-specific lexicon. However, their performance degrades significantly when only a subset of the questions are considered. Using only the first 14 questions, covering facts about the ordering of subjects, verbs and objects, adjectives, adverbs, auxiliaries, adpositions, possessives and relative markers, they achieve an accuracy of 68.2, which is almost identical to ours, even though we use significantly less initial knowledge. However, the lexicons we present below indicate that we are in fact learning many of the very exact details that in their system are constructed by hand. The remaining 14 questions in Boonkwan and Steedman's questionnaire cover less frequent phenomena such as the order of negative markers, dative shift, and pro-drop. The obvious advantage of this approach is that this allows them to define a much more fine-grained inventory of lexical categories than our system can automatically induce. We also stipulate that for certain languages knowledge of pro-drop could play a significant role in the success of their approach: if complete sentences are allowed to be of the form $\mathsf{S\backslash N}$ or $\mathsf{S/N}$, the same lexical category can be used for the verb regardless of whether the subject is present or has been dropped.

[7]Our earlier generative model showed similar behavior, although the results in Bisk and Hockenmaier (2012b) are not directly comparable due to differences in the data.

	Sl	Es	Da	Pt	Sv
#Tokens	3,857	4,230	9,549	15,015	24,021
G10	51.2	62.4	47.2	54.3	48.6
HDP	**57.9**	**65.4**	**49.3**	**73.5**	**73.2**
	Bg	**WSJ**	**Nl**	**Ja**	**De**
#Tokens	38,220	42,442	43,405	43,501	77,705
G10	59.8	64.4	47.5	60.2	47.4
HDP	**66.1**	**70.3**	**56.2**	**64.1**	**68.4**

Table 3: A comparison of our system with Gillenwater et al. (2010), both trained on the length 10 training data, and tested on the length 10 test data, from the CoNLL-X Shared task.

7.3 Additional Languages

In order to provide results on additional languages, we present in Table 3 a comparison to the work of Gillenwater et al. (2010) (G10), using the ConLL-X Shared Task data (Buchholz and Marsi, 2006). Following Gillenwater et al., we train only on sentences of length 10 from the training set and evaluate on the test set. Since this is a different training regime, and these corpora differ for many languages from that of the PASCAL challenge, numbers from Table 1 cannot be compared directly with those in Table 3. We have also applied our model to Goldberg (2011)'s Hebrew corpus, where it achieves an accuracy of 62.1 (trained and tested on all sentences length 10; 7,253) and 59.6 (length 15; 21,422 tokens).

	Arabic	%	Swedish	%	WSJ	%	Childes	%	Japanese	%	Czech	%
VERB	(S\N)/N	56	S	45	S\N	52	S/N	44	S	84	S	26
	(S/N)/N	29	S\N	20	(S\N)/N	19	S	37			S\N	25
ADP	N\N	68	(S\S)/N	49	(S\S)/N	46	(S\S)/N	45	(S/S)\N	44	(S\S)/N	42
	N/N	21	(N\N)/N	25	(N\N)/N	20	N/N	25	N\N	23	(S/S)/N	26
NOUN	N\N	50	N	91	N	79	N	89	N	73	N	74
	N	35			N/N	12						
ADJ	N\N	82	N/N	50	N/N	70	N/N	46	S/S	64	N/N	55

Figure 3: Partial lexicons demonstrating language specific knowledge learned automatically for five languages. For ease of comparison between languages, we use the universal tag label (Verb, Adposition, Noun and Adjective). Shown are the most common categories and the fraction of occurrences of the tag that are assigned this category (according to the Viterbi parses).

8 The Induced Lexicons

Since our approach is based on a lexicalized formalism such as CCG, our system automatically induces lexicons that pair words (or, in our case, POS-tags) with language-specific categories that capture their syntactic behavior. If our approach is successful, it should learn the basic syntactic properties of each language, which will be reflected in the corresponding lexicon. In Figure 3 one sees how verbs subcategorize differently, how word ordering differs by language, and how the attachment structures of prepositions are automatically discovered and differ across languages. In Arabic, for example, the system learns that word order is variable and therefore the verb must allow for both SVO and VOS style constructions. We generally learn that adpositions (prepositions or postpositions) take nouns as arguments. In Czech, PPs can appear before and after the verb, leading to two different categories ((S\S)/N and (S/S)/N). Japanese has postpositions that appear in preverbal position ((S/S)\N), but when this category is assigned to nominal particles that correspond to case markers, it effectively absorbs the noun, leading to a preference for verbs that do not take any arguments (S), and to a misanalysis of adjectives as verb modifiers (S/S). Our lexicons also reflect differences in style: while Childes and the WSJ are both English, they represent very different registers. We learn that subjects are mostly absent in the informal speech and child-directed instructions contained in Childes, while effectively mandatory in the Wall Street Journal.

9 Conclusions

This paper has introduced a novel factorization for CCG models and showed how when combined with non-parametric Bayesian statistics it can compete with every other grammar induction system currently available, including those that capture a significant amount of prior linguistic knowledge. The use of a powerful syntactic formalism proves beneficial both in terms of requiring very limited universal knowledge and robustness at longer sentence lengths. Unlike standard grammar induction systems that are based on dependency grammar, our system returns linguistically interpretable lexicons for each language that demonstrate it has discovered their basic word order. Of particular note is the simplicity of the model both algorithmically and in terms of implementation. By not faltering on longer sentences or requiring extensive tuning, the system can be easily and quickly deployed on a new language and return state of the art performance and easily interpretable lexicons. In this paper, we have applied this model only to a restricted fragment of CCG, but future work will address the impact of lexicalization and the inclusion of richer combinators.

10 Acknowledgements

This work is supported by NSF CAREER award 1053856 (Bayesian Models for Lexicalized Grammars).

References

Taylor Berg-Kirkpatrick and Dan Klein. 2010. Phylogenetic Grammar Induction. In *Proceedings of the 48th Annual Meeting of the Association for Computational Linguistics*, pages 1288–1297, Uppsala, Sweden, July.

Christopher Bishop. 2006. *Pattern Recognition and Machine Learning*. Springer-Verlag, August.

Yonatan Bisk and Julia Hockenmaier. 2012a. Induction of Linguistic Structure with Combinatory Categorial Grammars. In *NAACL HLT Workshop on Induction of Linguistic Structure*, pages 90–95, Montréal, Canada, June.

Yonatan Bisk and Julia Hockenmaier. 2012b. Simple Robust Grammar Induction with Combinatory Categorial Grammars. In *Proceedings of the Twenty-Sixth Conference on Artificial Intelligence (AAAI-12)*, pages 1643–1649, Toronto, Canada, July.

David M Blei and Michael I Jordan. 2004. Variational Methods for the Dirichlet Process. In *Proceedings of the Twenty-First International Conference on Machine Learning (ICML 2004)*, Banff, Alberta, Canada, July.

Phil Blunsom and Trevor Cohn. 2010. Unsupervised Induction of Tree Substitution Grammars for Dependency Parsing. *Proceedings of the 2010 Conference on Empirical Methods of Natural Language Processing*, pages 1204–1213, October.

Prachya Boonkwan and Mark Steedman. 2011. Grammar Induction from Text Using Small Syntactic Prototypes. In *Proceedings of 5th International Joint Conference on Natural Language Processing*, pages 438–446, Chiang Mai, Thailand, November.

Sabine Buchholz and Erwin Marsi. 2006. CoNLL-X Shared Task on Multilingual Dependency Parsing. In *Proceedings of the 10th Conference on Computational Natural Language Learning (CoNLL-X)*, pages 149–164, New York City, June.

Glenn Carroll and Eugene Charniak. 1992. Two Experiments on Learning Probabilistic Dependency Grammars from Corpora. *Working Notes of the Workshop Statistically-Based NLP Techniques*, pages 1–13.

Eugene Charniak. 1993. *Statistical Language Learning*. The MIT Press, Cambridge, Massachusetts.

Stephen Clark and James R Curran. 2007. Formalism-Independent Parser Evaluation with CCG and DepBank. In *Proceedings of the 45th Annual Meeting of the Association of Computational Linguistics*, pages 248–255, Prague, Czech Republic, June.

Alex Clark. 2001. *Unsupervised Language Acquisition: Theory and Practice*. Ph.D. thesis, University of Sussex, September.

Shay B Cohen and Noah A Smith. 2009. Variational Inference for Grammar Induction with Prior Knowledge. *Proceedings of the ACL-IJCNLP 2009 Conference Short Papers*, pages 1–4.

Shay B Cohen and Noah A Smith. 2010. Covariance in Unsupervised Learning of Probabilistic Grammars. *The Journal of Machine Learning Research*, pages 3117–3151, November.

Trevor Cohn, Phil Blunsom, and Sharon Goldwater. 2010. Inducing Tree-Substitution Grammars. *The Journal of Machine Learning Research*, 11:3053–3096, November.

Michael Collins. 2003. Head-Driven Statistical Models for Natural Language Parsing. *Computational Linguistics*, 29(4):589–637, December.

Gregory Druck, Gideon Mann, and Andrew McCallum. 2009. Semi-supervised Learning of Dependency Parsers using Generalized Expectation Criteria. In *Proceedings of the Joint Conference of the 47th Annual Meeting of the ACL and the 4th International Joint Conference on Natural Language Processing of the AFNLP*, pages 360–368, Suntec, Singapore, August.

Jason Eisner. 1996. Efficient Normal-Form Parsing for Combinatory Categorial Grammar. In *Proceedings of the 34th Annual Meeting of the Association for Computational Linguistics*, pages 79–86, Santa Cruz, California, USA, June.

Douwe Gelling, Trevor Cohn, Phil Blunsom, and João V Graca. 2012. The PASCAL Challenge on Grammar Induction. In *NAACL HLT Workshop on Induction of Linguistic Structure*, pages 64–80, Montréal, Canada, June.

Jennifer Gillenwater, Kuzman Ganchev, João V Graca, Fernando Pereira, and Ben Taskar. 2010. Sparsity in Dependency Grammar Induction. In *Proceedings of the 48th Annual Meeting of the Association for Computational Linguistics*, pages 194–199, Uppsala, Sweden, July.

Jennifer Gillenwater, Kuzman Ganchev, João V Graca, Fernando Pereira, and Ben Taskar. 2011. Posterior Sparsity in Unsupervised Dependency Parsing. *The Journal of Machine Learning Research*, 12:455–490, February.

Yoav Goldberg. 2011. *Automatic Syntactic Processing of Modern Hebrew*. Ph.D. thesis, Ben-Gurion University of the Negev, November.

William P Headden III, Mark Johnson, and David McClosky. 2009. Improving Unsupervised Dependency Parsing with Richer Contexts and Smoothing. In *Proceedings of Human Language Technologies: The 2009 Annual Conference of the North American Chapter of the Association for Computational Linguistics*, pages 101–109, Boulder, Colorado, June.

Julia Hockenmaier and Yonatan Bisk. 2010. Normal-form parsing for Combinatory Categorial Grammars with generalized composition and type-raising. In

Proceedings of the 23rd International Conference on Computational Linguistics (Coling 2010), pages 465–473, Beijing, China, August. Coling 2010 Organizing Committee.

Julia Hockenmaier and Mark Steedman. 2002. Generative Models for Statistical Parsing with Combinatory Categorial Grammar. In *Proceedings of 40th Annual Meeting of the Association for Computational Linguistics*, pages 335–342, Philadelphia, Pennsylvania, USA, July.

Julia Hockenmaier and Mark Steedman. 2007. CCGbank: A Corpus of CCG Derivations and Dependency Structures Extracted from the Penn Treebank. *Computational Linguistics*, 33(3):355–396, September.

Yun Huang, Min Zhang, and Chew Lim Tan. 2012. Improved Combinatory Categorial Grammar Induction with Boundary Words and Bayesian Inference. In *Proceedings of the 24rd International Conference on Computational Linguistics (Coling 2012)*, Mumbai, India, December.

Ray Jackendoff. 1977. *X-Bar Syntax: A Study of Phrase Structure*. The MIT Press.

Dan Klein and Christopher D Manning. 2004. Corpus-Based Induction of Syntactic Structure: Models of Dependency and Constituency. In *Proceedings of the 42nd Meeting of the Association for Computational Linguistics (ACL'04), Main Volume*, pages 478–485, Barcelona, Spain, July.

Kenichi Kurihara and Taisuke Sato. 2004. An Application of the Variational Bayesian Approach to Probabilistic Context-Free Grammars. *International Joint Conference on Natural Language Language Processing Workshop Beyond Shallow Analyses*, March.

Kenichi Kurihara, Max Welling, and Yee-Whye Teh. 2007. Collapsed Variational Dirichlet Process Mixture Models. In *Proceedings of the 20th International Joint Conference on Artificial Intelligence (IJCAI07)*, pages 2796–2801, Hyderabad, India, January.

Tom Kwiatkowski, Sharon Goldwater, Luke Zettlemoyer, and Mark Steedman. 2012. A probabilistic model of syntactic and semantic acquisition from child-directed utterances and their meanings. In *Proceedings of the 13th Conference of the European Chapter of the Association for Computational Linguistics*, pages 234–244, Avignon, France, April. Association for Computational Linguistics.

Karim Lari and Steve J Young. 1991. Applications of stochastic context-free grammars using the Inside-Outside algorithm. *Computer speech & language*, 5(3):237–257, January.

Percy Liang, Slav Petrov, Michael I Jordan, and Dan Klein. 2007. The Infinite PCFG Using Hierarchical Dirichlet Processes. In *Proceedings of the 2007 Joint Conference on Empirical Methods in Natural Language Processing and Computational Natural Language Learning (EMNLP-CoNLL)*, pages 688–697, Prague, Czech Republic.

Percy Liang, Michael I Jordan, and Dan Klein. 2009. Probabilistic Grammars and Hierarchical Dirichlet Processes. In *The Oxford Handbook of Applied Bayesian Analysis*. Oxford University Press.

Mitchell P Marcus, Beatrice Santorini, and Mary Ann Marcinkiewicz. 1993. Building a Large Annotated Corpus of English: The Penn Treebank. *Computational Linguistics*, 19(2):313–330, June.

David Marecek and Zdenek Zabokrtsky. 2012. Unsupervised Dependency Parsing using Reducibility and Fertility features. In *NAACL HLT Workshop on Induction of Linguistic Structure*, pages 84–89, Montréal, Canada, June.

Tahira Naseem, Harr Chen, Regina Barzilay, and Mark Johnson. 2010. Using Universal Linguistic Knowledge to Guide Grammar Induction. In *Proceedings of the 2010 Conference on Empirical Methods in Natural Language Processing*, pages 1234–1244, Cambridge, MA, October.

Tahira Naseem, Regina Barzilay, and Amir Globerson. 2012. Selective Sharing for Multilingual Dependency Parsing. In *Proceedings of the 50th Annual Meeting of the Association for Computational Linguistics (Volume 1: Long Papers)*, pages 629–637, Jeju, Republic of Korea, July.

Joakim Nivre. 2006. *Inductive Dependency Parsing*. Springer.

Slav Petrov, Dipanjan Das, and Ryan McDonald. 2012. A Universal Part-of-Speech Tagset. In *Proceedings of the 8th International Conference on Language Resources and Evaluation (LREC-2012)*, pages 2089–2096, Istanbul, Turkey, May.

Anders Søgaard. 2012. Two baselines for unsupervised dependency parsing. In *NAACL HLT Workshop on Induction of Linguistic Structure*, pages 81–83, Montréal, Canada, June.

Valentin I Spitkovsky, Hiyan Alshawi, and Daniel Jurafsky. 2010. From Baby Steps to Leapfrog: How "Less is More" in Unsupervised Dependency Parsing. In *Human Language Technologies: The 2010 Annual Conference of the North American Chapter of the Association for Computational Linguistics*, pages 751–759, Los Angeles, California, June.

Mark Steedman. 1996. *Surface Structure and Interpretation*. The MIT Press, January.

Mark Steedman. 2000. *The Syntactic Process*. The MIT Press, September.

Yee-Whye Teh, Michael I Jordan, Matthew J Beal, and David M Blei. 2006. Hierarchical Dirichlet Processes. *Journal of the American Statistical Association*, 101(476):1566–1581.

Yee-Whye Teh. 2006. A Hierarchical Bayesian Language Model based on Pitman-Yor Processes. In *Proceedings of the 21st International Conference on Computational Linguistics and 44th Annual Meeting of the Association for Computational Linguistics*, pages 985–992, Sydney, Australia, July.

Yee-Whye Teh. 2010. Dirichlet Process. In *Encyclopedia of Machine Learning*, pages 280–287. Springer.

Kewei Tu. 2012. Combining the Sparsity and Unambiguity Biases for Grammar Induction. In *NAACL HLT Workshop on Induction of Linguistic Structure*, pages 105–110, Montréal, Canada, June.

A Novel Feature-based Bayesian Model for Query Focused Multi-document Summarization

Jiwei Li
School of Computer Science
Carnegie Mellon University
bdlijiwei@gmail.com

Sujian Li
Laboratory of Computational Linguistics
Peking University
lisujian@pku.edu.cn

Abstract

Supervised learning methods and LDA based topic model have been successfully applied in the field of multi-document summarization. In this paper, we propose a novel supervised approach that can incorporate rich sentence features into Bayesian topic models in a principled way, thus taking advantages of both topic model and feature based supervised learning methods. Experimental results on DUC2007, TAC2008 and TAC2009 demonstrate the effectiveness of our approach.

1 Introduction

Query-focused multi-document summarization (Nenkova et al., 2006; Wan et al., 2007; Ouyang et al., 2010) can facilitate users to grasp the main idea of documents. In query-focused summarization, a specific topic description, such as a query, which expresses the most important topic information is proposed before the document collection, and a summary would be generated according to the given topic.

Supervised models have been widely used in summarization (Li, et al., 2009, Shen et al., 2007, Ouyang et al., 2010). Supervised models usually regard summarization as a classification or regression problem and use various sentence features to build a classifier based on labeled negative or positive samples. However, existing supervised approaches seldom exploit the intrinsic structure among sentences. This disadvantage usually gives rise to serious problems such as unbalance and low recall in summaries.

Recently, LDA-based (Blei et al., 2003) Bayesian topic models have widely been applied in multi-document summarization in that Bayesian approaches can offer clear and rigorous probabilistic interpretations for summaries(Daume and Marcu, 2006; Haghighi and Vanderwende, 2009; Jin et al., 2010; Mason and Charniak, 2011; Delort and Alfonseca, 2012). Exiting Bayesian approaches label sentences or words with topics and sentences which are closely related with query or can highly generalize documents are selected into summaries. However, LDA topic model suffers from the intrinsic disadvantages that it only uses word frequency for topic modeling and can not use useful text features such as position, word order etc (Zhu and Xing, 2010). For example, the first sentence in a document may be more important for summary since it is more likely to give a global generalization about the document. It is hard for LDA model to consider such information, making useful information lost.

It naturally comes to our minds that we can improve summarization performance by making full use of both useful text features and the latent semantic structures from by LDA topic model. One related work is from Celikyilmaz and Hakkani-Tur (2010). They built a hierarchical topic model called Hybhsum based on LDA for topic discovery and assumed this model can produce appropriate scores for sentence evaluation. Then the scores are used for tuning the weights of various features that helpful for summary generation. Their work made a good step of combining topic model with feature based supervised learning. However, what their approach confuses us is that whether a topic model only based on word frequency is good enough to generate an appropriate sentence score for regression. Actually, how to incorporate features into LDA topic model has been a open problem. Supervised topic models such as sLDA(Blei and MacAuliffe 2007) give us some inspiration. In sLDA, each document is associated with a labeled feature and sLDA can integrate such feature into LDA for topic modeling in a principled way.

With reference to the work of supervised LDA models, in this paper, we propose a novel sentence feature based Bayesian model S-sLDA for multi-document summarization. Our approach can naturally combine feature based supervised methods and topic models. The most important and challenging problem in our model is the tuning of feature weights. To solve this problem, we transform the problem of finding optimum feature weights into an optimization algorithm and learn these weights in a supervised way. A set of experiments are conducted based on the benchmark data of DUC2007, TAC2008 and TAC2009, and experimental results show the effectiveness of our model.

The rest of the paper is organized as follows. Section 2 describes some background and related works. Section 3 describes our details of S-sLDA model. Section 4 demonstrates details of our approaches, including learning, inference and summary generation. Section 5 provides experiments results and Section 6 concludes the paper.

2 Related Work

A variety of approaches have been proposed for query-focused multi-document summarizations such as unsupervised (semi-supervised) approaches, supervised approaches, and Bayesian approaches.

Unsupervised (semi-supervised) approaches such as Lexrank (Erkan and Radex, 2004), manifold (Wan et al., 2007) treat summarization as a graph-based ranking problem. The relatedness between the query and each sentence is achieved by imposing querys influence on each sentence along with the propagation of graph. Most supervised approaches regard summarization task as a sentence level two class classification problem. Supervised machine learning methods such as Support Vector Machine(SVM) (Li, et al., 2009), Maximum Entropy (Osborne, 2002) , Conditional Random Field (Shen et al., 2007) and regression models (Ouyang et al., 2010) have been adopted to leverage the rich sentence features for summarization.

Recently, Bayesian topic models have shown their power in summarization for its clear probabilistic interpretation. Daume and Marcu (2006) proposed Bayesum model for sentence extraction based on query expansion concept in information retrieval. Haghighi and Vanderwende (2009) proposed topic-sum and hiersum which use a LDA-like topic model and assign each sentence a distribution over background topic, doc-specific topic and content topics. Celikyilmaz and Hakkani-Tur (2010) made a good step in combining topic model with supervised feature based regression for sentence scoring in summarization. In their model, the score of training sentences are firstly got through a novel hierarchical topic model. Then a featured based support vector regression (SVR) is used for sentence score prediction. The problem of Celikyilmaz and Hakkani-Turs model is that topic model and feature based regression are two separate processes and the score of training sentences may be biased because their topic model only consider word frequency and fail to consider other important features. Supervised feature based topic models have been proposed in recent years to incorporate different kinds of features into LDA model. Blei (2007) proposed sLDA for document response pairs and Daniel et al. (2009) proposed Labeled LDA by defining a one to one correspondence between latent topic and user tags. Zhu and Xing (2010) proposed conditional topic random field (CTRF) which addresses feature and independent limitation in LDA.

3 Model description

3.1 LDA and sLDA

The hierarchical Bayesian LDA (Blei et al., 2003) models the probability of a corpus on hidden topics as shown in Figure 1(a). Let K be the number of topics , M be the number of documents in the corpus and V be vocabulary size. The topic distribution of each document θ_m is drawn from a prior Dirichlet distribution $Dir(\alpha)$, and each document word w_{mn} is sampled from a topic-word distribution ϕ^z specified by a drawn from the topic-document distribution θ_m. β is a $K \times M$ dimensional matrix and each β_k is a distribution over the V terms. The generating procedure of LDA is illustrated in Figure 2. θ_m is a mixture proportion over topics of document m and z_{mn} is a K dimensional variable that presents the topic assignment distribution of different words.

Supervised LDA (sLDA) (Blei and McAuliffe 2007) is a document feature based model and intro-

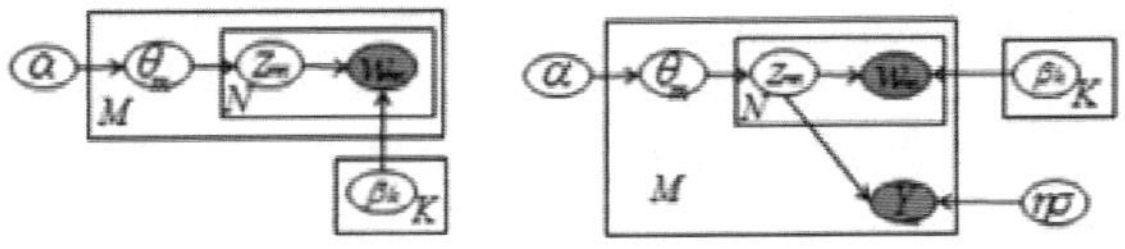

Figure 1: Graphical models for (a) LDA model and (b) sLDA model.

1. Draw a document proportion vector $\theta_m|\alpha \sim Dir(\alpha)$
2. For each word in m
   (a)draw topic assignment $z_{mn}|\theta \sim Multi(\theta_{z_{mn}})$
   (b)draw word $w_{mn}|z_{mn}, \beta \sim Multi(\beta_{z_{mn}})$

Figure 2: Generation process for LDA

duces a response variable to each document for topic discovering, as shown in Figure 1(b). In the generative procedure of sLDA, the document pairwise label is draw from $y|\overrightarrow{z_m}, \eta, \delta^2 \sim p(y|\overrightarrow{z_m}, \eta, \delta^2)$, where $\overrightarrow{z_m} = \frac{1}{N}\sum_{n=1}^{N} z_{m,n}$.

3.2 Problem Formulation

Here we firstly give a standard formulation of the task. Let K be the number of topics, V be the vocabulary size and M be the number of documents. Each document D_m is represented with a collection of sentence $D_m = \{S_s\}_{s=1}^{s=N_m}$ where N_m denotes the number of sentences in m^{th} document. Each sentence is represented with a collection of words $\{w_{msn}\}_{n=1}^{n=N_{ms}}$ where N_{ms} denotes the number of words in current sentence. $\overrightarrow{Y_{ms}}$ denotes the feature vector of current sentence and we assume that these features are independent.

3.3 S-sLDA

z_{ms} is the hidden variable indicating the topic of current sentence. In S-sLDA, we make an assumption that words in the same sentence are generated from the same topic which was proposed by Gruber (2007). z_{msn} denotes the topic assignment of current word. According to our assumption, $z_{msn} =$

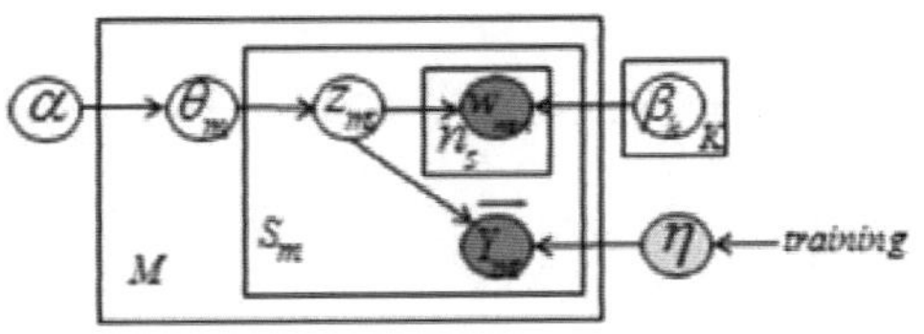

Figure 3: Graph model for S-sLDA model

1. Draw a document proportion vector $\theta_m|\alpha \sim Dir(\alpha)$
2. For each sentence in m
   (a)draw topic assignment $z_{ms}|\theta \sim Multi(\theta_{z_{mn}})$
   (b)draw feature vector $\overrightarrow{Y_{ms}}|z_{ms}, \eta \sim p(\overrightarrow{Y_{ms}}|z_{ms}, \eta)$
   (c)for each word w_{msn} in current sentence
      draw $w_{msn}|z_{ms}, \beta \sim Multi(\beta_{z_{ms}})$

Figure 4: generation process for S-sLDA

z_{ms} for any $n \in [1, N_{ms}]$. The generative approach of S-sLDA is shown in Figure 3 and Figure 4. We can see that the generative process involves not only the words within current sentence, but also a series of sentence features. The mixture weights over features in S-sLDA are defined with a generalized linear model (GLM).

$$p(\overrightarrow{Y_{ms}}|z_{ms}, \eta) = \frac{exp(z_{ms}^T \eta)\overrightarrow{Y_{ms}}}{\sum_{z_{ms}} exp(z_{ms}^T \eta)\overrightarrow{Y_{ms}}} \quad (1)$$

Here we assume that each sentence has T features and $\overrightarrow{Y_{ms}}$ is a $T \times 1$ dimensional vector. η is a $K \times T$ weight matrix of each feature upon topics, which largely controls the feature generation procedure. Unlike s-LDA where η is a latent variable estimated from the maximum likelihood estimation algorithm, in S-sLDA the value of η is trained through a supervised algorithm which will be illustrated in detail in Section 3.

3.4 Posterior Inference and Estimation

Given a document and labels for each sentence, the posterior distribution of the latent variables is:

$$p(\theta, z_{1:N}|w_{1:N}, Y, \alpha, \beta_{1:K}, \eta) = \frac{\prod_m p(\theta_m|\alpha) \prod_s [p(z_{ms}|\theta_m) p(\overrightarrow{Y_{ms}}|z_{ms}, \eta) \prod_n p(w_{msn}|z_{msn}, \beta_{z_{msn}}]}{\int d\theta p(\theta_m|\alpha) \sum_z \prod_s [p(z_{ms}|\theta_m) p(\overrightarrow{Y_{ms}}|z_{ms}, \eta) \prod_n p(w_{msn}|\beta_{z_{msn}})]} \quad (2)$$

Eqn. (2) cannot be efficiently computed. By applying the Jensens inequality, we obtain a lower bound of the log likelihood of document $p(\theta, z_{1:N}|w_{1:N}, \overrightarrow{Y_{ms}}, \alpha, \beta_{1:K}, \eta) \geq L$, where

$$L = \sum_{ms} E[logP(z_ms|\theta)] + \sum_{ms} E[logP(\overrightarrow{Y_{ms}}|z_{ms}, \eta)] + \sum_{m} E[logP(\theta|\alpha)] + \sum_{msn} E[logP(w_{msn}|z_{ms}, \beta)] + H(q) \quad (3)$$

where $H(q) = -E[logq]$ and it is the entropy of variational distribution q is defined as

$$q(\theta, z|\gamma, \phi) = \prod_{mk} q(\theta_m|\gamma) \prod_{sn} q(z_{msn}|\phi_{ms}) \quad (4)$$

here γ a K-dimensional Dirichlet parameter vector and multinomial parameters. The first, third and forth terms of Eqn. (3) are identical to the corresponding terms for unsupervised LDA (Blei et al., 2003). The second term is the expectation of log probability of features given the latent topic assignments.

$$E[logP(\overrightarrow{Y_{ms}}|z_{ms}, \eta)] = E(z_{ms})^T \eta \overrightarrow{Y_{ms}} - log \sum_{z_{ms}} exp(z_{ms}^T \eta \overrightarrow{Y_{ms}}) \quad (5)$$

where $E(z_{ms})^T$ is a $1 \times K$ dimensional vector $[\phi_{msk}]_{k=1}^{k=K}$. The Bayes estimation for S-sLDA model can be got via a variational EM algorithm. In EM procedure, the lower bound is firstly minimized with respect to γ and ϕ, and then minimized with α and β by fixing γ and ϕ.

E-step:

The updating of Dirichlet parameter γ is identical to that of unsupervised LDA, and does not involve feature vector $\overrightarrow{Y_{ms}}$.

$$\gamma_m^{new} \leftarrow \alpha + \sum_{s \in m} \phi_s \quad (6)$$

$$\phi_{sk}^{new} \propto exp\{E[log\theta_m|\gamma] + \sum_{n=1}^{N_{ms}} E[log(w_{msn}|\beta_{1:K})] + \sum_{t=1}^{T} \eta_{kt} Y_{st}\} = exp[\Psi(\gamma_{mk}) - \Psi(\sum_{k=1}^{K} \gamma_{mk}) + \sum_{t=1}^{T} \eta_{kt} Y_{st}] \quad (7)$$

where $\Psi(\cdot)$ denotes the log Γ function. m_s denotes the document that current sentence comes from and Y_{st} denotes the tth feature of sentence s.

M-step:

The M-step for updating β is the same as the procedure in unsupervised LDA, where the probability of a word generated from a topic is proportional to the number of times this word assigned to the topic.

$$\beta_{kw}^{new} = \sum_{m=1}^{M} \sum_{s=1}^{N_m} \sum_{n=1}^{N_{ms}} 1(w_{msn} = w) \phi_{ms}^k \quad (8)$$

4 Our Approach

4.1 Learning

In this subsection, we describe how we learn the feature weight η in a supervised way. The learning process of η is a supervised algorithm combined with variational inference of S-sLDA. Given a topic description Q[1] and a collection of training sentences S from related documents, human assessors assign a score $v(v = -2, -1, 0, 1, 1)$ to each sentence in S. The score is an integer between -2 (the least desired summary sentences) and $+2$ (the most desired summary sentences), and score 0 denotes neutral attitude. $O_v = \{o_{v1}, o_{v2}, ..., v_{vk}\}(v = -2, -1, 0, 1, 2)$ is the set containing sentences with score v. Let ϕ_{Qk} denote the probability that query is generated from topic k. Since query does not belong to any document, we use the following strategy to leverage ϕ_{Qk}

$$\phi_{Qk} = \prod_{w \in Q} \beta_{kw} \cdot \frac{1}{M} \sum_{m=1}^{M} exp[\Psi(\gamma_{mk}) - \Psi(\sum_{k=1}^{K} \gamma_{mk})] \quad (9)$$

In Equ.(9), $\prod_{w \in Q} \beta_{kw}$ denotes the probability that all terms in query are generated from topic k and $\frac{1}{M} \sum_{m=1}^{M} exp[\Psi(\gamma_{mk}) - \Psi(\sum_{k=1}^{K} \gamma_{mk})]$ can be seen as the average probability that all documents in the corpus are talking about topic k. Eqn. (9) is based on the assumption that query topic is relevant to the main topic discussed by the document corpus. This is a reasonable assumption and most previous LDA summarization models are based on similar assumptions.

Next, we define $\phi_{O_v,k}$ for sentence set O_v, which can be interpreted as the probability that all sentences in collection O_v are generated from topic k.

$$\phi_{O_v,k} = \frac{1}{|O_v|} \sum_{s \in O_v} \phi_{sk}, k \in [1, K], v \in [-2, 2] \quad (10)$$

$|O_v|$ denotes the number of sentences in set O_v. Inspired by the idea that desired summary sentences would be more semantically related with the query, we transform problem of finding optimum η to the following optimization problem:

$$min_\eta L(\eta) = \sum_{v=-2}^{v=2} v \cdot KL(O_v||Q); \quad \sum_{t=1}^{T} \eta_{kt} = 1 \quad (11)$$

[1] We select multiple queries and their related sentences for training

where $KL(O_v||Q)$ is the Kullback-Leibler divergence between the topic and sentence set O_v as shown in Eqn.(12).

$$KL(O_v||Q) = \sum_{k=1}^{K} \phi_{O_v k} log \frac{\phi_{O_v k}}{\phi_{Qk}} \quad (12)$$

In Eqn. (11), we can see that O_2, which contain desirable sentences, would be given the largest penalty for its KL divergence from Query. The case is just opposite for undesired set.

Our idea is to incorporate the minimization process of Eqn.(11) into variational inference process of S-sLDA model. Here we perform gradient based optimization method to minimize Eqn.(11). Firstly, we derive the gradient of $L(\eta)$ with respect to η.

$$\frac{\partial L(\eta)}{\eta_{xy}} = \sum_{v=-2}^{v=2} v \cdot \frac{\partial KL(Q_v||Q)}{\partial \eta_{xy}} \quad (13)$$

$$\frac{\partial KL(Q_v||Q)}{\partial \eta_{xy}} = \sum_{k=1}^{K} \frac{1}{|Q_v|}(1 + log \frac{\sum_{s \in Q_v}}{|Q_v|}) \sum_{s \in Q_v} \frac{\partial \phi_{sk}}{\partial \eta_{xy}}$$
$$- \sum_{k=1}^{K} \frac{1}{|Q_v|} \sum_{s \in Q_v} \frac{\partial Q_{sk}}{\eta_{xy}} - \sum_{k=1}^{K} \frac{1}{Q_v} \frac{\sum_{s \in Q_v \phi_{sk}}}{\phi_{Qk}} \frac{\partial \phi_{sk}}{\partial \eta_{xy}} \quad (14)$$

For simplification, we regard β and γ as constant during updating process of η, so $\frac{\partial \phi_{Qk}}{\partial \eta_{xy}} = 0$.[2] We can further get first derivative for each labeled sentence.

$$\frac{\partial \phi_{sk}}{\eta_{xy}} \propto \begin{cases} Y_{sy} exp[\Psi(\gamma_{m_s i}) - \Psi(\sum_{k=1}^{K} \gamma_{m_s k}) + \sum_{t=1}^{T} \eta_{kt} Y_{sy}] & \\ \times \prod_{w \in s} \beta_{kw} & if\ k = x \\ 0 & if\ k \neq x \end{cases} \quad (15)$$

4.2 Feature Space

Lots of features have been proven to be useful for summarization (Louis et al., 2010). Here we discuss several types of features which are adopted in S-sLDA model. The feature values are either binary or normalized to the interval [0,1]. The following features are used in S-sLDA:

Cosine Similarity with query: Cosine similarity is based on the tf-idf value of terms.

[2]This is reasonable because the influence of γ and β have been embodied in ϕ during each iteration.

Local Inner-document Degree Order: Local Inner document Degree Order is a binary feature which indicates whether Inner-document Degree (IDD) of sentence s is the largest among its neighbors. IDD means the edge number between s and other sentences in the same document.

Document Specific Word: 1 if a sentence contains document specific word, 0 otherwise.

Average Unigram Probability (Nenkova and Vanderwende, 2005; Celikyilmaz and Hakkani-Tur 2010): As for sentence s, $p(s) = \sum_{w \in s} \frac{1}{|s|} p_D(w)$, where $p_D(w)$ is the observed unigram probability in document collection.

In addition, we also use the commonly used features including **sentence position**, **paragraph position**, **sentence length** and **sentence bigram frequency**.

```
E-step
  initialize φ⁰_sk := 1/K for all i and s.
  initialize γ_mi := α_mi + N)m/K for all i.
  initialize η_kt = 0 for all k and t.
  while not convergence
  for m = 1 : M
    update γ^{t+1}_m according to Eqn.(6)
    for s = 1 : N_m
      for k = 1 : K
        update φ^{t+1}_sk according to Eqn.(7)
      normalize the sum of φ^{t+1}_sk to 1.
Minimize L(η) according to Eqn.(11)-(15).
M-step:
  update β according to Eqn.(8)
```

Figure 5: Learning process of η in S-sLDA

4.3 Sentence Selection Strategy

Next we explain our sentence selection strategy. According to our intuition that the desired summary should have a small KL divergence with query, we propose a function to score a set of sentences Sum. We use a decreasing logistic function $\zeta(x) = 1/(1 + e^x)$ to refine the score to the range of (0,1).

$$Score(Sum) = \zeta(KL(sum||Q)) \quad (16)$$

Let $Sum^\star$ denote the optimum update summary. We can get $Sum^\star$ by maximizing the scoring function.

$$Sum^\star = \underset{Sum \in S \&\& words(Sum) \leq L}{\arg\max} Score(Sum) \quad (17)$$

1. Learning: Given labeled set O_v, learn the feature weight vector η using algorithm in Figure 5.
2. Given new data set and η, use algorithm in section 3.3 for inference. (The only difference between this step and step (1) is that in this step we do not need minimize $L(\eta)$.
3. Select sentences for summarization from algorithm in Figure 6.

Figure 6: Summarization Generation by S-sLDA.

A greedy algorithm is applied by adding sentence one by one to obtain $Sum^{\star}$. We use G to denote the sentence set containing selected sentences. The algorithm first initializes G to Φ and X to SU. During each iteration, we select one sentence from X which maximize $Score(s_m \cup G)$. To avoid topic redundancy in the summary, we also revise the MMR strategy (Goldstein et al., 1999; Ouyang et al., 2007) in the process of sentence selection. For each s_m, we compute the semantic similarity between s_m and each sentence s_t in set Y in Eqn.(18).

$$cos-sem(s_m, s_t) = \frac{\sum_k \phi_{s_m k}\phi_{s_t k}}{\sqrt{\sum_k \phi^2_{s_m k}}\sqrt{\sum_k \phi^2_{s_t k}}} \quad (18)$$

We need to assure that the value of semantic similarity between two sentences is less than Th_{sem}. The whole procedure for summarization using S-sLDA model is illustrated in Figure 6. Th_{sem} is set to 0.5 in the experiments.

5 Experiments

5.1 Experiments Set-up

The query-focused multi-document summarization task defined in DUC[3](Document Understanding Conference) and TAC[4](Text Analysis Conference) evaluations requires generating a concise and well organized summary for a collection of related news documents according to a given query which describes the users information need. The query usually consists of a title and one or more narrative/question sentences. The system-generated summaries for DUC and TAC are respectively limited to 250 words and 100 words. Our experiment data is composed of DUC 2007, TAC[5] 2008 and TAC 2009 data which have 45, 48 and 44 collections respectively. In our experiments, DUC 2007 data is used as training data and TAC (2008-2009) data is used as the test data.

Stop-words in both documents and queries are removed using a stop-word list of 598 words, and the remaining words are stemmed by Porter Stemmer[6]. As for the automatic evaluation of summarization, ROUGE (Recall-Oriented Understudy for Gisting Evaluation) measures, including ROUGE-1, ROUGE-2, and ROUGE-SU4[7] and their corresponding 95% confidence intervals, are used to evaluate the performance of the summaries. In order to obtain a more comprehensive measure of summary quality, we also conduct manual evaluation on TAC data with reference to (Haghighi and Vanderwende, 2009; Celikyilmaz and Hakkani-Tur, 2011; Delort and Alfonseca, 2011).

5.2 Comparison with other Bayesian models

In this subsection, we compare our model with the following Bayesian baselines:

KL-sum: It is developed by Haghighi and Vanderwende (Lin et al., 2006) by using a KL-divergence based sentence selection strategy.

$$KL(P_s||Q_d) = \sum_w P(w) log \frac{P(w)}{Q(w)} \quad (19)$$

where P_s is the unigram distribution of candidate summary and Q_d denotes the unigram distribution of document collection. Sentences with higher ranking score is selected into the summary.

HierSum: A LDA based approach proposed by Haghighi and Vanderwende (2009), where unigram distribution is calculated from LDA topic model in Equ.(14).

Hybhsum: A supervised approach developed by Celikyilmaz and Hakkani-Tur (2010).

For fair comparison, baselines use the same propecessing methods with our model and all sum-

[3]http://duc.nist.gov/.

[4]http://www.nist.gov/tac/.

[5]Here, we only use the docset-A data in TAC, since TAC data is composed of docset-A and docset-B data, and the docset-B data is mainly for the update summarization task.

[6]http://tartarus.org/ martin/PorterStemmer/.

[7]Jackknife scoring for ROUGE is used in order to compare with the human summaries.

maries are truncated to the same length of 100 words. From Table 1 and Table 2, we can

Methods	ROUGE-1	ROUGE-2	ROUGE-SU4
Our approach	0.3724 (0.3660-0.3788)	0.1030 (0.0999-0.1061)	0.1342 (0.1290-0.1394)
Hybhsum	0.3703 (0.3600-0.3806)	0.1007 (0.0952-0.1059)	0.1314 (0.1241-0.1387)
HierSum	0.3613 (0.3374-0.3752)	0.0948 (0.0899-0.0998)	0.1278 (0.1197-0.1359)
KLsum	0.3504 (0.3411-0.3597)	0.0917 (0.0842-0.0992)	0.1234 (0.1155-0.1315)
StandLDA	0.3368 (0.3252-0.3386)	0.0797 (0.0758-0.0836)	0.1156 (0.1072-0.1240)

Table 1: Comparison of Bayesian models on TAC2008

Methods	ROUGE-1	ROUGE-2	ROUGE-SU4
Our approach	0.3903 (0.3819-0.3987)	0.1223 (0.1167-0.1279)	0.1488 (0.1446-0.1530)
Hybhsum	0.3824 (0.3686-0.3952)	0.1173 (0.1132-0.1214)	0.1436 (0.1358-0.1514)
HierSum	0.3706 (0.3624-0.3788)	0.1088 (0.0950-0.1144)	0.1386 (0.1312-0.1464)
KLsum	0.3619 (0.3510-0.3728)	0.0972 (0.0917-0.1047)	0.1299 (0.1213-0.1385)
StandLDA	0.3552 (0.3447-0.3657)	0.0847 (0.0813-0.0881)	0.1214 (0.1141-0.1286)

Table 2: Comparison of Bayesian models on TAC2009

see that among all the Bayesian baselines, Hybhsum achieves the best result. This further illustrates the advantages of combining topic model with supervised method. In Table 1, we can see that our S-sLDA model performs better than Hybhsum and the improvements are 3.4% and 3.7% with respect to ROUGE-2 and ROUGE-SU4 on TAC2008 data. The comparison can be extended to TAC2009 data as shown in Table 2: the performance of S-sLDA is above Hybhsum by 4.3% in ROUGE-2 and 5.1% in ROUGE-SU4. It is worth explaining that these achievements are significant, because in the TAC2008 evaluation, the performance of the top ranking systems are very close, i.e. the best system is only 4.2% above the 4th best system on ROUGE-2 and 1.2% on ROUGE-SU4.

5.3 Comparison with other baselines.

In this subsection, we compare our model with some widely used models in summarization.

Manifold: It is the one-layer graph based semi-supervised summarization approach developed by Wan et al.(2008). The graph is constructed only considering sentence relations using tf-idf and neglects topic information.

LexRank: Graph based summarization approach (Erkan and Radev, 2004), which is a revised version of famous web ranking algorithm PageRank. It is an unsupervised ranking algorithms compared with Manifold.

SVM: A supervised method - Support Vector Machine (SVM) (Vapnik 1995) which uses the same features as our approach.

MEAD: A centroid based summary algorithm by Radev et al. (2004). Cluster centroids in MEAD consists of words which are central not only to one article in a cluster, but to all the articles. Similarity is measure using tf-idf.

At the same time, we also present the top three participating systems with regard to ROUGE-2 on TAC2008 and TAC2009 for comparison, denoted as (denoted as SysRank 1st, 2nd and 3rd)(Gillick et al., 2008; Zhang et al., 2008; Gillick et al., 2009; Varma et al., 2009). The ROUGE scores of the top TAC system are directly provided by the TAC evaluation.

From Table 3 and Table 4, we can see that our approach outperforms the baselines in terms of ROUGE metrics consistently. When compared with the standard supervised method SVM, the relative improvements over the ROUGE-1, ROUGE-2 and ROUGE-SU4 scores are 4.3%, 13.1%, 8.3% respectively on TAC2008 and 7.2%, 14.9%, 14.3% on TAC2009. Our model is not as good as top participating systems on TAC2008 and TAC2009. But considering the fact that our model neither uses sentence compression algorithm nor leverage domain knowledge bases like Wikipedia or training data, such small difference in ROUGE scores is reasonable.

5.4 Manual Evaluations

In order to obtain a more accurate measure of summary quality for our S-sLDA model and Hybhsum, we performed a simple user study concerning the following aspects: (1) Overall quality: Which summary is better overall? (2) Focus: Which summary contains less irrelevant content? (3)Responsiveness: Which summary is more responsive to the query. (4) Non-Redundancy: Which summary is less redundant? 8 judges who specialize in NLP participated in the blind evaluation task. Evaluators are presented with two summaries generated by S-sLDA

Methods	ROUGE-1	ROUGE-2	ROUGE-SU4
Our approach	0.3724 (0.3660-0.3788)	0.1030 (0.0999-0.1061)	0.1342 (0.1290-0.1394)
SysRank 1st	0.3742 (0.3639-0.3845)	0.1039 (0.0974-0.1104)	0.1364 (0.1285-0.1443)
SysRank 2nd	0.3717 (0.3610-0.3824	0.0990 (0.0944-0.1038)	0.1326 (0.1269-0.1385)
SysRank 3rd	0.3710 (0.3550-0.3849)	0.0977 (0.0920-0.1034)	0.1329 (0.1267-0.1391)
PageRank	0.3597 (0.3499-0.3695)	0.0879 (0.0809-0.0950)	0.1221 (0.1173-0.1269)
Manifold	0.3621 (0.3506-0.3736)	0.0931 (0.0868-0.0994)	0.1243 (0.1206-0.1280)
SVM	0.3588 (0.3489-0.3687)	0.0921 (0.0882-0.0960)	0.1258 (0.1204-0.1302)
MEAD	0.3558 (0.3489-0.3627)	0.0917 (0.0882-0.0952)	0.1226 (0.1174-0.1278)

Table 3: Comparison with baselines on TAC2008

Methods	ROUGE-1	ROUGE-2	ROUGE-SU4
Our approach	0.3903 (0.3819-0.3987)	0.1223 (0.1167-0.1279)	0.1488 (0.1446-0.1530)
SysRank 1st	0.3917 (0.3778-0.4057)	0.1218 (0.1122-0.1314)	0.1505 (0.1414-0.1596)
SysRank 2nd	0.3914 (0.3808-0.4020)	0.1212 (0.1147-0.1277)	0.1513 (0.1455-0.1571)
SysRank 3rd	0.3851 (0.3762-0.3932)	0.1084 (0.1025-0.1144)	0.1447 (0.1398-0.1496)
PageRank	0.3616 (0.3532-0.3700)	0.0849 (0.0802-0.0896)	0.1249 (0.1221-0.1277)
Manifold	0.3713 (0.3586-0.3841)	0.1014 (0.0950-0.1178)	0.1342 (0.1299-0.1385)
SVM	0.3649 (0.3536-0.3762)	0.1028 (0.0957-0.1099)	0.1319 (0.1258-0.1380)
MEAD	0.3601 (0.3536-0.3666)	0.1001 (0.0953-0.1049)	0.1287 (0.1228-0.1346)

Table 4: Comparison with baselines on TAC2009

and Hybhsum, as well as the four questions above. Then they need to answer which summary is better (tie). We randomly select 20 document collections from TAC 2008 data and randomly assign two summaries for each collection to three different evaluators to judge which model is better in each aspect.

As we can see from Table 5, the two models almost tie with respect to Non-redundancy, mainly because both models have used appropriate MMR strategies. But as for Overall quality, Focus and Responsiveness, S-sLDA model outputs Hybhsum based on t-test on 95% confidence level. Table 6 shows the example summaries generated respectively by two models for document collection D0803A-A in TAC2008, whose query is "Describe the coal mine accidents in China and actions taken". From table 6, we can see that each sentence in these two summaries is somewhat related to topics of coal mines in China. We also observe that the summary in Table 6(a) is better than that in Table 6(b), tending to select shorter sentences and provide more information. This is because, in S-sLDA model, topic modeling is determined simultaneously by various features including terms and other ones such as sentence length, sentence position and so on, which can contribute to summary quality. As we can see, in Table 6(b), sentences (3) and (5) provide some unimportant information such as "somebody said", though they contain some words which are related to topics about coal mines.

	Our(win)	Hybhsum(win)	Tie
Overall	37	14	9
Focus	32	18	10
Responsiveness	33	13	14
Non-redundancy	13	11	36

Table 5: Comparison with baselines on TAC2009

(1)China to close at least 4,000 coal mines this year: official (2)By Oct. 10 this year there had been 43 coal mine accidents that killed 10 or more people, (3)Officials had stakes in coal mines. (4)All the coal mines will be closed down this year. (5) In the first eight months, the death toll of coal mine accidents rose 8.5 percent last year. (6) The government has issued a series of regulations and measures to improve the coun.try's coal mine safety situation. (7)The mining safety technology and equipments have been sold to countries. (8)More than 6,000 miners died in accidents in China

(1) In the first eight months, the death toll of coal mine accidents across China rose 8.5 percent from the same period last year. (2)China will close down a number of ill-operated coal mines at the end of this month, said a work safety official here Monday. (3) Li Yizhong, director of the National Bureau of Production Safety Supervision and Administration, has said the collusion between mine owners and officials is to be condemned. (4)from January to September this year, 4,228 people were killed in 2,337 coal mine accidents. (5) Chen said officials who refused to register their stakes in coal mines within the required time

Table 6: Example summary text generated by systems (a)S-sLDA and (b) Hybhsum. (D0803A-A, TAC2008)

6 Conclusion

In this paper, we propose a novel supervised approach based on revised supervised topic model for query-focused multi document summarization. Our approach naturally combines Bayesian topic model with supervised method and enjoy the advantages of both models. Experiments on benchmark demonstrate good performance of our model.

Acknowledgments

This research work has been supported by NSFC grants (No.90920011 and No.61273278), National Key Technology R&D Program (No:2011BAH1B0403), and National High Technology *R&D* Program (No.2012AA011101). We also thank the three anonymous reviewers for their helpful comments. Corresponding author: Sujian Li.

References

David Blei and Jon McAuliffe. Supervised topic models. 2007. In *Neural Information Processing Systems*

David Blei, Andrew Ng and Micheal Jordan. Latent dirichlet allocation. In *The Journal of Machine Learning Research*, page: 993-1022.

Charles Broyden. 1965. A class of methods for solving nonlinear simultaneous equations. In *Math. Comp.* volume 19, page 577-593.

Jaime Carbonell and Jade Goldstein. 1998. The use of MMR, diversity-based reranking for reordering documents and producing summaries. In *Proceedings of the 21st annual international ACM SIGIR conference on Research and development in information retrieval.*

Asli Celikyilmaz and Dilek Hakkani-Tur. 2010. A Hybrid hierarchical model for multi-document summarization. In *Proceedings of the 48th Annual Meeting of the Association for Computational Linguistics*. page: 815-825

Jade Goldstein, Mark Kantrowitz, Vibhu Mittal and Jaime Carbonell. 1999. Summarizing Text Documents: Sentence Selection and Evaluation Metrics. In *Proceedings of the 22nd annual international ACM SIGIR conference on Research and development in information retrieval*, page: 121-128.

Amit Grubber, Micheal Rosen-zvi and Yair Weiss. 2007. Hidden Topic Markov Model. *In Artificial Intelligence and Statistics.*

Hal Daume and Daniel Marcu H. 2006. Bayesian Query-Focused Summarization. In *Proceedings of the 21st International Conference on Computational Linguistics and the 44th annual meeting of the Association for Computational Linguistics*, page 305-312.

Gune Erkan and Dragomir Radev. 2004. Lexrank: graph-based lexical centrality as salience in text summarization. In *J. Artif. Intell. Res. (JAIR)*, page 457-479.

Dan Gillick, Benoit Favre, Dilek Hakkani-Tur, *The ICSI Summarization System at TAC*, TAC 2008.

Dan Gillick, Benoit Favre, and Dilek Hakkani-Tur, Berndt Bohnet, Yang Liu, Shasha Xie. *The ICSI/UTD Summarization System at TAC 2009*. TAC 2009

Aria Haghighi and Lucy Vanderwende. 2009. Exploring content models for multi-document summarization. In *Proceedings of Human Language Technologies: The 2009 Annual Conference of the North American Chapter of the Association for Computational Linguistics*, pages 362370.

Feng Jin, Minlie Huang, and Xiaoyan Zhu. 2010. The summarization systems at tac 2010. In *Proceedings of the third Text Analysis Conference*, TAC-2010.

Liangda Li, Ke Zhou, Gui-Rong Xue, Hongyuan Zha and Yong Yu. 2009. Enhancing diversity, coverage and balance for summarization through structure learning. In *Proceedings of the 18th international conference on World wide web*, page 71-80.

Chin-Yew Lin, Guihong Gao, Jianfeng Gao and Jian-Yun Nie. 2006. An information-theoretic approach to automatic evaluation of summaries. In *Proceedings of the main conference on Human Language Technology Conference of the North American Chapter of the Association of Computational Linguistics*, page:462-470.

Annie Louis, Aravind Joshi, Ani Nenkova. 2010. Discourse indicators for content selection in summarization. In *Proceedings of the 11th Annual Meeting of the Special Interest Group on Discourse and Dialogue*, page:147-156.

Tengfei Ma, Xiaojun Wan. 2010. Multi-document summarization using minimum distortion, in *Proceedings of International Conference of Data Mining*. page 354363.

Rebecca Mason and Eugene Charniak. 2011. Extractive multi-document summaries should explicitly not contain document-specific content. In *proceedings of ACL HLT*, page:49-54.

Ani Nenkova and Lucy Vanderwende. The impact of frequency on summarization. In *Tech. Report MSR-TR-2005-101*, Microsoft Research, Redwood, Washington, 2005.

Ani Nenkova, Lucy Vanderwende and Kathleen McKeown. 2006. A compositional context sensitive multi-document summarizer: exploring the factors that inuence summarization. In *Proceedings of the 29th annual International ACM SIGIR Conference on Re-*

search and Development in Information Retrieval, page 573-580.

Miles Osborne. 2002. Using maximum entropy for sentence extraction. In *Proceedings of the ACL-02 Workshop on Automatic Summarization*, Volume 4 page:1-8.

Jahna Otterbacher, Gunes Erkan and Dragomir Radev. 2005. Using random walks for question-focused sentence retrieval. In *Proceedings of the Conference on Human Language Technology and Empirical Methods in Natural Language Processing*, page 915-922

You Ouyang, Wenjie Li, Sujian Li and Qin Lua. 2011. Applying regression models to query-focused multi-document summarization. In *Information Processing and Management*, page 227-237.

You Ouyang, Sujian. Li, and Wenjie. Li. 2007, Developing learning strategies for topic-based summarization. In *Proceedings of the sixteenth ACM conference on Conference on information and knowledge management*, page: 7986.

Daniel Ramage, David Hall, Ramesh Nallapati and Christopher Manning. 2009. Labeled LDA: A supervised topic model for credit attribution in multi-labeled corpora. In *Proceedings of the 2009 Conference on Empirical Methods in Natural Language Processing*, Vol 1, page 248-256.

Dou She, Jian-Tao Sun, Hua Li, Qiang Yang and Zheng Chen. 2007. Document summarization using conditional random elds. In *Proceedings of International Joint Conference on Artificial Intelligence*, page: 28622867.

V. Varma, V. Bharat, S. Kovelamudi, P. Bysani, S. GSK, K. Kumar N, K. Reddy, N. Maganti , IIIT Hyderabad at *TAC 2009*. TAC2009

Xiaojun Wan and Jianwu Yang. 2008. Multi-document Summarization using cluster-based link analysis. In *Proceedings of the 31st annual international ACM SIGIR conference on Research and development in information retrieval*, page: 299-306.

Xiaojun Wan, Jianwu Yang and Jianguo Xiao. 2007. Manifold-ranking based topic-focused multi-document summarization. In *Proceedings of International Joint Conference on Artificial Intelligence*, page 2903-2908.

Furu Wei, Wenjie Li, Qin Lu and Yanxiang He. 2008. Exploiting Query-Sensitive Similarity for Graph-Based Query-Oriented Summarization. In *Proceedings of the 31st annual International ACM SIGIR Conference on Research and Development in Information Retrieval*, page 283-290.

Jin Zhang, Xueqi Cheng, Hongbo Xu, Xiaolei Wang, Yiling Zeng. ICTCAS's ICTGrasper at TAC 2008: Summarizing Dynamic Information with Signature Terms Based Content Filtering, TAC 2008.

Dengzhong Zhou, Jason Weston, Arthur Gretton, Olivier Bousquet and Bernhard Schlkopf. 2003. Ranking on Data Manifolds. In *Proceedings of the Conference on Advances in Neural Information Processing Systems*, page 169-176.

Jun Zhu and Eric Xing. 2010. Conditional Topic Random Fields. In *Proceedings of the 27th International Conference on Machine Learning.*

Xiaojin Zhu, Zoubin Ghahramani and John Lafferty. 2003. Semi-supervised Learning using Gaussian Fields and Harmonic Functions. In *Proceedings of International Conference of Machine Learning*, page: 912-919.

Using Pivot-Based Paraphrasing and Sentiment Profiles to Improve a Subjectivity Lexicon for Essay Data

Beata Beigman Klebanov, Nitin Madnani, Jill Burstein
Educational Testing Service
660 Rosedale Road, Princeton, NJ 08541, USA
{bbeigmanklebanov,nmadnani,jburstein@ets.org}

Abstract

We demonstrate a method of improving a seed sentiment lexicon developed on essay data by using a pivot-based paraphrasing system for lexical expansion coupled with sentiment profile enrichment using crowdsourcing. Profile enrichment alone yields up to 15% improvement in the accuracy of the seed lexicon on 3-way sentence-level sentiment polarity classification of essay data. Using lexical expansion in addition to sentiment profiles provides a further 7% improvement in performance. Additional experiments show that the proposed method is also effective with other subjectivity lexicons and in a different domain of application (product reviews).

1 Introduction

In almost any sub-field of computational linguistics, creation of working systems starts with an investment in manually-generated or manually-annotated data for computational exploration. In subjectivity and sentiment analysis, annotation of training and testing data and construction of subjectivity lexicons have been the loci of costly labor investment.

Many subjectivity lexicons are mentioned in the literature. The two large manually-built lexicons for English – the General Inquirer (Stone et al., 1966) and the lexicon provided with the Opinion-Finder distribution (Wiebe and Riloff, 2005) – are available for research and education only[1] and under GNU GPL license that disallows their incorporation into proprietary materials,[2] respectively. Those wishing to integrate sentiment analysis into products, along with those studying subjectivity in languages other than English, or for specific domains such as finance, or for particular genres such as MySpace comments, reported construction of lexicons (Taboada et al., 2011; Loughran and McDonald, 2011; Thelwall et al., 2010; Rao and Ravichandran, 2009; Jijkoun and Hofmann, 2009; Pitel and Grefenstette, 2008; Mihalcea et al., 2007).

In this paper, we address the step of expanding a small-scale, manually-built subjectivity lexicon (a seed lexicon, typically for a domain or language in question) into a much larger but noisier lexicon using an automatic procedure. We present a novel expansion method using a state-of-the-art paraphrasing system. The expansion yields a 4-fold increase in lexicon size; yet, the expansion alone is insufficient in order to improve performance on sentence-level sentiment polarity classification.

In this paper we test the following hypothesis. We suggest that the effectiveness of the expansion is hampered by (1) introduction of opposite-polarity items, such as introducing *resolute* as an expansion of *forceful*, or *remarkable* as an expansion of *peculiar*; (2) introduction of weakly polar, neutral, or ambiguous words as expansions of polar seed words, such as generating *concern* as an expansion of *anxiety* or *future* as an expansion of *aftermath*;[3] (3) inability to distinguish between stronger or clear-cut versus weaker or ambiguous sentiment and to make a differential use of those.

We address items (1) and (2) by enriching the lexicon with sentiment profiles (section 3), and propose

[1] http://www.wjh.harvard.edu/ inquirer/j1_1/manual/
[2] http://www.gnu.org/copyleft/gpl.html

[3] Table 2 and Figure 1 provide support to these assessments.

a way of effectively utilizing this information for the sentence-level sentiment polarity classification task (sections 5 and 6). Profile-enrichment alone yields up to 15% increase in performance for the seed lexicon when using different machine learning algorithms; paraphraser-based expansion with sentiment profiles improves performance by an additional 7%. Overall, we observe an improvement of up to 25% in classification accuracy over the seed lexicon without profiles.

In section 7, we present comparative evaluations, demonstrating the competitiveness of the expanded and profile-enriched lexicon, as well as the effectiveness of the expansion and enrichment paradigm presented here for different subjectivity lexicons, different lexical expansion methods, and in a different domain of application (product reviews).

2 Building Subjectivity Lexicons

The goal of our sentiment analysis project is to allow for the identification of sentiment in sentences that appear in essay responses to a variety of tasks designed to test English proficiency in both native- and non-native-speaker populations in a standardized assessment as well as in an instructional settings. In order to allow for the future use of the sentiment analyzer in a proprietory product and to ensure its fit to the test-taker essay domain, we began our work with the construction of a seed lexicon relying on our materials (section 2.1). We then used a statistical paraphrasing system to expand the seed lexicon (section 2.2).

2.1 Seed Lexicon

In order to inform the process of lexicon construction, we randomly sampled 5,000 essays from a corpus of about 100,000 essays containing writing samples across many topics. Essays were responses to several different writing assignments, including graduate school entrance exams, non-native English speaker proficiency exams, and professional licensure exams. Our seed lexicon is a combination of (1) positive and negative sentiment words manually selected from a full list of word types in these data, and (2) words marked in a small-scale annotation of a sample of sentences from these data for all positive and negative words. A more detailed description of the construction of seed lexicon can be found in Beigman Klebanov et al (2012). The seed lexicon contains 749 single words, 406 positive and 343 negative.

2.2 Expanded Lexicon

We used a pivot-based lexical and phrasal paraphrase generation system (Madnani and Dorr, 2013). The paraphraser implements the pivot-based method as described by Bannard and Callison-Burch (2005) with several additional filtering mechanisms to increase the precision of the extracted pairs. The pivot-based method utilizes the inherent monolingual semantic knowledge from bilingual corpora: We first identify phrasal correspondences between English and a given foreign language F, then map from English to English by following translation units from English to the other language and back. For example, if the two English phrases $e1$ and $e2$ both correspond to the same foreign phrase f, then they may be considered to be paraphrases of each other with the following probability:

$$p(e1|e2) \approx p(e1|f)p(f|e2)$$

If there are several pivot phrases that link the two English phrases, then they are all used in computing the probability:

$$p(e1|e2) \approx \sum_{f'} p(e1|f')p(f'|e2)$$

Seed	Expansion	Seed	Expansion
abuse	exploitation	costly	onerous
accuse	reproach	dangerous	unsafe
anxiety	disquiet	improve	reinforce
conflict	crisis	invaluable	precious

Table 1: Examples of paraphraser expansions.

Some examples of expansions generated by the paraphraser are shown in Table 1. More details about this kind of approach can be found in Bannard and Callison-Burch (2005). We use the French-English parallel corpus (approximately 1.2 million sentences) from the corpus of European parliamentary proceedings (Koehn, 2005) as the data on which pivoting is performed to extract the paraphrases. However, the base paraphrase system is susceptible to large amounts of noise due to the imperfect bilingual word alignments. Therefore, we implement additional heuristics in order to minimize the number of noisy paraphrase pairs (Madnani and Dorr, 2013). For example, one such heuristic filters out pairs where a function word may have been inferred as a paraphrase of a content word. For the lexicon expansion experiment reported here, we use the top 15 single-word paraphrases for every word from the seed lexicon, excluding morphological variants of the seed word. This process results in an expanded lexicon of 2,994 different words, 1,666 positive and 1,761 negative (433 words are in both the positive and the negative lists). The expanded lexicon includes the seed lexicon.

3 Inducing sentiment profiles

Let γ^w be the sentiment profile of the word w.

$$\gamma^w = (p_w^{pos}, p_w^{neg}, p_w^{neu}) \tag{1}$$

where $\Sigma_{i\in\{pos,neg,neu\}}\, p_w^i = 1$. Thus, a sentiment profile of a word is essentially a 3-sided coin, corresponding to its probability of coming out positive, negative, and neutral, respectively.

3.1 Estimating sentiment profiles

Our goal is to estimate the profile using outcomes of multiple trials as follows. For every word, a person is shown the word and asked whether it is positive, negative, or neutral. A person's decision is modeled as flipping the coin corresponding to the word, and recording the outcome – positive, negative, or neutral. We run N=20 such trials for every word in the expanded lexicon using the CrowdFlower crowdsourcing site,[4] for a total cost of $800. We use maximum likelihood estimate of sentiment profile:

$$\hat{p}_w^i = n_w^i \tag{2}$$

where n_w^i is the proportion of N trials on the word w that fell in cell $i \in \{pos, neg, neu\}$. Table 2 shows some estimated profiles.

Following Goodman (1965) and Quesenberry and Hurst (1964), we calculate confidence intervals for the parameters p_w^i:

$$(\hat{p}_w^i)^- = (B + 2n_w^i - T)/(2(N + B)) \tag{3}$$

[4]www.crowdflower.com

Word	$\hat{p}_w^{pos}$	$\hat{p}_w^{neu}$	$\hat{p}_w^{neg}$
forceful	0	0.15	0.85
resolute	0.8	0.15	0.05
peculiar	0.05	0.15	0.8
remarkable	1	0	0
anxiety	0	0	1
concern	0.25	0.4	0.35
absurd	0	0	1
laughable	0.5	0.05	0.45
deadly	0	0	1
fateful	0.25	0.45	0.3
consequence	0.05	0.15	0.8
outcome	0.15	0.85	0

Table 2: Examples of estimated sentiment profiles. Words in gray are expansions generated from words in the preceding row; note the difference in the profiles.

$$(\hat{p}_w^i)^+ = (B + 2n_w^i + T)/(2(N + B)) \tag{4}$$

where

$$T = \sqrt{B[B + 4n_w^i(N - n_w^i)/N])} \tag{5}$$

For confidence α that all p_w^i, $i \in \{pos, neg, neu\}$ are simultaneously within their respective intervals, the value of B is determined as the upper $\alpha/3\times 100^{th}$ percentile of the χ^2 distribution with one degree of freedom. We use α=0.1, resulting in B=4.55. The resulting interval is about 0.2 around the estimated value when $\hat{p}_w^i$ is close to 0.5, and somewhat narrower for $\hat{p}_w^i$ closer to 0 or 1. We will use this information when inducing features from the profiles.

3.2 Sentiment distributions of the lexicons

The estimated sentiment profiles per word allow us to visualize the distributions of the two lexicons. In Figure 1, we plot the number of entries in the lexicon as a function of the difference in positive and negative parts of the profile, in 0.2-wide bins. Thus, a word w would be in the second-leftmost bin if $-0.8 < (\hat{p}_w^{pos} - \hat{p}_w^{neg}) < -0.6$.

While the expansion process more than doubles the number of words in the highest bins for both the positive and the negative polarity, it clearly introduces a large number of words in the low- and medium bins into the lexicon. It is in this sense that the expansion process is noisy; apparently, seed words with clear and strong polarity

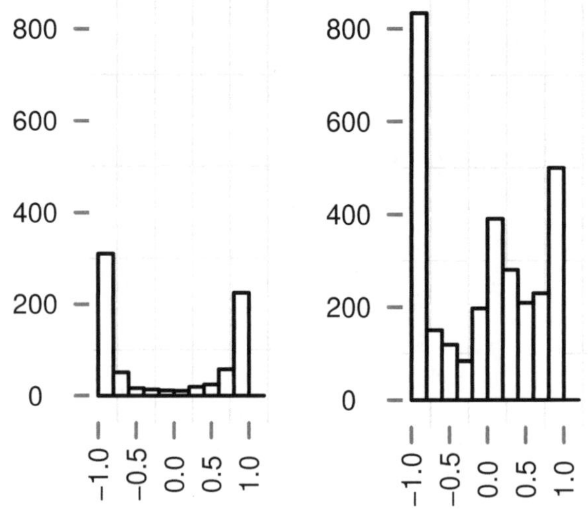

Figure 1: Sentiment distributions for the seed (left) and the expanded (right) lexicons.

are often expanded into low intensity, neutral, or ambiguous ones, as in pairs like *absurd/laughable*, *deadly/fateful*, *anxiety/concern* shown in Table 2.

4 Related Work

The most popular seed expansion methods discussed in the literature are based on WordNet (Miller, 1995) or another lexicographic resource, on distributional similarity with the seeds, or on a mixture thereof (Cruz et al., 2011; Baccianella et al., 2010; Velikovich et al., 2010; Qiu et al., 2009; Mohammad et al., 2009; Esuli and Sebastiani, 2006; Kim and Hovy, 2004; Andreevskaia and Bergler, 2006; Hu and Liu, 2004; Kanayama and Nasukawa, 2006; Strapparava and Valitutti, 2004; Kamps et al., 2004; Takamura et al., 2005; Turney and Littman, 2003; Hatzivassiloglou and McKeown, 1997). The paraphrase-based expansion method is in the distributional similarity camp; we also experimented with WordNet-based expansion as descibed in section 7.2.

The task of assigning sentiment profiles to words in a sentiment lexicon has been addressed in the literature. SentiWordNet assigns profiles to all words in WordNet based on a propagation algorithm from a small seed set manually annotated by a small number of judges (Baccianella et al., 2010; Cerini et al., 2007). Andreevskaia and Bergler (2006) use graph propagation algorithms on WordNet to assign centrality scores in positive and negative categories; a similar approach based on web-scale co-occurrence graphs is discussed in Velikovich et al (2010). Thelwall et al (2010) manually annotated a set of words for strength of sentiment and used machine learning to fine-tune it. Taboada et al (2011) produced an expert annotation of their lexicon with strength of sentiment. Subasic and Huettner (2001) manually built an affect lexicon with intensities. Wiebe and Riloff (2005) classifed lexicon entries into weakly and strongly subjective, based on their relative frequency of appearance in subjective versus objective contexts in a large annotated dataset.

Our sentiment profiles are best thought of as relatively fine-grained *priors* for the sentiment expressed by a given word out-of-context. These reflect a mixture of strength of sentiment ($\hat{p}^{pos}_{good} > \hat{p}^{pos}_{decent}$), contextual ambiguity (*concern* can be interpreted as similar to *worry* or to *care*, as in "Her condition was causing concern" versus "He showed genuine concern for her"), and dominance of a polar connotation (*abandon* is $\hat{p}^{neg}$=1; it has a negative overtone even if the actual sense is not that of *desert* but of *vacate*, as in "You must abandon your office").

To the best of our knowledge, this paper presents the first attempt to integrate judgements obtained through crowdsourcing on a large scale into a sentiment lexicon, showing the effectiveness of this lexicon-enrichment procedure for a sentiment classification task.

5 Using profiles for sentence-level sentiment polarity classification

To evaluate the usefulness of the lexicons, we use them to generate features for machine learning systems, and compare performance on 3-way sentence-level sentiment polarity classification. To ensure robustness of the observed trends, we experiment with a number of machine learning algorithms: SVM Linear and RBF, Naïve Bayes, Logistic Regression (using WEKA (Hall et al., 2009)), and c5.0 Decision Trees (Quinlan, 1993).[5]

5.1 Data

We generated the data for training and testing the machine learning systems as follows. We used our

[5]available from http://rulequest.com/

pool of 100,000 essays to sample a second, non-overlapping set of 5,000 essays, so that no essay used for lexicon development appears in this set. From these essays, we randomly sampled 550 sentences, and submitted them to sentiment polarity annotation by two experienced research assistants; 50 double-annotated sentenced showed κ=0.8. TEST set contains the 43 agreed double-annotated sentences, and additional 238 sampled from the 500 single-annotated sentences, 281 sentence in total. The category distribution in the TEST set is 46.6% neutral, 32.4% positive, and 21% negative.

The TRAIN set contains the remaining sentences, plus positive, negative, and neutral sentences annotated during lexicon development, for the total of 1,631 sentences. The category distribution in TRAIN is 39% neutral, 35% positive, 26% negative.

5.2 From lexicons to features

Our goal is to evaluate the impact of sentiment profiles on sentence-level sentiment polarity classification for the seed and the expanded lexicons, while also looking for the most effective ways to represent this information for machine learners.

We implement two baseline systems. One provides the machine learner with the most detailed information contained in a lexicon: **BL-full** has 2 features for every lexicon word, taking the values (1,0) for positive match in a sentence, (0,1) – for negative, (1,1) for a word in both positive and negative parts of the lexicon, and (0,0) otherwise.

The second baseline provides the machine learner with only summary information about the overall sentiment of the sentence. **BL-sum** uses only 2 features: (1) the total count of positive words in the sentence; (2) the total count of negative words in the sentence, according to the given lexicon.

For the sentiment-enriched runs, we construct a number of representations: Int-full, Int-sum, Int-bin, and Int-c. Int-full and Int-sum are parallel to the respective baseline systems. **Int-full** represents each lexicon word as 2 features corresponding to the word's estimated $\hat{p}_w^{pos}$ and $\hat{p}_w^{neg}$, providing the most detailed information to the machine learner. In the **Int-sum** condition, we use $\hat{p}_w^{pos}$ and $\hat{p}_w^{neg}$ for every word to induce 2 features: (1) the sum of positive probabilities of all words in the sentence; (2) the sum of negative probabilities for all words in the sentence, according to the given lexicon.

For **Int-bin** runs, we use bins of the size of 0.2 – half of the maximal confidence interval – to group together words with close estimates. We produce 10 features. For positive bins, the 5 features count the number of words in the sentence that fall in bin_i, $1 \leq i \leq 5$, respectively, that is, words with $0.2(i-1) < \hat{p}_w^{pos} \leq 0.2i$. Bin 1 also includes words with $\hat{p}_w^{pos} = 0$, since these cannot be distinguished with high confidence from $\hat{p}_w^{pos}$=0.1. Note that we do not provide a scale, we merely represent different ranges with different features. This should allow the machine learners the flexibility to weight the different bins differently when inducing classifiers.

The **Int-c** condition represents a coarse-grained setting. We produce 4 features, two for each polarity: (1) the number of words such that $0 \leq \hat{p}_w^{pos} < 0.4$; (2) the number of words such that $0.4 \leq \hat{p}_w^{pos} \leq 1$; similarity for the negative polarity.

Table 3 summarizes conditions and features.

Cond.	#F	Feature Description
BL-full	2|L|	$(\mathbf{1}_{L^{pos}\cap S}(w), \mathbf{1}_{L^{neg}\cap S}(w))$
BL-sum	2	$f_1=\|\{w : w \in L^{pos} \cap S\}\|$ $f_2=\|\{w : w \in L^{neg} \cap S\}\|$
Int-full	2|L|	$(\hat{p}_w^{pos}, \hat{p}_w^{neg})\ \forall w \in A$
Int-sum	2	$(\Sigma_{w\in A}\, \hat{p}_w^{pos}, \Sigma_{w\in A}\, \hat{p}_w^{neg})$
Int-bin	10	$f_1=\|\{w \in A : 0 \leq \hat{p}_w^{pos} \leq 0.2\}\|$ ... $f_{10}=\|\{w \in A : 0.8 < \hat{p}_w^{neg} \leq 1\}\|$
Int-c	4	$f_1=\|\{w \in A : 0 \leq \hat{p}_w^{pos} < 0.4\}\|$ ... $f_4=\|\{w \in A : 0.4 \leq \hat{p}_w^{neg} \leq 1\}\|$

Table 3: Description of conditions. Column 2 shows the number of features. In column 3: **1** is an indicator function; L is a lexicon; L^{pos} is the part of the lexicon containing positive words (same with negatives); S is a sentence for which a feature vector is built; $A = L \cap S$. For all $w \in L - S$ in the -full conditions, w is represented with (0,0).

6 Results

Table 4 shows classification accuracies for 5 machine learning systems across 6 conditions, for the seed and the expanded lexicons.

Let **BL** denote the best-performing baseline (BL-

Machine Learner	Condition	Seed	Expanded
–	Majority	0.466	0.466
c5.0	BL-full	0.441	0.498
	BL-sum	0.512	0.480
	Int-full	0.441	0.498
	Int-sum	0.566	0.616
	Int-bin	0.587	0.641
	Int-c	0.530	0.577
SVM RBF	BL-full	0.466	0.466
	BL-sum	0.527	0.495
	Int-full	0.466	0.466
	Int-sum	0.548	0.601
	Int-bin	0.573	**0.644**
	Int-c	0.530	0.562
SVM Linear	BL-full	0.584	0.566
	BL-sum	0.509	0.502
	Int-full	0.580	0.609
	Int-sum	0.601	0.580
	Int-bin	0.573	0.630
	Int-c	0.569	0.569
Logistic Regression	BL-full	0.545	0.509
	BL-sum	0.545	0.509
	Int-full	0.534	0.502
	Int-sum	0.555	0.584
	Int-bin	0.584	0.616
	Int-c	0.545	0.577
Naïve Bayes	BL-full	0.598	0.584
	BL-sum	0.509	0.473
	Int-full	0.598	0.580
	Int-sum	0.545	0.605
	Int-bin	0.559	0.626
	Int-c	0.537	0.601

Table 4: Classification accuracies on TEST set. Majority baseline corresponds to classifying all sentences as neutral. The best performance is boldfaced. Let BL stand for the best-performing baseline (BL-full or BL-sum) for a combination of machine learner and lexicon. We use Wilcoxon Signed-Rank test, reporting the number of signed ranks (N) and the sum of signed ranks (W). Statistically significant results at p=0.05 are: Int-sum > BL (N=10, W=43); Int-bin > BL (N=10, W=48); Int-bin > Int-sum (N=10, W=43); Int-bin > Int-full (N=10, W=47); Int-sum > Int-full (N=10, W=37); Int-bin > Int-c (N=10, W=55); Int-sum > Int-c (N=10, W=55); Expanded > Seed under Int condition (includes Int-full, Int-sum, Int-bin, Int-c) (N=18, W=152, z=3.3). Differences between Int-full, Int-c, and BL are not significant.

full or BL-sum) for a combination of machine learner and lexicon. The results show that (1) Int-bin > Int-sum > BL = Int-c = Int-full; (2) Expanded > Seed under Int condition. All inequalities are statistically significant at p=0.05 (see caption of Table 4 for details).

First, both the seed and the expanded lexicons benefit from profile enrichment, although, as predicted, the expanded lexicon yields larger gains due to its more varied profiles: The seed lexicon gains up to 15% in accuracy (c5.0 BL-sum vs Int-bin), while the expanded lexicon gains up to 30%, as SVM RBF scores go up from 0.495 to 0.644.

Second, observe that profiling allows the expanded lexicon to leverage its improved coverage: While it is inferior to the best baseline run with the seed lexicon for all systems, it succeeds in improving the seed lexicon accuracies by 5%-12% across the different systems for the Int-bin runs. The best run of the expanded lexicon (Int-bin for SVM RBF) improves upon the best run of the seed lexicon (Int-sum for SVM-linear) by 7%, demonstrating the success of the paraphraser-based expansion once profiles are taken into account. Overall, comparing the best baseline for the seed lexicon with Int-bin condition of the expanded lexicon, we observe an improvement between 5% (0.598 to 0.626 for Naïve Bayes) and 25% (0.512 to 0.641 for c5.0), proving the effectiviness of the paraphrase-based expansion with profile enrichment paradigm.

Third, representing profiles using 10 bins (Int-bin) provides a small but consistent improvement over the summary representation (Int-sum) that sums positivity and negativity of the sentiment-bearing words in a sentence, over a coarse-grained representation (Int-c), as well as over the full-information representation (Int-full). Even Naïve Bayes and SVM linear, known to work well with large feature sets, show better performance in the Int-bin condition for the expanded lexicon. The results indicate that an intermediate degree of detail – between summary-only and coarse-grained representation on the one hand and full-information representation on the other – is the best choice in our setting.

7 Comparative Evaluations

In this section, we present comparative evaluations of the work presented in this paper with respect to related work. This section shows that the paraphrase expansion+profile enrichment solution proposed in this paper is effective for our task beyond off-the-shelf solutions, and that its effectiveness generalizes to sentiment analysis in a different domain. We also show that profile enrichment can be effectively coupled with other methods of lexical expansion, although the paraphraser-based expansion receives a larger boost in performance from profile enrichment than the alternative expansion methods we consider.

In section 7.1, we demonstrate that the paraphrase-based expansion and profile enrichment yield superior performance on our data relative to state-of-art subjectivity lexicons – OpinionFinder, General Inquirer, and SentiWordNet. In section 7.2, we show that profile enrichment can be effectively coupled with other methods of lexical expansion, such as a WordNet-based expansion and an expansion that utilizes Lin's distributional thesaurus. However, we find that the paraphraser-based expansion benefits the most from profile enrichment, and attains better performance on our data than the alterantive expansion methods. In section 7.3, we show that the paraphrase-based expansion and profile enrichment paradigm is effective for other subjecitivy lexicons on other data. We use a dataset of product reviews annotated for sentence-level positivity and negativity as new data for evaluation (Hu and Liu, 2004). We use subsets of OpinionFinder, General Inquirer, and sentiment lexicon from Hu and Liu (2004). We demonstrate that paraphrase-based expansion and profile enrichment improve the accuracy of sentiment classification of product reviews *for every lexicon and machine learner combination*; the magnitude of improvement is 5% on average.

7.1 Competitiveness of the Expanded Lexicon

Had we been able to use the OpinionFinder or the General Inquirer lexicons (**OFL** and **GIL**) as-is, how would the results have compared to those attained using our lexicons? We performed the baseline runs with both lexicons; OFL accuracies were 0.544-0.594 across machine learning systems, GIL's – 0.491-0.584 (see GIL column in Table 5).

We also experimented with using the *weaksubj* and *strongsubj* labels in OFL as somewhat parallel distinctions to the ones presented here (see section 4 – Related Work – for a more detailed discussion). We used (1,0,0) profile for strong positives, (0.3,0,0.7) for weak positives, (0,1,0) for strong negatives, and (0,0.3,0.7) for weak negatives, and ran all the feature representations discussed in section 5.2. Table 5 column OFL shows the best run for every machine learning system, across the different feature representations, and choosing the better performing run between vanilla OFL and the version enriched with weak/strong distinctions.

Machine Learner	Seed BL	OFL	GIL	SWN	Exp.
c5.0	0.512	0.598	0.491	0.516	0.641
SVM-RBF	0.527	0.594	0.495	0.520	0.644
SVM-lin.	0.584	0.594	0.580	0.569	0.630
Log. Reg.	0.545	0.598	0.541	0.537	0.616
Naïve B.	0.598	0.573	0.584	0.587	0.626

Table 5: Performance of different lexicons on essay data using various machine learning systems. For each system and lexicon, the best performance across the applicable feature representations from section 5.2 and the variants (see text) is shown. **Seed BL** column shows the best baseline performance of our seed lexicon – before paraphraser expansion and profile enrichment were applied. **Exp.** column shows the performance of Int-bin feature representation for the expanded lexicon after profile enrichment.

Additionally, we experimented with SentiWordNet (Baccianella et al., 2010). SentiWordNet is a resource for opinion mining built on top of WordNet, which assigns each synset in WordNet a score triplet (positive, negative, and objective), indicating the strength of each of these three properties for the words in the synset. The SentiWordNet annotations were automatically generated, starting with a set of manually labeled synsets. Currently, SentiWordNet includes an automatic annotation for all the synsets in WordNet, totaling more than 100,000 words. It is therefore the largest-scale lexicon with intensity information that is currently available.

Since SentiWordNet assigns scores to synsets and since our data is not sense-tagged, we induced SentiWordNet scores in the following ways. We part-of-speech tagged our train and test data using Stanford tagger (Toutanova et al., 2003). Then, we took the SentiWordNet scores for the top sense for the given part-of-speech (SWN-1). In a different variant, we took a weighted average of the scores for the different senses, using the weighting algorithm provided on SentiWordNet website[6] (SWN-2). Table 5 column SWN shows the best performance figures between SWN-1 and SWN-2, across the feature representations in section 5.2.

The comparative results in Table 5 clearly show that while our vanilla seed lexicon performs comparably to off-the-shelf lexicons on our data, the paraphraser-expanded lexicon with sentitment profiles outperforms OpinionFinder, General Inquirer, and SentiWordNet.

7.2 Sentiment Profile Enrichment with Other Lexical Expansion Methods

We presented a novel lexicon expansion method using a paraphrasing system. We also experimented with more standard methods, using WordNet and distributional similarity (Beigman Klebanov et al., 2012; Esuli and Sebastiani, 2006; Kim and Hovy, 2004; Andreevskaia and Bergler, 2006; Hu and Liu, 2004; Kanayama and Nasukawa, 2006; Strapparava and Valitutti, 2004; Kamps et al., 2004; Takamura et al., 2005; Turney and Littman, 2003; Hatzivassiloglou and McKeown, 1997). Specifically, we implemented a WordNet (Miller, 1995) based expansion that uses the 3 most frequent synonyms of the top sense of the seed word (**WN-e**). We also implemented a method based on distributional similarity: Using Lin's proximity-based thesaurus (Lin, 1998) trained on our in-house essay data as well as on well-formed newswire texts, we took all words with the proximity score > 1.80 to any of the seed lexicon words (**Lin-e**). Just like the paraphraser lexicon, both perform worse than the seed lexicon in 9 out of 10 baseline runs (BL-sum and Bl-full conditions for the 5 machine learners).

To test the effect of profile enrichment, all words in WN-e and Lin-e underwent profile estimation as described in section 3.1, yielding lexicons **WN-e-p** and **Lin-e-p**, respectively. Figure 2 shows the distributions. WN-e-p and Lin-e-p exhibit similar trends to those of the paraphraser. Substituting WN-e-p for Expanded data in Table 4, we find the same relationships between the different feature sets: Int-bin>Int-sum>Int-full=BL. For Lin-e-p, Int-sum deteriorates: Int-bin>Int-sum=Int-full=BL. For the 20 runs in the Int condition, Paraphraser>WN-e-p>Lin-e-p.[7] Note that this is also the order of lexicon sizes: Lin-e is the most conservative expansion (1,907 words), WN-e is the second with 2,527 words, and the lexicon expanded using paraphrasing is the largest with 2,994 words. Table 6 shows the performance of Lin-e-p, WN-e-p, and of the Expanded lexicon from Table 4 using the Int-bin feature representation. The average relative improvements over the best baseline range between 6.6% to 14.6% for the different expansion methods.

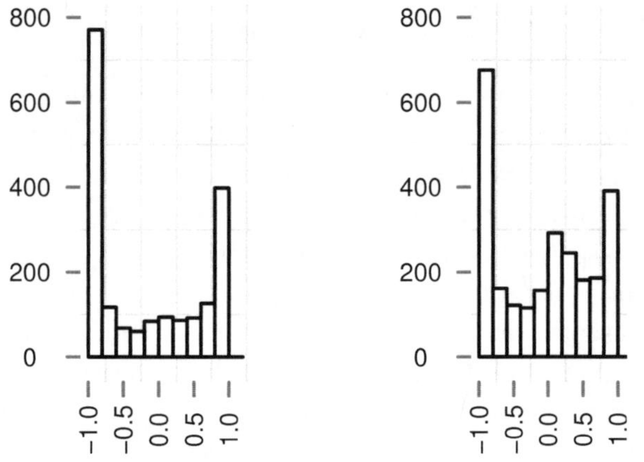

Figure 2: Sentiment profile distributions for Lin-e-p (left) and WN-e-p (right) lexicons.

Profile induction appears to be a powerful lexicon clean-up procedure that works especially well with more aggressive and thus potentially noisier expansions: The machine learners depress low-intensity and ambiguous expansions, thereby allowing the effective utilization of the improved coverage of sentiment-bearing vocabulary.

7.3 Effectiveness of the Paraphrase Expansion with Profile Enrichment Paradigm in a Different Domain

In order to check whether the paraphrase-based expasion and profile enrichment paradigm discussed in this paper generalizes to other subjectivity lexicons

[6]http://sentiwordnet.isti.cnr.it/, under "Sample code."

[7]All > are signficant at p=0.05 using Wilcoxon test.

Machine Learner	Seed BL	Lin-e-p	WN-e-p	Exp.
c5.0	0.512	0.584	0.616	0.641
SVM-RBF	0.527	0.598	0.601	0.644
SVM-lin.	0.584	0.577	0.569	0.630
Log. Reg.	0.545	0.587	0.580	0.616
Naïve B.	0.598	0.591	0.623	0.626
Av. Gain		0.066	0.085	0.146

Table 6: Performance of WordNet-based, Lin-based, and Paraphraser-based expansions with profile enrichment in the Int-bin condition. **Seed BL** column shows the best baseline performance of the seed lexicon – before expansion and profile enrichment were applied. The last line shows the average relative gain over the best baseline calculated as $AG_{lex} = \Sigma_{m \in M} \frac{Lex_m - SeedBL_m}{SeedBL_m}$, where M = {c5.0, SVM-RBF, SVM-linear, Logistic Regression, Naïve Bayes}, and $lex \in$ {Lin-e-p, Wn-e-p, Exp}.

and domains of application, we experimented with a product reviews dataset (Hu and Liu, 2004) and additional lexicons as follows.

7.3.1 Lexicons

We use the OpinionFinder and General Inquirer lexicons (OFL and GIL) as before, as well as the lexicon of positive and negative sentiment and opinion words available along with (Hu and Liu, 2004) product reviews dataset – **HL**.[8]

Since each of these lexicons contains more than 3,000 words, enrichment of the full lexicons with profiles is beyond the financial scope of our project. We therefore restrict each of the lexicons to the size of their overlap with our seed lexicon (see 2.1); the overlaps have between 415 and 467 words. These restricted lexicons are our initial lexicons for the new experiment that parallel the role of the seed lexicon in the experiments on essay data.

For each of the 3 initial lexicons **L**, L∈{OFL, GIL, HL}, we follow the paraphrase-based expansion as described in section 2.2. This results in about 4.5-fold expansion of each lexicon, the new lexicons **L-e**, L∈{OFL, GIL, HL}, numbering between 2,015 and 2,167 words. Both the initial and the expanded lexicons now undergo profile enrichment as described in section 3.1, producing lexicons **L-p** and **L-e-p**, L∈{OFL, GIL, HL}.

7.3.2 Data

We use the dataset from Hu and Liu (2004)[9] that contains reviews of 5 products from amazon.com: two digital cameras, a DVD player, an MP3 player, and a cellular phone. The reviews are annotated at sentence level with a label that desrcibes the particular feature that is the subject of the positive or negative evaluation and the polarity and extent of the evaluation. For example, the sentence "The phone book is very user-friendly and the speakerphone is excellent" is labeled as PHONE BOOK[+2], SPEAKERPHONE[+2], while the sentence "I am bored with the silver look" is labeled LOOK[−1]. We used all sentences that were labeled with a numerical score for at least one feature, removing a small number of sentences labeled with both positive and negative scores for different features.[10] We used the sign of the numerical score to label the sentences as positive or negative. The resulting dataset consists of 1,695 sentences, 1,061 positive and 634 negative; accuracy for a majority baseline on this dataset is 0.626. Our experiments on this dataset are done using 5-fold cross-validation.

7.3.3 Results

Table 7 shows classification accuracies for the product review data using different lexicons and machine learners. We observe that the combination of paraphrase-based expansion and profile enrichment (L-e-p column in the table) resulted in an improved performance over the initial lexicon (L column in the table) *in all cases*, with the average gain of 5% in accuracy.

Furthermore, the contributions of the expansion and the profile enrichment are complementary, since their combination performs better than each in isolation. We note that profile enrichment alone for the initial lexicon did not yield an improvement. This can be explained by the fact that the initial lexicons are highly polar, so profiles provide little additional information: The percentage of words with $\hat{p}^{pos} \geq 0.8$ or $\hat{p}^{neg} \geq 0.8$ is 84%, 86% and 91% for GIL,

[8]http://www.cs.uic.edu/~liub/FBS/sentiment-analysis.html#lexicon

[9]http://www.cs.uic.edu/~liub/FBS/sentiment-analysis.html#datasets, the link under "Customer Review Datasets (5 products)"

[10]such as "The headset that comes with the phone has good sound volume but it hurts the ears like you cannot imagine!"

Machine Learner	Lexicon Variant			
	L	L-p	L-e	L-e-p
L = OFL∩Seed, |L|=467, |L-e|=2,167				
c5.0	0.663	0.670	0.691	0.704
SVM-RBF	0.668	0.676	0.693	0.714
SVM-lin.	0.675	0.670	0.688	0.696
Log. Reg.	0.666	0.658	0.693	0.698
Naïve B.	0.668	0.668	0.686	0.695
L = GIL∩Seed, |L|=415,|L-e|=2,015				
c5.0	0.644	0.658	0.663	0.686
SVM-RBF	0.650	0.665	0.653	0.683
SVM-lin.	0.665	0.665	0.677	0.681
Log. Reg.	0.664	0.658	0.678	0.694
Naïve B.	0.669	0.666	0.678	0.703
L = HL∩Seed, |L|=434, |L-e|=2,054				
c5.0	0.676	0.675	0.689	0.706
SVM-RBF	0.673	0.674	0.700	0.713
SVM-lin.	0.676	0.664	0.703	0.710
Log. Reg.	0.668	0.661	0.703	0.699
Naïve B.	0.668	0.672	0.697	0.697

Table 7: Accuracies on product review data. For each machine learner and lexicon, the best baseline performance is shown as **L** for the initial lexicon and as **L-e** for the paraphrase-expanded lexicon. **L-p** and **L-e-p** show the performance of Int-bin feature set on the profile-enriched initial and paraphrase-expanded lexicons, respectively. The three initial lexicons L are OpinionFinder (OFL), General Inquirer (GIL), and (Hu and Liu, 2004) (HL), each intersected with our seed lexicon. Sizes of the intial and expanded lexicons are provided.

OFL, and HL-derived lexicons, respectively. In contrast, for the expanded lexicons, these percentages are 51%, 53%, and 56%; these lexicons benefit from profile enrichment.

8 Conclusions

We demonstrated a method of improving a seed sentiment lexicon by using a pivot-based paraphrasing system for lexical expansion and sentiment profile enrichment using crowdsourcing. Profile enrichment alone yielded up to 15% improvement in the performance of the seed lexicon on the task of 3-way sentence-level sentiment polarity classification of test-taker essay data. While the lexical expansion on its own failed to improve upon the performance of the seed lexicon, it became much more effective on top of sentiment profiles, generating a 7% performance boost over the best profile-enriched run with the seed lexicon. Overall, paraphrase-based expansion coupled with profile enrichment yields an up to 25% improvement in accuracy.

Additionally, we showed that our paraphrase-expanded and profile-enriched lexicon performs significantly better on our data than off-the-shelf subjectivity lexicons, namely, Opinion Finder, General Inquirer, and SentiWordNet. Furthermore, our results suggest that paraphrase-based expansion derives more benefit from profiles than two competing expansion mechanisms based on WordNet and on Lin's distributional thesaurus.

Finally, we demonstrated the effectiveness of the paraphraser-based expansion with profile enrichment paradigm on a different dataset. We used Hu and Liu (2004) product review data with sentence-level sentiment polarity labels. Paraphrase-based expansion with profile enrichment yielded an improved performance across all lexicons and machine learning algorithms we tried, with an average improvement rate of 5% in classification accuracy.

Recent literature argues that sentiment polarity is a property of word senses, rather than of words (Gyamfi et al., 2009; Su and Markert, 2008; Wiebe and Mihalcea, 2006), although Dragut et al (2012) successfully operate with "mostly negative" and "mostly positive" words based on the polarity distributions of word senses. We plan to address in future work sense disambiguation for words that have multiple senses with very different sentiment, such as *stress*, as either *anxiety* (negative) or *emphasis* (neutral).

References

Alina Andreevskaia and Sabine Bergler. 2006. Mining WordNet for a fuzzy sentiment: Sentiment tag extraction of WordNet glosses. In *Proceedings of EACL*, pages 209–216, Trento, Italy.

Stefano Baccianella, Andrea Esuli, and Fabrizio Sebastiani. 2010. SENTIWORDNET 3.0: An Enhanced Lexical Resource for Sentiment Analysis and Opinion Mining. In *Proceedings of LREC*, pages 2200–2204, Malta.

Colin Bannard and Chris Callison-Burch. 2005. Paraphrasing with bilingual parallel corpora. In *Proceedings of ACL*, pages 597–604, Ann Arbor, MI.

Beata Beigman Klebanov, Jill Burstein, Nitin Madnani, Adam Faulkner, and Joel Tetreault. 2012. Building sentiment lexicon(s) from scratch for essay data. In *Proceedings of the 13th International Conference on Intelligent Text Processing and Computational Linguistics (CICLing)*, New Delhi, India, March.

S. Cerini, V. Compagnoni, A. Demontis, M. Formentelli, and G. Gandini. 2007. Micro-WNOp: A gold standard for the evaluation of automatically compiled lexical resources for opinion mining. In Andrea Sanso, editor, *Language resources and linguistic theory: Typology, second language acquisition*, pages 200–210. Franco Angeli Editore, Milano, IT.

Fermín L. Cruz, José A. Troyano, F. Javier Ortega, and Fernando Enríquez. 2011. Automatic expansion of feature-level opinion lexicons. In *Proceedings of the 2nd Workshop on Computational Approaches to Subjectivity and Sentiment Analysis*, pages 125–131, Portland, Oregon, June.

Eduard Dragut, Hong Wang, Clement Yu, Prasad Sistla, and Weiyi Meng. 2012. Polarity consistency checking for sentiment dictionaries. In *Proceedings of the 50th Annual Meeting of the Association for Computational Linguistics (Volume 1: Long Papers)*, pages 997–1005, Jeju Island, Korea, July. Association for Computational Linguistics.

Andrea Esuli and Fabrizio Sebastiani. 2006. Determining term subjectivity and term orientation for opinion mining. In *Proceedings of EACL*, pages 193–200, Trento, Italy.

Leo A. Goodman. 1965. On Simultaneous Confidence Intervals for Multinomial Proportions. *Technometrics*, 7(2):247–254.

Yaw Gyamfi, Janyce Wiebe, Rada Mihalcea, and Cem Akkaya. 2009. Integrating knowledge for subjectivity sense labeling. In *Proceedings of NAACL*, pages 10–18, Boulder, CO.

Mark Hall, Eibe Frank, Geoffrey Holmes, Bernhard Pfahringer, Peter Reutemann, and Ian H. Witten. 2009. The WEKA Data Mining Software: An Update. *SIGKDD Explorations*, 11.

Vasileios Hatzivassiloglou and Kathleen McKeown. 1997. Predicting the semantic orientation of adjectives. In *Proceedings of ACL*, pages 174–181, Madrid, Spain.

Minqing Hu and Bing Liu. 2004. Mining and summarizing customer reviews. In *Proceedings of ACM SIGKDD International Conference on Knowledge Discovery and Data Mining*, pages 168–177, Seattle, WA.

Valentin Jijkoun and Katja Hofmann. 2009. Generating a Non-English Subjectivity Lexicon: Relations That Matter. In *Proceedings of EACL*, pages 398–405, Athens, Greece.

Jaap Kamps, Maarten Marx, Robert Mokken, and Maarten de Rijke. 2004. Using WordNet to measure semantic orientation of adjectives. In *Proceedings of LREC*, pages 1115–1118, Lisbon, Portugal.

Hiroshi Kanayama and Tetsuya Nasukawa. 2006. Fully automatic Lexicon Expansion for Domain-oriented Sentiment Analysis. In *Proceedings of EMNLP*, pages 355–363, Syndey, Australia.

Soo-Min Kim and Edward Hovy. 2004. Determining the sentiment of opinions. In *Proceedings of COLING*, pages 1367–1373, Geneva, Switzerland.

Philip Koehn. 2005. EUROPARL: A Parallel corpus for Statistical Machine Translation. In *Proceedings of the Machine Translation Summit*.

Dekang Lin. 1998. Automatic retrieval and clustering of similar words. In *Proceedings of ACL*, pages 768–774, Montreal, Canada.

Tim Loughran and Bill McDonald. 2011. When is a Liability not a Liability? Textual Analysis, Dictionaries, and 10-Ks. *Journal of Finance*, 66:35–65.

Nitin Madnani and Bonnie Dorr. 2013. Generating Targeted Paraphrases for Improved Translation. *ACM Transactions on Intelligent Systems and Technology, to appear*.

Rada Mihalcea, Carmen Banea, and Janyce Wiebe. 2007. Learning multilingual subjective language via cross-lingual projections. In *Proceedings of ACL*, pages 976–983, Prague, Czech Republic.

George Miller. 1995. WordNet: A lexical database. *Communications of the ACM*, 38:39–41.

Saif Mohammad, Cody Dunne, and Bonnie Dorr. 2009. Generating high-coverage semantic orientation lexicons from overtly marked words and a thesaurus. In *Proceedings of EMNLP*, pages 599–608, Singapore, August.

Guillaume Pitel and Gregory Grefenstette. 2008. Semi-automatic building method for a multidimensional affect dictionary for a new language. In *Proceedings of LREC*, Marrakech, Morocco.

Guang Qiu, Bing Liu, Jiajun Bu, and Chun Chen. 2009. Expanding domain sentiment lexicon through double propagation. In *Proceedings of the 21st international jont conference on Artifical intelligence*, IJCAI'09, pages 1199–1204.

C. Quesenberry and D. Hurst. 1964. Large sample simultaneous confidence intervals for multinomial proportions. *Technometrics*, 6:191–195.

J. R. Quinlan. 1993. *C4.5: Programs for machine learning*. Morgan Kaufmann Publishers.

Delip Rao and Deepak Ravichandran. 2009. Semi-supervised polarity lexicon induction. In *Proceedings of EACL*, pages 675–682, Athens.

Philip Stone, Dexter Dunphy, Marshall Smith, and Daniel Ogilvie. 1966. *The General Inquirer: A Computer Approach to Content Analysis*. MIT Press.

Carlo Strapparava and Alessandro Valitutti. 2004. WordNet-affect: an affective extension of WordNet. In *Proceedings of LREC*, pages 1083–1086, Lisbon, Portugal.

Fangzhong Su and Katja Markert. 2008. Eliciting Subjectivity and Polarity Judgements on Word Senses. In *Proceedings of COLING*, pages 825–832, Manchester, UK.

P. Subasic and A. Huettner. 2001. Affect analysis of text using fuzzy semantic typing. *IEEE Transactions on Fuzzy Systems*, 9(4).

Maite Taboada, Julian Brooke, Milan Tofiloski, Kimberly Voll, and Manfred Stede. 2011. Lexicon-Based Method for Sentiment Analysis. *Computational Linguistics*, 37(2):267–307.

Hiroya Takamura, Takashi Inui, and Manabu Okumura. 2005. Extracting semantic orientation of words using spin model. In *Proceedings of ACL*, pages 133–140, Ann Arbor, MI.

Mike Thelwall, Kevan Buckley, Georgios Paltoglou, Di Cai, and Arvid Kappas. 2010. Sentiment strength detection in short informal text. *Journal of the American Society for Information Science and Technology*, 61(12):2544–2558.

Kristina Toutanova, Dan Klein, Christopher Manning, and Yoram Singer. 2003. Feature-Rich Part-of-Speech Tagging with a Cyclic Dependency Network. In *Proceedings of HLT-NAACL*, pages 252–259.

Peter Turney and Michael Littman. 2003. Measuring praise and criticism: Inference of semantic orientation from association. *ACM Transactions on Information Systems*, 21(4):315346.

Leonid Velikovich, Sasha Blair-Goldensohn, Kerry Hannan, and Ryan McDonald. 2010. The viability of Web-derived polarity lexicons. In *Proceedings of NAACL*, pages 777–785, Los Angeles, CA.

Janyce Wiebe and Rada Mihalcea. 2006. Word sense and subjectivity. In *Proceedings of ACL*, pages 1065–1072, Sydney, Australia.

Janyce Wiebe and Ellen Riloff. 2005. Creating subjective and objective sentence classifiers from unannotated texts. In *Proceedings of CICLING (invited paper)*, pages 486–497, Mexico City.

Incremental Tree Substitution Grammar for Parsing and Sentence Prediction

Federico Sangati and **Frank Keller**
Institute for Language, Cognition, and Computation
School of Informatics, University of Edinburgh
10 Crichton Street, Edinburgh EH8 9AB, UK
federico.sangati@gmail.com keller@inf.ed.ac.uk

Abstract

In this paper, we present the first incremental parser for Tree Substitution Grammar (TSG). A TSG allows arbitrarily large syntactic fragments to be combined into complete trees; we show how constraints (including lexicalization) can be imposed on the shape of the TSG fragments to enable incremental processing. We propose an efficient Earley-based algorithm for incremental TSG parsing and report an F-score competitive with other incremental parsers. In addition to whole-sentence F-score, we also evaluate the partial trees that the parser constructs for sentence prefixes; partial trees play an important role in incremental interpretation, language modeling, and psycholinguistics. Unlike existing parsers, our incremental TSG parser can generate partial trees that include predictions about the upcoming words in a sentence. We show that it outperforms an n-gram model in predicting more than one upcoming word.

1 Introduction

When humans listen to speech, the input becomes available gradually as the speech signal unfolds. Reading happens in a similarly gradual manner when the eyes scan a text. There is good evidence that the human language processor is adapted to this and works incrementally, i.e., computes an interpretation for an incoming sentence on a word-by-word basis (Tanenhaus et al., 1995; Altmann and Kamide, 1999). Also language processing systems often deal with speech as it is spoken, or text as it is being typed. A dialogue system should start interpreting a sentence while it is being spoken, and a question answering system should start retrieving answers before the user has finished typing the question.

Incremental processing is therefore essential both for realistic models of human language processing and for NLP applications that react to user input in real time. In response to this, a number of incremental parsers have been developed, which use context-free grammar (Roark, 2001; Schuler et al., 2010), dependency grammar (Chelba and Jelinek, 2000; Nivre, 2007; Huang and Sagae, 2010), or tree-adjoining grammar (Demberg et al., 2014). Typical applications of incremental parsers include speech recognition (Chelba and Jelinek, 2000; Roark, 2001; Xu et al., 2002), machine translation (Schwartz et al., 2011; Tan et al., 2011), reading time modeling (Demberg and Keller, 2008), or dialogue systems (Stoness et al., 2004). Another potential use of incremental parsers is sentence prediction, i.e., the task of predicting upcoming words in a sentence given a prefix. However, so far only n-gram models and classifiers have been used for this task (Fazly and Hirst, 2003; Eng and Eisner, 2004; Grabski and Scheffer, 2004; Bickel et al., 2005; Li and Hirst, 2005).

In this paper, we present an incremental parser for Tree Substitution Grammar (TSG). A TSG contains a set of arbitrarily large tree fragments, which can be combined into new syntax trees by means of a substitution operation. An extensive tradition of parsing with TSG (also referred to as data-oriented parsing) exists (Bod, 1995; Bod et al., 2003), but none of the existing TSG parsers are incremental. We show how constraints can be imposed on the shape of the TSG fragments to enable incremental processing. We propose an efficient Earley-based algorithm for incremental TSG parsing and report an F-score competitive with other incremental parsers.

TSG fragments can be arbitrarily large and can contain multiple lexical items. This property enables our incremental TSG parser to generate partial parse trees that include predictions about the upcoming words in a sentence. It can therefore be applied directly to the task of sentence prediction, simply by reading off the predicted items in a partial tree. We show that our parser outperforms an n-gram model in predicting more than one upcoming word.

The rest of the paper is structured as follows. In Section 2, we introduce the ITSG framework and relate it to the original TSG formalism. Section 3 describes the chart-parser algorithm, while Section 4 details the experimental setup and results. Sections 5 and 6 present related work and conclusions.

2 Incremental Tree Substitution Grammar

The current work is based on Tree Substitution Grammar (TSG, Schabes 1990; for a recent overview see Bod et al. 2003). A TSG is composed of (i) a set of arbitrarily large *fragments*, usually extracted from an annotated phrase-structure treebank, and (ii) the *substitution operation* by means of which fragments can be combined into complete syntactic analyses (derivations) of novel sentences.

Every fragment's node is either a lexical node (word), a substitution site (a non-lexical node in the yield of the structure),[1] or an internal node. An internal node must always keep the same daughter nodes as in the original tree. For an example of a binarized[2] tree and a fragment extracted from it see Figure 1.

A TSG derivation is constructed in a top-down generative process starting from a fragment in the grammar rooted in S (the unique non-lexical node all syntactic analysis are rooted in). A partial derivation is extended by subsequently introducing more fragments: if X is the left-most substitution site in the yield of the current partial derivation, a fragment

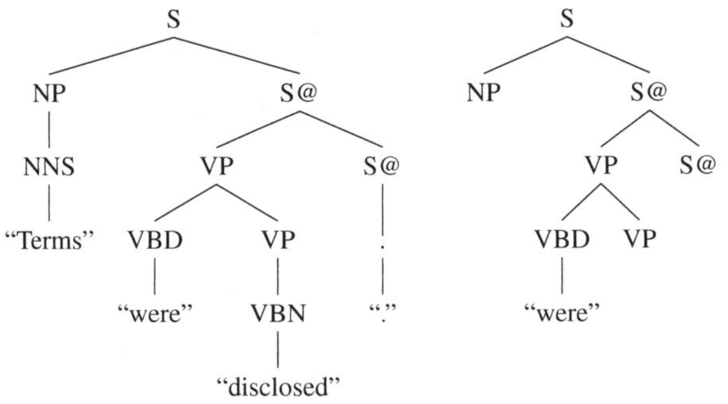

Figure 1: An example of a binarized[2] parse tree and a lexicalized fragment extracted from it.

rooted in X is chosen from the grammar and substituted into it. When there are no more substitution sites (all nodes in the yield are lexical items) the generative process terminates.

2.1 Incrementality

In this work we are interested in defining an *incremental* TSG (in short ITSG). The new generative process, while retaining the original mechanism for combining fragments (by means of the substitution operation), must ensure a way for deriving syntactic analyses of novel sentences in an incremental manner, i.e., one word at the time from left to right. More precisely, at each stage of the generative process, the partially derived structure must be connected (as in standard TSG) and have a prefix of the sentence at the beginning of its yield. A partial derivation is connected if it has tree shape, i.e., all the nodes are dominated by a common root node (which does not necessarily have to be the root node of the sentence). For instance, the right fragment in Figure 1 shows a possible way of starting a standard TSG derivation which does not satisfy the incrementality constraint: the partial derivation has a substitution site as the first element in its yield.

In order to achieve incrementality while maintaining connectedness, we impose one further constraint on the type of fragments which are allowed in an ITSG: each fragment should be *lexicalized*, i.e., contain at least one word (lexical anchor) at the first or the second position in its yield. Allowing more than one substitution site at the beginning of a fragment's yield would lead to a violation of the incrementality requirement (as will become clear in Section 2.2).

[1]For example nodes NP, VP, S@ are the substitution sites of the right fragment in Figure 1.

[2]The tree is right-binarized via artificial nodes with @ symbols, as explained in Section 4.1. The original tree is

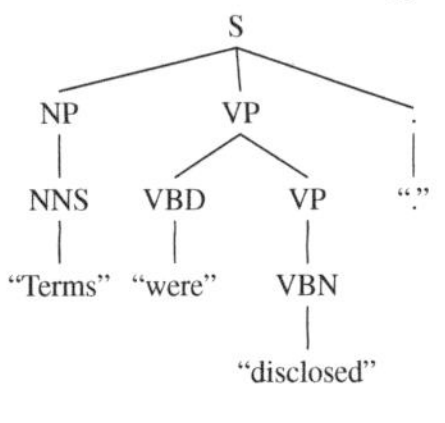

The generative process starts with a fragment anchored in the first word of the sentence being generated. At each subsequent step, a lexicalized fragment is introduced (by means of the substitution operation) to extend the current partial derivation in such a way that the prefix of the yield of the partial structure is lengthened by one word (the lexical anchor of the fragment being introduced). The lexicalization constraint allows a fragment to have multiple lexical items, not necessarily adjacent to one another. This is useful to capture the general ability of TSG to produce in one single step an arbitrarily big syntactic construction ranging from phrasal verbs (e.g., ask someone out), to parallel constructions (e.g., either X or Y), and idiomatic expressions (e.g., took me to the cleaners). For an example of a fragment with multiple lexical anchors see the fragment in the middle of Figure 2.

2.2 Symbolic Grammar

An ITSG is a tuple $\langle \mathscr{N}, \mathscr{L}, \mathscr{F}, \oslash, \obslash, \oplus \rangle$, where $\mathscr{N}$ and $\mathscr{L}$ are the set of non-lexical and lexical nodes respectively, $\mathscr{F}$ is a collection of lexicalized fragments, $\oslash$ and $\obslash$ are two variants of the substitution operation (backward and forward) used to combine fragments into derivations, and $\oplus$ is the stop operation which terminates the generative process.

Fragments A fragment $f \in \mathscr{F}$ belongs to one of the three sets $\mathscr{F}_{init}, \mathscr{F}^X_{lex}, \mathscr{F}^Y_{sub}$:

- An *initial fragment* (f_{init}) has the lexical anchor in the first position of the yield, being the initial word of a sentence (the left-most lexical node of the parse tree from which it was extracted).
- A *lex-first fragment* (f^X_{lex}) has the lexical anchor (non sentence-initial) in the first position of the yield, and is rooted in X.[3]
- A *sub-first fragment* (f^Y_{sub}) has the lexical anchor in the second position of its yield, and a substitution site Y in the first.

Fringes We will use fringes (Demberg et al., 2014) as a compressed representation of fragments,

[3]A fragment can be both an initial and a lex-first fragment (e.g., if the lexical anchor is a proper noun). We will make use of two separate instances of the same fragment in the two sets.

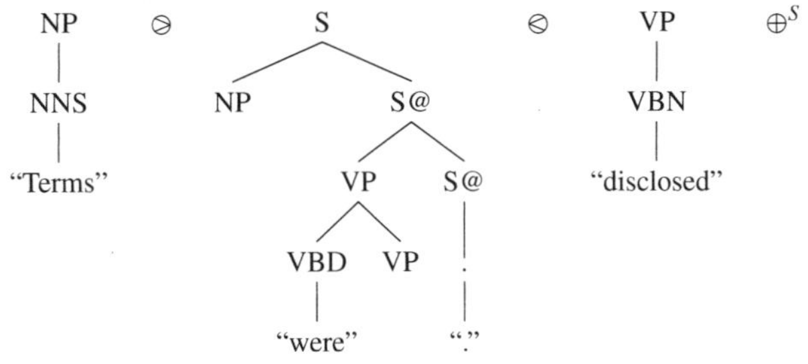

Figure 2: An example of an ITSG derivation yielding the tree on the left side of Figure 1. The second and third fragment are introduced by means of forward and backward substitution, respectively.

in which the internal structure is replaced by a triangle ($\triangle$ or $\lhd$) and only the root and the yield are visible. It is possible in a grammar that multiple fragments map to the same fringe; we will refer to those as *ambiguous fringes*. We use both vertical ($\triangle$, e.g., in Figure 3 and 4) and horizontal ($\lhd$) fringe notation. The latter is used for describing the states in our chart-parsing algorithm in Section 3. For instance, the horizontal fringe representation of the right fragment in Figure 1 is S $\lhd$ NP "were" VP S@.

Incremental Derivation An incremental derivation is a sequence of lexicalized fragments $\langle f_1, f_2, \ldots, f_n \rangle$ which, combined together in the specified order, give rise to a complete parse tree (see Figure 2 for an example). The first fragment f_1 being introduced in the derivation must be an initial fragment, and its lexical anchor constitutes the one-word prefix of the sentence being generated. Subsequent fragments are introduced by means of the substitution operation, which has two variants: backward substitution ($\oslash$), which is used to substitute lex-first fragments into the partial derivation generated so far, and forward substitution ($\obslash$), which is used to substitute sub-first fragments into the partial derivation. After a number of fragments are introduced, a stop operation ($\oplus$) may terminate the generative process.

Operations The three ITSG operations take place under specific conditions within an incremental derivation, as illustrated in Figure 3 and explained hereafter. At a given stage of the generative process (after an initial fragment has been inserted), the connected partial structure may or may not have sub-

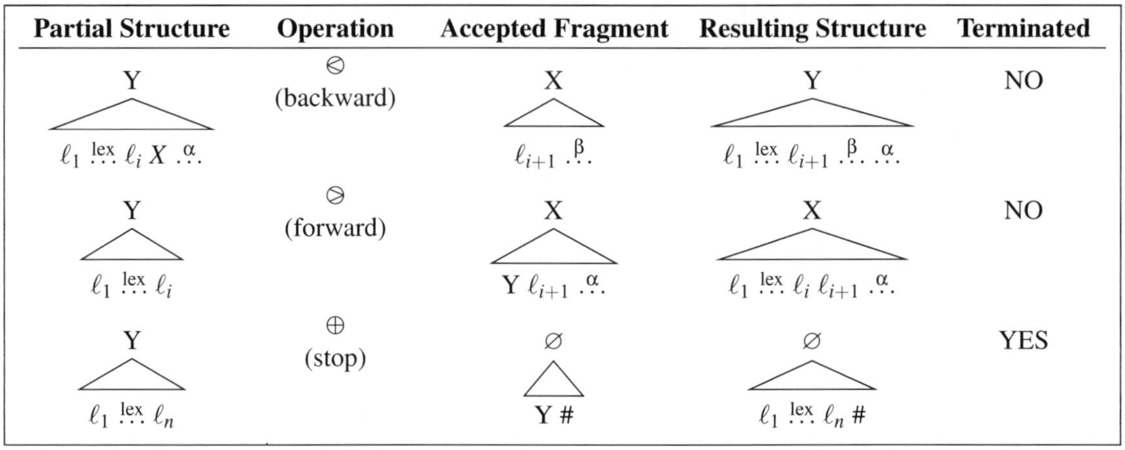

Figure 3: Schemata of the three ITSG operations. All tree structures (partial structure and fragments) are represented in a compact notation, which displays only the root nodes and the yields. The i-th words in the structure's yield is represented as ℓ_i, while α and β stands for any (possibly empty) sequence of words and substitution sites.

stitution sites present in its yield. In the first case, a backward substitution (⧀) must take place in the following generative step: if X is the left-most substitution site, a new fragment of type f^X_{lex} is chosen from the grammar and substituted into X. If the partially derived structure has no substitution site (all the nodes in its yield are lexical nodes) and it is rooted in Y, two possible choices exist: either the generative process terminates by means of the stop operation ($\oplus^Y$), or the generative process continues. In the latter case a forward substitution (⧁) is performed: a new f^Y_{sub} fragment is chosen from the grammar, and the partial structure is substituted into the left-most substitution site Y of the fragment.[4]

Multiple Derivations As in TSG, an ITSG may be able to generate the same parse tree in multiple ways: multiple incremental derivations yielding the same tree. Figure 4 shows one such example.

Generative Capacity It is useful to clarify the difference between ITSG and the more general TSG formalism in terms of generative capacity. Although both types of grammar make use of the substitution operation to combine fragments, an ITSG imposes more constraints on (i) the type of fragments which are allowed in the grammar (initial, lex-first, and sub-first fragments), and (ii) the generative process with which fragments are combined (incrementally left to right instead of top-down). If we compare a TSG and an ITSG on the same set of (ITSG-compatible) fragments, then there are cases in which the TSG can generate more tree structures than the ITSG.

In the following, we provide a more formal characterization of the strong and weak generative power

[4]A stop operation can be viewed as a forward substitution when using an artificial sub-first fragment $\varnothing \lhd Y\#$ (stop fragment), where # is an artificial lexical node indicating the termination of the sentence. For simplicity, stop fragments are omitted in Figure 2 and 4 and Y is attached to the stop symbol ($\oplus^Y$).

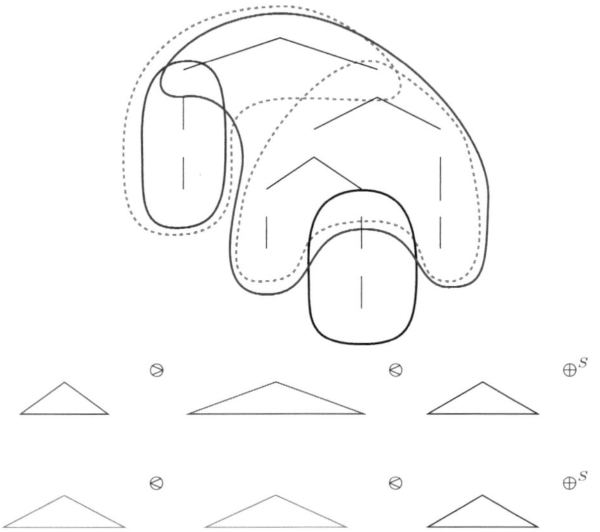

Figure 4: Above: an example of a set of fragments extracted from the tree in Figure 1. Below: two incremental derivations that generate it. Colors (and lines strokes) indicate which derivation fragments belong to.

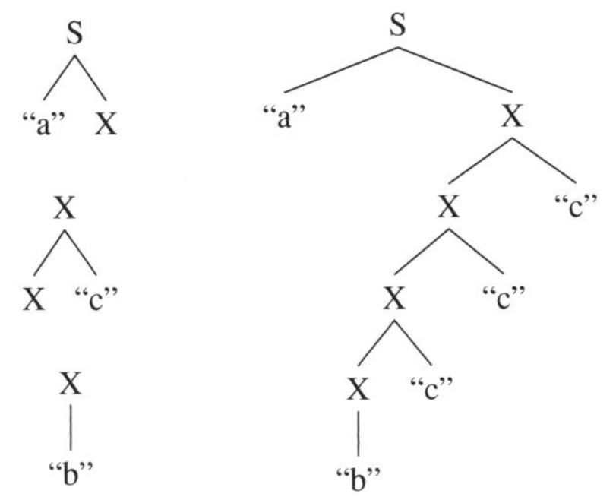

Figure 5: Left: an example of a CFG with left recursion. Right: one of the structures the CFG can generate.

of ITSG with respects to context-free grammar (CFG) and TSG. (However, a full investigation of this issue is beyond the scope of this paper.) We can limit our analysis to CFG, as TSG is strongly equivalent to CFG. The weak equivalence between ITSG and CFG is straightforward: for any CFG there is a way to produce a weakly equivalent grammar in Greibach Normal Form in which any production has a right side beginning with a lexical item (Aho and Ullman, 1972). The grammar that results from this transformation is an ITSG which uses only backward substitutions.

Left-recursion seems to be the main obstacle for strong equivalence between ITSG and CFG. As an example, the left side of Figure 5 shows a CFG that contains a left-recursive rule. The types of structures this grammar can generate (such as the one given on the right side of the same figure) are characterized by an arbitrarily long chain of rules that can intervene before the second word of the string, "b", is generated. Given the incrementality constraints, there is no ITSG that can generate the same set of structures that this CFG can generate. However, it may be possible to circumvent this problem by applying the left-corner transform (Rosenkrantz and Lewis, 1970; Aho and Ullman, 1972) to generate an equivalent CFG without left-recursive rules.

2.3 Probabilistic Grammar

In the generative process presented above there are a number of choices which are left open, i.e., which fragment is being introduced at a specific stage of a derivation, and when the generative process terminates. A symbolic ITSG can be equipped with a probabilistic component which deals with these choices. A proper probability model for ITSG needs to define three probability distributions over the three types of fragments in the grammar, such that:

$$\sum_{f_{init} \in \mathscr{F}_{init}} P(f_{init}) = 1 \quad (1)$$

$$\sum_{f_{lex}^{X} \in \mathscr{F}_{lex}^{X}} P(f_{lex}^{X}) = 1 \;\; (\forall X \in \mathscr{N}) \quad (2)$$

$$P(\oplus^{Y}) + \sum_{f_{sub}^{Y} \in \mathscr{F}_{sub}^{Y}} P(f_{sub}^{Y}) = 1 \;\; (\forall Y \in \mathscr{N}) \quad (3)$$

The probability that an ITSG generates a specific derivation d is obtained by multiplying the probabilities of the fragments taking part in the derivation:

$$P(d) = \prod_{f \in d} P(f) \quad (4)$$

Since the grammar may generate a tree t via multiple derivations $D(t) = d_1, d_2, \ldots, d_m$, the probability of the parse tree is the sum of the probabilities of the ITSG derivations in $D(t)$:

$$P(t) = \sum_{d \in D(t)} P(d) = \sum_{d \in D(t)} \prod_{f \in d} P(f) \quad (5)$$

3 Probabilistic ITSG Parser

We introduce a probabilistic chart-parsing algorithm to efficiently compute all possible incremental derivations that an ITSG can generate given an input sentence (presented one word at the time). The parsing algorithm is an adaptation of the Earley algorithm (Earley, 1970) and its probabilistic instantiation (Stolcke, 1995).

3.1 Parsing Chart

A TSG incremental derivation is represented in the chart as a sequence of chart states, i.e., a *path*.

For a given fringe in an incremental derivation, there will be one or more states in the chart, depending on the length of the fringe's yield. This is because we need to keep track of the extent to which the yield of each fringe has been consumed within a derivation as the sentence is processed incrementally.[5] At the given stage of the derivation, the states offer a compact representation over the partial structures generated so far.

[5]A fringe (state) may occur in multiple derivations (paths): for instance in Figure 4 the two derivations will correspond to two separate paths that will converge to the same fringe (state).

Start(ℓ_0)

$$\frac{X \triangleleft \ell_0 \nu}{0 : {}_0X \triangleleft \bullet \ell_0 \nu \; [\alpha, \gamma, \beta]}$$

$$\alpha = \gamma \;=\; P(X \triangleleft \ell_0 \nu) \qquad \beta \;=\; \beta(1 : {}_0X \triangleleft \ell_0 \bullet \nu)$$

Backward Substitution(ℓ_i)

$$\frac{i : {}_kX \triangleleft \lambda \bullet Y\mu \; [\alpha, \gamma, \beta] \qquad Y \triangleleft \ell_i \nu}{i : {}_iY \triangleleft \bullet \ell_i \nu \; [\alpha', \gamma', \beta']}$$

$$\alpha' \overset{\pm}{=} \alpha \cdot P(Y \triangleleft \ell_i \nu) \qquad \gamma' \;=\; P(Y \triangleleft \ell_i \nu)$$

Forward Substitution(ℓ_i)

$$\frac{i : {}_0Y \triangleleft \nu \bullet \; [\alpha, \gamma, \beta] \qquad X \triangleleft Y \ell_i \mu}{i : {}_0X \triangleleft Y \bullet \ell_i \mu \; [\alpha', \gamma', \beta']}$$

$$\begin{array}{ll} \alpha' \overset{\pm}{=} \alpha \cdot P(X \triangleleft Y \ell_i \mu) & \\ & \beta \overset{\pm}{=} \beta' \cdot P(X \triangleleft Y \ell_i \mu) \\ \gamma' \overset{\pm}{=} \gamma \cdot P(X \triangleleft Y \ell_i \mu) & \end{array}$$

Completion

$$\frac{i : {}_jY \triangleleft \ell_j \nu \bullet \; [\alpha, \gamma, \beta] \qquad j : {}_kX \triangleleft \lambda \bullet Y\mu \; [\alpha', \gamma', \beta']}{i : {}_kX \triangleleft \lambda Y \bullet \mu \; [\alpha'', \gamma'', \beta'']}$$

$$\begin{array}{ll} \alpha'' \overset{\pm}{=} \alpha' \cdot \gamma & \beta \overset{\pm}{=} \beta'' \cdot \gamma' \\ \gamma'' \overset{\pm}{=} \gamma' \cdot \gamma & \beta' \overset{\pm}{=} \beta'' \cdot \gamma'' \end{array}$$

Scan(ℓ_i)

$$\frac{i : {}_kX \triangleleft \lambda \bullet \ell_i \mu \; [\alpha, \gamma, \beta]}{i+1 : {}_kX \triangleleft \lambda \ell_i \bullet \mu \; [\alpha', \gamma', \beta']}$$

$$\begin{array}{ll} \alpha' = \alpha & \\ & \beta = \beta' \\ \gamma' = \gamma & \end{array}$$

Stop(#)

$$\frac{n : {}_0Y \triangleleft \nu \bullet \; [\alpha = \gamma, \beta] \qquad \emptyset \triangleleft Y\#}{n : {}_0\emptyset \triangleleft Y \bullet \# \; [\alpha', \gamma', \beta']}$$

$$\alpha' \;=\; \gamma' = \alpha \cdot P(\oplus^Y) \qquad \begin{array}{l} \beta' = 1 \\ \beta = P(\oplus^Y) \end{array}$$

Figure 6: Chart operations with forward (α), inner (γ), and outer (β) probabilities.

Each state is composed of a fringe and some additional information which keeps track of where the fringe is located within a path. A chart state can be generally represented as

$$i : {}_kX \triangleleft \lambda \bullet \mu \tag{6}$$

where $X \triangleleft \lambda\mu$ is the state's fringe, Greek letters are (possibly empty) sequences of words and substitution sites, and $\bullet$ is a placeholder indicating to which extent the fragment's yield has been consumed: all the elements in the yield preceding the dot have been already accepted. Finally, i and k are indices of words in the input sentence:

- i signifies that the current state is introduced after the first i words in the sentence have been scanned. All states in the chart will be grouped according to this index, and will constitute *state-set i*.
- k indicates that the fringe associated with the current state was first introduced in the chart after the first k words in the input sentence had been scanned. The index k is therefore called the *start index*.

For instance when generating the first incremental derivation in Figure 4, the parser will pass through state $1 : {}_1S \triangleleft$ NP $\bullet$ "were" VP "." indicating that the second fringe is introduced right after the parser has scanned the first word in the sentence and before having scanned the second word.

3.2 Parsing Algorithm

We will first introduce the symbolic part of the parsing algorithm, and then discuss its probabilistic component in Section 3.3. In line with the generative process illustrated in Section 2.2, the parser operates on the chart states in order to keep track of all possible ITSG derivations as new words are fed in. It *starts* by reading the first word ℓ_0 and introducing new states to state-set 0 in the chart, those mapping to initial fragments in the grammar with ℓ_0 as lexical anchor. At a given stage, after i words have been scanned, the parser reads the next word (ℓ_i) and introduces new states in state-sets i and $i+1$ by applying specific operations on states present in the chart, and fringes in the grammar.

Parser Operations The parser begins with the *start* operation just described, and continues with a cycle of four operations for every word in the input sentence ℓ_i (for $i \geq 0$). The order of the four operations is the following: completion, backward substitution ($\olessthan$), forward substitution ($\ogreaterthan$), and scan. When there are no more words in input, the parser terminates with a *stop* operation. We will now describe the parser operations (see Figure 6 for their formal definition), ignoring the probabilities for now.

Start(ℓ_0): For every *initial fringe* in the grammar anchored in ℓ_0, the parser inserts a (scan) state for that fringe in the state-set 0.

Backward Substitution(ℓ_i) applies to *acceptor states*, i.e., those with a substitution site following the dot, say X. For each acceptor state in state-set i, and any lex-first fringe in the grammar rooted in X and anchored in ℓ_i, the parser inserts a (scan) state for that fringe in state-set i.

Forward Substitution(ℓ_i) applies to *donor states*, i.e., those that have no elements following the dot and with start index 0. For each donor state in state-set i, rooted in Y, and any sub-first fringe in the grammar with Y as the left-most element in its yield, the parser inserts a (scan) state for that fringe in state-set i, with the dot placed after Y.

Completion applies to complete states, i.e., those with no elements following the dot and with start index $j > 0$. For every complete state in state-set i, rooted in Y, with starting index j, and every acceptor state in set j with Y following the dot, the parser inserts a copy of the acceptor state in state-set i, and advances the dot.

Scan(ℓ_i) applies to *scan states*, i.e., those with a word after the dot. For every scan state in state-set i having ℓ_i after the dot, the parser inserts a copy of that state in state-set $(i+1)$, and advances the dot.

Stop(#) is a special type of forward substitution and applies to donor states, but only when the input word is the terminal symbol #. For every donor state in state-set n (the length of the sentence), if the root of the fringe's state is Y, the parser introduces a *stop state* whose fringe is a stop fringe with Y as the left most substitution site.

Comparison with the Earley Algorithm It is useful to clarify the differences between the proposed ITSG parsing algorithm and the original Earley algorithm. Primarily, the ITSG parser is based on a left-right processing order, whereas the Earley algorithm uses a top-down generative process. Moreover, our parser presupposes a restricted inventory of fragments in the grammar (the ones allowed by an ITSG) as opposed to the general CFG rules allowed by the Earley algorithm. In particular, the *Backward Substitution* operation is more limited than the corresponding *Prediction* step of the Earley algorithm: only lex-first fragments can be introduced using Backward Substitution, and therefore left recursion (allowed by the Earley algorithm) is not possible here.[6] This restriction is compensated for by the existence of the *Forward Substitution* operation, which has no analog in the Earley algorithm.[7] The worst case complexity of Earley algorithm is dominated by the *Completion* operation which is identical to that in our parser, and therefore the original total time complexity applies, i.e., $O(l^3)$ for an input sentence of length l, and $O(n^3)$ in terms of the number of non-lexical nodes n in the grammar.

Derivations Incremental (partial) derivations are represented in the chart as (partial) paths along states. Each state can lead to one or more successors, and come from one or more antecedents. Scan is the only operation which introduces, for every scan state, a new single successor state (which can be of any of the four types) in the following state-set. Complete states may lead to several states within the current state-set, which may belong to any of the four types. An acceptor state may lead to a number of scan states via backward substitution (depending on the number of lex-first fringes that can combine with it). Similarly, a donor state may lead to a number of scan states via forward substitution.

After i words have been scanned, we can retrieve (partial) paths from the chart. This is done in a backward direction starting from scan states in state-set i all the way back to the initial states. This is possible since all the operations are reversible, i.e., given a state it is possible to retrieve its antecedent state(s).

As an example, consider the ITSG grammar consisting of the fragments in Figure 7 and the two derivations of the same parse tree in the same figure; Figure 7 represents the parsing chart of the same grammar, containing the two corresponding paths.

3.3 Probabilistic Parser

In the probabilistic version of the parser, each fringe in the grammar has a given probability, such that Equations (1)–(3) are satisfied.[8] In the probabilistic chart, every state $i : {}_kX \lhd \lambda \bullet \mu$ is decorated with three

[6] This further simplifies the probabilistic version of our parser, as there is no need to resort to the probabilistic reflexive, transitive left-corner relation described by Stolcke (1995).

[7] This operation would violate Earley's top-down constraint; donor states are in fact the terminal states in Earley algorithm.

[8] The probability of an ambiguous fringe is the marginal probability of the fragments mapping to it.

	0 – “Terms”	
S	| $_0NP \lhd \bullet$ “Terms” [1/2, 1/2, 1] || $_0S \lhd \bullet$ “Terms” $S@$ [1/2, 1/2, 1]	

	1 – “were”	
S	| $_0S \lhd NP\ \bullet$ “were” VP “.” [1/2, 1/2, 1] || $_1S@ \lhd \bullet$ “were” VP “.” [1/2, 1, 1/2]	
⧀	|| $_0S \lhd$ “Terms” $\bullet\ S@$ [1/2, 1/2, 1] $*$	|| $S@ \lhd$ “were” VP “.” [1]
⧁	| $_0NP \lhd$ “Terms” $\bullet$ [1/2, 1/2, 1]	| $S \lhd NP$ “were” VP “.” [1]

	2 – “disclosed”	
S	$_2VP \lhd \bullet$ “disclosed” [1, 1, 1]	
⧀	| $_0S \lhd NP$ “were” $\bullet\ VP$ “.” [1/2, 1/2, 1] $**$ || $_1S@ \lhd$ “were” $\bullet\ VP$ “.” [1/2, 1, 1/2] $***$	$VP \lhd$ “disclosed” [1]

	3 – “.”	
S	| $_0S \lhd NP$ “were” $VP\ \bullet$ “.” [1/2, 1/2, 1] || $_1S@ \lhd$ “were” $VP\ \bullet$ “.” [1/2, 1, 1/2]	
C	$_2VP \lhd$ “disclosed” $\bullet$ [1, 1, 1]	| $**$ || $***$

	4 – #	
S	$_0\varnothing \lhd S\ \bullet$ # [1, 1, 1]	
$\oplus$	|| $_0S \lhd$ “Terms” $S@\ \bullet$ [1/2, 1/2, 1] | $_0S \lhd NP$ “were” VP “.” $\bullet$ [1/2, 1/2, 1]	$\varnothing \lhd S$ # [1]
C	|| $_1S@ \lhd$ “were” VP “.” $\bullet$ [1/2, 1, 1/2]	|| $*$

Figure 7: The parsing chart of the two derivations in Figure 4. Blue states or fringes (also marked with |) are the ones in the first derivation, red (||) in the second, and yellow (no marks) are the ones in common. Each state-set is represented as a separate block in the chart, headed by the state-set index and the next word. Each row maps to a chart operation (specified in the first column, with S and C standing for ‘scan’ and ‘complete’ respectively) and follows the same notation of figure 6. Symbols $*$ are used as state placeholders.

probabilities $[\alpha, \gamma, \beta]$ as shown in the chart example in Figure 7.

- The *forward probability* α is the marginal probability of all the paths starting with an initial state, scanning all initial words in the sentence until ℓ_{i-1} included, and passing through the current state.
- The *inner probability* γ is the marginal probability of all the paths passing through the state $k : {}_kX \lhd \bullet\lambda\mu$, scanning words $\ell_k, \ldots, \ell_{i-1}$ and passing through the current state.
- The *outer probability* β is the marginal probability of all the paths starting with an initial state, scanning all initial words in the sentence until ℓ_{k-1} included, passing through the current state, and reaching a stop state.

Forward (α) and inner (γ) probabilities are propagated while filling the chart incrementally, whereas outer probabilities (β) are back-propagated from the stop states, for which $\beta = 1$ (see Figure 6). These probabilities are used for computing prefix and sentence probabilities, and for obtaining the most probable partial derivation (MPD) of a prefix, the MPD of a sentence, its minimum risk parse (MRP), and to approximate its most probable parse (MPP).

Prefix probabilities are obtained by summing over the forward probabilities of all scan states in state-set i having ℓ_i after the dot:[9]

$$P(\ell_0, \ldots, \ell_i) = \sum_{\substack{\text{state } s \\ i:{}_kX \lhd \lambda \bullet \ell_i \mu}} \alpha(s) \qquad (7)$$

3.4 Most Probable Derivation (MPD)

The Most Probable (partial) Derivation (MPD) can be obtained from the chart by backtracking the Viterbi path. Viterbi forward and inner probabilities

[9] *Sentence probability* is obtained by marginalizing the forward probabilities of the stop states in the last state-set n.

(α^*, γ^*) are propagated as standard forward and inner probabilities except that summation is replaced by maximization, and the probability of an ambiguous fringe is the maximum probability among all the fragments mapping into it (instead of the marginal one). The Viterbi partial path for the prefix $\ell_0, \dots, \ell_i$ can then be retrieved by backtracking from the scan state in state-set i with max α^*: for each state, the most probable preceding state is retrieved, i.e., the state among its antecedents with maximum α^*. The Viterbi complete path of a sentence can be obtained by backtracking the Viterbi path from the stop state with max α^*. Given a Viterbi path, it is possible to obtain the corresponding MPD. This is done by retrieving the associated sequence of fragments[10] and connecting them.

3.5 Most Probable Parse (MPP)

According to Equation (5), if we want to compute the MPP we need to retrieve all possible derivations of the current sentence, sum up the probabilities of those generating the same tree, and returning the tree with max marginal probability. Unfortunately the number of possible derivations grows exponentially with the length of the sentence, and computing the exact MPP is NP-hard (Sima'an, 1996). In our implementation, we approximate the MPP by performing this marginalization over the Viterbi-best derivations obtained from all stop states in the chart.

3.6 Minimum Risk Parse (MRP)

MPD and MPP aim at obtaining the structure of a sentence which is more likely *as a whole* under the current probabilistic model. Alternatively, we may want to focus on the single components of a tree structures, e.g., CFG rules covering a certain span of the sentence, and search for the structure which has the highest number of correct constituents, as proposed by Goodman (1996). Such structure is more likely to obtain higher results according to standard parsing evaluations, as the objective being maximized is closely related to the metric used for evaluation (recall/precision on the number of correct labeled constituents).

[10]For each scan state in the path, we obtain the fragment in the grammar that maps into the state's fringe. For ambiguous fringes the most probable fragment that maps into it is selected.

In order to obtain the minimum risk parse (MRP) we utilize both inner (γ) and outer (β) probabilities. The product of these two probabilities equals the marginal probability of all paths generating the entire current sentence and passing through the current state. We can therefore compute the probability of a fringe $f = X \lhd \lambda \bullet \mu$ covering a specific span $[s,t]$ of the sentence:

$$P(f, [s,t]) = \gamma(t : {}_s f \bullet) \cdot \beta(t : {}_s f \bullet) \tag{8}$$

We can then compute the probability of each fragment spanning $[s,t]$,[11] and the probability $P(r, [s,t])$ of a CFG-rule r spanning $[s,t]$.[12] Finally the MRP is computed as

$$MRP = \arg\max_T \prod_{r \in T} P(r, [s,t]) \tag{9}$$

4 Experiments

For training and evaluating the ITSG parser, we employ the Penn WSJ Treebank (Marcus et al., 1993). We use sections 2–21 for training, section 22 and 24 for development and section 23 for testing.

4.1 Grammar Extraction

Following standard practice, we start with some preprocessing of the treebank. After removing traces and functional tags, we apply right binarization on the training treebank (Klein and Manning, 2003), with no horizontal and vertical conditioning. This means that when a node X has more than two children, new artificial constituents labeled $X@$ are created in a right recursive fashion (see Figure 1).[13] We then replace words appearing less than five times in the training data by one of 50 unknown word categories based on the presence of lexical features as described in Petrov (2009).

Fragment Extraction In order to equip the grammar with a representative set of lexicalized fragments, we use the extraction algorithm of Sangati

[11]For an ambiguous fringe, the spanning probability of each fragment mapping into it is the fraction of the fringe's spanning probability with respect to the marginal fringe probability.

[12]Marginalizing the probabilities of all fragments having r spanning $[s,t]$.

[13]This shallow binarization (H0V1) was used based on gold coverage of the unsmoothed grammar (extracted from the training set) on trees in section 22: H0V1 binarization results on a coverage of 88.0% of the trees, compared to 79.2% for H1V1.

et al. (2010) which finds maximal fragments recurring twice or more in the training treebank. To ensure better coverage, we additionally extract one-word fragments from each training parse tree: for each lexical node ℓ in the parse tree we percolate up till the root node, and for every encountered internal node $X_0, X_1, \ldots, X_i$ we extract the lexicalized fragment whose spine is $X_i - X_{i-1} - \ldots - X_0 - \ell$, and where all the remaining children of the internal nodes are substitution sites (see for instance the right fragment in Figure 1). Finally, we remove all fragments which do not comply with the restrictions presented in Section 2.1.[14]

For each extracted fragment we keep track of its frequency, i.e., the number of times it occurs in the training corpus. Each fragment's probability is then derived according to its relative frequency in the corresponding set of fragments ($f_{init}, f^X_{lex}, f^Y_{sub}$), so that equations(1)–(3) are satisfied. The final grammar consists of 2.2M fragments mapping to 2.0M fringes.

Smoothing Two types of smoothing are performed over the grammar's fragments: *Open class smoothing* adds simple CFG rewriting rules to the grammar for open-class[15] $\langle \text{PoS}, \text{word} \rangle$ pairs not encountered in the training corpus, with frequency 10^{-6}. *Initial fragments smoothing* adds each lex-first fragment f to the initial fragment set with frequency $10^{-2} \cdot freq(f)$.[16]

All ITSG experiments we report used exhaustive search (no beam was used to prune the search space).

4.2 Evaluation

In addition to standard *full-sentence parsing results*, we propose a novel way of evaluating our ITSG on *partial trees*, i.e., those that the parser constructs for sentence prefixes. More precisely, for each prefix of the input sentence (length two words or longer) we compute the parsing accuracy on the minimal structure spanning that prefix. The minimal structure is obtained from the subtree rooted in the minimum common ancestor of the prefix nodes, after pruning those nodes not yielding any word in the prefix.

As observed in the example derivations of Figure 4, our ITSG generates partial trees for a given prefix which may include predictions about unseen parts of the sentence. We propose three new measures for evaluating sentence prediction:[17]

Word prediction PRD(m): For every prefix of each test sentence, if the model predicts $m' \geq m$ words, the prediction is correct if the first m predicted words are *identical* to the m words following the prefix in the original sentence.

Word presence PRS(m): For every prefix of each test sentence, if the model predicts $m' \geq m$ words, the prediction is correct if the first m predicted words are *present*, in the same order, in the words following the prefix in the original sentence (i.e., the predicted word sequence is a subsequence of the sequence of words following the prefix).[18]

Longest common subsequence LCS: For every prefix of each test sentence, it computes the longest common subsequence between the sequence of predicted words (possibly none) and the words following the prefix in the original sentence.

Recall and precision can be computed in the usual way for these three measures. Recall is the total number (over all prefixes) of correctly predicted words (as defined by PRD(m), PRS(m), or LCS) over the total number of words expected to be predicted (according to m), while precision is the number of correctly predicted words over the number of words predicted by the model.

We compare the ITSG parser with the incremental parsers of Schuler et al. (2010) and Demberg et al. (2014) for full-sentence parsing, with the Roark (2001) parser[19] for full-sentence and partial pars-

[14] The fragment with no lexical items, and those with more than one substitution site at the beginning of the yield.

[15] A PoS belongs to the open class if it rewrites to at least 50 different words in the training corpus. A word belongs to the open class if it has been seen only with open-class PoS tags.

[16] The parameters were tuned on section 24 of the WSJ.

[17] We also evaluated our ITSG model using perplexity; the results obtained were substantially worse than those obtained using Roark's parsers.

[18] Note that neither PRD(m) nor PRS(m) correspond to word error rate (WER). PRD requires the predicted word sequence to be identical to the original sequence, while PRS only requires the predicted words to be present in the original. In contrast, WER measures the minimum number of substitutions, insertions, and deletions needed to transform the predicted sequence into the original sequence.

[19] Apart from reporting the results in Roark (2001), we also run the latest version of Roark's parser, used in Roark et al. (2009), which has higher results compared to the original work.

	R	P	F1
Demberg et al. (2014)	79.4	79.4	79.4
Schuler et al. (2010)	83.4	83.7	83.5
Roark (2001)	86.6	86.5	86.5
Roark et al. (2009)	**87.7**	**87.5**	**87.6**
ITSG (MPD)	81.5	83.5	82.5
ITSG (MPP)	81.6	83.6	82.6
ITSG (MRP)	82.6	85.8	84.1
ITSG Smoothing (MPD)	83.0	83.5	83.2
ITSG Smoothing (MPP)	83.2	83.6	83.4
ITSG Smoothing (MRP)	**83.9**	**85.6**	**84.8**

Table 1: Full-sentence parsing results for sentences in the test set of length up to 40 words.

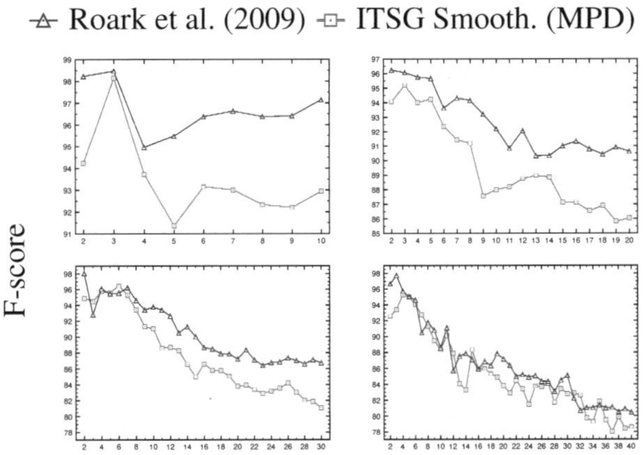

Figure 8: Partial parsing results for sentences of length 10, 20, 30, and 40 (from upper left to lower right).

ing, and with a language model built using SRILM (Stolcke, 2002) for sentence prediction. We used a standard 3-gram model trained on the sentences of the training set using the default setting and smoothing (Kneser-Ney) provided by the SRILM package. (Higher n-gram model do not seem appropriate, given the small size of the training corpus.) For every prefix in the test set we compute the most probable continuation predicted by the n-gram model.[20]

4.3 Results

Table 1 reports full-sentence parsing results for our parser and three comparable incremental parsers from the literature. While Roark (2001) obtains the best results, the ITSG parser without smoothing performs on a par with Schuler et al. (2010), and outperforms Demberg et al. (2014).[21] Adding smoothing results in a gain of 1.2 points F-score over the Schuler parser. When we compare the different parsing objectives of the ITSG parser, MRP is the best one, followed by MPP and MPD.

Incremental Parsing The graphs in Figure 8 compare the ITSG and Roark's parser on the incremental parsing evaluation, when parsing sentences of length 10, 20, 30 and 40. The performance of both models declines as the length of the prefix increases, with Roark's parser outperforming the ITSG parser on average, although the ITSG parser seems more competitive when parsing prefixes for longer (and therefore more difficult) sentences.

Sentence Prediction Table 2 compares the sentence prediction results of the ITSG and the language model (SRILM). The latter is outperforming the former when predicting the next word of a prefix, i.e. PRD(1), whereas ITSG is better than the language model at predicting a single future word, i.e. PRS(1). When more than one (consecutive) word is considered, the SRILM model exhibits a slightly better recall while ITSG achieves a large gain in precision. This illustrates the complementary nature of the two models: while the language model is better at predicting the next word, the ITSG predicts future words (rarely adjacent to the prefix) with high confidence (89.4% LCS precision). However, it makes predictions for only a small number of words (5.9% LCS recall). Examples of sentence predictions can be found in Table 3.

5 Related Work

To the best of our knowledge, there are no other incremental TSG parsers in the literature. The parser of Demberg et al. (2014) is closely related, but uses tree-adjoining grammar, which includes both substitution and adjunction. That parser makes predictions, but only for upcoming structure, not for upcoming words, and thus cannot be used directly for sentence prediction. The incremental parser of Roark (2001) uses a top-down algorithm and works

[20]We used a modified version of a script by Nathaniel Smith available at `https://github.com/njsmith/pysrilm`.

[21]Note that the scores reported by Demberg et al. (2014) are for TAG structures, not for the original Penn Treebank trees.

	ITSG			SRILM		
	Correct	R	P	Correct	R	P
PRD(1)	4,637	8.7	12.5	11,430	**21.5**	**21.6**
PRD(2)	864	1.7	**13.9**	2,686	**5.3**	5.7
PRD(3)	414	0.9	**20.9**	911	**1.9**	2.1
PRD(4)	236	0.5	**23.4**	387	**0.8**	1.0
PRS(1)	34,831	**65.4**	**93.9**	21,954	41.2	41.5
PRS(2)	4,062	8.0	**65.3**	5,726	**11.3**	12.2
PRS(3)	1,066	2.2	**53.7**	1,636	**3.4**	3.8
PRS(4)	541	1.2	**53.7**	654	**1.4**	1.7
LCS	44,454	5.9	**89.4**	92,587	**12.2**	18.4

Table 2: Sentence prediction results.

Prefix	Shares of UAL , the parent	PRD(3)	PRS(3)
ITSG	company of United Airlines ,	–	–
SRILM	company , which is the	–	–
Goldstd	of United Airlines , were extremely active all day Friday .		
Prefix	PSE said it expects to report earnings of $ 1.3 million to $ 1.7 million , or 14		
ITSG	cents a share ,	–	+
SRILM	% to $ UNK	–	–
Goldstd	cents to 18 cents a share .		

Table 3: Examples comparing sentence predictions for ITSG and SRILM (UNK: unknown word).

on the basis of context-free rules. These are augmented with a large number of non-local features (e.g., grandparent categories). Our approach avoids the need for such additional features, as TSG fragments naturally contain non-local information. Roark's parser outperforms ours in both full-sentence and incremental F-score (see Section 4), but cannot be used for sentence prediction straightforwardly: to obtain a prediction for the next word, we would need to compute an argmax over the whole vocabulary, then iterate this for each word after that (the same is true for the parsers of Schuler et al., 2010 and Demberg et al., 2014). Most incremental dependency parsers use a discriminative model over parse actions (Nivre, 2007), and therefore cannot predict upcoming words either (but see Huang and Sagae 2010).

Turning to the literature on sentence prediction, we note that ours is the first attempt to use a parser for this task. Existing approaches either use n-gram models (Eng and Eisner, 2004; Bickel et al., 2005) or a retrieval approach in which the best matching sentence is identified from a sentence collection given a set of features (Grabski and Scheffer, 2004). There is also work combining n-gram models with lexical semantics (Li and Hirst, 2005) or part-of-speech information (Fazly and Hirst, 2003).

In the language modeling literature, more sophisticated models than simple n-gram models have been developed in the past few years, and these could potentially improve sentence prediction. Examples include syntactic language models which have applied successfully for speech recognition (Chelba and Jelinek, 2000; Xu et al., 2002) and machine translation (Schwartz et al., 2011; Tan et al., 2011), as well as discriminative language models (Mikolov et al., 2010; Roark et al., 2007). Future work should evaluate these approaches against the ITSG model proposed here.

6 Conclusions

We have presented the first incremental parser for tree substitution grammar. Incrementality is motivated by psycholinguistic findings, and by the need for real-time interpretation in NLP. We have shown that our parser performs competitively on both full sentence and sentence prefix F-score. We also introduced sentence prediction as a new way of evaluating incremental parsers, and demonstrated that our parser outperforms an n-gram model in predicting more than one upcoming word.

The performance of our approach is likely to improve by implementing better binarization and more advanced smoothing. Also, our model currently contains no conditioning on lexical information, which is also likely to yield a performance gain. Finally, future work could involve replacing the relative frequency estimator that we use with more sophisticated estimation schemes.

Acknowledgments

This work was funded by EPSRC grant EP/I032916/1 "An integrated model of syntactic and semantic prediction in human language processing". We are grateful to Brian Roark for clarifying correspondence and for guidance in using his incremental parser. We would also like to thank Katja Abramova, Vera Demberg, Mirella Lapata, Andreas van Cranenburgh, and three anonymous reviewers for useful comments.

References

Alfred V. Aho and Jeffrey D. Ullman. 1972. *The theory of parsing, translation, and compiling*. Prentice-Hall, Inc., Upper Saddle River, NJ.

Gerry T. M. Altmann and Yuki Kamide. 1999. Incremental interpretation at verbs: Restricting the domain of subsequent reference. *Cognition*, 73:247–264.

Steffen Bickel, Peter Haider, and Tobias Scheffer. 2005. Predicting sentences using n-gram language models. In *Proceedings of the Conference on Human Language Technology and Empirical Methods in Natural Language Processing*, pages 193–200. Vancouver.

Rens Bod. 1995. The problem of computing the most probable tree in data-oriented parsing and stochastic tree grammars. In *Proceedings of the 7th Conference of the European Chapter of the Association for Computational Linguistics*, pages 104–111. Association for Computer Linguistics, Dublin.

Rens Bod, Khalil Sima'an, and Remko Scha. 2003. *Data-Oriented Parsing*. University of Chicago Press, Chicago, IL.

Ciprian Chelba and Frederick Jelinek. 2000. Structured language modeling. *Computer Speech and Language*, 14:283–332.

Vera Demberg and Frank Keller. 2008. Data from eye-tracking corpora as evidence for theories of syntactic processing complexity. *Cognition*, 101(2):193–210.

Vera Demberg, Frank Keller, and Alexander Koller. 2014. Parsing with psycholinguistically motivated tree-adjoining grammar. *Computational Linguistics*, 40(1). In press.

Jay Earley. 1970. An efficient context-free parsing algorithm. *Communications of the ACM*, 13(2):94–102.

John Eng and Jason M. Eisner. 2004. Radiology report entry with automatic phrase completion driven by language modeling. *Radiographics*, 24(5):1493–1501.

Afsaneh Fazly and Graeme Hirst. 2003. Testing the efficacy of part-of-speech information in word completion. In *Proceedings of the EACL Workshop on Language Modeling for Text Entry Methods*, pages 9–16. Budapest.

Joshua Goodman. 1996. Parsing algorithms and metrics. In *Proceedings of the 34th Annual Meeting on Association for Computational Linguistics*, pages 177–183. Association for Computational Linguistics, Santa Cruz.

Korinna Grabski and Tobias Scheffer. 2004. Sentence completion. In *Proceedings of the 27th Annual International ACM SIR Conference on Research and Development in Information Retrieval*, pages 433–439. Sheffield.

Liang Huang and Kenji Sagae. 2010. Dynamic programming for linear-time incremental parsing. In *Proceedings of the 48th Annual Meeting of the Association for Computational Linguistics*, pages 1077–1086. Association for Computational Linguistics, Uppsala.

Dan Klein and Christopher D. Manning. 2003. Accurate unlexicalized parsing. In *Proceedings of the 41st Annual Meeting on Association for Computational Linguistics*, pages 423–430. Association for Computational Linguistics, Sapporo.

Jianhua Li and Graeme Hirst. 2005. Semantic knowledge in a word completion task. In *Proceedings of the 7th International ACM SIGACCESS Conference on Computers and Accessibility*, pages 121–128. Baltimore.

Mitchell P. Marcus, Mary Ann Marcinkiewicz, and Beatrice Santorini. 1993. Building a large annotated corpus of english: The penn treebank. *Computational Linguistics*, 19(2):313–330.

Tomas Mikolov, Martin Karafiat, Jan Cernocky, and Sanjeev. 2010. Recurrent neural network based language model. In *Proceedings of the 11th Annual Conference of the International Speech Communication Association*, pages 2877–2880. Florence.

Joakim Nivre. 2007. Incremental non-projective dependency parsing. In *Proceedings of Human Language Technologies: The Annual Conference of the North American Chapter of the Association for Computational Linguistics*, pages 396–403. Association for Computational Linguistics, Rochester.

Slav Petrov. 2009. *Coarse-to-Fine Natural Language Processing*. Ph.D. thesis, University of California at Bekeley, Berkeley, CA.

Brian Roark. 2001. Probabilistic top-down parsing and language modeling. *Computational Linguististics*, 27:249–276.

Brian Roark, Asaf Bachrach, Carlos Cardenas, and Christophe Pallier. 2009. Deriving lexical and syntactic expectation-based measures for psycholinguistic modeling via incremental top-down parsing. In *Proceedings of the Conference on Empirical Methods in Natural Language Processing*, pages 324–333. Association for Computational Linguistics, Singapore.

Brian Roark, Murat Saraclar, and Michael Collins. 2007. Discriminative n-gram language modeling. *Computer Speech and Language*, 21(2):373–392.

D. J. Rosenkrantz and P. M. Lewis. 1970. Deterministic left corner parsing. In *Proceedings of the 11th Annual Symposium on Switching and Automata Theory*, pages 139–152. IEEE Computer Society, Washington, DC.

Federico Sangati, Willem Zuidema, and Rens Bod. 2010. Efficiently extract recurring tree fragments from large treebanks. In Nicoletta Calzolari, Khalid Choukri, Bente Maegaard, Joseph Mariani, Jan Odijk, Stelios Piperidis, Mike Rosner, and Daniel Tapias, editors, *Proceedings of the 7th InternationalConference on Language Resources and Evaluation*. European Language Resources Association, Valletta, Malta.

Yves Schabes. 1990. *Mathematical and Computational Aspects of Lexicalized Grammars*. Ph.D. thesis, University of Pennsylvania, Philadelphia, PA.

William Schuler, Samir AbdelRahman, Tim Miller, and Lane Schwartz. 2010. Broad-coverage parsing using human-like memory constraints. *Computational Linguististics*, 36(1):1–30.

Lane Schwartz, Chris Callison-Burch, William Schuler, and Stephen Wu. 2011. Incremental syntactic language models for phrase-based translation. In *Proceedings of the 49th Annual Meeting of the Association for Computational Linguistics: Human Language Technologies, Volume 1*, pages 620–631. Association for Computational Linguistics, Portland, OR.

Khalil Sima'an. 1996. Computational complexity of probabilistic disambiguation by means of tree-grammars. In *Proceedings of the 16th Conference on Computational Linguistics*, pages 1175–1180. Association for Computational Linguistics, Copenhagen.

Andreas Stolcke. 1995. An efficient probabilistic context-free parsing algorithm that computes prefix probabilities. *Computational Linguistics*, 21(2):165–201.

Andreas Stolcke. 2002. SRILM – an extensible language modeling toolkit. In *Proceedings International Conference on Spoken Language Processing*, pages 257–286. Denver, CO.

Scott C. Stoness, Joel Tetreault, and James Allen. 2004. Incremental parsing with reference interaction. In Frank Keller, Stephen Clark, Matthew Crocker, and Mark Steedman, editors, *Proceedings of the ACL Workshop Incremental Parsing: Bringing Engineering and Cognition Together*, pages 18–25. Association for Computational Linguistics, Barcelona.

Ming Tan, Wenli Zhou, Lei Zheng, and Shaojun Wang. 2011. A large scale distributed syntactic, semantic and lexical language model for machine translation. In *Proceedings of the 49th Annual Meeting of the Association for Computational Linguistics: Human Language Technologies, Volume 1*, pages 201–210. Association for Computational Linguistics, Portland, OR.

Michael K. Tanenhaus, Michael J. Spivey-Knowlton, Kathleen M. Eberhard, and Julie C. Sedivy. 1995. Integration of visual and linguistic information in spoken language comprehension. *Science*, 268:1632–1634.

Peng Xu, Ciprian Chelba, and Frederick Jelinek. 2002. A study on richer syntactic dependencies for structured language modeling. In *Proceedings of the 40th Annual Meeting on Association for Computational Linguistics*, pages 191–198. Association for Computational Linguistics, Philadelphia.

Modeling Child Divergences from Adult Grammar

Sam Sahakian
University of Wisconsin-Madison
sahakian@cs.wisc.edu

Benjamin Snyder
University of Wisconsin-Madison
bsnyder@cs.wisc.edu

Abstract

During the course of first language acquisition, children produce linguistic forms that do not conform to adult grammar. In this paper, we introduce a data set and approach for systematically modeling this child-adult grammar divergence. Our corpus consists of child sentences with corrected adult forms. We bridge the gap between these forms with a discriminatively reranked noisy channel model that translates child sentences into equivalent adult utterances. Our method outperforms MT and ESL baselines, reducing child error by 20%. Our model allows us to chart specific aspects of grammar development in longitudinal studies of children, and investigate the hypothesis that children share a common developmental path in language acquisition.

1 Introduction

Since the publication of the Brown Study (1973), the existence of standard stages of development has been an underlying assumption in the study of first language learning. As a child moves towards language mastery, their language use grows predictably to include more complex syntactic structures, eventually converging to full adult usage. In the course of this process, children may produce linguistic forms that do not conform to the grammatical standard. From the adult point of view these are language errors, a label which implies a faulty production. Considering the work-in-progress nature of a child language learner, these divergences could also be described as expressions of the structural differences between child and adult grammar. The predictability of these divergences has been observed by psychologists, linguists and parents (Owens, 2008).[1]

Our work leverages the differences between child and adult language to make two contributions towards the study of language acquisition. First, we provide a corpus of errorful child sentences annotated with adult-like rephrasings. This data will allow researchers to test hypotheses and build models relating the development of child language to adult forms. Our second contribution is a probabilistic model trained on our corpus that predicts a grammatical rephrasing given an errorful child sentence.

The generative assumption of our model is that sentences begin in underlying adult forms, and are then stochastically transformed into observed child utterances. Given an observed child utterance s, we calculate the probability of the corrected adult translation t as

$$P(t|s) \propto P(s|t)P(t),$$

where $P(t)$ is an adult language model and $P(s|t)$ is a noise model crafted to capture child grammar errors like omission of certain function words and corruptions of tense or declension. The parameters of this noise model are estimated using our corpus of child and adult-form utterances, using EM to handle unobserved word alignments. We use this generative model to produce n-best lists of candidate corrections which are then reranked using long range sentence features in a discriminative framework (Collins and Roark, 2004).

[1]For the remainder of this paper we use "error" and "divergence" interchangeably.

One could argue that our noisy channel model mirrors the cognitive process of child language production by appealing to the hypothesis that children rapidly learn adult-like grammar but produce errors due to performance factors (Bloom, 1990; Hamburger and Crain, 1984). That being said, our primary goal in this paper is not cognitive plausibility, but rather the creation of a practical tool to aid in the empirical study of language acquisition. By automatically inferring adult-like forms of child sentences, our model can highlight and compare developmental trends of children over time using large quantities of data, while minimizing the need for human annotation.

Besides this, our model's predictive success itself has theoretical implications. By aggregating training and testing data across children, our model instantiates the Brown hypothesis of a shared developmental path. Even when adequate per-child training data exists, using data only from other children leads to no degradation in performance, suggesting that the learned parameters capture general child language phenomena and not just individual habits. Besides aggregating across children, our model coarsely lumps together all stages of development, providing a frozen snapshot of child grammar. This establishes a baseline for more cognitively plausible and temporally dynamic models.

We compare our correction system against two baselines, a phrase-based Machine Translation (MT) system, and a model designed for English Second Language (ESL) error correction. Relative to the best performing baseline, our approach achieves a 30% decrease in word error-rate and a four point increase in BLEU score. We analyze the performance of our system on various child error categories, highlighting our model's strengths (correcting *be* drops and morphological overgeneralizations) as well as its weaknesses (correcting pronoun and auxiliary drops). We also assess the learning rate of our model, showing that very little annotation is needed to achieve high performance. Finally, to showcase a potential application, we use our model to chart one aspect of four children's grammar acquisition over time. While generally vindicating the Brown thesis of a common developmental path, the results point to subtleties in variation across individuals that merit further investigation.

2 Background and Related Work

While child error correction is a novel task, computational methods are frequently used to study first language acquisition. The computational study of speech is facilitated by TalkBank (MacWhinney, 2007), a large database of transcribed dialogues including CHILDES (MacWhinney, 2000), a subsection composed entirely of child conversation data. Computational tools have been developed specifically for the large-scale analysis of CHILDES. These tools enable further computational study such as the automatic calculation of the language development metrics IPSYN (Sagae et al., 2005) and D-Level (Lu, 2009), or the automatic formulation of novel language development metrics themselves (Sahakian and Snyder, 2012).

The availability of child language is also key to the design of computational models of language learning (Alishahi, 2010), which can support the plausibility of proposed human strategies for tasks like semantic role labeling (Connor et al., 2008) or word learning (Regier, 2005). To our knowledge this paper is the first work on error correction in the first language learning domain. Previous work has employed a classifier-based approach to identify speech errors indicative of language disorders in children (Morley and Prud'hommeaux, 2012).

Automatic correction of second language (L2) writing is a common objective in computer assisted language learning (CALL). These tasks generally target high-frequency error categories including article, word-form, and preposition choice. Previous work in CALL error correction includes identifying word choice errors in TOEFL essays based on context (Chodorow and Leacock, 2000), correcting errors with a generative lattice and PCFG reranking (Lee and Seneff, 2006), and identifying a broad range of errors in ESL essays by examining linguistic features of words in sequence (Gamon, 2011). In a 2011 shared ESL correction task (Dale and Kilgarriff, 2011), the best performing system (Rozovskaya et al., 2011) corrected preposition, article, punctuation and spelling errors by building classifiers for each category. This line of work is grounded in the practical application of automatic error correction as a learning tool for ESL students.

Statistical Machine Translation (SMT) has been

applied in diverse contexts including grammar correction as well as paraphrasing (Quirk et al., 2004), question answering (Echihabi and Marcu, 2003) and prediction of twitter responses (Ritter et al., 2011). In the realm of error correction, SMT has been applied to identify and correct spelling errors in internet search queries (Sun et al., 2010). Within CALL, Park and Levy (2011) took an unsupervised SMT approach to ESL error correction using Weighted Finite State Transducers (FSTs). The work described in this paper is inspired by that of Park and Levy, and in Section 6 we detail differences between our approaches. We also include their model as a baseline.

3 Data

To train and evaluate our translation system, we first collected a corpus of 1,000 errorful child-language utterances from the American English portion of the CHILDES database. To encourage diversity in the grammatical divergences captured by our corpus, our data is drawn from a large pool of studies (see bibliography for the full list of citations).

In the annotation process, candidate child sentences were randomly selected from the pool and classified by hand as either grammatically correct, divergent or unclassifiable (when it was not possible to tell what a child is trying to say). We continued this process until 1,000 divergent sentences were found. Along the way we also encountered 5,197 grammatically correct utterances and 909 that were unclassifiable.[2] Because CHILDES includes speech samples from children of diverse age, background and language ability, our corpus does not capture any specific stage of language development. Instead, the corpus represents a general snapshot of a learner who has not yet mastered English as their first language.

To provide the grammatically correct counterpart to child data, our errorful sentences were corrected by workers on Amazon's Mechanical Turk web service. Given a child utterance and its surrounding conversational context, annotators were instructed to translate the child utterance into adult-like English. We limited eligible workers to native English speakers residing in the US. We also required annotators to follow a brief tutorial in which they practice correcting sample utterances according to our guidelines. These guidelines instructed workers to minimally alter sentences to be grammatically consistent with a conversation or written letter, without altering underlying meaning. Annotators were evaluated on a worker-by-worker basis and rejected in the rare case that they ignored our guidelines. Accepted workers were paid 7 cents for correcting each set of 5 sentences. To achieve a consistent judgment, we posted each set of sentences for correction by 7 different annotators.

Error Type	Child Utterance
Insertion	I did locked it.
Inflection	More cookie?
Deletion	That not how.
Lemma Choice	I got grain.
Overgeneralization	I drawed it.

Table 1: Examples of error types captured by our model.

Once multiple reference translations were obtained we selected a single best correction by plurality, arbitrating ties as necessary. There were several cases in which corrections obtained by plurality decision did not perfectly follow instructions. These were manually corrected. Both the raw translations provided by individual annotators as well as the curated final adult forms are provided online as part of our data set.[3] Resulting pairs of errorful child sentences and their adult-like corrections were split into 73% training, 7% development and 20% test data, which we use to build, tune and evaluate our grammar correction system. In the final test phase, development data is included in the training set.

4 Model

According to our generative model, adult-like utterances are formed and then transformed by a noisy channel to become child sentences. The structure of our noise model is tailored to match our observations of common child errors. These include: function word insertions, function word deletions, swaps of function words and, inflectional changes to content words. Examples of each error type are given

[2]These hand-classified sentences are available online along with our set of errorful sentences.

[3]Data is available at
`http://pages.cs.wisc.edu/~bsnyder`

in Table 1. Our model does not allow reorderings, and can thus be described in terms of word-by-word stochastic transformations to the adult sentence.

We use 10 word classes to parameterize our model: pronouns, negators, wh-words, conjunctions, prepositions, determiners, modal verbs, "be" verbs, other auxiliary verbs, and lexical content words. The list of words in each class is provided as part of our data set. For each input adult word w, the model generates output word w' as a hierarchical series of draws from multinomial distributions, conditioned on the original word w and its class c.

All distributions receive an asymmetric Dirichlet prior which favors retention of the adult word. With the sole exception of word insertions, the distributions are parameterized and learned during training. Our model consists of 217 multinomial distributions, with 6,718 free parameters.

The precise form and parameterization of our model were handcrafted for performance on the development data, using trial and error. We also considered more fine-grained model forms (i.e. one parameter for each non-lexical input-output word pair), as well as coarser parameterizations (i.e. a single shared parameter denoting any inflection change). The model we describe here seemed to achieve the best balance of specificity and generalization.

We now present pseudocode describing the noise model's operation upon processing each word, along with a brief description of each step.

Action selection (lines 3-7): On reading an input word, an action category a is selected from a probability distribution conditioned on the input word's class. Our model allows up to two function word insertions or deletions in a row before a swap is required. Lexical content words may not be deleted or inserted, only swapped.

Insert and Delete (lines 8-15): The deletion case requires no decision after action selection. In the insertion case, the class of the inserted word, c', is selected conditioned on c_{PREV}, the class of the previous adult word. The precise identity of the inserted word is then drawn from a uniform distribution over words in class c'. It is important to note that in the insertion case, the input word at a given iteration will be re-processed at the next iteration (lines 33-35).

```
    insdel ← 0
    for word w with class c, inflection f, lemma ℓ
    do
3:      if insdel = 2 then
            a ← swap
        else
6:          a ∼ {insert, delete, swap} | c
        end if
        if a = delete then
9:          insdel++
            c' ← ε
            w' ← ε
12:     else if a = insert then
            insdel++
            c' ∼ classes | c_PREV, insert
15:         w' ∼ words in c' | insert
        else
            insdel ← 0
18:         c' ← c
            if c ∈ uninflected-classes then
                w' ∼ words in c | w, swap
21:         else if c = aux then
                ℓ' ∼ aux-lemmas | ℓ, swap
                f' ∼ inflections | f, swap
24:             w' ← COMBINE(ℓ', f')
            else
                f' ∼ inflections | f, swap
27:             w' ← COMBINE(ℓ, f')
            end if
        end if
30:     if w' ∈ irregular then
            w' ∼ OVERGEN(w') ∪ {w'}
        end if
33:     if a = insert then
            goto line 3
        end if
36: end for
```

Swap (lines 16 - 29): In the swap case, a word of given class is substituted for another word in the same class. Depending on the source word's class, swaps are handled in slightly different ways. If the word is a modal, conjunction, determiner, preposition, "wh-" word or negative, it is considered "uninflected." In these cases, a new word w' is selected from all words in class c, conditioned on the source word w.

If w is an auxiliary verb, the swap procedure consists of two parallel steps. A lemma is selected from possible auxiliary lemmas, conditioned on the lemma of the source word.[4] In the second step, an output inflection type is selected from a distribution conditioned on the source word's inflection. The precise output word is fully specified by the choice of lemma and conjugation.

If w is not in either of the above two categories, it is a lexical word, and our model only allows changes in conjugation or declension. If the source word is a noun it may swap to singular or plural form conditioned on the source form. If the word is a verb, it may swap to any conjugated or non-finite form, again conditioned on the source form. Lexical words that are not marked by CELEX (Baayen et al., 1996) as nouns or verbs may only swap to the exact same word.

Overgeneralization (lines 30-32): Finally, the noisy channel considers the possibility of producing overgeneralized word forms (like "maked" and "childs") in place of their correct irregular forms. The OVERGEN function produces the incorrect overgeneralized form. We draw from a distribution which chooses between this form and the correct original word. Our model maintains separate distributions for nouns (overgeneralized plurals) and verbs (overgeneralized past tense).

5 Implementation

In this section, we describe steps necessary to build, train and test our error correction model. Weighted Finite State Transducers (FSTs) used in our model are constructed with OpenFst (Allauzen et al., 2007).

5.1 Sentence FSTs

These FSTs provide the basis for our translation process. We represent sentences by building a simple linear chain FST, progressing from node to node with each arc accepting and yielding one word in the sentence. All arcs are weighted with probability one.

[4]Auxiliary lemmas include *have, do, go, will,* and *get.*

5.2 Noise FST

The noise model provides a conditional probability over child sentences given an adult sentence. We encode this model as a FST with several states, allowing us to track the number of consecutive insertions or deletions. We allow only two of these operations in a row, thereby constraining the length of the output sentence. This constraint results in three states ($insdel = 0, insdel = 1, insdel = 2$), along with an end state. In our training data, only 2 sentence pairs cannot be described by the noise model due to this constraint.

Each arc in the FST has an ϵ or adult-language word as input symbol, and a possibly errorful child-language word or ϵ as output symbol. Each arc weight is the probability of transducing the input word to the output word, determined according to the parameterized distributions described in Section 4. Arcs corresponding to insertions or deletions lead to a new state ($insdel$++) and are not allowed from state $insdel = 2$. Substitution arcs all lead back to state $insdel = 0$. Word class information is given by a set of word lists for each non-lexical class.[5] Inflectional information is derived from CELEX.

5.3 Language Model FST

The language model provides a prior distribution over adult form sentences. We build a a trigram language model FST with Kneser-Ney smoothing using OpenGRM (Roark et al., 2012). The language model is trained on all parent speech in the CHILDES studies from which our errorful sentences are drawn.

In the language model FST, the input and output words of each arc are identical. Arcs are weighted with the probability of the n-gram beginning with some prefix associated with the source node, and ending with the arc's input/output word. In this setup, the probability of a string is the total weight of the path accepting and emitting that string.

5.4 Training

As detailed in Section 4, our noise model consists of a series of multinomial distributions which govern

[5]Word lists are included for reference with our dataset.

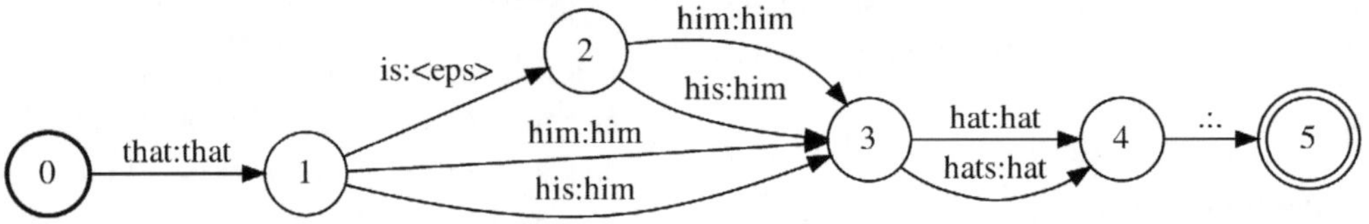

Figure 1: A simplified decoding FST for the child sentence "That him hat." In an actual decoding FST many more transduction arcs exist, including those translating "that" and "him" to any determiner and pronoun, respectively, and affording opportunities for many more deletions and insertions. Input and output strings given by FST paths correspond to possible adult-to-child translations.

the transformation from adult word to child word, allowing limited insertions and deletions. We estimate parameters θ for these distributions that maximize their posterior probability given the observed training sentences $\{(s,t)\}$. Since our language model $P(t)$ does not depend on on the noise model parameters, this objective is equivalent to jointly maximizing the prior and the conditional likelihoods of child sentences given adult sentences:

$$\operatorname*{argmax}_{\theta} P(\theta) \prod P(s|t,\theta)$$

To represent all possible derivations of each child sentence s from its adult translation t, we compose the sentence FSTs with the noise model, obtaining:

$$FST_{train} = FST_t \circ FST_{noise} \circ FST_s$$

Each path through FST_{train} corresponds to a single derivation d, with path weight $P(s,d|t,\theta)$. By summing all path weights, we obtain $P(s|t,\theta)$. We use a MAP-EM algorithm to maximize our objective while summing over all possible derivations.

Our training scheme relies on FSTs weighted in the V-expectation semiring (Eisner, 2001), implemented using code from fstrain (Dreyer et al., 2008). Besides carrying probabilities, arc weights are supplemented with a vector to indicate parameter counts involved in the arc traversal. The V-expectation semiring is designed so that the total arc weight of all paths through the FST yields both the probability $P(s|t,\theta)$, along with expected parameter counts. Our EM algorithm proceeds as follows: We start by initializing all parameters to uniform distributions with random noise. We then weight the arcs in FST_{noise} accordingly. For each sentence pair (s,t), we build FST_{train} by composition with our noise model, as described in the previous paragraph. We then compute the total arc weight of all paths through FST_{train} by relabeling all input and output symbols to ϵ and then reducing FST_{train} to a single state using epsilon removal (Mohri, 2008). The stopping weight of this single state is the sum of all paths through the original FST, yielding the probability $P(s|t,\theta)$, along with expected parameter counts according to our current distributions. We then reestimate θ using the expected counts plus pseudo-counts given by priors, and repeat this process until convergence.

Besides smoothing our estimated distributions, the pseudo-counts given by our asymmetric Dirichlet priors favor multinomials that retain the adult word form (swaps, identical lemmas, and identical inflections). Concretely, we use pseudo-counts of .5 for these favored outcomes, and pseudo-counts of .01 for all others.[6]

In practice, 109 of the child sentences in our data set cannot be translated into a corresponding adult version using our model. This is due to a range of rare phenomena like rephrasing, lexical word swaps and word-order errors. In these cases, the composed FST has no valid paths from start to finish and the sentence is removed from training. We run EM for 100 iterations, at which time the log likelihood of all sentences generally converges to within .01.

5.5 Decoding

After training our noise model, we apply the system to translate divergent child language to adult-like speech. As in training, the noise FST is composed with the FST for each child sentence s. In

[6]corresponding to Dirichlet hyperparameters of 1.5 and 1.01 respectively.

place of the adult sentence, the language model FST is used, yielding:

$$FST_{decode} = FST_{lm} \circ FST_{noise} \circ FST_s$$

Each path through FST_{decode} corresponds to an adult translation and derivation (t, d), with path weight $P(s, d|t, \theta)P(t)$. Thus, the highest-weight path corresponds to the most likely translation and derivation pair:

$$\underset{t,d}{\operatorname{argmax}} P(t, d|s, \theta)$$

We use a dynamic program to find the n highest-weight paths with distinct adult sentences t. This can be viewed as finding the n most likely adult translations, using a Viterbi approximation $P(t|s, \theta) = \operatorname{argmax}_d P(t, d|s, \theta)$. In our experiments we set $n = 50$. A simplified FST_{decode} example is shown in Figure 1.

5.6 Discriminative Reranking

To more flexibly capture long range syntactic features, we embed our noisy channel model in a discriminative reranking procedure. For each child sentence s, we take the n-best candidate translations $t_1, \ldots, t_n$ from the underlying generative model, as described in the previous section. We then map each candidate translation t_i to a d-dimensional feature vector $f(s, t_i)$. The reranking model then uses a d-dimensional weight vector λ to predict the candidate translation with highest linear score:

$$t^* = \underset{t_i}{\operatorname{argmax}} \lambda \cdot f(s, t_i)$$

To simulate test conditions, we train the weight vector on n-best lists from 8-fold cross-validation over training data, using the averaged perceptron reranking algorithm (Collins and Roark, 2004). Since the n-best list might not include the exact gold-standard correction, a target correction which maximizes our evaluation metric is chosen from the list. The n-best list is non-linearly separable, so perceptron training iterates for 1000 rounds, when it is terminated without converging.

Our feature function $f(s, t_i)$ yields nine boolean and real-valued features derived from (i) the FST that generates child sentence s from candidate adult-form t_i, and (ii) the POS sequence and dependency parse of candidate t_i obtained with the Stanford Parser (de Marneffe et al., 2006). Features were selected based on their performance in reranking held-out development data from the training set. Reranking features are given below:

Generative Model Probabilities: We first include the joint probability of the child sentence s and candidate translation t_i, given by the generative model: $P_{lm}(t_i)P_{noise}(s|t_i)$. We also isolate the candidate translation's language model and noise model probabilities as features. Since both of these probabilities naturally favor shorter sentences, we scale them to sentence length, yielding $\sqrt[n]{P_{lm}(t_i)}$ and $\sqrt[n]{P_{noise}(s|t_i)}$ respectively. By not scaling the joint probability, we allow the reranker to learn its own bias towards longer or shorter corrected sentences.

Contains Noun Subject, Accusative Noun Subject: The first boolean feature indicates whether the dependency parse of candidate translation t_i contains a "nsubj" relation. The second indicates if a "nsubj" relation exists where the dependent is an accusative pronoun (e.g. "Him ate the cookie"). These features and the one following have previously been used in classifier based error detection (Morley and Prud'hommeaux, 2012).

Contains Finite Verb: This boolean feature is true if the POS tags of t_i include a finite verb. This feature differentiates structures like "I am going" from "I going."

Question Template Features: We define templates for wh- and yes-no questions. A sentence fits the wh- question template if it begins with a wh-word, followed by an auxiliary or copula verb (e.g. "Who did..."). A sentence fits the yes-no template when it begins with an auxiliary or copula verb, then a noun subject followed by a verb or adjective (e.g. "Are you going..."). We include one boolean feature for each of these templates indicating when a template match is *inappropriate*, when the original child utterance terminates in a period instead of a question mark. In addition to the two features for inappropriate template matches, we have a single feature that signals *appropriate* matches of either question template — when the original child utterance terminates in a question mark.

Child Utterance	Human Correction	Machine Correction
I am not put in my mouth.	I am not putting it in my mouth.	I am not going to put it in my mouth.
This one have water?	Does this one have water?	This one has water?
Want to read the book.	I want to read the book.	You want to read the book.
Why you going to get two?	Why are you going to get two?	Why are you going to have two?
You very sticky.	You are very sticky.	You are very sticky.
He no like.	He does not like it.	He does not like that.
Yeah it looks a lady.	Yeah it looks like a lady	Yeah it looks like a lady.
Eleanor come too.	Eleanor came too.	Eleanor come too.
Desk in here.	The desk is in here	Desk is in here.
Why he's doc?	Why is he called doc?	He's up doc?

Table 2: Randomly selected test output generated by our complete error correction model, along with corresponding child utterances and human corrections.

6 Experiments and Analysis

Baselines We compare our system's performance with two pre-existing baselines. The first is a standard phrase-based machine translation system using MOSES (Koehn et al., 2007) with GIZA++ (Och and Ney, 2003) word alignments. We hold out 9% of the training data for tuning using the MERT algorithm with BLEU objective (Och, 2003).

The second baseline is our implementation of the ESL error correction system described by Park and Levy (2011). Like our system, this baseline trains FST noise models using EM in the V-expectation semiring. Our noise model is crafted specifically for the child language domain, and so differs from Park and Levy's in several ways: First, we capture a wider range of word-swaps, with richer parameterization allowing many more translation options. As a result, our model has 6,718 parameters, many more than the ESL model's 187. These parameters correspond to learned probability distributions, whereas in the ESL model many of the distributions are fixed as uniform. We also capture a larger class of errors, including deletions, change of auxiliary lemma, and inflectional overgeneralizations. Finally, we use a discriminative reranking step to model long-range syntactic dependencies. Although the ESL model is originally geared towards fully unsupervised training, we train this baseline in the same supervised framework as our model.

Evaluation and Performance We train all models on 80% of our child-adult sentence pairs and test on the remaining 20%. For illustration, selected output from our model is shown in Table 2.

Predictions are evaluated with BLEU score (Papineni et al., 2002) and Word Error Rate (WER), defined as the minimum string edit distance (in words) between reference and predicted translations, divided by length of the reference. As a control, we compare all results against scores for the uncorrected child sentences themselves. As reported in Table 3, our model achieves the best scores for both metrics. BLEU score increases from 50 for child sentences to 62, while WER is reduced from .271 to .224. Interestingly, MOSES achieves a BLEU score of 58 — still four points below our model — but actually increases WER to .449. For both metrics, the ESL system increases error. This is not surprising given that its intended application is in an entirely different domain.

Error Analysis We measured the performance of our model over the six most common categories of child divergence, including deletions of various function words and overgeneralizations of past tense forms (e.g. "maked" for "made"). We first identified model parameters associated with each category, and then counted the number of correct and incorrect parameter firings on the test sentences. As Table 4 indicates, our model performs reasonably well on "be" verb deletions, preposition deletions, and overgeneralizations, but has difficulty correcting pronoun and auxiliary deletions.

In general, hypothesizing dropped words burdens the noise model by adding additional draws from multinomial distributions to the derivation. To pre-

	BLEU	WER
WER reranking	**62.12**	**.224**
BLEU reranking	60.86	.231
No reranking	60.37	.233
Moses	58.29	.449
ESL	40.76	.318
Child Sentences	49.55	.271

Table 3: WER and BLEU scores. Our system's performance using various reranking schemes (BLEU objective, WER objective and none) is contrasted with Moses MT and ESL error correction baselines, as well as uncorrected test sentences. Best performance under each metric is shown in bold.

Error Type	Count	F_1	P	R
Be Deletions	63	.84	.84	.84
Pronoun Deletions	30	.15	.38	.1
Aux. Deletions	30	.21	.44	.13
Prep. Deletions	26	.65	.82	.54
Det. Deletions	22	.48	.73	.36
Overgen. Past	7	.92	1.0	.86

Table 4: Frequency of the six most common error types in test data, along with our model's corresponding F-measure, precision and recall. All counts are $\pm.12$ at $p = .05$ under a binomial normal approximation interval.

dict a deletion, either the language model or the reranker must strongly prefer including the omitted word. A syntax-based noise model may achieve better performance in detecting and correcting child word drops.

While our model parameterization and performance rely on the largely constrained nature of child language errors, we observe some instances in which it is overly restrictive. For 10% of utterances in our corpus, it is impossible to recover the exact gold-standard adult sentence. These sentences feature errors like reordering or lexical lemma swaps — for example "I talk Mexican" for "I speak Spanish." While our model may correct other errors in these sentences, a perfect correction is unattainable.

Sometimes, our model produces appropriate forms which by happenstance do not conform to the annotators' decision. For example, in the second row of Table 2, the model corrects "This one have water?" to "This one has water?", instead of the more verbose correction chosen by the annotators ("Does this one have water?"). Similarly, our model sometimes produces corrections which seem appropriate in isolation, but do not preserve the meaning implied by the larger conversational context. For example, in row three of Table 2, the sentence "Want to read the book." is recognized both by our human annotators and the system as requiring a pronoun subject. Unlike the annotators, however, the model has no knowledge of conversational context, so it chooses the highest probability pronoun — in this case "you" — instead of the contextually correct "I."

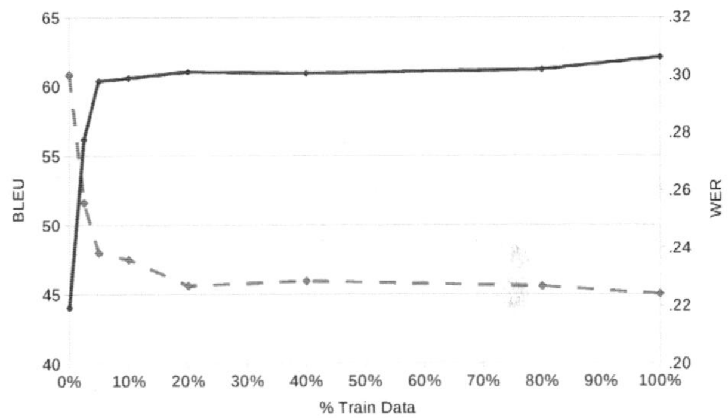

Figure 2: Performance with limited training data. WER is drawn as the dashed line, and BLEU as the solid line.

Learning Curves In Figure 2, we see that the learning curves for our model initially rise sharply, then remain relatively flat. Using only 10% of our training data (80 sentences), we increase BLEU from 44 (using just the language model) to almost 61. We only reach our reported BLEU score of 62 when adding the final 20% of training data. This result emphasizes the specificity of our parameterization. Because our model is so tailored to the child-language scenario, only a few examples of each error type are needed to find good parameter values. We suspect that more annotated data would lead to a continued but slow increase in performance.

Training and Testing across Children We use our system to investigate the hypothesis that language acquisition follows a similar path across children (Brown, 1973). To test this hypothesis, we train our model on all children excluding Adam, who alone is responsible for 21% of our sentences. We then test the learned model on the separated Adam

Trained on:	**BLEU**	**WER**
Adam	**72.58**	.226
All Others	69.83	**.186**
Uncorrected	45.54	.278

Table 5: Performance on Adam's sentences training on other children, versus training on himself. Best performance under each metric is shown in bold.

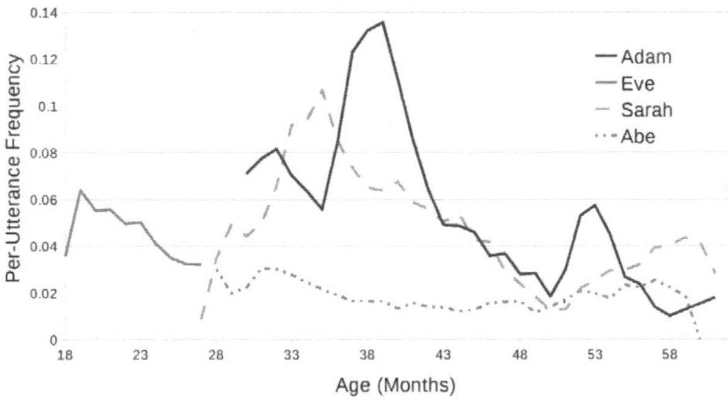

Figure 3: Automatically detected preposition omissions in un-annotated utterances from four children over time. Assuming perfect model predictions, frequencies are $\pm.002$ at $p = .05$ under a binomial normal approximation interval. Prediction error is given in Table 4.

data. These results are contrasted with performance of 8-fold cross validation training and testing solely on Adam's utterances. Performance statistics are given in Table 5.

We first note that models trained in both scenarios lead to large error reductions over the child sentences. This provides evidence that our model captures general, and not child-specific, error patterns. Although training exclusively on Adam does lead to increased BLEU score (72.58 vs 69.83), WER is minimized when using the larger volume of training data from other children (.186 vs .226). Taken as a whole, these results suggest that training and testing on separate children does not degrade performance. This finding supports the general hypothesis of shared developmental paths.

Plotting Child Language Errors over Time After training on annotated data, we predict divergences in all available data from the children in Roger Brown's 1973 study — Adam, Eve and Sarah — as well as Abe (Kuczaj, 1977), a child from a separate study over a similar age-range. We plot each child's per-utterance frequency of preposition omissions in Figure 3. Since we evaluate over 65,000 utterances and reranking has no impact on preposition drop prediction, we skip the reranking step to save computation.

In Figure 3, we see that Adam and Sarah's preposition drops spike early, and then gradually decrease in frequency as their preposition use moves towards that of an adult. Although Eve's data covers an earlier time period, we see that her pattern of preposition drops shows a similar spike and gradual decrease. This is consistent with Eve's general language precocity. Brown's conclusion — that the language development of these three children advanced in similar stages at different times — is consistent with our predictions. However, when we examine Abe we do not observe the same pattern.[7] This points to a degree of variance across children, and suggests the use of our model as a tool for further empirical refinement of language development hypotheses.

Discussion Our error correction system is designed to be more constrained than a full-scale MT system, focusing parameter learning on errors that are known to be common to child language learners. Reorderings are prohibited, lexical word swaps are limited to inflectional changes, and deletions are restricted to function word categories. By highly restricting our hypothesis space, we provide an inductive bias for our model that matches the child language domain. This is particularly important since the size of our training set is much smaller than that usually used in MT. Indeed, as Figure 2 shows, very little data is needed to achieve good performance.

In contrast, the ESL baseline suffers because its generative model is too restricted for the domain of transcribed child language. As shown above in Table 4, child deletions of function words are the most frequent error types in our data. Since the ESL model does not capture word deletions, and has a more restricted notion of word swaps, 88% of child sentences in our training corpus cannot be translated to their reference adult versions. The result is that the ESL model tends to rely too heavily on the language model. For example, on the sentence "I com-

[7]Though it is of course possible that a similar spike and drop-off occurred earlier in Abe's development.

ing to you," the ESL model improves n-gram probability by producing "I came to you" instead of the correct "I am coming to you". This increases error over the child sentence itself.

In addition to the domain-specific generative model, our approach has the advantage of long-range syntactic information encoded by reranking features. Although the perceptron algorithm places high weight on the generative model probability, it alters the predictions in 17 out of 201 test sentences, in all cases an improvement. Three of these reranking changes add a noun subject, five enforce question structure, and nine add a main verb.

7 Conclusion and Future Work

In this paper we introduce a corpus of divergent child sentences with corresponding adult forms, enabling the systematic computational modeling of child language by relating it to adult grammar. We propose a child-to-adult translation task as a means to investigate child language development, and provide an initial model for this task.

Our model is based on a noisy-channel assumption, allowing for the deletion and corruption of individual words, and is trained using FST techniques. Despite the debatable cognitive plausibility of our setup, our results demonstrate that our model captures many standard divergences and reduces the average error of child sentences by approximately 20%, with high performance on specific frequently occurring error types.

The model allows us to chart aspects of language development over time, without the need for additional human annotation. Our experiments show that children share common developmental stages in language learning, while pointing to child-specific subtleties in preposition use.

In future work, we intend to dynamically model child language ability as it grows and shifts in response to internal processes and external stimuli. We also plan to develop and train models specializing in the detection of specific error categories. By explicitly shifting our model's objective from child-adult translation to the detection of some particular error, we hope to improve our analysis of child divergences over time.

Acknowledgments

The authors thank the reviewers and acknowledge support by the NSF (grant IIS-1116676) and a research gift from Google. Any opinions, findings, or conclusions are those of the authors, and do not necessarily reflect the views of the NSF.

References

A. Alishahi. 2010. Computational modeling of human language acquisition. *Synthesis Lectures on Human Language Technologies*, 3(1):1–107.

C. Allauzen, M. Riley, J. Schalkwyk, W. Skut, and M. Mohri. 2007. OpenFst: A general and efficient weighted finite-state transducer library. *Implementation and Application of Automata*, pages 11–23.

R.H. Baayen, R. Piepenbrock, and L. Gulikers. 1996. CELEX2 (CD-ROM). Linguistic Data Consortium.

E. Bates, I. Bretherton, and L. Snyder. 1988. *From first words to grammar: Individual differences and dissociable mechanisms*. Cambridge University Press.

D.C. Bellinger and J.B. Gleason. 1982. Sex differences in parental directives to young children. *Sex Roles*, 8(11):1123–1139.

L. Bliss. 1988. The development of modals. *Journal of Applied Developmental Psychology*, 9:253–261.

L. Bloom, L. Hood, and P. Lightbown. 1974. Imitation in language development: If, when, and why. *Cognitive Psychology*, 6(3):380–420.

L. Bloom, P. Lightbown, L. Hood, M. Bowerman, M. Maratsos, and M.P. Maratsos. 1975. Structure and variation in child language. *Monographs of the Society for Research in Child Development*, pages 1–97.

L. Bloom. 1973. *One word at a time: The use of single word utterances before syntax*. Mouton.

P. Bloom. 1990. Subjectless sentences in child language. *Linguistic Inquiry*, 21(4):491–504.

J.N. Bohannon III and A.L. Marquis. 1977. Children's control of adult speech. *Child Development*, 48(3):1002–1008.

R. Brown. 1973. *A first language: The early stages*. Harvard University Press.

V. Carlson-Luden. 1979. *Causal understanding in the 10-month-old*. Ph.D. thesis, University of Colorado at Boulder.

E.C. Carterette and M.H. Jones. 1974. *Informal speech: Alphabetic & phonemic texts with statistical analyses and tables*. University of California Press.

M. Chodorow and C. Leacock. 2000. An unsupervised method for detecting grammatical errors. In *Proceedings of the North American Chapter of the Association for Computational Linguistics*, pages 140–147.

M. Collins and B. Roark. 2004. Incremental parsing with the perceptron algorithm. In *Proceedings of the Association for Computational Linguistics*, pages 111–118, Barcelona, Spain, July.

M. Connor, Y. Gertner, C. Fisher, and D. Roth. 2008. Baby SRL: Modeling early language acquisition. In *Proceedings of the Conference on Computational Natural Language Learning*, pages 81–88.

R. Dale and A. Kilgarriff. 2011. Helping our own: The HOO 2011 pilot shared task. In *Proceedings of the European Workshop on Natural Language Generation*, pages 242–249.

M.C. de Marneffe, B. MacCartney, and C.D. Manning. 2006. Generating typed dependency parses from phrase structure parses. In *Proceedings of The International Conference on Language Resources and Evaluation*, volume 6, pages 449–454.

M.J. Demetras, K.N. Post, and C.E. Snow. 1986. Feedback to first language learners: The role of repetitions and clarification questions. *Journal of Child Language*, 13(2):275–292.

M.J. Demetras. 1989. Working parents' conversational responses to their two-year-old sons.

M. Dreyer, J.R. Smith, and J. Eisner. 2008. Latent-variable modeling of string transductions with finite-state methods. In *Proceedings of the Conference on Empirical Methods in Natural Language Processing*, pages 1080–1089.

A. Echihabi and D. Marcu. 2003. A noisy-channel approach to question answering. In *Proceedings of the Association for Computational Linguistics*, pages 16–23.

J. Eisner. 2001. Expectation semirings: Flexible EM for learning finite-state transducers. In *Proceedings of the ESSLLI workshop on finite-state methods in NLP*.

M. Gamon. 2011. High-order sequence modeling for language learner error detection. In *Proceedings of the Workshop on Innovative Use of NLP for Building Educational Applications*, pages 180–189.

L.C.G. Haggerty. 1930. What a two-and-one-half-year-old child said in one day. *The Pedagogical Seminary and Journal of Genetic Psychology*, 37(1):75–101.

W.S. Hall, W.C. Tirre, A.L. Brown, J.C. Campoine, P.F. Nardulli, HO Abdulrahman, MA Sozen, W.C. Schnobrich, H. Cecen, J.G. Barnitz, et al. 1979. The communicative environment of young children: Social class, ethnic, and situational differences. *Bulletin of the Center for Children's Books*, 32:08.

W.S. Hall, W.E. Nagy, and R.L. Linn. 1980. *Spoken words: Effects of situation and social group on oral word usage and frequency*. University of Illinois at Urbana-Champaign, Center for the Study of Reading.

W.S. Hall, W.E. Nagy, and G. Nottenburg. 1981. Situational variation in the use of internal state words. Technical report, University of Illinois at Urbana-Champaign, Center for the Study of Reading.

H. Hamburger and S. Crain. 1984. Acquisition of cognitive compiling. *Cognition*, 17(2):85–136.

R.P. Higginson. 1987. *Fixing: Assimilation in language acquisition*. University Microfilms International.

M.H. Jones and E.C. Carterette. 1963. Redundancy in children's free-reading choices. *Journal of Verbal Learning and Verbal Behavior*, 2(5-6):489–493.

P. Koehn, H. Hoang, A. Birch, C. Callison-Burch, M. Federico, N. Bertoldi, B. Cowan, W. Shen, C. Moran, R. Zens, et al. 2007. Moses: Open source toolkit for statistical machine translation. In *Proceedings of the Association for Computational Linguistics (Interactive Poster and Demonstration Sessions)*, pages 177–180.

S. A. Kuczaj. 1977. The acquisition of regular and irregular past tense forms. *Journal of Verbal Learning and Verbal Behavior*, 16(5):589–600.

J. Lee and S. Seneff. 2006. Automatic grammar correction for second-language learners. In *Proceedings of the International Conference on Spoken Language Processing*.

X. Lu. 2009. Automatic measurement of syntactic complexity in child language acquisition. *International Journal of Corpus Linguistics*, 14(1):3–28.

B. MacWhinney. 2000. *The CHILDES project: Tools for analyzing talk*, volume 2. Psychology Press.

B. MacWhinney. 2007. The TalkBank project. *Creating and digitizing language corpora: Synchronic Databases*, 1:163–180.

M. Mohri. 2008. System and method of epsilon removal of weighted automata and transducers, June 3. US Patent 7,383,185.

E. Morley and E. Prud'hommeaux. 2012. Using constituency and dependency parse features to identify errorful words in disordered language. In *Proceedings of the Workshop on Child, Computer and Interaction*.

A. Ninio, C.E. Snow, B.A. Pan, and P.R. Rollins. 1994. Classifying communicative acts in children's interactions. *Journal of Communication Disorders*, 27(2):157–187.

F.J. Och and H. Ney. 2003. A systematic comparison of various statistical alignment models. *Computational Linguistics*, 29(1):19–51.

F.J. Och. 2003. Minimum error rate training in statistical machine translation. In *Proceedings of the Association for Computational Linguistics*, pages 160–167.

R.E. Owens. 2008. *Language development: An introduction*. Pearson Education, Inc.

K. Papineni, S. Roukos, T. Ward, and W.J. Zhu. 2002. BLEU: a method for automatic evaluation of machine translation. In *Proceedings of the Association for Computational Linguistics*, pages 311–318.

Y.A. Park and R. Levy. 2011. Automated whole sentence grammar correction using a noisy channel model. *Proceedings of the Association for Computational Linguistics*, pages 934–944.

A.M. Peters. 1987. The role of imitation in the developing syntax of a blind child in perspectives on repetition. *Text*, 7(3):289–311.

K. Post. 1992. *The language learning environment of laterborns in a rural Florida community*. Ph.D. thesis, Harvard University.

C. Quirk, C. Brockett, and W. Dolan. 2004. Monolingual machine translation for paraphrase generation. In *Proceedings of the Conference on Empirical Methods in Natural Language Processing*, pages 142–149.

T. Regier. 2005. The emergence of words: Attentional learning in form and meaning. *Cognitive Science*, 29(6):819–865.

A. Ritter, C. Cherry, and W.B. Dolan. 2011. Data-driven response generation in social media. In *Proceedings of the Conference on Empirical Methods in Natural Language Processing*, pages 583–593.

B. Roark, R. Sproat, C. Allauzen, M. Riley, J. Sorensen, and T. Tai. 2012. The OpenGrm open-source finite-state grammar software libraries. In *Proceedings of the Association for Computational Linguistics (System Demonstrations)*, pages 61–66.

A. Rozovskaya, M. Sammons, J. Gioja, and D. Roth. 2011. University of Illinois system in HOO text correction shared task. In *Proceedings of the European Workshop on Natural Language Generation*, pages 263–266.

J. Sachs. 1983. Talking about the there and then: The emergence of displaced reference in parent-child discourse. *Children's Language*, 4.

K. Sagae, A. Lavie, and B. MacWhinney. 2005. Automatic measurement of syntactic development in child language. In *Proceedings of the Association for Computational Linguistics*, pages 197–204.

S. Sahakian and B. Snyder. 2012. Automatically learning measures of child language development. *Proceedings of the Association for Computational Linguistics (Volume 2: Short Papers)*, pages 95–99.

C.E. Snow, F. Shonkoff, K. Lee, and H. Levin. 1986. Learning to play doctor: Effects of sex, age, and experience in hospital. *Discourse Processes*, 9(4):461–473.

E.L. Stine and J.N. Bohannon. 1983. Imitations, interactions, and language acquisition. *Journal of Child Language*, 10(03):589–603.

X. Sun, J. Gao, D. Micol, and C. Quirk. 2010. Learning phrase-based spelling error models from clickthrough data. In *Proceedings of the Association for Computational Linguistics*, pages 266–274.

P. Suppes. 1974. The semantics of children's language. *American Psychologist*, 29(2):103.

T.Z. Tardif. 1994. *Adult-to-child speech and language acquisition in Mandarin Chinese*. Ph.D. thesis, Yale University.

V. Valian. 1991. Syntactic subjects in the early speech of American and Italian children. *Cognition*, 40(1-2):21–81.

L. Van Houten. 1986. Role of maternal input in the acquisition process: The communicative strategies of adolescent and older mothers with their language learning children. In *Boston University Conference on Language Development*.

A. Warren-Leubecker and J.N. Bohannon III. 1984. Intonation patterns in child-directed speech: Mother-father differences. *Child Development*, 55(4):1379–1385.

A. Warren. 1982. *Sex differences in speech to children*. Ph.D. thesis, Georgia Institute of Technology.

B. Wilson and A.M. Peters. 1988. What are you cookin' on a hot?: A three-year-old blind child's 'violation' of universal constraints on constituent movement. *Language*, 64:249–273.

Efficient Stacked Dependency Parsing by Forest Reranking

Katsuhiko Hayashi and Shuhei Kondo and Yuji Matsumoto
Graduate School of Information Science Nara Institute of Science and Technology
8916-5, Takayama, Ikoma, Nara 630-0192, Japan
{katsuhiko-h,shuhei-k,matsu}@is.naist.jp

Abstract

This paper proposes a discriminative forest reranking algorithm for dependency parsing that can be seen as a form of efficient stacked parsing. A dynamic programming shift-reduce parser produces a packed derivation forest which is then scored by a discriminative reranker, using the 1-best tree output by the shift-reduce parser as guide features in addition to third-order graph-based features. To improve efficiency and accuracy, this paper also proposes a novel shift-reduce parser that eliminates the spurious ambiguity of arc-standard transition systems. Testing on the English Penn Treebank data, forest reranking gave a state-of-the-art unlabeled dependency accuracy of 93.12.

1 Introduction

There are two main approaches of data-driven dependency parsing – one is graph-based and the other is transition-based.

In the graph-based approach, global optimization algorithms find the highest-scoring tree with locally factored models (McDonald et al., 2005). While third-order graph-based models achieve state-of-the-art accuracy, it has $O(n^4)$ time complexity for a sentence of length n. Recently, some pruning techniques have been proposed to improve the efficiency of third-order models (Rush and Petrov, 2012; Zhang and McDonald, 2012).

The transition-based approach usually employs the shift-reduce parsing algorithm with linear-time complexity (Nivre, 2008). It greedily chooses the transition with the highest score and the resulting transition sequence is not always globally optimal. The beam search algorithm improves parsing flexibility in deterministic parsing (Zhang and Clark, 2008; Zhang and Nivre, 2011), and dynamic programming makes beam search more efficient (Huang and Sagae, 2010).

There is also an alternative approach that integrates graph-based and transition-based models (Sagae and Lavie, 2006; Zhang and Clark, 2008; Nivre and McDonald, 2008; Martins et al., 2008). Martins et al. (2008) formulated their approach as stacking of parsers where the output of the first-stage parser is provided to the second as guide features. In particular, they used a transition-based parser for the first stage and a graph-based parser for the second stage. The main drawback of this approach is that the efficiency of the transition-based parser is sacrificed because the second-stage employs full parsing.

This paper proposes an efficient stacked parsing method through discriminative reranking with higher-order graph-based features, which works on the forests output by the first-stage dynamic programming shift-reduce parser and integrates non-local features efficiently with cube-pruning (Huang and Chiang, 2007). The advantages of our method are as follows:

- Unlike the conventional stacking approach, the first-stage shift-reduce parser prunes the search space of the second-stage graph-based parser.
- In addition to guide features, the second-stage graph-based parser can employ the scores of the first-stage parser which cannot be incorpo-

$$\text{axiom}(c_0): \quad 0 : (0, 1, \mathbf{w}_0) : \emptyset$$

$$\text{goal}(c_{2n}): \quad 2n : (0, n, \mathbf{s}_0) : \emptyset$$

$$\text{shift}: \quad \frac{\overbrace{\ell : (\_, j, \mathbf{s}_d|\mathbf{s}_{d-1}|\ldots|\mathbf{s}_1|\mathbf{s}_0) : \_}^{\text{state } p}}{\ell + 1 : (j, j+1, \mathbf{s}_{d-1}|\mathbf{s}_{d-2}|\ldots|\mathbf{s}_0|\mathbf{w}_j) : (p)} \; i < n$$

$$\text{reduce}_{\curvearrowleft}: \quad \frac{\overbrace{\_ : (i, j, \mathbf{s}'_d|\mathbf{s}'_{d-1}|\ldots|\mathbf{s}'_1|\mathbf{s}'_0) : \pi'}^{\text{state } p} \quad \overbrace{\ell : (j, k, \mathbf{s}_d|\mathbf{s}_{d-1}|\ldots|\mathbf{s}_1|\mathbf{s}_0) : \pi}^{\text{state } q}}{\ell + 1 : (i, k, \mathbf{s}'_d|\mathbf{s}'_{d-1}|\ldots|\mathbf{s}'_1|\mathbf{s}'_0 \curvearrowleft \mathbf{s}_0) : \pi'} \; \mathbf{s}'_0.\text{h}.\mathbf{w} \neq \mathbf{w}_0 \wedge p \in \pi$$

$$\text{reduce}_{\curvearrowright}: \quad \frac{\overbrace{\_ : (i, j, \mathbf{s}'_d|\mathbf{s}'_{d-1}|\ldots|\mathbf{s}'_1|\mathbf{s}'_0) : \pi'}^{\text{state } p} \quad \overbrace{\ell : (j, k, \mathbf{s}_d|\mathbf{s}_{d-1}|\ldots|\mathbf{s}_1|\mathbf{s}_0) : \pi}^{\text{state } q}}{\ell + 1 : (i, k, \mathbf{s}'_d|\mathbf{s}'_{d-1}|\ldots|\mathbf{s}'_1|\mathbf{s}'_0 \curvearrowright \mathbf{s}_0) : \pi'} \; p \in \pi$$

Figure 1: The arc-standard transition-based dependency parsing system with dynamic programming: _ means "take anything". $\mathbf{a} \curvearrowright \mathbf{b}$ denotes that a tree $\mathbf{b}$ is attached to a tree $\mathbf{a}$.

rated in standard graph-based models.

- In contrast to joint transition-based/graph-based approaches (Zhang and Clark, 2008; Bohnet and Kuhn, 2012) which require a large beam size and make dynamic programming impractical, our two-stage approach can integrate both models with little loss of efficiency.

In addition, the elimination of spurious ambiguity from the arc-standard shift-reduce parser improves the efficiency and accuracy of our approach.

$\mathbf{s}_0.\text{h.t} \circ \mathbf{s}_0.\text{lc.t} \circ \mathbf{s}_0.\text{lc2.t}$	$\mathbf{s}_0.\text{h.t} \circ \mathbf{s}_0.\text{rc.t} \circ \mathbf{s}_0.\text{rc2.t}$
$\mathbf{s}_1.\text{h.t} \circ \mathbf{s}_1.\text{lc.t} \circ \mathbf{s}_1.\text{lc2.t}$	$\mathbf{s}_1.\text{h.t} \circ \mathbf{s}_1.\text{rc.t} \circ \mathbf{s}_1.\text{rc2.t}$
$\mathbf{s}_0.\text{h.t} \circ \mathbf{s}_0.\text{lc.t} \circ \mathbf{s}_0.\text{lc2.t} \circ \mathbf{q}_0.\text{t}$	
$\mathbf{s}_0.\text{h.t} \circ \mathbf{s}_0.\text{rc.t} \circ \mathbf{s}_0.\text{rc2.t} \circ \mathbf{q}_0.\text{t}$	
$\mathbf{s}_0.\text{h.t} \circ \mathbf{s}_1.\text{h.t} \circ \mathbf{q}_0.\text{t} \circ \mathbf{q}_1.\text{t}$	
$\mathbf{s}_0.\text{h.w} \circ \mathbf{s}_1.\text{h.t} \circ \mathbf{q}_0.\text{t} \circ \mathbf{q}_1.\text{t}$	

Table 1: Additional feature templates for shift-reduce parsers: $\mathbf{q}$ denotes input queue. h, lc and rc are head, leftmost child and rightmost child of a stack element $\mathbf{s}$. lc2 and rc2 denote the second leftmost and rightmost children. t and w are a part-of-speech (POS) tag and a word.

2 Arc-Standard Shift-Reduce Parsing

We use a beam search shift-reduce parser with dynamic programming as our baseline system. Figure 1 shows it as a deductive system (Shieber et al., 1995). A state is defined as the following:

$$\ell : (i, j, \mathbf{s}_d|\mathbf{s}_{d-1}|\ldots|\mathbf{s}_1|\mathbf{s}_0) : \pi$$

where ℓ is the step size, $[i, j]$ is the span of the topmost stack element $\mathbf{s}_0$, and $\mathbf{s}_d|\mathbf{s}_{d-1}|\ldots|\mathbf{s}_1$ shows a stack with d elements at the top, where d is the window size used for defining features. The axiom is initialized with an input sentence of length n, $x = \mathbf{w}_0 \ldots \mathbf{w}_n$ where $\mathbf{w}_0$ is a special root symbol $\$_0$. The system takes $2n$ steps for a complete analysis.

π is a set of pointers to the predictor states, each of which is the state just before shifting the root word of $\mathbf{s}_0$ into stack[1]. Dynamic programming merges equivalent states in the same step if they have the same feature values. We add the feature templates shown in Table 1 to Huang and Sagae (2010)'s feature templates.

Dynamic programming not only makes the shift-reduce parser with beam search more efficient but also produces a packed forest that encodes an exponential number of dependency trees. A packed dependency forest can be represented by a weighted (directed) hypergraph. A weighted hypergraph is a pair $H = \langle V, E \rangle$, where V is the set of vertices and E is the set of hyperedges. Each hyperedge $e \in E$ is a tuple $e = \langle T(e), h(e), f_e \rangle$, where $h(e) \in V$ is

[1] Huang and Sagae (2010)'s dynamic programming is based on a notion of a *push computation* (Kuhlmann et al., 2011). The details are out of scope here and readers may refer to the paper.

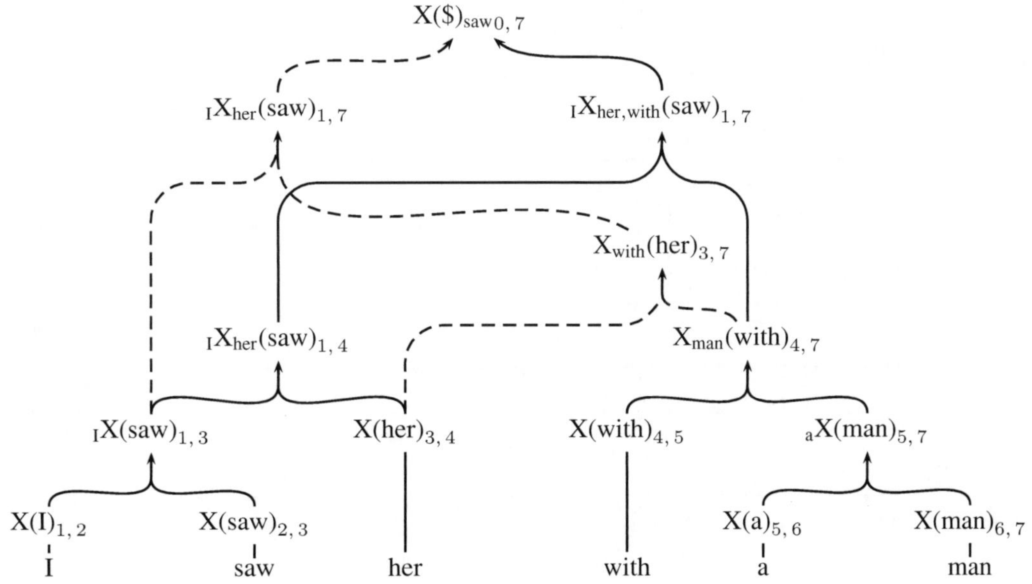

Figure 2: An example of packed dependency (derivation) forest: each vertex has information about the topmost stack element of the corresponding state to it.

its head vertex, $T(e) \in V^+$ is an ordered list of tail vertices, and f_e is a weight for e.

Figure 2 shows an example of a packed forest. Each binary hyperedge corresponds to a reduce action, and each leaf vertex corresponds to a shift action. Each vertex also corresponds to a state, and parse histories on the states can be encoded into the vertices. In the example, information about the topmost stack element is attached to the corresponding vertex marked with a non-terminal symbol X.

Weights are omitted in the example. In practice, we attach each reduction weight to the corresponding hyperedge, and add the shift weight to the reduction weight when a shifted word is reduced.

3 Arc-Standard Shift-Reduce Parsing without Spurious Ambiguity

One solution to remove spurious ambiguity in the arc-standard transition system is to give priority to the construction of left arcs over that of right arcs (or vice versa) like Eisner (1997). For example, an Earley dependency parser (Hayashi et al., 2012) attaches all left dependents to a word before right dependents. The parser uses a scan action to stop the construction of left arcs.

We apply this idea to the arc-standard transition system and show the resulting transition system in Figure 3. We introduce the $*$ symbol to indicate that the root node of the topmost element on the stack has not been scanned yet. The shift and reduce$_\curvearrowright$ actions can be used only when the root of the topmost element on the stack has already been scanned, and all left arcs are always attached to the head before the head is scanned.

The arc-standard shift-reduce parser without spurious ambiguity takes $3n$ steps to finish parsing, and the additional n scan actions add surplus vertices and (unary) hyperedges to a packed forest. However, it is easy to remove them from the packed forest because the consequent state of a scan action has a unique antecedent state and all the hyperedges going out from a vertex corresponding to the consequent state can be attached to the vertex corresponding to the antecedent state. The scan weight of the removed unary hyperedge is added to each weight of the hyperedges attached to the antecedent.

4 Experiments (Spurious Ambiguity vs. Non-Spurious Ambiguity)

We conducted experiments on the English Penn Treebank (PTB) data to compare spurious and non-spurious shift-reduce parsers. We split the WSJ part of PTB into sections 02-21 for training, section 22 for development, and section 23 for test. We used the head rules (Yamada and Matsumoto, 2003) to convert phrase structure to dependency structure.

$$
\begin{array}{rl}
\text{axiom}(c_0): & 0 : (0, 1, \mathbf{w}_0) : \emptyset \\
\text{goal}(c_{3n}): & 3n : (0, n, \mathbf{s}_0) : \emptyset
\end{array}
$$

$$
\text{shift}: \quad \frac{\overbrace{\ell : (\_, j, \mathbf{s}_d|\mathbf{s}_{d-1}|\ldots|\mathbf{s}_1|\mathbf{s}_0) : \_}^{\text{state } p}}{\ell + 1 : (j, j+1, \mathbf{s}_{d-1}|\mathbf{s}_{d-2}|\ldots|\mathbf{s}_0|\mathbf{w}_j^*) : (p)} \; j < n
$$

$$
\text{scan}: \quad \frac{\ell : (i, j, \mathbf{s}_d|\mathbf{s}_{d-1}|\ldots|\mathbf{s}_1|\mathbf{s}_0^*) : \pi}{\ell + 1 : (i, j, \mathbf{s}_d|\mathbf{s}_{d-1}|\ldots|\mathbf{s}_1|\mathbf{s}_0) : \pi}
$$

$$
\text{reduce}_{\curvearrowleft}: \quad \frac{\overbrace{\_ : (i, j, \mathbf{s}'_d|\mathbf{s}'_{d-1}|\ldots|\mathbf{s}'_0|\mathbf{s}'_0) : \pi'}^{\text{state } p} \quad \overbrace{\ell : (j, k, \mathbf{s}_d|\mathbf{s}_{d-1}|\ldots|\mathbf{s}_1|\mathbf{s}_0^*) : \pi}^{\text{state } q}}{\ell + 1 : (i, k, \mathbf{s}'_d|\mathbf{s}'_{d-1}|\ldots|\mathbf{s}'_1|\mathbf{s}'_0{\curvearrowleft}\mathbf{s}_0^*) : \pi'} \; \mathbf{s}'_0.\mathrm{h}.\mathbf{w} \neq \mathbf{w}_0 \wedge p \in \pi
$$

$$
\text{reduce}_{\curvearrowright}: \quad \frac{\overbrace{\_ : (i, j, \mathbf{s}'_d|\mathbf{s}'_{d-1}|\ldots|\mathbf{s}'_1|\mathbf{s}'_0) : \pi'}^{\text{state } p} \quad \overbrace{\ell : (j, k, \mathbf{s}_d|\mathbf{s}_{d-1}|\ldots|\mathbf{s}_1|\mathbf{s}_0) : \pi}^{\text{state } q}}{\ell + 1 : (i, k, \mathbf{s}'_d|\mathbf{s}'_{d-1}|\ldots|\mathbf{s}'_1|\mathbf{s}'_0{\curvearrowright}\mathbf{s}_0) : \pi'} \; p \in \pi
$$

Figure 3: The dynamic programming arc-standard transition-based deductive system without spurious ambiguity: the symbol represents that the root node of the topmost element on the stack has not been scanned yet.

			8	16	32	64	128
dev.	spurious	UAS (w/o punc.)	92.5 (93.5)	**92.7** (93.6)	92.6 (93.6)	92.6 (93.6)	92.6 (93.6)
		sec. (per sent.)	0.01	**0.017**	0.03	**0.06**	0.13
	non-sp.	UAS (w/o punc.)	92.5 (**93.6**)	92.6 (93.6)	92.6 (93.6)	92.6 (93.6)	92.6 (93.6)
		sec. (per sent.)	0.01	0.018	0.03	0.07	0.13
test	spurious	UAS (w/o punc.)	92.7 (93.3)	92.7 (93.3)	92.7 (93.3)	92.8 (93.3)	92.8 (93.3)
		sec. (per sent.)	0.01	**0.017**	0.03	0.06	0.13
	non-sp.	UAS (w/o punc.)	**92.8 (93.4)**	**92.9 (93.5)**	**92.9 (93.5)**	**92.9 (93.5)**	**92.9 (93.5)**
		sec. (per sent.)	0.01	0.018	0.03	0.06	0.13

Table 2: Unlabeled accuracy scores (UAS) and parsing times (+forest dumping times, second per sentence) for parsing development (WSJ22) and test (WSJ23) data with spurious shift-reduce and proposed shift-reduce parser (non-sp.) using several beam sizes.

We used an early update version of the averaged perceptron algorithm (Collins and Roark, 2004; Huang et al., 2012) to train two shift-reduce dependency parsers with beam size of 12.

Table 2 shows experimental results of parsing the development and test datasets with each of the spurious and non-spurious shift-reduce parsers using several beam sizes. Parsing accuracies were evaluated by unlabeled accuracy scores (UAS) with and without punctuations. The parsing times were measured on an Intel Core i7 2.8GHz. The average cpu time (per sentence) includes that of dumping packed forests. This result indicates that the non-spurious parser achieves better accuracies than the spurious parser without loss of efficiency.

beam size	8	32	128
% of distinct trees (10)	93.5	94.8	95.0
% of distinct trees (100)	81.8	84.9	87.2
% of distinct trees (1000)	70.6	73.1	77.6
% of distinct trees (10000)	62.1	64.3	65.6

Table 3: The percentages of distinct dependency trees in 10, 100, 1000 and 10000 best trees extracted from spurious forests with several beam sizes.

Figure 4 shows oracle unlabeled accuracies of spurious k-best lists, non-spurious k-best lists, spurious forests, and non-spurious forests. We extract an oracle tree from each packed forest using the for-

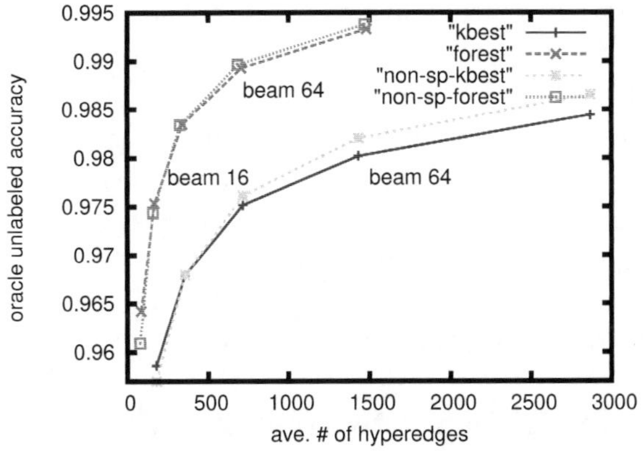

Figure 4: Each plot shows oracle unlabeled accuracies of spurious k-best lists, spurious forests, and non-spurious forests. The oracle accuracies are evaluated using UAS with punctuations.

est oracle algorithm (Huang, 2008). Both forests produce much better results than the k-best lists, and non-spurious forests have almost the same oracle accuracies as spurious forests.

However, as shown in Table 3, spurious forests encode a number of non-unique dependency trees while all dependency trees in non-spurious forests are distinct from each other.

5 Forest Reranking

5.1 Discriminative Reranking Model

We define a reranking model based on the graph-based features as the following:

$$\hat{y} = \operatorname*{argmax}_{y \in H} \alpha \cdot \mathbf{f}_{\mathrm{g}}(x, y) \quad (1)$$

where α is a weight vector, $\mathbf{f}_{\mathrm{g}}$ is a feature vector (g indicates "graph-based"), x is the input sentence, y is a dependency tree and H is a dependency forest. This model assumes a hyperedge factorization which induces a decomposition of the feature vector as the following:

$$\alpha \cdot \mathbf{f}_{\mathrm{g}}(x, y) = \sum_{e \in y} \alpha \cdot \mathbf{f}_{\mathrm{g},e}(e). \quad (2)$$

The search problem can be solved by simply using the (generalized) Viterbi algorithm (Klein and Manning, 2001). When using non-local features, the hyperedge factorization is redefined to the following:

$$\alpha \cdot \mathbf{f}_{\mathrm{g}}(x, y) = \sum_{e \in y} \alpha \cdot \mathbf{f}_{\mathrm{g},e}(e) + \alpha \cdot \mathbf{f}_{\mathrm{g},e,N}(e) \quad (3)$$

where $\mathbf{f}_{\mathrm{g},e,N}$ is a non-local feature vector. Though the cube-pruning algorithm (Huang and Chiang, 2007) is an approximate decoding technique based on a k-best Viterbi algorithm, it can calculate the non-local scores efficiently.

The baseline score can be taken into the reranker as a linear interpolation:

$$\hat{y} = \operatorname*{argmax}_{y \in H} \beta \cdot \mathbf{sc}_{\mathrm{tr}}(x, y) + \alpha \cdot \mathbf{f}_{\mathrm{g}}(x, y) \quad (4)$$

where $\mathbf{sc}_{\mathrm{tr}}$ is the score from the baseline parser (tr indicates "transition-based"), and β is a scaling factor.

5.2 Features for Discriminative Model

5.2.1 Local Features

While the inference algorithm is a simple Viterbi algorithm, the discriminative model can use all tri-sibling features and some grand-sibling features[2] (Koo and Collins, 2010) as a local scoring factor in addition to the first- and sibling second-order graph-based features. This is because the first stage shift-reduce parser uses features described in Section 2 and this information can be encoded into vertices of a hypergraph.

The reranking model also uses guide features extracted from the 1-best tree predicted by the first stage shift-reduce parser. We define the guide features as first-order relations like those used in Nivre and McDonald (2008) though our parser handles only unlabeled and projective dependency structures. We summarize the features for discriminative reranking model as the following:

- First- and second-order features: these features are the same as those used in MST parser[3].
- Grand-child features: we define tri-gram POS features with POS tags of grand parent, parent, and rightmost or leftmost child.
- Tri-sibling features: we define tri-gram features with three POS-tags of child, sibling, and tri-sibling. We also define tri-gram features with one word and two POS tags of the above.

[2]The grand-child and grand-sibling features can be used only when interacting with the leftmost or rightmost child and sibling. In case of local reranking, we did not use grand-sibling features because in our experiments, they were not effective.

[3]http://www.seas.upenn.edu/~strctlrn/MSTParser/MSTParser.html

- Guide feaures: we define a feature indicating whether an arc from a child to its parent is present in the 1-best tree predicted by the first-stage shift-reduce parser, conjoined with the POS tags of the parent and child.

- PP-Attachment features: when a parent word is a preposition, we define tri-gram features with the parent word and POS tags of grand parent and the rightmost child.

5.2.2 Non-local Features

To define richer features as a non-local factor, we extend a local reranking algorithm by augmenting each k-best item with all child vertices of its head vertex[4]. Information about all children enables the reranker to calculate the following features when reducing the head vertex:

- Grand-child features: we define tri-gram features with one word and two POS tags of grand parent, parent, and child.

- Grand-sibling features: we define 4-gram POS features with POS tags of grand parent, parent, child and sibling. We also define coordination features with POS tags of grand parent, parent and child when the sibling word is a coordinate conjunction.

- Valency features: we define a feature indicating the number of children of a head, conjoined with each of its word and POS tag.

When using non-local features, we removed the local grand-child features from the model.

5.3 Oracle for Discriminative Training

A discriminative reranking model is trained on packed forests by using their oracle trees as the correct parse. More accurate oracles are essential to train a discriminative reranking model well.

While large size forests have much more accurate oracles than small size forests, large forests have too many hyperedges to train a discriminative model on them, as shown in Figure 4. The usual forest reranking algorithms (Huang, 2008; Hayashi et al., 2011) remove low quality hyperedges from large forests by using inside-outside forest pruning.

However, producing large forests and pruning them is computationally very expensive. Instead, we propose a simpler method to produce small forests which have more accurate oracles by forcing the beam search shift-reduce parser to keep the correct state in the beam buffer. As a result, the correct tree will always be encoded in a packed forest.

6 Experiments (Discriminative Reranking)

6.1 Experimental Setting

Following (Huang, 2008), the training set (WSJ02-21) is split into 20 folds, and each fold is parsed by each of the spurious and non-spurious shift-reduce parsers using beam size 12 with the model trained on sentences from the remaining 19 folds, dumping the outputs as packed forests.

The reranker is modeled by either equation (1) or (4). By our preliminary experiments using development data (WSJ22), we modeled the reranker with equation (1) when training, and with equation (4) when testing[5] (i.e., the scores of the first-stage parser are not considered during training of the reranking model). This prevents the discriminative reranking features from *under-training* (Sutton et al., 2006; Hollingshead and Roark, 2008).

A discriminative reranking model is trained on the packed forests by using the averaged perceptron algorithm with 5 iterations. When training non-local reranking models, we set k-best size of cube-pruning to 5.

For dumping packed forests for test data, spurious and non-spurious shift-reduce parsers are trained by the averaged perceptron algorithm. In all experiments on English data, we fixed beam size to 12 for training both parsers.

6.2 Test with Gold POS tags

We show the comparison of dumped spurious and non-spurious packed forests for training data in Table 4. Both oracle accuracies are 100.0 due to the

[4]If each item is augmented with richer information, even features based on the entire subtree can be defined.

[5]The scaling factor β was tuned by minimum error rate training (MERT) algorithm (Och, 2003) using development data. The MERT algorithm is suited to tune low-dimensional parameters. The β was set to about 1.2 in case of local reranking, and to about 1.5 in case of non-local reranking.

system	w/ rerank.	sec. (per sent.)	UAS (w/o punc.)
sr (12)	–	0.011	92.8 (93.3)
(8)	w/ local	0.009 + 0.0056	93.03 (93.69)
(12)	w/ local	0.011 + 0.0079	93.03 (93.68)
(32)	w/ local	0.03 + 0.019	93.07 (93.67)
(64)	w/ local	0.06 + 0.039	93.0 (93.61)
(12, k=3)	w/ non-local	0.011 + 0.0085	93.17 (93.78)
(64, k=3)	w/ non-local	0.06 + 0.046	93.19 (93.78)
non-sp sr (12)	–	0.012	92.9 (93.5)
(8)	w/ local	0.01 + 0.005	93.05 (93.73)
(12)	w/ local	0.012 + 0.0074	93.21 (93.87)
(32)	w/ local	0.031 + 0.0184	93.22 (93.84)
(64)	w/ local	0.061 + 0.0375	93.23 (93.83)
(12, k=3)	w/ non-local	0.012 + 0.0083	93.28 (93.9)
(64, k=3)	w/ non-local	0.061 + 0.045	93.39 (93.96)

Table 7: Unlabeled accuracy scores and cpu times per sentence (parsing+reranking) when parsing and reranking test data (WSJ23) with gold POS tags: shift-reduce parser is denoted as sr (beam size, k: k-best size of cube pruning).

	sp.	non-sp.
ave. # of hyperedges	141.9	133.3
ave. # of vertices	199.1	187.6
ave. % of distinct trees	82.5	100.0
1-best UAS w/ punc.	92.5	92.6
oracle UAS w/ punc.	100.0	100.0

Table 4: Comparison of spurious (sp.) and non-spurious (non-sp.) forests: each forest is produced by baseline and proposed shift-reduce parsers using beam size 12 for 39832 training sentences with gold POS tags.

reranker	pre-comp.	training
spurious	16.4 min.	34.9 min.
non-spurious	15.5 min.	32.9 min.
spurious non-local	17.3 min.	64.3 min.
non-spurious non-local	16.2 min.	60.3 min.

Table 5: Training times on both spurious and non-spurious packed forests (beam 12): pre-comp. denotes cpu time for feature extraction and attaching features to all hyperedges. The non-local models were trained setting k-best size of cube-pruning to 5, and non-local features were calculated on-the-fly while training.

method described in Section 5.3. The 1-best accuracy of the non-spurious forests is higher than that of the spurious forests. As we expected, the results show that there are many non-unique dependency trees in the spurious forests. The spurious forests also get larger than the non-spurious forests.

Table 5 shows how long the training on spurious and non-spurious forests took on an Opteron 8356 2.3GHz. It is clear from the results that training on non-spurious forests is more efficient than that on spurious forests.

Table 6 shows the statistics of spurious and non-spurious packed forests dumped by shift-reduce parsers using beam size 12 for test data. The trends are similar to those for training data shown in Table 4. We show the results of the forest reranking algorithms for test data in Table 7. Each spurious and non-spurious shift-reduce parser produces packed forests using four beam sizes 8, 12, 32, and 64. The reranking on non-spurious forests achieves better accuracies and is slightly faster than that on spurious forests consistently.

6.3 Test with Automatic POS tags

To compare the proposed reranking system with other systems, we evaluate its parsing accuracy on test data with automatic POS tags. We used the Stanford POS tagger[6] with a model trained on sections 02-21 to tag development and test data, and used 10-way jackknifing to tag training data. The tagging accuracies on training, development, and test data were 97.1, 97.2, and 97.5.

Table 8 lists the accuracy and parsing speed of

[6] `http://nlp.stanford.edu/software/tagger.shtml`

	sp.	non-sp.
ave. # of hyperedges	127.0	119.1
ave. # of vertices	178.6	168.5
ave. % of distinct trees	82.4	100.0
1-best UAS w/ punc.	92.8	92.9
oracle UAS w/ punc.	97.0	97.0

Table 6: Comparison of spurious (sp.) and non-spurious (non-sp.) forests: each forest is produced by baseline and proposed shift-reduce parsers using beam size 12 for test data (WSJ23) with gold POS tags.

system	tok./sec.	UAS w/o punc.
sr (12)	2130	92.5
w/ local (12)	1290	92.8
non-sp sr (12)	1950	92.6
w/ local (12)	1300	92.98
w/ non-local (12, k=1)	1280	93.1
w/ non-local (12, k=3)	1180	**93.12**
w/ non-local (12, k=12)	1060	**93.12**
Huang10 sr (8)	782	92.1
Rush12 sr (16)	4780	92.5
Rush12 sr (64)	1280	92.7
Koo10	–	93.04
Rush12 third	20	93.3
Rush12 vine	4400	93.1
H-Zhang12 third	50	92.81
H-Zhang12 (label)	220	93.06
Y-Zhang11 (64, label)	680	92.9
Bohnet12 (80, label)	120	93.39

Table 8: Comparison with other systems: the results were evaluated on testing data (WSJ23) with automatic POS tags: label means labeled dependency parsing and the cpu times of our systems were taken on Intel Core i7 2.8GHz.

our proposed systems together with results from related work. The parsing times are reported in tokens/second for comparison. Note that, however, the difference of the parsing time does not represent the efficiency of the algorithm directly because each system was implemented in different programming language and the times were measured on different environments.

The accuracy of local reranking on non-spurious forests is the best among unlabeled shift-reduce parsers, but slightly behind the third-order graph-based systems (Koo and Collins, 2010; Zhang and McDonald, 2012; Rush and Petrov, 2012). It is likely that the difference comes from the fact that our local reranking model can define only some of the grand-child related features.

UAS / feature	w/ guide.	w/o guide.
UAS	**92.98**	92.86
Linear (first)	89,330	89,215
CorePos (first)	1,047,948	1,053,796
TwoObs (first)	1,303,911	1,325,990
Sibling (second)	290,291	292,849
Trip (second)	19,333	19,267
Grand-child	16,975	16,951
Guide	4,934	–
Tri-sibling	277,770	279,720
PP-Attachment	32,695	32,993
total	3,083,187	3,110,781

Table 9: Accuracy and the number of non-zero weighted features of the local reranking models with and without guide features: the first- and second-order features are named for MSTParser.

To define all grand-child features and other non-local features, we also experimented with the non-local reranking algorithm on non-spurious packed forests. It achieved almost the same accuracy as the previous third-order graph-based algorithms. Moreover, the computational overhead is very small when setting k-best size of cube-pruning small.

6.4 Analysis

One advantage of our reranking approach is that guide features can be defined as in stacked parsing. To analyze the effect of the guide features on parsing accuracy, we remove the guide features from baseline reranking models with and without non-local features used in Section 6.3. The results are shown in Table 9 and 10. The parsing accuracies of the baseline reranking models are better than those of the models without guide features though the number of guide features is not large. Additionally, each model with guide features is smaller than that without guide features. This indicates that stacking has a good effect on training the models.

To further investigate the effects of guide features, we tried to define unlabeled versions of the second-order guide features used in (Martins et al., 2008; McClosky et al., 2012). However, these features did not produce good results, and investigation to find the cause is an important future work.

We also examined parsing errors in more detail. Table 11 shows root and sentence complete rates of three systems, the non-spurious shift-reduce

UAS / feature	w/ guide.	w/o guide.
	93.12	93.04
Linear (first)	88,634	88,934
CorePos (first)	1,035,897	1,045,242
TwoObs (first)	1,274,834	1,301,103
Sibling (second)	284,341	288,796
Trip (second)	19,201	19,219
Guide	4,916	–
Tri-sibling	272,418	276,025
PP-Attachment	32,085	32,577
Grand-child	718,064	730,663
Grand-sibling	72,865	73,103
Valency	49,262	49,677
total	3,852,517	3,905,339

Table 10: Accuracy and the number of non-zero weighted features of the non-local reranking models with and without guide features: the first- and second-order features are named for MSTParser.

system	UAS	root	comp.
non-sp sr	92.6	95.8	45.6
local	92.98	96.1	48.1
non-local	**93.12**	**96.3**	**48.2**

Table 11: Unlabeled accuracy, root correct rate, and sentence complete rate: these scores are measured on test data (WSJ23) without punctuations.

parser, local reranking, and non-local reranking. The two reranking systems outperform the shift-reduce parser significantly, and the non-local reranking system is the best among them.

Part of the difference between the shift-reduce parser and reranking systems comes from the correction of coordination errors. Table 12 shows the head correct rate, recall, precision, F-measure and complete rate of coordination structures, by which we mean the head and siblings of a token whose POS tag is CC. The head correct rate denotes how correct a head of the CC token is. The recall, precision, F-measure are measured by counting arcs between the head and siblings. When the head of the CC token is incorrect, all arcs of the coordination structure are counted as incorrect. Therefore, the recall, precision, F-measure are greatly affected by the head correct rate, and though the complete rate of non-local reranking is higher than that of local reranking, the results of the first three measures are lower.

	non-sp sr	local	non-local
head correct	87.73	**88.97**	88.83
recall	82.38	**84.35**	84.11
precision	83.07	**84.57**	83.98
F-measure	82.72	**84.46**	84.05
comp.	62.92	64.52	**65.18**

Table 12: Head correct rate, recall, precision, F-measure, and complete rate of coordination strutures: these are measured on test data (WSJ23).

system	recall	precision	F-measure
non-sp sr	91.58	92.5	92.04
local	91.96	92.95	92.45
non-local	**92.44**	**93.07**	**92.75**

Table 13: Recall, precision, and F-measure of grand-child structures whose grand parent is an artificial root symbol: these are measured on test data (WSJ23).

We assume that the improvements of non-local reranking over the others can be mainly attributed to the better prediction of the structures around the sentence root because most of the non-local features are useful for predicting these structures. Table 13 shows the recall, precision and F-measure of grand-child structures whose grand parent is a sentence root symbol \$. The results support the above assumption. The root correct rate directly influences on prediction of the overall structures of a sentence, and it is likely that the reduction of root prediction errors brings better results.

6.5 Experiments on Chinese

We also experiment on the Penn Chinese Treebank (CTB5). Following Huang and Sagae (2010), we split it into training (secs 001-815 and 1001-1136), development (secs 886-931 and 1148-1151), and test (secs 816-885 and 1137-1147) sets, and use the head rules of Zhang and Clark (2008). The training set is split into 10 folds to dump packed forests for training of reranking models.

We set the beam size of both spurious and non-spurious parsers to 12, and the number of perceptron training iterations to 25 for the parsers and to 8 for both rerankers. Table 14 shows the results for the test sets. As we expected, reranking on non-spurious forests outperforms that on spurious forests.

system	UAS	root	comp.
sr (12)	85.3	78.6	33.4
w/ non-local (12, k=3)	85.8	79.4	34.2
non-sp sr (12)	85.3	78.4	33.7
w/ non-local (12, k=3)	**85.9**	**79.6**	**34.3**

Table 14: Results on Chinese Treebank data (CTB5): evaluations are performed without punctuations.

7 Related Works

7.1 How to Handle Spurious Ambiguity

The graph-based approach employs Eisner and Satta (1999)'s algorithm where spurious ambiguities are eliminated by the notion of split head automaton grammars (Alshawi, 1996).

However, the arc-standard transition-based parser has the spurious ambiguity problem. Cohen et al. (2012) proposed a method to eliminate the spurious ambiguity of shift-reduce transition systems. Their method covers existing systems such as the arc-standard and non-projective transition-based parsers (Attardi, 2006). Our system copes only with the projective case, but is simpler than theirs and we show its efficacy empirically through some experiments.

The arc-eager shift-reduce parser also has a spurious ambiguity problem. Goldberg and Nivre (2012) addressed this problem by not only training with a canonical transition sequence but also with alternate optimal transitions that are calculated dynamically for a current state.

7.2 Methods to Improve Dependency Parsing

Higher-order features like third-order dependency relations are essential to improve dependency parsing accuracy (Koo and Collins, 2010; Rush and Petrov, 2012; Zhang and McDonald, 2012). A reranking approach is one effective solution to introduce rich features to a parser model in the context of constituency parsing (Charniak and Johnson, 2005; Huang, 2008).

Hall (2007) applied a k-best maximum spanning tree algorithm to non-projective dependency analysis, and showed that k-best discriminative reranking improves parsing accuracy in several languages. Sangati et al. (2009) proposed a k-best dependency reranking algorithm using a third-order generative model, and Hayashi et al. (2011) extended it to a forest algorithm. Though forest reranking requires some approximations such as cube-pruning to integrate non-local features, it can explore larger search space than k-best reranking.

The stacking approach (Nivre and McDonald, 2008; Martins et al., 2008) uses the output of one dependency parser to provide guide features for another. Stacking improves the parsing accuracy of second stage parsers on various language datasets. The joint graph-based and transition-based approach (Zhang and Clark, 2008; Bohnet and Kuhn, 2012) uses an arc-eager shift-reduce parser with a joint graph-based and transition-based model. Though it improves parsing accuracy significantly, the large beam size of the shift-reduce parser harms its efficiency. Sagae and Lavie (2006) showed that combining the outputs of graph-based and transition-based parsers can improve parsing accuracies.

8 Conclusion

We have presented a discriminative forest reranking algorithm for dependency parsing. This can be seen as a kind of joint transition-based and graph-based approach because the first-stage parser is a shift-reduce parser and the second-stage reranker uses a graph-based model.

Additionally, we have proposed a dynamic programming arc-standard transition-based dependency parser without spurious ambiguity, along with a heuristic that encodes the correct tree in the output packed forest for reranker training, and shown that forest reranking works well on packed forests produced by the proposed parser.

To improve the accuracy of reranking, we will engage in feature engineering. We need to further investigate effective higher-order guide and non-local features. It also seems promising to extend the unlabeled reranker to a labeled one because labeled information often improves unlabeled accuracy.

In this paper, we adopt a reranking approach, but a rescoring approach is more promising to improve efficiency because it does not have the overhead of dumping packed forests.

Acknowledgments

We would like to thank the anonymous reviewers for their valuable comments. This work was partly supported by Grant-in-Aid for Japan Society for the Promotion of Science (JSPS) Research Fellowship for Young Scientists.

References

H. Alshawi. 1996. Head automata for speech translation. In *Proc. the ICSLP*.

G. Attardi. 2006. Experiments with a multilanguage non-projective dependency parser. In *Proc. of the 10th Conference on Natural Language Learning*, pages 166–170.

B. Bohnet and J. Kuhn. 2012. The best of bothworlds – a graph-based completion model for transition-based parsers. In *Proceedings of the 13th Conference of the European Chapter of the Association for Computational Linguistics*, pages 77–87.

E. Charniak and M. Johnson. 2005. Coarse-to-fine n-best parsing and maxent discriminative reranking. In *Proceedings of the 43rd Annual Meeting of the Association for Computational Linguistics*, pages 173–180.

S. B. Cohen, C. Gómez-Rodríguez, and G. Satta. 2012. Elimination of spurious ambiguity in transition-based dependency parsing. Technical report.

M. Collins and B. Roark. 2004. Incremental parsing with the perceptron algorithm. In *Proceedings of the 42nd Annual Meeting of the Association for Computational Linguistics (ACL'04)*.

J. M. Eisner and G. Satta. 1999. Efficient parsing for bilexical context-free grammars and head automaton grammars. In *Proceedings of the 37th Annual Meeting of the Association for Computational Linguistics*, pages 457–464.

J. Eisner. 1997. Bilexical grammars and a cubic-time probabilistic parser. In *Proceedings of the 5th International Workshop on Parsing Technologies (IWPT)*, pages 54–65.

Y. Goldberg and J. Nivre. 2012. A dynamic oracle for arc-eager dependency parsing. In *Proceedings of the 24rd International Conference on Computational Linguistics (Coling 2012)*.

K. Hall. 2007. K-best spanning tree parsing. In *Proceedings of the 45th Annual Meeting of the Association of Computational Linguistics*, pages 392–399.

K. Hayashi, T. Watanabe, M. Asahara, and Y. Matsumoto. 2011. The third-order variational reranking on packed-shared dependency forests. In *Proceedings of the 2011 Conference on Empirical Methods in Natural Language Processing*, pages 1479–1488.

K. Hayashi, T. Watanabe, M. Asahara, and Y. Matsumoto. 2012. Head-driven transition-based parsing with top-down prediction. In *Proceedings of the 50th Annual Meeting of the Association for Computational Linguistics*, pages 657–665.

K. Hollingshead and B. Roark. 2008. Reranking with baseline system scores and ranks as features. In *CSLU-08-001, Center for Spoken Language Understanding, Oregon Health and Science University*.

L. Huang and D. Chiang. 2007. Forest rescoring: Faster decoding with integrated language models. In *Proceedings of the 45th Annual Meeting of the Association of Computational Linguistics*, pages 144–151.

L. Huang and K. Sagae. 2010. Dynamic programming for linear-time incremental parsing. In *Proceedings of the 48th Annual Meeting of the Association for Computational Linguistics (ACL'10)*, pages 1077–1086.

L. Huang, S. Fayong, and Y. Guo. 2012. Structured perceptron with inexact search. In *Proceedings of the 2012 Conference of the North American Chapter of the Association for Computational Linguistics: Human Language Technologies*, pages 142–151.

L. Huang. 2008. Forest reranking: Discriminative parsing with non-local features. In *Proceedings of the 46th Annual Meeting of the Association for Computational Linguistics*, pages 586–594.

D. Klein and C. D. Manning. 2001. Parsing and hypergraphs. In *Proceedings of the 7th International Workshop on Parsing Technologies*.

T. Koo and M. Collins. 2010. Efficient third-order dependency parsers. In *Proceedings of the 48th Annual Meeting of the Association for Computational Linguistics (ACL'10)*, pages 1–11.

M. Kuhlmann, C. Gómez-Rodríguez, and G. Satta. 2011. Dynamic programming algorithms for transition-based dependency parsers. In *Proceedings of the 49th Annual Meeting of the Association for Computational Linguistics*, pages 673–682.

André F. T. Martins, D. Das, N. A. Smith, and E. P. Xing. 2008. Stacking dependency parsers. In *Proceedings of the 2008 Conference on Empirical Methods in Natural Language Processing*, pages 157–166.

D. McClosky, W. Che, M. Recasens, M. Wang, R. Socher, and C. D. Manning. 2012. Stanfords system for parsing the english web. In *Proceedings of First Workshop on Syntactic Analysis of Non-Canonical Language (SANCL) at NAACL 2012*.

R. McDonald, K. Crammer, and F. Pereira. 2005. Online large-margin training of dependency parsers. In *Proceedings of the 43rd Annual Meeting of the Association for Computational Linguistics (ACL'05)*, pages 91–98.

J. Nivre and R. McDonald. 2008. Integrating graph-based and transition-based dependency parsers. In *Proceedings of ACL-08: HLT*, pages 950–958.

J. Nivre. 2008. Algorithms for deterministic incremental dependency parsing. *Computational Linguistics*, 34:513–553.

F. J. Och. 2003. Minimum error rate training in statistical machine translation. In *Proc. the 41st ACL*, pages 160–167.

A. Rush and S. Petrov. 2012. Vine pruning for efficient multi-pass dependency parsing. In *Proceedings of the 2012 Conference of the North American Chapter of the Association for Computational Linguistics: Human Language Technologies*, pages 498–507.

K. Sagae and A. Lavie. 2006. Parser combination by reparsing. In *Proc. HLT*, pages 129–132.

F. Sangati, W. Zuidema, and R. Bod. 2009. A generative re-ranking model for dependency parsing. In *Proceedings of the 11th International Conference on Parsing Technologies (IWPT'09)*, pages 238–241.

S. M. Shieber, Y. Schabes, and F. C. N. Pereira. 1995. Principles and implementation of deductive parsing. *J. Log. Program.*, 24(1&2):3–36.

C. Sutton, M. Sindelar, and A. McCallum. 2006. Reducing weight undertraining in structured discriminative learning. In *Conference on Human Language Technology and North American Association for Computational Linguistics (HLT-NAACL)*.

H. Yamada and Y. Matsumoto. 2003. Statistical dependency analysis with support vector machines. In *Proceedings of the 10th International Conference on Parsing Technologies (IWPT'03)*, pages 195–206.

Y. Zhang and S. Clark. 2008. A tale of two parsers: Investigating and combining graph-based and transition-based dependency parsing using beam-search. In *Proceedings of the 2008 Conference on Empirical Methods in Natural Language Processing*, pages 562–571.

H. Zhang and R. McDonald. 2012. Generalized higher-order dependency parsing with cube pruning. In *Proceedings of the 2012 Joint Conference on Empirical Methods in Natural Language Processing and Computational Natural Language Learning*, pages 320–331.

Y. Zhang and J. Nivre. 2011. Transition-based dependency parsing with rich non-local features. In *Proceedings of the 49th Annual Meeting of the Association for Computational Linguistics: Human Language Technologies*, pages 188–193.

Dijkstra-WSA: A Graph-Based Approach to Word Sense Alignment

Michael Matuschek [‡] **and Iryna Gurevych** [†‡]
† Ubiquitous Knowledge Processing Lab (UKP-DIPF),
German Institute for Educational Research and Educational Information
Schloßstr. 29, 60486 Frankfurt, Germany
‡Ubiquitous Knowledge Processing Lab (UKP-TUDA),
Department of Computer Science, Technische Universität Darmstadt
Hochschulstr. 10, 64289 Darmstadt, Germany
http://www.ukp.tu-darmstadt.de

Abstract

In this paper, we present Dijkstra-WSA, a novel graph-based algorithm for word sense alignment. We evaluate it on four different pairs of lexical-semantic resources with different characteristics (WordNet-OmegaWiki, WordNet-Wiktionary, GermaNet-Wiktionary and WordNet-Wikipedia) and show that it achieves competitive performance on 3 out of 4 datasets. Dijkstra-WSA outperforms the state of the art on every dataset if it is combined with a back-off based on gloss similarity. We also demonstrate that Dijkstra-WSA is not only flexibly applicable to different resources but also highly parameterizable to optimize for precision or recall.

1 Introduction

Lexical-semantic resources (LSRs) are a cornerstone for many Natural Language Processing (NLP) applications such as word sense disambiguation (WSD) and information extraction. However, the growing demand for large-scale resources in different languages is hard to meet. The Princeton WordNet (WN) (Fellbaum, 1998) is widely used for English, but for most languages corresponding resources are considerably smaller or missing. Collaboratively constructed resources like Wiktionary (WKT) and OmegaWiki (OW) provide a viable option for such cases and seem especially suitable for smaller languages (Matuschek et al., 2013), but there are still considerable gaps in coverage which need to be filled. A related problem is that there usually does not exist a single resource which works best for all purposes, as different LSRs cover different words, senses and information types.

These considerations have sparked increasing research efforts in the area of word sense alignment (WSA). It has been shown that aligned resources can indeed lead to better performance than using the resources individually. Examples include semantic parsing using FrameNet (FN), WN, and VerbNet (VN) (Shi and Mihalcea, 2005), word sense disambiguation using an alignment of WN and Wikipedia (WP) (Navigli and Ponzetto, 2012) and semantic role labeling using a combination of PropBank, VN and FN in the *SemLink* project (Palmer, 2009). Some of these approaches to WSA either rely heavily on manual labor (e.g. Shi and Mihalcea (2005)) or on information which is only present in few resources such as the most frequent sense (MFS) (Suchanek et al., 2008). This makes it difficult to apply them to a larger set of resources.

In earlier work, we presented the large-scale resource UBY (Gurevych et al., 2012). It contains nine resources in two languages which are mapped to a uniform representation using the LMF standard (Eckle-Kohler et al., 2012). They are thus structurally interoperable. UBY contains pairwise sense alignments between a subset of these resources, and this work also presented a framework for creating alignments based on the similarity of glosses (Meyer and Gurevych, 2011). However, it is not clear to what extent this approach can be applied to resources which lack this kind of information (see Section 3).

In summary, aligning senses is a key requirement for semantic interoperability of LSRs to increase the coverage and effectiveness in NLP tasks. Still, existing efforts are mostly focused on specific types of resources (most often requiring glosses) or application scenarios. In this paper, we propose an approach to alleviate this and present Dijkstra-WSA, a novel, robust algorithm for word sense alignment which is applicable to a wide variety of resource pairs and languages. For the first time, we apply a graph-based algorithm which works on full graph representations of both resources to word sense alignment. This enables us to take a more abstract perspective and reduce the problem of identifying equivalent senses to the problem of matching nodes in these graphs. Also for the first time, we comparatively evaluate a WSA algorithm on a variety of different datasets with different characteristics.

The key properties of Dijkstra-WSA are:

Robustness The entities within the LSRs which are to be aligned (usually senses or synsets) are modeled as nodes in the graph. These nodes are connected by an edge if they are semantically related. While, for instance, semantic relations lend themselves very well to deriving edges, different possibilities for graph construction are equally valid as the algorithm is agnostic to the origin of the edges.

Language-independence No external resources such as corpora or other dictionaries are needed; the graph construction and alignment only rely on the information from the considered LSRs.

Flexibility The graph construction as well as the actual alignment are highly parameterizable to accommodate different requirements regarding precision or recall.

The rest of this paper is structured as follows: In Section 2 we give a precise problem description and introduce the resources covered in our experiments, in Section 3 we discuss some related work, while our graph-based algorithm Dijkstra-WSA is presented in Section 4. We describe an evaluation on four datasets with different properties, including an error analysis, in Section 5 and conclude in Section 6, pointing out directions for future work.

2 Notation and Resources

2.1 Problem Description

A *word sense alignment*, or *alignment* for short, is formally defined as a list of pairs of senses from two LSRs. A pair of aligned senses denote the same meaning. E.g., the two senses of *letter* "The conventional characters of the alphabet used to represent speech" and "A symbol in an alphabet, bookstave" (taken from WN and WKT, respectively) are clearly equivalent and should be aligned.

2.2 Evaluation Resources

For the evaluation of Dijkstra-WSA, we align four pairs of LSRs used in previous work, namely WN-OW (Gurevych et al., 2012), WN-WKT (Meyer and Gurevych, 2011), GN-WKT (Henrich et al., 2011) and WN-WP (Niemann and Gurevych, 2011). Our goal is to cover resources with different characteristics: Expert-built (WN, GN) and collaboratively constructed LSRs (WP, WKT, OW), resources in different languages (English and German) and also resources with few sense descriptions (GN) or semantic relations (WKT). We contrastively discuss the results of the Dijkstra-WSA algorithm on these different datasets and relate the results to the properties of the LSRs involved. Moreover, using existing datasets ensures comparability to previous work which discusses only one dataset at a time.

WordNet (WN) (Fellbaum, 1998) is a lexical resource for the English language created at Princeton University. The resource is organized in sets of synonymous words (synsets) which are represented by glosses (sometimes accompanied by example sentences) and organized in a hierarchy. The latest version 3.0 contains 117,659 synsets.

Wikipedia (WP) is a freely available, multilingual online encyclopedia. WP can be edited by every Web user, which causes rapid growth: By February 2013 the English WP contained over 4,000,000 article pages. Each article usually describes a distinct concept, and articles are connected by hyperlinks within the article texts.

Wiktionary (WKT) is the dictionary pendant to WP. By February 2013 the English WKT contained over 3,200,000 article pages, while the German edition contained over 200,000 ones. For each word, multiple senses can be encoded. Similar to WN, they are represented by a gloss and usage examples. There also exist hyperlinks to synonyms, hypernyms, meronyms etc. The targets of these relations are not senses, however, but merely lexemes (i.e. the relations are not disambiguated).

	LSRs	$P/R/F_1/Acc.$	Approach
Meyer and Gurevych (2011)	WN-WKT	0.67/0.65/0.66/0.91	Gloss similarity + Machine learning
Niemann and Gurevych (2011)	WN-WP	0.78/0.78/0.78/0.95	Gloss similarity + Machine learning
Henrich et al. (2011)	GN-WKT	0.84/0.85/0.84/0.94	Pseudo-gloss overlap
de Melo and Weikum (2010)	WN-WP	0.86/NA/NA/NA	Gloss/article overlap
Laparra et al. (2010)	FN-WN	0.79/0.79/0.79/NA	Dijkstra-SSI+ (WSD algorithm)
Navigli (2009)	WN	0.64/0.64/0.64/NA	Graph-based WSD of WN glosses
Ponzetto and Navigli (2009)	WN-WP	NA/NA/NA/0.81	Graph-based, only for WP categories
Navigli and Ponzetto (2012)	WN-WP	0.81/0.75/0.78/0.83	Graph-based WSA using WN relations

Table 1: Summary of various approaches to WSA. "NA" stands for "Not Available".

OmegaWiki (OW) is a freely editable online dictionary like WKT. However, there do not exist distinct language editions as OW is organized in language-independent concepts ("Defined Meanings") to which lexicalizations in various languages are attached. These can be considered as multilingual synsets, and they are interconnected by unambiguous relations just like WN. As of February 2013, OW contains over 46,000 of these concepts and lexicalizations in over 400 languages.

GermaNet (GN) is the German counterpart to WN (Hamp and Feldweg, 1997). It is also organized in synsets (around 70,000 in the latest version 7.0) which are connected via semantic relations.

3 Related Work

The are two strands of closely related work: Similarity-based and graph-based approaches to word sense alignment. To our knowledge, there exists no previous work which fully represents both LSRs involved in an alignment as graphs. We give a summary of different approaches in Table 1.

3.1 Similarity-based Approaches

Niemann and Gurevych (2011) and Meyer and Gurevych (2011) created WN-WP and WN-WKT alignments using a framework which first calculates the similarity of glosses (or glosses and articles in the case of WN-WP) using either cosine or personalized page rank (PPR) similarity (Agirre and Soroa, 2009) and then learns a threshold on the gold standard to classify each pair of senses as a (non-)valid alignment. This approach was later extended to cross-lingual alignment between the German OW and WN (Gurevych et al., 2012) using a machine translation component. However, its applicability depends on the availability and quality of the glosses, which are not present in every case (e.g. for VN). Moreover, as it involves supervised machine learning, it requires the initial effort of manually annotating a sufficient amount of training data. Henrich et al. (2011) use a similar approach for aligning GN and WKT. However, they use word overlap as a similarity measure and do not require a machine learning component as they align to the candidate sense with the highest similarity regardless of the absolute value. The alignment of WP articles and WN synsets reported by de Melo and Weikum (2010) also relies on word overlap.

Although these approaches give reasonable results (with precision in the range of 0.67-0.84), they all depend on the lexical knowledge contained in the glosses, yielding low recall if there is insufficient lexical overlap (known as the "lexical gap", see for instance (Meyer and Gurevych, 2011)). Consider these two senses of *Thessalonian* in WKT and WN: "A native or inhabitant of Thessalonica" and "Someone or something from, or pertaining to, Thessaloniki". These are (mostly) identical and should be aligned, but there is no word overlap due to the interchangeable usage of the synonyms *Thessalonica* and *Thessaloniki*.

3.2 Graph-based Approaches

Laparra et al. (2010) utilize the SSI-Dijkstra+ algorithm to align FN lexical units (LUs) with WN synsets. The basic idea is to align monosemous LUs first and, based on this, find the closest synset in WN for the other LUs in the same frame. However, as SSI-Dijkstra+ is a word sense disambiguation (not alignment) algorithm, the LUs are merely considered as texts which are to be disambiguated; there is no attempt made to build a global graph structure for FN. Moreover, the algorithm solely relies on the semantic relations found in WN and eXtended WN (Mihalcea and Moldovan, 2001). Thus, it is not applicable to other resources which have no or only few relations such as WKT.

Navigli (2009) aims at disambiguating WN glosses, i.e. assigning the correct senses to all non-stopwords in each WN gloss. His approach is to find the shortest possible circles in the WN relation graph to identify the correct disambiguation. In later work, this idea was extended to the disambiguation of translations in a bilingual dictionary (Flati and Navigli, 2012). However, there is no discussion of how this idea could be applied to word sense alignment of two or more resources. We build upon this idea of finding shortest paths (circles are a special kind of path) and extend it to multiple resources and edges other than semantic relations, in particular WP links and links to senses of monosemous lexemes appearing in glosses.

Ponzetto and Navigli (2009) propose a graph-based method to tackle the related, but slightly different problem of aligning WN synsets and WP categories (not articles). Using semantic relations, they build WN subgraphs for each WP category and then align those synsets which best match the category structure. In later work, Navigli and Ponzetto (2012) also align WN with the full WP. They build "disambiguation contexts" for the senses in both resources by using, for instance, WP redirects or WN glosses and then compute the similarity between these contexts. Again, a graph structure is built from WN semantic relations covering all possible senses in these contexts. The goal is to determine which WN sense is closest to the WP sense to be aligned. While these approaches are in some respects similar to Dijkstra-WSA, they do not take the global structure of both resources into account. Instead, they merely rely on a (locally restricted) subset of WN relations for creating the alignment. Thus, applying these approaches to resources in different languages might be difficult if WN relations are not applicable.

4 Dijkstra-WSA

In this section, we discuss our approach to aligning lexical-semantic resources based on the graph structure. This includes two steps: (i) the initial construction of the graphs using appropriate parameters, and (ii) the alignment itself.

4.1 Graph Construction

We represent the set of senses (or synsets, if applicable) of an LSR L as a set of nodes V where the set of edges $E, E \subseteq V \times V$ between these nodes represents semantic relatedness between them. We call this a *resource graph*. A WP article is considered a sense as it represents a distinct concept.

There are multiple options for deriving the edges from the resource. The most straightforward approach is to directly use the existing semantic relations (such as hyponymy), as it has been reported in previous work (Laparra et al., 2010; Navigli, 2009). For WP, we can directly use the given hyperlinks between articles as they also express a certain degree of relatedness (Milne and Witten, 2008). However, for many LSRs no or only few semantic relations exist. Consider WKT: Its relations are not sense disambiguated (Meyer and Gurevych, 2012). We thus cannot determine the correct target sense if a relation is pointing to an ambiguous word.

Our solution to this is twofold: First, for each sense s, we create an edge (s, t) for those semantic relations which have a monosemous target t, as in this case the target sense is unambiguous. This approach, however, only recovers a subset of the relations, and it is not applicable to resources where no sense relations exist at all, e.g. FN. For this case, we propose to use the glosses of senses in the LSR to derive additional edges in the following way: For each monosemous, non-stopword lexeme l (a combination of lemma and part of speech) in the gloss of a sense s_1 with a sense s_l, we introduce an edge (s_1, s_l). Moreover, if there is another sense s_2 with l in its gloss, we also introduce an edge (s_1, s_2). This technique will be called *linking of monosemous lexemes* or *monosemous linking* throughout the rest of this paper. The intuition behind this is that monosemous lexemes usually have a rather specific meaning, and thus it can be expected that the senses in whose description they appear have at least a certain degree of semantic relationship. This directly relates to the notion of "information content" (Resnik, 1995), stating that senses in an LSR which are more specific (and hence more likely to be monosemous) are more useful for evaluating semantic similarity. Note that this step requires part of speech tagging of the glosses, which we perform as a preprocessing step. Thereby we filter out stopwords and words tagged as "unknown" by the POS tagger.

As an example, consider the gloss of *Java*: "An object-oriented programming language". Even in the absence of any semantic relations, we could unambiguously derive an edge between this sense of *Java* and the multiword noun *programming language* if the latter is monosemous, i.e. if there exists exactly one sense for this lexeme in the LSR. Also, if *programming language* appears in the gloss of one of the senses of *Python*, we can derive an edge between these senses of *Java* and *Python*, expressing that they are semantically related.

An important factor to keep in mind, however, is the density of the resulting graph. In preliminary experiments, we discovered that linking every monosemous lexeme yielded very dense graphs with short paths between most senses. In turn, we decided to exclude "common" lexemes and focus on more specific ones in order to increase the graph's meaningfulness. The indicator for this is the frequency of a lexeme in the LSR, i.e. how often it occurs in the glosses. Our experiments on small development sets (100 random samples of each gold standard) indeed show that a strict filter leads to discriminative edges resulting in high precision, while at the same time graph sparsity decreases recall. Independently of the resource pair, we discovered that setting this frequency limit value ϕ to about 1/100 of the graph size (e.g. 1,000 for a graph containing 100,000 senses) gives the best balance between precision and recall; larger values of ϕ usually led to no significant improvement[1] in recall while the precision was continuously degrading. Note that WP was excluded from these experiments as the identification and linking of monosemous lexemes in all WP articles proved too time-consuming; instead, we decided to use only the already given links (see Section 5.3).

4.2 Computing Sense Alignments

Initialization After resource graphs for both LSRs A and B are created, the trivial alignments are retrieved and introduced as edges between them. Trivial alignments are those between senses which have

[1]All significance statements throughout the paper are based on McNemar's test and the confidence level of 1%.

```
Dijkstra-WSA(A,B)
ASenseSet = A.senses
BSenseSet = B.senses
UnalignableSenses = ∅

foreach sense s ∈ ASenseSet
  if(s.isMonosemous)
    t = findTrivialMatch(s, BSenseSet)
    if(t != null)
        ASenseSet.remove(s)
        BSenseSet.remove(t)
        createEdge(s,t)

foreach sense s' ∈ ASenseSet
  ASenseSet.remove(s')
  T=findCandidatesWithSameLexeme(s', B)
  if(T!= ∅)
    t'=findShortestPathToCandidates(s', T)
    if(t' != null)
        createEdge(s', t')
    else
        UnalignableSenses.put(s')
  else
    UnalignableSenses.put(s')
```

Table 2: Pseudocode of the Dijkstra-WSA algorithm.

the same attached lexeme in A and B and where this lexeme is also monosemous within either resource. E.g., if the noun phrase *programming language* is contained in either resource and has exactly one sense in each one, we can directly infer the alignment. For WP, a lexeme was considered monosemous if there was exactly one article with this title, also counting titles with a bracketed disambiguation (e.g., *Java (programming language)* and *Java (island)* are two distinct senses of *Java*). While this method does not work perfectly, we observed a precision > 0.95 for monosemous gold standard senses, which is in line with the observations by Henrich et al. (2011).

Alignment We consider each sense $s \in A$ which has not been aligned in the initialization step. For this, we first retrieve the set of possible target senses $T \subset B$ (those with matching lemma and part of speech) and compute the shortest path to each of them with Dijkstra's shortest path algorithm (Dijkstra, 1959). The candidate $t \in T$ with the shortest distance is then assigned as the alignment target, and the algorithm continues with the next still unaligned sense in A until either all senses are aligned or no path can be found for the remaining senses. The intuition behind this is that the trivial alignments from the initialization serve as "bridges" between A and B, such that a path starting from a sense s_1 in A traverses edges to find a nearby already aligned sense s_2, "jumps" to B using a cross-resource edge leading to t_2 and then ideally finds an appropriate target sense t_1 in the vicinity of t_2. Note that with each successful alignment, edges are added to the graph so that, in theory, a different ordering of the considered senses would lead to different results. While we observed slight differences for repeated runs using the same configuration, these were in no case statistically significant. The pseudo code of this algorithm can be found in Table 2, while an example can be found in Figure 1.

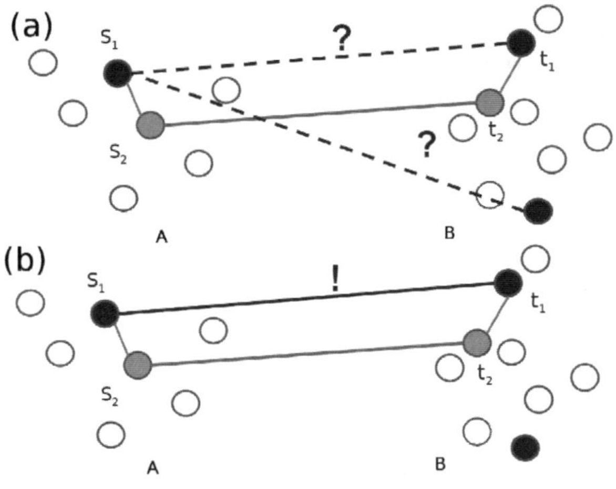

Figure 1: An example of how Dijkstra-WSA works. While there exist 2 candidates for aligning a sense $s_1 \in A$ (dashed lines) (a), the correct one $t_1 \in B$ can be determined by finding the shortest path using an already established edge between two monosemous senses $s_2 \in A$ and $t_2 \in B$ (solid line) (b).

Parameter Influence Apart from the already mentioned parameter ϕ for limiting the number of edges in the graph, another important variable is the maximum allowed path length λ of Dijkstra's algorithm. In general, allowing an unbounded search for the candidate senses is undesirable as long paths, while increasing recall, usually also lead to a decrease in precision, as the nodes which can be reached in many steps are usually also semantically distant from the source sense. In this respect, we found significant differences between the optimal configuration for individual resource pairs. However, the general observation is that short paths ($\lambda \leq 3$) lead to a very high precision, while paths longer than 10 do not increase recall significantly any more.

A modification of the algorithm is to not only align the closest target sense, but all senses which can be reached with a certain number of steps. This caters to the fact that, due to different sense granularities, one coarser sense in A can be represented by several senses in B and vice versa (see Table 3 for the fraction of 1:n alignments in the datasets). Regarding this modification, we made the observation that the recall improved (sometimes considerably), but at the same time the precision decreased, sometimes to an extent where the overall F-Measure (the harmonic mean of precision and recall) got worse. In the evaluation section, we state which setting is used for which datasets and configurations.

5 Experimental Work

5.1 Datasets and their Characteristics

WN 3.0-English OW The previous alignment between these two resources reported in Gurevych et al. (2012) is based on the German OW (database dump from 2010/01/03) and WN 3.0 and utilizes gloss similarities using machine translation as an intermediate component. This does not pose a problem since for each synset in the German part of OW, there is a translation in the English part. This makes the German-English gold standard directly usable for our purposes.[2] Table 3 presents the details about this as well as the other evaluation datasets, including the observed inter-rater agreement A_O (where available) which can be considered as an upper bound for automatic alignment accuracy and the degree of polysemy (i.e. the number of possible alignment targets per sense) which is a hint towards the difficulty of the alignment task.

WN 3.0-English WKT We use the gold standard dataset from Meyer and Gurevych (2011) without any modification, thus for comparability to this

[2]Cross-lingual alignment is left to future work.

work, we use the same WKT dump version (from 2010/02/01) which contains around 421,000 senses.

GN 7.0-German WKT Henrich et al. (2011) aligned the German WKT (dump from 2011/04/02, 72,000 senses) and GN 7.0. This is the only existing alignment between these two resources so far, and we use their freely available dataset[3] to test Dijkstra-WSA on a language other than English. As this alignment is fairly large (see Table 3), we created a random sample as a gold standard to keep the computation time at bay. However, the datasets are still similar enough to allow direct comparison of the results. Note that no inter-annotator agreement is available for this study.

WN 3.0-English WP We use the gold standard from Niemann and Gurevych (2011). For comparability, we use the same Wikipeda dump version (from 2009/08/22) with around 2,921,000 articles.

5.2 Baselines

WN-OW We used the same configuration as in Gurevych et al. (2012) to calculate a similarity-based alignment for the monolingual case (i.e. without the translation step) as a baseline and achieved comparable results.

WN-WKT As stated above, the alignment[4] presented in Meyer and Gurevych (2011) was created by calculating the similarity of glosses and training a machine-learning classifier on the gold standard to classify each pair of senses.

GN-WKT The automatic alignment results (i.e. the outcome of the algorithm without manual post-correction) reported by Henrich et al. (2011) were unavailable for us as a baseline. Thus, we utilize the alignment approach by Meyer and Gurevych (2011) to create a similarity-based baseline, with minor modifications. Unlike the original approach, we directly align senses regardless of their similarity if the decision is trivial (see Section 4.2). We also do not train a machine learning component on a gold standard. Instead, we adapt the idea of Henrich et al. (2011) to align the most similar candidate regardless of the absolute value.

WN-WP The alignment reported in Niemann and Gurevych (2011) was created in the same way as the WN-WKT alignment described in Meyer and Gurevych (2011). Note that while the full alignment results[5] proved incomplete, the correct alignment results on the gold standard were available and thus used in our experiments.

We will henceforth mark these similarity-based results with *SB*.

5.3 System Configurations

For the construction of the resource graphs we experimented with three options:

Semantic relations only (SR) OW, WN and GN all feature disambiguated sense relations which can be directly used as edges between senses. Note that in the expert-built resources, the majority of nodes are connected by sense relations, while this is not the case for OW. For WKT, only the unambiguous semantic relations can be used (see Section 4.1), resulting in graphs less dense and with many isolated nodes. However, as we reported in Matuschek et al. (2013), the English WKT is almost 6 times as large as the German one for the versions we used in our experiments (421,000 senses vs. 72,000 senses), while it contains not even twice as many relations (720,000 vs. 430,000). This is directly reflected in the fewer isolated nodes for the German WKT. WP links are also unambiguous as they lead to a distinct article. However, intuitively not all links in an article are equally meaningful. Thus, for the SR configuration, we decided to retain only the category links and the links within the first paragraph of the article. We assume that the targets of these links are most closely related to the sense an article represents as the first paragraph usually includes a concise definition of a concept, and the category links allow determining the topic an article belongs to.

Linking of monosemous lexemes only (LM) For this configuration, the limiting parameter ϕ was set to 1/100 of the graph size for every resource except WP as described in section 4.1. As our experiments show, linking the monosemous lexemes in the glosses while disregarding semantic relations results in well-connected graphs for all resources but GN and WKT. Only about 10% of the GN senses have a gloss, thus this option was completely disre-

[3] http://www.sfs.uni-tuebingen.de/GermaNet/wiktionary.shtml

[4] Available at http://www.ukp.tu-darmstadt.de/data/lexical-resources/wordnet-wiktionary-alignment/

[5] Available at http://www.ukp.tu-darmstadt.de/data/lexical-resources/wordnet-wikipedia-alignment/

Pair	Aligned	Not Aligned	Sum	1:n Alignments %	Polysemy	Sampling	A_0
WN-OW	210	473	683	10.7%	1.50	Random	0.85
WN-WKT	313	2,110	2,423	2.7%	4.76	Balanced	0.93
GN-WKT (full)	27,127	18,509	45,636	5.6%	1.78	All	N/A
GN-WKT (sample)	1,000	751	1,751	4.8%	1.84	Random	N/A
WN-WP	227	1,588	1,815	5.2%	5.7	Balanced	0.97

Table 3: Characteristics of the gold standards used in the evaluation. A_0 is the observed inter-rater agreement which can be considered as an upper bound for alignment accuracy. The degree of polysemy (i.e. the number of possible alignment targets per sense) hints towards the difficulty of the alignment task.

garded in this case. For both WKTs, an analysis of the graphs revealed that the reason for the relatively high number of isolated nodes are very short glosses, containing many polysemous lexemes. For WP, we refrained from monosemous linking due to the prohibitive computation time. Instead, we decided to use the fully linked WP (excluding the links used for the SR configuration) in this case. The rationale is that in the majority of articles many meaningful terms link to the corresponding articles anyway, so that the resulting graph is comparable with those for the other LSRs.

Combining both (SR+LM) This configuration yields the maximum number of available edges. We report the results for GN only for this configuration and omit the SR results for the sake of brevity as the influence on the F-Measure for the GN-WKT alignment (see Section 5.4) is not statistically significant. For WKT, this configuration only increases the number of connected nodes slightly (as insufficient glosses often coincide with missing semantic relations), while for OW an almost connected graph can be constructed.

Table 4 gives an overview of the fraction of isolated nodes for each resource in every configuration.

Note again that for each alignment task (i.e. each pair of resources), we tuned the parameters on 100 random samples from each gold standard for a result balancing precision and recall as discussed above. Individual tuning of parameters was necessary for each pair due to the greatly varying properties of the LSRs (e.g. the number of senses). While it would have been ideal to train and test on disjoint sets, we calculated the overall results on the full gold standards including the development sets to ensure comparability with the previous work.

Hybrid Approach Manual inspection of the results revealed that the alignments found by Dijkstra-WSA are usually different from those based on the gloss similarity. While the latter precisely recognizes alignments with similar wording of glosses, Dijkstra-WSA is advantageous if the glosses are different but the senses are still semantically close in the graph. Section 5.5 will analyze this in greater detail. Exploiting this fact, we experimented with a hybrid approach: We perform an alignment using Dijkstra-WSA, tuned for high precision (i.e. using shorter path lengths) and fall back to using the results of the similarity-based approaches for those cases where no alignment target could be found in the graph. These results are marked with *+SB* in the result overview (Table 5).

Resource	SR	LM	SR+LM
WN	0.25	0.07	0.02
GN	0.0	0.92	0.0
WKT-en	0.98	0.32	0.30
WKT-de	0.69	0.18	0.15
OW	0.41	0.33	0.04
WP	0.06	0.05	0.04

Table 4: This table describes what percentage of nodes remains isolated (i.e. with 0 attached edges) in different graph configurations using semantic relations (SR), monosemous linking (LM) ($\phi = 1/100$) or both (SR+LM). Note that this number is highest for the English WKT as the few semantic relations and short glosses do not offer many possibilities for connecting nodes, while the German WKT and OW do not suffer from this problem as much. GN is fully linked via relations, but has only few glosses which makes monosemous linking ineffective. WN and WP are relatively well-linked in all configurations. Also note that for WP, SR means that we used category links and links from the first paragraph, while links from the rest of the article were used for the LM configuration.

	WordNet-OmegaWiki				WordNet-Wiktionary				GermaNet-Wiktionary				WordNet-Wikipedia			
	P	R	F_1	$Acc.$	P	R	F_1	$Acc.$	P	R	F_1	$Acc.$	P	R	F_1	$Acc.$
Random	0.46	0.35	0.40	0.51	0.21	0.59	0.31	0.67	0.44	0.51	0.47	0.54	0.49	0.62	0.53	0.86
SB	0.55	0.53	0.54	0.73	0.67	0.65	0.66	0.91	0.93	0.74	0.83	0.83	0.78	0.78	0.78	**0.95**
SR	**0.66**	0.45	0.53	0.76	**0.95**	0.13	0.23	0.89	**0.94**	0.65	0.77	0.78	**0.82**	0.63	0.71	0.93
LM	0.62	0.54	0.58	**0.77**	0.72	0.24	0.36	0.89	0.89	0.75	0.81	0.80	0.65	0.66	0.65	0.91
SR+LM	0.56	0.69	0.62	0.74	0.68	0.27	0.39	0.89	0.90	0.78	0.83	0.82	0.75	0.67	0.71	0.93
SR+SB	0.60	0.65	0.63	0.76	0.68	0.67	0.68	0.92	0.90	0.82	0.86	0.84	0.75	**0.87**	**0.81**	**0.95**
LM+SB	0.60	0.70	0.64	0.76	0.68	0.70	**0.69**	**0.92**	0.86	0.87	**0.87**	**0.85**	0.70	**0.87**	0.78	0.94
SR+LM+SB	0.57	**0.75**	**0.65**	0.75	0.68	**0.71**	**0.69**	**0.92**	0.87	**0.88**	**0.87**	**0.85**	0.75	**0.87**	**0.81**	**0.95**
A_0	-	-	-	0.85	-	-	-	0.93	-	-	-	N/A	-	-	-	0.97

Table 5: Alignment results for all datasets and configurations: Using semantic relations (SR), monosemous links (LM) or both (SR+LM). The similarity-based (SB) baselines, also used as a back-off for the hybrid approaches (+SB), were created using the approach reported in Gurevych et al. (2012). Note that for GN, the SR+LM configuration was always used. The different configurations given for this alignment thus only apply to WKT. For WP, SR means that only category links and links within the first paragraph were used, while LM uses links from the full article. A random baseline and the inter-annotator agreement A_0 of the gold standard annotation (if available) are given for reference.

5.4 Experimental Results

WN-OW When using only semantic relations (SR), we achieved an F-Measure of 0.53 which is comparable with the 0.54 from Gurevych et al. (2012). Notably, our approach has a high precision, while the recall is considerably worse due to the relative sparsity of the resulting OW resource graph. When adding more edges to the graph by linking monosemous lexemes (SR+LM), we can drastically improve the recall, leading to an overall F-Measure of 0.62, which is a significant improvement over our previous results (Gurevych et al., 2012). Using monosemous links only (LM), the result of 0.58 still outperforms Gurevych et al. (2012) due to the higher precision. Building a graph from glosses alone is thus a viable approach if no or only few semantic relations are available. Regarding the path lengths, $\lambda = 10$ works best when semantic relations are included in the graph, while for the LM configuration shorter paths ($\lambda \leq 5$) were more appropriate. The intuition behind this is that for semantic relations, unlike monosemous links, even longer paths still express a high degree of semantic relatedness. Also, when semantic relations are involved allowing multiple alignments increases the overall results (which is in line with the relatively high number of 1:n alignments in the gold standard), while this is not the case for the LM configuration; here, the edges again do not sufficiently express relatedness.

Using the hybrid approach (+SB), we can increase the F-Measure up to 0.65 if semantic relations and monosemous linking are combined (SR+LM) and the parameters are tuned for high precision ($\lambda \leq 3$, 1:1 alignments). This is significantly better than Dijkstra-WSA alone in any configuration. In this scenario, we also observe the best overall recall.

WN-WKT Experiments using only the semantic relations (SR) yield a very low recall - the small number of sense relations with monosemous targets in WKT leaves the graph very sparse. Nevertheless, the alignment targets which Dijkstra-WSA finds are mostly correct, with a precision greater than 0.95 even when allowing 1:n alignments. Using only monosemous links (LM) improves the recall considerably, but unlike the WN-OW alignment, it stays fairly low. Consequently, even when using semantic relations and monosemous links in conjunction (SR+LM), the recall can only be increased slightly, leading to an overall F-Measure of 0.39. As mentioned above, this is due to the WKT glosses. In many cases, they are very short, often consisting of only 3-5 words, many of which are polysemous. This leads to many isolated nodes in the graph with no or only very few connecting edges. The ideal, rather short path length λ of 2-3 stems from the relatively high polysemy of the gold standard (see Table 3). We experimented with $\lambda \geq 4$, achieving reasonable recall, but in this case the precision was so low that this configuration, in conclusion, does not increase the F-Measure. However, 1:n alignments work well with these short paths as the correct alignments are mostly in the close vicinity of a sense, hence we achieve an increase in recall in this case without too much loss of precision.

For the hybrid approach, we achieve an F-Measure of 0.69 when using all edges (SR+LM+SB), setting the path length to 2, and also allowing 1:n alignments. This is a statistically significant improvement over Meyer and Gurevych (2011) which again confirms the effectiveness of the hybrid approach.

GN-WKT As stated above, we used the SR+LM configuration for GN in every case. For the German WKT, the much greater number of relations compared to its English counterpart is directly reflected in the results, as using the semantic relations only (SR) not only yields the best precision of 0.94 but also a good recall of 0.65. Using the semantic relations together with monosemous links (SR+LM) yields the F-Measure of 0.83, which is on par with the similarity-based (SB) approach.

In the hybrid configuration, we can increase the performance to an F-Measure of up to 0.87 (SR+LM+SB), significantly outperforming all graph-based and similarity-based configurations.

In general, results for this pair of LSRs are higher in comparison with the others. We attribute this to the fact that the German WKT and GN both are densely linked with semantic relations which is especially beneficial for the recall of Dijkstra-WSA. This is also reflected in the ideal λ of 10-12: Many high-confidence edges allow long paths which still express a considerable degree of relatedness. However, while the results for 1:n alignments are already good, restricting oneself to 1:1 alignments gives the best overall results as the precision can then be pushed towards 0.90 without hurting recall too much. An important factor in this respect is that the GN-WKT dataset has a relatively low degree of polysemy (compared to WN-WKT) and only few 1:n alignments (compared to WN-OW), two facts which make the task significantly easier.

WN-WP The SR configuration (WN relations + WP category/first paragraph links) yields the best precision (0.82), even outperforming the SB approach, and an F-Measure of 0.71. This again shows that using an appropriate parametrization ($\lambda \leq 4$ in this case) Dijkstra-WSA can detect alignments with high confidence. The relatively low recall of 0.63 could be increased by allowing longer paths, however, as hyperlinks do not express relatedness as reliably as semantic relations, this introduces many false positives and thus hurts precision considerably. This issue of "misleading" WP links becomes even more prominent when the links from the full articles are used as edges (LM); while the increase in recall is relatively small the precision drops substantially. However, using all possible links (SR+LM) allows us to balance out precision and recall to some extent, while yielding the same F-Measure as the SR configuration. Note that 1:1 alignments were enforced in any case, as the high polysemy of the dataset in conjunction with the dense WP link structure rendered 1:n alignments very imprecise.

Using the hybrid approach, we can increase the F-Measure up to 0.81 (SR+SB), outperforming the results reported in Niemann and Gurevych (2011) by a significant margin. The F-Measure for LM+SB is slightly worse due to the lower precision. Combining all edges (SR+LM+SB) does not influence the results any more, but in any case the hybrid configuration achieves the best overall recall (0.87).

In conclusion, our experiments on all four datasets consistently demonstrate that combining Dijkstra-WSA with a similarity-based approach as a back-off yields the strongest performance. The results of these best alignments will be made freely available to the research community on our website (http://www.ukp.tu-darmstadt.de).

5.5 Error Analyis

The by far most significant error source, reflected in the relatively low recall for different configurations, is the high number of false negatives, i.e. sense pairs which were not aligned although they should have been. This is especially striking for the WN-WKT alignment. As discussed earlier, WKT contains a significant number of short glosses, which in many cases also contain few or no monosemous terms. A prototypical example is the first sense of *seedling*: "A young plant grown from seed". This gloss has no monosemous words which could be linked, and as there are also no semantic relations attached to this sense which could be exploited, the node is isolated in the graph. Our experiments show that for the English WKT, even when optimizing the parameters for recall, around 30% of the senses remain isolated, i.e. without edges. This is by far the highest value across all resources (see Table 4). Solving this problem would require making the graph more dense, and especially finding ways to include isolated nodes as well. However, this example also shows why the hybrid approach works so well: The correct WN sense "young plant or tree grown from a seed" was recognized by the similarity-based approach with high confidence.

With regard to false positives, Dijkstra-WSA and the similarity-based approaches display very similar performance. This is because senses with very similar wording are likely to share the same monosemous words, leading to a close vicinity in the graph and the false alignment. As an example, consider two senses of *bowdlerization* in WN ("written material that has been bowdlerized") and WKT ("The action or instance of bowdlerizing; the omission or removal of material considered vulgar or indecent."). While these senses are clearly related, they are not identical and should not be aligned, nevertheless the similar wording (and especially the use of the highly specific verb "bowdlerize") results in an alignment. Similarly to the similarity-based approaches, it is an open question how this kind of error can be effectively avoided (Meyer and Gurevych, 2011).

There is a considerable number of examples where Dijkstra-WSA recognizes an alignment which similarity-based approaches do not. The two senses of *Thessalonian* from the introductory example (Section 3) contain the terms *Thessalonica* and *Thessaloniki* in their glosses which are both monosemous in WN as well as in WKT, sharing the also monosemous noun *Greece* in their glosses. This yields the bridge between the resources to find a path and correctly derive the alignment.

6 Conclusions and Future Work

In this work, we present Dijkstra-WSA, a graph-based algorithm for word sense alignment. We show that this algorithm performs competitively on 3 out of 4 evaluation datasets. A hybrid approach leads to a statistically significant improvement over similarity-based state of the art results on every dataset. Dijkstra-WSA can operate on glosses or semantic relations alone (although it is beneficial if both are combined), and it does not require any external knowledge in the form of annotated training data or corpora. Additionally, it is flexibly configurable for different pairs of LSRs in order to optimize for precision or recall.

An important task for future work is to evaluate Dijkstra-WSA on LSRs which structurally differ from the ones discussed here. It is important to determine how resources like FN or VN can be meaningfully transformed into a graph representation. Another idea is to extend the approach to cross-lingual resource alignment, which would require a machine translation component to identify sense alignment candidates with the correct lexeme.

Regarding the algorithm itself, the main direction for future work is to increase recall while keeping high precision. One possible way would be to not only link monosemous lexemes, but also to create edges for polysemous ones. Laparra et al. (2010) discuss a possibility to do this with high precision. The main idea is to focus on lexemes with a low degree of polysemy and align if one of the possible senses is clearly more similar to the source sense than the other(s). If recall is still low, more polysemous lexemes can be examined.

A weighting of edges (e.g. based on gloss similarities) has not been considered at all, but would be easily applicable to the existing framework.

A more elaborate idea would be to investigate entirely different graph-based algorithms, e.g. for matching nodes in bipartite graphs. Also, we plan to investigate if and how our approach can be extended to align more than two resources at once using the graph representations. This might improve alignment results as more information about the overall alignment topology becomes available.

Acknowledgements

This work has been supported by the Volkswagen Foundation as part of the Lichtenberg Professorship Program under grant No. I/82806 and by the Hessian research excellence program "Landes-Offensive zur Entwicklung Wissenschaftlich-ökonomischer Exzellenz (LOEWE)" as part of the research center "Digital Humanities". We would like to thank Christian M. Meyer, Wolfgang Stille, Karsten Weihe and Tristan Miller for insightful discussions and comments. We also thank the anonymous reviewers for their helpful remarks.

References

Eneko Agirre and Aitor Soroa. 2009. Personalizing PageRank for Word Sense Disambiguation. In *Proceedings of the 12th Conference of the European Chapter of the Association for Computational Linguistics*, pages 33–41, Athens, Greece.

Gerard de Melo and Gerhard Weikum. 2010. Providing Multilingual, Multimodal Answers to Lexical Database Queries. In *Proceedings of the 7th Language Resources and Evaluation Conference (LREC 2010)*, pages 348–355, Valetta, Malta.

Edsger. W. Dijkstra. 1959. A note on two problems in connexion with graphs. *Numerische Mathematik*, 1:269–271. 10.1007/BF01386390.

Judith Eckle-Kohler, Iryna Gurevych, Silvana Hartmann, Michael Matuschek, and Christian M. Meyer. 2012. UBY-LMF - A Uniform Model for Standardizing Heterogeneous Lexical-Semantic Resources in ISO-LMF. In *Proceedings of the 8th International Conference on Language Resources and Evaluation (LREC'12)*, pages 275–282, Istanbul, Turkey.

Christiane Fellbaum. 1998. *WordNet: An Electronic Lexical Database*. MIT Press.

Tiziano Flati and Roberto Navigli. 2012. The CQC algorithm: Cycling in graphs to semantically enrich and enhance a bilingual dictionary. *Journal of Artificial Intelligence Research (JAIR)*, 43:135–171.

Iryna Gurevych, Judith Eckle-Kohler, Silvana Hartmann, Michael Matuschek, Christian M. Meyer, and Christian Wirth. 2012. UBY - A Large-Scale Unified Lexical-Semantic Resource Based on LMF. In *Proceedings of the 13th Conference of the European Chapter of the Association for Computational Linguistics (EACL'12)*, pages 580–590, Avignon, France.

Birgit Hamp and Helmut Feldweg. 1997. Germanet - a lexical-semantic net for german. In *In Proceedings of ACL workshop Automatic Information Extraction and Building of Lexical Semantic Resources for NLP Applications*, pages 9–15.

Verena Henrich, Erhard Hinrichs, and Tatiana Vodolazova. 2011. Semi-Automatic Extension of GermaNet with Sense Definitions from Wiktionary. In *Proceedings of the 5th Language and Technology Conference (LTC 2011)*, pages 126–130, Poznan, Poland.

Egoitz Laparra, German Rigau, and Montse Cuadros. 2010. Exploring the integration of WordNet and FrameNet. In *Proceedings of the 5th Global WordNet Conference (GWC'10)*, Mumbai, India.

Michael Matuschek, Christian M. Meyer, and Iryna Gurevych. 2013. Multilingual Knowledge in Aligned Wiktionary and OmegaWiki for Computer-Aided Translation. *Translation: Computation, Corpora, Cognition. Special Issue on "Language Technology for a Multilingual Europe"*, to appear.

Christian M. Meyer and Iryna Gurevych. 2011. What Psycholinguists Know About Chemistry: Aligning Wiktionary and WordNet for Increased Domain Coverage. In *Proceedings of the 5th International Joint Conference on Natural Language Processing (IJCNLP)*, pages 883–892, Chiang Mai, Thailand.

Christian M. Meyer and Iryna Gurevych. 2012. Wiktionary: A new rival for expert-built lexicons? Exploring the possibilities of collaborative lexicography. In Sylviane Granger and Magali Paquot, editors, *Electronic Lexicography*, chapter 13, pages 259–291. Oxford University Press.

Rada Mihalcea and Dan I. Moldovan. 2001. eXtended WordNet: progress report. In *Proceedings of NAACL Workshop on WordNet and Other Lexical Resources*, pages 95–100, Pittsburgh, PA, USA.

David Milne and Ian H. Witten. 2008. An effective, low-cost measure of semantic relatedness obtained from Wikipedia links. In *Proceedings of the AAAI Workshop on Wikipedia and Artificial Intelligence: an Evolving Synergy*, pages 25–30, Chicago, IL, USA.

Roberto Navigli and Simone Paolo Ponzetto. 2012. BabelNet: The automatic construction, evaluation and application of a wide-coverage multilingual semantic network. *Artificial Intelligence*, 193:217–250.

Roberto Navigli. 2009. Using Cycles and Quasi-Cycles to Disambiguate Dictionary Glosses. In *Proceedings of the 12th Conference of the European Chapter of the Association for Computational Linguistics (EACL'09)*, pages 594–602, Athens, Greece.

Elisabeth Niemann and Iryna Gurevych. 2011. The People's Web meets Linguistic Knowledge: Automatic Sense Alignment of Wikipedia and WordNet. In *Proceedings of the 9th International Conference on Computational Semantics (IWCS)*, pages 205–214, Oxford, UK.

Martha Palmer. 2009. SemLink: Linking PropBank, VerbNet and FrameNet. In *Proceedings of the Generative Lexicon ConferenceGenLex-09*, pages 9–15, Pisa, Italy.

Simone Paolo Ponzetto and Roberto Navigli. 2009. Large-scale taxonomy mapping for restructuring and integrating Wikipedia. In *Proceedings of the* 21st *International Joint Conference on Artificial Intelligence*, pages 2083–2088, Pasadena, CA, USA.

Philip Resnik. 1995. Using Information Content to Evaluate Semantic Similarity in a Taxonomy. In *International Joint Conference for Artificial Intelligence (IJCAI-95)*, pages 448–453, Montreal, Canada.

Lei Shi and Rada Mihalcea. 2005. Putting Pieces Together: Combining FrameNet, VerbNet and WordNet for Robust Semantic Parsing. In *Computational Linguistics and Intelligent Text Processing: 6th International Conference*, volume 3406 of *Lecture Notes in*

Computer Science, pages 100–111. Berlin/Heidelberg: Springer.

Fabian M. Suchanek, Gjergji Kasneci, and Gerhard Weikum. 2008. YAGO: A Large Ontology from Wikipedia and WordNet. *Web Semantics*, 6(3):203–217.

Learning to translate with products of novices: a suite of open-ended challenge problems for teaching MT

Adam Lopez[1], Matt Post[1], Chris Callison-Burch[1,2], Jonathan Weese, Juri Ganitkevitch, Narges Ahmidi, Olivia Buzek, Leah Hanson, Beenish Jamil, Matthias Lee, Ya-Ting Lin, Henry Pao, Fatima Rivera, Leili Shahriyari, Debu Sinha, Adam Teichert, Stephen Wampler, Michael Weinberger, Daguang Xu, Lin Yang, and **Shang Zhao***
Department of Computer Science, Johns Hopkins University
[1]Human Language Technology Center of Excellence, Johns Hopkins University
[2]Computer and Information Science Department, University of Pennsylvania

Abstract

Machine translation (MT) draws from several different disciplines, making it a complex subject to teach. There are excellent pedagogical texts, but problems in MT and current algorithms for solving them are best learned by doing. As a centerpiece of our MT course, we devised a series of open-ended challenges for students in which the goal was to improve performance on carefully constrained instances of four key MT tasks: alignment, decoding, evaluation, and reranking. Students brought a diverse set of techniques to the problems, including some novel solutions which performed remarkably well. A surprising and exciting outcome was that student solutions or their combinations fared competitively on some tasks, demonstrating that even newcomers to the field can help improve the state-of-the-art on hard NLP problems while simultaneously learning a great deal. The problems, baseline code, and results are freely available.

1 Introduction

A decade ago, students interested in natural language processing arrived at universities having been exposed to the idea of machine translation (MT) primarily through science fiction. Today, incoming students have been exposed to services like Google Translate since they were in secondary school or earlier. For them, MT is science fact. So it makes sense to teach statistical MT, either on its own or as a unit in a class on natural language processing (NLP), machine learning (ML), or artificial intelligence (AI). A course that promises to show students how Google Translate works and teach them how to build something like it is especially appealing, and several universities and summer schools now offer such classes. There are excellent introductory texts—depending on the level of detail required, instructors can choose from a comprehensive MT textbook (Koehn, 2010), a chapter of a popular NLP textbook (Jurafsky and Martin, 2009), a tutorial survey (Lopez, 2008), or an intuitive tutorial on the IBM Models (Knight, 1999b), among many others.

But MT is not just an object of academic study. It's a real application that isn't fully perfected, and the best way to learn about it is to build an MT system. This can be done with open-source toolkits such as Moses (Koehn et al., 2007), cdec (Dyer et al., 2010), or Joshua (Ganitkevitch et al., 2012), but these systems are not designed for pedagogy. They are mature codebases featuring tens of thousands of source code lines, making it difficult to focus on their core algorithms. Most tutorials present them as black boxes. But our goal is for students to learn the key techniques in MT, and ideally to **learn by doing**. Black boxes are incompatible with this goal.

We solve this dilemma by presenting students with concise, fully-functioning, self-contained components of a statistical MT system: word alignment, decoding, evaluation, and reranking. Each implementation consists of a naïve baseline algorithm in less than 150 lines of Python code. We assign them to students as open-ended challenges in which the goal is to improve performance on objective evaluation metrics as much as possible. This setting mirrors evaluations conducted by the NLP research

* The first five authors were instructors and the remaining authors were students in the worked described here. This research was conducted while Chris Callison-Burch was at Johns Hopkins University.

community and by the engineering teams behind high-profile NLP projects such as Google Translate and IBM's Watson. While we designate specific algorithms as benchmarks for each task, we encourage creativity by awarding more points for the best systems. As additional incentive, we provide a web-based leaderboard to display standings in real time.

In our graduate class on MT, students took a variety of different approaches to the tasks, in some cases devising novel algorithms. A more exciting result is that some student systems or combinations of systems rivaled the state of the art on some datasets.

2 Designing MT Challenge Problems

Our goal was for students to freely experiment with different ways of solving MT problems on real data, and our approach consisted of two separable components. First, we provided a framework that strips key MT problems down to their essence so students could focus on understanding classic algorithms or invent new ones. Second, we designed incentives that motivated them to improve their solutions as much as possible, encouraging experimentation with approaches beyond what we taught in class.

2.1 Decoding, Reranking, Evaluation, and Alignment for MT (DREAMT)

We designed four assignments, each corresponding to a real subproblem in MT: alignment, decoding, evaluation, and reranking.[1] From the more general perspective of AI, they emphasize the key problems of unsupervised learning, search, evaluation design, and supervised learning, respectively. In real MT systems, these problems are highly interdependent, a point we emphasized in class and at the end of each assignment—for example, that alignment is an exercise in parameter estimation for translation models, that model choice is a tradeoff between expressivity and efficient inference, and that optimal search does not guarantee optimal accuracy. However, presenting each problem independently and holding all else constant enables more focused exploration.

For each problem we provided data, a naïve solution, and an evaluation program. Following Bird et al. (2008) and Madnani and Dorr (2008), we implemented the challenges in Python, a high-level programming language that can be used to write very concise programs resembling pseudocode.[2,3] By default, each baseline system reads the test data and generates output in the evaluation format, so setup required zero configuration, and students could begin experimenting immediately. For example, on receipt of the alignment code, aligning data and evaluating results required only typing:

```
> align | grade
```

Students could then run experiments within minutes of beginning the assignment.

Three of the four challenges also included unlabeled test data (except the decoding assignment, as explained in §4). We evaluated test results against a hidden key when assignments were submitted.

2.2 Incentive Design

We wanted to balance several pedagogical goals: understanding of classic algorithms, free exploration of alternatives, experience with typical experimental design, and unhindered collaboration.

Machine translation is far from solved, so we expected more than reimplementation of prescribed algorithms; we wanted students to really explore the problems. To motivate exploration, we made the assignments competitive. Competition is a powerful force, but must be applied with care in an educational setting.[4] We did not want the consequences of ambitious but failed experiments to be too dire, and we did not want to discourage collaboration.

For each assignment, we guaranteed a passing grade for matching the performance of a specific target algorithm. Typically, the target was important but not state-of-the-art: we left substantial room for improvement, and thus competition. We told students the exact algorithm that produced the target accuracy (though we expected them to derive it themselves based on lectures, notes, or literature). We did not specifically require them to implement it, but the guarantee of a passing grade provided a powerful incentive for this to be the first step of each assignment. Submissions that beat this target received additional credit. The top five submissions received full credit, while the top three received extra credit.

[1] http://alopez.github.io/dreamt

[2] http://python.org

[3] Some well-known MT systems have been implemented in Python (Chiang, 2007; Huang and Chiang, 2007).

[4] Thanks to an anonymous reviewer for this turn of phrase.

This scheme provided strong incentive to continue experimentation beyond the target algorithm.[5]

For each assignment, students could form teams of any size, under three rules: each team had to publicize its formation to the class, all team members agreed to receive the same grade, and teams could not drop members. Our hope was that these requirements would balance the perceived competitive advantage of collaboration against a reluctance to take (and thus support) teammates who did not contribute to the competitive effort.[6] This strategy worked: out of sixteen students, ten opted to work collaboratively on at least one assignment, always in pairs.

We provided a web-based leaderboard that displayed standings on the test data in real time, identifying each submission by a pseudonymous handle known only to the team and instructors. Teams could upload solutions as often as they liked before the assignment deadline. The leaderboard displayed scores of the default and target algorithms. This incentivized an early start, since teams could verify for themselves when they met the threshold for a passing grade. Though effective, it also detracted from realism in one important way: it enabled hill-climbing on the evaluation metric. In early assignments, we observed a few cases of this behavior, so for the remaining assignments, we modified the leaderboard so that changes in score would only be reflected once every twelve hours. This strategy trades some amount of scientific realism for some measure of incentive, a strategy that has proven effective in other pedagogical tools with real-time feedback (Spacco et al., 2006).

To obtain a grade, teams were required to submit their results, share their code privately with the instructors, and publicly describe their experimental process to the class so that everyone could learn from their collective effort. Teams were free (but not required) to share their code publicly at any time. Some did so after the assignment deadline.

3 The Alignment Challenge

The first challenge was word alignment: given a parallel text, students were challenged to produce word-to-word alignments with low alignment error rate (AER; Och and Ney, 2000). This is a variant of a classic assignment not just in MT, but in NLP generally. Klein (2005) describes a version of it, and we know several other instructors who use it.[7] In most of these, the object is to implement IBM Model 1 or 2, or a hidden Markov model. Our version makes it open-ended by asking students to match or beat an IBM Model 1 baseline.

3.1 Data

We provided 100,000 sentences of parallel data from the Canadian Hansards, totaling around two million words.[8] This dataset is small enough to align in a few minutes with our implementation—enabling rapid experimentation—yet large enough to obtain reasonable results. In fact, Liang et al. (2006) report alignment accuracy on data of this size that is within a fraction of a point of their accuracy on the complete Hansards data. To evaluate, we used manual alignments of a small fraction of sentences, developed by Och and Ney (2000), which we obtained from the shared task resources organized by Mihalcea and Pedersen (2003). The first 37 sentences of the corpus were development data, with manual alignments provided in a separate file. Test data consisted of an additional 447 sentences, for which we did not provide alignments.[9]

3.2 Implementation

We distributed three Python programs with the data. The first, `align`, computes Dice's coefficient (1945) for every pair of French and English words, then aligns every pair for which its value is above an adjustable threshold. Our implementation (most of

[5]Grades depend on institutional norms. In our case, high grades in the rest of class combined with matching all assignment target algorithms would earn a B+; beating two target algorithms would earn an A-; top five placement on any assignment would earn an A; and top three placement compensated for weaker grades in other course criteria. Everyone who completed all four assignments placed in the top five at least once.

[6]The equilibrium point is a single team, though this team would still need to decide on a division of labor. One student contemplated organizing this team, but decided against it.

[7]Among them, Jordan Boyd-Graber, John DeNero, Philipp Koehn, and Slav Petrov (personal communication).

[8]http://www.isi.edu/natural-language/download/hansard/

[9]This invited the possibility of cheating, since alignments of the test data are publicly available on the web. We did not advertise this, but as an added safeguard we obfuscated the data by distributing the test sentences randomly throughout the file.

Listing 1 The default aligner in DREAMT: thresholding Dice's coefficient.

```
for (f, e) in bitext:
  for f_i in set(f):
    f_count[f_i] += 1
    for e_j in set(e):
      fe_count[(f_i,e_j)] += 1
  for e_j in set(e):
    e_count[e_j] += 1

for (f_i, e_j) in fe_count.keys():
  dice[(f_i,e_j)] = \
    2.0 * fe_count[(f_i, e_j)] / \
    (f_count[f_i] + e_count[e_j])

for (f, e) in bitext:
  for (i, f_i) in enumerate(f):
    for (j, e_j) in enumerate(e):
      if dice[(f_i,e_j)] >= cutoff:
        print "%i-%i " % (i,j)
```

which is shown in Listing 1) is quite close to pseudocode, making it easy to focus on the algorithm, one of our pedagogical goals. The `grade` program computes AER and optionally prints an alignment grid for sentences in the development data, showing both human and automatic alignments. Finally the `check` program verifies that the results represent a valid solution, reporting an error if not—enabling students to diagnose bugs in their submissions.

The default implementation enabled immediate experimentation. On receipt of the code, students were instructed to align the first 1,000 sentences and compute AER using a simple command.

`> align -n 1000 | grade` By varying the number of input sentences and the threshold for an alignment, students could immediately see the effect of various parameters on alignment quality.

We privately implemented IBM Model 1 (Brown et al., 1993) as the target algorithm for a passing grade. We ran it for five iterations with English as the target language and French as the source. Our implementation did not use null alignment or symmetrization—leaving out these common improvements offered students the possibility of discovering them independently, and thereby rewarded.

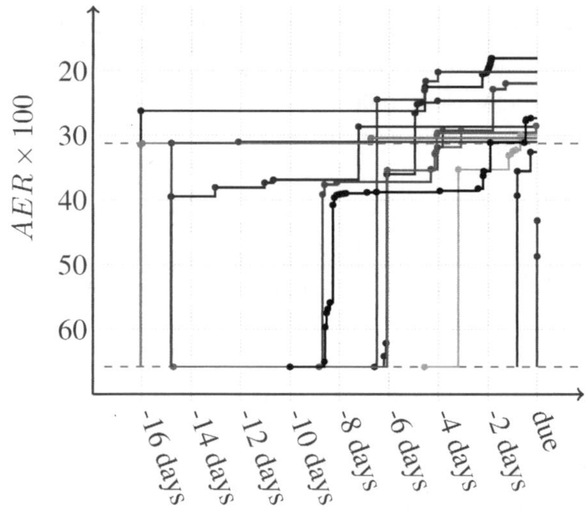

Figure 1: Submission history for the alignment challenge. Dashed lines represent the default and baseline system performance. Each colored line represents a student, and each dot represents a submission. For clarity, we show only submissions that improved the student's AER.

3.3 Challenge Results

We received 209 submissions from 11 teams over a period of two weeks (Figure 1). Everyone eventually matched or exceeded IBM Model 1 AER of 31.26. Most students implemented IBM Model 1, but we saw many other solutions, indicating that many truly experimented with the problem:

- Implementing heuristic constraints to require alignment of proper names and punctuation.
- Running the algorithm on stems rather than surface words.
- Initializing the first iteration of Model 1 with parameters estimated on the observed alignments in the development data.
- Running Model 1 for many iterations. Most researchers typically run Model 1 for five iterations or fewer, and there are few experiments in the literature on its behavior over many iterations, as there are for hidden Markov model taggers (Johnson, 2007). Our students carried out these experiments, reporting runs of 5, 20, 100, and even 2000 iterations. No improvement was observed after 20 iterations.

- Implementing various alternative approaches from the literature, including IBM Model 2 (Brown et al., 1993), competitive linking (Melamed, 2000), and smoothing (Moore, 2004).

One of the best solutions was competitive linking with Dice's coefficient, modified to incorporate the observation that alignments tend to be monotonic by restricting possible alignment points to a window of eight words around the diagonal. Although simple, it acheived an AER of 18.41, an error reduction over Model 1 of more than 40%.

The best score compares unfavorably against a state-of-the-art AER of 3.6 (Liu et al., 2010). But under a different view, it still represents a significant amount of progress for an effort taking just over two weeks: on the original challenge from which we obtained the data (Mihalcea and Pedersen, 2003) the best student system would have placed fifth out of fifteen systems. Consider also the *combined* effort of all the students: when we trained a perceptron classifier on the development data, taking each student's prediction as a feature, we obtained an AER of 15.4, which would have placed fourth on the original challenge. This is notable since *none* of the systems incorporated first-order dependencies on the alignments of adjacent words, long noted as an important feature of the best alignment models (Och and Ney, 2003). Yet a simple system combination of student assignments is as effective as a hidden Markov Model trained on a comparable amount of data (Och and Ney, 2003).

It is important to note that AER does not necessarily correlate with downstream performance, particularly on the Hansards dataset (Fraser and Marcu, 2007). We used the conclusion of the assignment as an opportunity to emphasize this point.

4 The Decoding Challenge

The second challenge was decoding: given a fixed translation model and a set of input sentences, students were challenged to produce translations with the highest model score. This challenge introduced the difficulties of combinatorial optimization under a deceptively simple setup: the model we provided was a simple phrase-based translation model (Koehn et al., 2003) consisting only of a phrase table and trigram language model. Under this simple model, for a French sentence f of length I, English sentence e of length J, and alignment a where each element consists of a span in both e and f such that every word in both e and f is aligned exactly once, the conditional probability of e and a given f is as follows.[10]

$$p(e,a|f) = \prod_{\langle i,i',j,j'\rangle \in a} p(f_i^{i'}|e_j^{j'}) \prod_{j=1}^{J+1} p(e_j|e_{j-1},e_{j-2}) \quad (1)$$

To evaluate output, we compute the conditional probability of e as follows.

$$p(e|f) = \sum_a p(e,a|f) \quad (2)$$

Note that this formulation is different from the typical Viterbi objective of standard beam search decoders, which do not sum over all alignments, but approximate $p(e|f)$ by $\max_a p(e,a|f)$. Though the computation in Equation 2 is intractable (DeNero and Klein, 2008), it can be computed in a few minutes via dynamic programming on reasonably short sentences. We ensured that our data met this criterion. The corpus-level probability is then the product of all sentence-level probabilities in the data.

The model includes no distortion limit or distortion model, for two reasons. First, leaving out the distortion model slightly simplifies the implementation, since it is not necessary to keep track of the last word translated in a beam decoder; we felt that this detail was secondary to understanding the difficulty of search over phrase permutations. Second, it actually makes the problem more difficult, since a simple distance-based distortion model prefers translations with fewer permutations; without it, the model may easily prefer any permutation of the target phrases, making even the Viterbi search problem exhibit its true NP-hardness (Knight, 1999a; Zaslavskiy et al., 2009).

Since the goal was to find the translation with the highest probability, we did not provide a held-out test set; with access to both the input sentences and

[10] For simplicity, this formula assumes that e is padded with two sentence-initial symbols and one sentence-final symbol, and ignores the probability of sentence segmentation, which we take to be uniform.

the model, students had enough information to compute the evaluation score on any dataset themselves. The difficulty of the challenge lies simply in finding the translation that maximizes the evaluation. Indeed, since the problem is intractable, even the instructors did not know the true solution.[11]

4.1 Data

We chose 48 French sentences totaling 716 words from the Canadian Hansards to serve as test data. To create a simple translation model, we used the Berkeley aligner to align the parallel text from the first assignment, and extracted a phrase table using the method of Lopez (2007), as implemented in cdec (Dyer et al., 2010). To create a simple language model, we used SRILM (Stolcke, 2002).

4.2 Implementation

We distributed two Python programs. The first, `decode`, decodes the test data monotonically—using both the language model and translation model, but without permuting phrases. The implementation is completely self-contained with no external dependencies: it implements both models and a simple stack decoding algorithm for monotonic translation. It contains only 122 lines of Python—orders of magnitude fewer than most full-featured decoders. To see its similarity to pseudocode, compare the decoding algorithm (Listing 2) with the pseudocode in Koehn's (2010) popular textbook (reproduced here as Algorithm 1). The second program, `grade`, computes the log-probability of a set of translations, as outline above.

We privately implemented a simple stack decoder that searched over permutations of phrases, similar to Koehn (2004). Our implementation increased the codebase by 44 lines of code and included parameters for beam size, distortion limit, and the maximum number of translations considered for each input phrase. We posted a baseline to the leaderboard using values of 50, 3, and 20 for these, respectively.

[11]We implemented a version of the Lagrangian relaxation algorithm of Chang and Collins (2011), but found it difficult to obtain tight (optimal) solutions without iteratively reintroducing all of the original constraints. We suspect this is due to the lack of a distortion penalty, which enforces a strong preference towards translations with little reordering. However, the solution found by this algorithm is only approximates the objective implied by Equation 2, which sums over alignments.

We also posted an oracle containing the most probable output for each sentence, selected from among all submissions received so far. The intent of this oracle was to provide a lower bound on the best possible output, giving students additional incentive to continue improving their systems.

4.3 Challenge Results

We received 71 submissions from 10 teams (Figure 2), again exhibiting variety of solutions.

- Implementation of greedy decoder which at each step chooses the most probable translation from among those reachable by a single swap or retranslation (Germann et al., 2001; Langlais et al., 2007).
- Inclusion of heuristic estimates of future cost.
- Implementation of a private oracle. Some students observed that the ideal beam setting was not uniform across the corpus. They ran their decoder under different settings, and then selected the most probable translation of each sentence.

Many teams who implemented the standard stack decoding algorithm experimented heavily with its pruning parameters. The best submission used extremely wide beam settings in conjunction with a reimplementation of the future cost estimate used in Moses (Koehn et al., 2007). Five of the submissions beat Moses using its standard beam settings after it had been configured to decode with our model.

We used this assignment to emphasize the importance of good models: the model score of the submissions was generally inversely correlated with BLEU, possibly because our simple model had no distortion limits. We used this to illustrate the difference between model error and search error, including *fortuitous search error* (Germann et al., 2001) made by decoders with less accurate search.

5 The Evaluation Challenge

The third challenge was evaluation: given a test corpus with reference translations and the output of several MT systems, students were challenged to produce a ranking of the systems that closely correlated with a human ranking.

Listing 2 The default decoder in DREAMT: a stack decoder for monotonic translation.

```
stacks = [{} for _ in f] + [{}]
stacks[0][lm.begin()] = initial_hypothesis
for i, stack in enumerate(stacks[:-1]):
  for h in sorted(stack.itervalues(),key=lambda h: -h.logprob)[:alpha]:
    for j in xrange(i+1,len(f)+1):
      if f[i:j] in tm:
        for phrase in tm[f[i:j]]:
          logprob = h.logprob + phrase.logprob
          lm_state = h.lm_state
          for word in phrase.english.split():
            (lm_state, word_logprob) = lm.score(lm_state, word)
            logprob += word_logprob
          logprob += lm.end(lm_state) if j == len(f) else 0.0
          new_hypothesis = hypothesis(logprob, lm_state, h, phrase)
          if lm_state not in stacks[j] or \
            stacks[j][lm_state].logprob < logprob:
              stacks[j][lm_state] = new_hypothesis
winner = max(stacks[-1].itervalues(), key=lambda h: h.logprob)
def extract_english(h):
  return "" if h.predecessor is None else "%s%s " %
    (extract_english(h.predecessor), h.phrase.english)
print extract_english(winner)
```

Algorithm 1 Basic stack decoding algorithm, adapted from Koehn (2010), p. 165.

```
place empty hypothesis into stack 0
for all stacks 0...n − 1 do
  for all hypotheses in stack do
    for all translation options do
      if applicable then
        create new hypothesis
        place in stack
        recombine with existing hypothesis
        prune stack if too big
```

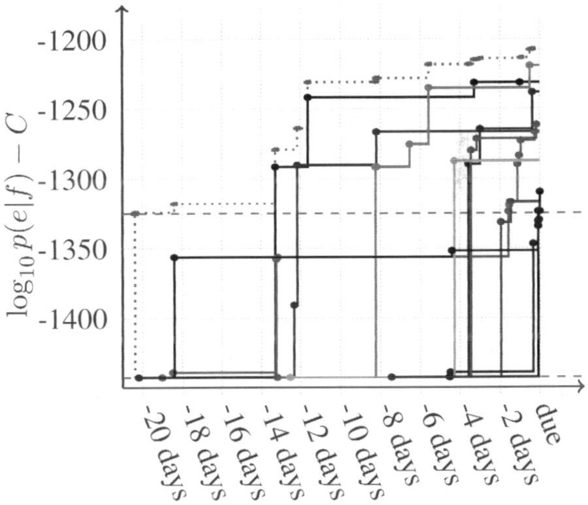

Figure 2: Submission history for the decoding challenge. The dotted green line represents the oracle over submissions.

5.1 Data

We chose the English-to-German translation systems from the 2009 and 2011 shared task at the annual Workshop for Machine Translation (Callison-Burch et al., 2009; Callison-Burch et al., 2011), providing the first as development data and the second as test data. We chose these sets because BLEU (Papineni et al., 2002), our baseline metric, performed particularly poorly on them; this left room for improvement in addition to highlighting some deficiencies of BLEU. For each dataset we provided the source and reference sentences along with anonymized system outputs. For the development data we also provided the human ranking of the systems, computed from pairwise human judgements according to a formula recommended by Bojar et al. (2011).[12]

5.2 Implementation

We provided three simple Python programs: `evaluate` implements a simple ranking of the systems based on position-independent word error rate (PER; Tillmann et al., 1997), which computes a bag-of-words overlap between the system translations and the reference. The `grade` program computes Spearman's ρ between the human ranking and an output ranking. The `check` program simply ensures that a submission contains a valid ranking.

We were concerned about hill-climbing on the test data, so we modified the leaderboard to report new results only twice a day. This encouraged students to experiment on the development data before posting new submissions, while still providing intermittent feedback.

We privately implemented a version of BLEU, which obtained a correlation of 38.6 with the human rankings, a modest improvement over the baseline of 34.0. Our implementation underperforms the one reported in Callison-Burch et al. (2011) since it performs no tokenization or normalization of the data. This also left room for improvement.

5.3 Evaluation Challenge Results

We received 212 submissions from 12 teams (Figure 3), again demonstrating a wide range of techniques.

- Experimentation with the maximum n-gram length and weights in BLEU.
- Implementation of smoothed versions of BLEU (Lin and Och, 2004).
- Implementation of weighted F-measure to balance both precision and recall.
- Careful normalization of the reference and machine translations, including lowercasing and punctuation-stripping.

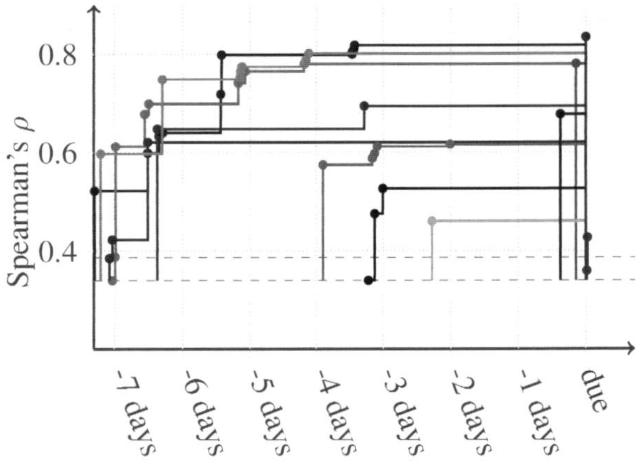

Figure 3: Submission history for the evaluation challenge.

- Implementation of several techniques used in AMBER (Chen and Kuhn, 2005).

The best submission, obtaining a correlation of 83.5, relied on the idea that the reference and machine translation should be good paraphrases of each other (Owczarzak et al., 2006; Kauchak and Barzilay, 2006). It employed a simple paraphrase system trained on the alignment challenge data, using the pivot technique of Bannard and Callison-Burch (2005), and computing the optimal alignment between machine translation and reference under a simple model in which words could align if they were paraphrases. When compared with the 20 systems submitted to the original task from which the data was obtained (Callison-Burch et al., 2011), this system would have ranked fifth, quite near the top-scoring competitors, whose correlations ranged from 88 to 94.

6 The Reranking Challenge

The fourth challenge was reranking: given a test corpus and a large N-best list of candidate translations for each sentence, students were challenged to select a candidate translation for each sentence to produce a high corpus-level BLEU score. Due to an error our data preparation, this assignment had a simple solution that was very difficult to improve on. Nevertheless, it featured several elements that may be useful for future courses.

[12]This ranking has been disputed over a series of papers (Lopez, 2012; Callison-Burch et al., 2012; Koehn, 2012). The paper which initiated the dispute, written by the first author, was directly inspired by the experience of designing this assignment.

6.1 Data

We obtained 300-best lists from a Spanish-English translation system built with the Joshua toolkit (Ganitkevitch et al., 2012) using data and resources from the 2011 Workshop on Machine Translation (Callison-Burch et al., 2011). We provided 1989 training sentences, consisting of source and reference sentences along with the candidate translations. We also included a test set of 250 sentences, for which we provided only the source and candidate translations. Each candidate translation included six features from the underlying translation system, out of an original 21; our hope was that students might rediscover some features through experimentation.

6.2 Implementation

We conceived of the assignment as one in which students could apply machine learning or feature engineering to the task of reranking the systems, so we provided several tools. The first of these, `learn`, was a simple program that produced a vector of feature weights using pairwise ranking optimization (PRO; Hopkins and May, 2011), with a perceptron as the underlying learning algorithm. A second, `rerank`, takes a weight vector as input and reranks the sentences; both programs were designed to work with arbitrary numbers of features. The `grade` program computed the BLEU score on development data, while `check` ensured that a test submission is valid. Finally, we provided an `oracle` program, which computed a lower bound on the achievable BLEU score on the development data using a greedy approximation (Och et al., 2004). The leaderboard likewise displayed an oracle on test data. We did not assign a target algorithm, but left the assignment fully open-ended.

6.3 Reranking Challenge Outcome

For each assignment, we made an effort to create room for competition above the target algorithm. However, we did not accomplish this in the reranking challenge: we had removed most of the features from the candidate translations, in hopes that students might reinvent some of them, but we left one highly predictive *implicit* feature in the data: the rank order of the underlying translation system. Students discovered that simply returning the first candidate earned a very high score, and most of them quickly converged to this solution. Unfortunately, the high accuracy of this baseline left little room for additional competition. Nevertheless, we were encouraged that most students discovered this by accident while attempting other strategies to rerank the translations.

- Experimentation with parameters of the PRO algorithm.
- Substitution of alternative learning algorithms.
- Implementation of a simplified minimum Bayes risk reranker (Kumar and Byrne, 2004).

Over a baseline of 24.02, the latter approach obtained a BLEU of 27.08, nearly matching the score of 27.39 from the underlying system despite an impoverished feature set.

7 Pedagogical Outcomes

Could our students have obtained similar results by running standard toolkits? Undoubtedly. However, our goal was for students to learn by doing: they obtained these results by *implementing* key MT algorithms, observing their behavior on real data, and improving them. This left them with much more insight into how MT systems actually work, and in this sense, DREAMT was a success. At the end of class, we requested written feedback on the design of the assignments. Many commented positively on the motivation provided by the challenge problems:

- *The immediate feedback of the automatic grading was really nice.*
- *Fast feedback on my submissions and my relative position on the leaderboard kept me both motivated to start the assignments early and to constantly improve them. Also knowing how well others were doing was a good way to gauge whether I was completely off track or not when I got bad results.*
- *The homework assignments were very engaging thanks to the clear yet open-ended setup and their competitive aspects.*

Students also commented that they learned a lot about MT and even research in general:

Question	1	2	3	4	5	N/A
Feedback on my work for this course is useful	-	-	-	4	9	3
This course enhanced my ability to work effectively in a team	1	-	5	8	2	-
Compared to other courses at this level, the workload for this course is high	-	1	7	6	1	1

Table 1: Response to student survey questions on a Likert scale from 1 (strongly disagree) to 5 (strongly agree).

- *I learned the most from the assignments.*
- *The assignments always pushed me one step more towards thinking out loud how the particular task can be completed.*
- *I appreciated the setup of the homework problems. I think it has helped me learn how to set up and attack research questions in an organized way. I have a much better sense for what goes into an MT system and what problems aren't solved.*

We also received feedback through an anonymous survey conducted at the end of the course before posting final grades. Each student rated aspects of the course on a five point Likert scale, from 1 (strongly disagree) to 5 (strongly agree). Several questions pertained to assignments (Table 1), and allay two possible concerns about competition: most students felt that the assignments enhanced their collaborative skills, and that their open-endedness did not result in an overload of work. For all survey questions, student satisfaction was higher than average for courses in our department.

8 Discussion

DREAMT is inspired by several different approaches to teaching NLP, AI, and computer science. Eisner and Smith (2008) teach NLP using a competitive game in which students aim to write fragments of English grammar. Charniak et al. (2000) improve the state-of-the-art in a reading comprehension task as part of a group project. Christopher et al. (1993) use NACHOS, a classic tool for teaching operating systems by providing a rudimentary system that students then augment. DeNero and Klein (2010) devise a series of assignments based on Pac-Man, for which students implement several classic AI techniques. A crucial element in such approaches is a highly functional but simple scaffolding. The DREAMT codebase, including grading and validation scripts, consists of only 656 lines of code (LOC) over four assignments: 141 LOC for alignment, 237 LOC for decoding, 86 LOC for evaluation, and 192 LOC for reranking. To simplify implementation further, the optional leaderboard could be delegated to Kaggle.com, a company that organizes machine learning competitions using a model similar to the Netflix Challenge (Bennet and Lanning, 2007), and offers pro bono use of its services for educational challenge problems. A recent machine learning class at Oxford hosted its assignments on Kaggle (Phil Blunsom, personal communication).

We imagine other uses of DREAMT. It could be used in an inverted classroom, where students view lecture material outside of class and work on practical problems in class. It might also be useful in massive open online courses (MOOCs). In this format, course material (primarily lectures and quizzes) is distributed over the internet to an arbitrarily large number of interested students through sites such as coursera.org, udacity.com, and khanacademy.org. In many cases, material and problem sets focus on specific techniques. Although this is important, there is also a place for open-ended problems on which students apply a full range of problem-solving skills. Automatic grading enables them to scale easily to large numbers of students.

On the scientific side, the scale of MOOCs might make it possible to empirically measure the effectiveness of hands-on or competitive assignments, by comparing course performance of students who work on them against that of those who do not. Though there is some empirical work on competitive assignments in the computer science education literature (Lawrence, 2004; Garlick and Akl, 2006; Regueras et al., 2008; Ribeiro et al., 2009), they generally measure student satisfaction and retention rather than the more difficult question of whether such assignments actually improve student learning. However, it might be feasible to answer such questions in large, data-rich virtual classrooms offered by MOOCs. This is an interesting potential avenue for future work.

Because our class came within reach of state-of-the-art on each problem within a matter of weeks, we wonder what might happen with a very large body of competitors. Could real innovation occur? Could we solve large-scale problems? It may be interesting to adopt a different incentive structure, such as one posed by Abernethy and Frongillo (2011) for crowdsourcing machine learning problems: rather than competing, everyone works together to solve a shared task, with credit awarded proportional to the contribution that each individual makes. In this setting, everyone stands to gain: students learn to solve problems as they are found in the real world, instructors learn new insights into the problems they pose, and, in the long run, users of AI technology benefit from overall improvements. Hence it is possible that posing open-ended, real-world problems to students might be a small piece of the puzzle of providing high-quality NLP technologies.

Acknowledgments

We are grateful to Colin Cherry and Chris Dyer for testing the assignments in different settings and providing valuable feedback, and to Jessie Young for implementing a dual decomposition solution to the decoding assignment. We thank Jason Eisner, Frank Ferraro, Yoav Goldberg, Matt Gormley, Ann Irvine, Rebecca Knowles, Ben Mitchell, Courtney Napoles, Michael Rushanan, Joanne Selinski, Svitlana Volkova, and the anonymous reviewers for lively discussion and helpful comments on previous drafts of this paper. Any errors are our own.

References

J. Abernethy and R. M. Frongillo. 2011. A collaborative mechanism for crowdsourcing prediction problems. In *Proc. of NIPS*.

C. Bannard and C. Callison-Burch. 2005. Paraphrasing with bilingual parallel corpora. In *Proc. of ACL*.

J. Bennet and S. Lanning. 2007. The netflix prize. In *Proc. of the KDD Cup and Workshop*.

S. Bird, E. Klein, E. Loper, and J. Baldridge. 2008. Multidisciplinary instruction with the natural language toolkit. In *Proc. of Workshop on Issues in Teaching Computational Linguistics*.

O. Bojar, M. Ercegovčević, M. Popel, and O. Zaidan. 2011. A grain of salt for the WMT manual evaluation. In *Proc. of WMT*.

P. E. Brown, S. A. D. Pietra, V. J. D. Pietra, and R. L. Mercer. 1993. The mathematics of statistical machine translation: Parameter estimation. *Computational Linguistics*, 19(2).

C. Callison-Burch, P. Koehn, C. Monz, and J. Schroeder. 2009. Findings of the 2009 workshop on statistical machine translation. In *Proc. of WMT*.

C. Callison-Burch, P. Koehn, C. Monz, and O. Zaidan. 2011. Findings of the 2011 workshop on statistical machine translation. In *Proc. of WMT*.

C. Callison-Burch, P. Koehn, C. Monz, M. Post, R. Soricut, and L. Specia. 2012. Findings of the 2012 workshop on statistical machine translation. In *Proc. of WMT*.

Y.-W. Chang and M. Collins. 2011. Exact decoding of phrase-based translation models through Lagrangian relaxation. In *Proc. of EMNLP*.

E. Charniak, Y. Altun, R. de Salvo Braz, B. Garrett, M. Kosmala, T. Moscovich, L. Pang, C. Pyo, Y. Sun, W. Wy, Z. Yang, S. Zeiler, and L. Zorn. 2000. Reading comprehension programs in a statistical-language-processing class. In *Proc. of Workshop on Reading Comprehension Tests as Evaluation for Computer-Based Language Understanding Systems*.

B. Chen and R. Kuhn. 2005. AMBER: A modified BLEU, enhanced ranking metric. In *Proc. of WMT*.

D. Chiang. 2007. Hierarchical phrase-based translation. *Computational Linguistics*, 33(2).

W. A. Christopher, S. J. Procter, and T. E. Anderson. 1993. The nachos instructional operating system. In *Proc. of USENIX*.

J. DeNero and D. Klein. 2008. The complexity of phrase alignment problems. In *Proc. of ACL*.

J. DeNero and D. Klein. 2010. Teaching introductory articial intelligence with Pac-Man. In *Proc. of Symposium on Educational Advances in Artificial Intelligence*.

L. R. Dice. 1945. Measures of the amount of ecologic association between species. *Ecology*, 26(3):297–302.

C. Dyer, A. Lopez, J. Ganitkevitch, J. Weese, F. Ture, P. Blunsom, H. Setiawan, V. Eidelman, and P. Resnik. 2010. cdec: A decoder, alignment, and learning framework for finite-state and context-free translation models. In *Proc. of ACL*.

J. Eisner and N. A. Smith. 2008. Competitive grammar writing. In *Proc. of Workshop on Issues in Teaching Computational Linguistics*.

A. Fraser and D. Marcu. 2007. Measuring word alignment quality for statistical machine translation. *Computational Linguistics*, 33(3).

J. Ganitkevitch, Y. Cao, J. Weese, M. Post, and C. Callison-Burch. 2012. Joshua 4.0: Packing, PRO, and paraphrases. In *Proc. of WMT*.

R. Garlick and R. Akl. 2006. Intra-class competitive assignments in CS2: A one-year study. In *Proc. of International Conference on Engineering Education*.

U. Germann, M. Jahr, K. Knight, D. Marcu, and K. Yamada. 2001. Fast decoding and optimal decoding for machine translation. In *Proc. of ACL*.

L. Huang and D. Chiang. 2007. Forest rescoring: Faster decoding with integrated language models. In *Proc. of ACL*.

M. Johnson. 2007. Why doesn't EM find good HMM POS-taggers? In *Proc. of EMNLP*.

D. Jurafsky and J. H. Martin. 2009. *Speech and Language Processing*. Prentice Hall, 2nd edition.

D. Kauchak and R. Barzilay. 2006. Paraphrasing for automatic evaluation. In *Proc. of HLT-NAACL*.

D. Klein. 2005. A core-tools statistical NLP course. In *Proc. of Workshop on Effective Tools and Methodologies for Teaching NLP and CL*.

K. Knight. 1999a. Decoding complexity in word-replacement translation models. *Computational Linguistics*, 25(4).

K. Knight. 1999b. A statistical MT tutorial workbook.

P. Koehn, F. J. Och, and D. Marcu. 2003. Statistical phrase-based translation. In *Proc. of NAACL*.

P. Koehn, H. Hoang, A. Birch, C. Callison-Burch, M. Federico, N. Bertoldi, B. Cowan, W. Shen, C. Moran, R. Zens, C. Dyer, O. Bojar, A. Constantin, and E. Herbst. 2007. Moses: Open source toolkit for statistical machine translation. In *Proc. of ACL*.

P. Koehn. 2004. Pharaoh: a beam search decoder for phrase-based statistical machine translation models. In *Proc. of AMTA*.

P. Koehn. 2010. *Statistical Machine Translation*. Cambridge University Press.

P. Koehn. 2012. Simulating human judgment in machine translation evaluation campaigns. In *Proc. of IWSLT*.

S. Kumar and W. Byrne. 2004. Minimum bayes-risk decoding for statistical machine translation. In *Proc. of HLT-NAACL*.

P. Langlais, A. Patry, and F. Gotti. 2007. A greedy decoder for phrase-based statistical machine translation. In *Proc. of TMI*.

R. Lawrence. 2004. Teaching data structures using competitive games. *IEEE Transactions on Education*, 47(4).

P. Liang, B. Taskar, and D. Klein. 2006. Alignment by agreement. In *Proc. of NAACL*.

C.-Y. Lin and F. J. Och. 2004. ORANGE: a method for evaluating automatic evaluation metrics for machine translation. In *Proc. of COLING*.

Y. Liu, Q. Liu, and S. Lin. 2010. Discriminative word alignment by linear modeling. *Computational Linguistics*, 36(3).

A. Lopez. 2007. Hierarchical phrase-based translation with suffix arrays. In *Proc. of EMNLP*.

A. Lopez. 2008. Statistical machine translation. *ACM Computing Surveys*, 40(3).

A. Lopez. 2012. Putting human assessments of machine translation systems in order. In *Proc. of WMT*.

N. Madnani and B. Dorr. 2008. Combining open-source with research to re-engineer a hands-on introductory NLP course. In *Proc. of Workshop on Issues in Teaching Computational Linguistics*.

I. D. Melamed. 2000. Models of translational equivalence among words. *Computational Linguistics*, 26(2).

R. Mihalcea and T. Pedersen. 2003. An evaluation exercise for word alignment. In *Proc. on Workshop on Building and Using Parallel Texts*.

R. C. Moore. 2004. Improving IBM word alignment model 1. In *Proc. of ACL*.

F. J. Och and H. Ney. 2000. Improved statistical alignment models. In *Proc. of ACL*.

F. J. Och and H. Ney. 2003. A systematic comparison of various statistical alignment models. *Computational Linguistics*, 29.

F. J. Och, D. Gildea, S. Khudanpur, A. Sarkar, K. Yamada, A. Fraser, S. Kumar, L. Shen, D. Smith, K. Eng, V. Jain, Z. Jin, and D. Radev. 2004. A smorgasbord of features for statistical machine translation. In *Proc. of NAACL*.

K. Owczarzak, D. Groves, J. V. Genabith, and A. Way. 2006. Contextual bitext-derived paraphrases in automatic MT evaluation. In *Proc. of WMT*.

K. Papineni, S. Roukos, T. Ward, and W.-J. Zhu. 2002. Bleu: a method for automatic evaluation of machine translation. In *Proc. of ACL*.

L. Regueras, E. Verdú, M. Verdú, M. Pérez, J. de Castro, and M. Muñoz. 2008. Motivating students through on-line competition: An analysis of satisfaction and learning styles.

P. Ribeiro, M. Ferreira, and H. Simões. 2009. Teaching artificial intelligence and logic programming in a competitive environment. *Informatics in Education*, (Vol 8_1):85.

J. Spacco, D. Hovemeyer, W. Pugh, J. Hollingsworth, N. Padua-Perez, and F. Emad. 2006. Experiences with marmoset: Designing and using an advanced submission and testing system for programming courses. In *Proc. of Innovation and technology in computer science education*.

A. Stolcke. 2002. SRILM - an extensible language modeling toolkit. In *Proc. of ICSLP*.

C. Tillmann, S. Vogel, H. Ney, A. Zubiaga, and H. Sawaf. 1997. Accelerated DP based search for statistical translation. In *Proc. of European Conf. on Speech Communication and Technology*.

M. Zaslavskiy, M. Dymetman, and N. Cancedda. 2009. Phrase-based statistical machine translation as a traveling salesman problem. In *Proc. of ACL*.

Combined Distributional and Logical Semantics

Mike Lewis
School of Informatics
University of Edinburgh
Edinburgh, EH8 9AB, UK
mike.lewis@ed.ac.uk

Mark Steedman
School of Informatics
University of Edinburgh
Edinburgh, EH8 9AB, UK
steedman@inf.ed.ac.uk

Abstract

We introduce a new approach to semantics which combines the benefits of distributional and formal logical semantics. Distributional models have been successful in modelling the meanings of content words, but logical semantics is necessary to adequately represent many function words. We follow formal semantics in mapping language to logical representations, but differ in that the relational constants used are induced by offline distributional clustering at the level of predicate-argument structure. Our clustering algorithm is highly scalable, allowing us to run on corpora the size of Gigaword. Different senses of a word are disambiguated based on their induced types. We outperform a variety of existing approaches on a wide-coverage question answering task, and demonstrate the ability to make complex multi-sentence inferences involving quantifiers on the FraCaS suite.

1 Introduction

Mapping natural language to meaning representations is a central challenge of NLP. There has been much recent progress in unsupervised distributional semantics, in which the meaning of a word is induced based on its usage in large corpora. This approach is useful for a range of key applications including question answering and relation extraction (Lin and Pantel, 2001; Poon and Domingos, 2009; Yao et al., 2011). Because such a semantics can be automically induced, it escapes the limitation of depending on relations from hand-built training data, knowledge bases or ontologies, which have proved of limited use in capturing the huge variety of meanings that can be expressed in language.

However, distributional semantics has largely developed in isolation from the formal semantics literature. Whilst distributional semantics has been effective in modelling the meanings of content words such as nouns and verbs, it is less clear that it can be applied to the meanings of function words. Semantic operators, such as determiners, negation, conjunctions, modals, tense, mood, aspect, and plurals are ubiquitous in natural language, and are crucial for high performance on many practical applications—but current distributional models struggle to capture even simple examples. Conversely, computational models of formal semantics have shown low recall on practical applications, stemming from their reliance on ontologies such as WordNet (Miller, 1995) to model the meanings of content words (Bobrow et al., 2007; Bos and Markert, 2005).

For example, consider what is needed to answer a question like *Did Google buy YouTube?* from the following sentences:

1. Google purchased YouTube
2. Google's acquisition of YouTube
3. Google acquired every company
4. YouTube may be sold to Google
5. Google will buy YouTube or Microsoft
6. Google didn't takeover YouTube

All of these require knowledge of lexical semantics (e.g. that *buy* and *purchase* are synonyms), but some also need interpretation of quantifiers, negatives, modals and disjunction. It seems unlikely that distributional or formal approaches can accomplish the task alone.

We propose a method for mapping natural language to first-order logic representations capable of capturing the meanings of function words such as *every*, *not* and *or*, but which also uses distributional statistics to model the meaning of content words. Our approach differs from standard formal semantics in that the non-logical symbols used in the logical form are cluster identifiers. Where standard semantic formalisms would map the verb *write* to a *write'* symbol, we map it to a cluster identifier such as *relation37*, which the noun *author* may also map to. This mapping is learnt by offline clustering.

Unlike previous distributional approaches, we perform clustering at the level of predicate-argument structure, rather than syntactic dependency structure. This means that we abstract away from many syntactic differences that are not present in the semantics, such as conjunctions, passives, relative clauses, and long-range dependencies. This significantly reduces sparsity, so we have fewer predicates to cluster and more observations for each.

Of course, many practical inferences rely heavily on background knowledge about the world—such knowledge falls outside the scope of this work.

2 Background

Our approach is based on Combinatory Categorial Grammar (CCG; Steedman, 2000), a strongly lexicalised theory of language in which lexical entries for words contain all language-specific information. The lexical entry for each word contains a *syntactic category*, which determines which other categories the word may combine with, and a *semantic interpretation*, which defines the compositional semantics. For example, the lexicon may contain the entry: $write \vdash (S\backslash NP)/NP : \lambda y \lambda x.write'(x,y)$

Crucially, there is a transparent interface between the syntactic category and the semantics. For example the transitive verb entry above defines the verb syntactically as a function mapping two noun-phrases to a sentence, and semantically as a binary relation between its two argument entities. This means that it is relatively straightforward to deterministically map parser output to a logical form, as in the Boxer system (Bos, 2008). This form of semantics captures the underlying predicate-argument structure, but fails to license many important inferences—as, for example, *write* and *author* do not map to the same predicate.

In addition to the lexicon, there is a small set of binary combinators and unary rules, which have a syntactic and semantic interpretation. Figure 1 gives an example CCG derivation.

Every	dog	barks
$NP^{\uparrow}/N$ $\lambda p \lambda q.\forall x[p(x) \implies q(x)]$	N $\lambda x.dog'(x)$	$S\backslash NP$ $\lambda x.bark'(x)$
$NP^{\uparrow}$ (>) $\lambda q.\forall x[dog'(x) \implies q(x)]$		
S (>) $\forall x[dog'(x) \implies bark'(x)]$		

Figure 1: A standard logical form derivation using CCG. The $NP^{\uparrow}$ notation means that the subject is type-raised, and taking the verb-phrase as an argument—so is an abbreviation of $S/(S\backslash NP)$. This is necessary in part to support a correct semantics for quantifiers.

Input Sentence
Shakespeare wrote Macbeth
⇓
Intial semantic analysis
$write_{arg0,arg1}$*(shakespeare, macbeth)*
⇓
Entity Typing
$write_{arg0:PER,arg1:BOOK}$*(shakespeare:PER, macbeth:BOOK)*
⇓
Distributional semantic analysis
relation37(shakespeare:PER, macbeth:BOOK)

Figure 2: Layers used in our model.

3 Overview of Approach

We attempt to learn a CCG lexicon which maps equivalent words onto the same logical form—for example learning entries such as:
$author \vdash N/PP[of] : \lambda x \lambda y.relation37(x,y)$
$write \vdash (S\backslash NP)/NP : \lambda x \lambda y.relation37(x,y)$
The only change to the standard CCG derivation is that the symbols used in the logical form are arbitrary relation identifiers. We learn these by first mapping to a deterministic logical form (using predicates

such as *author'* and *write'*), using a process similar to Boxer, and then clustering predicates based on their arguments. This lexicon can then be used to parse new sentences, and integrates seamlessly with CCG theories of formal semantics.

Typing predicates—for example, determining that *writing* is a relation between people and books—has become standard in relation clustering (Schoenmackers et al., 2010; Berant et al., 2011; Yao et al., 2012). We demonstate how to build a typing model into the CCG derivation, by subcategorizing all terms representing entities in the logical form with a more detailed type. These types are also induced from text, as explained in Section 5, but for convenience we describe them with human-readable labels, such as *PER*, *LOC* and *BOOK*.

A key advantage of typing is that it allows us to model ambiguous predicates. Following Berant et al. (2011), we assume that different type signatures of the same predicate have different meanings, but given a type signature a predicate is unambiguous. For example a different lexical entry for the verb *born* is used in the contexts *Obama was born in Hawaii* and *Obama was born in 1961*, reflecting a distinction in the semantics that is not obvious in the syntax[1]. Typing also greatly improves the efficiency of clustering, as we only need to compare predicates with the same type during clustering (for example, we do not have to consider clustering a predicate between people and places with predicates between people and dates).

In this work, we focus on inducing binary relations. Many existing approaches have shown how to produce good clusterings of (non-event) nouns (Brown et al., 1992), any of which could be simply integrated into our semantics—but relation clustering remains an open problem (see Section 9). N-ary relations are binarized, by creating a binary relation between each pair of arguments. For example, for the sentence *Russia sold Alaska to the United States*, the system creates three binary relations— corresponding to *sellToSomeone(Russia, Alaska)*, *buyFromSomeone(US, Alaska)*, *sellSomethingTo(Russia, US)*. This transformation does not exactly preserve meaning, but still captures the most important relations. Note that this allows us to compare semantic relations across different syntactic types—for example, both transitive verbs and argument-taking nouns can be seen as expressing binary semantic relations between entities.

Figure 2 shows the layers used in our model.

4 Initial Semantic Analysis

The initial semantic analysis maps parser output onto a logical form, in a similar way to Boxer. The semantic formalism is based on Steedman (2012).

The first step is syntactic parsing. We use the C&C parser (Clark and Curran, 2004), trained on CCGBank (Hockenmaier and Steedman, 2007), using the refined version of Honnibal et al. (2010) which brings the syntax closer to the predicate-argument structure. An automatic post-processing step makes a number of minor changes to the parser output, which converts the grammar into one more suitable for our semantics. PP (prepositional phrase) and PR (phrasal verb complement) categories are sub-categorised with the relevant preposition. Noun compounds with the same MUC named-entity type (Chinchor and Robinson, 1997) are merged into a single non-compositional node[2] (we otherwise ignore named-entity types). All argument NPs and PPs are type-raised, allowing us to represent quantifiers. All prepositional phrases are treated as core arguments (i.e. given the category *PP*, not adjunct categories like $(N\backslash N)/NP$ or $((S\backslash NP)\backslash(S\backslash NP))/NP$), as it is difficult for the parser to distinguish arguments and adjuncts.

Initial semantic lexical entries for almost all words can be generated automatically from the syntactic category and POS tag (obtained from the parser), as the syntactic category captures the underlying predicate-argument structure. We use a Davidsonian-style representation of arguments (Davidson, 1967), which we binarize by creating a separate predicate for each pair of arguments of a word. These predicates are labelled with the lemma of the head word and a Propbank-style argument key (Kingsbury and Palmer, 2002), e.g. *arg0*, *argIn*. We distinguish noun and verb predicates based on POS

[1] Whilst this assumption is very useful, it does not always hold—for example, the genitive in *Shakespeare's book* is ambiguous between ownership and authorship relations even given the types of the arguments.

[2] For example, this allows us to give *Barack Obama* the semantics $\lambda x.barack\_obama(x)$ instead of $\lambda x.barack(x) \wedge obama(x)$, which is more convenient for collecting distributional statistics.

	Word	Category	Semantics
Automatic	author	$N/PP[of]$	$\lambda x \lambda y.author_{arg0,argOf}(y,x)$
	write	$(S\backslash NP)/NP$	$\lambda x \lambda y.write_{arg0,arg1}(y,x)$
Manual	every	$NP^{\uparrow}/N$	$\lambda p \lambda q.\forall x[p(x) \rightarrow q(x)]$
	not	$(S\backslash NP)/(S\backslash NP)$	$\lambda p \lambda x.\neg p(x)$

Figure 3: Example initial lexical entries

tag—so, for example, we have different predicates for *effect* as a noun or verb.

This algorithm can be overridden with manual lexical entries for specific closed-class function words. Whilst it may be possible to learn these from data, our approach is pragmatic as there are relatively few such words, and the complex logical forms required would be difficult to induce from distributional statistics. We add a small number of lexical entries for words such as negatives (*no*, *not* etc.), and quantifiers (numbers, *each*, *every*, *all*, etc.).

Some example initial lexical entries are shown in Figure 3.

5 Entity Typing Model

Our entity-typing model assigns types to nouns, which is useful for disambiguating polysemous predicates. Our approach is similar to O'Seaghdha (2010) in that we aim to cluster entities based on the noun and unary predicates applied to them (it is simple to convert from the binary predicates to unary predicates). For example, we want the pair *(*$born_{argIn}$*, 1961)* to map to a DAT type, and *(*$born_{argIn}$*, Hawaii)* to map to a LOC type. This is non-trivial, as both the predicates and arguments can be ambiguous between multiple types—but topic models offer a good solution (described below).

5.1 Topic Model

We assume that the type of each argument of a predicate depends only on the predicate and argument, although Ritter et al. (2010) demonstrate an advantage of modelling the joint probability of the types of multiple arguments of the same predicate. We use the standard Latent Dirichlet Allocation model (Blei et al., 2003), which performs comparably to more complex models proposed in O'Seaghdha (2010).

In topic-modelling terminology, we construct a document for each unary predicate (e.g. $born_{argIn}$), based on all of its argument entities (words). We assume that these arguments are drawn from a small number of types (topics), such as PER, DAT or LOC[3]. Each type j has a multinomial distribution ϕ_j over arguments (for example, a LOC type is more likely to generate *Hawaii* than *1961*). Each unary predicate i has a multinomial distribution θ_i over topics, so the $born_{argIn}$ predicate will normally generate a DAT or LOC type. Sparse Dirichlet priors α and β on the multinomials bias the distributions to be peaky. The parameters are estimated by Gibbs sampling, using the Mallet implementation (McCallum, 2002).

The generative story to create the data is:

For every type k:
  Draw the $p(arg|k)$ distribution ϕ_k from $Dir(\beta)$
For every unary predicate i:
  Draw the $p(type|i)$ distribution θ_i from $Dir(\alpha)$
  For every argument j:
    Draw a type z_{ij} from $Mult(\theta_i)$
    Draw an argument w_{ij} from $Mult(\phi_{\theta_i})$

5.2 Typing in Logical Form

In the logical form, all constants and variables representing entities x can be assigned a distribution over types $p_x(t)$ using the type model. An initial type distribution is applied in the lexicon, using the ϕ distributions for the types of nouns, and the θ_i distributions for the type of arguments of binary predicates (inverted using Bayes' rule). Then at each β-reduction in the derivation, we update probabilities of the types to be the product of the type distributions of the terms being reduced. If two terms x and

[3]Types are induced from the text, but we give human-readable labels here for convenience.

$$\frac{\text{file}}{(S\backslash NP)/NP \quad \lambda y{:}\left\{\begin{matrix} DOC{=}0.5 \\ LEGAL{=}0.4 \\ CLOTHES{=}0.01 \\ \ldots \end{matrix}\right\} \lambda x{:}\left\{\begin{matrix} PER{=}0.7 \\ ORG{=}0.2 \\ \ldots \end{matrix}\right\}.file_{arg0,arg1}(x,y)} \quad \frac{\text{a suit}}{NP^{\uparrow} \quad \lambda p.\exists y{:}\left\{\begin{matrix} CLOTHES{=}0.6 \\ LEGAL{=}0.3 \\ DOC{=}0.001 \\ \ldots \end{matrix}\right\}[suit'(y) \wedge p(y)]}$$

$$\overline{S\backslash NP \quad \lambda x{:}\left\{\begin{matrix} PER{=}0.7 \\ ORG{=}0.2 \\ \ldots \end{matrix}\right\} \exists y{:}\left\{\begin{matrix} LEGAL{=}0.94 \\ CLOTHES{=}0.05 \\ DOC{=}0.004 \\ \ldots \end{matrix}\right\})[suit'(y) \wedge file_{arg0,arg1}(x,y)]}^{\;<}$$

Figure 4: Using the type model for disambiguation in the derivation of *file a suit*. Type distributions are shown after the variable declarations. Both *suit* and the object of *file* are lexically ambiguous between different types, but after the β-reduction only one interpretation is likely. If the verb were *wear*, a different interpretation would be preferred.

y combine to a term z:

$$p_z(t) = \frac{p_x(t)p_y(t)}{\sum_{t'} p_x(t')p_y(t')}$$

For example, in *wore a suit* and *file a suit*, the variable representing *suit* may be lexically ambiguous between CLOTHES and LEGAL types, but the variables representing the objects of *wear* and *file* will have preferences that allow us to choose the correct type when the terms combine. Figure 4 shows an example derivation using the type model for disambiguation[4].

6 Distributional Relation Clustering Model

The typed binary predicates can be grouped into clusters, each of which represents a distinct semantic relation. Note that because we cluster typed predicates, $born_{arg0:PER,argIn:LOC}$ and $born_{arg0:PER,argIn:DAT}$ can be clustered separately.

6.1 Corpus statistics

Typed binary predicates are clustered based on the expected number of times they hold between each argument-pair in the corpus. This means we create a single vector of argument-pair counts for each predicate (not a separate vector for each argument). For example, the vector for the typed predicate $write_{arg0:PER,arg1:BOOK}$ may contain non-zero counts for entity-pairs such as *(Shakespeare, Macbeth)*, *(Dickens, Oliver Twist)* and *(Rowling, Harry Potter)*. The entity-pair counts for $author_{arg0:PER,argOf:BOOK}$ may be similar, on the assumption that both are samples from the same underlying semantic relation.

To find the expected number of occurrences of argument-pairs for typed binary predicates in a corpus, we first apply the type model to the derivation of each sentence, as described in Section 5.2. This outputs untyped binary predicates, with distributions over the types of their arguments. The type of the predicate must match the type of its arguments, so the type distribution of a binary predicate is simply the joint distribution of the two argument type distributions.

For example, if the arguments in a $born_{arg0,argIn}(obama,hawaii)$ derivation have the respective type distributions *(PER=0.9, LOC=0.1)* and *(LOC=0.7, DAT=0.3)*, the distribution over binary typed predicates is ($born_{arg0:PER,argIn:LOC}$=0.63, $born_{arg0:PER,argIn:DAT}$=0.27, etc.) The expected counts for $(obama,hawaii)$ in the vectors for $born_{arg0:PER,argIn:LOC}$ and $born_{arg0:PER,argIn:DAT}$ are then incremented by these probabilities.

6.2 Clustering

Many algorithms have been proposed for clustering predicates based on their arguments (Poon and Domingos, 2009; Yao et al., 2012). The number of relations in the corpus is unbounded, so the clustering algorithm should be non-parametric. It is also important that it remains tractable for very large numbers of predicates and arguments, in order to give us a greater coverage of language than can be achieved by hand-built ontologies.

We cluster the typed predicate vectors using the Chinese Whispers algorithm (Biemann, 2006)—

[4]Our implementation follows Steedman (2012) in using Generalized Skolem Terms rather than existential quantifiers, in order to capture quantifier scope alternations monotonically, but we omit these from the example to avoid introducing new notation.

although somewhat ad-hoc, it is both non-parametric and highly scalable[5]. This has previously been used for noun-clustering by Fountain and Lapata (2011), who argue it is a cognitively plausible model for language acquisition. The collection of predicates and arguments is converted into a graph with one node per predicate, and edge weights representing the similarity between predicates. Predicates with different types have zero-similarity, and otherwise similarity is computed as the cosine-similarity of the tf-idf vectors of argument-pairs. We prune nodes occurring fewer than 20 times, edges with weights less than 10^{-3}, and a short list of stop predicates.

The algorithm proceeds as follows:

1. Each predicate p is assigned to a different semantic relation r_p
2. Iterate over the predicates p in a random order
3. Set $r_p = \arg\max_r \sum_{p'} \mathbb{1}_{r=r_{p'}} sim(p,p')$, where $sim(p,p')$ is the distributional similarity between p and p', and $\mathbb{1}_{r=r'}$ is 1 iff r=r' and 0 otherwise.
4. Repeat (2.) to convergence.

7 Semantic Parsing using Relation Clusters

The final phase is to use our relation clusters in the lexical entries of the CCG semantic derivation. This is slightly complicated by the fact that our predicates are lexically ambiguous between all the possible types they could take, and hence the relations they could express. For example, the system cannot tell whether *born in* is expressing a *birthplace* or *birthdate* relation until later in the derivation, when it combines with its arguments. However, all the possible logical forms are identical except for the symbols used, which means we can produce a packed logical form capturing the full distribution over logical forms. To do this, we make the predicate a function from argument types to relations.

For each word, we first take the lexical semantic definition produced by the algorithm in Section 4. For binary predicates in this definition (which will be untyped), we perform a deterministic lookup in the cluster model learned in Section 6, using all possible corresponding typed predicates. This allows us to represent the binary predicates as *packed predicates*: functions from argument types to relations.

For example, if the clustering maps $born_{arg0:PER,argIn:LOC}$ to *rel49* ("birthplace") and $born_{arg0:PER,argIn:DAT}$ to *rel53* ("birthdate"), our lexicon contains the following packed lexical entry (type-distributions on the variables are suppressed):

$$born \vdash (S\backslash NP)/PP[in] :$$
$$\lambda y \lambda x. \begin{Bmatrix} (x:PER, y:LOC) \Rightarrow rel49 \\ (x:PER, y:DAT) \Rightarrow rel53 \end{Bmatrix} (x,y)$$

The distributions over argument types then imply a distribution over relations. For example, if the packed-predicate for $born_{arg0,argIn}$ is applied to arguments *Obama* and *Hawaii*, with respective type distributions *(PER=0.9, LOC=0.1)* and *(LOC=0.7, DAT=0.3)*[6], the distribution over relations will be (*rel49*=0.63, *rel53*=0.27, etc.).

If *1961* has a type-distribution *(LOC=0.1, DAT=0.9)*, the output packed-logical form for *Obama was born in Hawaii in 1961* will be:

$$\begin{Bmatrix} rel49{=}0.63 \\ rel53{=}0.27 \\ \ldots \end{Bmatrix} (ob,hw) \wedge \begin{Bmatrix} rel49{=}0.09 \\ rel53{=}0.81 \\ \ldots \end{Bmatrix} (ob,1961)$$

The probability of a given logical form can be read from this packed logical form.

8 Experiments

Our approach aims to offer a strong model of both formal and lexical semantics. We perform two evaluations, aiming to target each of these separately, but using the same semantic representations in each.

We train our system on Gigaword (Graff et al., 2003), which contains around 4 billion words of newswire. The type-model is trained using 15 types[7], and 5,000 iterations of Gibbs sampling (using the distributions from the final sample). Table 1

[5]We also experimented with a Dirichlet Process Mixture Model (Neal, 2000), but even with the efficient A* search algorithms introduced by Daumé III (2007), the cost of inference was found to be prohibitively high when run at large scale.

[6]These distributions are composed from the type-distributions for both the predicate and argument, as explained in Section 5

[7]This number was chosen by examination of models trained with different numbers of types. The algorithm produces semantically coherent clusters for much larger numbers of types, but many of these are fine-grained categories of people, which introduces sparsity in the relation clustering.

Type	Top Words
1	suspect, assailant, fugitive, accomplice
2	author, singer, actress, actor, dad
5	city, area, country, region, town, capital
8	subsidiary, automaker, airline, Co., GM
10	musical, thriller, sequel, special

Table 1: Most probable terms in some clusters induced by the Type Model.

shows some example types. The relation clustering uses only proper nouns, to improve precision (sparsity problems are partly offset by the large input corpus). Aside from parsing, the pipeline takes around a day to run using 12 cores.

8.1 Question Answering Experiments

As yet, there is no standard way of evaluating lexical semantics. Existing tasks like Recognising Textual Entailment (RTE; Dagan et al., 2006) rely heavily on background knowledge, which is beyond the scope of this work. Intrinsic evaluations of entailment relations have low inter-annotator agreement (Szpektor et al., 2007), due to the difficulty of evaluating relations out of context.

Our evaluation is based on that performed by Poon and Domingos (2009). We automatically construct a set of questions by sampling from text, and then evaluate how many answers can be found in a different corpus. From dependency-parsed newswire, we sample either $X \stackrel{nsubj}{\leftarrow} verb \stackrel{dobj}{\rightarrow} Y$, $X \stackrel{nsubj}{\leftarrow} verb \stackrel{pobj}{\rightarrow} Y$ or $X \stackrel{nsubj}{\leftarrow} be \stackrel{dobj}{\rightarrow} noun \stackrel{pobj}{\rightarrow} Y$ patterns, where X and Y are proper nouns and the verb is not on a list of stop verbs, and deterministically convert these to questions. For example, from *Google bought YouTube* we create the questions *What did Google buy?* and *What bought YouTube?*. The task is to find proper-noun answers to these questions in a different corpus, which are then evaluated by human annotators based on the sentence the answer was retrieved from[8]. Systems can return multiple answers to the same question (e.g. *What did Google buy?* may have many valid answers), and all of these contribute to the result. As none of the systems model tense or temporal semantics, annotators were instructed to annotate answers as correct if they were true at any time. This approach means we evaluate on relations in proportion to corpus frequency. We sample 1000 questions from the New York Times subset of Gigaword from 2010, and search for answers in the New York Times from 2009.

We evaluate the following approaches:

- **CCG-Baseline** The logical form produced by our CCG derivation, without the clustering.
- **CCG-WordNet** The CCG logical form, plus WordNet as a model of lexical semantics.
- **CCG-Distributional** The logical form including the type model and clusters.
- **Relational LDA** An LDA based model for clustering dependency paths (Yao et al., 2011). We train on New York Times subset of Gigaword[9], using their setup of 50 iterations with 100 relation types.
- **Reverb** A sophisticated Open Information Extraction system (Fader et al., 2011).

Unsupervised Semantic Parsing (USP; Poon and Domingos, 2009; USP; Poon and Domingos, 2010; USP; Titov and Klementiev, 2011) would be another obvious baseline. However, memory requirements mean it is not possible to run at this scale (our system is trained on 4 orders of magnitude more data than the USP evaluation). Yao et al. (2011) found it had comparable performance to Relational LDA.

For the CCG models, rather than performing full first-order inference on a large corpus, we simply test whether the question predicate subsumes a candidate answer predicate, and whether the arguments match[10]. In the case of CCG-Distributional, we calculate the probability that the two packed-predicates

[8]Common nouns are filtered automatically. To focus on evaluating the semantics, annotators ignored garbled sentences due to errors pre-processing the corpus (these are excluded from the results). We also automatically exclude weekday and month answers, which are overwhelmingly syntax errors for all systems—e.g. treating *Tuesday* as an object in *Obama announced Tuesday that...*

[9]This is around 35% of Gigaword, and was the largest scale possible on our resources.

[10]We do this as it is much more efficient than full first-order theorem-proving. We could in principle make additional inferences with theorem-proving, such as answering *What did Google buy?* from *Google bought the largest video website* and *YouTube is the largest video website.*

System	Answers	Correct
Relational-LDA	7046	11.6%
Reverb	180	89.4%
CCG-Baseline	203	95.8%
CCG-WordNet	211	94.8%
CCG-Distributional@250	250	94.1%
CCG-Distributional@500	500	82.0%

Table 2: Results on wide-coverage Question Answering task. CCG-Distributional ranks question/answer pairs by confidence—@250 means we evaluate the top 250 of these. It is not possible to give a recall figure, as the total number of correct answers in the corpus is unknown.

are in the same cluster, marginalizing over their argument types. Answers are ranked by this probability. For CCG-WordNet, we check if the question predicate is a hypernym of the candidate answer predicate (using any WordNet sense of either term).

Results are shown in Table 2. Relational-LDA induces many meaningful clusters, but predicates must be assigned to one of 100 relations, so results are dominated by large, noisy clusters (it is not possible to take the N-best answers as the cluster assignments do not have a confidence score). The CCG-Baseline errors are mainly caused by parser errors, or relations in the scope of non-factive operators. CCG-WordNet adds few answers to CCG-Baseline, reflecting the limitations of hand-built ontologies.

CCG-Distributional substantially improves recall over other approaches whilst retaining good precision, demonstrating that we have learnt a powerful model of lexical semantics. Table 3 shows some correctly answered questions. The system improves over the baseline by mapping expressions such as *merge with* and *acquisition of* to the same relation cluster. Many of the errors are caused by conflating predicates where the entailment only holds in one direction, such as *was elected to* with *ran for*. Hierarchical clustering could be used to address this.

8.2 Experiments on the FraCaS Suite

We are also interested in evaluating our approach as a model of formal semantics—demonstrating that it is possible to integrate the formal semantics of Steedman (2012) with our distributional clusters.

The FraCaS suite (Cooper et al., 1996)[11] contains a hand-built set of entailment problems designed to be challenging in terms of formal semantics. We use Section 1, which contains 74 problems requiring an understanding of quantifiers[12]. They do not require any knowledge of lexical semantics, meaning we can evaluate the formal component of our system in isolation. However, we use the same representations as in our previous experiment, even though the clusters provide no benefit on this task. Figure 5 gives an example problem.

The only previous work we are aware of on this dataset is by MacCartney and Manning (2007). This approach learns the monotonicity properties of words from a hand-built training set, and uses this to transform a sentence into a polarity annotated string. The system then aims to transform the premise string into a hypothesis. Positively polarized words can be replaced with less specific ones (e.g. by deleting adjuncts), whereas negatively polarized words can be replaced with more specific ones (e.g. by adding adjuncts). Whilst this is high-precision and often useful, this logic is unable to perform inferences with multiple premise sentences (in contrast to our first-order logic).

Development consists of adding entries to our lexicon for quantifiers. For simplicity, we treat multiword quantifiers like *at least a few*, as being multiword expressions—although a more compositional analysis may be possible. Following MacCartney and Manning (2007), we do not use held-out data—each problem is designed to test a different issue, so it is not possible to generalize from one subset of the suite to another. As we are interested in evaluating the semantics, not the parser, we manually supply gold-standard lexical categories for sentences with parser errors (any syntactic mistake causes incorrect semantics). Our derivations produce a distribution over logical forms—we license the inference if it holds in any interpretation with non-zero probability. We use the Prover9 (McCune, 2005) theorem prover for inference, returning *yes* if the premise implies the hypothesis, *no* if it implies the negation of the hypothesis, and *unknown* otherwise.

Results are shown in Table 4. Our system im-

[11]We use the version converted to machine readable format by MacCartney and Manning (2007)

[12]Excluding 6 problems without a defined solution.

Question	Answer	Sentence
What did Delta merge with?	Northwest	The 747 freighters came with Delta's acquisition of Northwest
What spoke with Hu Jintao?	Obama	Obama conveyed his respect for the Dalai Lama to China's president Hu Jintao during their first meeting...
What arrived in Colorado?	Zazi	Zazi flew back to Colorado...
What ran for Congress?	Young	... Young was elected to Congress in 1972

Table 3: Example questions correctly answered by CCG-Distributional.

Premises:	Every European has the right to live in Europe. Every European is a person. Every person who has the right to live in Europe can travel freely within Europe.
Hypothesis:	Every European can travel freely within Europe
Solution:	Yes

Figure 5: Example problem from the FraCaS suite.

System	Single Premise	Multiple Premises
MacCartney&Manning 07	84%	-
MacCartney&Manning 08	98%	-
CCG-Dist (parser syntax)	70%	50%
CCG-Dist (gold syntax)	89%	80%

Table 4: Accuracy on Section 1 of the FraCaS suite. Problems are divided into those with one premise sentence (44) and those with multiple premises (30).

proves on previous work by making multi-sentence inferences. Causes of errors include missing a distinct lexical entry for plural *the*, only taking existential interpretations of bare plurals, failing to interpret mass-noun determiners such as *a lot of*, and not providing a good semantics for non-monotone determiners such as *most*. We believe these problems will be surmountable with more work. Almost all errors are due to incorrectly predicting *unknown* — the system makes just one error on *yes* or *no* predictions (with or without gold syntax). This suggests that making first-order logic inferences in applications will not harm precision. We are less robust than MacCartney and Manning (2007) to syntax errors but, conversely, we are able to attempt more of the problems (i.e. those with multi-sentence premises). Other approaches based on distributional semantics seem unable to tackle any of these problems, as they do not represent quantifiers or negation.

9 Related Work

Much work on semantics has taken place in a supervised setting—for example the GeoQuery (Zelle and Mooney, 1996) and ATIS (Dahl et al., 1994) semantic parsing tasks. This approach makes sense for generating queries for a specific database, but means the semantic representations do not generalize to other datasets. There have been several attempts to annotate larger corpora with semantics—such as Ontonotes (Hovy et al., 2006) or the Groningen Meaning Bank (Basile et al., 2012). These typically map words onto senses in ontologies such as WordNet, VerbNet (Kipper et al., 2000) and FrameNet (Baker et al., 1998). However, limitations of these ontologies mean that they do not support inferences such as *X is the author of Y* $\rightarrow$ *X wrote Y*.

Given the difficulty of annotating large amounts of text with semantics, various approaches have attempted to learn meaning without annotated text. Distant Supervision approaches leverage existing knowledge bases, such as Freebase (Bollacker et al., 2008), to learn semantics (Mintz et al., 2009; Krishnamurthy and Mitchell, 2012). Dependency-based Compositional Semantics (Liang et al., 2011) learns the meaning of questions by using their answers as denotations—but this appears to be specific to question parsing. Such approaches can only learn the pre-specified relations in the knowledge base.

The approaches discussed so far in this section have all attempted to map language onto some pre-specified set of relations. Various attempts have been made to instead induce relations from text by clustering predicates based on their arguments. For example, Yao et al. (2011) propose a series of LDA-based models which cluster relations between entities based on a variety of lexical, syntactic and semantic features. Unsupervised Semantic Parsing (Poon and Domingos, 2009) recursively clusters fragments of dependency trees based on their arguments. Although USP is an elegant model, it is too computationally expensive to run on large corpora. It is also based on frame semantics, so does not cluster equivalent predicates with different frames. To our knowledge, our work is the first such approach to be integrated within a linguistic theory supporting formal semantics for logical operators.

Vector space models represent words by vectors based on co-occurrence counts. Recent work has tackled the problem of composing these matrices to build up the semantics of phrases or sentences (Mitchell and Lapata, 2008). Another strand (Coecke et al., 2010; Grefenstette et al., 2011) has shown how to represent meanings as tensors, whose order depends on the syntactic category, allowing an elegant correspondence between syntactic and semantic types. Socher et al. (2012) train a composition function using a neural network—however their method requires annotated data. It is also not obvious how to represent logical relations such as quantification in vector-space models. Baroni et al. (2012) make progress towards this by learning a classifier that can recognise entailments such as *all dogs* $\Longrightarrow$ *some dogs*, but this remains some way from the power of first-order theorem proving of the kind required by the problem in Figure 5.

An alternative strand of research has attempted to build computational models of linguistic theories based on formal compositional semantics, such as the CCG-based Boxer (Bos, 2008) and the LFG-based XLE (Bobrow et al., 2007). Such approaches convert parser output into formal semantic representations, and have demonstrated some ability to model complex phenomena such as negation. For lexical semantics, they typically compile lexical resources such as VerbNet and WordNet into inference rules—but still achieve only low recall on open-domain tasks, such as RTE, mostly due to the low coverage of such resources. Garrette et al. (2011) use distributional statistics to determine the probability that a WordNet-derived inference rule is valid in a given context. Our approach differs in that we learn inference rules not present in WordNet. Our lexical semantics is integrated into the lexicon, rather than being implemented as additional inference rules, meaning that inference is more efficient, as equivalent statements have the same logical form.

Natural Logic (MacCartney and Manning, 2007) offers an interesting alternative to symbolic logics, and has been shown to be able to capture complex logical inferences by simply identifying the scope of negation in text. This approach achieves similar precision and much higher recall than Boxer on the RTE task. Their approach also suffers from such limitations as only being able to make inferences between two sentences. It is also sensitive to word order, so cannot make inferences such as *Shakespeare wrote Macbeth* $\Longrightarrow$ *Macbeth was written by Shakespeare*.

10 Conclusions and Future Work

This is the first work we are aware of that combines a distributionally induced lexicon with formal semantics. Experiments suggest our approach compares favourably with existing work in both areas.

Many potential areas for improvement remain. Hierachical clustering would allow us to capture hypernym relations, rather than the synonyms captured by our flat clustering. There is much potential for integrating existing hand-built resources, such as Ontonotes and WordNet, to improve the accuracy of clustering. There are cases where the existing CCGBank grammar does not match the required predicate-argument structure—for example in the case of light verbs. It may be possible to rebank CCGBank, in a way similar to Honnibal et al. (2010), to improve it on this point.

Acknowledgements

We thank Christos Christodoulopoulos, Tejaswini Deoskar, Mark Granroth-Wilding, Ewan Klein, Katrin Erk, Johan Bos and the anonymous reviewers for their helpful comments, and Limin Yao for sharing code. This work was funded by ERC Advanced Fellowship 249520 GRAMPLUS and IP EC-FP7-270273 Xperience.

References

C.F. Baker, C.J. Fillmore, and J.B. Lowe. 1998. The berkeley framenet project. In *Proceedings of the 36th Annual Meeting of the Association for Computational Linguistics and 17th International Conference on Computational Linguistics-Volume 1*, pages 86–90. Association for Computational Linguistics.

M. Baroni, R. Bernardi, N.Q. Do, and C. Shan. 2012. Entailment above the word level in distributional semantics. In *Proceedings of EACL*, pages 23–32. Citeseer.

V. Basile, J. Bos, K. Evang, and N. Venhuizen. 2012. Developing a large semantically annotated corpus. In *Proceedings of the Eighth International Conference on Language Resources and Evaluation (LREC12). To appear*.

Jonathan Berant, Ido Dagan, and Jacob Goldberger. 2011. Global learning of typed entailment rules. In *Proceedings of the 49th Annual Meeting of the Association for Computational Linguistics: Human Language Technologies - Volume 1*, HLT '11, pages 610–619. Association for Computational Linguistics.

C. Biemann. 2006. Chinese whispers: an efficient graph clustering algorithm and its application to natural language processing problems. In *Proceedings of the First Workshop on Graph Based Methods for Natural Language Processing*, pages 73–80. Association for Computational Linguistics.

D.M. Blei, A.Y. Ng, and M.I. Jordan. 2003. Latent dirichlet allocation. *the Journal of machine Learning research*, 3:993–1022.

D. G. Bobrow, C. Condoravdi, R. Crouch, V. De Paiva, L. Karttunen, T. H. King, R. Nairn, L. Price, and A. Zaenen. 2007. Precision-focused textual inference. In *Proceedings of the ACL-PASCAL Workshop on Textual Entailment and Paraphrasing*, RTE '07, pages 16–21. Association for Computational Linguistics.

Kurt Bollacker, Colin Evans, Praveen Paritosh, Tim Sturge, and Jamie Taylor. 2008. Freebase: a collaboratively created graph database for structuring human knowledge. In *Proceedings of the 2008 ACM SIGMOD international conference on Management of data*, SIGMOD '08, pages 1247–1250, New York, NY, USA. ACM.

J. Bos and K. Markert. 2005. Recognising textual entailment with logical inference. In *Proceedings of the conference on Human Language Technology and Empirical Methods in Natural Language Processing*, pages 628–635. Association for Computational Linguistics.

Johan Bos. 2008. Wide-coverage semantic analysis with boxer. In Johan Bos and Rodolfo Delmonte, editors, *Semantics in Text Processing. STEP 2008 Conference Proceedings*, Research in Computational Semantics, pages 277–286. College Publications.

P.F. Brown, P.V. Desouza, R.L. Mercer, V.J.D. Pietra, and J.C. Lai. 1992. Class-based n-gram models of natural language. *Computational linguistics*, 18(4):467–479.

N. Chinchor and P. Robinson. 1997. Muc-7 named entity task definition. In *Proceedings of the 7th Conference on Message Understanding*.

Stephen Clark and James R. Curran. 2004. Parsing the WSJ using CCG and log-linear models. In *Proceedings of the 42nd Annual Meeting on Association for Computational Linguistics*, ACL '04. Association for Computational Linguistics.

Bob Coecke, Mehrnoosh Sadrzadeh, and Stephen Clark. 2010. Mathematical foundations for a compositional distributional model of meaning. *Linguistic Analysis: A Festschrift for Joachim Lambek*, 36(1-4):345–384.

Robin Cooper, Dick Crouch, Jan Van Eijck, Chris Fox, Johan Van Genabith, Jan Jaspars, Hans Kamp, David Milward, Manfred Pinkal, Massimo Poesio, et al. 1996. Using the framework. *FraCaS Deliverable D*, 16.

Ido Dagan, O. Glickman, and B. Magnini. 2006. The PASCAL recognising textual entailment challenge. *Machine Learning Challenges. Evaluating Predictive Uncertainty, Visual Object Classification, and Recognising Tectual Entailment*, pages 177–190.

D.A. Dahl, M. Bates, M. Brown, W. Fisher, K. Hunicke-Smith, D. Pallett, C. Pao, A. Rudnicky, and E. Shriberg. 1994. Expanding the scope of the ATIS task: The ATIS-3 corpus. In *Proceedings of the workshop on Human Language Technology*, pages 43–48. Association for Computational Linguistics.

Hal Daumé III. 2007. Fast search for dirichlet process mixture models. In *Proceedings of the Eleventh International Conference on Artificial Intelligence and Statistics (AIStats)*, San Juan, Puerto Rico.

D. Davidson. 1967. 6. the logical form of action sentences. *Essays on actions and events*, 1(9):105–149.

Anthony Fader, Stephen Soderland, and Oren Etzioni. 2011. Identifying relations for open information extraction. In *Proceedings of the Conference on Empirical Methods in Natural Language Processing*, EMNLP '11, pages 1535–1545. Association for Computational Linguistics.

T. Fountain and M. Lapata. 2011. Incremental models of natural language category acquisition. In *Proceedings of the 32st Annual Conference of the Cognitive Science Society*.

D. Garrette, K. Erk, and R. Mooney. 2011. Integrating logical representations with probabilistic information using markov logic. In *Proceedings of the Ninth International Conference on Computational Semantics*, pages 105–114. Association for Computational Linguistics.

D. Graff, J. Kong, K. Chen, and K. Maeda. 2003. English gigaword. *Linguistic Data Consortium, Philadelphia.*

Edward Grefenstette, Mehrnoosh Sadrzadeh, Stephen Clark, Bob Coecke, and Stephen Pulman. 2011. Concrete sentence spaces for compositional distributional models of meaning. *Computational Semantics IWCS 2011*, page 125.

Julia Hockenmaier and Mark Steedman. 2007. CCGbank: a corpus of CCG derivations and dependency structures extracted from the penn treebank. *Computational Linguistics*, 33(3):355–396.

M. Honnibal, J.R. Curran, and J. Bos. 2010. Rebanking CCGbank for improved NP interpretation. In *Proceedings of the 48th Annual Meeting of the Association for Computational Linguistics*, pages 207–215. Association for Computational Linguistics.

E. Hovy, M. Marcus, M. Palmer, L. Ramshaw, and R. Weischedel. 2006. Ontonotes: the 90% solution. In *Proceedings of the Human Language Technology Conference of the NAACL, Companion Volume: Short Papers*, pages 57–60. Association for Computational Linguistics.

P. Kingsbury and M. Palmer. 2002. From treebank to propbank. In *Proceedings of the 3rd International Conference on Language Resources and Evaluation (LREC-2002)*, pages 1989–1993. Citeseer.

K. Kipper, H.T. Dang, and M. Palmer. 2000. Class-based construction of a verb lexicon. In *Proceedings of the National Conference on Artificial Intelligence*, pages 691–696. Menlo Park, CA; Cambridge, MA; London; AAAI Press; MIT Press; 1999.

Jayant Krishnamurthy and Tom M. Mitchell. 2012. Weakly supervised training of semantic parsers. In *Proceedings of the 2012 Joint Conference on Empirical Methods in Natural Language Processing and Computational Natural Language Learning*, EMNLP-CoNLL '12, pages 754–765. Association for Computational Linguistics.

P. Liang, M.I. Jordan, and D. Klein. 2011. Learning dependency-based compositional semantics. In *Proc. Association for Computational Linguistics (ACL).*

Dekang Lin and Patrick Pantel. 2001. DIRT - Discovery of Inference Rules from Text. In *In Proceedings of the ACM SIGKDD Conference on Knowledge Discovery and Data Mining*, pages 323–328.

Bill MacCartney and Christopher D. Manning. 2007. Natural logic for textual inference. In *Proceedings of the ACL-PASCAL Workshop on Textual Entailment and Paraphrasing*, RTE '07, pages 193–200. Association for Computational Linguistics.

Andrew Kachites McCallum. 2002. Mallet: A machine learning for language toolkit. http://mallet.cs.umass.edu.

W. McCune. 2005. Prover9 and Mace4. `http://cs.unm.edu/~mccune/mace4/`.

G.A. Miller. 1995. Wordnet: a lexical database for english. *Communications of the ACM*, 38(11):39–41.

M. Mintz, S. Bills, R. Snow, and D. Jurafsky. 2009. Distant supervision for relation extraction without labeled data. In *Proceedings of the Joint Conference of the 47th Annual Meeting of the ACL and the 4th International Joint Conference on Natural Language Processing of the AFNLP: Volume 2-Volume 2*, pages 1003–1011. Association for Computational Linguistics.

J. Mitchell and M. Lapata. 2008. Vector-based models of semantic composition. *proceedings of ACL-08: HLT*, pages 236–244.

R.M. Neal. 2000. Markov chain sampling methods for dirichlet process mixture models. *Journal of computational and graphical statistics*, 9(2):249–265.

D.O. O'Seaghdha. 2010. Latent variable models of selectional preference. In *Proceedings of the 48th Annual Meeting of the Association for Computational Linguistics*, pages 435–444. Association for Computational Linguistics.

Hoifung Poon and Pedro Domingos. 2009. Unsupervised semantic parsing. In *Proceedings of the 2009 Conference on Empirical Methods in Natural Language Processing: Volume 1 - Volume 1*, EMNLP '09, pages 1–10. Association for Computational Linguistics.

Hoifung Poon and Pedro Domingos. 2010. Unsupervised ontology induction from text. In *Proceedings of the 48th Annual Meeting of the Association for Computational Linguistics*, ACL '10, pages 296–305. Association for Computational Linguistics.

A. Ritter, O. Etzioni, et al. 2010. A latent dirichlet allocation method for selectional preferences. In *Proceedings of the 48th Annual Meeting of the Association for Computational Linguistics*, pages 424–434. Association for Computational Linguistics.

Stefan Schoenmackers, Oren Etzioni, Daniel S. Weld, and Jesse Davis. 2010. Learning first-order horn clauses from web text. In *Proceedings of the 2010 Conference on Empirical Methods in Natural Language Processing*, EMNLP '10, pages 1088–1098. Association for Computational Linguistics.

R. Socher, B. Huval, C.D. Manning, and A.Y. Ng. 2012. Semantic compositionality through recursive matrix-vector spaces. In *Proceedings of the 2012 Joint Conference on Empirical Methods in Natural Language Processing and Computational Natural Language Learning*, pages 1201–1211. Association for Computational Linguistics.

Mark Steedman. 2000. *The Syntactic Process*. MIT Press.

Mark Steedman. 2012. *Taking Scope: The Natural Semantics of Quantifiers*. MIT Press.

Idan Szpektor, Eyal Shnarch, and Ido Dagan. 2007. Instance-based evaluation of entailment rule acquisition. In *In Proceedings of ACL 2007*, volume 45, page 456.

Ivan Titov and Alexandre Klementiev. 2011. A bayesian model for unsupervised semantic parsing. In *Proceedings of the 49th Annual Meeting of the Association for Computational Linguistics: Human Language Technologies*, pages 1445–1455, Portland, Oregon, USA, June. Association for Computational Linguistics.

Limin Yao, Aria Haghighi, Sebastian Riedel, and Andrew McCallum. 2011. Structured relation discovery using generative models. In *Proceedings of the Conference on Empirical Methods in Natural Language Processing*, EMNLP '11, pages 1456–1466. Association for Computational Linguistics.

Limin Yao, Sebastian Riedel, and Andrew McCallum. 2012. Unsupervised relation discovery with sense disambiguation. In *ACL (1)*, pages 712–720.

J.M. Zelle and R.J. Mooney. 1996. Learning to parse database queries using inductive logic programming. In *Proceedings of the National Conference on Artificial Intelligence*, pages 1050–1055.

Jointly Learning to Parse and Perceive: Connecting Natural Language to the Physical World

Jayant Krishnamurthy
Computer Science Department
Carnegie Mellon University
jayantk@cs.cmu.edu

Thomas Kollar
Computer Science Department
Carnegie Mellon University
tkollar@andrew.cmu.edu

Abstract

This paper introduces Logical Semantics with Perception (LSP), a model for grounded language acquisition that learns to map natural language statements to their referents in a physical environment. For example, given an image, LSP can map the statement "blue mug on the table" to the set of image segments showing blue mugs on tables. LSP learns physical representations for both categorical ("blue," "mug") and relational ("on") language, and also learns to compose these representations to produce the referents of entire statements. We further introduce a weakly supervised training procedure that estimates LSP's parameters using annotated referents for entire statements, without annotated referents for individual words or the parse structure of the statement. We perform experiments on two applications: scene understanding and geographical question answering. We find that LSP outperforms existing, less expressive models that cannot represent relational language. We further find that weakly supervised training is competitive with fully supervised training while requiring significantly less annotation effort.

1 Introduction

Learning the mapping from natural language to physical environments is a central problem for natural language semantics. Understanding this mapping is necessary to enable natural language interactions with robots and other embodied systems. For example, for an autonomous robot to understand the sentence "The blue mug is on the table," it must be able to identify (1) the objects in its environment corresponding to "blue mug" and "table," and (2) the objects which participate in the spatial relation denoted by "on." If the robot can successfully identify these objects, it understands the meaning of the sentence.

The problem of learning to map from natural language expressions to their referents in an environment is known as *grounded language acquisition*. In embodied settings, environments consist of raw sensor data – for example, an environment could be an image collected from a robot's camera. In such applications, grounded language acquisition has two subproblems: *parsing*, learning the compositional structure of natural language; and *perception*, learning the environmental referents of individual words. Acquiring both kinds of knowledge is necessary to understand novel language in novel environments.

Unfortunately, perception is often ignored in work on language acquisition. Other variants of grounded language acquisition eliminate the need for perception by assuming access to a logical representation of the environment (Zettlemoyer and Collins, 2005; Wong and Mooney, 2006; Matuszek et al., 2010; Chen and Mooney, 2011; Liang et al., 2011). The existing work which has jointly addressed both parsing and perception has significant drawbacks, including: (1) fully supervised models requiring large amounts of manual annotation and (2) limited semantic representations (Kollar et al., 2010; Tellex et al., 2011; Matuszek et al., 2012).

This paper introduces Logical Semantics with Perception (LSP), a model for grounded language acquisition that jointly learns to semantically parse language and perceive the world. LSP models a mapping from natural language queries to sets of objects in a real-world environment. The input to LSP is an environment containing objects, such as a seg-

(a) An environment containing 4 objects (image segments).

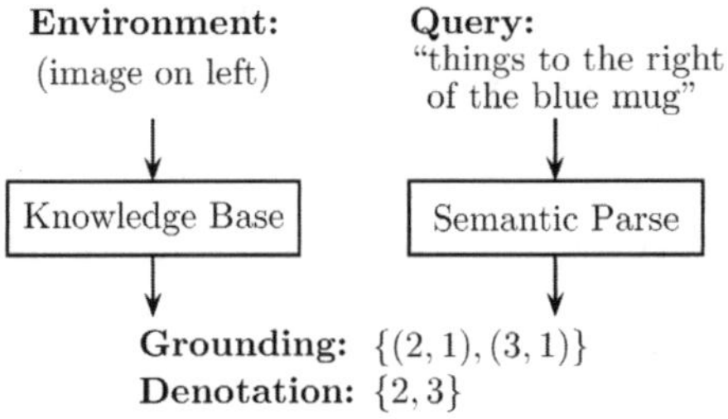

(b) LSP predicting the environmental referents of a natural language query.

Language	Denotation
The mugs	$\{1, 3\}$
The objects on the table	$\{1, 2, 3\}$
There is an LCD monitor	$\{2\}$
Is the blue mug right of the monitor?	$\{\}$
The monitor is behind the blue cup.	$\{2\}$

(c) Training examples for weakly supervised training.

Figure 1: LSP applied to scene understanding. Given an environment containing a set of objects (left), and a natural language query, LSP produces a semantic parse, logical knowledge base, grounding and denotation (middle), using only language/denotation pairs (right) for training.

mented image (Figure 1a), and a natural language query, such as "the things to the right of the blue mug." Given these inputs, LSP produces (1) a logical knowledge base describing objects and relationships in the environment and (2) a semantic parse of the query capturing its compositional structure. LSP combines these two outputs to produce the query's *grounding*, which is the set of object referents of the query's noun phrases, and its *denotation*, which is the query's answer (Figure 1b).[1] Weakly supervised training estimates parameters for LSP using queries annotated with their denotations in an environment (Figure 1c).

This work has two contributions. The first contribution is LSP, which is more expressive than previous models, representing both one-argument categories and two-argument relations over sets of objects in the environment. The second contribution is a weakly supervised training procedure that estimates LSP's parameters without annotated semantic parses, noun phrase/object mappings, or manually-constructed knowledge bases.

We perform experiments on two different applications. The first application is scene understanding, where LSP grounds descriptions of images in image segments. The second application is geographical question answering, where LSP learns to answer questions about locations, represented as polygons on a map. In geographical question answering, LSP correctly answers 34% more questions than the most comparable state-of-the-art model (Matuszek et al., 2012). In scene understanding, accuracy similarly improves by 16%. Furthermore, weakly supervised training achieves an accuracy within 6% of that achieved by fully supervised training, while requiring significantly less annotation effort.

2 Prior Work

Logical Semantics with Perception (LSP) is related to work from planning, natural language processing, computer vision and robotics. Much of the related work focuses on interpreting natural language using a fixed formal representation. Some work constructs integrated systems which execute plans in response to natural language commands (Winograd, 1970; Hsiao et al., 2003; Roy et al., 2003; Skubic et al., 2004; MacMahon et al., 2006; Levit and Roy, 2007; Kruijff et al., 2007). These systems parse natural language to a formal representation which can be executed using a set of fixed control programs. Similarly, work on semantic parsing learns to map natural language to a given formal representation. Semantic parsers can be trained using sentences annotated with their formal representation (Zelle and Mooney, 1996; Zettlemoyer and Collins, 2005; Kate and Mooney, 2006; Kwiatkowski et al., 2010) or various less restrictive annotations (Clarke et al., 2010; Liang et al., 2011; Krishnamurthy and Mitchell, 2012). Finally, work on grounded language acquisition leverages semantic parsing to map from natural language to a formal representation of an environment (Kate and Mooney, 2007; Chen and Mooney, 2008; Shimizu and Haas, 2009; Matuszek

[1]We treat declarative sentences as if they were queries about their subject, e.g., the denotation of "the mug is on the table" is the set of mugs on tables. Typically, the denotation of a sentence is either true or false; our treatment is strictly more general, as a sentence's denotation is nonempty if and only if the sentence is true.

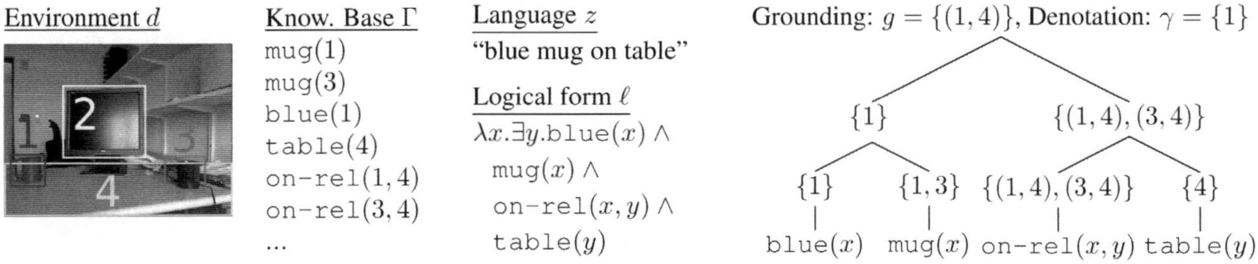

(a) Perception f_{per} produces a logical knowledge base Γ from the environment d using an independent classifier for each category and relation.

(b) Semantic parsing f_{prs} maps language z to a logical form ℓ.

(c) Evaluation f_{eval} evaluates a logical form ℓ on a logical knowledge base Γ to produce a grounding g and denotation γ.

Figure 2: Overview of Logical Semantics with Perception (LSP).

et al., 2010; Dzifcak et al., 2009; Cantrell et al., 2010; Chen and Mooney, 2011). All of this work assumes that the formal environment representation is given, while LSP learns to produce this formal representation from raw sensor input.

Most similar to LSP is work on simultaneously understanding natural language and perceiving the environment. This problem has been addressed in the context of robot direction following (Kollar et al., 2010; Tellex et al., 2011) and visual attribute learning (Matuszek et al., 2012). However, this work is less semantically expressive than LSP and trained using more supervision. The G^3 model (Kollar et al., 2010; Tellex et al., 2011) assumes a one-to-one mapping from noun phrases to entities and is trained using full supervision, while LSP allows one-to-many mappings from noun phrases to entities and can be trained using minimal annotation. Matuszek et al. (2012) learns only one-argument categories ("attributes") and requires a fully supervised initial training phase. In contrast, LSP models two-argument relations and allows for weakly supervised supervised training throughout.

3 Logical Semantics with Perception

Logical Semantics with Perception (LSP) is a model for grounded language acquisition. LSP accepts as input a natural language statement and an environment and outputs the objects in the environment denoted by the statement. The LSP model has three components: perception, parsing and evaluation (see Figure 2). The perception component constructs logical knowledge bases from low-level feature-based representations of environments. The parsing component semantically parses natural language into lambda calculus queries against the constructed knowledge base. Finally, the evaluation component deterministically executes this query against the knowledge base to produce LSP's output.

The output of LSP can be either a *denotation* or a *grounding*. A denotation is the set of entity referents for the phrase as a whole, while a grounding is the set of entity referents for each component of the phrase. The distinction between these two outputs is shown in Figure 1b. In this example, the denotation is the set of "things to the right of the blue mug," which does not include the blue mug itself. On the other hand, the grounding includes both the referents of "things" and "blue mug." Only denotations are used during training, so we ignore groundings in the following model description. However, groundings are used in our evaluation, as they are a more complete description of the model's understanding.

Formally, LSP is a linear model f that predicts a denotation γ given a natural language statement z in an environment d. As shown in Figure 3, the structure of LSP factors into perception (f_{per}), semantic parsing (f_{prs}) and evaluation (f_{eval}) components using several latent variables:

$$f(\gamma, \Gamma, \ell, t, z, d; \theta) = f_{per}(\Gamma, d; \theta_{per}) + f_{prs}(\ell, t, z; \theta_{prs}) + f_{eval}(\gamma, \Gamma, \ell)$$

LSP assumes access to a set of predicates that take either one argument, called categories ($c \in C$) or two arguments, called relations ($r \in R$).[2] These predicates are the interface between LSP's perception and parsing components. The perception function f_{per} takes an environment d and produces a log-

[2]The set of predicates are derived from our training data. See Section 5.3.

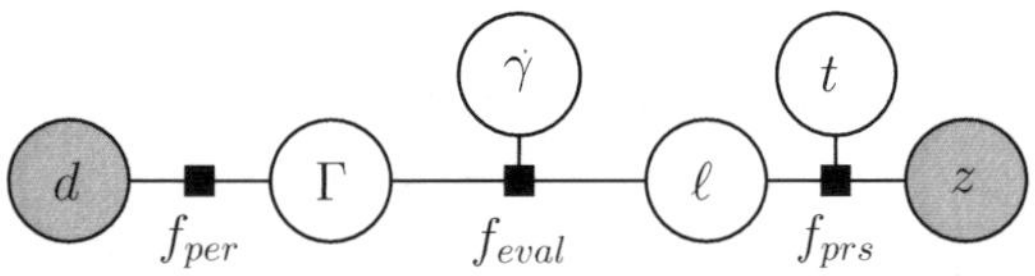

Figure 3: Factor graph of LSP. The environment d and language z are given as input, from which the model predicts a logical knowledge base Γ, logical form ℓ, syntactic tree t and denotation γ.

ical knowledge base Γ that assigns truth values to instances of these predicates using parameters θ_{per}. This function uses an independent classifier to predict the instances of each predicate. The semantic parser f_{prs} takes a natural language statement z and produces a logical form ℓ and syntactic parse t using parameters θ_{prs}. The logical form ℓ is a database query expressed in lambda calculus notation, constructed by logically combining the given predicates. Finally, the evaluation function f_{eval} deterministically evaluates the logical form ℓ on the knowledge base Γ to produce a denotation γ. These components are illustrated in Figure 2.

The following sections describe the perception function (Section 3.1), semantic parser (Section 3.2), evaluation function (Section 3.3), and inference (Section 3.4) in more detail.

3.1 Perception Function

The perception function f_{per} constructs a logical knowledge base Γ given an environment d. The perception function assumes that an environment contains a collection of entities $e \in E_d$. The knowledge base produced by perception is a collection of ground predicate instances using these entities. For example, in Figure 2a, the entire image is the environment, and each image segment is an entity. The logical knowledge base Γ contains the shown predicate instances, where the categories include `blue`, `mug` and `table`, and the relations include `on-rel`.

The perception function scores logical knowledge bases using a set of per-predicate binary classifiers. These classifiers independently assign a score to whether each entity (entity pair) is an element of each category (relation). Let $\gamma^c \in \Gamma$ denote the set of entities which are elements of category c; similarly, let $\gamma^r \in \Gamma$ denote the set of entity pairs which are elements of the relation r. Given these sets, the score of a logical knowledge base Γ factors into per-relation and per-category scores h:

$$f_{per}(\Gamma, d; \theta_{per}) = \sum_{c \in C} h(\gamma^c, d; \theta^c_{per}) + \sum_{r \in R} h(\gamma^r, d; \theta^r_{per})$$

The per-predicate scores are in turn given by a sum of per-element classification scores:

$$h(\gamma^c, d; \theta^c_{per}) = \sum_{e \in E_d} \gamma^c(e)(\theta^c_{per})^T \phi_{cat}(e)$$

$$h(\gamma^r, d; \theta^r_{per}) = \sum_{(e_1,e_2) \in E_d} \gamma^r(e_1, e_2)(\theta^r_{per})^T \phi_{rel}(e_1, e_2)$$

Each term in the above sums represents a single binary classification, determining the score for a single entity (entity pair) belonging to a particular category (relation). We treat γ^c and γ^r as indicator functions for the sets they denote, i.e., $\gamma^c(e) = 1$ for entities e in the set, and 0 otherwise. Similarly, $\gamma^r(e_1, e_2) = 1$ for entity pairs (e_1, e_2) in the set, and 0 otherwise. The features of these classifiers are given by ϕ_{cat} and ϕ_{rel}, which are feature functions that map entities and entity pairs to feature vectors. The parameters of these classifiers are given by θ^c_{per} and θ^r_{per}. The perception parameters θ_{per} contain one such set of parameters for every category and relation, i.e., $\theta_{per} = \{\theta^c_{per} : c \in C\} \cup \{\theta^r_{per} : r \in R\}$.

3.2 Semantic Parser

The goal of semantic parsing is to identify which portions of the input natural language denote entities and relationships between entities in the environment. Semantic parsing accomplishes this goal by mapping from natural language to a logical form that explicitly describes the language's entity referents using one- and two-argument predicates. The logical form is combined with instances of these predicates to produce the statement's denotation.

LSP's semantic parser is defined using Combinatory Categorial Grammar (CCG) (Steedman, 1996). The grammar of the parser is given by a lexicon Λ which maps words to syntactic categories and logical forms. For example, "mug" may have the syntactic category N for noun, and the logical form $\lambda x.\texttt{mug}(x)$, denoting the set of all entities x such that `mug` is true. During parsing, the logical forms for adjacent phrases are combined to produce the logical form for the complete statement.

the	mugs	are	right	of	the	monitor
N/N	N	$(S\backslash N)/N$	N/PP	PP/N	N/N	N
$\lambda f.f$	$\lambda x.\texttt{mug}(x)$	$\lambda f.\lambda g.\lambda x.g(x) \wedge f(x)$	$\lambda f.\lambda x.\exists y.\texttt{right-rel}(x,y) \wedge f(y)$	$\lambda f.f$	$\lambda f.f$	$\lambda x.\texttt{monitor}(x)$

$N : \lambda x.\texttt{monitor}(x)$

$PP : \lambda x.\texttt{monitor}(x)$

$N : \lambda x.\exists y.\texttt{right-rel}(x,y) \wedge \texttt{monitor}(y)$

$N : \lambda x.\texttt{mug}(x)$ $\quad$ $S\backslash N : \lambda g.\lambda x.\exists y.g(x) \wedge \texttt{right-rel}(x,y) \wedge \texttt{monitor}(y)$

$S : \lambda x.\exists y.\texttt{mug}(x) \wedge \texttt{right-rel}(x,y) \wedge \texttt{monitor}(y)$

Figure 4: Example parse of "the mugs are right of the monitor." The first row of the derivation retrieves lexical categories from the lexicon, while the remaining rows represent applications of CCG combinators.

Figure 4 illustrates how CCG parsing produces a syntactic tree t and a logical form ℓ. The top row of the parse represents retrieving a lexicon entry for each word. Each successive row combines a pair of entries by applying a logical form to an adjacent argument. A given sentence may have multiple parses like the one shown, using a different set of lexicon entries or a different order of function applications. The semantic parser scores each such parse, learning to distinguish correct and incorrect parses.

The semantic parser in LSP is a linear model over CCG parses (ℓ, t) given language z:

$$f_{prs}(\ell, t, z; \theta_{prs}) = \theta_{prs}^T \phi_{prs}(\ell, t, z)$$

Here, $\phi_{prs}(\ell, t, z)$ represents a feature function mapping CCG parses to vectors of feature values. ϕ_{prs} factorizes according to the tree structure of the CCG parse; it contains features for local parsing operations which are summed to produce the feature values for a tree. If the parse tree is a terminal, then:

$$\phi_{prs}(\ell, t, z) = \mathbb{1}(\text{lexicon entry})$$

The notation $\mathbb{1}(x)$ denotes a vector with a single one entry whose position is determined by x. The terminal features are indicator features for each lexicon entry, as shown in the top row of Figure 4. These features allow the model to learn the correct syntactic and semantic function of each word. If the parse tree is a nonterminal, then:

$$\phi_{prs}(\ell, t, z) = \phi_{prs}(\text{left}(\ell, t, z)) + \phi_{prs}(\text{right}(\ell, t, z)) + \mathbb{1}(\text{combinator})$$

These nonterminal features are defined over combinator rules in the parse tree, as in the remaining rows of Figure 4. These features allow the model to learn which adjacent parse trees are likely to combine. We refer the reader to Zettlemoyer and Collins (2005) for more information about CCG semantic parsing.

3.3 Evaluation Function

The evaluation function f_{eval} deterministically scores denotations given a logical form ℓ and a logical knowledge base Γ. Intuitively, the evaluation function simply evaluates the query ℓ on the database Γ to produce a denotation. The evaluation function then assigns score 0 to this denotation, and score $-\infty$ to all other denotations.

We describe f_{eval} by giving a recurrence for computing the denotation γ of a logical form ℓ on a logical knowledge base Γ. This evaluation takes the form of a tree, as in Figure 2c. The base cases are:

- If $\ell = \lambda x.c(x)$ then $\gamma = \gamma^c$.
- If $\ell = \lambda x.\lambda y.r(x, y)$, then $\gamma = \gamma^r$.

The denotations for more complex logical forms are computed recursively by decomposing ℓ according to its logical structure. Our logical forms contain only conjunctions and existential quantifiers; the corresponding recursive computations are:

- If $\ell = \lambda x.\ell_1(x) \wedge \ell_2(x)$, then $\gamma(e) = 1$ iff $\gamma_1(e) = 1 \wedge \gamma_2(e) = 1$.
- If $\ell = \lambda x.\exists y.\ell_1(x, y)$, then $\gamma(e_1) = 1$ iff $\exists e_2.\gamma_1(e_1, e_2) = 1$.

Note that a similar recurrence can be used to compute groundings: simply retain the satisfying assignments to existentially-quantified variables.

3.4 Inference

The basic inference problem in LSP is to predict a denotation γ given language z and an environment d. This inference problem is straightforward due to the deterministic structure of f_{eval}. The highest-scoring γ can be found by independently maximizing f_{prs} and f_{per} to find the highest-scoring logical form ℓ and logical knowledge base Γ. Deterministically evaluating the recurrence for f_{eval} using these values yields the highest-scoring denotation.

Another inference problem occurs during training: identify the highest-scoring logical form and knowledge base which produce a particular denotation. Our approximate inference algorithm for this problem is described in Section 4.2.

4 Weakly Supervised Parameter Estimation

This section describes a weakly supervised training procedure for LSP, which estimates parameters using a corpus of sentences with annotated denotations. The algorithm jointly trains both the parsing and the perception components of LSP to best predict the denotations of the observed training sentences. Our approach trains LSP as a maximum margin Markov network using the stochastic subgradient method. The main difficulty is computing the subgradient, which requires computing values for the model's hidden variables, i.e., the logical knowledge base Γ and semantic parse ℓ that are responsible for the model's prediction.

4.1 Stochastic Subgradient Method

The training procedure trains LSP as a maximum margin Markov network (Taskar et al., 2004), a structured analog of a support vector machine. The training data for our weakly supervised algorithm is a collection $\{(z^i, \gamma^i, d^i)\}_{i=1}^n$, consisting of language z^i paired with its denotation γ^i in environment d^i. Given this data, the parameters $\theta = [\theta_{prs}, \theta_{per}]$ are estimated by minimizing the following objective function:

$$O(\theta) = \frac{\lambda}{2}||\theta||^2 + \frac{1}{n}\left[\sum_{i=1}^{n} \zeta_i\right] \quad (1)$$

where λ is a regularization parameter that controls the trade-off between model complexity and slack penalties. The slack variable ζ_i represents a margin violation penalty for the ith training example, defined as:

$$\zeta_i = \max_{\gamma,\Gamma,\ell,t} \left[f(\gamma, \Gamma, \ell, t, z^i, d^i; \theta) + \text{cost}(\gamma, \gamma^i)\right] - \max_{\Gamma,\ell,t} f(\gamma^i, \Gamma, \ell, t, z^i, d^i; \theta)$$

The above expression is the structured counterpart of the hinge loss, where $\text{cost}(\gamma, \gamma^i)$ is the margin by which γ^i's score must exceed γ's score. We let $\text{cost}(\gamma, \gamma^i)$ be the Hamming cost; it adds a cost of 1 for each entity e such that $\gamma^i(e) \neq \gamma(e)$.

We optimize this objective using the stochastic subgradient method (Ratliff et al., 2006). To compute the subgradient g^i, first compute the highest-scoring assignments to the model's hidden variables:

$$\hat{\gamma}, \hat{\Gamma}, \hat{\ell}, \hat{t} \leftarrow \arg\max_{\gamma,\Gamma,\ell,t} f(\gamma, \Gamma, \ell, t, z^i, d^i; \theta^j) + \text{cost}(\gamma, \gamma^i) \quad (2)$$

$$\Gamma^*, \ell^*, t^* \leftarrow \arg\max_{\Gamma,\ell,t} f(\gamma^i, \Gamma, \ell, t, z^i, d^i; \theta^j) \quad (3)$$

The first set of values (e.g., $\hat{\ell}$) are the best explanation for the denotation $\hat{\gamma}$ which most violates the margin constraint. The second set of values (e.g., ℓ^*) are the best explanation for the true denotation γ^i. The subgradient update increases the weights of features that explain the true denotation, while decreasing the weights of features that explain the denotation violating the margin. The subgradient factors into parsing and perception components: $g^i = [g^i_{prs}, g^i_{per}]$. The parsing subgradient is:

$$g^i_{prs} = \phi_{prs}(\hat{\ell}, \hat{t}, z^i) - \phi_{prs}(\ell^*, t^*, z^i)$$

The subgradient of the perception parameters θ_{per} factors into subgradients of the category and relation classifier parameters. Recall that $\theta_{per} = \{\theta^c_{per} : c \in C\} \cup \{\theta^r_{per} : r \in R\}$. Let $\hat{\gamma}^c \in \hat{\Gamma}$ be the best margin-violating set of entities for c, and $\gamma^{c*} \in \Gamma^*$ be the best truth-explaining set of entities. Similarly define $\hat{\gamma}^r$ and γ^{r*}. The subgradients of the category and relation classifier parameters are:

$$g^{i,c}_{per} = \sum_{e \in E_{d^i}} (\hat{\gamma}^c(e) - \gamma^{c*}(e))\, \phi_{cat}(e)$$

$$g^{i,r}_{per} = \sum_{(e_1,e_2) \in E_{d^i}} (\hat{\gamma}^r(e_1, e_2) - \gamma^{r*}(e_1, e_2))\, \phi_{rel}(e_1, e_2)$$

4.2 Inference: Computing the Subgradient

Solving the maximizations in Equations 2 and 3 is challenging because the weights placed on the denotation γ couple f_{prs} and f_{per}. Due to this coupling, exactly solving these problems requires (1) enumerating all possible logical forms ℓ, and (2) for each logical form, finding the highest-scoring logical knowledge base Γ by propagating the weights on γ back through f_{eval}.

We use a two-step approximate inference algorithm for both maximizations. The first step performs a beam search over CCG parses, producing

k possible logical forms $\ell_1, ..., \ell_k$. The second step uses an integer linear program (ILP) to find the best logical knowledge base Γ given each parse ℓ_i. In our experiments, we parse with a beam size of 1000, then solve an ILP for each of the 10 highest-scoring logical forms. The highest-scoring parse/logical knowledge base pair is the approximate maximizer.

Given a logical form ℓ output by beam search, the second step of inference computes the best values for the logical knowledge base Γ and denotation γ:

$$\max_{\Gamma,\gamma} f_{per}(\Gamma, d; \theta_{per}) + f_{eval}(\gamma, \ell, \Gamma) + \psi(\gamma) \quad (4)$$

Here, $\psi(\gamma) = \sum_{e \in E_d} \psi_e \gamma(e)$ represents a set of weights on the entities in the predicted denotation γ. For Equation 2, ψ represents $\text{cost}(\gamma, \gamma^i)$. For Equation 3, ψ is a hard constraint encoding $\gamma = \gamma^i$ (i.e., $\psi(\gamma) = -\infty$ when $\gamma \neq \gamma^i$ and 0 otherwise).

We encode the maximization in Equation 4 as an ILP. For each category c and relation r, we create binary variables $\gamma^c(e_1)$ and $\gamma^r(e_1, e_2)$ for each entity in the environment, $e_1, e_2 \in E_d$. We similarly create binary variables $\gamma(e)$ for the denotation γ. Using the fact that f_{per} is a linear function of these variables, we write the ILP objective as:

$$f_{per}(\Gamma, d; \theta_{per}) + \psi(\gamma) = \sum_{e_1 \in E_d} \sum_{c \in C} w^c_{e_1} \gamma^c(e_1)$$
$$+ \sum_{e_1, e_2 \in E_d} \sum_{r \in R} w^r_{e_1,e_2} \gamma^r(e_1, e_2) + \sum_{e_1 \in E_d} \psi_{e_1} \gamma(e_1)$$

where the weights $w^c_{e_1}$ and $w^r_{e_1,e_2}$ determine how likely it is that each entity or entity pair belongs to the predicates c and r:

$$w^c_{e_1} = (\theta^c_{per})^T \phi_{cat}(e_1)$$
$$w^r_{e_1,e_2} = (\theta^r_{per})^T \phi_{rel}(e_1, e_2)$$

The ILP also includes constraints and additional auxiliary variables that represent f_{eval}. These constraints couple the denotation γ and the logical knowledge base Γ such that γ is the result of evaluating ℓ on Γ. ℓ is recursively decomposed as in Section 3.3, and each intermediate set of entities in the recurrence is given its own set of $|E_d|$ (or $|E_d|^2$) variables. These variables are then logically constrained to enforce ℓ's structure.

5 Evaluation

Our evaluation performs three major comparisons. First, we examine the performance impact of weakly supervised training by comparing weakly and fully supervised variants of LSP. Second, we examine the performance impact of modelling relations by comparing against a category-only baseline, which is an ablated version of LSP similar to the model of Matuszek et al. (2012). Finally, we examine the causes of errors by performing an error analysis of LSP's semantic parser and perceptual classifiers.

Before describing our results, we first describe some necessary set-up for the experiments. These sections describe the data sets, features, construction of the CCG lexicon, and details of the models. Our data sets and additional evaluation resources are available online from `http://rtw.ml.cmu.edu/tacl2013_lsp/`.

5.1 Data Sets

We evaluate LSP on two applications: scene understanding (SCENE) and geographical question answering (GEOQA). These data sets are collections $\{(z^i, \gamma^i, d^i, \ell^i, \Gamma^i)\}_{i=1}^n$, consisting of a number of natural language statements z^i with annotated denotations γ^i in environments d^i. For fully supervised training, each statement is annotated with a gold standard logical form ℓ^i, and each environment with a gold standard logical knowledge base Γ^i. Statistics of these data sets are shown in Table 1, and example environments and statements are shown in Figure 5.

The SCENE data set consists of segmented images of indoor environments containing a number of ordinary objects such as mugs and monitors. Each image is an environment, and each image segment (bounding box) is an entity. We collected natural language descriptions of each scene from members of our lab and Amazon Mechanical Turk, asking subjects to describe the objects in each scene. The authors then manually annotated the collected statements with their denotations and logical forms. In this data set, each image contains the same set of objects; note that this does not trivialize the task, as the model only observes visual features of the objects, which are not consistent across environments.

The GEOQA data set consists of several maps containing entities such as cities, states, national parks, lakes and oceans. Each map is an environment, and its component entities are given by polygons of latitude/longitude coordinates marking

Data Set Statistics	SCENE	GEOQA
# of environments	15	10
Mean entities / environment d	4.1	6.9
Mean # of entities in denotation γ	1.5	1.2
# of statements	284	263
Mean words / statement	6.3	6.3
Mean predicates / log. form	2.6	2.8
# of preds. in annotated worlds	46	38
Lexicon Statistics		
# of words in lexicon	169	288
# of lexicon entries	712	876
Mean parses / statement	15.0	8.9

Table 1: Statistics of the two data sets used in our evaluation, and of the generated lexicons.

their boundaries.[3] Furthermore, each entity has one known name (e.g., "Greenville"). In this data set, distinct entities occur on average in 1.25 environments; repeated entities are mostly large locations, such as states and oceans. The language for this data set was contributed by members of our research group, who were instructed to provide a mixture of simple and complex geographical questions. The authors then manually annotated each question with a denotation (its answer) and a logical form.

5.2 Features

The features of both applications are intended to capture properties of entities and relations between them. As such, both applications share a set of physical features which are functions of the bounding polygons of each entity. Example category features (ϕ_{cat}) are the area and perimeter of the entity, and an example relation feature (ϕ_{rel}) is the distance between entity centroids.

The SCENE data set additionally includes visual appearance features in ϕ_{cat} to capture visual properties of objects. These features include a Histogram of Oriented Gradients (HOG) (Dalal and Triggs, 2005) and an RGB color histogram.

The GEOQA data set additionally includes distributional semantic features to distinguish between different types of entities (e.g., states vs. lakes) and to capture non-spatial relations (e.g., capitals of states). These features are derived from phrase co-occurrences with entity names in the Clueweb09 web corpus.[4] The category features ϕ_{cat} include indicators for the 20 contexts which most frequently occur with an entity's name (e.g., "X is a city"). Similarly, the relation features ϕ_{rel} include indicators for the 20 most frequent contexts between two entities' names (e.g., "X in eastern Y").

5.3 Lexicon Induction

One of the inputs to the semantic parser (Section 3.2) is a lexicon that lists possible syntactic and semantic functions for each word. Together, these per-word entries define the set of possible logical forms for every statement. Each word may have multiple lexicon entries to capture uncertainty about its meaning. For example, the word "right" may have entries $N : \lambda x.\texttt{right}(x)$ and $N/PP : \lambda f.\lambda x.\exists y.\texttt{right-rel}(x, y) \wedge f(y)$. The semantic parser learns to distinguish among these interpretations to produce good logical forms.

We automatically generated lexicons for both applications using part-of-speech tag heuristics.[5] These heuristics map words to lexicon entries containing category and relation predicates derived from the word's lemma. Nouns and adjectives produce lexicon entries containing either categories or relations (as shown above for "right"). Mapping these parts-of-speech to relations is necessary for phrases like "to the right of," where the noun "right" denotes a relation. Verbs and prepositions produce lexicon entries containing relations. Additional heuristics generate semantically-empty lexicon entries, allowing words like determiners to have no physical interpretation. Finally, there are special heuristics for forms of "to be" and, in GEOQA, to handle known entity names. The complete set of lexicon induction heuristics is available online.

The automatically generated lexicon makes it difficult to compare semantic parses across models, since the correctness of a semantic parse depends on the learned perceptual classifiers. To facilitate such a comparison (Section 5.6), we filtered out lexicon entries containing predicates which were not used in any of the annotated logical forms. Statistics of the filtered lexicons are shown in Table 1.

[3]Polygons were extracted from OpenStreetMap, `http://www.openstreetmap.org/`.

[4]`http://www.lemurproject.org/clueweb09/`

[5]We used the Stanford POS tagger (Toutanova et al., 2003).

Environment d	Language z and predicted logical form ℓ	Predicted grounding	True grounding
	monitor to the left of the mugs $\lambda x.\exists y.\mathtt{monitor}(x) \wedge \mathtt{left\text{-}rel}(x, y) \wedge \mathtt{mug}(y)$	$\{(2, 1), (2, 3)\}$	$\{(2, 1), (2, 3)\}$
	mug to the left of the other mug $\lambda x.\exists y.\mathtt{mug}(x) \wedge \mathtt{left\text{-}rel}(x, y) \wedge \mathtt{mug}(y)$	$\{(3, 1)\}$	$\{(3, 1)\}$
	objects on the table $\lambda x.\exists y.\mathtt{object}(x) \wedge \mathtt{on\text{-}rel}(x, y) \wedge \mathtt{table}(y)$	$\{(1, 4), (2, 4)$ $(3, 4)\}$	$\{(1, 4), (2, 4),$ $(3, 4)\}$
	two blue cups are placed near to the computer screen $\lambda x.\mathtt{blue}(x) \wedge \mathtt{cup}(x) \wedge \mathtt{comp.}(x) \wedge \mathtt{screen}(x)$	$\{(1)\}$	$\{(1, 2), (3, 2)\}$
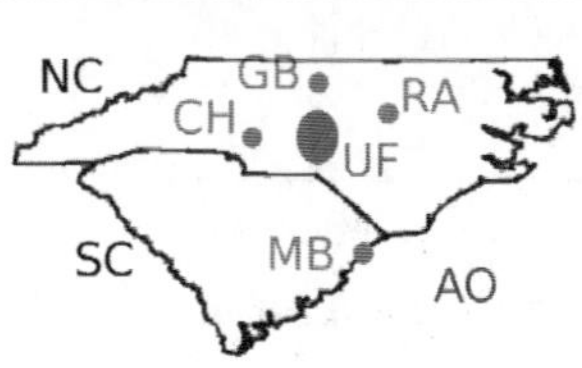	What cities are in North Carolina? $\lambda x.\exists y.\mathtt{city}(x) \wedge \mathtt{in\text{-}rel}(x, y) \wedge y = \mathtt{NC}$	$\{(\mathtt{CH}, \mathtt{NC}), (\mathtt{GB}, \mathtt{NC})$ $(\mathtt{RA}, \mathtt{NC})\}$	$\{(\mathtt{CH}, \mathtt{NC}), (\mathtt{GB}, \mathtt{NC})$ $(\mathtt{RA}, \mathtt{NC})\}$
	What city is east of Greensboro in North Carolina? $\lambda x.\exists y, z.\mathtt{city}(x) \wedge \mathtt{east\text{-}rel}(x, y)$ $\wedge\ y = \mathtt{GB} \wedge \mathtt{in\text{-}rel}(y, z) \wedge z = \mathtt{NC}$	$\{(\mathtt{RA}, \mathtt{GB}, \mathtt{NC}),$ $(\mathtt{MB}, \mathtt{GB}, \mathtt{NC})\}$	$\{(\mathtt{RA}, \mathtt{GB}, \mathtt{NC})\}$
	What cities are on the ocean? $\lambda x.\exists y.\mathtt{city}(x) \wedge \mathtt{on\text{-}rel}(x, y) \wedge \mathtt{ocean}(y)$	$\{(\mathtt{CH}, \mathtt{AO}), (\mathtt{GB}, \mathtt{AO}),$ $(\mathtt{MB}, \mathtt{AO}), (\mathtt{RA}, \mathtt{AO})\}$	$\{(\mathtt{MB}, \mathtt{AO})\}$

Figure 5: Example environments, statements, and model predictions from the SCENE and GEOQA data sets.

5.4 Models and Training

The evaluation compares three models. The first model is LSP-W, which is LSP trained using the weakly supervised algorithm described in Section 4. The second model, LSP-CAT, replicates the model of Matuszek et al. (2012) by restricting LSP to use category predicates. LSP-CAT is constructed by removing all relation predicates in lexicon entries, mapping entries like $\lambda f.\lambda g.\lambda x.\exists y.r(x, y) \wedge g(x) \wedge f(y)$ to $\lambda f.\lambda g.\lambda x.\exists y.g(x) \wedge f(y)$. This model is also trained using our weakly supervised algorithm. The third model, LSP-F, is LSP trained with full supervision, using the manually annotated semantic parses and logical knowledge bases in our data sets. Given these annotations, training LSP amounts to independently training a semantic parser (using sentences with annotated logical forms, $\{(z^i, \ell^i)\}$) and a set of perceptual classifiers (using environments with annotated logical knowledge bases, $\{(d^i, \Gamma^i)\}$). This model measures the performance achievable with LSP given significantly more supervision.

All three variants of LSP were trained using the same hyperparameters. For SCENE, we computed subgradients in 5 example minibatches and performed 100 passes over the data using $\lambda = 0.03$. For GEOQA, we computed subgradients in 8 example minibatches, again performing 100 passes over the data using $\lambda = 0.02$. We tried varying the regularization parameter, but found that performance was relatively stable under $\lambda \leq 0.05$. All experiments use leave-one-environment-out cross-validation to estimate model performance. We hold out each environment in turn, train each model on the remaining environments, then test on the held-out environment.

5.5 Results

We consider two prediction problems in the evaluation. The first problem is to predict the correct denotation γ^i for a statement z^i in an environment d^i. A correct prediction on this task corresponds to a correctly answered question. A weakness of this task is that it is possible to guess the right denotation without fully understanding the language. For example, given a query like "mugs on the table," it might be possible to guess the denotation based solely on "mugs," ignoring "table" altogether. The grounding prediction task corrects for this problem. Here, each model predicts a grounding, which is the set of all satisfying assignments to the variables in a logical form. For example, for the logical form $\lambda x.\exists y.\mathtt{left\text{-}rel}(x, y) \wedge \mathtt{mug}(y)$, the grounding is the set of (x, y) tuples for which both $\mathtt{left\text{-}rel}(x, y)$ and $\mathtt{mug}(y)$ return true. Note that, if the predicted semantic parse is incorrect, the predicted grounding for a statement may contain a different number of variables than the true grounding; such groundings are incorrect. Figure 5 shows model predictions for the grounding task.

Performance on both tasks is measured using exact match accuracy. This metric is the fraction of examples for which the predicted set of entities (be it the denotation or grounding) exactly equals the annotated set. This is a challenging metric, as the

Denotation γ	0 rel.	1 rel.	other	total
LSP-CAT	**0.94**	0.45	**0.20**	0.51
LSP-F	0.89	**0.81**	**0.20**	**0.70**
LSP-W	0.89	0.77	0.16	0.67
Grounding g	0 rel.	1 rel.	other	total
LSP-CAT	**0.94**	0.37	0.00	0.42
LSP-F	0.89	**0.80**	0.00	**0.65**
LSP-W	0.89	0.70	0.00	0.59
% of data	23	56	21	100

(a) Results on the SCENE data set.

Denotation γ	0 rel.	1 rel.	other	total
LSP-CAT	0.22	0.19	0.07	0.17
LSP-F	**0.64**	0.53	**0.21**	0.48
LSP-W	**0.64**	**0.58**	**0.21**	**0.51**
Grounding g	0 rel.	1 rel.	other	total
LSP-CAT	0.22	0.19	0.00	0.16
LSP-F	0.64	0.53	**0.17**	0.47
LSP-W	**0.64**	**0.58**	0.15	**0.50**
% of data	8	72	20	100

(b) Results on the GEOQA data set.

Table 2: Model performance on the SCENE and GEOQA datasets. LSP-CAT is an ablated version of LSP that only learns categories (similar to Matuszek et al. (2012)), LSP-F is LSP trained with annotated semantic parses and logical knowledge bases, and LSP-W is LSP trained on sentences with annotated denotations. Results are separated by the number of relations in each test natural language statement.

number of possible sets grows exponentially in the number of entities in the environment. Say an environment has 5 entities and a logical form has two variables; then there are 2^5 possible denotations and 2^{25} possible groundings. To quantify this difficulty, note that selecting a denotation uniformly at random achieves 6% accuracy on SCENE, and 1% accuracy on GEOQA; selecting a random grounding achieves 1% and 0% accuracy, respectively.

Table 2 shows results for both applications using exact match accuracy. To better understand the performance of each model, we break down performance according to linguistic complexity. We compute the number of relations in the annotated logical form for each statement, and show separate results for 0 and 1 relations. We also include an "other" category to capture sentences with more than one relation (very infrequent), or that include quantifiers, comparatives, or other linguistic phenomena not captured by LSP.

The results from these experiments suggest three conclusions. First, we find that modelling relations is important for both applications, as (1) the majority of examples contain relational language, and (2) LSP-W and LSP-F dramatically outperform LSP-CAT on these examples. The low performance of LSP-CAT suggests that many denotations cannot be predicted from only the first noun phrase in a statement, demonstrating that both applications require an understanding of relations. Second, we find that weakly supervised training and fully supervised training perform similarly, with accuracy differences in the range of 3%-6%. Finally, we find that LSP-W performs similarly on both the denotation and complete grounding tasks; this result suggests that when LSP-W predicts a correct denotation, it does so because it has identified the correct entity referents of each portion of the statement.

5.6 Component Error Analysis

We performed an error analysis of each model component to better understand the causes of errors. Table 3 shows the accuracy of the semantic parser from each trained model. Each held-out sentence z^i is parsed to produce a logical form ℓ, which is marked correct if it exactly matches our manual annotation ℓ^i. A correct logical form implies a correct grounding for the statement when the parse is evaluated in the gold standard logical knowledge base. These results show that both LSP-W and LSP-F have reasonably accurate semantic parsers, given the restrictions on possible logical forms. Common mistakes include missing lexicon entries (e.g., "borders" is POS-tagged as a noun, so the GEOQA lexicon does not include a verb for it) and prepositional phrase attachments (e.g., 6th example in Figure 5).

Table 4 shows the precision and recall of the individual perceptual classifiers. We computed these metrics by comparing each annotated predicate in the held-out environment with the model's predictions for the same predicate, treating each entity (or entity pair) as an independent example for classifi-

	SCENE	GEOQA
LSP-CAT	0.21	0.17
LSP-W	0.72	0.71
LSP-F	**0.73**	**0.75**
Upper Bound	0.79	0.87

Table 3: Accuracy of the semantic parser from each trained model. Upper bound is the highest accuracy achievable without modelling comparatives and other linguistic phenomena not captured by LSP.

cation. Fully supervised training appears to produce better perceptual classifiers than weakly supervised training; however, this result conflicts with the full system evaluation in Table 2, where both systems perform equally well. There are two causes for this phenomenon: uninformative adjectives and unimportant relation instances.

Uninformative adjective predicates are responsible for the low performance of the category classifiers in SCENE. Phrases like "LCD screen" in this domain are annotated with logical forms such as $\lambda x.\texttt{lcd}(x) \wedge \texttt{screen}(x)$. Here, lcd is uninformative, since screen already denotes a unique object in the environment. Therefore, it is not important to learn an accurate classifier for lcd. Weakly supervised training learns that lcd is meaningless, yet predicts the correct denotation for $\lambda x.\texttt{lcd}(x) \wedge \texttt{screen}(x)$ using its screen classifier.

The discrepancy in relation performance occurs because the relation evaluation weights every relation equally, whereas in reality some relations are more frequent. Furthermore, even within a single relation, each entity pair is not equally important – for example, people tend to ask what is in a state, but not what is in an ocean. To account for these factors, we define a reweighted relation metric using the annotated logical forms containing only one relation, of the form $\lambda x.\exists y.c_1(x) \wedge r(x, y) \wedge c_2(y)$. Using these logical forms, we measure the performance of r on the set of x, y pairs such that $c_1(x) \wedge c_2(y)$, then average this over all examples. Table 4 shows that, using this metric, both training regimes have similar performance. This result suggests that weakly supervised training adapts LSP's relation classifiers to the relation instances which are empirically important for grounding natural language.

	SCENE			GEOQA		
Categories	P	R	F1	P	R	F1
LSP-CAT	0.40	0.86	0.55	0.78	0.25	0.38
LSP-W	0.40	0.84	0.54	0.85	**0.63**	0.73
LSP-F	**0.98**	**0.96**	**0.97**	**0.89**	**0.63**	**0.74**
Relations	P	R	F1	P	R	F1
LSP-W	0.40	0.42	0.41	0.34	**0.51**	0.41
LSP-F	**0.99**	**0.87**	**0.92**	**0.70**	0.46	**0.55**
Relations (rw)	P	R	F1	P	R	F1
LSP-W	**0.98**	**0.98**	**0.98**	0.86	**0.72**	**0.79**
LSP-F	**0.98**	0.95	0.96	**0.89**	0.66	0.76

Table 4: Perceptual classifier performance, measured against the gold standard logical knowledge bases. LSP-CAT is excluded from the relation evaluations, since it does not learn relations. Relations (rw) is the reweighted metric (see text for details).

6 Conclusions

This paper introduces Logical Semantics with Perception (LSP), a model for mapping natural language statements to their referents in a physical environment. LSP jointly models perception and language understanding, simultaneously learning (1) to map from environments to logical knowledge bases containing instances of both one-argument categories and two-argument relations, and (2) to semantically parse natural language. Furthermore, we introduce a weakly supervised training procedure that trains LSP using only sentences with annotated denotations, without annotated semantic parses or noun phrase/entity mappings. An experimental evaluation reveals that this procedure performs nearly as well fully supervised training, while requiring significantly less annotation effort. Our experiments also find that LSP's ability to learn relations improves performance over comparable prior work (Matuszek et al., 2012).

Acknowledgments

This research has been supported in part by DARPA under award FA8750-13-2-0005, and in part by a gift from Google. We also gratefully acknowledge the CMU Read the Web group for assistance with data set construction, and Tom Mitchell, Manuela Veloso, Brendan O'Connor, Felix Duvallet, Robert Fisher and the anonymous reviewers for helpful discussions and comments on the paper.

References

Rehj Cantrell, Matthias Scheutz, Paul Schermerhorn, and Xuan Wu. 2010. Robust spoken instruction understanding for HRI. In *Proceedings of the 5th ACM/IEEE International Conference on Human-Robot Interaction*.

David L. Chen and Raymond J. Mooney. 2008. Learning to sportscast: a test of grounded language acquisition. In *Proceedings of the 25th International Conference on Machine learning*.

David L. Chen and Raymond J. Mooney. 2011. Learning to interpret natural language navigation instructions from observations. In *Proceedings of the 25th AAAI Conference on Artificial Intelligence*.

James Clarke, Dan Goldwasser, Ming-Wei Chang, and Dan Roth. 2010. Driving semantic parsing from the world's response. In *Proceedings of the Fourteenth Conference on Computational Natural Language Learning*.

Navneet Dalal and Bill Triggs. 2005. Histograms of oriented gradients for human detection. In *Proceedings of the 2005 IEEE Computer Society Conference on Computer Vision and Pattern Recognition*.

Juraj Dzifcak, Matthias Scheutz, Chitta Baral, and Paul Schermerhorn. 2009. What to do and how to do it: translating natural language directives into temporal and dynamic logic representation for goal management and action execution. In *Proceedings of the 2009 IEEE International Conference on Robotics and Automation*.

Kai-yuh Hsiao, Nikolaos Mavridis, and Deb Roy. 2003. Coupling perception and simulation: Steps towards conversational robotics. In *Proceedings of the IEEE/RSJ International Conference on Intelligent Robots and Systems*.

Rohit J. Kate and Raymond J. Mooney. 2006. Using string-kernels for learning semantic parsers. In *Proceedings of the 21st International Conference on Computational Linguistics and the 44th annual meeting of the ACL*.

Rohit J. Kate and Raymond J. Mooney. 2007. Learning language semantics from ambiguous supervision. In *Proceedings of the 22nd Conference on Artificial Intelligence*.

Thomas Kollar, Stefanie Tellex, Deb Roy, and Nicholas Roy. 2010. Toward understanding natural language directions. In *Proceedings of the 5th ACM/IEEE International Conference on Human-Robot Interaction*.

Jayant Krishnamurthy and Tom M. Mitchell. 2012. Weakly supervised training of semantic parsers. In *Proceedings of the 2012 Joint Conference on Empirical Methods in Natural Language Processing and Computational Natural Language Learning*.

Geert-Jan M. Kruijff, Hendrik Zender, Patric Jensfelt, and Henrik I. Christensen. 2007. Situated dialogue and spatial organization: What, where... and why. *International Journal of Advanced Robotic Systems*.

Tom Kwiatkowski, Luke Zettlemoyer, Sharon Goldwater, and Mark Steedman. 2010. Inducing probabilistic CCG grammars from logical form with higher-order unification. In *Proceedings of the 2010 Conference on Empirical Methods in Natural Language Processing*.

Michael Levit and Deb Roy. 2007. Interpretation of spatial language in a map navigation task. *IEEE Transactions on Systems, Man, and Cybernetics, Part B*.

Percy Liang, Michael I. Jordan, and Dan Klein. 2011. Learning dependency-based compositional semantics. In *Proceedings of the Association for Computational Linguistics*.

Matthew MacMahon, Brian Stankiewicz, and Benjamin Kuipers. 2006. Walk the talk: connecting language, knowledge, and action in route instructions. In *Proceedings of the 21st National Conference on Artificial Intelligence*.

Cynthia Matuszek, Dieter Fox, and Karl Koscher. 2010. Following directions using statistical machine translation. In *Proceedings of the 5th ACM/IEEE International Conference on Human-Robot Interaction*.

Cynthia Matuszek, Nicholas FitzGerald, Luke Zettlemoyer, Liefeng Bo, and Dieter Fox. 2012. A joint model of language and perception for grounded attribute learning. In *Proceedings of the 29th International Conference on Machine Learning*.

Nathan D. Ratliff, J. Andrew Bagnell, and Martin A. Zinkevich. 2006. (online) subgradient methods for structured prediction. *Artificial Intelligence and Statistics*.

Deb Roy, Kai-Yuh Hsiao, and Nikolaos Mavridis. 2003. Conversational robots: building blocks for grounding word meaning. In *Proceedings of the HLT-NAACL 2003 Workshop on Learning Word Meaning from Non-linguistic Data*.

Nobuyuki Shimizu and Andrew Haas. 2009. Learning to follow navigational route instructions. In *Proceedings of the 21st international joint conference on artifical intelligence*.

Marjorie Skubic, Dennis Perzanowski, Sam Blisard, Alan Schultz, William Adams, Magda Bugajska, and Derek Brock. 2004. Spatial language for human-robot dialogs. *IEEE Transactions on Systems, Man, and Cybernetics, Part C: Applications and Reviews*.

Mark Steedman. 1996. *Surface Structure and Interpretation*.

Ben Taskar, Carlos Guestrin, and Daphne Koller. 2004. Max-margin markov networks. In *Advances in Neural Information Processing Systems*.

Stefanie Tellex, Thomas Kollar, Steven Dickerson, Matthew Walter, Ashis Banerjee, Seth Teller, and Nicholas Roy. 2011. Understanding natural language commands for robotic navigation and mobile manipulation. In *AAAI Conference on Artificial Intelligence*.

Kristina Toutanova, Dan Klein, Christopher D. Manning, and Yoram Singer. 2003. Feature-rich part-of-speech tagging with a cyclic dependency network. In *Proceedings of the 2003 Conference of the North American Chapter of the Association for Computational Linguistics on Human Language Technology*.

Terry Winograd. 1970. *Procedures as a representation for data in a computer program for understanding natural language.* Ph.D. thesis, Massachusetts Institute of Technology.

Yuk Wah Wong and Raymond J. Mooney. 2006. Learning for semantic parsing with statistical machine translation. In *Proceedings of the main conference on Human Language Technology Conference of NAACL.*

John M. Zelle and Raymond J. Mooney. 1996. Learning to parse database queries using inductive logic programming. In *Proceedings of the Thirteenth National Conference on Artificial Intelligence*.

Luke S. Zettlemoyer and Michael Collins. 2005. Learning to map sentences to logical form: Structured classification with probabilistic categorial grammars. In *Proceedings of the 21st Conference in Uncertainty in Artificial Intelligence*.

Dual Coordinate Descent Algorithms for Efficient Large Margin Structured Prediction

Ming-Wei Chang **Wen-tau Yih**
Microsoft Research
Redmond, WA 98052, USA
{minchang,scottyih}@microsoft.com

Abstract

Due to the nature of complex NLP problems, *structured prediction algorithms* have been important modeling tools for a wide range of tasks. While there exists evidence showing that linear Structural Support Vector Machine (SSVM) algorithm performs better than structured Perceptron, the SSVM algorithm is still less frequently chosen in the NLP community because of its relatively slow training speed.

In this paper, we propose a fast and easy-to-implement dual coordinate descent algorithm for SSVMs. Unlike algorithms such as Perceptron and stochastic gradient descent, our method keeps track of dual variables and updates the weight vector more aggressively. As a result, this training process is as efficient as existing online learning methods, and yet derives consistently better models, as evaluated on four benchmark NLP datasets for part-of-speech tagging, named-entity recognition and dependency parsing.

1 Introduction

Complex natural language processing tasks are inherently structured. From sequence labeling problems like *part-of-speech tagging* and *named entity recognition* to tree construction tasks like *syntactic parsing*, strong dependencies exist among the labels of individual components. By modeling such relations in the output space, structured output prediction algorithms have been shown to outperform significantly simple binary or multi-class classifiers (Lafferty et al., 2001; Collins, 2002; McDonald et al., 2005).

Among the existing structured output prediction algorithms, the linear Structural Support Vector Machine (SSVM) algorithm (Tsochantaridis et al., 2004; Joachims et al., 2009) has shown outstanding performance in several NLP tasks, such as bilingual word alignment (Moore et al., 2007), constituency and dependency parsing (Taskar et al., 2004b; Koo et al., 2007), sentence compression (Cohn and Lapata, 2009) and document summarization (Li et al., 2009). Nevertheless, as a learning method for NLP, the SSVM algorithm has been less than popular algorithms such as the structured Perceptron (Collins, 2002). This may be due to the fact that current SSVM implementations often suffer from several practical issues. First, state-of-the-art implementations of SSVM such as cutting plane methods (Joachims et al., 2009) are typically complicated.[1] Second, while methods like stochastic gradient descent are simple to implement, tuning learning rates can be difficult. Finally, while SSVM models can achieve superior accuracy, this often requires long training time.

In this paper, we propose a novel optimization method for efficiently training linear SSVMs. Our method not only is easy to implement, but also has excellent training speed, competitive with both structured Perceptron (Collins, 2002) and MIRA (Crammer et al., 2005). When evaluated on several NLP tasks, including POS tagging, NER and dependency parsing, this optimization method also outperforms other approaches in terms of prediction accuracy. Our final algorithm is a dual coordinate

[1]Our algorithm is easy to implement mainly because we use the square hinge loss function.

descent (DCD) algorithm for solving a structured output SVM problem with a 2-norm hinge loss function. The algorithm consists of two main components. One component behaves analogously to online learning methods and updates the weight vector immediately after inference is performed. The other component is similar to the cutting plane method and updates the dual variables (and the weight vector) without running inference. Conceptually, this hybrid approach operates at a balanced trade-off point between inference and weight update, performing better than with either component alone.

Our contributions in this work can be summarized as follows. Firstly, our proposed algorithm shows that even for structured output prediction, an SSVM model can be trained as efficiently as a structured Perceptron one. Secondly, we conducted a careful experimental study on three NLP tasks using four different benchmark datasets. When compared with previous methods for training SSVMs (Joachims et al., 2009), our method achieves similar performance using less training time. When compared to commonly used learning algorithms such as Perceptron and MIRA, the model trained by our algorithm performs consistently better when given the same amount of training time. We believe our method can be a powerful tool for many different NLP tasks.

The rest of our paper is organized as follows. We first describe our approach by formally defining the problem and notation in Sec. 2, where we also review some existing, closely-related structured-output learning algorithms and optimization techniques. We introduce the detailed algorithmic design in Sec. 3. The experimental comparisons of variations of our approach and the existing methods on several NLP benchmark tasks and datasets are reported in Sec. 4. Finally, Sec. 5 concludes the paper.

2 Background and Related Work

We first introduce notations used throughout this paper. An input example is denoted by $\mathbf{x}$ and an output structure is denoted by $\mathbf{y}$. The feature vector $\Phi(\mathbf{x}, \mathbf{y})$ is a function defined over an input-output pair $(\mathbf{x}, \mathbf{y})$. We focus on linear models with predictions made by solving the *decoding* problem:

$$\arg\max_{\mathbf{y} \in \mathcal{Y}(\mathbf{x}_i)} \mathbf{w}^T \Phi(\mathbf{x}_i, \mathbf{y}). \tag{1}$$

The set $\mathcal{Y}(\mathbf{x}_i)$ represents all possible (exponentially many) structures that can be generated from the example $\mathbf{x}_i$. Let $\mathbf{y}_i$ be the true structured label of $\mathbf{x}_i$. The difference between the feature vectors of the correct label $\mathbf{y}_i$ and $\mathbf{y}$ is denoted as $\Phi_{\mathbf{y}_i,\mathbf{y}}(\mathbf{x}_i) \equiv \Phi(\mathbf{x}_i, \mathbf{y}_i) - \Phi(\mathbf{x}_i, \mathbf{y})$. We define $\Delta(\mathbf{y}_i, \mathbf{y})$ as a distance function between two structures.

2.1 Perceptron and MIRA

Structured Perceptron First introduced by Collins (2002), the structured Perceptron algorithm runs two steps iteratively: first, it finds the best structured prediction $\mathbf{y}$ for an example with the current weight vector using Eq. (1); then the weight vector is updated according to the difference between the feature vectors of the true label and the prediction: $\mathbf{w} \leftarrow \mathbf{w} + \Phi_{\mathbf{y}_i,\mathbf{y}}(\mathbf{x}_i)$. Inspired by Freund and Schapire (1999), Collins (2002) also proposed the *averaged* structured Perceptron, which maintains an averaged weight vector throughout the training procedure. This technique has been shown to improve the generalization ability of the model.

MIRA The *Margin Infused Relaxed Algorithm (MIRA)*, which was introduced by Crammer et al. (2005), explicitly uses the notion of margin to update the weight vector. The MIRA updates the weight vector by calculating the step size using

$$\min_{\mathbf{w}} \frac{1}{2} \|\mathbf{w} - \mathbf{w}_0\|^2$$
$$\text{S.T. } \mathbf{w}^T \Phi_{\mathbf{y}_i,\mathbf{y}}(\mathbf{x}_i) \geq \Delta(\mathbf{y}, \mathbf{y}_i), \forall \mathbf{y} \in \mathcal{H}_k,$$

where $\mathcal{H}_k$ is a set containing the best-k structures according to the weight vector $\mathbf{w}_0$. MIRA is a very popular method in the NLP community and has been applied to NLP tasks like word segmentation and part-of-speech tagging (Kruengkrai et al., 2009), NER and chunking (Mejer and Crammer, 2010) and dependency parsing (McDonald et al., 2005).

2.2 Structural SVM

Structural SVM (SSVM) is a maximum margin model for the structured output prediction setting. Training SSVM is equivalent to solving the following global optimization problem:

$$\min_{\mathbf{w}} \frac{\|\mathbf{w}\|^2}{2} + C \sum_{i=1}^{l} L(\mathbf{x}_i, \mathbf{y}_i, \mathbf{w}), \tag{2}$$

where l is the number of labeled examples and

$$L(\mathbf{x}_i, \mathbf{y}_i, \mathbf{w}) = \ell \left(\max_{\mathbf{y}} \left[\Delta(\mathbf{y}_i, \mathbf{y}) - \mathbf{w}^T \Phi_{\mathbf{y}_x i, \mathbf{y}}(\mathbf{x}_i) \right] \right)$$

The typical choice of ℓ is $\ell(a) = a^t$. If $t = 2$ is used, we refer to the SSVM defined in Eq. (2) as the L2-Loss SSVM. If hinge loss ($t = 1$) is used in Eq. (2), we refer to it as the L1-Loss SSVM. Note that the function Δ is not only necessary,[2] but also enables us to use more information on the differences between the structures in the training phase. For example, using Hamming distance for sequence labeling is a reasonable choice, as the model can express finer distinctions between structures $\mathbf{y}_i$ and $\mathbf{y}$.

When training an SSVM model, we often need to solve the loss-augmented inference problem,

$$\arg\max_{\mathbf{y} \in \mathcal{Y}(\mathbf{x}_i)} \left[\mathbf{w}^T \Phi(\mathbf{x}_i, \mathbf{y}) + \Delta(\mathbf{y}_i, \mathbf{y}) \right]. \quad (3)$$

Note that it is a *different* inference problem than the decoding problem in Eq. (1).

Algorithms for training SSVM Cutting plane (CP) methods (Tsochantaridis et al., 2004; Joachims et al., 2009) have been the dominant method for learning the L1-Loss SSVM. Eq. (2) contains an exponential number of constraints. The cutting plane (CP) methods iteratively select a subset of active constraints for each example then solve a sub-problem which contains active constraints to improve the model. CP has proven useful for solving SSVMs. For instance, Yu and Joachims (2009) proposed using CP methods to solve a 1-slack variable formulation, and showed that solving for a 1-slack variable formulation is much faster than solving the l-slack variable one (Eq. (2)). Chang et al. (2010) also proposed a variant of cutting plane method for solving the L2-Loss SSVM. This method uses a dual coordinate descent algorithm to solve the sub-problems. We call their approach the CPD method.

Several other algorithms also aim at solving the L1-Loss SSVM. Stochastic gradient descent (SGD) (Bottou, 2004; Shalev-Shwartz et al., 2007) is a technique for optimizing general convex functions and has been applied to solving the L1-Loss SSVM (Ratliff et al., 2007). Taskar et al. (2004a) proposed a structured SMO algorithm. Because the algorithm solves the dual formulation of the L1-Loss SSVM, it requires picking a violation pair for each update. In contrast, because each dual variable can be updated independently in our DCD algorithm, the implementation is relatively simple. The extragradient algorithm has also been applied to solving the L1-Loss SSVM (Taskar et al., 2005). Unlike our DCD algorithm, the extragradient method requires the learning rate to be specified.

The connections between dual methods and the online algorithms have been previously discussed. Specifically, Shalev-Shwartz and Singer (2006) connects the dual methods to a wide range of online learning algorithms. In (Martins et al., 2010), the authors apply similar techniques on L1-Loss SSVMs and show that the proposed algorithm can be faster than the SGD algorithm.

Exponentiated Gradient (EG) descent (Kivinen and Warmuth, 1995; Collins et al., 2008) has recently been applied to solving the L1-Loss SSVM. Compared to other SSVM learners, EG requires manual tuning of the step size. In addition, EG requires solution of the sum-product inference problem, which can be more expensive than solving Eq. (3) (Taskar et al., 2006). Very recently, Lacoste-Julien et al. (2013) proposed a block-coordinate descent algorithm for the L1-Loss SSVM based on the Frank-Wolfe algorithm (FW-Struct), which has been shown to outperform the EG algorithm significantly. Similar to our DCD algorithm, FW calculates the optimal learning rate when updating the dual variables.

The Sequential Dual Method (SDM) (Shevade et al., 2011) is probably the most related to this paper. SDM solves the L1-Loss SSVM problem using multiple updating policies, which is similar to our approach. However, there are several important differences in the detailed algorithmic design. As will be clear in Sec. 3, our dual coordinate descent (DCD) algorithm is very simple, while SDM (which is not a DCD algorithm) uses a complicated procedure to balance different update policies. By targeting the L2-Loss SSVM formulation, our methods can update the weight vector more efficiently, since there are no equality constraints in the dual.

[2] Without $\Delta(\mathbf{y}, \mathbf{y}_i)$ in Eq. 2, the optimal $\mathbf{w}$ would be zero.

3 Dual Coordinate Descent Algorithms for Structural SVM

In this work, we focus on solving the dual of linear L2-Loss SSVM, which can be written as follows:

$$\min_{\alpha_{i,\mathbf{y}}\geq 0} \frac{1}{2}\|\sum_{i,\mathbf{y}} \alpha_{i,\mathbf{y}} \Phi_{\mathbf{y}_i,\mathbf{y}}(\mathbf{x}_i)\|^2 + \frac{1}{4C}\sum_i (\sum_{\mathbf{y}\in\mathcal{Y}(\mathbf{x}_i)} \alpha_{i,\mathbf{y}})^2 - \sum_{i,\mathbf{y}} \Delta(\mathbf{y},\mathbf{y}_i)\alpha_{i,\mathbf{y}}. \tag{4}$$

In the above equation, a dual variable $\alpha_{i,\mathbf{y}}$ is associated with a structure $\mathbf{y} \in \mathcal{Y}(\mathbf{x}_i)$. Therefore, the total number of dual variables can be quite large: its upper bound is lB, where $B = \max_i |\mathcal{Y}(\mathbf{x}_i)|$.

The connection between the dual variables and the weight vector $\mathbf{w}$ at optimal solutions is through the following equation:

$$\mathbf{w} = \sum_{i=1}^{l} \sum_{\mathbf{y}\in\mathcal{Y}(\mathbf{x}_i)} \alpha_{i,\mathbf{y}} \Phi_{\mathbf{y}_i,\mathbf{y}}(\mathbf{x}_i). \tag{5}$$

Advantages of L2-Loss SSVM The use of the 2-norm hinge loss function eliminates the need of equality constraints[3]; only non-negative constraints ($\alpha_{i,\mathbf{y}} \geq 0$) remain. This is important because now each dual variable can be updated without changing values of the other dual variables. We can then update one single dual variable at a time. As a result, this dual formulation allows us to design a simple and principled dual coordinate descent (DCD) optimization method.

DCD algorithms consist of two iterative steps:

1. Pick a dual variable $\alpha_{i,\mathbf{y}}$.
2. Update the dual variable and the weight vector. Go to 1.

In the normal binary classification case, how to select dual variables to solve is not an issue as choosing them randomly works effectively in practice (Hsieh et al., 2008). However, this is not a practical scheme for training SSVM models given that the number of dual variables in Eq. (4) can be very large because of the exponentially many legitimate output structures. To address this issue, we introduce the concept of *working set* below.

Working Set The number of non-zero variables in the optimal α can be small when solving Eq. (4). Hence, it is often feasible to use a small working set $\mathcal{W}_i$ for each example to keep track of the structures for non-zero α's. More formally,

$$\mathcal{W}_i = \{\mathbf{y} \mid \forall \mathbf{y} \in \mathcal{Y}(\mathbf{x}_i), \alpha_{i,\mathbf{y}} > 0\}.$$

Intuitively, the working set $\mathcal{W}_i$ records the output structures that are similar to the true structure $\mathbf{y}_i$.We set all dual variables to be zero initially (therefore, $\mathbf{w} = 0$ as well), so $\mathcal{W}_i = \emptyset$ for all i. Then the algorithm starts to build the working set in the training procedure. After training, the weight vector is computed using dual variables in the working set and thus equivalent to

$$\mathbf{w} = \sum_{i=1}^{l} \sum_{\mathbf{y}\in\mathcal{W}_i} \alpha_{i,\mathbf{y}} \Phi_{\mathbf{y}_i,\mathbf{y}}(\mathbf{x}_i). \tag{6}$$

Connections to Structured Perceptron The process of updating a dual variable is in fact very similar to the update rule used in Perceptron and MIRA. Take structured Perceptron for example, its weight vector can be determined using the following equation:

$$\mathbf{w}_{\text{perc}} = \sum_{i=1}^{l} \sum_{\mathbf{y}\in\Gamma(\mathbf{x}_i)} \beta_{i,\mathbf{y}} \Phi_{\mathbf{y}_i,\mathbf{y}}(\mathbf{x}_i), \tag{7}$$

where $\Gamma(\mathbf{x}_i)$ is the set containing all structures Perceptron predicts for $\mathbf{x}_i$ during training, and $\beta_{i,\mathbf{y}}$ is the number of times Perceptron predicts $\mathbf{y}$ for $\mathbf{x}_i$ during training. By comparing Eq. (6) and Eq. (7), it is clear that SSVM is just a more principled way to update the weight vector, as α's are computed based on the notion of margin.[4]

Updating Dual Variables and Weights After picking a dual variable $\alpha_{i,\bar{\mathbf{y}}}$, we first show how to update it optimally. Recall that a dual variable $\alpha_{i,\bar{\mathbf{y}}}$ is associated with the i-th example and a structure $\bar{\mathbf{y}}$. The optimal update size d for $\alpha_{i,\bar{\mathbf{y}}}$ can be calculated analytically from the following optimization prob-

[3]For L1-Loss SSVM, there are the equality constraints: $\sum_{\mathbf{y}\in\mathcal{Y}(\mathbf{x}_i)} \alpha_{i,\mathbf{y}} = C, \forall i$.

[4]Of course, $\mathcal{W}_i$ could be very different from $\Gamma(\mathbf{x}_i)$, the construction of the working sets will be discussed in Sec. 3.1.

Algorithm 1 UPDATEWEIGHT(i, $\mathbf{w}$):
Update the weight vector $\mathbf{w}$ and the dual variables in the working set of the i-th example. C is the regularization parameter defined in Eq. (2).

1: Shuffle the elements in $\mathcal{W}_i$ (but retain the newest member of the working set to be updated first. See Theorem 1 for the reasons.)
2: **for** $\bar{\mathbf{y}} \in \mathcal{W}_i$ **do**
3: $\quad d \leftarrow \frac{\Delta(\bar{\mathbf{y}},\mathbf{y}_i) - \mathbf{w}^T \Phi_{\mathbf{y}_i,\bar{\mathbf{y}}}(\mathbf{x}_i) - \frac{\sum_{\mathbf{y}\in\mathcal{W}_i} \alpha_{i,\mathbf{y}}}{2C}}{\|\Phi_{\mathbf{y}_i,\bar{\mathbf{y}}}(\mathbf{x}_i)\|^2 + \frac{1}{2C}}$
4: $\quad \alpha' \leftarrow \max(\alpha_{i,\bar{\mathbf{y}}} + d, 0)$
5: $\quad \mathbf{w} \leftarrow \mathbf{w} + (\alpha' - \alpha_{i,\bar{\mathbf{y}}})\Phi_{\mathbf{y}_i,\bar{\mathbf{y}}}(\mathbf{x}_i)$
6: $\quad \alpha_{i,\bar{\mathbf{y}}} \leftarrow \alpha'$
7: **end for**

lem (derived from Eq. (4)):

$$\min_{d \geq -\alpha_{i,\bar{\mathbf{y}}}} \frac{1}{2}\|\mathbf{w} + d\Phi_{\mathbf{y}_i,\bar{\mathbf{y}}}(\mathbf{x})\|^2 + \frac{1}{4C}(d + \sum_{\mathbf{y}\in\mathcal{W}_i} \alpha_{i,\mathbf{y}})^2 - d\Delta(\mathbf{y}_i, \bar{\mathbf{y}}), \quad (8)$$

where the $\mathbf{w}$ is defined in Eq. (6). Compared to stochastic gradient descent, DCD algorithms keep track of dual variables and do not need to tune the learning rate.

Instead of updating one dual variable at a time, our algorithm updates all dual variables once in the working set. This step is important for the convergence of the DCD algorithms.[5] The exact update algorithm is presented in Algorithm 1. Line 3 calculates the optimal step size (the analytical solution to the above optimization problem). Line 4 makes sure that dual variables are non-negative. Lines 5 and 6 update the weight vectors and the dual variables. Note that every update ensures Eq. (4) to be no greater than the original value.

3.1 Two DCD Optimization Algorithms

Now we are ready to present two novel DCD algorithms for L2-Loss SSVM: *DCD-Light* and *DCD-SSVM*.

3.1.1 DCD-Light

The basic idea of DCD-Light is just like online learning algorithms. Instead of doing inference for the whole batch of examples before updating the weight vector in each iteration, as done in CPD and 1-slack variable formulation of SVM-Struct, DCD-Light updates the model weights after solving the inference problem for each individual example. Algorithm 2 depicts the detailed steps. In Line 5, the loss-augmented inference (Eq. (3)) is performed; then the weight vector is updated in Line 9 – all of the structures and dual variables in the working set are used to update the weight vector. Note that there is a δ parameter in Line 6 to control how precise we would like to solve this SSVM problem. As suggested in (Hsieh et al., 2008), we shuffle the examples in each iteration (Line 3) as it helps the algorithm converge faster.

DCD-Light has several noticeable differences when compared to the most popular online learning method, averaged Perceptron. First, DCD-Light performs the loss-augmented inference (Eq. (3)) at Line 5 instead of the argmax inference (Eq. (1)). Second, the algorithm updates the weight vector with all structures in the working set. Finally, DCD-light does not average the weight vectors.

3.1.2 DCD-SSVM

Observing that DCD-Light does not fully utilize the saved dual variables in the working set, we propose a *hybrid* approach called DCD-SSVM, which combines ideas from DCD-Light and cutting plane methods. In short, after running the updates on a batch of examples, we refine the model by solving the dual variables further in the current working sets. The key advantage of keeping track of these dual variables is that it allows us to *update* the saved dual variables *without* performing any inference, which is often an expensive step in structured prediction algorithms.

DCD-SSVM is summarized in Algorithm 3. Lines 10 to 16 are from DCD-Light. In Lines 3 to 8, we grab the idea from cutting plane methods by updating the weight vector using the saved dual variables in the working sets without any inference (note that Lines 3 to 8 do not have any effect at the first iteration). By revisiting the dual variables, we can derive a better intermediate model, resulting in running the inference procedure less frequently. Similar to DCD-Light, we also shuffle the examples in each iteration.

[5] Specifically, updating all of the structures in the working set is a necessary condition for our algorithms to converge.

Algorithm 2 DCD-Light: The lightweight dual coordinate descent algorithm for optimizing Eq. (4).

1: $\mathbf{w} \leftarrow 0, \mathcal{W}_i \leftarrow \emptyset, \forall i$
2: **for** $t = 1 \dots T$ **do**
3: Shuffle the order of the training examples
4: **for** $i = 1 \dots l$ **do**
5: $\bar{\mathbf{y}} \leftarrow \arg\max_{\mathbf{y}} \mathbf{w}^T \Phi(\mathbf{x}_i, \mathbf{y}) + \Delta(\mathbf{y}, \mathbf{y}_i)$
6: **if** $\Delta(\bar{\mathbf{y}}, \mathbf{y}_i) - \mathbf{w}^T \Phi_{\mathbf{y}_i, \bar{\mathbf{y}}}(\mathbf{x}_i) - \frac{\sum_{\mathbf{y} \in \mathcal{W}_i} \alpha_{i,\mathbf{y}}}{2C} \geq \delta$ **then**
7: $\mathcal{W}_i \leftarrow \mathcal{W}_i \cup \{\bar{\mathbf{y}}\}$
8: **end if**
9: UPDATEWEIGHT$(i, \mathbf{w})$ {Algo. 1}
10: **end for**
11: **end for**

DCD algorithms are similar to column generation algorithms for linear programming (Desrosiers and Lübbecke, 2005), where the master problem is to solve the dual problem that focuses on the variables in the working sets, and the subproblem is to find new variables for the working sets. In Sec. 4, we will demonstrate the importance of balancing these two problems by comparing DCD-SSVM and DCD-Light.

3.2 Convergence Analysis

We now present the theoretic analysis of both DCD-Light and DCD-SSVM, and address two main topics: (1) whether the working sets will grow exponentially and (2) the convergence rate. Due to the lack of space, we show only the main theorems.

Leveraging Theorem 5 in (Joachims et al., 2009), we can prove that the DCD algorithms only add a limited number of variables in the working sets, and have the following theorem.

Theorem 1. *The number of times that DCD-Light or DCD-SSVM adds structures into working sets is bounded by* $O\left(\frac{2(R^2+\frac{1}{2C})lC\Delta^2}{\delta^2}\right)$, *where* R^2 *is defined as* $\max_{i,\bar{\mathbf{y}}} \|\Phi_{\mathbf{y}_i,\bar{\mathbf{y}}}(\mathbf{x}_i)\|^2$, *and* Δ *is the upper bound of* $\Delta(y_i, y'), \forall y_i, y' \in \mathcal{Y}(x_i)$.

We discuss next the convergence rates of our DCD algorithms under two different conditions – when the working sets are fixed and the general case. If the working sets are fixed in DCD algorithms, they become cyclic dual coordinate descent methods. In this case, we denote the minimization problem Eq. (4) as $F(\alpha)$. For fixed working sets $\{\mathcal{W}_i\}$, we denote $F_S(\alpha)$ as the minimization problem that focuses on the dual variables in the working set only. By applying the results from (Luo and Tseng, 1993; Wang and Lin, 2013) to L2-Loss SSVM, we have the following theorem.

Algorithm 3 DCD-SSVM: a *hybrid* dual coordinate descent algorithm that combines ideas from DCD-Light and cutting plane algorithms.

1: $\mathbf{w} \leftarrow 0, \mathcal{W}_i \leftarrow \emptyset, \forall i$
2: **for** $t = 1 \dots T$ **do**
3: **for** $j = 1 \dots r$ **do**
4: Shuffle the order of the training examples
5: **for** $i = 1 \dots l$ **do**
6: UPDATEWEIGHT$(i, \mathbf{w})$ {Algo. 1}
7: **end for**
8: **end for**
9: Shuffle the order of the training examples
10: **for** $i = 1 \dots l$ **do**
11: $\bar{\mathbf{y}} \leftarrow \arg\max_{\mathbf{y}} \mathbf{w}^T \Phi(\mathbf{x}_i, \mathbf{y}) + \Delta(\mathbf{y}, \mathbf{y}_i)$
12: **if** $\Delta(\bar{\mathbf{y}}, \mathbf{y}_i) - \mathbf{w}^T \Phi_{\mathbf{y}_i, \bar{\mathbf{y}}}(\mathbf{x}_i) - \frac{\sum_{\mathbf{y} \in \mathcal{W}_i} \alpha_{i,\mathbf{y}}}{2C} \geq \delta$ **then**
13: $\mathcal{W}_i \leftarrow \mathcal{W}_i \cup \{\bar{\mathbf{y}}\}$
14: **end if**
15: UPDATEWEIGHT$(i, \mathbf{w})$ {Algo. 1}
16: **end for**
17: **end for**

Theorem 2. *For any given non-empty working sets* $\{\mathcal{W}_i\}$, *if the DCD algorithms do not extend the working sets (i.e., line 6-8 in Algorithm 2 are not executed), then the DCD algorithms will obtain the* ϵ*-optimal solution for* $F_S(\alpha)$ *in* $O(\log(\frac{1}{\epsilon}))$ *iterations.*

Based on Theorem 1 and Theorem 2, we have the following theorem.

Theorem 3. *DCD-SSVM obtains an* ϵ*-optimal solution in* $O(\frac{1}{\epsilon^2}\log(\frac{1}{\epsilon}))$ *iterations.*

To the best of our knowledge, this is the first convergence analysis result for L2-Loss SSVM. Compared to other theoretic analysis results for L1-Loss SSVM, a tighter bound might exist given a better theoretic analysis. We leave this for future work.[6]

[6]Noticeably, the use of working sets complicates the theo-

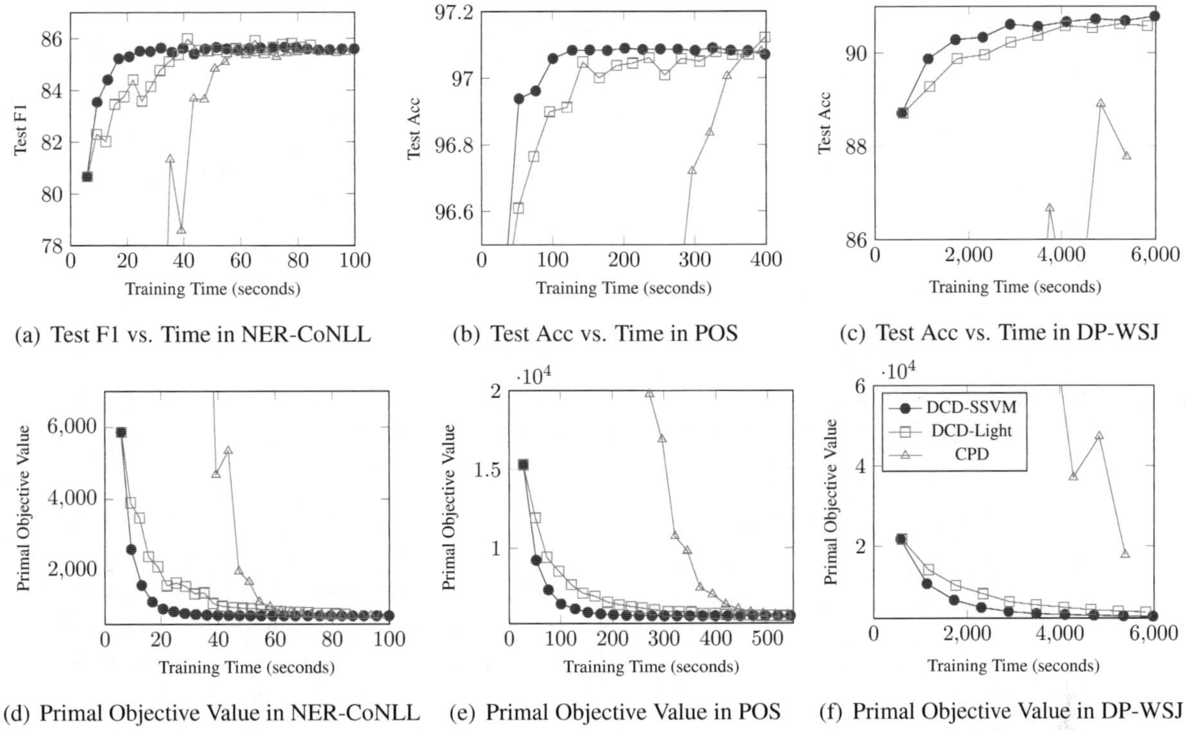

(a) Test F1 vs. Time in NER-CoNLL (b) Test Acc vs. Time in POS (c) Test Acc vs. Time in DP-WSJ

(d) Primal Objective Value in NER-CoNLL (e) Primal Objective Value in POS (f) Primal Objective Value in DP-WSJ

Figure 1: We plot the testing performance (top row) and the primal objective function (bottom row) versus training time for three optimization methods for learning the L2-Loss SSVM. In general, DCD-SSVM is the best algorithm for both the objective function and the testing performance.

4 Experiments

In order to verify the effectiveness of the proposed algorithm, we conduct a set of experiments on different optimization and learning algorithms. Before going to the experimental results, we first introduce the tasks and settings used in the experiments.

4.1 Tasks and Data

We evaluated our method and existing structured output learning approaches on named entity recognition (NER), part-of-speech tagging (POS) and dependency parsing (DP) on four benchmark datasets.

NER-MUC7 MUC-7 data contains a subset of North American News Text Corpora annotated with many types of entities. We followed the settings in (Ratinov and Roth, 2009) and consider three main entities categories: PER, LOC and ORG. We evaluated the results using phrase-level F_1.

---

retic analysis significantly. Also note that Theorem 2 shows that if we put all possible structures in the working sets (i.e., $F(\alpha) = F_S(\alpha)$), then the DCD algorithms can obtain ϵ-optimal solution in $O(\log(\frac{1}{\epsilon}))$ iterations.

NER-CoNLL This is the English dataset from the CoNLL 2003 shared task (T. K. Sang and De Meulder, 2003). The data set labels sentences from the Reuters Corpus, Volume 1 (Lewis et al., 2004) with four different entity types: PER, LOC, ORG and MISC. We evaluated the results using phrase-level F_1.

POS-WSJ The standard set for evaluating the performance of a part-of-speech tagger. The training, development and test sets consist of sections 0-18, 19-21 and 22-24 of the Penn Treebank data (Marcus et al., 1993), respectively. We evaluated the results by token-level accuracy.

DP-WSJ We took sections 02-21 of Penn Treebank as the training set, section 00 as the development set and section 23 as the test set. We implement a simple version of hash kernel to speed up of training procedure for this task (Bohnet, 2010). We reported the unlabeled attachment accuracy for this task (McDonald et al., 2005).

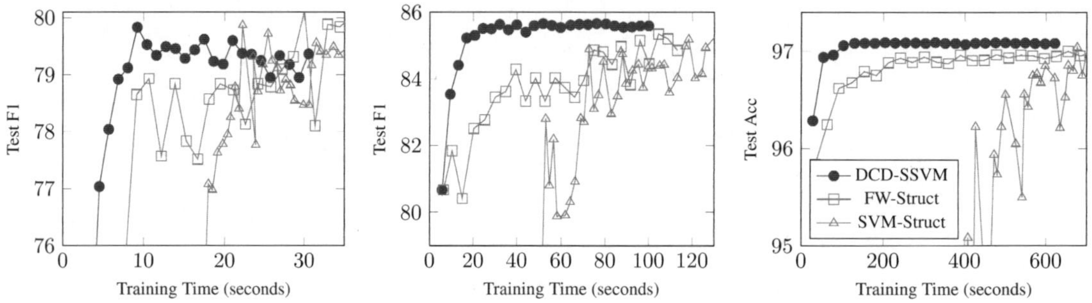

(a) Test F1 vs. Time in NER-MUC7 (b) Test F1 vs. Time in NER-CoNLL (c) Test Acc vs. Time in POS-WSJ

Figure 2: Comparisons between the testing performance of DCD-SSVM, FW-Struct and SVM-Struct. Note that DCD-SSVM often obtain a better model with much less training time when comparing to SVM-Struct.

4.2 Features and Inference Algorithms

For the sequence labeling tasks, NER and POS, we followed the discriminative HMM settings used in (Joachims et al., 2009) and defined the features as

$$\Phi(\mathbf{x}, \mathbf{y}) = \sum_{i=l}^{N} \begin{bmatrix} \Phi_{\text{emi}}(x_i, y_i) \\ [y_i = 1][y_{i-1} = 1] \\ [y_i = 1][y_{i-1} = 2] \\ \cdots \\ [y_i = k][y_{i-1} = k] \end{bmatrix},$$

where Φ_{emi} is the feature vector dedicated to the i-th token (or, the emission features), N represents the number of tokens in this sequence, y_i represents the i-th token in the sequence $\mathbf{y}$, $[y_i = 1]$ is the indictor variable and k is the number of tags.

The inference problems are solved by the Viterbi algorithm. The emission features used in both POS and NER are the standard ones, including word features, word-shape features, etc. For NER, we used additional simple gazetteer features[7] and word cluster features (Turian et al., 2010)

For dependency parsing, we followed the setting described in (McDonald et al., 2005) and used similar features. The decoding algorithm is the first-order Eisner's algorithm (Eisner, 1997).

4.3 Algorithms and Implementation Detail

For all SSVM algorithms (including SGD), C was chosen among the set $\{0.01, 0.05, 0.1, 0.5, 1, 5\}$ according to the accuracy/F_1 on the development set. For each task, the same features were used by all algorithms. For NER-MUC7, NER-CoNLL and POS-WSJ, we ran the online algorithms and DCD-SSVM for 25 iterations. For DP-WSJ, we only let the algorithms run for 10 iterations as the inference procedure is very expensive computationally. The algorithms in the experiments are:

DCD Our dual coordinate descent method on the L2-Loss SSVM. For DCD-SSVM, r is set to be 5. For both DCD-Light and DCD-SSVM , we follow the suggestion in (Joachims et al., 2009): if the value of a dual variable becomes zero, its corresponding structure will be removed from the working set to improve the speed.

SVM-Struct We used the latest (v3.10) of SVM-HMM.[8] This version uses the cutting plane method on a 1-slack variable formulation (Joachims et al., 2009) for the L1-Loss SSVM. SVM-Struct was implemented in C and all the other algorithms are implemented in C#. We did not apply SVM-Struct to DP-WSJ because there is no native implementation.

Perceptron This refers to the averaged structured Perceptron method introduced by Collins (2002). To speed up the convergence rate, we shuffle the training examples at each iteration.

MIRA *Margin Infused Relaxed Algorithm (MIRA)* (Crammer et al., 2005) is the online learning algorithm that explicitly uses the notion of margin to update the weight vector. We use 1-best MIRA in our experiments. To increase

[7] Adding Wikipedia gazetteers would likely increase the performance significantly (Ratinov and Roth, 2009).

[8] `http://www.cs.cornell.edu/People/tj/svm_light/svm_hmm.html`

the convergence speed, we shuffle the training examples at each iteration. Following (McDonald et al., 2005), we did not tune the C parameter for the MIRA algorithm.

SGD Stochastic gradient descent (SGD) (Bottou, 2004) is a technique for optimizing general convex functions. In this paper, we use SGD as an alternative baseline for optimizing the L1-Loss SSVM objective function (Eq. (2) with higne loss).[9] When using SGD, the learning rate must be carefully tuned. Following (Bottou, 2004), the learning rate is obtained by

$$\frac{\eta_0}{(1.0 + (\eta_0 T/C))^{0.75}},$$

where C is the regularization parameter, T is the number of updates so far and η_0 is the initial step size. The parameter η_0 was selected among the set $\{2^{-1}, 2^{-2}, 2^{-3}, 2^{-4}, 2^{-5}\}$ by running the SGD algorithm on a set of 1000 randomly sampled examples, and then choosing the η_0 with lowest primal objective function on these examples.

FW-Struct FW-Struct represents the Frank-Wolfe algorithm for the L1-Loss SSVM (Lacoste-Julien et al., 2013).

In order to improve the training speed, we cached all the feature vectors generated by the gold labeled data once computed. This applied to all algorithms except SVM-Struct, which has its own caching mechanism. We report the performance of the averaged weight vectors for Perceptron and MIRA.

4.4 Results

We present the experimental results below on comparing different dual coordinate descent methods, as well as comparing our main algorithm, DCD-SSVM, with other structured learning approaches.

4.4.1 Comparisons of DCD Methods

We compared three DCD methods: DCD-Light, DCD-SSVM and CPD. CPD is a cutting plane method proposed by Chang et al. (2010), which uses a dual coordinate descent algorithm to solve the internal sub-problems. We specifically included CPD as it also targets at the L2-Loss SSVM.

Because different optimization strategies will reach the same objective values eventually, comparing them on prediction accuracy of the final models is not meaningful. Instead, here we compare how fast each algorithm converges as shown in Figure 1. Each marker on the line in this figure represents one iteration of the corresponding algorithm. Generally speaking, CPD improves the model very slowly in the early stages, but much faster after several iterations. In comparison, DCD-Light often behaves much better initially, and DCD-SSVM is generally the most efficient algorithm here.

The reason behind the slow performance of CPD is clear. During early rounds of the algorithm, the weight vector is far from optimal, so it spends too much time using "bad" weight vectors to find the most violated structures. On the other hand, DCD-Light updates the weight vector more frequently, so it behaves much better in general. DCD-SSVM spends more time on updating models during each batch, but keeps the same amount of time doing inference as DCD-Light. As a result, it finds a better trade-off between inference and learning.

4.4.2 DCD-SSVM, SVM-Struct and FW-Struct

Joachims et al. (2009) proposed a 1-slack variable method for the L1-Loss SSVM. They showed that solving a 1-slack variable formulation is an order-of-magnitude faster than solving the original formulation (l-slack variables formulation). Nevertheless, from Figure 2, we can see the clear advantage of DCD-SSVM over SVM-Struct. Although using 1-slack variable has improved the learning speed, SVM-Struct still converges slower than DCD-SSVM. In addition, the performance of models trained by SVM-Struct in the early stage is quite unstable, which makes early stopping an ineffective strategy in practice when training time is limited.

We also compared our algorithms to FW-Struct. Our results agree with (Lacoste-Julien et al., 2013), which shows that the FW-Struct outperforms the SVM-Struct. In our experiments, we found that our DCD algorithms were competitive, sometimes converged faster than the FW-Struct.

[9] To compare with SGD using its best setting, we report only the results of SGD on the L1-Loss SSVM as we found tuning the step size for the L2-Loss SSVM is more difficult.

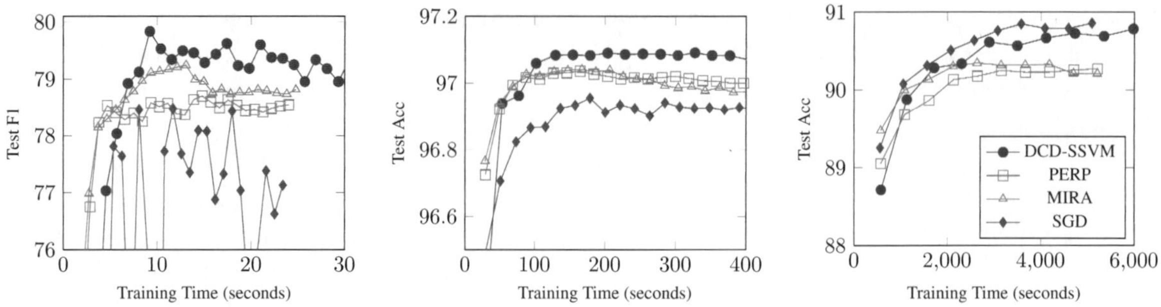

(a) Test F1 vs. Time in NER-MUC7 (b) Test Acc vs. Time in POS-WSJ (c) Test Acc vs. Time in DP-WSJ

Figure 3: Comparisons between DCD-SSVM and popular online learning algorithms. Note that the results diverge when comparing Perceptron and MIRA. In general, DCD-SSVM is the most stable algorithm.

Task/Data	DCD	Percep	MIRA	SGD
NER-MUC7	**79.4**	78.5	78.8	77.8
NER-CoNLL	**85.6**	85.3	85.1	84.2
POS-WSJ	**97.1**	96.9	96.9	96.9
DP-WSJ	90.8	90.3	90.2	**90.9**

Table 1: Performance of online learning algorithms and the DCD-SSVM algorithm on the testing sets. NER is measured by F_1 while others by accuracy.

4.4.3 DCD-SSVM, MIRA, Perceptron and SGD

As in binary classification, large-margin methods like SVMs often perform better than algorithms like Perceptron and SGD (Hsieh et al., 2008; Shalev-Shwartz and Zhang, 2013), here we observe similar behaviors in the structured output domain. Table 1 shows the final test accuracy numbers or F_1 scores of models trained by algorithms including Perceptron, MIRA and SGD, compared to those of the SSVM models trained by DCD-SSVM. Among the benchmark datasets and tasks we have experimented with, DCD-SSVM derived the most accurate models, except for DP-WSJ when compared to SGD.

Perhaps a more interesting comparison is on the training speed, which can be observed in Figure 3. Compared to other online algorithms, DCD-SSVM can take advantage of cached dual variables and structures. We show that the training speed of DCD-SSVM can be competitive to that of the online learning algorithms, unlike SVM-Struct. Note that SGD is not very stable for NER-MUC7, even though we tuned the step size very carefully.

5 Conclusion

In this paper, we present a novel approach for learning the L2-Loss SSVM model. By combining the ideas of dual coordinate descent and cutting plane methods, the hybrid approach, DCD-SSVM outperforms other SSVM training methods both in terms of objective value reduction and testing error rate reduction. As demonstrated in our experiments on several NLP tasks, our approach also tends to learn more accurate models than commonly used structured learning algorithms, including structured Perceptron, MIRA and SGD. Perhaps more interestingly, our SSVM learning method is very efficient: the model training time is competitive to online learning algorithms such as structured Perceptron and MIRA. These unique qualities make DCD-SSVM an excellent choice for solving a variety of complex NLP problems.

In the future, we would like to compare our algorithm to other structured prediction approaches, such as conditional random fields (Lafferty et al., 2001) and exponential gradient descent methods (Collins et al., 2008). Expediting the learning process further by leveraging approximate inference is also an interesting direction to investigate.

Acknowledgments

We sincerely thank John Platt, Lin Xiao and Kaiwei Chang for the discussions and feedback. We are grateful to Po-Wei Wang and Chih-Jen Lin for providing their work on convergence rate analysis on feasible descent methods. We also thank the reviewers for their detailed comments on this paper.

References

B. Bohnet. 2010. Very high accuracy and fast dependency parsing is not a contradiction. In *Proceedings of the 23rd International Conference on Computational Linguistics*, Proceedings the International Conference on Computational Linguistics (COLING).

L. Bottou. 2004. Stochastic learning. In Olivier Bousquet and Ulrike von Luxburg, editors, *Advanced Lectures on Machine Learning*, Lecture Notes in Artificial Intelligence, LNAI 3176, pages 146–168. Springer Verlag, Berlin.

M. Chang, V. Srikumar, D. Goldwasser, and D. Roth. 2010. Structured output learning with indirect supervision. In *Proceedings of the International Conference on Machine Learning (ICML)*.

T. Cohn and M. Lapata. 2009. Sentence compression as tree transduction. *Journal of AI Research*, 34:637–674, April.

M. Collins, A. Globerson, T. Koo, X. Carreras, and P. L. Bartlett. 2008. Exponentiated gradient algorithms for conditional random fields and max-margin Markov networks. *Journal of Machine Learning Research*, 9.

M. Collins. 2002. Discriminative training methods for hidden Markov models: Theory and experiments with perceptron algorithms. In *Proceedings of the Conference on Empirical Methods for Natural Language Processing (EMNLP)*.

K. Crammer, R. Mcdonald, and F. Pereira. 2005. Scalable large-margin online learning for structured classification. Technical report, Department of Computer and Information Science, University of Pennsylvania.

J. Desrosiers and M. E. Lübbecke. 2005. A primer in column generation. In *Column Generation*, pages 1–32. Springer.

J. M. Eisner. 1997. Three new probabilistic models for dependency parsing: An exploration. In *Proceedings the International Conference on Computational Linguistics (COLING)*, pages 340–345.

Y. Freund and R. Schapire. 1999. Large margin classification using the Perceptron algorithm. *Machine Learning*, 37(3):277–296.

C.-J. Hsieh, K.-W. Chang, C.-J. Lin, S. S. Keerthi, and S. Sundararajan. 2008. A dual coordinate descent method for large-scale linear SVM. In *Proceedings of the International Conference on Machine Learning (ICML)*, New York, NY, USA. ACM.

T. Joachims, T. Finley, and Chun-Nam Yu. 2009. Cutting-plane training of structural SVMs. *Machine Learning*, 77(1):27–59.

J. Kivinen and M. K. Warmuth. 1995. Exponentiated gradient versus gradient descent for linear predictors. In *ACM Symp. of the Theory of Computing*.

T. Koo, A. Globerson, X. Carreras, and M. Collins. 2007. Structured prediction models via the matrix-tree theorem. In *Proceedings of the 2007 Joint Conference of EMNLP-CoNLL*, pages 141–150.

C. Kruengkrai, K. Uchimoto, J. Kazama, Y. Wang, K. Torisawa, and H. Isahara. 2009. An error-driven word-character hybrid model for joint chinese word segmentation and pos tagging. In *Proceedings of the Annual Meeting of the Association for Computational Linguistics (ACL)*, pages 513–521.

S. Lacoste-Julien, M. Jaggi, M. W. Schmidt, and P. Pletscher. 2013. Stochastic block-coordinate Frank-Wolfe optimization for structural SVMs. In *Proceedings of the International Conference on Machine Learning (ICML)*.

J. Lafferty, A. McCallum, and F. Pereira. 2001. Conditional random fields: Probabilistic models for segmenting and labeling sequence data. In *Proceedings of the International Conference on Machine Learning (ICML)*.

D. D. Lewis, Y. Yang, T. Rose, and F. Li. 2004. RCV1: A new benchmark collection for text categorization research. *Journal of Machine Learning Research*, 5:361–397.

L. Li, K. Zhou, G.-R. Xue, H. Zha, and Y. Yu. 2009. Enhancing diversity, coverage and balance for summarization through structure learning. In *Proceedings of the 18th international conference on World wide web*, The International World Wide Web Conference, pages 71–80, New York, NY, USA. ACM.

Z.-Q. Luo and P. Tseng. 1993. Error bounds and convergence analysis of feasible descent methods: A general approach. *Annals of Operations Research*, 46(1):157–178.

M. P. Marcus, B. Santorini, and M. Marcinkiewicz. 1993. Building a large annotated corpus of English: The Penn Treebank. *Computational Linguistics*, 19(2):313–330, June.

A. F. Martins, K. Gimpel, N. A. Smith, E. P. Xing, M. A. Figueiredo, and P. M. Aguiar. 2010. Learning structured classifiers with dual coordinate ascent. Technical report, Technical report CMU-ML-10-109.

R. McDonald, K. Crammer, and F. Pereira. 2005. Online large-margin training of dependency parsers. In *Proceedings of the Annual Meeting of the Association for Computational Linguistics (ACL)*, pages 91–98, Ann Arbor, Michigan.

A. Mejer and K. Crammer. 2010. Confidence in structured-prediction using confidence-weighted models. In *Proceedings of the 2010 Conference on Empirical Methods in Natural Language Processing*, Proceedings of the Conference on Empirical Methods for Natural Language Processing (EMNLP), pages 971–981.

R. C. Moore, W. Yih, and A. Bode. 2007. Improved discriminative bilingual word alignment. In *Proceedings of the Annual Meeting of the Association for Computational Linguistics (ACL).*

L. Ratinov and D. Roth. 2009. Design challenges and misconceptions in named entity recognition. In *Proc. of the Annual Conference on Computational Natural Language Learning (CoNLL)*, Jun.

N. Ratliff, J. Andrew (Drew) Bagnell, and M. Zinkevich. 2007. (Online) subgradient methods for structured prediction. In *Proceedings of the International Workshop on Artificial Intelligence and Statistics*, March.

S. Shalev-Shwartz and Y. Singer. 2006. Online learning meets optimization in the dual. In *Proceedings of the Annual ACM Workshop on Computational Learning Theory (COLT).*

S. Shalev-Shwartz and T. Zhang. 2013. Stochastic dual coordinate ascent methods for regularized loss minimization. *Journal of Machine Learning Research*, 14:567–599.

S. Shalev-Shwartz, Y. Singer, and N. Srebro. 2007. Pegasos: primal estimated sub-gradient solver for SVM. In Zoubin Ghahramani, editor, *Proceedings of the International Conference on Machine Learning (ICML)*, pages 807–814. Omnipress.

S. Shevade, P. Balamurugan, S. Sundararajan, and S. Keerthi. 2011. A sequential dual method for structural SVMs. In *IEEE International Conference on Data Mining(ICDM).*

E. F. T. K. Sang and F. De Meulder. 2003. Introduction to the CoNLL-2003 shared task: Language-independent named entity recognition. In Walter Daelemans and Miles Osborne, editors, *Proceedings of CoNLL-2003*, pages 142–147. Edmonton, Canada.

B. Taskar, C. Guestrin, and D. Koller. 2004a. Max-margin markov networks. In *The Conference on Advances in Neural Information Processing Systems (NIPS).*

B. Taskar, D. Klein, M. Collins, D. Koller, and C. Manning. 2004b. Max-margin parsing. In *Proceedings of the Conference on Empirical Methods for Natural Language Processing (EMNLP).*

B. Taskar, S. Lacoste-julien, and M. I. Jordan. 2005. Structured prediction via the extragradient method. In *The Conference on Advances in Neural Information Processing Systems (NIPS).*

B. Taskar, S. Lacoste-Julien, and M. I Jordan. 2006. Structured prediction, dual extragradient and bregman projections. *Journal of Machine Learning Research*, 7:1627–1653.

I. Tsochantaridis, T. Hofmann, T. Joachims, and Y. Altun. 2004. Support vector machine learning for interdependent and structured output spaces. In *Proceedings of the International Conference on Machine Learning (ICML).*

J. Turian, L. Ratinov, and Y. Bengio. 2010. Word representations: a simple and general method for semi-supervised learning. In *Proceedings of the Annual Meeting of the Association for Computational Linguistics (ACL)*, pages 384–394, Stroudsburg, PA, USA. Association for Computational Linguistics.

Po-Wei Wang and Chih-Jen Lin. 2013. Iteration complexity of feasible descent methods for convex optimization. Technical report, National Taiwan University.

C. Yu and T. Joachims. 2009. Learning structural SVMs with latent variables. In *Proceedings of the International Conference on Machine Learning (ICML).*

Joint Arc-factored Parsing of Syntactic and Semantic Dependencies

Xavier Lluís and **Xavier Carreras** and **Lluís Màrquez**
TALP Research Center
Universitat Politècnica de Catalunya
Jordi Girona 1–3, 08034 Barcelona
{xlluis,carreras,lluism}@lsi.upc.edu

Abstract

In this paper we introduce a joint arc-factored model for syntactic and semantic dependency parsing. The semantic role labeler predicts the full syntactic paths that connect predicates with their arguments. This process is framed as a linear assignment task, which allows to control some well-formedness constraints. For the syntactic part, we define a standard arc-factored dependency model that predicts the full syntactic tree. Finally, we employ dual decomposition techniques to produce consistent syntactic and predicate-argument structures while searching over a large space of syntactic configurations. In experiments on the CoNLL-2009 English benchmark we observe very competitive results.

1 Introduction

Semantic role labeling (SRL) is the task of identifying the arguments of lexical predicates in a sentence and labeling them with semantic roles (Gildea and Jurafsky, 2002; Màrquez et al., 2008). SRL is an important shallow semantic task in NLP since predicate-argument relations directly represent semantic properties of the type "who" did "what" to "whom", "how", and "why" for events expressed by predicates (typically verbs and nouns).

Predicate-argument relations are strongly related to the syntactic structure of the sentence: the majority of predicate arguments correspond to some syntactic constituent, and the syntactic structure that connects an argument with the predicate is a strong indicator of its semantic role. Actually, semantic roles represent an abstraction of the syntactic form of a predicative event. While syntactic functions of arguments change with the form of the event (e.g., active vs. passive forms), the semantic roles of arguments remain invariant to their syntactic realization.

Consequently, since the first works, SRL systems have assumed access to the syntactic structure of the sentence (Gildea and Jurafsky, 2002; Carreras and Màrquez, 2005). A simple approach is to obtain the parse trees as a pre-process to the SRL system, which allows the use of unrestricted features of the syntax. However, as in other pipeline approaches in NLP, it has been shown that the errors of the syntactic parser severely degrade the predictions of the SRL model (Gildea and Palmer, 2002). A common approach to alleviate this problem is to work with multiple alternative syntactic trees and let the SRL system optimize over any input tree or part of it (Toutanova et al., 2008; Punyakanok et al., 2008). As a step further, more recent work has proposed parsing models that predict syntactic structure augmented with semantic predicate-argument relations (Surdeanu et al., 2008; Hajič et al., 2009; Johansson, 2009; Titov et al., 2009; Lluís et al., 2009), which is the focus of this paper. These joint models should favor the syntactic structure that is most consistent with the semantic predicate-argument structures of a sentence. In principle, these models can exploit syntactic and semantic features simultaneously, and could potentially improve the accuracy for both syntactic and semantic relations.

One difficulty in the design of joint syntactic-semantic parsing models is that there exist important structural divergences between the two layers.

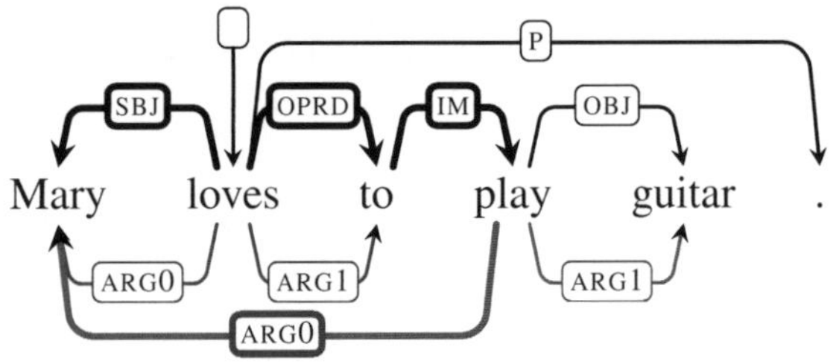

Figure 1: A sentence with syntactic dependencies (top) and semantic dependencies for the predicates "loves" and "play" (bottom). The thick arcs illustrate a structural divergence where the argument "Mary" is linked to "play" with a path involving three syntactic dependencies.

This is clearly seen in dependency-based representations of syntax and semantic roles (Surdeanu et al., 2008), such as in the example in Figure 1: the construct "loves to" causes the argument "Mary" to be syntactically distant from the predicate "play". Linguistic phenomena such as auxiliary verbs, control and raising, typically result in syntactic structures where semantic arguments are not among the direct dependants of their predicate —e.g., about 25% of arguments are *distant* in the English development set of the CoNLL-2009 shared task. Besides, standard models for dependency parsing crucially depend on arc factorizations of the dependency structure (McDonald et al., 2005; Nivre and Nilsson, 2005), otherwise their computational properties break. Hence, it is challenging to define efficient methods for syntactic and semantic dependency parsing that can exploit features of both layers simultaneously. In this paper we propose a method for this joint task.

In our method we define predicate-centric semantic models that, rather than predicting just the argument that realizes each semantic role, they predict the full syntactic path that connects the predicate with the argument. We show how efficient predictions with these models can be made using assignment algorithms in bipartite graphs. Simultaneously, we use a standard arc-factored dependency model that predicts the full syntactic tree of the sentence. Finally, we employ dual decomposition techniques (Koo et al., 2010; Rush et al., 2010; Sontag et al., 2010) to find agreement between the full dependency tree and the partial syntactic trees linking each predicate with its arguments. In summary, the main contributions of this paper are:

- We frame SRL as a weighted assignment problem in a bipartite graph. Under this framework we can control assignment constraints between roles and arguments. Key to our method, we can efficiently search over a large space of syntactic realizations of semantic arguments.
- We solve joint inference of syntactic and semantic dependencies with a dual decomposition method, similar to that of Koo et al. (2010). Our system produces consistent syntactic and predicate-argument structures while searching over a large space of syntactic configurations.

In the experimental section we compare joint and pipeline models. The final results of our joint syntactic-semantic system are competitive with the state-of-the-art and improve over the best results published by a joint method on the CoNLL-2009 English dataset.

2 A Syntactic-Semantic Dependency Model

We first describe how we represent structures of syntactic and semantic dependencies like the one in Figure 1. Throughout the paper, we will assume a fixed input sentence $\mathbf{x}$ with n tokens where lexical predicates are marked. We will also assume fixed sets of syntactic functions $\mathcal{R}_{\text{syn}}$ and semantic roles $\mathcal{R}_{\text{sem}}$. We will represent depencency structures using vectors of binary variables. A variable $y_{h,m,l}$ will indicate the presence of a syntactic dependency from head token h to dependant token m labeled with syntactic function l. Then, a syntactic tree will be denoted as a vector $\mathbf{y}$ of variables indexed by syntactic dependencies. Similarly, a variable $z_{p,a,r}$ will indicate the presence of a semantic dependency between predicate token p and argument token a labeled with semantic role r. We will represent a semantic role structure as a vector $\mathbf{z}$ indexed by semantic dependencies. Whenever we enumerate syntactic dependencies $\langle h, m, l\rangle$ we will assume that they are in the valid range for $\mathbf{x}$, i.e. $0 \leq h \leq n$, $1 \leq m \leq n$, $h \neq m$ and $l \in \mathcal{R}_{\text{syn}}$, where $h = 0$ stands for a special *root* token. Similarly, for semantic dependencies $\langle p, a, r\rangle$ we will assume that p points to a predicate of $\mathbf{x}$, $1 \leq a \leq n$ and $r \in \mathcal{R}_{\text{sem}}$.

A joint model for syntactic and semantic dependency parsing could be defined as:

$$\underset{\mathbf{y},\mathbf{z}}{\text{argmax}} \ \text{s\_syn}(\mathbf{x},\mathbf{y}) + \text{s\_srl}(\mathbf{x},\mathbf{z},\mathbf{y}) \quad . \tag{1}$$

In the equation, $\text{s\_syn}(\mathbf{x},\mathbf{y})$ gives a score for the syntactic tree $\mathbf{y}$. In the literature, it is standard to use arc-factored models defined as

$$\text{s\_syn}(\mathbf{x},\mathbf{y}) = \sum_{y_{h,m,l}=1} \text{s\_syn}(\mathbf{x},h,m,l) \quad , \tag{2}$$

where we overload s_syn to be a function that computes scores for individual syntactic dependencies. In linear discriminative models one has $\text{s\_syn}(\mathbf{x},h,m,l) = \mathbf{w}_{\text{syn}} \cdot \mathbf{f}_{\text{syn}}(\mathbf{x},h,m,l)$, where $\mathbf{f}_{\text{syn}}$ is a feature vector for a syntactic dependency and $\mathbf{w}_{\text{syn}}$ is a vector of parameters (McDonald et al., 2005). In Section 6 we describe how we trained score functions with discriminative methods.

The other term in Eq. 1, $\text{s\_srl}(\mathbf{x},\mathbf{z},\mathbf{y})$, gives a score for a semantic dependency structure $\mathbf{z}$ using features of the syntactic structure $\mathbf{y}$. Previous work has empirically proved the importance of exploiting syntactic features in the semantic component (Gildea and Jurafsky, 2002; Xue and Palmer, 2004; Punyakanok et al., 2008). However, without further assumptions, this property makes the optimization problem computationally hard. One simple approximation is to use a pipeline model: first compute the optimal syntactic tree $\mathbf{y}$, and then optimize for the best semantic structure $\mathbf{z}$ given $\mathbf{y}$. In the rest of the paper we describe a method that searches over syntactic and semantic dependency structures jointly.

We first note that for a fixed semantic dependency, the semantic component will typically restrict the syntactic features representing the dependency to a specific subtree of $\mathbf{y}$. For example, previous work has restricted such features to the syntactic path that links a predicate with an argument (Moschitti, 2004; Johansson, 2009), and in this paper we employ this restriction. Figure 1 gives an example of a subtree, where we highlight the syntactic path that connects the semantic dependency between "play" and "Mary" with role ARG0.

Formally, for a predicate p, argument a and role r we define a *local* syntactic subtree $\boldsymbol{\pi}^{p,a,r}$ represented as a vector: $\pi^{p,a,r}_{h,m,l}$ indicates if a dependency $\langle h,m,l\rangle$ is part of the syntactic path that links predicate p with token a and role r.[1] Given full syntactic and semantic structures $\mathbf{y}$ and $\mathbf{z}$ it is trivial to construct a vector $\boldsymbol{\pi}$ that concatenates vectors $\boldsymbol{\pi}^{p,a,r}$ for all $\langle p,a,r\rangle$ in $\mathbf{z}$. The semantic model becomes

$$\text{s\_srl}(\mathbf{x},\mathbf{z},\boldsymbol{\pi}) = \sum_{z_{p,a,r}=1} \text{s\_srl}(\mathbf{x},p,a,r,\boldsymbol{\pi}^{p,a,r}) \quad , \tag{3}$$

where s_srl computes a score for a semantic dependency $\langle p,a,r\rangle$ *together* with its syntactic path $\boldsymbol{\pi}^{p,a,r}$. As in the syntactic component, this function is typically defined as a linear function over a set of features of the semantic dependency and its path.

The inference problem of our joint model is:

$$\underset{\mathbf{y},\mathbf{z},\boldsymbol{\pi}}{\text{argmax}} \ \text{s\_syn}(\mathbf{x},\mathbf{y}) + \text{s\_srl}(\mathbf{x},\mathbf{z},\boldsymbol{\pi}) \tag{4}$$

subject to

cTree : $\mathbf{y}$ is a valid dependency tree

cRole : $\forall p,r : \sum_a z_{p,a,r} \leq 1$

cArg : $\forall p,a : \sum_r z_{p,a,r} \leq 1$

cPath : $\forall p,a,r :$ if $z_{p,a,r} = 1$ then $\boldsymbol{\pi}^{p,a,r}$ is a path from p to a, otherwise $\boldsymbol{\pi}^{p,a,r} = \mathbf{0}$

cSubtree : $\forall p,a,r : \boldsymbol{\pi}^{p,a,r}$ is a subtree of $\mathbf{y}$

Constraint **cTree** dictates that $\mathbf{y}$ is a valid dependency tree; see (Martins et al., 2009) for a detailed specification. The next two sets of constraints concern the semantic structure only. **cRole** imposes that each semantic role is realized at most once.[2] Conversely, **cArg** dictates that an argument can realize at most one semantic role in a predicate. The final two sets of constraints model the syntactic-semantic interdependencies. **cPath** imposes that each $\boldsymbol{\pi}^{p,a,r}$ represents a syntactic path between p and a whenever there exists a semantic relation. Finally, **cSubtree** imposes that the paths in $\boldsymbol{\pi}$ are consistent with the full syntactic structure, i.e. they are subtrees.

[1]In this paper we say that structures $\boldsymbol{\pi}^{p,a,r}$ are paths from predicates to arguments, but they could be more general subtrees. The condition to build a joint system is that these subtrees must be parseable in the way we describe in Section 3.1.

[2]In general a semantic role can be realized with more than one argument, though it is rare. It is not hard to modify our framework to allow for a maximum number of occurrences of a semantic role.

In Section 3 we define a process that optimizes the semantic structure ignoring constraint **cSubtree**. Then in Section 4 we describe a dual decomposition method that uses the first process repeatedly to solve the joint problem.

3 SRL as Assignment

In this section we frame the problem of finding semantic dependencies as a linear assignment task. The problem we optimize is:

$$\underset{\mathbf{z},\boldsymbol{\pi}}{\operatorname{argmax}}\ \text{s\_srl}(\mathbf{x},\mathbf{z},\boldsymbol{\pi}) \quad \text{subject to} \quad \textbf{cRole}, \textbf{cArg}, \textbf{cPath} \tag{5}$$

In this case we dropped the full syntactic structure $\mathbf{y}$ from the optimization in Eq. 4, as well as the corresponding constraints **cTree** and **cSubtree**. As a consequence, we note that the syntactic paths $\boldsymbol{\pi}$ are not tied to any consistency constraint other than each of the paths being a well-formed sequence of dependencies linking the predicate to the argument. In other words, the optimal solution in this case does not guarantee that the set of paths from a predicate to all of its arguments satisfies tree constraints. We first describe how these paths can be optimized locally. Then we show how to find a solution $\mathbf{z}$ satisfying **cRole** and **cArg** using an assignment algorithm.

3.1 Local Optimization of Syntactic Paths

Let $\widehat{\mathbf{z}}$ and $\widehat{\boldsymbol{\pi}}$ be the optimal values of Eq. 5. For any $\langle p, a, r\rangle$, let

$$\tilde{\boldsymbol{\pi}}^{p,a,r} = \underset{\boldsymbol{\pi}^{p,a,r}}{\operatorname{argmax}}\ \text{s\_srl}(\mathbf{x}, p, a, r, \boldsymbol{\pi}^{p,a,r})\,. \tag{6}$$

For any $\langle p, a, r\rangle$ such that $\widehat{z}_{p,a,r} = 1$ it has to be that $\widehat{\boldsymbol{\pi}}^{p,a,r} = \tilde{\boldsymbol{\pi}}^{p,a,r}$. If this was not true, replacing $\widehat{\boldsymbol{\pi}}^{p,a,r}$ with $\tilde{\boldsymbol{\pi}}^{p,a,r}$ would improve the objective of Eq. 5 without violating the constraints, thus contradicting the hypothesis about optimality of $\widehat{\boldsymbol{\pi}}$. Therefore, for each $\langle p, a, r\rangle$ we can optimize its best syntactic path locally as defined in Eq. 6.

In this paper, we will assume access to a list of likely syntactic paths for each predicate p and argument candidate a, such that the optimization in Eq. 6 can be solved explicitly by looping over each path in the list. The main advantage of this method is that, since paths are precomputed, our model can make unrestricted use of syntactic path features.

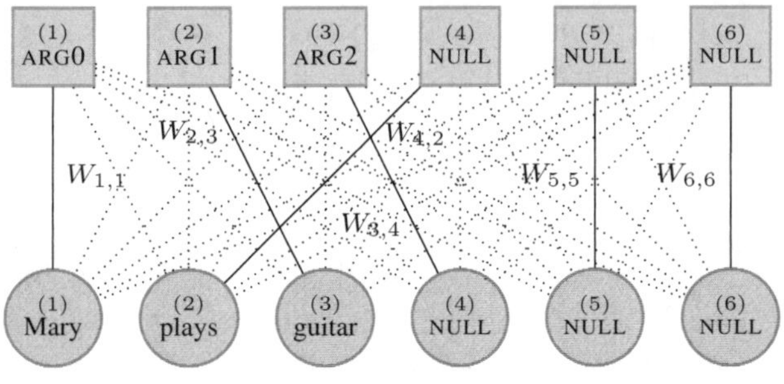

Figure 2: Illustration of the assignment graph for the sentence "Mary plays guitar", where the predicate "plays" can have up to three roles: ARG0 (agent), ARG1 (theme) and ARG2 (benefactor). Nodes labeled NULL represent a null role or token. Highlighted edges are the correct assignment.

It is simple to employ a probabilistic syntactic dependency model to create the list of likely paths for each predicate-argument pair. In the experiments we explore this approach and show that with an average of 60 paths per predicate we recover 97% of correct paths to arguments.

We leave for future work the development of efficient methods to recover the most likely syntactic structure linking an argument with its predicate.

3.2 The Assignment Algorithm

Coming back to solving Eq. 5, it is easy to see that an optimal solution satisfying constraints **cRole** and **cArg** can be found with a linear assignment algorithm. The process we describe determines the predicate-argument relations separately for each predicate. Assume a bipartite graph of size N with *role* nodes $r_1 \ldots r_N$ on one side and *argument* nodes $a_1 \ldots a_N$ on the other side. Assume also a matrix of non-negative scores $W_{i,j}$ corresponding to assigning argument a_j to role r_i. A linear assignment algorithm finds a bijection $f : i \rightarrow j$ from roles to arguments that maximizes $\sum_{i=1}^{N} W_{i,f(i)}$. The Hungarian algorithm finds the exact solution to this problem in $\mathcal{O}(N^3)$ time (Kuhn, 1955; Burkard et al., 2009).

All that is left is to construct a bipartite graph representing predicate roles and sentence tokens, such that some roles and tokens can be left unassigned, which is a common setting for assignment tasks. Algorithm 1 describes a procedure for constructing a weighted bipartite graph for SRL, and Figure 2 illustrates an example of a bipartite graph. We then

Algorithm 1 Construction of an Assignment Graph for Semantic Role Labeling

Let p be a predicate with k possible roles. Let n be the number of argument candidates in the sentence. This algorithm creates a bipartite graph with $N = n+k$ vertices on each side.

1. Create *role* vertices r_i for $i = 1 \ldots N$, where
   - for $1 \leq i \leq k$, r_i is the i-th role,
   - for $1 \leq i \leq n$, r_{k+i} is a special NULL role.
2. Create *argument* vertices a_j for $j = 1 \ldots N$, where
   - for $1 \leq j \leq n$, a_j is the j-th argument candidate,
   - for $1 \leq j \leq k$, a_{n+j} is a special NULL argument.
3. Define a matrix of model scores $S \in \mathbb{R}^{(k+1)\times n}$:
   (a) Optimization of syntactic paths:
   For $1 \leq i \leq k, 1 \leq j \leq n$
   $S_{i,j} = \max_{\boldsymbol{\pi}^{p,a_j,r_i}} \text{s\_srl}(\mathbf{x}, p, a_j, r_i, \boldsymbol{\pi}^{p,a_j,r_i})$
   (b) Scores of NULL assignments[3]:
   For $1 \leq j \leq n$
   $S_{k+1,j} = 0$
4. Let $S_0 = \min_{i,j} S_{i,j}$, the minimum of any score in S. Define a matrix of *non-negative* scores $W \in \mathbb{R}^{N\times N}$ as follows:
   (a) for $1 \leq i \leq k, \ \ 1 \leq j \leq n$
   $W_{i,j} = S_{i,j} - S_0$
   (b) for $k < i \leq N, \ \ 1 \leq j \leq n$
   $W_{i,j} = S_{k+1,j} - S_0$
   (c) for $1 < i \leq N, \ \ n < j \leq N$
   $W_{i,j} = 0$

run the Hungarian algorithm on the weighted graph and obtain a bijection $f : r_i \to a_j$, from which it is trivial to recover the optimal solution of Eq. 5. Finally, we note that it is simple to allow for multiple instances of a semantic role by adding more role nodes in step 1; it would be straightforward to add penalties in step 3 for multiple instances of roles.

4 A Dual Decomposition Algorithm

We now present a dual decomposition method to optimize Eq. 4, that uses the assignment algorithm presented above as a subroutine. Our method is similar to that of Koo et al. (2010), in the sense that our joint optimization can be decomposed into two sub-problems that need to agree on the syntactic dependencies they predict. For a detailed description of dual decomposition methods applied to NLP see (Sontag et al., 2010; Rush et al., 2010).

We note that in Eq. 4 the constraint **cSubtree** ties the syntactic and semantic structures, imposing that any path $\boldsymbol{\pi}^{p,a,r}$ that links a predicate p with an argument a must be a subtree of the full syntactic structure $\mathbf{y}$. Formally the set of constraints is:

$$y_{h,m,l} \geq \pi^{p,a,r}_{h,m,l} \quad \forall\, p, a, r, h, m, l \ .$$

These constraints can be compactly written as

$$c \cdot y_{h,m,l} \geq \sum_{p,a,r} \pi^{p,a,r}_{h,m,l} \quad \forall\, h, m, l \ ,$$

where c is a constant equal to the number of distinct semantic dependencies $\langle p, a, r\rangle$. In addition, we can introduce a vector non-negative slack variables $\boldsymbol{\xi}$ with a component for each syntactic dependency $\xi_{h,m,l}$, turning the constraints into:

$$c \cdot y_{h,m,l} - \sum_{p,a,r} \pi^{p,a,r}_{h,m,l} - \xi_{h,m,l} = 0 \quad \forall\, h, m, l$$

We can now rewrite Eq. 4 as:

$$\begin{aligned} &\operatorname*{argmax}_{\mathbf{y},\mathbf{z},\boldsymbol{\pi},\boldsymbol{\xi}\geq\mathbf{0}} \ \text{s\_syn}(\mathbf{x}, \mathbf{y}) + \text{s\_srl}(\mathbf{x}, \mathbf{z}, \boldsymbol{\pi}) \\ &\quad \text{subject to} \\ &\quad \textbf{cTree, cRole, cArg, cPath} \\ &\quad \forall h, m, l : c \cdot y_{h,m,l} - \sum_{p,a,r} \pi^{p,a,r}_{h,m,l} - \xi_{h,m,l} = 0 \end{aligned} \tag{7}$$

As in Koo et al. (2010), we will relax subtree constraints by introducing a vector of Lagrange multipliers $\boldsymbol{\lambda}$ indexed by syntactic dependencies, i.e. each coordinate $\lambda_{h,m,l}$ is a Lagrange multiplier for the constraint associated with $\langle h, m, l\rangle$. The Lagrangian of the problem is:

$$\begin{aligned} L(\mathbf{y}, \mathbf{z}, \boldsymbol{\pi}, \boldsymbol{\xi}, \boldsymbol{\lambda}) =& \ \text{s\_syn}(\mathbf{x}, \mathbf{y}) + \text{s\_srl}(\mathbf{x}, \mathbf{z}, \boldsymbol{\pi}) \\ &+ \boldsymbol{\lambda} \cdot \left(c \cdot \mathbf{y} - \sum_{p,a,r} \boldsymbol{\pi}^{p,a,r} - \boldsymbol{\xi} \right) \end{aligned} \tag{8}$$

We can now formulate Eq. 7 as:

$$\max_{\substack{\mathbf{y},\mathbf{z},\boldsymbol{\pi},\boldsymbol{\xi}\geq\mathbf{0} \\ \text{s.t. } \textbf{cTree,cRole,cArg,cPath} \\ c\cdot\mathbf{y} - \sum_{p,a,r} \boldsymbol{\pi}^{p,a,r} - \boldsymbol{\xi} = \mathbf{0}}} L(\mathbf{y}, \mathbf{z}, \boldsymbol{\pi}, \boldsymbol{\xi}, \boldsymbol{\lambda}) \tag{9}$$

[3] In our model we fix the score of null assignments to 0. It is straightforward to compute a discriminative score instead.

This optimization problem has the property that its optimum value is the same as the optimum of Eq. 7 for any value of $\boldsymbol{\lambda}$. This is because whenever the constraints are satisfied, the terms in the Lagrangian involving $\boldsymbol{\lambda}$ are zero. If we remove the subtree constraints from Eq. 9 we obtain the dual objective:

$$\begin{aligned} D(\boldsymbol{\lambda}) &= \max_{\substack{\mathbf{y},\mathbf{z},\boldsymbol{\pi},\boldsymbol{\xi}\geq \mathbf{0} \\ \text{s.t. } \mathbf{cTree},\mathbf{cRole},\mathbf{cArg},\mathbf{cPath}}} L(\mathbf{y},\mathbf{z},\boldsymbol{\pi},\boldsymbol{\xi},\boldsymbol{\lambda}) \qquad (10) \\ &= \max_{\mathbf{y} \text{ s.t. } \mathbf{cTree}} \left(\text{s\_syn}(\mathbf{x},\mathbf{y}) + c\cdot \mathbf{y}\cdot\boldsymbol{\lambda}\right) \\ &+ \max_{\substack{\mathbf{z},\boldsymbol{\pi} \\ \text{s.t. } \mathbf{cRole},\mathbf{cArg},\mathbf{cPath}}} \left(\text{s\_srl}(\mathbf{x},\mathbf{z},\boldsymbol{\pi}) - \boldsymbol{\lambda}\cdot\sum_{p,a,r}\boldsymbol{\pi}^{p,a,r}\right) \\ &+ \max_{\boldsymbol{\xi}\geq\mathbf{0}} (-\boldsymbol{\lambda}\cdot\boldsymbol{\xi}) \qquad (11) \end{aligned}$$

The dual objective is an upper bound to the optimal value of primal objective of Eq. 7. Thus, we are interested in finding the minimum of the dual in order to tighten the upper-bound. We will solve

$$\min_{\boldsymbol{\lambda}} D(\boldsymbol{\lambda}) \qquad (12)$$

using a subgradient method. Algorithm 2 presents pseudo-code. The algorithm takes advantage of the *decomposed* form of the dual in Eq. 11, where we have rewritten the Lagrangian such that syntactic and semantic structures appear in separate terms. This will allow to compute subgradients efficiently. In particular, the subgradient of D at a point $\boldsymbol{\lambda}$ is:

$$\Delta(\boldsymbol{\lambda}) = c\cdot\widehat{\mathbf{y}} - \sum_{p,a,r}\widehat{\boldsymbol{\pi}}^{p,a,r} - \widehat{\boldsymbol{\xi}} \qquad (13)$$

where

$$\widehat{\mathbf{y}} = \operatorname*{argmax}_{\mathbf{y} \text{ s.t. } \mathbf{cTree}} \left(\text{s\_syn}(\mathbf{x},\mathbf{y}) + c\cdot\mathbf{y}\cdot\boldsymbol{\lambda}\right) \qquad (14)$$

$$\widehat{\mathbf{z}},\widehat{\boldsymbol{\pi}} = \operatorname*{argmax}_{\substack{\mathbf{z},\boldsymbol{\pi} \text{ s.t.} \\ \mathbf{cRole},\mathbf{cArg},\mathbf{cPath}}} \text{s\_srl}(\mathbf{x},\mathbf{z},\boldsymbol{\pi}) - \boldsymbol{\lambda}\cdot\sum_{p,a,r}\boldsymbol{\pi}^{p,a,r} \qquad (15)$$

$$\widehat{\boldsymbol{\xi}} = \operatorname*{argmax}_{\boldsymbol{\xi}\geq\mathbf{0}} -\boldsymbol{\lambda}\cdot\boldsymbol{\xi} \qquad (16)$$

Whenever $\widehat{\boldsymbol{\pi}}$ is consistent with $\widehat{\mathbf{y}}$ the subgradient will be zero and the method will converge. When paths $\widehat{\boldsymbol{\pi}}$ contain a dependency $\langle h,m,l\rangle$ that is inconsistent with $\widehat{\mathbf{y}}$, the associated dual $\lambda_{h,m,l}$ will increase, hence lowering the score of all paths that use $\langle h,m,l\rangle$ at the next iteration; at same time, the total score for that dependency will increase, favoring syntactic dependency structures alternative to $\widehat{\mathbf{y}}$. As in previous work, in the algorithm a parameter α_t controls the size of subgradient steps at iteration t.

Algorithm 2 A dual-decomposition algorithm for syntactic-semantic dependency parsing

Input: $\mathbf{x}$, a sentence; T, number of iterations;
Output: syntactic and semantic structures $\widehat{\mathbf{y}}$ and $\widehat{\mathbf{z}}$
Notation: we use **cSem**= **cRole** $\wedge$ **cArg** $\wedge$ **cPath**

```
λ^1 = 0 # initialize dual variables
c = number of distinct ⟨h, m, l⟩ in x
for t = 1 ... T do
    ŷ = argmax_{y s.t. cTree} (s_syn(x, y) + c · λ^t · y)
    ẑ, π̂ = argmax_{z,π s.t. cSem} (s_srl(x, z, π)
                                   − λ^t · Σ_{p,a,r} π^{p,a,r})
    λ^{t+1} = λ^t # dual variables for the next iteration
    Set α_t, the step size of the current iteration
    for each ⟨h, m, l⟩ do
        q = Σ_{p,a,r} π̂^{p,a,r}_{h,m,l} # num. paths using ⟨h, m, l⟩
        if q > 0 and ŷ_{h,m,l} = 0 then
            λ^{t+1}_{h,m,l} = λ^{t+1}_{h,m,l} + α_t q
    break if λ^{t+1} = λ^t # convergence
return ŷ, ẑ
```

The key point of the method is that solutions to Eq. 14 and 15 can be computed efficiently using separate processes. In particular, Eq. 14 corresponds to a standard dependency parsing problem, where for each dependency $\langle h,m,l\rangle$ we have an additional score term $c\cdot\lambda_{h,m,l}$ —in our experiments we use the projected dependency parsing algorithm by (Eisner, 2000). To calculate Eq. 15 we use the assignment method described in Section 3, where it is straightforward to introduce additional score terms $-\lambda_{h,m,l}$ to every factor $\pi^{p,a,r}_{h,m,l}$. It can be shown that whenever the subgradient method converges, the solutions $\widehat{\mathbf{y}}$ and $\widehat{\mathbf{z}}$ are the optimal solutions to our original problem in Eq. 4 (see (Koo et al., 2010) for a justification). In practice we run the subgradient method for a maximum number of iterations, and return the solutions of the last iteration if it does not converge.

5 Related Work

Recently, there have been a number of approaches to joint parsing of syntactic and semantic dependencies, partly because of the availability of treebanks in this format popularized by the CoNLL shared tasks (Surdeanu et al., 2008; Hajič et al., 2009).

Like in our method, Johansson (2009) defined a model that exploits features of a semantic dependency together with the syntactic path connecting the predicate and the argument. That method uses an approximate parsing algorithm that employs k-best inference and beam search. Similarly, Lluís et al. (2009) defined a joint model that forces the predicate structure to be represented in the syntactic dependency tree, by enriching arcs with semantic information. The semantic component uses features of pre-computed syntactic structures that may diverge from the joint structure. In contrast, our joint parsing method is exact whenever the dual decomposition algorithm converges.

Titov et al. (2009) augmented a transition-based dependency parser with operations that produce synchronous derivations of syntactic and semantic structures. Instead of explicitly representing semantic dependencies together with a syntactic path, they induce latent representations of the interactions between syntactic and semantic layers.

In all works mentioned the model has no control of assignment constraints that disallow labeling multiple arguments with the same semantic role. Punyakanok et al. (2008) first introduced a system that explicitly controls these constraints, as well as other constraints that look at pairwise assignments which we can not model. They solve SRL using general-purpose Integer Linear Programming (ILP) methods. In similar spirit, Riedel and McCallum (2011) presented a model for extracting structured events that controls interactions between predicate-argument assignments. They take into account pairwise assignments and solve the optimization problem with dual decomposition. More recently, Das et al. (2012) proposed a dual decomposition method that deals with several assignment constraints for predicate-argument relations. Their method is an alternative to general ILP methods. To our knowledge, our work is the first that frames SRL as a linear assignment task, for which simple and exact algorithms exist. We should note that these works model predicate-argument relations with assignment constraints, but none of them predicts the underlying syntactic structure.

Our dual decomposition method follows from that of Koo et al. (2010). In both cases two separate processes predict syntactic dependency structures, and the dual decomposition algorithm seeks agreement at the level of individual dependencies. One difference is that our semantic process predicts partial syntax (restricted to syntactic paths connecting predicates and arguments), while in their case each of the two processes predicts the full set of dependencies.

6 Experiments

We present experiments using our syntactic-semantic parser on the CoNLL-2009 Shared Task English benchmark (Hajič et al., 2009). It consists of the usual WSJ training/development/test sections mapped to dependency trees, augmented with semantic predicate-argument relations from PropBank (Palmer et al., 2005) and NomBank (Meyers et al., 2004) also represented as dependencies. It also contains a PropBanked portion of the Brown corpus as an out-of-domain test set.

Our goal was to evaluate the contributions of parsing algorithms in the following configurations:

Base Pipeline Runs a syntactic parser and then runs an SRL parser constrained to paths of the best syntactic tree. In the SRL it only enforces constraint **cArg**, by simply classifying the candidate argument in each path into one of the possible semantic roles or as NULL.

Pipeline with Assignment Runs the assignment algorithm for SRL, enforcing constraints **cRole** and **cArg**, but constrained to paths of the best syntactic tree.

Forest Runs the assignment algorithm for SRL on a large set of precomputed syntactic paths, described below. This configuration corresponds to running Dual Decomposition for a single iteration, and is not guaranteed to predict consistent syntactic and semantic structures.

Dual Decomposition (DD) Runs dual decomposition using the assignment algorithm on the set of precomputed paths. Syntactic and semantic structures are consistent when it reaches convergence.

All four systems used the same type of discriminative scorers and features. Next we provide details about these systems. Then we present the results.

6.1 Implementation

Syntactic model We used two discriminative arc-factored models for labeled dependency parsing: a first-order model, and a second-order model with grandchildren interactions, both reimplementations of the parsers by McDonald et al. (2005) and Carreras (2007) respectively. In both cases we used projective dependency parsing algorithms based on (Eisner, 2000).[4] To learn the models, we used a log-linear loss function following Koo et al. (2007), which trains probabilistic discriminative parsers. At test time, we used the probabilistic parsers to compute marginal probabilities $p(h, m, l \mid \mathbf{x})$, using inside-outside algorithms for first/second-order models. Hence, for either of the parsing models, we always obtain a table of first-order marginal scores, with one score per labeled dependency. Then we run first-order inference with these marginals to obtain the best tree. We found that the higher-order parser performed equally well on development using this method as using second-order inference to predict trees: since we run the parser multiple times within *Dual Decomposition*, our strategy results in faster parsing times.

Precomputed Paths Both *Forest* and *Dual Decomposition* run the assignment on a set of precomputed paths, and here we explain how we build it. We first observed that 98.4% of the correct arguments in development data are either direct descendants of the predicate, direct descendants of an ancestor of the predicate, or an ancestor of the predicate.[5] All methods we test are restricted to this syntactic scope. To generate a list of paths, we did as follows:

- Calculate marginals of *unlabeled* dependencies using the first-order parser: $p(h, m \mid \mathbf{x}) = \sum_l p(h, m, l \mid \mathbf{x})$. Note that for each m, the probabilities $p(h, m|\mathbf{x})$ for all h form a distribution (i.e. they sum to one). Then, for each m, keep the most-likely dependencies that cover at least 90% of the mass, and prune the rest.
- Starting from a predicate p, generate a path by taking any number of dependencies that ascend, and optionally adding one dependency that descends. We constrained paths to be projective, and to have a maximum number of 6 ascendant dependencies.
- Label each unlabeled edge (h, m) in the paths with $l = \mathrm{argmax}_l \, p(h, m, l \mid \mathbf{x})$.

This procedure generated an average of 61.3 paths per predicate that covers 97% of the correct paths. In contrast, enumerating paths of the single-best tree covers 91.9% of the correct paths for the first-order parser, and 93% for the second-order parser.

SRL model We used a discriminative model with similar features to those in the system of Johansson (2009). In addition, we included the following:

- Unigram/bigram/trigram path features. For every such n-gram in the syntactic path, patterns of words and POS tags (e.g., mary+loves+to, mary+VB+to).
- Voice features. The predicate voice together with the word/POS of the argument (e.g., passive+mary).
- Path continuity. Count of the number of non-consecutive tokens in a predicate-argument path.

To train SRL models we used the averaged perceptron (Collins, 2002). For the base pipeline we trained standard SRL classifiers. For the rest of models we used the structured Perceptron running the assignment algorithm as inference routine. In this case, we generated a large set of syntactic paths for training using the procedure described above, and we set the loss function to penalize mistakes in predicting the semantic role of arguments and their syntactic path.

Dual Decomposition We added a parameter β weighting the syntactic and semantic components of the model as follows:

$$(1 - \beta)\,\mathrm{s\_syn}(\mathbf{x}, \mathbf{y}) + \beta\,\mathrm{s\_srl}(\mathbf{x}, \mathbf{z}, \boldsymbol{\pi}) \quad .$$

As syntactic scores we used normalized marginal probabilities of dependencies, either from the first or the higher-order parser. The scores of all factors of the SRL model were normalized at every sentence to be between -1 and 1. The rest of details of the method were implemented following Koo et al. (2010), including the strategy for decreasing the step size α_t. We ran the algorithm for up to 500 iterations, with initial step size of 0.001.

[4]Our method allows to use non-projective dependency parsing methods seamlessly.

[5]This is specific to CoNLL-2009 data for English. In general, for other languages the coverage of these rules may be lower. We leave this question to future work.

	o	LAS	UAS	sem_p	sem_r	sem_{F_1}	sem_{pp}
Pipeline	1	85.32	88.86	**86.23**	67.67	75.83	45.64
w. Assig.	1	85.32	88.86	84.08	71.82	**77.47**	51.17
Forest	-	-	-	80.67	**73.60**	76.97	**51.33**
Pipeline	2	87.77	90.96	**87.07**	68.65	76.77	47.07
w. Assig.	2	87.77	90.96	85.21	73.41	**78.87**	**53.80**

Table 1: Results on development for the baseline and assignment pipelines, running first and second-order syntactic parsers, and the Forest method. *o* indicates the order of syntactic inference.

o	β	LAS	UAS	sem_p	sem_r	sem_{F_1}	sem_{pp}	%conv
1	0.1	85.32	88.86	84.09	71.84	77.48	51.77	100
1	0.4	85.36	88.91	84.07	71.94	77.53	51.85	100
1	0.5	85.38	88.93	84.08	72.03	77.59	51.96	100
1	0.6	85.41	88.95	84.05	72.19	77.67	52.03	99.8
1	0.7	85.44	89.00	84.10	72.42	77.82	52.24	99.7
1	0.8	**85.48**	**89.02**	**83.99**	72.69	**77.94**	**52.57**	99.5
1	0.9	85.39	88.93	83.68	**72.82**	77.88	52.49	99.8
2	0.1	87.78	90.96	85.20	73.11	78.69	53.74	100
2	0.4	87.78	90.96	**85.21**	73.12	78.70	53.74	100
2	0.5	87.78	90.96	85.19	73.12	78.70	53.72	100
2	0.6	87.78	90.96	85.20	73.13	78.70	53.72	99.9
2	0.7	87.78	90.96	85.19	73.13	78.70	53.72	99.8
2	0.8	87.80	90.98	85.20	73.18	78.74	53.77	99.8
2	0.9	**87.84**	**91.02**	85.20	**73.23**	**78.76**	**53.82**	100

Table 2: Results of the dual decomposition method on development data, for different values of the β parameter. *o* is the order of the syntactic parser. %conv is the percentage of examples that converged.

6.2 Results

To evaluate syntactic dependencies we use *unlabeled attachment score* (UAS), i.e., the percentage of words with the correct head, and *labeled attachment scores* (LAS), i.e., the percentage of words with the correct head and syntactic label. Semantic predicate-argument relations are evaluated with precision (sem_p), recall (sem_r) and F_1 measure (sem_{F_1}) at the level of labeled semantic dependencies. In addition, we measure the percentage of perfectly predicted predicate structures (sem_{pp}).[6]

Table 1 shows the results on the development set for our three first methods. We can see that the pipeline methods running assignment improve over the baseline pipelines in semantic F_1 by about 2 points, due to the application of the **cRole** constraint. The *Forest* method also shows an improvement in recall of semantic roles with respect to the pipeline methods. Presumably, the set of paths available in the *Forest* model allows to recognize a higher number of arguments at an expense of a lower precision. Regarding the percentage of perfect predicate-argument structures there is a remarkable improvement in the systems that apply the full set of constraints using the assignment algorithm. We believe that the **cRole** constraint that ensures no repeated roles for a given predicate is a key factor to predict the full set of arguments of a predicate.

The *Forest* configuration is the starting point to run the dual decomposition algorithm. We ran experiments for various values of the β parameter. Table 2 shows the results. We see that as we increase β, the SRL component has more relative weight, and the syntactic structure changes. The *DD* methods are always able to improve over the *Forest* methods, and find convergence in more than 99.5% of sentences. Compared to the pipeline running assignment, *DD* improves semantic F_1 for first-order inference, but not for higher-order inference, suggesting that 2nd order predictions of paths are quite accurate. We also observe slight benefits in syntactic accuracy.

Table 3 presents results of our system on the test sets, where we run *Pipeline with Assignment* and *Dual Decomposition* with our best configuration ($\beta = 0.8/0.9$ for $1^{st}/2^{nd}$ order syntax). For comparison, the table also reports the results of the best CoNLL–2009 joint system, *Merlo09* (Gesmundo et al., 2009), which proved to be very competitive ranking third in the closed challenge. We also include *Lluís09* (Lluís et al., 2009), which is another joint syntactic-semantic system from CoNLL–2009.[7] In the WSJ test *DD* obtains the best syntactic accuracies, while the *Pipeline* obtains the best semantic F_1. The bottom part of Table 3 presents re-

[6]Our evaluation metrics differ slightly from the official metric at CoNLL-2009. That metric considers predicate senses as special semantic dependencies and, thus, it includes them in the calculation of the evaluation metrics. In this paper, we are not addressing predicate sense disambiguation and, consequently, we ignore predicate senses when presenting evaluation results. When we report the performance of CoNLL systems, their scores will be noticeably lower than the scores reported at the shared task. This is because predicate disambiguation is a reasonably simple task with a very high baseline around 90%.

[7]Another system to compare to is the joint system by Johansson (2009). Unfortunately, a direct comparison is not possible because it is evaluated on the CoNLL-2008 datasets, which are slightly different. However, note that *Merlo09* is an application of the system by Titov et al. (2009). In that paper authors report results on the CoNLL-2008 datasets, and they are comparable to Johansson's.

WSJ	LAS	UAS	sem_p	sem_r	sem_{F_1}	sem_pp
Lluís09	87.48	89.91	73.87	67.40	70.49	39.68
Merlo09	88.79	91.26	81.00	**76.45**	78.66	54.80
Pipe-Assig 1st	86.85	89.68	85.12	73.78	79.05	54.12
DD 1st	87.04	89.89	85.03	74.56	79.45	54.92
Pipe-Assig 2nd	89.19	91.62	**86.11**	75.16	**80.26**	**55.96**
DD 2nd	**89.21**	**91.64**	86.01	74.84	80.04	55.73

Brown	LAS	UAS	sem_p	sem_r	sem_{F_1}	sem_pp
Lluís09	80.92	85.96	62.29	59.22	60.71	29.79
Merlo09	80.84	86.32	68.97	**63.06**	65.89	38.92
Pipe-Assig 1st	80.96	86.58	72.91	60.16	65.93	38.44
DD 1st	81.18	86.86	72.53	60.76	66.12	38.13
Pipe-Assig 2nd	82.56	87.98	73.94	61.63	67.23	**38.99**
DD 2nd	**82.61**	**88.04**	**74.12**	61.59	**67.28**	38.92

Table 3: Comparative results on the CoNLL–2009 English test sets, namely the WSJ test (top table) and the out of domain test from the Brown corpus (bottom table).

sults on the out-of-domain Brown test corpus. In this case, *DD* obtains slightly better results than the rest, both in terms of syntactic accuracy and semantic F_1.

Table 4 shows statistical significance tests for the syntactic LAS and semantic F_1 scores of Table 3. We have applied the sign test (Wackery et al., 2007) and approximate randomization tests (Yeh, 2000) to all pairs of systems outputs. The differences between systems in the WSJ test can be considered significant in almost all cases with $p = 0.05$. In the Brown test set, results are more unstable and differences are not significant in general, probably because of the relatively small size of that test.

Regarding running times, our implementation of the baseline pipeline with 2nd order inference parses the development set (1,334 sentences) in less than 7 minutes. Running assignment in the pipeline increases parsing time by $\sim$8% due to the overhead from the assignment algorithm. The *Forest* method, with an average of 61.3 paths per predicate, is $\sim$13% slower than the pipeline due to the exploration of the space of precomputed paths. Finally, *Dual Decomposition* with 2nd order inference converges in 36.6 iterations per sentence on average. The first iteration of *DD* has to perform roughly the same work as *Forest*, while subsequent iterations only need to re-parse the sentence with respect to the dual updates, which are extremely sparse. Our current implementation did not take advantage of the sparsity of updates, and overall, *DD* was on average 13 times slower than the pipeline running assignment and 15 times slower than the baseline pipeline.

	WSJ ME	WSJ PA1	WSJ DD1	WSJ PA2	WSJ DD2	Brown ME	Brown PA1	Brown DD1	Brown PA2	Brown DD2
LL	○●□■	○●□■	●□■	○●□■	○●□■	□■	□■	□■	○●□■	○●□■
ME		○●	○●□■	○●□■	○●□■				●	●
PA1			○●□■	○●□■	○●□■			●	○●■	○●□■
DD1				○●□■	○●□■				○●■	○●□■
PA2					●□■					

Table 4: Statistical tests of significance for LAS and sem_{F_1} differences between pairs of systems from Table 3. ○/● = LAS difference is significant by the sign/ approximate randomization tests at 0.05 level. □/■ = same meaning for sem_{F_1}. The legend for systems is: LL: *Lluís09*, ME: *Merlo09*, PA1/2: *Pipeline with Assignment, $1^{st}/2^{nd}$ order*, DD1/2: *Dual Decomposition, $1^{st}/2^{nd}$ order*.

7 Conclusion

We have introduced efficient methods to parse syntactic dependency structures augmented with predicate-argument relations, with two key ideas. One is to predict the local syntactic structure that links a predicate with its arguments, and seek agreement with the full syntactic structure using dual decomposition techniques. The second is to control linear assignment constraints in the predicate-argument structure.

In experiments we observe large improvements resulting from the assignment constraints. As for the dual decomposition technique for joint parsing, it does improve over the pipelines when we use a first order parser. This means that in this configuration the explicit semantic features help to find a solution that is better in both layers. To some extent, this empirically validates the research objective of joint models. However, when we move to second-order parsers the differences with respect to the pipeline are insignificant. It is to be expected that as syntactic parsers improve, the need of joint methods is less critical. It remains an open question to validate if large improvements can be achieved by integrating syntactic-semantic features. To study this question, it is necessary to have efficient parsing algorithms for joint dependency structures. This paper contributes with a method that has optimality guarantees whenever it converges.

Our method can incorporate richer families of features. It is straightforward to incorporate better semantic representations of predicates and arguments than just plain words, e.g. by exploiting WordNet or distributional representations as in (Zapirain et al.,

2013). Potentially, this could result in larger improvements in the performance of syntactic and semantic parsing.

It is also necessary to experiment with different languages, where the performance of syntactic parsers is lower than in English, and hence there is potential for improvement. Our treatment of local syntactic structure that links predicates with arguments, based on explicit enumeration of likely paths, was simplistic. Future work should explore methods that model the syntactic structure linking predicates with arguments: whenever this structure can be parsed efficiently, our dual decomposition algorithm can be employed to define an efficient joint system.

Acknowledgments

We thank the editor and the anonymous reviewers for their valuable feedback. This work was financed by the European Commission for the XLike project (FP7-288342); and by the Spanish Government for project OpenMT-2 (TIN2009-14675-C03-01), project Skater (TIN2012-38584-C06-01), and a Ramón y Cajal contract for Xavier Carreras (RYC-2008-02223).

References

Rainer Burkard, Mario Dell'Amico, and Silvano Martello. 2009. *Assignment Problems*. Society for Industrial and Applied Mathematics.

Xavier Carreras and Lluís Màrquez. 2005. Introduction to the CoNLL-2005 shared task: Semantic role labeling. In *Proceedings of the Ninth Conference on Computational Natural Language Learning (CoNLL-2005)*, pages 152–164, Ann Arbor, Michigan, June. Association for Computational Linguistics.

Xavier Carreras. 2007. Experiments with a higher-order projective dependency parser. In *Proceedings of the CoNLL Shared Task Session of EMNLP-CoNLL 2007*, pages 957–961, Prague, Czech Republic, June. Association for Computational Linguistics.

Michael Collins. 2002. Discriminative training methods for Hidden Markov Models: Theory and experiments with Perceptron algorithms. In *Proceedings of the 2002 Conference on Empirical Methods in Natural Language Processing*, pages 1–8. Association for Computational Linguistics, July.

Dipanjan Das, André F. T. Martins, and Noah A. Smith. 2012. An exact dual decomposition algorithm for shallow semantic parsing with constraints. In **SEM 2012: The First Joint Conference on Lexical and Computational Semantics – Volume 1: Proceedings of the main conference and the shared task, and Volume 2: Proceedings of the Sixth International Workshop on Semantic Evaluation (SemEval 2012)*, pages 209–217, Montréal, Canada, 7-8 June. Association for Computational Linguistics.

Jason Eisner. 2000. Bilexical grammars and their cubic-time parsing algorithms. In Harry Bunt and Anton Nijholt, editors, *Advances in Probabilistic and Other Parsing Technologies*, pages 29–62. Kluwer Academic Publishers, October.

Andrea Gesmundo, James Henderson, Paola Merlo, and Ivan Titov. 2009. A latent variable model of synchronous syntactic-semantic parsing for multiple languages. In *Proceedings of the Thirteenth Conference on Computational Natural Language Learning (CoNLL 2009): Shared Task*, pages 37–42, Boulder, Colorado, June. Association for Computational Linguistics.

Daniel Gildea and Daniel Jurafsky. 2002. Automatic labeling of semantic roles. *Computational Linguistics*, 28(3):245–288, September.

Daniel Gildea and Martha Palmer. 2002. The necessity of parsing for predicate argument recognition. In *Proceedings of 40th Annual Meeting of the Association for Computational Linguistics*, pages 239–246, Philadelphia, Pennsylvania, USA, July. Association for Computational Linguistics.

Jan Hajič, Massimiliano Ciaramita, Richard Johansson, Daisuke Kawahara, Maria Antònia Martí, Lluís Màrquez, Adam Meyers, Joakim Nivre, Sebastian Padó, Jan Štěpánek, Pavel Straňák, Mihai Surdeanu, Nianwen Xue, and Yi Zhang. 2009. The CoNLL-2009 shared task: Syntactic and semantic dependencies in multiple languages. In *Proceedings of the 13th Conference on Computational Natural Language Learning (CoNLL-2009), June 4-5*, Boulder, Colorado, USA.

Richard Johansson. 2009. Statistical bistratal dependency parsing. In *Proceedings of the 2009 Conference on Empirical Methods in Natural Language Processing*, pages 561–569, Singapore, August. Association for Computational Linguistics.

Terry Koo, Amir Globerson, Xavier Carreras, and Michael Collins. 2007. Structured prediction models via the matrix-tree theorem. In *Proceedings of the 2007 Joint Conference on Empirical Methods in Natural Language Processing and Computational Natural Language Learning (EMNLP-CoNLL)*, pages 141–150, Prague, Czech Republic, June. Association for Computational Linguistics.

Terry Koo, Alexander M. Rush, Michael Collins, Tommi Jaakkola, and David Sontag. 2010. Dual decomposition for parsing with non-projective head automata.

In *Proceedings of the 2010 Conference on Empirical Methods in Natural Language Processing*, pages 1288–1298, Cambridge, MA, October. Association for Computational Linguistics.

Harold W. Kuhn. 1955. The Hungarian method for the assignment problem. *Naval Research Logistics Quarterly*, (2):83–97.

Xavier Lluís, Stefan Bott, and Lluís Màrquez. 2009. A second-order joint eisner model for syntactic and semantic dependency parsing. In *Proceedings of the Thirteenth Conference on Computational Natural Language Learning (CoNLL 2009): Shared Task*, pages 79–84, Boulder, Colorado, June. Association for Computational Linguistics.

Lluís Màrquez, Xavier Carreras, Kenneth C. Litkowski, and Suzanne Stevenson. 2008. Semantic Role Labeling: An Introduction to the Special Issue. *Computational Linguistics*, 34(2):145–159, June.

André Martins, Noah Smith, and Eric Xing. 2009. Concise integer linear programming formulations for dependency parsing. In *Proceedings of the Joint Conference of the 47th Annual Meeting of the ACL and the 4th International Joint Conference on Natural Language Processing of the AFNLP*, pages 342–350, Suntec, Singapore, August. Association for Computational Linguistics.

Ryan McDonald, Koby Crammer, and Fernando Pereira. 2005. Online large-margin training of dependency parsers. In *Proceedings of the 43rd Annual Meeting of the Association for Computational Linguistics (ACL'05)*, pages 91–98, Ann Arbor, Michigan, June. Association for Computational Linguistics.

Adam Meyers, Ruth Reeves, Catherine Macleod, Rachel Szekely, Veronika Zielinska, Brian Young, and Ralph Grishman. 2004. The NomBank Project: An interim report. In A. Meyers, editor, *HLT-NAACL 2004 Workshop: Frontiers in Corpus Annotation*, pages 24–31, Boston, Massachusetts, USA, May. Association for Computational Linguistics.

Alessandro Moschitti. 2004. A study on convolution kernels for shallow statistic parsing. In *Proceedings of the 42nd Meeting of the Association for Computational Linguistics (ACL'04), Main Volume*, pages 335–342, Barcelona, Spain, July.

Joakim Nivre and Jens Nilsson. 2005. Pseudo-projective dependency parsing. In *Proceedings of the 43rd Annual Meeting of the Association for Computational Linguistics (ACL'05)*, pages 99–106, Ann Arbor, Michigan, June. Association for Computational Linguistics.

Martha Palmer, Daniel Gildea, and Paul Kingsbury. 2005. The Proposition Bank: An annotated corpus of semantic roles. *Computational Linguistics*, 31(1):71–105, March.

Vasin Punyakanok, Dan Roth, and Wen tau Yih. 2008. The importance of syntactic parsing and inference in semantic role labeling. *Computational Linguistics*, 34(3):257–287, June.

Sebastian Riedel and Andrew McCallum. 2011. Fast and robust joint models for biomedical event extraction. In *Proceedings of the 2011 Conference on Empirical Methods in Natural Language Processing*, pages 1–12, Edinburgh, Scotland, UK., July. Association for Computational Linguistics.

Alexander M Rush, David Sontag, Michael Collins, and Tommi Jaakkola. 2010. On dual decomposition and linear programming relaxations for natural language processing. In *Proceedings of the 2010 Conference on Empirical Methods in Natural Language Processing*, pages 1–11, Cambridge, MA, October. Association for Computational Linguistics.

David Sontag, Amir Globerson, and Tommi Jaakkola. 2010. Introduction to dual decomposition for inference. In S. Sra, S. Nowozin, and S. J. Wright, editors, *Optimization for Machine Learning*. MIT Press.

Mihai Surdeanu, Richard Johansson, Adam Meyers, Lluís Màrquez, and Joakim Nivre. 2008. The conll 2008 shared task on joint parsing of syntactic and semantic dependencies. In *CoNLL 2008: Proceedings of the Twelfth Conference on Computational Natural Language Learning*, pages 159–177, Manchester, England, August. Coling 2008 Organizing Committee.

Ivan Titov, James Henderson, Paola Merlo, and Gabriele Musillo. 2009. Online graph planarisation for synchronous parsing of semantic and syntactic dependencies. In *Proceedings of ICJAI*, pages 1562–1567.

Kristina Toutanova, Aria Haghighi, and Christopher D. Manning. 2008. Towards Robust Semantic Role Labeling. *Computational Linguistics*, 34(2):162–191, June.

Dennis D. Wackery, William Mendenhall, and Richard L. Scheaffer, 2007. *Mathematical Statistics with Applications*, chapter 15: Nonparametric statistics. Duxbury Press.

Nianwen Xue and Martha Palmer. 2004. Calibrating features for semantic role labeling. In Dekang Lin and Dekai Wu, editors, *Proceedings of EMNLP 2004*, pages 88–94, Barcelona, Spain, July. Association for Computational Linguistics.

Alexander S. Yeh. 2000. More accurate tests for the statistical significance of result differences. In *Proceedings of the 18th conference on Computational linguistics*.

Beñat Zapirain, Eneko Agirre, Lluís Màrquez, and Mihai Surdeanu. 2013. Selectional preferences for semantic role classification. *Computational Linguistics*, 39(3).

Modeling Semantic Relations Expressed by Prepositions

Vivek Srikumar and **Dan Roth**
University of Illinois, Urbana-Champaign
Urbana, IL. 61801.
{vsrikum2, danr}@illinois.edu

Abstract

This paper introduces the problem of predicting semantic relations expressed by prepositions and develops statistical learning models for predicting the relations, their arguments and the semantic types of the arguments. We define an inventory of 32 relations, building on the word sense disambiguation task for prepositions and collapsing related senses across prepositions. Given a preposition in a sentence, our computational task to jointly model the preposition relation and its arguments along with their semantic types, as a way to support the relation prediction. The annotated data, however, only provides labels for the relation label, and not the arguments and types. We address this by presenting two models for preposition relation labeling. Our generalization of latent structure SVM gives close to 90% accuracy on relation labeling. Further, by jointly predicting the relation, arguments, and their types along with preposition sense, we show that we can not only improve the relation accuracy, but also significantly improve sense prediction accuracy.

1 Introduction

This paper addresses the problem of predicting semantic relations conveyed by prepositions in text. Prepositions express many semantic relations between their governor and object. Predicting these can help advancing text understanding tasks like question answering and textual entailment. Consider the sentence:

(1) The book of Prof. Alexander on primary school methods is a valuable teaching resource.

Here, the preposition *on* indicates that *the book* and *primary school methods* are connected by the relation `Topic` and *of* indicates the `Creator-Creation` relation between *Prof. Alexander* and *the book*. Predicting these relations can help answer questions about the subject of the book and also recognize the entailment of sentences like *Prof. Alexander has written about primary school methods.*

Being highly polysemous, the same preposition can indicate different kinds of relations, depending on its governor and object. Furthermore, several prepositions can indicate the same semantic relation. For example, consider the sentence:

(2) Poor care led to her death from pneumonia.

The preposition *from* in this sentence expresses the relation `Cause`(*death, pneumonia*). In a different context, it can denote other relations, as in the phrases *copied from the film* (`Source`) and *recognized from the start* (`Temporal`). On the other hand, the relation `Cause` can be expressed by several prepositions; for example, the following phrases express a `Cause` relation: *died of pneumonia* and *tired after the surgery*.

We characterize semantic relations expressed by transitive prepositions and develop accurate models for predicting the relations, identifying their arguments and recognizing the semantic types of the arguments. Building on the word sense disambiguation task for prepositions, we collapse semantically related senses across prepositions to derive our relation inventory. These relations act as predicates in a predicate-argument representation, where the arguments are the governor and the object of the preposition. While ascertaining the arguments is a largely syntactic decision, we point out that syntactic parsers do not always make this prediction correctly. However, as illustrated in the examples above, identifying the relation depends on the governor and object of the preposition.

Given a sentence and a preposition, our goal is to model the predicate (i.e. the preposition relation) and its arguments (i.e. the governor and object). Very often, the relation label is not influenced by the surface form of the arguments but rather by their *semantic types*. In sentence (2) above, we want the predicate to be `Cause` when the object of the preposition is any illness. We thus suggest to model the argument types along with the preposition relations and arguments, using different notions of types. These three related aspects of the relation prediction task are further explained in Section 3 leading up to the problem definition.

Though we wish to predict relations, arguments and types, there is no corpus which annotates all three. The SemEval 2007 shared task of word sense disambiguation for prepositions provides sense annotations for prepositions. We use this data to generate training and test corpora for the relation labels. In Section 4, we present two models for the prepositional relation identification problem. The first model considers all possible argument candidates from various sources along with all argument types to predict the preposition relation label. The second model treats the arguments and types as latent variables during learning using a generalization of the latent structural SVM of (Yu and Joachims, 2009). We show in Section 5 that this model not only predicts the arguments and types, but also improves relation prediction performance.

The primary contributions of this paper are:

1. We introduce a new inventory of preposition relations that covers the 34 prepositions that formed the basis of the SemEval 2007 task of preposition sense disambiguation.

2. We model preposition relations, arguments and their types jointly and propose a learning algorithm that learns to predict all three using training data that annotates only relation labels.

3. We show that jointly predicting relations with word sense not only improves the relation predictor, but also gives a significant improvement in sense prediction.

2 Prepositions & Predicate-Argument Semantics

Semantic role labeling (cf. (Gildea and Jurafsky, 2002; Palmer et al., 2010; Punyakanok et al., 2008) and others) is the task of converting text into a predicate-argument representation. Given a trigger word or phrase in a sentence, this task solves two related prediction problems: (a) identifying the relation label, and (b) identifying and labeling the arguments of the relation.

This problem has been studied in the context of verb and nominal triggers using the PropBank (Palmer et al., 2005) and NomBank (Meyers et al., 2004) annotations over the Penn Treebank, and also using the FrameNet lexicon (Fillmore et al., 2003), which allows arbitrary words to trigger semantic frames.

This paper focuses on semantic relations expressed by transitive prepositions[1]. We can define the two prediction tasks for prepositions as follows: identifying the relation label for a preposition, and predicting the arguments of the relation. Prepositions can mark arguments (both core and adjunct) for verbal and nominal predicates. In addition, they can also trigger relations that are not part of other predicates. For example, in sentence (3) below, the prepositional phrase starting with *to* is an argument of the verb *visit*, but the *in* triggers an independent relation indicating the location of the aquarium.

(3) The children enjoyed the visit to the aquarium in Coney Island.

FrameNet covers some prepositional relations, but allows only temporal, locative and directional senses of prepositions to evoke frames, accounting for only 3% of the targets in the SemEval 2007 shared task of FrameNet parsing. In fact, the state-of-the-art FrameNet parser of (Das et al., 2010) does not consider any frame inducing prepositions.

(Baldwin et al., 2009) highlights the importance of studying prepositions for a complete linguistic

[1] By transitive prepositions we refer to the standard usage of prepositions that take an object. In particular, we do not consider prepositional particles in our analysis.

analysis of sentences and surveys work in the NLP literature that addresses the syntax and semantics of prepositions. One line of work (Ye and Baldwin, 2006) addressed the problem of preposition semantic role labeling by considering prepositional phrases that act as arguments of verbs according to the PropBank annotation. They built a system that predicts the labels of these prepositional phrases alone. However, by definition, this covered only verb-attached prepositions. (Zapirain et al., 2012) studied the impact of automatically learned selectional preferences for predicting arguments of verbs and showed that modeling prepositional phrases separately improves the performance of argument prediction.

Preposition semantics has also been studied via the Preposition Project (Litkowski and Hargraves, 2005) and the related SemEval 2007 shared task of word sense disambiguation of prepositions (Litkowski and Hargraves, 2007). The Preposition Project identifies preposition senses based on their definitions in the Oxford Dictionary of English. There are 332 different labels to be predicted with a wide variance in the number of senses per preposition ranging from 2 (*during* and *as*) to 25 (*on*). For example, according to the preposition sense inventory, the preposition *from* in sentence (2) above will be labeled with the sense **from:12(9)** to indicate a cause. (Dahlmeier et al., 2009) added sense annotation to seven prepositions in four sections of the Penn Treebank with the goal of studying their interaction with verb arguments.

Using the SemEval data, (Tratz and Hovy, 2009) and (Hovy et al., 2010) showed that the arguments offer an important cue to identify the sense of the preposition and (Tratz, 2011) showed further improvements by refining the sense inventory. However, though these works used a dependency parser to identify arguments, in order to overcome parsing errors, they augment the parser's predictions using part-of-speech based heuristics.

We argue that, while disambiguating the sense of a preposition does indeed reveal nuances of its meaning, it leads to a proliferation of labels to be predicted. Most importantly, sense labels do not transfer to other prepositions that express the same meaning. For example, both *finish lunch before noon* and *finish lunch by noon* express a `Temporal` relation. According to the Preposition Project, the sense label for the first preposition is **before:1(1)**, and that for the second is **by:17(4)**. This both defeats the purpose of identifying the relations to aid natural language understanding and makes the prediction task harder than it should be: using the standard word sense classification approach, we need to train a separate classifier for each word because the labels are defined per-preposition. In other words, we cannot share features across the different prepositions. This motivates the need to combine such senses of prepositions into the same class label.

In this direction, (O'Hara and Wiebe, 2009) describes an inventory of preposition relations obtained using Penn Treebank function tags and frame elements from FrameNet. (Srikumar and Roth, 2011) merged preposition senses of seven prepositions into relation labels. (Litkowski, 2012) also suggests collapsing the definitions of prepositions into a smaller set of semantic classes. To aid better generalization and to reduce the label complexity, we follow this line of work to define a set of relation labels which abstract word senses across prepositions[2].

3 Preposition-triggered Relations

This section describes the inventory of preposition relations introduced in this paper, and then identifies the components of the preposition relation extraction problem.

3.1 Preposition Relation Inventory

We build our relation inventory using the sense annotation in the Preposition Project, focusing on the 34 prepositions[3] annotated for the SemEval-2007 shared task of preposition sense disambiguation.

As discussed in Section 2, we construct the inventory of preposition relations by collapsing semantically related preposition senses across differ-

[2]Since the preposition sense data is annotated over FrameNet sentences, sense annotation can be used to extend FrameNet (Litkowski, 2012). We believe that the abstract labels proposed in this paper can further help in this effort.

[3]We consider the following prepositions: about, above, across, after, against, along, among, around, as, at, before, behind, beneath, beside, between, by, down, during, for, from, in, inside, into, like, of, off, on, onto, over, round, through, to, towards, and with. This does not include multi-word prepositions such as *because of* and *due to*.

ent prepositions. For each sense that is defined, the Preposition Project also specifies related prepositions. These definitions and related prepositions provide a starting point to identify senses that can be merged across prepositions. We followed this with a manual cleanup phase. Some senses do not cleanly align with a single relation because the definitions include idiomatic or figurative usage. For example, the sense **in:7(5)** of the preposition *in*, according to the definition, includes both spatial and figurative notions of the spatial sense (that is, both *in London* and *in a film*). In such cases, we sampled 20 examples from the SemEval 2007 training set and assigned the relation label based on majority. If sufficient examples could not be sampled, these senses were added to the label `Other`, which is not a semantically coherent category and represents the 'overflow' case.

Overall, we have 32 labels, which are listed in Table 1[4]. A companion publication (available on the authors' website) provides detailed definitions of each relation and the senses that were merged to create each label. Since we define relations to be groups of preposition sense labels, each sense can be uniquely mapped to a relation label. Hence, we can use the annotated sense data from SemEval 2007 to obtain a corpus of relation-labeled sentences.

To validate the labeling scheme, two native speakers of English annotated 200 sentences from the SemEval training corpus using only the definitions of the labels as the annotation guidelines. We measured Cohen's kappa coefficient (Cohen, 1960) between the annotators to be 0.75 and also between each annotator and the original corpus to be 0.76 and 0.74 respectively.

3.2 Preposition Relation Extraction

The input to the prediction problem consists of a preposition in a sentence and the goal is to jointly model the following: (i) The relation expressed by the preposition, and (ii) The arguments of the relation, namely the governor and the object.

We use sentence (2) in the introduction as our running example the following discussion. In our running example, the relation label is `Cause`. We represent the predicted relation label by r.

[4]Note that, even though we do not consider intransitive prepositions, the definitions of some relations in Table 1 could be extended apply to prepositional particles such *drive down* (`Direction`) and *run about* (`Manner`).

Relation Name	**Example**
Activity	good at boxing
Agent	opened by Annie
Attribute	walls of stone
Beneficiary	fight for Napoleon
Cause	died of cancer
Co-Participants	pick one among these
Destination	leaving for London
Direction	drove towards the border
EndState	driven to tears
Experiencer	warm towards her
Instrument	cut with a knife
Journey	travel by road
Location	living in London
Manner	scream like an animal
MediumOfCommunication	new show on TV
Numeric	increase by 10%
ObjectOfVerb	murder of the boys
Opponent/Contrast	fight with him
Other	*all others*
Participant/Accompanier	steak with wine
PartWhole	member of gang
PhysicalSupport	lean against the wall
Possessor	son of a friend
ProfessionalAspect	works in publishing
Purpose	tools for making it
Recipient	unkind to her
Separation	ousted from power
Source	purchased from the shop
Species	city of Prague
StartState	recover from illness
Temporal	arrived on Monday
Topic	books on Shakespeare

Table 1: List of preposition relations

Arguments The relation label crucially depends on correctly identifying the arguments of the preposition, which are *death* and *pneumonia* in our running example. While a parser can identify the arguments of a preposition, simply relying on the parser may impose an upper limit on the accuracy of relation prediction.

We build an oracle experiment to highlight this limitation. Table 2 shows the recall of the easy-first dependency parser of (Goldberg and Elhadad, 2010) on Section 23 of the Penn Treebank for identifying the governor and object of prepositions.

We define heuristics that generate a candidate governors and objects for a preposition. For the governor, this set includes the previous verb or noun and for the object, it includes only the next noun. The row labeled Best(Parser, Heuristics) shows the performance of an oracle predictor which selects the true governor/object if present among the parser's prediction and the heuristics. We see that, even for the in-domain case, if we are able to re-rank the candidates, we could achieve a big improvement in argument identification.

	Recall	
	Governor	**Object**
Parser	88.88	92.37
Best(Parser, Heuristics)	92.50	93.06

Table 2: Identifying governor and object of prepositions in the Penn Treebank data. Here, Best(Parser, Heuristics) reports the performance of an oracle that picks the true governor and object, if present among the candidates presented by the parser and the heuristic. This presents an in-domain upper bound for governor and object detection. See text for further details.

To overcome erroneous parser decisions, we entertain governor and object candidates proposed both by the parser and the heuristics. In the following discussion, we denote the chosen governor and object by g and o respectively.

Argument types While the primary purpose of this work is to model preposition relations and their arguments, the relation prediction is strongly dependent on the *semantic type* of the arguments. To illustrate this, consider the following incomplete sentence: *The message was delivered at* $\cdots$. This preposition can express both a `Temporal` or a `Location` relation depending on the object (for example, *noon* vs. *the doorstep*).

(Agirre et al., 2008) shows that modeling the semantic type of the arguments jointly with attachment can improve PP attachment accuracy. In this work, we point out that argument types should be modeled jointly with both aspects of the problem of preposition relation labeling.

Types are an abstraction that capture common properties of groups of entities. For example, WordNet provides generalizations of words in the form of their hypernyms. In our running example, we wish to generalize the relation label for *death from pneumonia* to include cases such as *suffering from flu*. Figure 1 shows the hypernym hierarchy for the word *pneumonia*. In this case, synsets in the hypernym hierarchy, like *pathological state* or *physical condition*, would also include ailments like flu.

```
pneumonia
  => respiratory disease
    => disease
      => illness
        => ill health
          => pathological state
            => physical condition
              => condition
                => state
                  => attribute
                    => abstraction
                      => entity
```

Figure 1: Hypernym hierarchy for the word *pneumonia*

We define a semantic type to be a cluster of words. In addition to WordNet hypernyms, we also cluster verbs, nouns and adjectives using the dependency-based word similarity of (Lin, 1998) and treat cluster membership as types. These are described in detail in Section 5.1.

Relation prediction involves not only identifying the arguments, but also selecting the right semantic type for them, which together, help predicting the relation label. Given an argument candidate and a collection of possible types (given by WordNet or the similarity based clusters), we need to select one of the types. For example, in the WordNet case, we need to pick one of the hypernyms in the hypernym hierarchy. Thus, for the governor and object, we have a set of type labels, comprised of one element for each type category. We denote this by $\mathbf{t}^g$ (governor type) and $\mathbf{t}^o$ (object type) respectively.

3.3 Problem definition

The input to our prediction task is a preposition in a sentence. Our goal is to jointly model the relation it expresses, the governor and the object of the relation and the types of each argument (both WordNet hypernyms and cluster membership). We denote the input by $\mathbf{x}$, which consists not only of the preposition but also a set of candidates for the governor and the object and, for each type category, the list of types for the governor and candidate.

The prediction, which we denote by $\mathbf{y}$, consists of the relation r, which can be one of the valid relation labels in Table 1 and the governor and object, denoted by g and o, each of which is one of text segments proposed by the parser or the heuristics. Additionally, $\mathbf{y}$ also consists of type predictions for the governor and object, denoted by $\mathbf{t}^g$ and $\mathbf{t}^o$ respectively, each of which is a vector of labels, one for each type category. Table 3 summarizes the notation described above. We refer to the ith element of vectors using subscripts and use the superscript * to denote gold labels. Recall that we have gold labels only for the relation labels and not for arguments and their types.

Symbol	Meaning
$\mathbf{x}$	Input (pre-processed sentence and preposition)
r	relation label for the preposition
g, o	governor and object of the relation
$\mathbf{t}^g, \mathbf{t}^o$	vectors of type assignments for governor and object respectively
$\mathbf{y}$	Full structure $(r, g, o, \mathbf{t}^g, \mathbf{t}^o)$

Table 3: Summary of notation

4 Learning preposition relations

A key challenge in modeling preposition relations is that our training data only annotates the relation labels and not the arguments and types. In this section, we introduce two approaches for predicting preposition relations using this data.

4.1 Feature Representation

We use the notation $\Phi(\mathbf{x}, \mathbf{y})$ to indicate the feature function for an input $\mathbf{x}$ and the full output $\mathbf{y}$. We build Φ using the features of the components of $\mathbf{y}$:

1. **Arguments**: For g and o, which represent an assignment to the governor and object, we denote the features extracted from the arguments as $\phi_A(\mathbf{x}, g)$ and $\phi_A(\mathbf{x}, o)$ respectively.

2. **Types**: Given a type assignment t_i^g to the ith type category of the governor, we define features $\phi_T(\mathbf{x}, g, t_i^g)$. Similarly, we define features $\phi_T(\mathbf{x}, o, t_i^o)$ for the types of the object.

We combine the argument and their type features to define the features for classifying the relation, which we denote by $\phi(\mathbf{x}, g, o, \mathbf{t}^g, \mathbf{t}^o)$:

$$\phi = \sum_{a \in \{g,o\}} \left(\phi_A(\mathbf{x}, a) + \sum_i \phi_T(\mathbf{x}, a, t_i^a) \right) \quad (1)$$

Section 5 describes the actual features used in our experiments.

Observe that given the arguments and their types, the task of predicting relations is simply a multiclass classification problem. Thus, following the standard convention for multiclass classification, the overall feature representation for the relation *and* argument prediction is defined by conjoining the relation r with features for the corresponding arguments and types, ϕ. This gives us the full feature representation, $\Phi(\mathbf{x}, \mathbf{y})$.

4.2 Model 1: Predicting only relations

The first model aims at predicting only the relation labels and not the arguments and types. This falls into the standard multiclass classification setting, where we wish to predict one of 32 labels. To do so, we sum over all the possible assignments to the rest of the structure and define features for the inputs as

$$\hat{\phi}(\mathbf{x}) = \sum_{g,o,\mathbf{t}^g,\mathbf{t}^o} \phi(\mathbf{x}, g, o, \mathbf{t}^g, \mathbf{t}^o) \quad (2)$$

Effectively, doing so uses all the governor and object candidates and all their semantic types to get a feature representation for the relation classification problem. Once again, for a relation label r, the overall feature representation is defined by conjoining the relation r with the features for that relation $\hat{\phi}$, which we write as $\phi_R(\mathbf{x}, r)$. Note that this summation is computationally inexpensive in our case because the sum decomposes according to equation (1). With a learned weight vector $\mathbf{w}$, the relation label is predicted as

$$r = \arg\max_{r'} \mathbf{w}^T \phi_R(\mathbf{x}, r') \quad (3)$$

We use a structural SVM (Tsochantaridis et al., 2004) to train a weight vector $\mathbf{w}$ that predicts the relation label as above. The training is parameterized by C, which represents the tradeoff between generalization and the hinge loss.

4.3 Model 2: Learning from partial annotations

In the second model, even though our annotation does not provide gold labels for arguments and types, our goal is to predict them. At inference time, if we had a weight vector $\mathbf{w}$, we could predict the full structure using inference as follows:

$$\mathbf{y} = \arg\max_{\mathbf{y}'} \mathbf{w}^T \Phi(\mathbf{x}, \mathbf{y}) \quad (4)$$

We propose an iterative learning algorithm to learn this weight vector.

In the following discussion, for a labeled example $(\mathbf{x}, \mathbf{y}^*)$, we refer to the missing part of its structure as $h(\mathbf{y}^*)$. That is, $h(\mathbf{y}^*)$ is the assignment to the arguments of the relation and their types. We use the notation $r(\mathbf{y})$ to denote the relation label specified by a structure $\mathbf{y}$.

Our learning algorithm is closely related to recently developed latent variable based frameworks (Yu and Joachims, 2009; Chang et al., 2010a; Chang et al., 2010b), where the supervision provides only partial annotation. We begin by defining two additional inference procedures:

1. **Latent Inference**: Given a weight vector $\mathbf{w}$ and a partially labeled example $(\mathbf{x}, \mathbf{y}^*)$, we can 'complete' the rest of the structure by inferring the highest scoring assignment to the missing parts. In the algorithm, we call this procedure $LatentInf(\mathbf{w}, \mathbf{x}, \mathbf{y}^*)$, which solves the following maximization problem:

$$\begin{aligned} \hat{\mathbf{y}} = \quad & \arg\max_{\mathbf{y}} \quad \mathbf{w}^T \Phi(\mathbf{x}, \mathbf{y}), \\ & \text{s.t.} \qquad r(\mathbf{y}) = r(\mathbf{y}^*). \end{aligned} \quad (5)$$

2. **Loss augmented inference**: This is a variant of the the standard loss augmented inference for structural SVMs, which solves the following maximization problem for a given $\mathbf{x}$ and *fully labeled* $\mathbf{y}^*$:

$$\arg\max_{\mathbf{y}} \mathbf{w}^T \Phi(\mathbf{x}, \mathbf{y}) + \Delta(\mathbf{y}, \mathbf{y}^*) \quad (6)$$

Here, $\Delta(\mathbf{y}, \mathbf{y}^*)$ denotes the loss function. In the standard structural SVMs, the loss is over the entire structure. In the Latent Structural SVM formulation of (Yu and Joachims, 2009), the loss is defined only over the part of the structure with the gold label. In this work, we use the standard Hamming loss over the entire structure, but scale the loss for the elements of $h(\mathbf{y})$ by a parameter $\alpha < 1$. This is a generalization of the latent structural SVM, which corresponds to the setting $\alpha = 0$. The intuition behind having a non-zero α is that in addition to penalizing the learning algorithm if it violates the annotated part of the structure, we also incorporate a small penalty for the rest of the structure.

Using these two inference procedures, we define the learning algorithm as Algorithm 1. The weight vector is initialized using Model 1. The algorithm then finds the best arguments and types for all examples in the training set (steps 3-5). Doing so gives an estimate of the arguments and types for each example, giving us 'fully labeled' structured data. The algorithm then proceeds to use this data to train a new weight vector using the standard structural SVM with the loss augmented inference listed above (step 6). These two steps are repeated several times. Note that as with the summation in Model 1, solving the inference problems described above is computationally inexpensive.

Algorithm 1 Algorithm for learning Model 2

Input: Examples $D = \{\mathbf{x}_i, r(\mathbf{y}_i^*)\}$, where examples are labeled only with the relation labels.

1: Initialize weight vector $\mathbf{w}$ using Model 1
2: **for** $t = 1, 2, \cdots$ **do**
3: **for** $(\mathbf{x}_i, \mathbf{y}_i^*) \in D$ **do**
4: $\hat{\mathbf{y}}_i \leftarrow LatentInf(\mathbf{w}, \mathbf{x}_i, \mathbf{y}_i^*)$ (Eq. 5)
5: **end for**
6: $\mathbf{w} \leftarrow LearnSSVM(\{\mathbf{x}_i, \hat{\mathbf{y}}_i\})$ with the loss augmented inference of Eq. 6
7: **end for**
8: **return** $\mathbf{w}$

Algorithm 1 is parameterized by C and α. The parameter α controls the extent to which the hypothesized labels according to the previous iteration's weight vector influence the learning.

4.4 Joint inference between preposition senses and relations

By defining preposition relations as disjoint sets of preposition senses, we effectively have a hierarchical relationship between senses and relations. This suggests that joint inference can be employed between sense and relation predictions with a validity constraint connecting the two. The idea of employing inference to combine independently trained predictors to obtain a coherent output structure has been used for various NLP tasks in recent years, starting with the work of (Roth and Yih, 2004; Roth and Yih, 2007).

We use the features defined by (Hovy et al., 2010), which we write as $\phi_s(\mathbf{x}, s)$ for a given input $\mathbf{x}$ and sense label s, and train a separate preposition sense model on the SemEval data with features $\phi_s(\mathbf{x}, s)$ using the structural SVM algorithm. Thus, we have two weight vectors – the one for predicting preposition relations described earlier, and the preposition sense weight vector. At prediction time, for a given input, we find the highest scoring *joint* assignment to the relation, arguments and types and the sense, subject to the constraint that the sense and the relation agree according to the definition of the relations.

5 Experiments and Results

The primary research goal of our experiments is to evaluate the different models (Model 1, Model 2 and joint relation-sense inference) for predicting preposition relations. In additional analysis experiments, we also show that the definition of preposition relations indeed captures cross-preposition semantics by taking advantage of shared features and also highlight the need for going beyond the syntactic parser.

5.1 Types and Features

Types As described in Section 3, we use WordNet hypernyms as one of the type categories. We use all hypernyms within four levels in the hypernym hierarchy for all senses.

The second type category is defined by word-similarity driven clusters. We briefly describe the clustering process here. The thesaurus of (Lin, 1998) specifies similar lexical items for a given word along with a similarity score from 0 to 1. It treats nouns, verbs and adjectives separately. We use the score to cluster groups of similar words using a greedy set-covering approach. Specifically, we randomly select a word which is not yet in a cluster as the center of a new cluster and add all words whose score is greater than σ to it. We repeat this process till all words are in some cluster. A word can appear in more than one cluster because *all* words similar to the cluster center are added to the cluster. We repeat this process for $\sigma \in \{0.1, 0.125, 0.15, 0.175, 0.2, 0.25\}$. By increasing the value of σ, the clusters become more selective and hence smaller. Table 4 shows example noun clusters created using $\sigma = 0.15$. For a given word, identifiers for clusters to which the word belongs serve as type label candidates for this type category[5].

Features Our argument features, denoted by ϕ_A in Section 4.1, are derived from the preposition sense feature set of (Hovy et al., 2010) and extract the following from the argument: 1. Word, part-of-speech, lemma and capitalization indicator, 2. Conflated part-of-speech (one of Noun, Verb, Adjective, Adverb, and Other), 3. Indicator for existence in WordNet, 4. WordNet synsets for the first and all senses, 5. WordNet lemma, lexicographer file names and part, member and substance holonyms, 6. Roget thesaurus divisions for the word, 7. The first and last two and three letters, and 8. Indicators for known affixes. Our type features (ϕ_T) are simply indicators for the type label, conjoined with the type category.

One advantage of abstracting word senses into relations is that we can share features across different prepositions. The base feature set (for both types and arguments) defined above does not encode information about the preposition to be classified. We do so by conjoining the features with the preposition. In addition, since the relation labels are shared across all prepositions, we include the base features as a shared representation between prepositions.

We consider two variants of our feature sets. We refer to the features described above as the **typed** features. In addition, we define the **typed+gen** features by conjoining argument and type features of **typed** with the name of the generator that proposes the argument. Recall that governor candidates are proposed by the dependency parser, or by the heuristics described earlier. Hence, for

[5]The clusters can be downloaded from the authors' website.

Jimmy Carter; Ronald Reagan; richard nixon; George Bush; Lyndon Johnson; Richard M. Nixon; Gerald Ford
metalwork; porcelain; handicraft; jade; bronzeware; carving; pottery; ceramic; earthenware; jewelry; stoneware; lacquerware
degradation; erosion; pollution; logging; desertification; siltation; urbanization; felling; poaching; soil erosion; depletion; water pollution; deforestation
expert; Wall Street analyst; analyst; economist; telecommunications analyst; strategist; media analyst
fox news channel; NBC News; MSNBC; Fox News; CNBC; CNNfn; C-Span
Tuesdays; Wednesdays; weekday; Mondays; Fridays; Thursdays; sundays; Saturdays

Table 4: Examples of noun clusters generated using the set-covering approach for $\sigma = 0.15$

a governor, the **typed+gen** features would conjoin the corresponding **typed** features with one of *parser*, *previous-verb*, *previous-noun*, *previous-adjective*, or *previous-word*.

5.2 Experimental setup and data

All our experiments are based on the SemEval 2007 data for preposition sense disambiguation (Litkowski and Hargraves, 2007) comprising word sense annotation over 16176 training and 8058 examples of prepositions labeled with their senses. We pre-processed sentences with part-of-speech tags using the Illinois POS tagger and dependency graphs using the parser of (Goldberg and Elhadad, 2010)[6]. For the experiments described below, we used the relation-annotated training set to train the models and evaluate accuracy of prediction on the test set.

We chose the structural SVM parameter C using five-fold cross-validation on a 1000 random examples chosen from the training set. For Model 2, we picked $\alpha = 0.1$ using a validation set consisting of a separate set of 1000 training examples. We ran Algorithm 1 for 20 rounds.

Predicting the most frequent relation for a preposition gives an accuracy of 21.18%. Even though the performance of the most-frequent relation label is poor, it does not represent the problem's difficulty and is not a good baseline. To compare, for preposition senses, using features from the neighboring words, (Ye and Baldwin, 2007) obtained an accuracy of 69.3%, and with features designed for the preposition sense task, (Hovy et al., 2010) get up to 84.8% accuracy for the task. Our re-implementation of the latter system using a different set of pre-processing tools gets an accuracy of 83.53%.

For preposition relations, our baseline system for relation labeling uses the **typed** feature set, but without any type information. This produces an accuracy of 88.01% with Model 1 and 88.64% with Model 2. We report statistical significance of results using our implementation of Dan Bikel's stratified-shuffling based statistical significance tester[7].

5.3 Main results: Relation prediction

Our main result, presented in Table 5, compares the baseline model (without types) against other systems, using both models described in Section 4. First, we see that adding type information (**typed**) improves performance over the baseline. Expanding the feature space (**typed+gen**) gives further improvements. Finally, jointly predicting the relations with preposition senses gives another improvement.

Setting	Accuracy	
	Model 1	Model 2
No types	88.01	88.64
typed	**88.77**	89.14
typed+gen	**89.90***	**89.43***
Joint **typed+gen** & sense	**89.99***	**90.26***†

Table 5: **Main results**: Accuracy of relation labeling. Results in bold are statistically significant ($p < 0.01$) improvements over the system that is unaware of types. Superscripts $*$ and $\dagger$ indicate significant improvements over **typed** and **typed+gen** respectively at $p < 0.01$. For Model 2, the improvement of **typed** over the model without types is significant at $p < 0.05$.

Our objective is not predicting preposition sense. However, we observe that with Model 2, jointly predicting the sense and relations improves not only the performance of relation identification, but via joint inference between relations and senses also leads to a large improvement in sense prediction accuracy. Table 6 shows the accuracy for sense prediction. We

[6]We used the Curator (Clarke et al., 2012) for all preprocessing.

[7]http://www.cis.upenn.edu/~dbikel/software.html

see that while Model 1 does not lead to a significant improvement in the accuracy, Model 2 gives an absolute improvement of over 1%.

Setting	Sense accuracy
Hovy (re-implementation)	83.53
Joint + Model 1	83.78
Joint + Model 2	**84.78***

Table 6: Sense prediction performance. Joint inference with Model 1, while improving relation performance, does not help sense accuracy in comparison to our re-implementation of the Hovy sense disambiguation system. However, with Model 2, the improvement is statistically significant at $p < 0.01$.

5.4 Ablation experiments

Feature sharing across prepositions In our first analysis experiment, we seek to highlight the utility of sharing features between different prepositions. To do so, we compare the performance of a system trained without shared features against the type-independent system, which uses shared features. To discount the influence of other factors, we use Model 1 in the **typed** setting without any types. Table 7 reports the accuracy of relation prediction for these two feature sets. We observed a similar improvement in performance even when type features are added or the setting is changed to **typed+gen** or with Model 2.

Setting	Accuracy
Independent	87.17
+ Shared	**88.01**

Table 7: Comparing the effect of feature sharing across prepositions. We see that having a shared representation that goes across prepositions improves accuracy of relation prediction ($p < 0.01$).

Different argument candidate generators Our second ablation study looks at the effect of the various argument candidate generators. Recall that in addition to the dependency governor and object, our models also use the previous word, the previous noun, adjective and verb as governor candidates and the next noun as object candidate. We refer to the candidates generated by the parser as *Parser only* and the others as *Heuristics only*. Table 8 compares the performance of these two argument candidate generators against the full set using Model 1 in both the **typed** and **typed+gen** settings.

We see that the heuristics give a better accuracy than the parser based system. This is because the heuristics often contain the governor/object predicted by the dependency. This is not always the case, though, because using all generators gives a slightly better performing system (not statistically significant). In the overall system, we retain the dependency parser as one of the generators in order to capture long-range governor/object candidates that may not be in the set selected by the heuristics.

	Feature sets	
Generator	**typed**	**typed+gen**
Parser only	87.12	87.12
Heuristics only	87.63	88.84
All	88.01	89.12

Table 8: The performance of different argument candidate generators. We see that considering a larger set of candidate generators gives a big accuracy improvement.

6 Discussion

There are two key differences between Model 1 and 2. First, the former predicts only the relation label, while the latter predicts the entire structure. Table 9 shows example predictions of Model 2 for relation label and WordNet argument types. These examples show how the argument types can be thought of as an explanation for the choice of relation label.

Input	Relation	Hypernyms	
		governor	**object**
died of pneumonia	`Cause`	experience	disease
suffered from flu	`Cause`	experience	disease
recovered from flu	`StartState`	change	disease

Table 9: Example predictions according to Model 2. The hypernyms column shows a representative of the synset chosen for the WordNet types. We see that in the combination of *experience* and *disease* suggests the relation `Cause` while the *change* and *disease* indicate the relation `StartState`.

The main difference between the two models is in the treatment of the unlabeled (or latent) parts of the structure (namely, the arguments and the types) during training and inference. During training, for each example, Model 1 aggregates features from all governors and objects even if they are possibly irrelevant, which may lead to a much bigger model in terms of the number of active weights. On the other hand, for Model 2, Algorithm 1 uses the *single* highest scoring prediction of the latent variables, according to the current parameters, to refine the parameters. Indeed, in our experiments, we observed that the number of non-zero weights in the weight vector of Model 2 is much smaller than that of Model 1. For instance, in the **typed** setting, the weight vector for Model 1 had 2.57 million elements while that for Model 2 had only 1.0 million weights. Similarly, for the **typed+gen** setting, Model 1 had 5.41 million non-zero elements in the weight vector while Model 2 had only 2.21 million non-zero elements.

The learning algorithm itself is a generalization of the latent structural SVM of (Yu and Joachims, 2009). By setting α to zero, we get the latent structure SVM. However, we found via cross-validation that this is not the best setting of the parameter. A theoretical understanding of the sparsity of weights learned by the algorithm and a study of its convergence properties is an avenue of future research.

7 Conclusion

We addressed the problem of modeling semantic relations expressed by prepositions. We approached this task by defining a set of preposition relations that combine preposition senses across prepositions. Doing so allowed us to leverage existing annotated preposition sense data to induce a corpus for preposition labels. We modeled preposition relations in terms of its arguments, namely the governor and object of the preposition, *and* the semantic types of the arguments. Using a generalization of the latent structural SVM, we trained a relation, argument and type predictor using only annotated relation labels. This allowed us to get an accuracy of 89.43% on relation prediction. By employing joint inference with a preposition sense predictor, we further improved the relation accuracy to 90.23%.

Acknowledgments

The authors wish to thank Martha Palmer, Nathan Schneider, the anonymous reviewers and the editor for their valuable feedback. The authors gratefully acknowledge the support of the Defense Advanced Research Projects Agency (DARPA) Machine Reading Program under Air Force Research Laboratory (AFRL) prime contract no. FA8750-09-C-0181. This material is also based on research sponsored by DARPA under agreement number FA8750-13-2-0008. The U.S. Government is authorized to reproduce and distribute reprints for Governmental purposes notwithstanding any copyright notation thereon. The views and conclusions contained herein are those of the authors and should not be interpreted as necessarily representing the official policies or endorsements, either expressed or implied, of DARPA, AFRL or the U.S. Government.

References

E. Agirre, T. Baldwin, and D. Martinez. 2008. Improving parsing and PP attachment performance with sense information. In *Proceedings of the Annual Meeting of the Association for Computational Linguistics (ACL)*, pages 317–325, Columbus, USA.

T. Baldwin, V. Kordoni, and A. Villavicencio. 2009. Prepositions in applications: A survey and introduction to the special issue. *Computational Linguistics*, 35(2):119–149.

M. Chang, D. Goldwasser, D. Roth, and V. Srikumar. 2010a. Discriminative learning over constrained latent representations. In *Proceedings of the Annual Meeting of the North American Association of Computational Linguistics (NAACL)*, pages 429–437, Los Angeles, USA.

M. Chang, V. Srikumar, D. Goldwasser, and D. Roth. 2010b. Structured output learning with indirect supervision. In *Proceedings of the International Conference on Machine Learning (ICML)*, pages 199–206, Haifa, Israel.

J. Clarke, V. Srikumar, M. Sammons, and D. Roth. 2012. An NLP Curator (or: How I Learned to Stop Worrying and Love NLP Pipelines). In *Proceedings of the International Conference on Language Resources and Evaluation (LREC)*, pages 3276–3283, Istanbul, Turkey.

J. Cohen. 1960. A coefficient of agreement for nominal scales. *Educational and Psychological Measurement*, 20:37–46.

D. Dahlmeier, H. T. Ng, and T. Schultz. 2009. Joint learning of preposition senses and semantic roles of prepositional phrases. In *Proceedings of the Conference on Empirical Methods for Natural Language Processing (EMNLP)*, pages 450–458, Singapore.

D. Das, N. Schneider, D. Chen, and N. Smith. 2010. Probabilistic frame-semantic parsing. In *Proceedings of Human Language Technologies: The 2010 Annual*

Conference of the North American Chapter of the Association for Computational Linguistics, pages 948–956, Los Angeles, USA.

C. Fillmore, C. Johnson, and M. Petruck. 2003. Background to FrameNet. *International Journal of Lexicography*, 16(3):235–250.

D. Gildea and D. Jurafsky. 2002. Automatic labeling of semantic roles. *Computational Linguistics*, 28(3):245–288.

Y. Goldberg and M. Elhadad. 2010. An efficient algorithm for easy-first non-directional dependency parsing. In *Proceedings of Human Language Technologies: The 2010 Annual Conference of the North American Chapter of the Association for Computational Linguistics*, pages 742–750, Los Angeles, USA.

D. Hovy, S. Tratz, and E. Hovy. 2010. What's in a preposition? dimensions of sense disambiguation for an interesting word class. In *Coling 2010: Posters*, pages 454–462, Beijing, China.

D. Lin. 1998. Automatic retrieval and clustering of similar words. In *Proceedings of the Annual Meeting of the Association for Computational Linguistics (ACL)*, pages 768–774, Montreal, Canada.

K. Litkowski and O. Hargraves. 2005. The Preposition Project. In *ACL-SIGSEM Workshop on the Linguistic Dimensions of Prepositions and their Use in Computational Linguistics Formalisms and Applications*, pages 171–179, Colchester, UK.

K. Litkowski and O. Hargraves. 2007. SemEval-2007 Task 06: Word-Sense Disambiguation of Prepositions. In *Proceedings of the Fourth International Workshop on Semantic Evaluations (SemEval-2007)*, pages 24–29, Prague, Czech Republic.

K. Litkowski. 2012. Proposed Next Steps for The Preposition Project. Technical Report 12-01, CL Research.

A. Meyers, R. Reeves, C. Macleod, R. Szekely, V. Zielinska, B. Young, and R. Grishman. 2004. The NomBank project: An interim report. In *HLT-NAACL 2004 Workshop: Frontiers in Corpus Annotation*, pages 24–31, Boston, USA.

T. O'Hara and J. Wiebe. 2009. Exploiting semantic role resources for preposition disambiguation. *Computational Linguistics*, 35(2):151–184.

M. Palmer, D. Gildea, and P. Kingsbury. 2005. The Proposition Bank: An Annotated Corpus of Semantic Roles. *Computational Linguistics*, 31(1):71–106.

M. Palmer, D. Gildea, and N. Xue. 2010. *Semantic Role Labeling*, volume 3. Morgan & Claypool Publishers.

V. Punyakanok, D. Roth, and W. Yih. 2008. The importance of syntactic parsing and inference in semantic role labeling. *Computational Linguistics*, 34(2).

D. Roth and W. Yih. 2004. A linear programming formulation for global inference in natural language tasks. In *Proceedings of the Annual Conference on Computational Natural Language Learning (CoNLL)*, pages 1–8, Boston, USA.

D. Roth and W. Yih. 2007. Global inference for entity and relation identification via a linear programming formulation. *Introduction to Statistical Relational Learning*.

V. Srikumar and D. Roth. 2011. A joint model for extended semantic role labeling. In *Proceedings of the Conference on Empirical Methods in Natural Language Processing (EMNLP)*, Edinburgh, Scotland.

S. Tratz and D. Hovy. 2009. Disambiguation of preposition sense using linguistically motivated features. In *Proceedings of Human Language Technologies: The 2009 Annual Conference of the North American Chapter of the Association for Computational Linguistics, Companion Volume: Student Research Workshop and Doctoral Consortium*, pages 96–100, Boulder, USA.

S. Tratz. 2011. *Semantically-enriched Parsing for Natural Language Understanding*. Ph.D. thesis, University of Southern California.

I. Tsochantaridis, T. Hofmann, T. Joachims, and Y. Altun. 2004. Support vector machine learning for interdependent and structured output spaces. In *Proceedings of the International Conference on Machine Learning (ICML)*, pages 104–111, Banff, Canada.

P. Ye and T. Baldwin. 2006. Semantic role labeling of prepositional phrases. *ACM Transactions on Asian Language Information Processing (TALIP)*, 5(3):228–244.

P. Ye and T. Baldwin. 2007. MELB-YB: Preposition sense disambiguation using rich semantic features. In *Proceedings of the Fourth International Workshop on Semantic Evaluations (SemEval-2007)*, pages 241–244, Prague, Czech Republic.

C. Yu and T. Joachims. 2009. Learning structural SVMs with latent variables. In *Proceedings of the International Conference on Machine Learning (ICML)*, pages 1–8, Montreal, Canada.

B. Zapirain, E. Agirre, L. Màrquez, and M. Surdeanu. 2012. Selectional preferences for semantic role classification. *Computational Linguistics*, pages 1–33.

Unsupervised Tree Induction for Tree-based Translation

Feifei Zhai, Jiajun Zhang, Yu Zhou and Chengqing Zong
National Laboratory of Pattern Recognition, Institute of Automation,
Chinese Academy of Sciences, Beijing, China
{ffzhai,jjzhang,yzhou,cqzong}@nlpr.ia.ac.cn

Abstract

In current research, most tree-based translation models are built directly from parse trees. In this study, we go in another direction and build a translation model with an unsupervised tree structure derived from a novel non-parametric Bayesian model. In the model, we utilize synchronous tree substitution grammars (STSG) to capture the bilingual mapping between language pairs. To train the model efficiently, we develop a Gibbs sampler with three novel Gibbs operators. The sampler is capable of exploring the infinite space of tree structures by performing local changes on the tree nodes. Experimental results show that the string-to-tree translation system using our Bayesian tree structures significantly outperforms the strong baseline string-to-tree system using parse trees.

1 Introduction

In recent years, tree-based translation models[1] are drawing more and more attention in the community of statistical machine translation (SMT). Due to their remarkable ability to incorporate context structure information and long distance reordering into the translation process, tree-based translation models have shown promising progress in improving translation quality (Liu et al., 2006, 2009; Quirk et al., 2005; Galley et al., 2004, 2006; Marcu et al., 2006; Shen et al., 2008; Zhang et al., 2011b).

However, tree-based translation models always suffer from two major challenges: 1) They are usually built directly from parse trees, which are generated by supervised linguistic parsers. However, for many language pairs, it is difficult to acquire such corresponding linguistic parsers due to the lack of Tree-bank resources for training. 2) Parse trees are actually only used to model and explain the monolingual structure, rather than the bilingual mapping between language pairs. This indicates that parse trees are usually not the optimal choice for training tree-based translation models (Wang et al., 2010).

Based on the above analysis, we can conclude that the tree structure that is independent from Tree-bank resources and simultaneously considers the bilingual mapping inside the bilingual sentence pairs would be a good choice for building tree-based translation models.

Therefore, complying with the above conditions, we propose an unsupervised tree structure for tree-based translation models in this study. In the structures, tree nodes are labeled by combining the word classes of their boundary words rather than by syntactic labels, such as NP, VP. Furthermore, using these node labels, we design a generative Bayesian model to infer the final tree structure based on synchronous tree substitution grammars (STSG)[2]. STSG is derived from the word alignments and thus can grasp the bilingual mapping effectively.

Training the Bayesian model is difficult due to the exponential space of possible tree structures for each training instance. We therefore develop an efficient Gibbs sampler with three novel Gibbs operators for training. The sampler is capable of exploring the infinite space of tree structures by performing local changes on the tree nodes.

[1] A tree-based translation model is defined as a model using tree structures on one side or both sides.

[2] We believe it is possible to design a model to infer the node label and tree structure jointly. We plan this as future work, and here, we focus only on inferring the tree structure in terms of the node labels derived from word classes.

The tree structure formed in this way is independent from the Tree-bank resources and simultaneously exploits the bilingual mapping effectively. Experiments show that the proposed unsupervised tree (U-tree) is more effective and reasonable for tree-based translation than the parse tree.

The main contributions of this study are as follows:

1) Instead of the parse tree, we propose a Bayesian model to induce a U-tree for tree-based translation. The U-tree exploits the bilingual mapping effectively and does not rely on any Tree-bank resources.
2) We design a Gibbs sampler with three novel Gibbs operators to train the Bayesian model efficiently.

The remainder of the paper is organized as follows. Section 2 introduces the related work. Section 3 describes the STSG generation process, and Section 4 depicts the adopted Bayesian model. Section 5 describes the Gibbs sampling algorithm and Gibbs operators. In Section 6, we analyze the achieved U-trees and evaluate their effectiveness. Finally, we conclude the paper in Section 7.

2 Related Work

In this study, we move in a new direction to build a tree-based translation model with effective unsupervised U-tree structures.

For unsupervised tree structure induction, DeNero and Uszkoreit (2011) adopted a parallel parsing model to induce unlabeled trees of source sentences for syntactic pre-reordering. Our previous work (Zhai et al., 2012) designed an EM-based method to construct unsupervised trees for tree-based translation models. This work differs from the above work in that we design a novel Bayesian model to induce unsupervised U-trees, and prior knowledge can be encoded into the model more freely and effectively.

Blunsom et al. (2008, 2009, 2010) utilized Bayesian methods to learn synchronous context free grammars (SCFG) from a parallel corpus. The obtained SCFG is further used in a phrase-based and hierarchical phrase-based system (Chiang, 2007). Levenberg et al. (2012) employed a Bayesian method to learn discontinuous SCFG rules. This study differs from their work because we concentrate on constructing tree structures for tree-based translation models. Our U-trees are learned based on STSG, which is more appropriate for tree-based translation models than SCFG.

Burkett and Klein (2008) and Burkett et al. (2010) focused on joint parsing and alignment. They utilized the bilingual Tree-bank to train a joint model for both parsing and word alignment. Cohn and Blunsom (2009) adopted a Bayesian method to infer an STSG by exploring the space of alignments based on parse trees. Liu et al. (2012) re-trained the linguistic parsers bilingually based on word alignment. Burkett and Klein (2012) utilized a transformation-based method to learn a sequence of monolingual tree transformations for translation. Compared to their work, we do not rely on any Tree-bank resources and focus on generating effective unsupervised tree structures for tree-based translation models.

Zollmann and Venugopal (2006) substituted the non-terminal X in hierarchical phrase-based model by extended syntactic categories. Zollmann and Vogel (2011) further labeled the SCFG rules with POS tags and unsupervised word classes. Our work differs from theirs in that we present a Bayesian model to learn effective STSG translation rules and U-tree structures for tree-based translation models, rather than designing a labeling strategy for translation rules.

3 The STSG Generation Process

In this work, we induce effective U-trees for the string-to-tree translation model, which is based on a synchronous tree substitution grammar (STSG) between source strings and target tree fragments. We take STSG as the generation grammar to match the translation model. Typically, such an STSG[3] is a 5-tuple as follows:

$$G = (\Sigma_s, \Sigma_t, N_t, S_t, P)$$

where:

- Σ_s and Σ_t represent the set of source and target words, respectively,
- N_t is the set of target non-terminals,
- $S_t \in N_t$ is the start root non-terminal, and
- P is the production rule set.

[3] Generally, an STSG involves tree fragments on both sides. Here we only consider the special case where the source side is actually a string.

Apart from the start non-terminal S_t, we define all the other non-terminals in N_t by word classes. Inspired by (Zollmann and Vogel, 2011), we divide these non-terminals into three categories: one-word, two-word and multi-word non-terminals. The one-word non-terminal is a word class, such as *C*, meaning that it dominates a word whose word class is *C*. Two-word non-terminals are used to stand for two word strings. They are labeled in the form of C_1+C_2, where C_1 and C_2 are the word classes of the two words separately. Accordingly, multi-word non-terminals represent the strings containing more than two words. They are labeled as $C_1...C_n$, demanding that the word classes of the leftmost word and the rightmost word are C_1 and C_n, respectively.

We use POS tag to play the role of word class[4]. For example, the head node of the rule in Figure 1 is a multi-word non-terminal *PRP...RB*. It requires that the POS tags of the leftmost and rightmost word must be *PRP* and *RB*, respectively. Xiong et al. (2006) showed that the boundary word is an effective indicator for phrase reordering. Thus, we believe that combining the word class of boundary words can denote the whole phrase well.

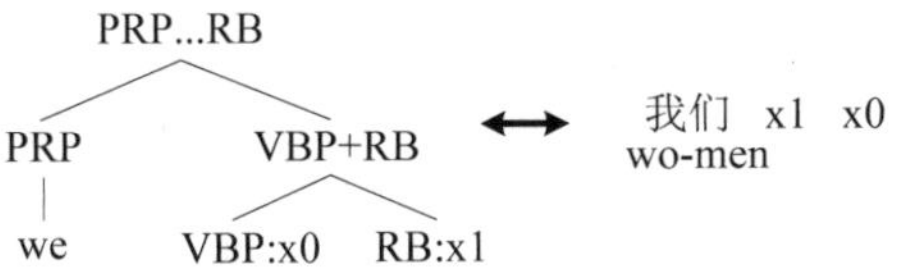

Figure 1. An example of an STSG production rule.

Each production rule in *P* consists of a source string and a target tree fragment. In the target tree fragment, each internal node is labeled with a non-terminal in N_t, and each leaf node is labeled with either a target word in Σ_t or a non-terminal in N_t. The source string in a production rule comprises source words and *variables*. Each variable corresponds to a leaf non-terminal in the target tree fragment. In the STSG, the production rule is used to rewrite the root node into a string and a tree fragment. For example, in Figure 1, the rule rewrites the head node *PRP...RB* into the corresponding string and fragment.

An STSG *derivation* refers to the process of generating a specific source string and target tree structure by production rules. This process begins with the start non-terminal S_t and an empty source string. We repeatedly choose production rules to rewrite the leaf non-terminals and expand the string until no leaf non-terminal is left. Finally, we acquire a source string and a target tree structure defined by the derivation. The probability of a derivation is given as follows:

$$p(d) = \prod_{i=1}^{n} p(r_i \mid N_i) \tag{1}$$

where the derivation comprises a sequence of rules $d=(r_1,\ldots,r_n)$, and N_i represents the root node of rule r_i. Hence, for a specific bilingual sentence pair, we can generate the best target-side tree structure based on the STSG, independent from the Tree-bank resources. The STSG used in the above process is learned by the Bayesian model that is detailed in the next section.

Actually, SCFG can also be used to build the U-trees. We do not use SCFG because most of the tree-based models are based on STSG. In our Bayesian model, the U-trees are optimized through selecting a set of STSG rules. These STSG rules are consistent with the translation rules used in the tree-based models.

Another reason is that STSG has a stronger expressive power on tree construction than SCFG. In a STSG-based U-tree or a STSG rule, although not linguistically informed, the nodes labeled by POS tags are also effective on distinguishing different ones. However, with SCFG, we have to discard all the internal nodes (i.e., flattening the U-trees or rules) to express the same sequence, leading to a poor ability of distinguishing different U-trees and production rules. Thus, using STSG, we can build more specific U-trees for translation.

In addition, we find that the Bayesian SCFG grammar cannot even significantly outperform the heuristic SCFG grammar (Blunsom et al. 2009)[5]. This would indicate that the SCFG-based derivation tree as by-product is also not such good for tree-based translation models. Considering the above reasons, we believe that the STSG-based learning procedure would result in a better translation grammar for tree-based models.

[4] The demand of a POS tagger impairs the independence from manual resources to some extent. In future, we plan to design a method to learn effective unsupervised labels for the non-terminals.

[5] In (Blunsom et al., 2009), for Chinese-to-English translation, the Bayesian SCFG grammar only outperform the heuristic SCFG grammar by 0.1 BLEU points on NIST MT 2004 and 0.6 BLEU points on NIST MT 2005 in the NEWS domain.

4 Bayesian Model

In this section, we present a Bayesian model to learn STSG defined in section 3. In the model, we use θ_N to denote the probability distribution $p(r \mid N)$ in Equation (1). θ_N follows a multinomial distribution and we impose a Dirichlet prior (DP) on it:

$$\begin{aligned} r \mid N &\sim Multi(\theta_N) \\ \theta_N \mid \alpha_N, P_0 &\sim DP(\alpha_N, P_0(\bullet \mid N)) \end{aligned} \tag{2}$$

where $P_0(\bullet \mid N)$ (*base distribution*) is used to assign prior probabilities to the STSG production rules. α_N controls the model's tendency to either reuse existing rules or create new ones using the base distribution $P_0(\bullet \mid N)$.

Instead of denoting the multinomial distribution explicitly with a specific θ_N, we integrate over all possible values of θ_N to achieve the probabilities of rules. This integration results in the following conditional probability for rule r_i given the previously observed rules $r^{-i} = r_1, \ldots, r_{i-1}$:

$$p(r_i \mid r^{-i}, N, \alpha_N, P_0) = \frac{n_{r_i}^{-i} + \alpha_N P_0(r_i \mid N)}{n_N^{-i} + \alpha_N} \tag{3}$$

Where $n_{r_i}^{-i}$ denotes the number of r_i in r^{-i}, and n_N^{-i} represents the total count of rules rewriting non-terminal N in r^{-i}. Thanks to the exchangeability of the model, all permutations of the rules are actually equiprobable. This means that we can compute the probability of each rule based on the previous and subsequent rules (i.e. consider each rule as the last one). This characteristic allows us to design an efficient Gibbs sampling algorithm to train the Bayesian model.

4.1 Base Distribution

The base distribution $P_0(r \mid N)$ is designed to assign prior probabilities to the STSG production rules. Because each rule r consists of a target tree fragment *frag* and a source string *str* in the model, we follow Cohn and Blunsom (2009) and decompose the prior probability $P_0(r \mid N)$ into two factors as follows:

$$P_0(r \mid N) = P(frag \mid N) \cdot P(str \mid frag) \tag{4}$$

where $P(frag \mid N)$ is the probability of producing the target tree fragment *frag*. To generate *frag*, Cohn and Blunsom (2009) used a geometric prior to decide how many child nodes to assign each node. Differently, we require that each multi-word non-terminal node must have two child nodes. This is because the binary structure has been verified to be very effective for tree-based translation (Wang et al., 2007; Zhang et al., 2011a).

The generation process starts at root node N. At first, root node N is expanded into two child nodes. Then, each newly generated node will be checked to expand into two new child nodes with probability p_{expand}. This process repeats until all the new non-terminal nodes are checked. Obviously, p_{expand} controls the scale of tree fragments, where a large p_{expand} corresponds to large fragments[6]. The new terminal nodes (words) are drawn uniformly from the target-side vocabulary, and the non-terminal nodes are created by asking two questions as follows:

1) What type is the node, one-word, two-word or multi-word non-terminal?
2) What tag is used to label the node?

The answer to question 1) is chosen from a uniform distribution, i.e., the probability is 1/3 for each type of non-terminal. The entire generation process is in a top-down manner, i.e., generating a parent node first and then its children.

With respect to question 2), because the father node has determined the POS tags of boundary words, we only need one POS tag to generate the label of the current node. For example, in Figure 1, as the father node *PRP...RB* demands that the POS tag of the rightmost word is *RB*, the right child of *PRP...RB* must also satisfy this condition. Therefore, we choose a POS tag *VBP* and obtain the label *VBP+RB*. The POS tag is drawn uniformly from the POS tag set. If the current node is a one-word non-terminal, question 2) is unnecessary. Similarly, with respect to the two-word non-terminal node, questions 1) and 2) are both unnecessary for its two child nodes because they have already been defined by their father node.

As an example of the generative process, the tree fragment in Figure 1 is created as follows:

a. Determine that the left child of *PRP...RB* is a one-word non-terminal (labeled with *PRP*);
b. Expand *PRP* and generate the word "we" for *PRP*;

[6] In our experiment, we set p_{expand} to 1/3 to encourage small tree fragments.

c. Determine that the right child of *PRP...RB* is a two-word non-terminal;
d. Utilize the predetermined *RB* and a POS tag *VBP* to form the tag of the two-word non-terminal: *VBP+RB*;
e. Expand *VBP+RB* (to *VBP* and *RB*);
f. Do not expand *VBP* and *RB*.

$P(str \mid frag)$ in Equation (4) is the probability of generating the source string, which contains several source words and variables. Inspired by (Blunsom et al., 2009) and (Cohn and Blunsom, 2009), we define $P(str \mid frag)$ as follows:

$$P(str \mid frag) = P_{poisson}(c_{sw};1) \times \frac{1}{|\sum_s|^{c_{sw}}} \times \prod_{i=1}^{c_{var}} \frac{1}{c_{sw}+i} \quad (5)$$

where c_{sw} is the number of words in the source string. $\sum_s$ means the source vocabulary set. Further, c_{var} denotes the number of variables, which is determined by the tree fragment *frag*.

As shown in Equation(5), we first determine how many source words to generate using a Poisson distribution $P_{poisson}(c_{sw};1)$, which imposes a stable preference for short source strings. Then, we draw each source word from a uniform distribution over $\sum_s$. Afterwards, we insert the variables into the string. The variables are inserted one at a time using a uniform distribution over the possible positions. This factor discourages more variables.

For the example rule in Figure 1, the generative process of the source string is:

a. Decide to generate one source word;
b. Generate the source word "我们 (wo-men) ";
c. Insert the first variable after the word;
d. Insert the second variable between the word and the first variable.

Intuitively, a good translation grammar should carry both small translation rules with enough generality and large rules with enough context information. DeNero and Klein (2007) proposed this statement, and Cohn and Blunsom (2009) has verified it in their experiments with parse trees.

Our base distribution is also designed based on this intuition. Considering the two factors in our base distribution, we penalize both large target tree fragments with many nodes and long source strings with many words and variables. The Bayesian model tends to select both small and frequent STSG production rules to construct the U-trees. With these types of trees, we can extract small rules with good generality and simultaneously obtain large rules with enough context information by composition. We will show the effectiveness of our U-trees in the verification experiment.

5 Model Training by Gibbs Sampling

In this section, we introduce a collapsed Gibbs sampler, which enables us to train the Bayesian model efficiently.

5.1 Initialization State

At first, we use random binary trees to initialize the sampler. To get the initial U-trees, we recursively and randomly segment a sentence into two parts and simultaneously create a tree node to dominate each part. The created tree nodes are labeled by the non-terminals described in section 3.

Using the initial target U-trees, source sentences and word alignment, we extract minimal GHKM translation rules[7] in terms of frontier nodes (Galley et al., 2004). Frontier nodes are the tree nodes that can map onto contiguous substrings on the source side via word alignment. For example, the bold italic nodes with shadows in Figure 2 are frontier nodes. In addition, it should be noted that the word alignment is fixed[8], and we only explore the entire space of tree structures in our sampler. Differently, Cohn and Blunsom (2009) designed a sampler to infer an STSG by fixing the tree structure and exploring the space of alignment. We believe that it is possible to investigate the space of both tree structure and alignment simultaneously. This subject will be one of our future work topics.

For each training instance (a pair of source sentence and target U-tree structure), the extracted GHKM minimal translation rules compose a unique STSG derivation[9]. Moreover, all the rules developed from the training data constitute an initial STSG for the Gibbs sampler.

[7] We attach the unaligned word to the lowest frontier node that can cover it in terms of word alignment.

[8] The sampler might reinforce the frequent alignment errors (AE), which would harm the translation model (TM). Actually, the frequent AEs also greatly impair the conventional TM. Besides, our sampler encourages the correct alignments and simultaneously discourages the infrequent AEs. Thus, compared with the conventional TMs, we believe that our final TM would not be worse due to AEs. Our final experiments verify this point and we will conduct a much detailed analysis in future.

[9] We only use the minimal GHKM rules (Galley et al., 2004) here to reduce the complexity of the sampler.

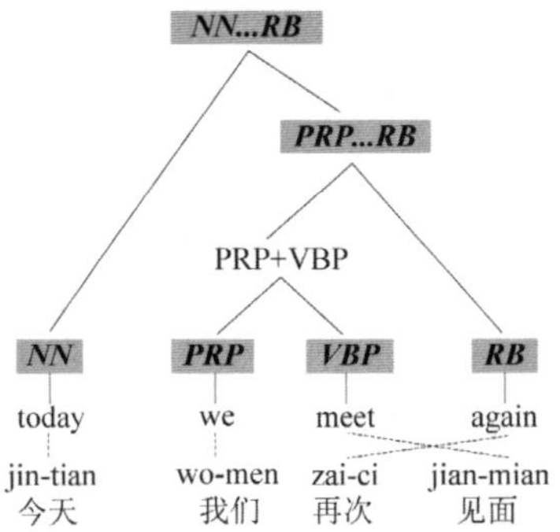

Figure 2. Illustration of an initial U-tree structure. The bold italic nodes with shadows are frontier nodes.

Under this initial STSG, the sampler modifies the initial U-trees (initial sample) to create a series of new ones (new samples) by the Gibbs operators. Consequently, new STSGs are created based on the new U-trees simultaneously and used for the next sampling operation. Repeatedly and after a number of iterations, we can obtain the final U-trees for building translation models.

5.2 The Gibbs Operators

In this section, we develop three novel Gibbs operators for the sampler. They explore the entire space of the U-tree structures by performing local changes on the tree nodes.

For a U-tree of a given sentence, we define ***s-node*** as the non-root node covering at least two words. Thus, the set of s-node contains all the tree nodes except the root node, the pre-terminal nodes and leaf nodes, which we call ***non-s-node***. For example, in Figure 2, *PRB...RB* and *PRP+VBP* are s-nodes, while *NN* and *NN...RB* are non-s-nodes. Since the POS tag sequence of the sentence is fixed, all non-s-nodes would stay unchanged in all possible U-trees of the sentence. Based on this fact, our Gibbs operators work only on s-nodes.

Further, we assign 3 descendant candidates (DC) for each s-node: its left child, right child and its sibling. For example, in Figure 3, the 3 DCs for the s-node are node *PRP*, *VBP* and *RB* respectively. According to the different DCs it governs, every s-node might be in one of the two different states:

1) ***Left state***: as Figure 3(a) shows, the s-node governs the left two DCs, *PRP* and *VBP*, and is labeled *PRP+VBP*.
2) ***Right state***: as Figure 3(b) shows, the s-node governs the right two DCs, *VBP* and *RB*, and is labeled *VBP+RB*.

For a specific U-tree, the states of s-nodes are fixed. Thus, by changing an s-node's state, we can easily transform this U-tree to another one, i.e., from the current sample to a new one.

To formulate the U-tree transformation process, we associate a binary variable $\Psi \in \{0,1\}$ with each s-node, indicating whether the s-node is in the left (Ψ=0) or right state (Ψ=1). Then we can change the U-tree by changing value of the Ψ parameters.

Our first Gibbs operator, ***Rotate***, just works by sampling value of the Ψ parameters, one at a time, and changing the U-tree accordingly. For example, in Figure 3(a), the s-node is currently in the left state (Ψ=0). We sample the Ψ of this node, and if the sampled value of Ψ is 0, we keep the structure unchanged, i.e., in the left state. Otherwise, we change its state to the right state (Ψ=1), and transform the U-tree to Figure 3(b) accordingly.

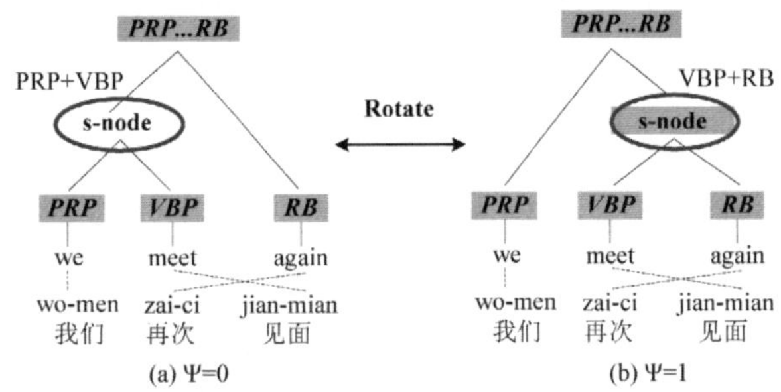

Figure 3. Illustration of the *Rotate* operator. In the figure, (a) and (b) denote the s-node's left state and right state respectively. The bold italic nodes with shadows in the figure are frontier nodes.

Obviously, towards an s-node for sampling, the two values of Ψ would define two different U-trees. Using the GHKM algorithm (Galley et al. 2004), we can get two different STSG derivations from the two U-trees based on the fixed word alignment. Each derivation carries a set of STSG rules (i.e., minimal GHKM translation rules) of its own. In the two derivations, the STSG rules defined by the two states include the one rooted at the s-node's lowest ancestor frontier node, and the one rooted at the s-node if it is a frontier node. For instance, in Figure 3(a), as the s-node is not a frontier node, the left state (Ψ=0) defines only one rule:

$$r_{left}: x_0\ x_2\ x_1 \rightarrow$$
$$PRP...RB(PRP+VBP(x_0: PRP\ x_1: VBP)\ x_2: RB)$$

Differently, in Figure 3(b), the s-node is a frontier node and thus the right state (Ψ=1) defines two rules:

$$r_{right\text{-}0}: x_0\ x_1 \rightarrow PRP...RB(x_0: PRP\ x_1: VBP+RB)$$
$$r_{right\text{-}1}: x_1\ x_0 \rightarrow VBP+RB(x_0: VBP\ x_1: RB)$$

Using these STSG rules, the two derivations are evaluated as follows (We use the value of Ψ to denote the corresponding STSG derivation):

$$p(\Psi=0) \propto p(r_{left} \mid r^{-})$$
$$p(\Psi=1) \propto p(r_{right\text{-}0}, r_{right\text{-}1} \mid r^{-})$$
$$= p(r_{right\text{-}0} \mid r^{-})\, p(r_{right\text{-}1} \mid r_{right\text{-}0}, r^{-})$$

Where r^{-} refers to the conditional context, i.e., the set of all other rules in the training data. All the probabilities in the above formulas are computed by Equation(3). We then normalize the two scores and sample a value of Ψ based on them. With the Bayesian model described in section 4, the sampler will prefer the Ψ that produces small and frequent STSG rules. This tendency results in more frontier nodes in the U-tree (i.e., the s-node tends to be in the state that is a frontier node), which will factor the training instance into more small STSG rules. In this way, the overall likelihood of the bilingual data is improved by the sampler.

Theoretically, the *Rotate* operator is capable of arriving at any possible U-tree from the initial U-tree. This is because we can first convert the initial U-tree to a left branch tree by the *Rotate* operator, and then transform it to any other U-tree. However, it may take a long time to do so. Thus, to speed up the structure transformation process, we employ a ***Two-level-Rotate*** operator, which takes a pair of s-nodes in a parent-child relationship as a unit for sampling. Similar to the *Rotate* operator, we also assign a binary variable $\xi \in \{0,1\}$ to each unit and update the U-tree by sampling the value of ξ. The method of sampling ξ is similar to the one used for Ψ. Figure 4 shows an example of the operator. As shown in Figure 4(a), the unit *NN...VBP* and *PRP+VBP* is in the left state (ξ=0), and governs the left three descendants: *NN*, *PRP*, and *VBP*. By the *Two-level-Rotate* operator, we can convert the unit to Figure 4(b), i.e., the right state (ξ=1). Just as Figure 4(b) shows, the governed descendants of the unit are turned to *PRP*, *VBP*, and *RB*.

It may be confusing when choosing the parent-child s-node pair for sampling because the parent node always faces two choices: combining the left child or right child for sampling. To avoid confusion, we split the *Two-level-Rotate* operator into two operators: ***Two-level-left-Rotate*** operator, which works with the parent node and its left child, and ***Two-level-right-Rotate*** operator, which only considers the parent node and its right child[10]. Therefore, the operator used in Figure 4 is a *Two-level-right-Rotate* operator.

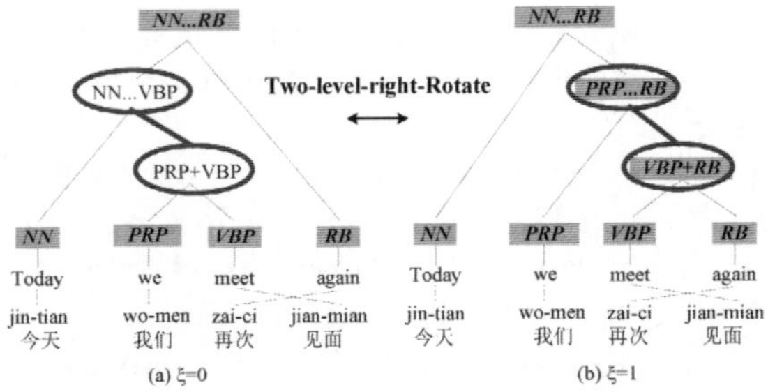

Figure 4. Illustration of the *Two-level-Rotate* operator. The bold italic nodes with shadows in the Figure are frontier nodes.

During sampling, for each training instance, the sampler first applies the *Two-level-left-Rotate* operator to all candidate pairs of s-nodes (parent s-node and its left child s-node) in the U-tree. After that, the *Two-level-right-Rotate* operator is applied to all the candidate pairs of s-nodes (parent s-node and its right child s-node). Then, we use the *Rotate* operator on every s-node in the U-tree. By utilizing the operators separately, we can guarantee that our sampler satisfies detailed balance. We visit all the training instances in a random order (one iteration). After a number of iterations, we can obtain the final U-tree structures and build the tree-based translation model accordingly.

6 Experiments

6.1 Experimental Setup

The experiments are conducted on Chinese-to-English translation. The training data are the FBIS corpus with approximately 7.1 million Chinese words and 9.2 million English words. We obtain the bidirectional word alignment with GIZA++, and then adopt the *grow-diag-final-and* strategy to obtain the final symmetric alignment. We train a 5-gram language model on the Xinhua portion of the English Gigaword corpus and the English part of

[10] We can also take more nodes as a unit for sampling, but this would make the algorithm much more complex.

the training data. For tuning and testing, we use the NIST MT 2003 evaluation data as the development set, and use the NIST MT04 and MT05 data as the test set. We use MERT (Och, 2004) to tune parameters. Since MERT is prone to search errors, we run MERT 5 times and select the best tuning parameters in the tuning set. The translation quality is evaluated by case-insensitive BLEU-4 with the shortest length penalty. The statistical significance test is performed by the re-sampling approach (Koehn, 2004).

To create the baseline system, we use the open-source Joshua 4.0 system (Ganitkevitch et al., 2012) to build a hierarchical phrase-based (HPB) system, and a syntax-augmented MT (SAMT) [11] system (Zollmann and Venugopal, 2006) respectively.

The translation system used for testing the effectiveness of our U-trees is our in-house string-to-tree system (abbreviated as ***s2t***). The system is implemented based on (Galley et al., 2006) and (Marcu et al. 2006). In the system, we extract both the minimal GHKM rules (Galley et al., 2004), and the rules of SPMT Model 1 (Galley et al., 2006) with phrases up to length *L=5* on the source side. We then obtain the composed rules by composing two or three adjacent minimal rules.

To build the above *s2t* system, we first use the parse tree, which is generated by parsing the English side of the bilingual data with the Berkeley parser (Petrov et al., 2006). Then, we binarize the English parse trees using the head binarization approach (Wang et al., 2007) and use the resulting binary parse trees to build another *s2t* system.

For the U-trees, we run the Gibbs sampler for 1000 iterations on the whole corpus. The sampler uses 1,087s per iteration, on average, using a single core, 2.3 GHz Intel Xeon machine. For the hyperparameters, we set α to 0.1 and p_{expand} = 1/3 to give a preference to the rules with small fragments. We built an *s2t* translation system with the achieved U-trees after the 1000th iteration. We only use one sample to extract the translation grammar because multiple samples would result in a grammar that would be too large.

[11] From (Zollmann and Vogel, 2011), we find that the performance of SAMT system is similar with the method of labeling SCFG rules with POS tags. Thus, to be convenient, we only conduct experiments with the SAMT system.

6.2 Analysis of The Gibbs Sampler

To evaluate the effectiveness of the Gibbs sampler, we explore the change of the training data's likelihood with increasing sampling iterations.

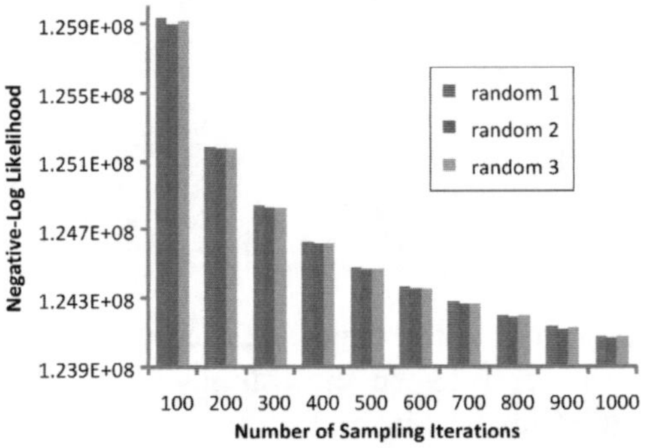

Figure 5. Histograms of the training data's likelihood vs. the number of sampling iterations. In the figure, random 1 to 3 refers to three independent runs of the sampler with different initial U-trees as initialization states.

Figure 5 depicts the negative-log likelihood of the training data after several sampling iterations. The results show that the overall likelihood of the training data is improved by the sampler. Moreover, comparing the three independent runs, we see that although the sampler begins with different initial U-trees, the training data's likelihood is always similar during sampling. This demonstrates that our sampler is not sensitive to the random initial U-trees and can always arrive at a good final state beginning from different initialization states. Thus, we only utilize the U-trees from random 1 for further analysis hereafter.

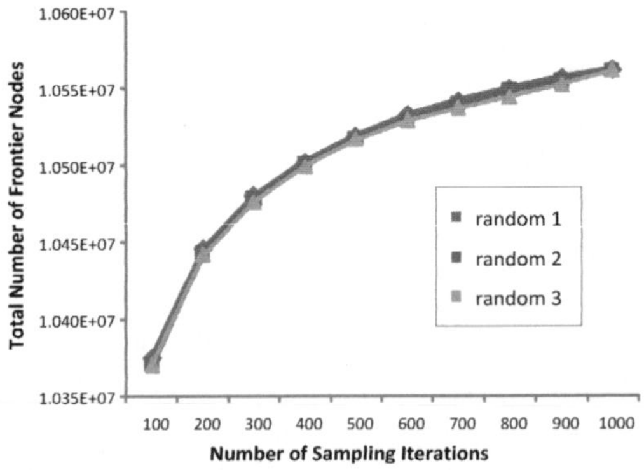

Figure 6. The total number of frontier nodes for the three independent runs.

6.3 Analysis of the U-tree Structure

Acquiring better U-trees for translation is our final purpose. However, are the U-trees achieved by the

Gibbs sampler appropriate for the tree-based translation model?

To answer this question, we first analyze the effect of the sampler on the U-trees. Figure 6 shows the total number of frontier nodes in the training data during sampling. The results show that the number of frontier nodes increases with increased sampling. This tendency indicates that our sampler prefers the tree structure with more frontier nodes. Consequently, the final U-tree structures can always be factored into many small minimal translation rules. Just as we have argued in section 4.1, this is beneficial for a good translation grammar.

To demonstrate the above analysis, Figure 7 shows a visual comparison between our U-tree (from random 1) and the binary parse tree (found by head binarization). Because the traditional parse tree is not binarized, we do not consider it for this analysis. Figure 7 shows that whether it is the target tree fragment or the source string of the rule, our U-trees always tend to obtain the smaller ones[12]. This comparison verifies that our Bayesian tree induction model is effective in shifting the tree structures away from complex minimal rules, which tend to negatively affect translation.

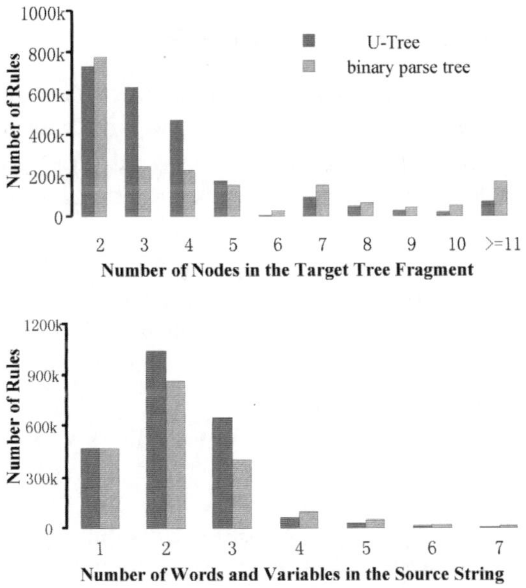

Figure 7. Histograms over minimal translation rule statistics comparing our U-trees and binary parse trees.

[12] Binary parse trees get more tree fragments with two nodes than U-trees. This is because there are many unary edges in the binary parse trees, while no unary edge exists in our U-trees.

Specifically, we show an example of a binary parse tree and our U-tree in Figure 8. The example U-tree is more conducive to extracting effective translation rules. For example, to translate the Chinese phrase "仅 为", we can extract a rule (R2 in Figure 9) directly from the U-tree because the phrase "仅 为" is governed by a frontier node, i.e., node "VBD+RB". However, because no node governs "仅 为" in the binary parse tree, we can only obtain a rule (R1 in Figure 9) with many extra nodes and edges, such as node CD in R1. Due to these extra things, R1 is too large to show good generality.

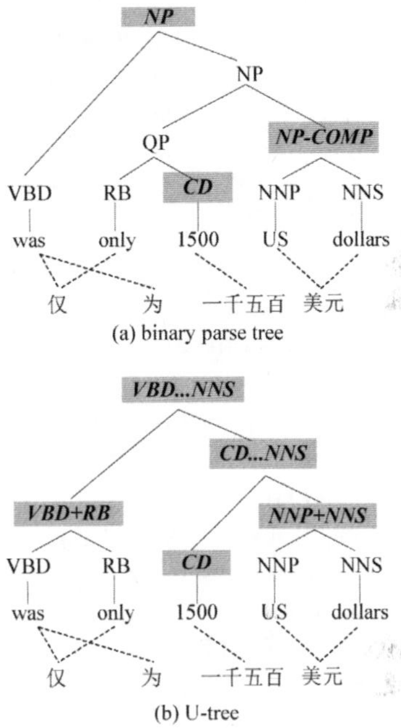

Figure 8. Example of different tree structures. The node NP-COMP is achieved by head binarization. The bold italic nodes with shadows denote frontier nodes.

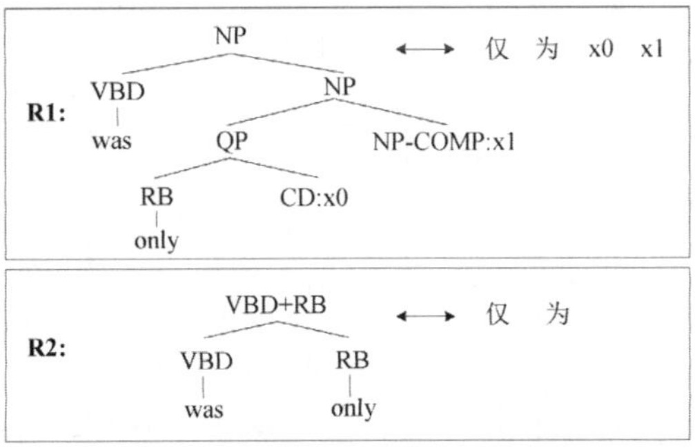

Figure 9. Example rules to translate the Chinese phrase "仅 为." R1 is extracted from Figure 8(a), i.e., the binary parse tree. R2 is from Figure 8(b), i.e., the U-tree.

Based on the above analysis, we can conclude that our proposed U-tree structures are conducive to extracting small, minimal translation rules. This indicates that the U-trees are more consistent with the word alignment and are good at capturing bilingual mapping information. Therefore, because parse trees are always constrained by cross-lingual structure divergence, we believe that the proposed U-trees would result in a better translation grammar. We demonstrate this conclusion in the next sub-section.

6.4 Final Translation Results

The final translation results are shown in Table 1. In the table, lines 3-6 refer to the string-to-tree systems built with different types of tree structures.

Table 1 shows that all our *s2t* systems outperform the *Joshua (HPB)* and *Joshua (SAMT)* system significantly. This comparison verifies the superiority of our in-house *s2t* system. Moreover, the results shown in Table 1 also demonstrate the effectiveness of head binarization, which helps to improve the *s2t* system using parse trees in all translation tasks.

To test the effectiveness of our U-trees, we give the *s2t* translation system using the U-trees (from random 1). The results show that the system using U-trees achieves the best translation result from all of the systems. It surpasses the *s2t* system using parse trees by 1.47 BLEU points on MT04 and 1.44 BLEU points on MT05. Moreover, even using the binary parse trees, the achieved *s2t* system is still lower than our U-tree-based *s2t* system by 0.97 BLEU points on the combined test set. From the translation results, we can validate our former analysis that the U-trees generated by our Bayesian tree induction model are more appropriate for string-to-tree translation than parse trees.

System	MT04	MT05	All
Joshua (HPB)	31.73	28.82	30.64
Joshua (SAMT)	32.48	29.77	31.56
s2t *(parse-tree)*	33.73*	30.25*	32.75*
s2t *(binary-parse-tree)*	34.09*	30.99*#	32.92*
s2t *(U-tree)*	**35.20***#	**31.69***#	**33.89***#

Table 1. Results (in case-insensitive BLEU-4 scores) of *s2t* systems using different types of trees. The "*" and "#" denote that the results are significantly better than the Joshua (SAMT) system and the *s2t* system using parse trees (p<0.01).

6.5 Large Data

We also conduct an experiment on a larger bilingual training data from the LDC corpus[13]. The training corpus contains 2.1M sentence pairs with approximately 27.7M Chinese words and 31.9M English words. Similarly, we train a 5-gram language model using the Xinhua portion of the English Gigaword corpus and the English part of the training corpus. With the same settings as before, we run the Gibbs sampler for 1000 iterations and utilize the final U-tree structure to build a string-to-tree translation system.

The final BLEU score results are shown in Table 2. In the scenario with a large data, the string-to-tree system using our U-trees still significantly outperforms the system using parse trees.

System	MT04	MT05	All
Joshua (HPB)	34.55	33.11	34.01
Joshua (SAMT)	34.76	33.72	34.37
s2t *(parse-tree)*	36.40*	34.53*	35.70*
s2t *(binary-parse-tree)*	37.38*#	35.14*#	36.54*#
s2t *(U-tree)*	**38.02***#	**36.12***#	**37.34***#

Table 2. Results (in case-insensitive BLEU-4 scores) for the large training data. The meaning of "*" and "#" are similar to Table 1.

7 Conclusion and Future Work

In this paper, we explored a new direction to build a tree-based model based on unsupervised Bayesian trees rather than supervised parse trees. To achieve this purpose, we have made two major efforts in this paper:

(1) We have proposed a novel generative Bayesian model to induce effective U-trees for tree-based translation. We utilized STSG in the model to grasp bilingual mapping information. We further imposed a reasonable hierarchical prior on the tree structures, encouraging small and frequent minimal rules for translation.

(2) To train the Bayesian tree induction model efficiently, we developed a Gibbs sampler with three novel Gibbs operators. The operators are designed specifically to explore the infinite space of tree structures by performing local changes on the tree structure.

[13] LDC category number : LDC2000T50, LDC2002E18, LDC2003E07, LDC2004T07, LDC2005T06, LDC2002L27, LDC2005T10 and LDC2005T34.

Experiments on the string-to-tree translation model demonstrated that our U-trees are better than the parse trees. The translation results verify that the well-designed unsupervised trees are actually more appropriate for tree-based translation than parse trees. Therefore, we believe that the unsupervised tree structure would be a promising research direction for tree-based translation.

In future, we plan to testify our sampler with various initial trees, such as the tree structure formed by (Zhang et al., 2008). We also plan to perform a detailed empirical comparison between STST and SCFG under our settings. Moreover, we will further conduct experiments to compare our methods with other relevant works, such as (Cohn and Blunsom, 2009) and (Burkett and Klein, 2012).

Acknowledgments

We would like to thank Philipp Koehn and three anonymous reviewers for their valuable comments and suggestions. The research work has been funded by the Hi-Tech Research and Development Program ("863" Program) of China under Grant No. 2011AA01A207, 2012AA011101, and 2012AA011102.

References

Phil Blunsom, Trevor Cohn, Miles Osborne. 2008. Bayesian synchronous grammar induction. In *Advances in Neural Information Processing Systems*, volume 21, pages 161-168.

Phil Blunsom, Trevor Cohn, Chris Dyer, and Miles Osborne. 2009. A gibbs sampler for phrasal synchronous grammar induction. In *Proc. of ACL 2009*, pages 782-790.

Phil Blunsom and Trevor Cohn. 2010. Inducing synchronous grammars with slice sampling. In *Proc. of NAACL 2010*, pages 238-241.

David Burkett and Dan Klein. 2008. Two languages are better than one (for syntactic Parsing). In *Proc. of EMNLP 2008*, pages 877-886.

David Burkett, John Blitzer, and Dan Klein. 2010. Joint parsing and alignment with weakly synchronized grammars. In Proc. of *NAACL 2010*, pages 127-135.

David Burkett and Dan Klein. 2012. Transforming trees to improve syntactic convergence. In *Proc. of EMNLP 2012*, pages 863-872.

David Chiang. 2007. Hierarchical phrase-based translation. *Computational Linguistics*, 33 (2). pages 201-228.

Dekai Wu. 1996. A polynomial-time algorithm for statistical machine translation. In *Proc. of ACL 1996*, pages 152-158.

Dekai Wu. 1997. Stochastic inversion transduction grammars and bilingual parsing of parallel corpora. *Computational Linguistics*, 23:377-404.

Trevor Cohn and Phil Blunsom. 2009. A bayesian model of syntax-directed tree to string grammar induction. In *Proc. of EMNLP 2009*, pages 352-361.

Trevor Cohn, Phil Blunsom, and Sharon Goldwater. 2010. Inducing tree-substitution grammars. *Journal of Machine Learning Research*, pages 3053-3096.

Brooke Cowan, Ivona Kucerova and Michael Collins. 2006. A discriminative model for tree-to-tree translation. In *Proc. of EMNLP 2006*, pages 232-241.

John DeNero and Dan Klein. 2007. Tailoring word alignments to syntactic machine translation. In *Proc. of ACL 2007*, pages 17-24.

John DeNero and Jakob Uszkoreit. 2011. Inducing sentence structure from parallel corpora for reordering. In *Proc. of EMNLP 2011*, pages 193-203.

Chris Dyer. 2010. Two monolingual parses are better than one (synchronous parse). In *Proc. of NAACL 2010*, pages 263-266.

Jason Eisner. 2003. Learning non-isomorphic tree mappings for machine translation. In *Proc. of ACL 2003*, pages 205-208.

Michel Galley, Mark Hopkins, Kevin Knight and Daniel Marcu. 2004. What's in a translation rule. In *Proc. of HLT-NAACL 2004*, pages 273–280.

Michel Galley, Jonathan Graehl, Kevin Knight, Daniel Marcu, Steve DeNeefe, Wei Wang and Ignacio Thayer. 2006. Scalable inference and training of context-rich syntactic translation models. In *Proc. of ACL-COLING 2006*, pages 961-968.

Jonathan Weese, Juri Ganitkevitch, Chris Callison-Burch, Matt Post and Adam Lopez. 2011. Joshua 3.0: syntax-based machine translation with the thrax Grammar Extractor. In *Proc of WMT11*, pages 478-484.

Liang Huang, Kevin Knight and Aravind Joshi. 2006. A syntax-directed translator with extended domain of locality. In *Proc. of AMTA 2006*, pages 65-73.

Philipp Koehn, Franz Och, and Daniel Marcu. 2003. Statistical phrase-based translation, In *Proc. of HLT/NAACL 2003*, pages 48-54.

Philipp Koehn. 2004. Statistical significance tests for machine translation evaluation. In *Proc. of EMNLP 2004*, pages 388–395.

Philipp Koehn, Hieu Hoang, Alexandra Birch, Chris Callison-Burch, Marcello Federico, Nicola Bertoldi, Brooke Cowan, Wade Shen, Christine Moran, Richard Zens, Chris Dyer and Ondřej Bojar. 2007. Moses: open source toolkit for statistical machine translation. In *Proc. of ACL 2007*, pages 177-180.

Abby Levenberg, Chris Dyer and Phil Blunsom. 2012. A bayesian model for learning SCFGs with discontiguous Rules. In *Proc. of EMNLP 2012*, pages 223-232.

Zhifei Li, Chris Callison-Burch, Chris Dyer, Juri Ganitkevitch, Sanjeev Khudanpur, Lane Schwartz, Wren N.G. Thornton, Jonathan Weese and Omar F. Zaidan. 2009. Joshua: An open source toolkit for parsing-based machine translation. In *Proc. of ACL 2009*, pages 135-139.

Shujie Liu, Chi-Ho Li, Mu Li, Ming Zhou. 2012. Re-training monolingual parser bilingually for syntactic SMT. In *Proc. of EMNLP 2012*, pages 854-862.

Yang Liu, Qun Liu and Shouxun Lin. 2006. Tree-to-string alignment template for statistical machine translation. In *Proc. of ACL-COLING 2006*, pages 609-616.

Yang Liu, Yajuan Lv and Qun Liu. 2009. Improving tree-to-tree translation with packed forests. In *Proc. of ACL-IJCNLP 2009*, pages 558-566.

Daniel Marcu, Wei Wang, Abdessamad Echihabi and Kevin Knight. 2006. SPMT: Statistical machine translation with syntactified target language phrases. In *Proc. of EMNLP 2006*, pages 44-52.

Franz Och, 2003. Minimum error rate training in statistical machine translation. In *Proc. of ACL 2003*, pages 160-167.

Kishore Papineni, Salim Roukos, Todd Ward, and Wei-Jing Zhu. 2002. BLEU: A method for automatic evaluation of machine translation. In *Proc. of ACL 2002*, pages 311-318.

Slav Petrov, Leon Barrett, Romain Thibaux and Dan Klein. 2006. Learning accurate, compact, and interpretable tree annotation. In *Proc. of COLING-ACL 2006*, pages 433-440.

Chris Quirk, Arul Menezes and Colin Cherry. 2005. Dependency treelet translation: syntactically informed phrasal SMT. In *Proc. of ACL 2005*, pages 271-279.

Libin Shen, Jinxi Xu and Ralph Weischedel. 2008. A new string-to-dependency machine translation algorithm with a target dependency language model. In *Proc. of ACL-08*, pages 577-585.

Wei Wang, Kevin Knight, and Daniel Marcu. 2007. Binarizing syntax trees to improve syntax-based machine translation accuracy. In *Proc. of EMNLP 2007*, pages 746-754.

Wei Wang, Jonathan May, Kevin Knight, and Daniel Marcu. 2010. Re-structuring, re-labeling, and re-aligning for syntax-based machine translation. *Computational Linguistics*, 36(2):247–277.

Feifei Zhai, Jiajun Zhang, Yu Zhou and Chengqing Zong. 2012. Tree-based translation without using parse trees. In *Proc. of COLING 2012*, pages 3037-3054.

Hao Zhang, Liang Huang, Daniel Gildea and Kevin Knight. 2006. Synchronous binarization for machine translation. In *Proc. of HLT-NAACL 2006*, pages 256-263.

Hao Zhang, Daniel Gildea, and David Chiang. 2008. Extracting synchronous grammars rules from word level alignments in linear time. In *Proc. of COLING 2008*, pages 1081-1088.

Hao Zhang, Licheng Fang, Peng Xu, Xiaoyun Wu. 2011a. Binarized forest to string translation. In *Proc. of ACL 2011*, pages 835-845.

Hui Zhang, Min Zhang, Haizhou Li, Aiti Aw, Chew Lim Tan. 2009. Forest-based tree sequence to string translation model. In *Proc. of ACL-IJCNLP 2009*, pages 172-180.

Jiajun Zhang, Feifei Zhai and Chengqing Zong. 2011b. Augmenting string-to-tree translation models with fuzzy use of source-side syntax. In *Proc. of EMNLP 2011*, pages 204-215.

Min Zhang, Hongfei Jiang, Ai Ti Aw, Jun Sun, Chew Lim Tan and Sheng Li. 2007. A tree-to-tree alignment-based model for statistical Machine translation. *MT-Summit-07*. pages 535-542

Min Zhang, Hongfei Jiang, Ai ti Aw, Haizhou Li, Chew Lim Tan and Sheng Li. 2008. A tree sequence alignment-based tree-to-tree translation model. In *Proc. of ACL 2008*, pages 559-567.

Andreas Zollmann and Ashish Venugopal. 2006. Syntax augmented machine translation via chart parsing. In *Proc. of Workshop on Statistical Machine Translation 2006*, pages 138-141.

Andreas Zollmann and Stephan Vogel. 2011. A word-class approach to labeling PSCFG rules for machine translation. In *Proc. of ACL 2011*, pages 1-11.

Minimally-Supervised Morphological Segmentation using Adaptor Grammars

Kairit Sirts
Institute of Cybernetics
Tallinn University of Technology
sirts@phon.ioc.ee

Sharon Goldwater
School of Informatics
The University of Edinburgh
sgwater@inf.ed.ac.uk

Abstract

This paper explores the use of Adaptor Grammars, a nonparametric Bayesian modelling framework, for minimally supervised morphological segmentation. We compare three training methods: unsupervised training, semi-supervised training, and a novel model selection method. In the model selection method, we train unsupervised Adaptor Grammars using an over-articulated *metagrammar*, then use a small labelled data set to select which potential morph boundaries identified by the metagrammar should be returned in the final output. We evaluate on five languages and show that semi-supervised training provides a boost over unsupervised training, while the model selection method yields the best average results over all languages and is competitive with state-of-the-art semi-supervised systems. Moreover, this method provides the potential to tune performance according to different evaluation metrics or downstream tasks.

1 Introduction

Research into unsupervised learning of morphology has a long history, starting with the work of Harris (1951). While early research was mostly motivated by linguistic interests, more recent work in NLP often aims to reduce data sparsity in morphologically rich languages for tasks such as automatic speech recognition, statistical machine translation, or automatic text generation. For these applications, however, completely unsupervised systems may not be ideal if even a small amount of segmented training data is available. In this paper, we explore the use of Adaptor Grammars (Johnson et al., 2007) for minimally supervised morphological segmentation.

Adaptor Grammars (AGs) are a nonparametric Bayesian modelling framework that can learn latent tree structures over an input corpus of strings. For example, they can be used to define a morphological grammar where each word consists of zero or more prefixes, a stem, and zero or more suffixes; the actual forms of these morphs (and the segmentation of words into morphs) are learned from the data. In this general approach AGs are similar to many other unsupervised morphological segmentation systems, such as Linguistica (Goldsmith, 2001) and the Morfessor family (Creutz and Lagus, 2007). A major difference, however, is that the morphological grammar is specified as an input to the program, rather than hard-coded, which allows different grammars to be explored easily. For the task of segmenting utterances into words, for example, Johnson and colleagues have experimented with grammars encoding different kinds of sub-word and super-word structure (e.g., syllables and collocations), showing that the best grammars far outperform other systems on the same corpora (Johnson, 2008a; Johnson and Goldwater, 2009; Johnson and Demuth, 2010).

These word segmentation papers demonstrated both the power of the AG approach and the synergistic behavior that occurs when learning multiple levels of structure simultaneously. However, the best-performing grammars were selected using the same corpus that was used for final testing, and each paper dealt with only one language. The ideal unsupervised learner would use a single grammar tuned on one or more development languages and still perform well on other languages where development data is unavailable. Indeed, this is the basic principle behind Linguistica and Morfessor. However, we know that different languages can have very different morphological properties, so using a single grammar for all languages may not be the best approach if there is a principled way to choose between grammars. Though AGs make it easy to try many different possible grammars, the process of proposing and testing plausible options can still be time-consuming.

In this paper, we propose a novel method for automatically selecting good morphological grammars for different languages (English, Finnish, Turkish, German, and Estonian) using a small amount of gold-segmented data (1000 word types). We use the AG framework to specify a very general binary-branching grammar of depth four with which we learn a parse tree of each word that contains several possible segmentation splits for the word. Then, we use the gold-segmented data to learn, for each language, which of the proposed splits from the original grammar should actually be used in order to best segment that language.

We evaluate our approach on both a small development set and the full Morpho Challenge test set for each language—up to three million word types. In doing so, we demonstrate that using the posterior grammar of an AG model to decode unseen data is a feasible way to scale these models to large data sets. We compare to several baselines which use the annotated data to different degrees: parameter tuning, grammar tuning, supervised training, or no use of annotated data. In addition to existing approaches—unsupervised and semi-supervised Morfessor, unsupervised Morsel (Lignos, 2010), and unsupervised AGs—we also show how to use the annotated data to train semi-supervised AGs (using the data to accumulate rule statistics rather than for grammar selection). The grammar selection method yields comparable results to the best of these other approaches.

To summarize, our contributions in this paper are: 1) scaling AGs to large data sets by using the posterior grammar to define an inductive model; 2) demonstrating how to train semi-supervised AG models, and showing that this improves morphological segmentation over unsupervised training; and 3) introducing a novel grammar selection method for AG models whose segmentation results are competitive with the best existing systems.

Before providing details of our methods and results, we first briefly review Adaptor Grammars. For a formal definition, see Johnson et al. (2007).

2 Adaptor Grammars

Adaptor Grammars are a framework for specifying nonparametric Bayesian models that can be used to learn latent tree structures from a corpus of strings. There are two components to an AG model: the *base distribution*, which is just a PCFG, and the *adaptor*, which "adapts" the probabilities assigned to individual subtrees under the PCFG model, such that the probability of a subtree under the complete model may be considerably higher than the product of the probabilities of the PCFG rules required to construct it. Although in principle the adaptor can be any function that maps one distribution onto another, Johnson et al. (2007) use a Pitman-Yor Process (PYP) (Pitman and Yor, 1997) as the adaptor because it acts as a caching model. Under a PYP AG model, the posterior probability of a particular subtree will be roughly proportional to the number of times that subtree occurs in the current analysis of the data (with the probability of unseen subtrees being computed under the base PCFG distribution).

An AG model can be defined by specifying the CFG rules (the support for the base distribution) and indicating which non-terminals are "adapted", i.e., can serve as the root of a cached subtree. Given this definition and an input corpus of strings, Markov chain Monte Carlo samplers can be used to infer the posterior distribution over trees (and all hyperparameters of the model, including PCFG probabilities in the base distribution and PYP hyperparameters). Any frequently recurring substring (e.g., a common prefix) will tend to be parsed consistently, as this permits the model to treat the subtree spanning that string as a cached subtree, assigning it higher probability than under the PCFG distribution.

Adaptor Grammars have been applied to a wide variety of tasks, including segmenting utterances into words (Johnson, 2008a; Johnson and Goldwater, 2009; Johnson and Demuth, 2010), classifying documents according to perspective (Hardisty et al., 2010), machine transliteration of names (Huang et al., 2011), native language identification (Wong et al., 2012), and named entity clustering (Elsner et al., 2009). There have also been AG experiments with morphological segmentation, but more as a proof of concept than an attempt to achieve state-of-the-art results (Johnson et al., 2007; Johnson, 2008b).

3 Using AGs for Learning Morphology

Originally, the AG framework was designed for unsupervised learning. This section first describes how AGs can be used for unsupervised morphological segmentation, and then introduces two ways to use a small labelled data set to improve performance: semi-supervised learning and grammar selection.

3.1 Unsupervised Adaptor Grammars

We define three AG models to use as unsupervised baselines in our segmentation experiments. The first of these is very simple:

$$\begin{aligned} \text{Word} &\rightarrow \underline{\text{Morph}}^{+} \\ \underline{\text{Morph}} &\rightarrow \text{Char}^{+} \end{aligned} \tag{1}$$

The underline notation indicates an adapted non-terminal, and $^{+}$ abbreviates a set of recursive rules, e.g., Word $\rightarrow \underline{\text{Morph}}^{+}$ is short for

$$\begin{aligned} \text{Word} &\rightarrow \text{Morphs} \\ \text{Morphs} &\rightarrow \underline{\text{Morph}}\ \text{Morphs} \\ \text{Morphs} &\rightarrow \underline{\text{Morph}} \end{aligned}$$

Grammar 1 (**MorphSeq**) is just a unigram model over morphs: the Morph symbol is adapted, so the probability of each Morph will be roughly proportional to its (inferred) frequency in the corpus. The grammar specifies no further structural relationships between morphs or inside of morphs (other than a geometric distribution on their length in characters).

Experiments with AGs for unsupervised word segmentation suggest that adding further latent structure can help with learning. Here, we add another layer of structure below the morphs,[1] calling the resulting grammar **SubMorphs**:

$$\begin{aligned} \text{Word} &\rightarrow \underline{\text{Morph}}^{+} \\ \underline{\text{Morph}} &\rightarrow \underline{\text{SubMorph}}^{+} \\ \underline{\text{SubMorph}} &\rightarrow \text{Char}^{+} \end{aligned} \tag{2}$$

For capturing the rules of morphotactics, a grammar with linguistically motivated non-terminals can be created. There are many plausible options and the best-performing grammar may be somewhat language-dependent. Rather than experimenting extensively, we designed our third grammar to replicate as closely as possible the grammar that is implicitly implemented in the Morfessor system. This **Compounding** grammar distinguishes between prefixes, stems and suffixes, allows compounding, defines the order in which the morphs can occur and also allows the morphs to have inner latent structure:

$$\begin{aligned} \text{Word} &\rightarrow \underline{\text{Compound}}^{+} \\ \underline{\text{Compound}} &\rightarrow \underline{\text{Prefix}}^{*}\ \underline{\text{Stem}}\ \underline{\text{Suffix}}^{*} \\ \underline{\text{Prefix}} &\rightarrow \underline{\text{SubMorph}}^{+} \\ \underline{\text{Stem}} &\rightarrow \underline{\text{SubMorph}}^{+} \\ \underline{\text{Suffix}} &\rightarrow \underline{\text{SubMorph}}^{+} \\ \underline{\text{SubMorph}} &\rightarrow \text{Char}^{+} \end{aligned} \tag{3}$$

3.2 Semi-Supervised Adaptor Grammars

The first new use of AGs we introduce is the *semi-supervised* AG, where we use the labelled data to extract counts of the different rules and subtrees used in the gold-standard analyses. We then run the MCMC sampler as usual over both the unlabelled and labelled data, treating the counts from the labelled data as fixed.

We assume that the labelled data provides a consistent bracketing (no two spans in the bracketing can partially overlap) and the labels of the spans must be compatible with the grammar. However, the bracketing may not specify all levels of structure in the grammar. In our case, we have morpheme bracketings but not, e.g., submorphs. Thus, using the SubMorphs grammar in semi-supervised mode will constrain the sampler so that Morph spans in the labelled data will remain fixed, while the SubMorphs inside those Morphs will be resampled.

[1] Because the nonterminal labels are arbitrary, this grammar can also be interpreted as adding another layer on top of morphs, allowing the model to learn morph *collocations* that encode dependencies between morphs (which themselves have no substructure). However preliminary experiments showed that the morph-submorph interpretation scored better than the collocation-morph interpretation, hence we chose the corresponding nonterminal names.

The main change made to the AG inference process[2] for implementing the semi-supervised AG was to prune out from the sampling distribution any non-terminals that are inconsistent with the spans/labels in the given labelling.

3.3 AG Select

Both the unsupervised and semi-supervised methods described above assume the definition of a grammar that adequately captures the phenomena being modelled. Although the AG framework makes it easy to experiment with different grammars, these experiments can be time-consuming and require some good guesses as to what a plausible grammar might be. These problems can be overcome by automating the grammar development process to systematically evaluate different grammars and find the best one.

We propose a minimally supervised model selection method AG Select that uses the AG framework to automatically identify the best grammar for different languages and data sets. We first define a very general binary-branching CFG grammar for AG training that we call the *metagrammar*. The metagrammar learns a parse tree for each word where each branch contains a different structure in the word. The granularity of these structures is determined by the depth of this tree. For example, Grammar 4 generates binary trees of depth two and can learn segmentations of up to four segments.

$$\begin{array}{llll} \text{Word} \rightarrow \underline{\text{M1}} & & \\ \text{Word} \rightarrow \underline{\text{M1}}\ \underline{\text{M2}} & \underline{\text{M11}} \rightarrow \text{Chars}^{+} & \\ \underline{\text{M1}} \rightarrow \underline{\text{M11}} & \underline{\text{M12}} \rightarrow \text{Chars}^{+} & \\ \underline{\text{M1}} \rightarrow \underline{\text{M11}}\ \underline{\text{M12}} & \underline{\text{M21}} \rightarrow \text{Chars}^{+} & (4) \\ \underline{\text{M2}} \rightarrow \underline{\text{M21}} & \underline{\text{M22}} \rightarrow \text{Chars}^{+} & \\ \underline{\text{M2}} \rightarrow \underline{\text{M21}}\ \underline{\text{M22}} & & \end{array}$$

Next we introduce the notion of a *morphological template*, which is an ordered sequence of non-terminals whose concatenated yields constitute the word and which are used to parse out a specific segmentation of the word. For example, using Grammar 4 the parse tree of the word *saltiness* is shown in Figure 1. There are four possible templates with four

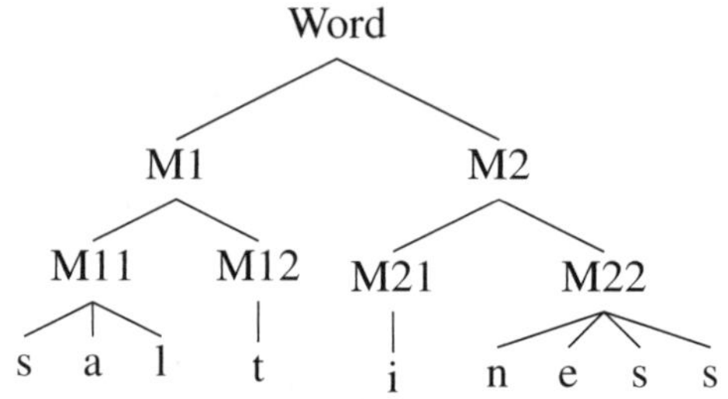

Figure 1: The parse tree generated by the metagrammar of depth 2 for the word *saltiness*.

different segmentations: **M1 M2** (*salt_iness*), **M11 M12 M2** (*sal_t_iness*), **M1 M21 M22** (*salt_i_ness*), and **M11 M12 M21 M22** (*sal_t_i_ness*).

The morphological template consisting only of non-terminals from the lowest cached level of the parse tree is expected to have high recall, whereas the template containing the non-terminals just below the Word is expected to have high precision. Our goal is to find the optimal template by using a small labelled data set. The grammar selection process iterates over the set of all templates. For each template, the segmentations of the words in the labelled data set are parsed out and the value of the desired evaluation metric is computed. The template that obtained the highest score is then chosen.

For each language we use a single template to segment all the words in that language. However, even using (say) a four-morph template such as **M11 M12 M21 M22**, some words may contain fewer morphs because the metagrammar permits either unary or binary branching rules, so some parses may not contain **M12** or **M2** (and thus **M21 M22**) spans. Thus, we can represent segmentations of different lengths (from 1 to 2^n, where n is the depth of the metagrammar) with a single template.[3]

For our experiments we use a metagrammar of depth four. This grammar allows words to consist of up to 16 segments, which we felt would be enough for any word in the training data. Also, iterating over all the templates of a grammar with bigger depth would not be feasible as the number of different templates increases very rapidly.[4]

[2]We started with Mark Johnson's PYAG implementation, http://web.science.mq.edu.au/~mjohnson/code/py-cfg.tgz, which we also used for our unsupervised and grammar selection experiments.

[3]We also experimented with selecting different templates for words of different length but observed no improvements over the single template approach.

[4]The number of templates of each depth can be expressed recursively as $N_i = (N_{i-1} + 1)^2$, where N_{i-1} is the number of

3.4 Inductive Learning

Previous work on AGs has used relatively small data sets and run the sampler on the entire input corpus (some or all of which is also used for evaluation)—a *transductive* learning scenario. However, our larger data sets contain millions of word types, where sampling over the whole set is not feasible. For example, 1000 training iterations on 50k word types took about a week on one 2.67 GHz CPU. To solve this problem, we need an *inductive* learner that can be trained on a small set of data and then used to segment a different larger set.

To create such a learner, we run the sampler on up to 50k word types, and then extract the *posterior grammar* as a PCFG.[5] This grammar contains all the initial CFG rules, plus rules to generate each of the cached subtrees inferred by the sampler. The sampler counts of all rules are normalized to obtain a PCFG, and we can then use a standard CKY parser to decode the remaining data using this PCFG.

4 Experiments

4.1 Data

We test on languages with a range of morphological complexity: English, Finnish, Turkish, German, and Estonian. For each language we use two small sets of gold-annotated data—a *labelled set* for semi-supervised training or model selection and a *dev set* for development results—and one larger gold-annotated dataset for final tests. We also have a large *unlabelled* training set for each language. Table 1 gives statistics.

The data sets for English, Finnish, Turkish and German are from the Morpho Challenge 2010 competition[6] (MC2010). We use the MC2010 training set of 1000 annotated word types as our labelled data, and for our dev sets we collate together the development data from all years of the MC competition. Final evaluation is done on the official MC2010 test sets, which are not public, so we rely on the MC organizers to perform the evaluation. The words in each test set are an unknown subset of the words in the unlabelled corpus, so to evaluate we segmented the entire unlabelled corpus and sent the results to the MC team, who then computed scores on the test words.

	Unlab.	Lab.	Dev	Test
English	0.9M	1000	1212	16K
Finnish	2.9M	1000	1494	225K
Turkish	0.6M	1000	1531	64K
German	2.3M	1000	785	62K
Estonian	2.1M	1000	1500	74K

Table 1: Number of word types in our data sets.

The Estonian wordlist is gathered from the newspaper texts of a mixed corpus of Estonian.[7] Gold standard segmentations of some of these words are available from the Estonian morphologically disambiguated corpus;[8] we used these for the test set, with small subsets selected randomly for the labelled and dev sets.

For semi-supervised tests of the AG Compounding grammar we annotated the morphemes in the English, Finnish and Estonian labelled sets as prefixes, stems or suffixes. We could not do so for Turkish because none of the authors knows Turkish.

4.2 Evaluation

We evaluate our results with two measures: segment border F1-score (SBF1) and EMMA (Spiegler and Monson, 2010). SBF1 is one of the simplest and most popular evaluation metrics for morphological segmentations. It computes F1-score from the precision and recall of ambiguous segment boundaries—i.e., word edges are not counted. It is easy and quick to compute but has the drawback that it gives no credit for one-morpheme words that have been segmented correctly (i.e., are assigned no segment borders). Also it can only be used on systems and gold standards where the output is just a segmentation of the surface string (e.g., *availabil+ity*) rather than a morpheme analysis (e.g., *available+ity*). For this reason we cannot report SBF1 on our German data, which annotations contain only analyses.

EMMA is a newer measure that addresses both

templates in the grammar of depth one less and $N_0 = 0$.

[5]This can be seen as a form of Structure Compilation (Liang et al., 2008), where the solution found by a more costly model is used to define a less costly model. However in Liang et al.'s case both models were already inductive.

[6]http://research.ics.aalto.fi/events/morphochallenge2010/datasets.shtml

[7]http://www.cl.ut.ee/korpused/segakorpus/epl

[8]http://www.cl.ut.ee/korpused/morfkorpus/

of these issues—correctly segmented one-morpheme words are reflected in the score, and it can evaluate both concatenative and non-concatenative morphology. EMMA works by finding the best one-to-one mapping between the hypothesized and true segments. The induced segments are then replaced with their mappings and based on that, F1-score on matching segments is calculated. Using EMMA we can evaluate the induced segmentations of German words against gold standard analyses. EMMA has a freely available implementation,[9] but is slow to compute because it uses Integer Linear Programming.

For our dev results, we computed both scores using the entire dev set, but for the large test sets, the evaluation is done on batches of 1000 word types selected randomly from the test set. This procedure is repeated 10 times and the average is reported, just as in the MC2010 competition (Kohonen et al., 2010a).

4.3 Baseline Models

We compare our AG models to several other morphology learning systems. We were able to obtain implementations of two of the best unsupervised systems from MC2010, Morfessor (Creutz and Lagus, 2007) and Morsel (Lignos, 2010), and we use these for comparisons on both the dev and test sets. We also report test results from MC2010 for the only semi-supervised system in the competition, semi-supervised Morfessor (Kohonen et al., 2010a; Kohonen et al., 2010b). No dev results are reported on this system since we were unable to obtain an implementation. This section briefly reviews the systems.

4.3.1 Morfessor Categories-MAP

Morfessor Categories-MAP (Morfessor) is a state-of-the-art unsupervised morphology learning system. Its implementation is freely available[10] so it is widely used both as a preprocessing step in tasks requiring morphological segmentations, and as a baseline for evaluating morphology learning systems.

Morfessor uses the Minimum Description Length (MDL) principle to choose the optimal segment lexicon and the corpus segmentation. Each morph in the segment lexicon is labelled as a stem, prefix, suffix or non-morph. The morphotactic rules are encoded as an HMM, which specifies the allowed morph sequences with respect to the labels (e.g., a suffix cannot directly follow a prefix).

The morphs in the segment lexicon can have a hierachical structure, containing submorphs which themselves can consist of submorphs etc. We hypothesize that this hierarchical structure is one of the key reasons why Morfessor has been so successful, as the experiments also in this paper with different grammars show that the ability to learn latent structures is crucial for learning good segmentations.

One essential difference between Morfessor and the proposed AG Select is that while we use the labelled data to choose which levels of the hierarchy are to be used as morphs, Morfessor makes this decision based on the labels of the segments, choosing the most fine-grained morph sequence that does not contain the non-morph label.

Morfessor includes a free parameter, perplexity threshold, which we found can affect the SBF1 score considerably (7 points or more). The best value for this parameter depends on the size of the training set, characteristics of the language being learned, and also the evaluation metric being used, as in some cases the best SBF1 and EMMA scores are obtained with completely different values.

Thus, we tuned the value of the perplexity threshold on the labelled set for each language and evaluation metric for different unlabelled training set sizes.

4.3.2 Semi-Supervised Morfessor

Recently, the Morfessor system has been adapted to allow semi-supervised training. Four versions of the system were evaluated in MC2010, using different degrees of supervision. Results reported here are from the Morfessor S+W system, which performed best of those that use the same kind of labelled data as we do.[11] This system uses the Morfessor Baseline model (not Cat-MAP), which incorporates a lexicon prior and data likelihood term. The semi-supervised version maintains separate likelihoods for the labelled and unlabelled data, and uses the development set to tune two parameters that weight these terms with respect to each other and the prior.

[9] http://www.cs.bris.ac.uk/Research/MachineLearning/Morphology/resources.jsp#eval

[10] http://www.cis.hut.fi/projects/morpho/morfessorcatmapdownloadform.shtml

[11] Morfessor S+W+L performs better, but uses training data with morpheme analyses rather than surface segmentations.

4.3.3 Morsel

Morsel (Lignos, 2010) is an unsupervised morphology learning system introduced in MC2010; we obtained the implementation from the author. Morsel learns morphological analyses rather than segmentations, so it can be evaluated only using EMMA. There are two options provided for running Morsel: aggressive and conservative. We used the development set to choose the best in each experimental case.

The MC data sets contain gold standard morphological analyses (as well as segmentations) so we could compute Morsel's EMMA scores using the analyses. However, we found that Morsel obtains higher EMMA scores when evaluated against gold standard segmentations and thus we used this option in all the experiments. (EMMA scores for other systems were also computed using the segmentations.)

4.4 Method

The experiments were conducted in two parts. First, we evaluated different aspects of the AG models and compared to all baseline models using the dev set data. Then we evaluated the most competitive models on the final test data.

For the development experiments, we compiled unlabelled training sets with sizes ranging from 10k to 50k word types (using the most frequent word types in each case). For the AG results, we report the average of five different runs made on the same training set. We let the sampler run for 1000 iterations. No annealing was used as it did not seem to help. The table label resampling option was turned on and the hyperparameter values were inferred.

We trained all AG and baseline models on each of these training sets. For AG Select, the words from the labelled data set were added to the training set to allow for template selection.[12] To compute results in transductive mode, the words from the dev set were also added to the training data. In inductive mode, the dev set was instead parsed with the CKY parser.

Preliminary experiments showed that the performance of unsupervised AG and AG Select improved with larger training sets, though the effect is small (see Figure 2 for results of AG Select in transductive mode; the trend in inductive mode is similar). Based on these and similar results with other baseline systems, all results reported later for unsupervised models (AG and baseline) and AG Select were obtained using training sets of 50k words.

In contrast to the above models, the semi-supervised AG does not always improve with more unlabelled data (see Figure 2) and in the limit, it will match the performance of the same grammar in the unsupervised setting. Other semi-supervised approaches often solve this problem by weighting the labelled data more heavily than the unlabelled data when estimating model parameters—effectively, assuming that each labelled item has actually been observed more than once. However, duplicating the labelled data does not make sense in the AG framework, because duplicate items will in most cases just be cached at the root (Word) node, providing no additional counts of Morphs (which are where the useful information is). It might be possible to come up with a different way to weight the labelled data more heavily when larger unlabelled sets are used, however for this paper we instead kept the labelled data the same and tuned the amount of unlabelled data. We used the dev set to choose the amount of unlabelled data (in the range from 10k to 50k types); results for semi-supervised AG are reported using the optimal amount of unlabelled data for each experiment.

For test set experiments with semi-supervised AG, we evaluated each language using whichever grammar performed best on that language's dev set. For test set experiments with AG Select, we chose the templates with a two-pass procedure. First, we trained 5 samplers on the 50k training set with labelled set added, and used the labelled data to choose the best template for each inferred grammar. Then, we decoded the dev set using each of the 5 grammar/template pairs and based on these results, chose the best of these pairs to decode the test set.

4.5 Results

We present the dev set results in Table 2(a) for transductive and in Table 2(b) for inductive learning. In each table, unsupervised models are shown in the upper section and the semi-supervised models and AG Select below. Morsel appears only in Table 2(a) since it only works transductively. Semi-supervised grammars cannot be trained on German, since we

[12] We also experimented with smaller sets of labelled data. In most cases, the template selected based on only 300 word types was the same than the one selected with 1000 word types.

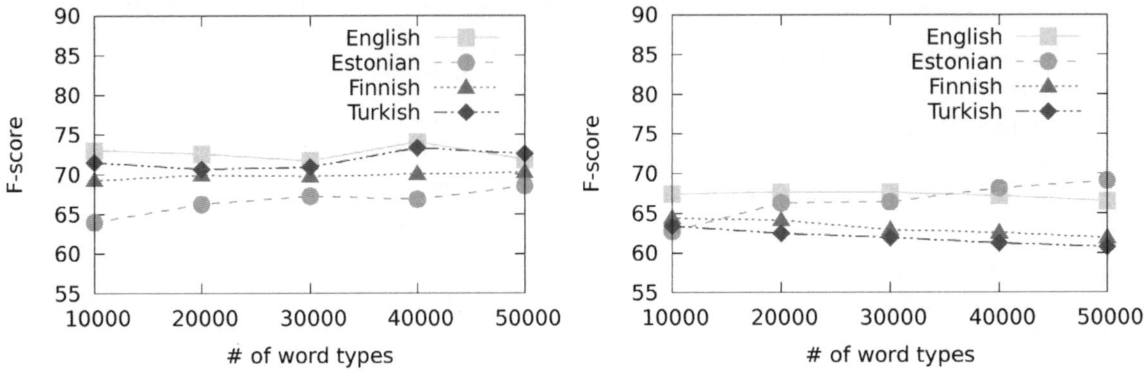

Figure 2: Effect of training data size on dev set SBF1 for AG Select (left) and semi-supervised SubMorphs grammar (right) in transductive mode.

only have gold standard analyses, not segmentations.

The SubMorphs grammar performs the best of the unsupervised AG models, with the Compounding grammar being only slightly worse. We also tried the Compounding grammar without the sub-morph structures but the results were even worse than those of MorphSeq. This shows that the latent structures are important for learning good segmentations.

In all cases, the semi-supervised AGs perform better (ofen much better) than the corresponding unsupervised grammars. Even though their average scores are not as high as AG Select's, they give the best dev set results in many cases. This shows that although for semi-supervised AG the grammar must be chosen manually, with a suitable choice of the grammar and only a small set of labelled data it can improve considerably over unsupervised AG.

In transductive mode, the AG Select performs the best in several cases. In both transductive and inductive mode, the results of AG Select are close to the best results obtained and are consistently good across all languages—it achieves the best average scores of all models, suggesting that the model selection method is robust to different types of morphology and annotation schemes.

Table 3 presents the test set results. We include scores for unsupervised Morfessor in both transductive and inductive mode, where transductive mode trains on the entire unlabelled corpus and inductive mode trains on the 50k subset. The semi-supervised Morfessor scores are taken from the MC results page[13] after verifying that the evaluation methodology and labelled data used is the same as ours.[14]

There is a good deal of variation between development and test results, indicating that the dev sets may not be a representative sample. The most notable differences are in Turkish, where all models perform far worse on the test than dev set. However, AG Select performs slightly better on the test set for the other languages. Thus its average SBF1 score actually improves on the test set and is not much worse than semi-supervised Morfessor. While its average performance drops somewhat on test set EMMA, it is still as good as any other model on that measure. Again, these results support the idea that AG Select is robust to variations in language and data set.

We also note the surprisingly good performance of Morfessor in transductive mode on Estonian; this could possibly be due to the larger amount of training data used for the test set results, but it is not clear why this would improve performance so much on Estonian and not on the other languages.

5 Discussion

To give a sense of what the AG Select model is learning, we provide some examples of both correctly and incorrectly induced segmentations in Table 4. These examples suggest that for example in English, M1 is used to model the stem, M21 is for the suffix or the second stem in the compound word, and the rest of the elements in the template are for the remaining suffixes (if any).

Table 5 presents examples of some of the most frequently used metagrammar rules and cached rules

[13] http://research.ics.aalto.fi/events/morphochallenge/

[14] Sami Virpioja, personal communication.

(a) Transductive mode	Border F1-score					EMMA					
	Eng	Est	Fin	Tur	Avg	Eng	Est	Fin	Tur	Ger	Avg
AG MorphSeq	61.5	54.0	56.9	59.5	58.0	74.7	74.1	63.7	53.5	59.4	65.1
AG SubMorphs	66.2	66.9	60.5	59.5	63.3	79.1	83.4	66.8	53.4	57.4	68.0
AG Compounding	63.0	64.8	60.9	60.9	62.4	75.4	81.6	65.5	53.7	62.2	67.7
Morfessor	69.5	55.7	65.0	69.3	64.9	**81.3**	75.3	67.8	62.2	**62.7**	69.9
Morsel	-	-	-	-	-	76.8	74.4	66.1	50.1	55.9	64.7
AG ssv MorphSeq	64.4	57.3	63.0	68.9	63.4	74.4	75.9	65.6	59.6	-	-
AG ssv SubMorphs	67.6	**69.1**	64.4	63.4	66.1	79.5	**84.4**	69.2	56.1	-	-
AG ssv Compounding	70.0	67.5	**71.8**	-	-	79.5	82.8	**74.0**	-	-	-
AG Select	**71.9**	68.5	70.2	**72.6**	**70.8**	77.5	81.8	73.2	**63.0**	62.4	**71.6**

(b) Inductive mode	Border F1-score					EMMA					
	Eng	Est	Fin	Tur	Avg	Eng	Est	Fin	Tur	Ger	Avg
AG MorphSeq	57.6	54.0	55.4	59.8	56.7	72.0	73.8	62.6	53.7	58.9	64.2
AG SubMorphs	66.1	67.5	61.6	59.8	63.7	78.6	**83.7**	67.4	53.4	56.0	67.8
AG Compounding	62.0	64.8	57.4	61.1	61.3	73.5	81.1	61.9	53.2	61.0	66.2
Morfessor	68.9	51.1	63.5	68.2	62.9	**80.9**	72.0	68.1	60.6	60.8	68.5
AG ssv MorphSeq	64.6	56.9	63.1	**70.3**	63.8	72.7	73.3	65.9	**61.2**	-	-
AG ssv SubMorphs	70.1	**69.7**	66.3	67.9	68.4	80.4	**83.7**	70.5	59.0	-	-
AG ssv Compounding	**70.5**	67.2	**70.0**	-	-	77.3	81.9	70.5	-	-	-
AG Select	69.8	68.8	67.5	70.1	**69.1**	77.3	81.9	**71.1**	59.7	**62.6**	**70.5**

Table 2: Dev set results for all models in (a) transductive and (b) inductive mode. Unsupervised AG models and baselines are shown in the top part of each table; semi-supervised AG models and grammar selection method are below.

	Border F1-score						EMMA						
	Eng	Est	Fin	Tur	Avg	-Est	Eng	Est	Fin	Tur	Ger	Avg	-Est/Ger
Morf. trans	67.3	**73.9**	61.2	57.1	64.9	61.9	78.4	78.8	61.8	49.8	**65.2**	66.8	63.3
Morf. ind	65.7	57.7	60.8	60.1	61.1	62.2	76.5	70.5	59.6	47.0	64.1	63.5	61.0
Morsel	-	-	-	-	-	-	**81.9**	77.2	63.3	47.8	59.0	65.8	**64.3**
Morf. ssv	**77.8**	-	**71.7**	**68.9**	-	**72.8**	80.6	-	62.1	**49.9**	-	-	64.2
AG ssv best	70.3*	68.6†	64.9*	58.2*	65.5	64.5	75.9*	80.3†	61.3*	46.1*	-	-	61.1
AG Select	74.4	71.7	70.0	61.4	**69.4**	68.6	81.3	**81.0**	**64.0**	47.5	63.8	**67.5**	**64.3**

Table 3: Test set results for unsupervised baselines Morfessor CatMAP (in transductive and inductive mode) and Morsel; semi-supervised Morfessor; and AG semi-supervised ($\star$ marks the Compounding grammar, $\dagger$ denotes SubMorphs grammar, and $*$ is the MorphSeq grammar) and grammar selection methods. Results are shown for each language, averaged over all languages (when possible: Avg), and averaged over just the languages where scores are available for all systems (-Est, -Est/Ger).

for English, together with their relative frequencies. It shows that at the Word level the binary rule is selected over three times more frequently than the unary rule. Also, most of the more frequently used grammar rules expand the first branch (rooted in M1) into more finegrained structures. The second branch (M2) is mostly modelled with the unary rule.

Among the frequently cached rules we see the common English prefixes and suffixes. One of the most frequent cached rule stores the single letter *e* at the end of a word, which often causes oversegmentation of words ending in *e* (as seen in the incorrect examples in Table 4). This problem is common in unsupervised morphological segmentation of English (Goldwater et al., 2006; Goldsmith, 2001).

We also took a look at the most frequent cached rules learned by the semi-supervised AG with the SubMorphs grammar, and observed that Morphs

Correct Segmentations		Incorrect Segmentations	
Word	**Segmentation**	**Induced**	**Correct**
treatable	[tr.ea.t]$_{M1}$ [a.b.le]$_{M21}$	disagree_s	dis_agree_s
disciplined	[dis.cip.l.i.n]$_{M1}$ [e.d]$_{M21}$	reduc_e	reduce
monogamous	[mon.o.g.a.m]$_{M1}$ [o.u.s]$_{M21}$	revalu_e	re_value
streakers	[st.r.e.a.k]$_{M1}$ [e.r]$_{M21}$ [s]$_{M2211}$	derid_e	deride
tollgate	[t.o.l.l.]$_{M1}$ [g.a.t.e]$_{M21}$ [s]$_{M2211}$	accompani_ed	ac_compani_ed
foxhunting	[f.o.x]$_{M1}$ [h.u.n.t]$_{M21}$ [ing]$_{M2211}$	war_y	wary
muscovites	[m.u.sc.o.v]$_{M1}$ [i.t.e]$_{M21}$ [s]$_{M2211}$	indescrib_able	in_describ_able
standardizes	[st.a.n.d.a.rd]$_{M1}$ [i.z.e]$_{M21}$ [s]$_{M2211}$	orat_es	orate_s
slavers'	[sl.a.v]$_{M1}$ [e.r]$_{M21}$ [s]$_{M2211}$ [']$_{M2212}$	alger_ian_s	algeri_an_s
earthiness'	[e.ar.th]$_{M1}$ [i]$_{M2111}$ [ness]$_{M2211}$ [']$_{M2212}$	disput_e_s	dispute_s
instinkt	[in.st.in.kt]$_{M1}$	meister_likkust	meisterlikkus_t
rebis	[re.b.i]$_{M1}$ [s]$_{M2}$	min_a	mina
toitsid	[to.it]$_{M1}$ [s.id]$_{M2}$	teiste	teis_te
armuavaldus	[a.rm.u]$_{M11}$ [ava.ld.u.s]$_{M12}$	kuritegu_de_sse	kuri_tegu_desse
määgivale	[mää.g.i]$_{M11}$ [v.a]$_{M12}$ [l.e]$_{M2}$	liharoa_ga	liha_roa_ga
keskuskoulussa	[kesk.us]$_{M11}$ [koul.u]$_{M12}$ [s.sa]$_{M2}$	polte_tti_in	polte_tt_i_in
peruslähteille	[per.u.s]$_{M11}$ [l.ä.ht.e]$_{M12}$ [i]$_{M211}$ [ll.e]$_{M212}$	kulttuuri_se_lt_a_kin	kulttuurise_lta_kin
perunakaupoista	[per.u.n.a]$_{M11}$ [k.au.p.o]$_{M12}$ [i]$_{M211}$ [st.a]$_{M212}$	tuote_palki_ntoja	tuote_palkinto_j_a
yöpaikkaani	[yö]$_{M11}$ [p.ai.kk.a]$_{M12}$ [a]$_{M21}$ [n.i]$_{M22}$	veli_puo_lt_a	veli_puol_ta
nimettäköön	[ni.m.e]$_{M11}$ [tt.ä]$_{M12}$ [k.ö]$_{M21}$ [ö.n]$_{M22}$	ota_ttava	otatta_va

Table 4: Examples of segmented words in English (top), Estonian (middle) and Finnish (bottom). Correctly segmented words are in the left part of the table. The identified segments are in brackets indexed by the respective template nonterminal; dots separate the metagrammar generated parse tree leaves. Examples of incorrectly segmented words together with the correct segmentation are on the right.

Freq (%)	Rule	Freq (%)	Cached Rule
9.9	Word → M1 M2	1.2	(M2 (M21 (M211 (M2111 s)))))
5.7	M1 → M11 M12	0.9	(M2 (M21 (M211 (M2111 e)) (M212 (M2121 d))))
3.1	Word → M1	0.7	(M2 (M21 (M211 (M2111 i)) (M212 (M2121 n g))))
2.5	M11 → M111	0.6	(M2 (M21 (M211 (M2111 e)))
1.8	M2 → M21	0.4	(M2 (M21 (M211 (M2111 '))) (M22 (M221 (M2211 s))))
1.4	M12→ M121 M122	0.3	(M1112 a)
1.4	M111 → M1111 M1112	0.3	(M2 (M21 (M211 (M2111 y))))
0.9	M12 → M121	0.3	(M2 (M21 (M211 (M2111 e))) (M212 (M2121 r)))
0.9	M11 → M111 M112	0.2	(M2 (M21 (M211 (M2111 a))))

Table 5: Examples from English most frequently used metagrammar rules and cached rules together with their relative occurrence frequencies (in percentages).

tended to contain only a single SubMorph. This helps to explain why the SubMorphs grammar in semi-supervised AG improved less over the unsupervised AG as compared to the MorphSeq grammar—the rules with only a single SubMorph under the Morph are essentially the same as they would be in the MorphSeq grammar.

Finally, we examined the consistency of the templates chosen for each of the 5 samplers during model selection for the test set (Section 4.4). We found that there was some variability in the templates, but in most experiments the same template was chosen for the majority of the samplers (see Table 6). While this majority template is not always the optimal one on the dev set, we observed that it does produce consistently good results. It is possible that using the majority template, rather than the optimal template for the dev set, would actually produce better results

	Majority template
English	M1 M21 M2211 M2212 M222
Finnish	M11 M12 M211 M212 M22
Turkish	M11 M12 M211 M212 M22
German	M11 M121 M122 M21 M221 M222
Estonian	M11 M12 M2

Table 6: Majority templates for each language. Note that the Estonian gold standard contains less fine-grained segmentations than some of the other languages.

on the test set, especially if (as appears to be the case here, and may often be the case in real applications) the dev and test sets are from somewhat different distributions.

It must be noted that both AG Select and semi-supervised AG are computationally more demanding than the comparison systems. Since we do inference over tree structures, the complexity is cubic in the input word length, while most segmentation systems are quadratic or linear. Even compared to the unsupervised AG, AG Select is more expensive, because of the larger grammar and number of cached symbols. Nevertheless, our systems can feasibly be run on the large Morpho Challenge datasets.

Other recent unsupervised systems have reported state-of-the art results by incorporating additional information from surrounding words (Lee et al., 2011), multilingual alignments (Snyder and Barzilay, 2008), or overlapping context features in a log-linear model (Poon et al., 2009), but they have only been run on Semitic languages and English (and in the latter case, a very small corpus). Since they explicitly enumerate and sample from all possible segmentations of each word (often with some heuristic constraints), they could have trouble with the much longer words of the agglutinative languages tested here. In any case the results are not directly comparable to ours.

6 Conclusion

In this paper we have introduced three new methods for Adaptor Grammars and demonstrated their usefulness for minimally supervised morphological segmentation. First, we showed that AG models can be scaled to large data sets by using the posterior grammar for defining an inductive model, that on average results in the same accuracy as compared to full transductive training.

Second, we implemented semi-supervised AG inference, which uses labelled data to constrain the sampler, and showed that in all cases it performs much better than the unsupervised AG on the same grammar. Semi-supervised AG could benefit from labelled data reweighting techniques frequently used in semi-supervised learning, and studying the proper ways of doing so within the AG framework would be a potential topic for future research.

Our final contribution is the AG Select method, where the initial model is trained using a very general grammar that oversegments the data, and the labelled data is used to select which granularity of segments to use. Unlike other morphological segmentation models, this method can adapt its grammar to languages with different structures, rather than having to use the same grammar for every language. Indeed, we found that AG Select performs well across a range of languages and also seems to be less sensitive to differences between data sets (here, dev vs. test). In addition, it can be trained on either morphological analyses or segmentations. Although we tuned all results to optimize the SBF1 metric, in principle the same method could be used to optimize other measures, including extrinsic measures on downstream applications such as machine translation or information retrieval. In future we hope to show that this method can be used to improve performance on such applications, and also to explore its use for related segmentation tasks such as stemming or syllabification. Also, the method itself could potentially be improved by designing a classifier to determinine the best template for each word based on a set of features, rather than using a single template for all words in the language.

Acknowledgments

This work was supported by the Tiger University program of Estonian Information Technology Foundation for the first author. We thank Constantine Lignos for releasing his Morsel code to us, Sami Virpioja for evaluating test set results, and Federico Sangati for providing useful scripts.

References

Mathias Creutz and Krista Lagus. 2007. Unsupervised models for morpheme segmentation and morphology learning. *ACM Transactions of Speech and Language Processing*, 4(1):1–34, February.

Micha Elsner, Eugene Charniak, and Mark Johnson. 2009. Structured generative models for unsupervised named-entity clustering. In *Proceedings of NAACL*, pages 164–172. Association for Computational Linguistics.

John Goldsmith. 2001. Unsupervised learning of the morphology of a natural language. *Computational Linguistics*, 27(2):153–198, June.

Sharon Goldwater, Thomas L. Griffiths, and Mark Johnson. 2006. Interpolating between types and tokens by estimating power-law generators. In *Advances in Neural Information Processing Systems 18*, pages 459–466, Cambridge, MA. MIT Press.

Eric A. Hardisty, Jordan Boyd-Graber, and Philip Resnik. 2010. Modeling perspective using adaptor grammars. In *Proceedings of EMNLP*, pages 284–292. Association for Computational Linguistics.

Zellig Harris. 1951. *Structural Linguistics*. University of Chicago Press.

Yun Huang, Min Zhang, and Chew Lim Tan. 2011. Nonparametric bayesian machine transliteration with synchronous adaptor grammars. In *Proceedings of ACL: short papers - Volume 2*, pages 534–539. Association for Computational Linguistics.

Mark Johnson and Katherine Demuth. 2010. Unsupervised phonemic chinese word segmentation using adaptor grammars. In *Proceedings of COLING*, pages 528–536. Association for Computational Linguistics.

Mark Johnson and Sharon Goldwater. 2009. Improving nonparameteric bayesian inference: experiments on unsupervised word segmentation with adaptor grammars. In *Proceedings of NAACL*, pages 317–325. Association for Computational Linguistics.

Mark Johnson, Thomas L. Griffiths, and Sharon Goldwater. 2007. Adaptor grammars: A framework for specifying compositional nonparametric bayesian models. In B. Schölkopf, J. Platt, and T. Hoffman, editors, *Advances in Neural Information Processing Systems 19*, pages 641–648. MIT Press, Cambridge, MA.

Mark Johnson. 2008a. Unsupervised word segmentation for sesotho using adaptor grammars. In *Proceedings of ACL Special Interest Group on Computational Morphology and Phonology*, pages 20–27. Association for Computational Linguistics.

Mark Johnson. 2008b. Using adaptor grammars to identify synergies in the unsupervised acquisition of linguistic structure. In *Proceedings of ACL*, pages 398–406. Association for Computational Linguistics.

Oskar Kohonen, Sami Virpioja, and Krista Lagus. 2010a. Semi-supervised learning of concatenative morphology. In *Proceedings of ACL Special Interest Group on Computational Morphology and Phonology*, pages 78–86. Association for Computational Linguistics.

Oskar Kohonen, Sami Virpioja, Laura Leppänen, and Krista Lagus. 2010b. Semi-supervised extensions to morfessor baseline. In *Proceedings of the Morpho Challenge 2010 Workshop*, pages 30–34. Aalto University School of Science and Technology.

Yoong Keok Lee, Aria Haghighi, and Regina Barzilay. 2011. Modeling syntactic context improves morphological segmentation. In *Proceedings of CoNLL*, pages 1–9. Association for Computational Linguistics.

Percy Liang, Hal Daumé, III, and Dan Klein. 2008. Structure compilation: trading structure for features. In *Proceedings of ICML*, pages 592–599. Association for Computing Machinery.

Constantine Lignos. 2010. Learning from Unseen Data. In Mikko Kurimo, Sami Virpioja, and Ville T. Turunen, editors, *Proceedings of the Morpho Challenge 2010 Workshop*, pages 35–38. Aalto University School of Science and Technology.

Jim Pitman and Marc Yor. 1997. The two-parameter Poisson-Dirichlet distribution derived from a stable subordinator. *Annals of Probability*, 25(2):855–900.

Hoifung Poon, Colin Cherry, and Kristina Toutanova. 2009. Unsupervised morphological segmentation with log-linear models. In *Proceedings of NAACL*, pages 209–217. Association for Computational Linguistics.

Benjamin Snyder and Regina Barzilay. 2008. Unsupervised multilingual learning for morphological segmentation. In *Proceedings of ACL*, pages 737–745. Association for Computational Linguistics.

Sebastian Spiegler and Christian Monson. 2010. Emma: A novel evaluation metric for morphological analysis. In *Proceedings of COLING*, pages 1029–1037. Association for Computational Linguistics.

Sze-Meng Jojo Wong, Mark Dras, and Mark Johnson. 2012. Exploring adaptor grammars for native language identification. In *Proceedings of EMNLP*, pages 699–709. Association for Computational Linguistics.

AUTHOR INDEX

Association for Computational Linguistics
209 N. Eighth Street
Stroudsburg, Pennsylvania 18360

CURRAN ASSOCIATES INC
proceedings.com

Workshop on Biomedical Natural Language Processing 2011

(BioNLP 2011)

Held at ACL HLT 2011

Portland, Oregon, USA
23-24 June 2011

ISBN: 978-1-61839-233-6